Check for CD-ROM in back of book.

JUN -- 2014

REF
W9-BON-956
Princeton Review (Firm)
Cracking the LSAT

Georgia Law requires Library materials to be returned or replacement costs paid. Failure to comply with this law is a misdemeanor. (O.C.G.A. 20-5-53)

# Cracking the LSAT®

## 2015 Edition

Adam Robinson and Kevin Blemel
Updated by Mindy Eve Myers,
Bob Spruill, and Andrew Brody

PrincetonReview.com

PENGUIN RANDOM HOUSE

CLAYTON COUNTY LIBRARY SYSTEM
FOREST PARK BRANCH
4812 WEST STREET
FOREST PARK, GEORGIA 30297-1824

The Princeton Review
24 Prime Parkway, Suite 201
Natick, MA 01760
E-mail: editorialsupport@review.com

Copyright © 2014 by TPR Education IP Holdings, LLC

All rights reserved. Published in the United States by Random House LLC New York, and in Canada by Random House of Canada Limited, Toronto. Originally published by Villard Books, a division of Random House, Inc., 1989

A Penguin Random House Company..

Terms of Service: The Princeton Review Online Companion Tools ("Online Companion Tools") for the *Cracking* book series and *11 Practice Tests for the SAT & PSAT* are available for the two most recent editions of each book title. Online Companion Tools may be activated only once per eligible book purchased. Activation of Online Companion Tools more than once per book is in direct violation of these Terms of Service and may result in discontinuation of access to Online Companion Tools services.

LSAT directions copyright © 1989 Law School Admission Council, Inc. All rights reserved. Reprinted by permission of Law School Admission Council, Inc.

Permission has been granted to reprint portions of the following:
"The Export of Hazardous Wastes: Issues and Policy Implications," by C. E. Davis and J. D. Hagen, taken from *International Journal of Public Affairs*, Vol. 8, No. 4, 1986.
"Employee Drug-Testing Issues Facing Private Sector Employees," by Steven O. Todd, taken from *North Carolina Law Review*, Vol. 65, No. 4, 1987.
"The Right of Publicity Revisited: Reconciling Fame, Fortune and Constitutional Rights," by Jane Gross, taken from *Boston University Law Review*, Vol. 62, No. 4, 1982.
"An Economist's Perspective on the Theory of the Firm," by Oliver Hart, 89 *Columbia Law Review* 1957. © 1989 by the Directors of the Columbia Law Review Association, Inc. All rights reserved. Used by kind permission from Professor Hart and *Columbia Law Review*. Several minor editorial changes were made to make the excerpts conform to LSAT passage specifications. Mr. Hart is a professor of economics at M.I.T.

The Princeton Review is not affiliated with Princeton University.

ISBN: 978-0-8041-2495-9
ISSN: 1062-5542

Editor: Kristen O'Toole
Production Editor: Beth Hanson
Production Coordinator: Sandra Schmeil

Printed in the United States of America on partially recycled paper.

10 9 8 7 6 5 4 3 2 1

2015 Edition

**Editorial**
Robert Franek, Senior VP Publisher
Casey Cornelius, VP, Content Development
Selena Coppock, Senior Editor
Calvin Cato, Editor
Meave Shelton, Editor
Kristen O'Toole, Editor
Alyssa Wolff, Editorial Assistant

**Random House Publishing Team**
Tom Russell, Publisher
Alison Stoltzfus, Publishing Manager
Dawn Ryan, Associate Managing Editor
Ellen Reed, Production Manager
Erika Pepe, Associate Production Manager
Kristin Lindner, Production Supervisor
Andrea Lau, Designer

# Acknowledgments

A successful LSAT program is a collaborative effort. We'd especially like to thank Andrew Brody, Akhil Sheth, Chad Chasteen, and Jennifer Wooddell for their expertise.

A very special thanks to Oliver Hart, professor of economics at M.I.T., and to Debora Davies and the folks at *Columbia Law Review* for their generous permission to quote an excerpt from an article by Professor Hart.

Special thanks to Adam Robinson, who conceived of and perfected the Joe Bloggs approach to standardized tests and many of the other successful techniques used by The Princeton Review.

# Contents

# Foreword

Dear Prospective Law Student,

Congratulations on your decision to purchase The Princeton Review's *Cracking the LSAT.* This self-study guide will help you achieve your highest possible score on the LSAT—arguably the single most significant factor in law school admissions decisions.

While most applicants understand the importance that the LSAT plays in their law school applications, many are unaware that the score they receive can have far-reaching consequences—often determining much more than just which law school they will attend. For example, many law schools consider LSAT scores when awarding merit scholarships and grants. Given that the average full-time Juris Doctor degree costs more than $150,000, a high score on the LSAT may well translate into tens of thousands of dollars in financial aid that can significantly reduce your law school debt upon graduation.

The LSAT purports to gauge your reading comprehension, reasoning, and analytical skills in an effort to predict your ability to survive a demanding law school curriculum. Those who hone their LSAT test-taking skills usually score the highest. Indeed, a strong LSAT score can be as much an indication of a strong work ethic as it is of intellect.

So invest the time and master The Princeton Review's proven test-taking strategies. While that investment begins with *Cracking the LSAT,* it should not end here. To get the most out of your self-study, take advantage of the many resources that accompany this book. By registering your book at **PrincetonReview.com/cracking**, you can gain access to additional practice tests, personalized score reports, online exercises, tutorials, and more.

The Princeton Review's master instructors are devoted to sharing their wisdom and inspiration so that you can conquer the LSAT. *Cracking the LSAT* and its online supplement are the fruits of their efforts. I firmly believe that The Princeton Review, with its personalized instruction and test-taking techniques, is the very best way for you to prepare comprehensively for the LSAT.

Good luck!

Sincerely,

Donald W. Macaulay, Esq.
President and Founder, Law Preview

# ...So Much More Online!

## Register your book now!

- Go to PrincetonReview.com and scroll down to the bottom right corner where you'll see a box that says "Register Books." Alternately, you can go to www.PrincetonReview.com/cracking.
- You'll see a Welcome page where you should register your book using the book's ISBN number: 9780804124959. Simply type this into the window and go on to the next page!
- Next you will see a Sign Up/Sign In page where you will type in your e-mail address (username) and choose a password.
- Now you're good to go!

## Once you've registered, you can...

- Take 1 full-length practice test
- Access detailed profiles for hundreds of law schools help you find the school that is right for you
- Find information about financial aid and scholarships to help you pay for law school
- Check out top 10 ranking lists including Best Professors, Most Competitive Students, Best Career Prospects, and tons more

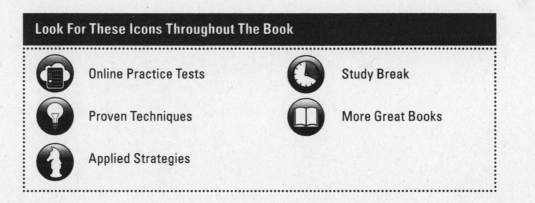

**Look For These Icons Throughout The Book**

Online Practice Tests

Study Break

Proven Techniques

More Great Books

Applied Strategies

PrincetonReview.com

# Chapter 1
# General Information and Strategies

In this chapter, we're going to give you an overall preparation plan for the LSAT. Before we hit you with some test-taking techniques, we want to make sure that you know all that we know about the LSAT itself. We'll start with a few pages' worth of information on the test. Make sure you read all this info carefully so you'll know exactly what you're up against.

## "CRACKING" THE LAW SCHOOL ADMISSION TEST

We hope you've bought this book at least a few months before the date of the LSAT you plan to take, so you'll have time to (a) actually follow the suggestions we make, including working on actual LSAT tests released by the Law School Admission Council (LSAC); (b) work through the specific problems in Chapters 2, 3, and 4 (at least twice); and (c) complete both practice tests at the end of this book.

If you've bought this book only a few weeks before the LSAT, read through this chapter and absorb the test-taking tips that we give you; then work through Chapters 2, 3, and 4. Finally, try to take at least one of the tests in the back of the book.

If you've bought (or are merely opening) this book for the first time only a few *days* before the LSAT, well, we admire your bravado. Take a complete test to see approximately what you would score on a real LSAT. If it's more than five or six points below where you want to be, consider skipping the test and taking it at a later date. The best way to improve your score dramatically is to work steadily on hundreds of problems throughout the course of a few months. Remember: The title of this book is *Cracking the LSAT,* not *Crashing the LSAT.*

## WHAT IS THE LSAT?

The LSAT is a tightly timed, multiple-choice test that almost always consists of 99 to 102 questions. By *tightly timed*, we mean that the test is designed so that the "average" test taker (someone scoring around the fiftieth percentile) should not be able to comfortably complete all the questions in the time allotted. The LSAT also includes a 35-minute essay. The LSAT is required by every American Bar Association (ABA)–certified law school in the United States—if you want to go to a U.S. law school, you not only have to take the LSAT, but you must do pretty well on it to boot.

The LSAC Website

You should go to **www.lsac.org** as soon as you decide to take the test. Spend some time exploring the website. On the site, you can sign up for the LSAT and for the Credential Assembly Service (CAS), you can order previously released LSATs, and you can obtain information about law schools and the application process. Some testing sites fill up very quickly, so you should register for a location as soon as possible.

## WHEN IS THE LSAT GIVEN?

The LSAT is administered four times a year—February, June, September/October, and December. Typically, students applying for regular fall admission to a law program take the test during June or September/October of the previous calendar year. You can take the test in December or February, but many schools will have filled at least a portion of their seats by the time your scores hit the admissions office. See Chapter 7 on Law School Admissions for more information about when and how to apply to law school.

## HOW IMPORTANT IS THE LSAT?

The LSAT is not only required by every single ABA-approved U.S. law school, but also weighted very heavily in the admissions process. For many schools, it is weighted just as heavily as (or even more heavily than) your undergraduate grade point average (GPA). That's the number that you worked very hard on in college, remember? The fact that a four-hour, multiple-choice test—one that is a questionable indicator of how well you'll do in law school—is considered as important as your undergraduate performance over the course of four *years* seems unjust. If you feel this way, you are not alone, but there isn't anything you can do about it. Instead, you need to focus on reaching your highest potential score.

## HOW IS THE LSAT SCORED?

The LSAT is scored on a scale of 120 to 180, with the median score being approximately 152. You need to get about 60 questions right (out of 99–102) to get that median score of 152, which means you need to bat about 60 percent. Very few people get a perfect score, mainly because the test is designed so that very few people can correctly answer all the questions, let alone do so in the time allotted.

Along with your LSAT score, you will receive a percentile ranking. This ranking compares your performance with that of everyone else who has taken the LSAT for the previous three years. Because a 152 is the median LSAT score, it would give you a percentile ranking of approximately 50. A score of 156 moves you up to a ranking of about 70. A 164 pulls you up to a ranking of 90. And any score over 167 puts you above 95 percent of all the LSAT takers.

As you can see, small numerical jumps (five points or so) can lead to a huge difference in percentile points. That means you're jumping over 20 percent of all test takers if, on your first practice test, you score a 150, but on the real test, you score a 155. Small gains can net big results.

The following table summarizes the number of questions you can skip or miss and still reach your LSAT goal. Notice that 93 percent of those taking the test make *more* than 15 errors. Take this into consideration as you develop your strategy of exactly how many questions you intend to answer or skip.

| Approximate Number of Errors (Out of 102) | LSAT Score | Percentile Rank |
|---|---|---|
| 1 | 180 | approx. 99++ |
| 4 | 175 | approx. 99+ |
| 8 | 170 | approx. 98+ |
| 15 | 165 | approx. 93+ |
| 22 | 160 | approx. 82+ |
| 32 | 155 | approx. 66+ |
| 43 | 150 | approx. 46+ |
| 52 | 145 | approx. 27+ |
| 62 | 140 | approx. 14+ |
| 69 | 135 | approx. 5+ |

### What Is a Good Score?

A good score on the LSAT is one that gets you into the law school you want to attend. Many people feel that they have to score at least a 160 to get into a "good" law school. That's pure myth. Remember: Any ABA-approved law school has to meet very strict standards in terms of its teaching staff, library, and facilities. Most schools use the Socratic method to teach students basic law. Therefore, a student's fundamental law school experience can be very similar no matter where he or she goes to school—be it NYU or Quinnipiac Law School. Read through Chapter 7 for a much more comprehensive discussion of "good" scores and where to go to law school.

## WHO'S RESPONSIBLE FOR THIS, ANYWAY?

The LSAT is brought to you by the wonderful folks at LSAC, based in Newtown, Pennsylvania. They work with the law schools and the ABA on many facets of the admissions process. You will register for the Credential Assembly Service (CAS), and that too is run by LSAC. See Chapter 7 for a full discussion of this alphabet soup.

## WHAT EXACTLY IS ON THE LSAT?

The LSAT is made up of five 35-minute multiple-choice sections and one 35-minute essay. Two of the five multiple-choice sections will be Logical Reasoning (Arguments), one will be Analytical Reasoning (Games), and one will be Reading Comprehension. The remaining section (which is almost always one of the first three to be administered) will be an experimental section that will not count toward your score. During this section you will do 35 minutes of unpaid work for LSAC, allowing them to test out new types of questions on a representative audience. This experimental section can be Arguments, Games, or Reading Comprehension. The Writing Sample, will not count toward your score either, though the schools you apply to will receive a scanned copy of it.

For instance, your LSAT could look as follows:

Section 1: Games (35 minutes)

Section 2: Experimental Reading Comprehension (35 minutes)

Section 3: Arguments (35 minutes)

10-minute break

Section 4: Reading Comprehension (35 minutes)

Section 5: Arguments (35 minutes)

35-minute Writing Sample

As you can see, it's nearly four hours of focused work. And because administrators check your ID and admissions ticket before the test begins, you can add another hour's worth of administrative mumbo-jumbo to that number. That's why we say that you should prepare very well for this test—so you only have to take it once.

### The Structure of an Arguments Section

There will be two scored Arguments sections, each lasting 35 minutes, on your LSAT. Each section has between 24 and 26 questions. Tests in the past frequently attached two questions to one argument, but LSAC has more or less phased out this style of question; you will almost certainly see one question per argument. Typically, the argument passages are no more than three or four sentences in length, but they can still be very dense and every word is potentially important, making critical reading the key skill on this section. The arguments are not arranged in strict order of difficulty, although the questions near the beginning of a section are generally easier than those at the end.

## The Structure of a Games Section

You will be given four "logic games" in a 35-minute section. Each game will have a setup and a set of conditions or clues that are attached to it. Then five to seven questions will ask you about various possible arrangements of the elements in the game. The four games are not arranged in order of difficulty.

## The Structure of a Reading Comprehension Section

In this 35-minute section, you will be given four reading comprehension passages, of about 60 to 80 lines each. Three of the passages will be written by one author; the fourth will be a combination of two shorter passages from two different sources discussing the same general subject. In each case, between five and eight questions will be attached to each passage. This is probably something you're familiar with from the SAT, the ACT, or any of the other myriad standardized tests you might have taken over the years. These passages are not arranged in any order of difficulty.

# WHAT DOES ALL THIS TEST?

According to the LSAC, "The LSAT is designed to measure skills that are considered essential for success in law school: the reading and comprehension of complex texts with accuracy and insight; the organization and management of information and the ability to draw reasonable inferences from it; the ability to think critically; and the analysis and evaluation of the reasoning and arguments of others." This means that the LSAT tests a few different things in order to measure your ability to think like a lawyer. The most important is your ability to read a passage or argument very closely and figure out what the author is and is not saying. On some questions, you'll have to figure out what the author is *implying*, and on others, what the author is *assuming to be true*. You'll find that the ability to read efficiently and identify the salient parts of a passage will be very useful on the test. Games test your ability to work with certain types of analytical reasoning, including conditional logic and logical deduction.

The schools all have access to your complete undergraduate transcript, your academic and professional recommendations, and your essays. They could also ask for some of your undergraduate papers if they wanted to. However, all this reading would take too much time and cost admissions offices too much money—hence, they've got a neat little shortcut in the form of the LSAT. When they combine this with your undergraduate GPA, they generate your index, a number that allows them to quickly sort your application into one of a few preliminary piles to make the process of evaluating the increasing number of applications more efficient.

The overriding point is that whatever it's testing, your goal is to do as well as possible on the LSAT and take it only once. That's exactly what we're going to show you how to do.

## GENERAL STRATEGIES

Following are several key things you should do when taking any multiple-choice test, especially the LSAT. Make sure you follow all of these mantras—they are the sum of more than 20 years' worth of our experience in researching and preparing hundreds of thousands of test takers to take the LSAT.

### Technique #1: Don't Rush

Most test takers believe that the key to success on the LSAT is to go faster. Realize, though, that your *accuracy*—your likelihood of getting a question right when you work it—is also a key factor in how well you perform. Generally speaking, the faster you work, the lower your accuracy will be. What this means is that there's a pacing "sweet spot" somewhere between working as fast as you can and working as carefully as you can. Practice on real LSAT sections is important, because you need to find the proper balance for yourself on each of the three section types.

Don't let the tight timing of the LSAT scare you into rushing. Most test takers do their best when they don't try to answer every question on every section.

On most LSAT questions, you'll find that you can eliminate two or three answer choices relatively easily. Some test takers simply pick the best-looking answer from the remaining ones and move on; this is poor strategy. It's only once you're down to two or three remaining choices that the real work on this test begins. Don't let the clock force you into bad decisions.

Your mantra: *I will fight the urge to rush and will work more deliberately, making choices about where to concentrate my energies so I can answer questions more accurately and end up with a higher score.*

### Technique #2: Fill in Every Bubble

Unlike some tests, the SAT for instance, the LSAT has no penalty for guessing, meaning that no points are subtracted for wrong answers. Therefore, even if you don't get to work on every question in a section, you want to make sure to fill in the rest of the bubbles before time is called. Even if you do only 75 percent of the test, you'll get an average of five more questions correct by picking a "letter of the day" and bubbling it in on the remaining 25 questions. Make sure you watch the time carefully. Just to be safe, assume the proctor will cut you off two minutes early, and stop yourself when five minutes remain to bubble in every remaining blank space in the section. Then, during the remaining minutes, you can change your answers on any questions you have time to work through.

This is a key concept that you should remember when you're taking the practice tests in the back of this book and when you're taking previously administered LSATs for practice. Some people want to wait until test day to bubble in questions they don't get to, thinking that they should see what their "real" score will be on practice tests.

However, if you bubble in questions you didn't get to on your practice tests, you *are* finding out what your "real" score would be. And this will ensure that you won't forget to do it on test day—bubbling in could be the difference between a 159 and a 161, for instance.

Your mantra: *I will always remember to bubble in answers for any questions I don't get to, thereby getting a higher score.*

## Technique #3: Use Process of Elimination

One solace (perhaps) on multiple-choice tests is the fact that all of the correct answers will be in front of you. Naturally, they will each be camouflaged by four incorrect answers, some of which will look just as good as, and often better than, the credited response. But the fact remains that if you can clear away some of that distraction, you'll be left staring at the credited response. Don't expect that the correct answers will just leap off the page at you. They won't. In fact, those choices that leap off the page at you are often very attractive *wrong* answers. Remember that the test writers have to be sure that they end up with a normal, curve when they administer the test. Making a wrong answer look very appealing (with a small, camouflaged flaw) is a great way to make sure that not everyone gets all the questions right.

Process of Elimination (POE) may be a very different test-taking strategy from what you are used to. If you look first at the answer choices critically, with an eye toward trying to see what's wrong with them, you'll do better on almost any standardized test than by always trying to find the right answer. This is because, given enough time and creativity, you can justify the correctness of any answer choice that you find appealing. That skill may be useful in certain situations, but on the LSAT, creativity of that sort is dangerous.

Your mantra: *I will always try to eliminate answer choices using Process of Elimination, thereby increasing my chances on each question and getting a higher score.*

## Technique #4: Be Prepared for Anything

You will be. Honest. You might not always feel that way, but you will be. True, you'll be nervous on test day, but a little nervousness is good because it can keep you focused. Just don't let this test psych you out. Remember that when you go into the test, you'll have worked through reams of LSAT problems and be a lot more prepared than all the other people who didn't put in the same amount of work you did. You'll have absorbed all the techniques we've given you, and you'll be wise to all the tricks and traps that the LSAT can throw at you.

Therefore, don't let anything get to you. If the room is too cold for you, you've brought along a sweater. If the room gets too warm, you've layered your clothing and can get comfortable. If the people sitting next to you are scratching away loudly or coughing nervously, you've practiced working in an environment with similar distractions and know how to tune them out and stay focused on the task at hand. If the proctor cuts your time short by a minute on one of the sections, you've already bubbled in the remaining choices with five minutes left. Relax and stay focused; you're prepared for anything.

No matter how prepared you are, it may happen that you lose focus temporarily. If you find yourself getting distracted or anxious, take a moment to focus and move on with confidence.

Your mantra: *I'm fully prepared to succeed. Nothing will distract me on test day. Nothing.*

## Technique #5: Practice Consistently, on Real LSATs

We've given you two full sample tests, plus explanations, to work through in the back of this book. Many Logical Reasoning and Analytical Reasoning questions that appear in this book are closely based on actual LSAT questions, with the permission of the Law School Admission Council. Unfortunately, that's just the tip of the iceberg. You should be ordering *at least* six recent real tests from LSAC (**www.lsac.org** or 215-968-1001), if not more. Here's a rough study plan for you, over a two-month period.

Week 1: Order at least six real LSATs (the most recent ones) from LSAC. Take one of the LSATs timed. Have a friend proctor the test for you so it's as legitimate as possible.

Week 2: Work through the Arguments chapter in this book; redo the Arguments questions from the test you took in week 1.

Week 3: Work through the Games chapter in this book; redo the games from the test you took in week 1. Take one of the two practice LSATs in the back of this book.

Week 4: Work through the Reading Comprehension chapter in this book; redo the reading comprehension passages from the test you took in week 1 and from the practice LSAT you took in week 3.

### Practice Material

If possible, order the 10 most recent real LSATs from LSAC—5 to take as full-length practice tests and 5 to use for timed section practice. If you're beginning the preparation process more than two months in advance, order more than 10 tests.

In addition to the questions in this book and the real LSATs you've purchased, you should also check out the material available to you free on our website (**PrincetonReview.com/cracking**). For practice with more complicated LSAT questions, pick up a copy of our *LSAT Workout*, or *LSAT Logic Games Workout*, which contain more practice drills and timed sections.

Week 5: Read through Chapter 6 in this book for pacing tips. Work untimed through one of the real LSATs you've ordered from LSAC; time yourself on another one.

Week 6: Review your mistakes in the work you did in week 5 and review the Arguments, Games, and Reading Comprehension chapters in this book. Work the specific problems again. Take the second test in this book.

Week 7: Work untimed through another real LSAT you've ordered from LSAC; time yourself on another one (this should be the fifth real LSAT you've looked at).

Week 8: Review all the general techniques in this book, and review any specific problems you might be having in Arguments, Games, and Reading Comprehension. Read the Writing Sample chapter in this book (Chapter 5). Take one more real LSAT timed (using a friend as a proctor again) and analyze your performance thoroughly.

If you follow this plan, you'll be well prepared for the LSAT when it comes around. Don't worry too much about your scores on any of these practice tests. Your performance on the real LSAT should be a bit higher than any of your practice tests if you've been working steadily; you should be taking the LSAT at the culmination of your studies, and if you follow the plan above, you will be. Never let more than one two days, pass without looking at LSAT problems once you've started this workout. You'll waste valuable study time relearning techniques that you would have remembered if you had been practicing steadily. The best athletes and musicians are the ones who practice all the time—follow their example and you'll be totally prepared for the LSAT on test day.

Your mantra: *I will work steadily and consistently to master the techniques in this manual by practicing them on real LSATs that I've ordered from LSAC.*

## Technique #6: Choose Your Battles

Not all questions on the LSAT are created equal, yet each is worth the same one raw point. Also, most test takers won't have enough time to finish all the questions and still maintain a high level of accuracy. Clearly, it is in your best interest to choose carefully which questions to work through and, even more important, which questions to skip if you don't have time for them all. By knowing the test and by knowing yourself, you will be able to make good *predictions* about which questions are your friends and which are your enemies before you start working on them; this will save you time, prevent frustration, and ultimately get you more points.

Your mantra: *I will fight my urge to work aimlessly through all of the questions in the order they are presented. Instead, I will make good decisions based on sound reasoning that will ultimately get me the most points.*

## Technique #7: Keep Your Pencil Moving

During almost any standardized test, you can find people who have just completely lost their concentration. Losing concentration can take different forms, but we've all experienced it—staring at the same question for too long, reading and rereading without really having anything sink in. Needless to say, you don't want to join this group of test zombies.

Using your pencil is a surprisingly easy way to stay focused and on task, and it can help to ensure that you're sticking with the method and visualizing information.

You should constantly be crossing out incorrect answers, circling the right answer before transferring the information to your bubble sheet, underlining and jotting down key pieces of information, taking notes, drawing diagrams, and so on. Don't let the test take *you*—take the test on your own terms; attack the test. Keeping your pencil involved in the process prevents you from getting passive and losing touch. Stay engaged, stay aggressive, and stay confident.

Your mantra: *I will use my pencil to stay engaged with the test and maximize my performance.*

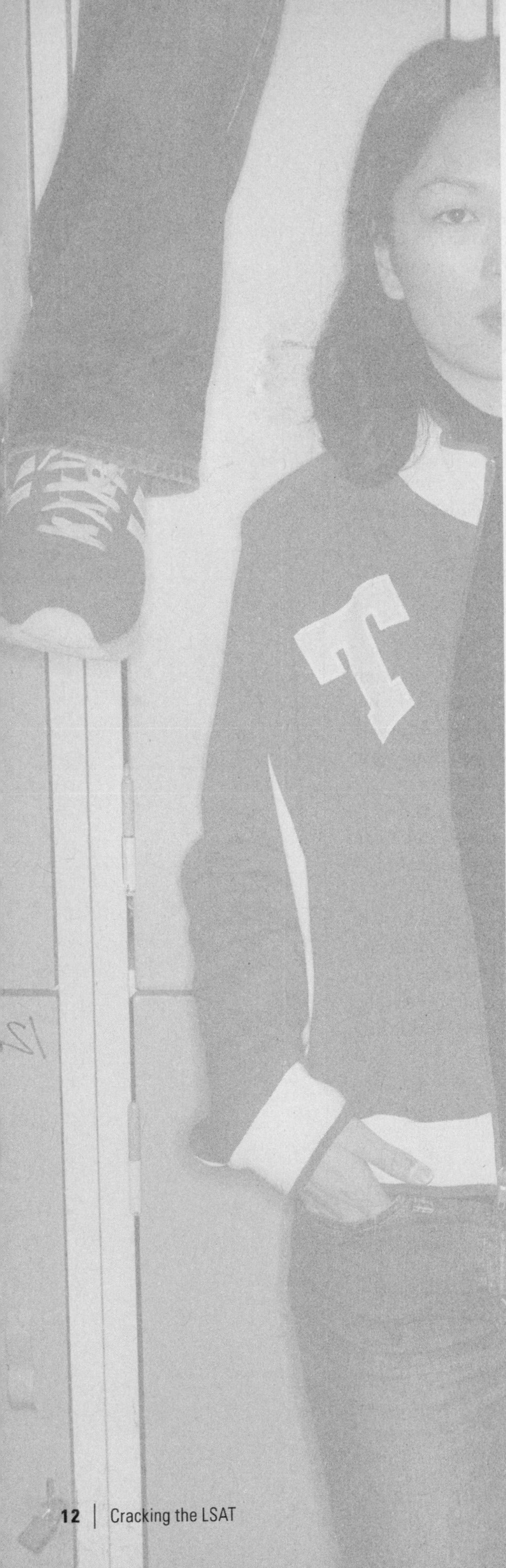

# Summary: General Strategies

Take the mantras from this chapter, learn them well, and—most importantly—use them. They are the distilled wisdom of much test-taking expertise. Here they are again.

- I will fight the urge to rush and will work more deliberately, making choices about where to concentrate my energies so I can answer questions more accurately and end up with a higher score.
- I will always remember to bubble in answers for any questions I don't get to, thereby getting a higher score.
- I will always try to eliminate answer choices using Process of Elimination, thereby increasing my chances on each question and getting a higher score.
- I'm fully prepared to succeed. Nothing will distract me on test day. Nothing.
- I will work steadily and consistently to master the techniques in this manual by practicing them on real LSATs that I've ordered from LSAC.
- I will fight my urge to work aimlessly through all of the questions in the order they are presented. Instead, I will make good decisions based on sound reasoning that will ultimately get me the most points.
- I will use my pencil to stay engaged with the test and maximize my performance.

Got 'em? Good. Now let's break the test down section by section.

# Chapter 2
# Arguments

For better or for worse, Arguments (logical reasoning, in LSAT-speak) questions make up half of the LSAT. For the past six years, there have been between 50 and 52 Arguments questions on the LSAT. The good news is that if you can substantially increase your Arguments performance, you will take a major step toward achieving the LSAT score you need. How do you go about improving your Arguments score? Well, let's get right to it.

## WHAT DOES THIS SECTION TEST?

The Arguments section of the LSAT tests a very useful skill: the ability to read closely and critically. It also tests your ability to break down an argument into parts, to identify flaws and methods of reasoning, and to find assumptions. Many arguments contain flaws that you have to identify to be able to get the correct answer. It's a minefield.

## WHY IS THIS SECTION ON THE LSAT?

Of all the sections on the test, this section relates the most to your future career as a lawyer. Evaluating an argument for its completeness, identifying assumptions, and making sound inferences are skills that will be useful to you in law school and beyond.

### Memorize the Instructions

If you took the advice in Chapter 1, you've already completed a real LSAT (preferably one from the last year or two), and you're familiar with the directions that appear at the start of each Arguments section. Here they are again.

> Directions: The questions in this section are based on the reasoning contained in brief statements or passages. For some questions, more than one of the choices could conceivably answer the question. However, you are to choose the best answer; that is, the response that most accurately and completely answers the question. You should not make assumptions that are by common sense standards implausible, superfluous, or incompatible with the passage. After you have chosen the best answer, blacken the corresponding space on your answer sheet.

When you're ready to take the real LSAT, you'll no longer need to read these directions—in fact, doing so would be a waste of time—but you can learn something from them. First, they tell you that the tasks you will be asked to perform will revolve around the reasoning used in each argument. They also indirectly tell you how important it is to stick only to the information presented on the page and not to consider any outside information. As for the part about picking the best answer, we'll get to that a little later on—first you'll learn how to simply and efficiently understand the reasoning of an LSAT argument.

## THE SECTION ITSELF

There are two scored Arguments sections on the LSAT. Each one will have between 24 and 26 questions, for a total of 48 to 52 Arguments questions. Some Arguments passages may be followed by two questions, although most Arguments passages, especially on recent tests, are followed by a single question. The fact that you are presented with 25 or so arguments to do in a 35-minute period indicates that the Arguments section is just as time intensive as the Games or Reading Comprehension sections.

## ARGUMENTS: STRATEGIES

The next few pages cover the general strategies you need to use during the Arguments sections of the LSAT. These pages contain a few simple rules that you must take to heart. We've taught hundreds of thousands of students how to work through arguments, and these strategies reflect some of the wisdom we have gained in the process.

## Always Read the Question First

Why should you read the question first? Because often the question will tell you what you should be looking for when you read the argument — whether it be the conclusion of the argument, a weak spot in the argument, how to diagram the argument, or something else. If you don't read the question until after you've read the argument, you'll often find that you need to read the argument *again*—wasting valuable time—after you learn what your task is. The question is a tip-off, so use it.

Your mantra: *I will always read the question first.*

## Pay Close Attention

Reading arguments too quickly is a recipe for disaster, even though they appear short and simple. Usually the arguments are merely three sentences, and the answer choices are just a sentence each. But their brevity can be deceptive because very often complex ideas are presented in these sentences. The answers often hinge on whether you've read each word correctly, especially words like *not*, *but*, or *some*. You should be reading as closely as if you were deconstructing Shakespeare, not as if you were reading the latest thriller on the beach. Slow down, and pay attention!

Your mantra: *I will slow down and read the arguments and answer choices carefully the first time.*

## Choose Your Battles

**Strategy**
Each question is worth the same number of points, so focus first on questions you can do without struggling.

What should you do if you read the first sentence of the argument and you don't understand what it's saying? Should you read sentence two? The answer is NO. Sentence two is not there to help you understand sentence one. Neither is sentence three. Neither are the answer choices—the answer choices exist to generate a bell curve, not to get you a 180. If you start reading an argument and you are confused, make sure you're focused and read the first sentence again more slowly. If this still doesn't help, skip that question. There are 24 to 26 arguments in the section—do another one! It doesn't matter which Arguments questions you work on, just that you do good work on those that you choose to do. Focus your time first on the questions you know you can get right. The LSAT rewards confidence, so it's important to maintain a confident mindset. Working through difficult questions when there are other, more manageable ones still available is not good form. Yes, you will feel as if you should finish the argument once you've invested the time to read part of it. But trust us; you'll benefit by leaving it. Remember: You can always come back to it later when there are no better opportunities to get points. Just mark the argument so you can find it if you have time later. Come back to it when it won't affect other questions that are more likely to yield points. After all, that's what you're after—points.

Your mantra: *If I don't understand the first sentence of an argument, I will skip to another argument that I do understand.*

## Transfer Your Answers in Groups

A classic question about standardized tests: Should I transfer my answers to the bubble sheet in groups, or transfer each answer after I've solved it? Our response: This section will have two or three arguments on the left-hand page and another two or three arguments on the right-hand page; work on all those questions and then transfer your answers before you turn the page. If you've left one blank, circle the argument you left blank on your test page, but bubble in an answer on your answer sheet anyway (remember: there's no guessing penalty). Why should you do this? Because if you don't have time to come back to it, you've still remembered to put an answer on your sheet (pick your favorite "letter of the day," and stick with it; there's no best letter, so just be consistent). And if you do have time to go back and work on arguments you skipped the first time around, you've got them handily marked in your test booklet; go back and change the answer (if necessary) for that question on the answer sheet.

Your mantra: *I will transfer my answers in groups, even bubbling in answers to questions that I'm skipping for the time being.*

## With Five Minutes Left, Transfer Answers One at a Time

When there are five minutes left, begin to transfer your answers one at a time. You can even skip ahead for a moment and bubble in your "letter of the day" for all the remaining questions. That way, if the proctor erroneously calls time before he or she is supposed to, or if you simply know you aren't going to finish in time, you've still got an answer on your sheet for every question.

Your mantra: *When five minutes are left, I will transfer answers one at a time and make sure I have bubbled in an answer to every remaining question.*

## Breathe

Please remember to do this! You will of course feel some anxiety, but this energy can actually be helpful, because it keeps your adrenaline pumping and can help keep you focused. So, don't get so stressed out that you lose the thread of reality. After finishing each two-page spread of arguments and transferring your answers, take 10 seconds, close your eyes, and inhale deeply three times. You'll invest only about a minute over the course of the entire section for these short breaks, but the payback will be enormous because they will help you to stay focused and to avoid careless errors. Trust us on this one.

Your mantra: *I will take a 10-second break after every five or six arguments.*

Here Are Your Arguments Mantras

*I will always read the question first.*

*I will slow down and read the arguments and answer choices carefully the first time.*

*If I don't understand the first sentence of an argument, I will skip to another argument that I do understand.*

*I will transfer my answers in groups, even bubbling in answers to questions that I'm skipping for the time being.*

*When five minutes are left, I will transfer answers one at a time and make sure I have bubbled in an answer to every remaining question.*

*I will take a 10-second break after every five or six arguments.*

## ARGUMENTS: HOW TO READ THEM

The first step in tackling LSAT arguments is to make sure you're thinking critically when you read. Maybe you've had a lot of practice reading critically (philosophy and literature majors, please stand up) or maybe you haven't. Perhaps you haven't been in an academic environment for a while and you're out of practice. The next few pages show you on what level you need to be reading arguments to be able to answer questions correctly.

### Argument Basics

So, what is an argument? When people hear the term *argument* they often think of a debate between two people, with each party trying to advance his or her own view. People often are emotionally invested in an argument, and thus arguments can become heated quickly. On the LSAT, it's crucial that you don't develop such an emotional response to the information.

Here's a definition of arguments that applies to the LSAT: "An argument is the *reasoned presentation* of *an idea* that is *supported by evidence* that is *assumed to be true*." Notice that we've italicized certain words for emphasis. We explain these phrases in detail below.

**Reasoned presentation:** The author of an LSAT argument has organized the information presented according to some kind of logical structure, however flawed the end result may be.

**An idea:** The conclusion of the author's argument is really nothing more than an idea. Just because it's on the LSAT doesn't mean it's valid. In fact, the only way to evaluate the validity of an author's conclusion is to examine the evidence in support of it and decide whether the author makes any leaps of logic between the evidence and his or her conclusion.

**Supported by evidence:** All of the arguments on the test in which an author is advancing a conclusion—there are a few exceptions to this, which we'll refer to as "passages" rather than "arguments"—have some kind of evidence presented in support of the author's conclusion.

**Assumed to be true:** On the LSAT, you are not allowed to question the validity of the *evidence* presented in support of a claim. In other words, you have to assume that whatever information the author presents as evidence is, in fact, true, even when the evidence includes arguable statements. You can question the validity of the *argument* by evaluating whether the evidence alone is able to support the conclusion without making a large leap.

> Arguments and Flaws
>
> Keep in mind that it is generally difficult to make an airtight case for a point of view if you have only three or four sentences in which to get that point across. Yet that's exactly the format of an argument on the LSAT. What can you take from that? The vast majority of the arguments you run across on this test are flawed in some way. That's a valuable thing to know because it reminds you to maintain a critical stance when evaluating these arguments. As you read an argument, always pay attention to *what* the author is trying to persuade you of, *how* the author is making the case, and *where* the author has lapsed in that attempt.

## Your Goal: Conclusions and Premises

Remember that arguments are constructed to persuade you of the author's idea. Thus you should always get a firm grasp on the argument's conclusion (whether or not you think it's valid) and how the arguer structured the evidence to reach that conclusion. If you understand the conclusion and the reasoning behind it, you've won half the battle because most of the questions in Arguments revolve around the hows and whys of the arguer's reasoning.

### Sample Argument #1

Let's start with something fairly simple. Although this argument is simple, its structure is similar to that of many real LSAT arguments that you will see. Here it is.

> Serena has to move to Kentucky. She lost the lease on her New York apartment, and her company is moving to Kentucky.

Okay, now what? You've got to make sure you understand the following things about this argument:

- the point that the author is trying to make (we'll call this the author's conclusion)
- the evidence or reasons the author presents in support of his or her argument (we'll refer to these as the author's premises)

If you are able to identify the conclusion and premises, you are well on your way to being able to tackle an LSAT question about the argument. After reading the argument again, try to identify the following elements:

- author's conclusion
- author's premises

**Careful!**
Though a great starting point, signal words can sometimes be a trap. Not all signal words introduce a conclusion.

**What's the author's conclusion?** When looking for the author's conclusion, try to figure out what the author is attempting to persuade us of. Ultimately, the author is trying to persuade you that Serena has to move to Kentucky. The rest of the information (about the lease and her company's move) is given in support of that conclusion. Often, the author's conclusion is signalled by words such as *thus*, *therefore*, or *so*, or is a recommendation, a prediction, or an explanation of the evidence presented.

**What if I didn't properly identify the author's conclusion?** Getting the author's conclusion and understanding the reasoning behind it is crucial to tackling an argument effectively and performing whatever task the question demands of you. But let's face it: Not every argument will be as simplistic as this one. It would be a good idea to have a technique to use when you aren't sure of an argument's conclusion. This technique is called the Why Test.

## The Why Test

The Why Test should be applied to verify that you have found the author's conclusion. Let's take the previous example and see how it works. If you had said that the author's conclusion was that she had lost her lease, the next step is to ask *Why did the author lose her lease?* There is absolutely no evidence in the argument to answer that question. Therefore, that statement can't be the author's conclusion.

Now, let's say that you had chosen the fact that the author's company was moving to Kentucky as the proper conclusion. You would ask *Why is the author's company moving to Kentucky?* Once again, the argument does not answer that question. But notice what happens when you use the Why Test on the author's conclusion: that she has to move to Kentucky. *Why does she have to move to Kentucky?* Now you have some answers: because she lost the lease on her New York apartment, and because her company is moving to Kentucky. In this case, the Why Test works perfectly. You have identified the author's conclusion.

**What are the author's premises?** So, why does the author think that Serena has to move to Kentucky? (1) She lost the lease on her apartment in New York, and (2) her company is relocating to Kentucky. Each of these is a premise in support of the conclusion. Now you know the author's conclusion and the premises behind it. This should be the first step you take in analyzing almost every argument on the LSAT. After taking a look at this argument, however, you might be thinking that Serena may not have thought this whole thing through. After all, couldn't she get another apartment in New York? And does she really have to stick with this company even though it's moving halfway across the country? If you're asking these kinds of questions, good! Hold onto those thoughts for another few minutes—we'll come back to these questions soon.

> Use the Why Test to determine whether you've properly identified the conclusion of the argument.

Later we'll see that this is an argument with a "causal" flaw.

## Sample Argument #2

Now let's take a look at another argument that deals with a slightly more complicated subject, one that's closer to what you'll see on the LSAT.

> The mayor of the town of Shasta sent a letter to the townspeople instructing them to burn less wood. A few weeks after the letter was delivered, there was a noticeable decrease in the amount of wood the townspeople of Shasta were burning on a daily basis. Therefore, it is obvious that the letter was successful in helping the mayor achieve his goal.

Now, let's identify the conclusion and premises in this argument.

**What's the author's conclusion?** The author is trying to persuade you that the letter was, in fact, the cause of the townspeople's burning less wood. Notice the phrase "it is obvious that," which indicates that a point is being made and that the point is debatable. Is there enough information preceding this statement to completely back it up? Can two short sentences persuade us that there is an "obvious" conclusion that you should come to when evaluating this information? Not if you're thinking about the issue critically and thinking about some of the other possible causes for this effect.

**What are the author's premises?** Use the Why Test here. If you've identified the right conclusion, asking "why" will provide the author's premises. *Why did the author conclude that the letter was successful in getting the townspeople of Shasta to burn less wood?* The author's premises are that the mayor sent a letter, and that the townspeople started burning less wood a few weeks later.

**What's missing?** Remember when we said that you need to be critical and ask questions? Well, here's your chance. Arguments on the LSAT are full of holes. Remember—it's difficult to make a solid, airtight case in just three sentences. Be skeptical and poke holes in this author's reasoning.

What do you think about the author's conclusion that the letter was responsible for helping the mayor achieve his or her goal? In evaluating the author's argument, you should start with his or her premises—they're the only facts that you have to go on. The mayor sends a letter to the townspeople, urging them to burn less wood, and a few weeks later, the townspeople start to burn less wood. (Remember that you have to accept these facts at face value. You have to accept that, for instance, there was in fact a noticeable decrease in the amount of wood being burned in Shasta.) Now, do you know *for certain* that the mayor's letter is what caused the decline in burning? Couldn't it have been something else? This author evidently doesn't think so— he or she thinks it's the letter and nothing else. You could probably come up with a hundred possible reasons that might explain why the residents of Shasta started to burn less wood, other than the mayor's letter. (For example, the price of firewood could have doubled right before the decline in burning.) But by asking these questions, you know the important thing—that this author *assumes* that there wasn't any other cause.

**What is an assumption?** An assumption, both in life and on the LSAT, is a leap of logic that we make to get from one piece of information to another. For instance, if you see a friend of yours wearing a yellow shirt and you conclude that your friend likes yellow, you would be making the following assumptions:

- Your friend isn't wearing the yellow shirt only as his or her work uniform.
- Your friend was not threatened by a madman who said that, unless he or she wore a yellow shirt for one month straight, his or her house would be burned to the ground.
- Your friend was not down to his or her last clean shirt, the one that he or she wears only when everything else needs to be washed.
- Your friend...

You get the point. You make these assumptions because you've seen a particular effect (in this case, your friend wearing a yellow shirt), and you think you've identified the proper cause (in this case, that your friend likes yellow and not that he or she is wearing a uniform or needs to do some laundry). Then, whether or not it's true, you *assume a connection* between the cause and the effect. You've made a leap of logic.

## Assumptions on the LSAT

The assumptions made in the arguments on the LSAT are also leaps of logic. Sometimes, the logic is so simple that it looks as if the author has actually stated it but really hasn't. The author's assumption is never explicitly stated in the passage. By definition, it is always unstated.

In LSAT terms, an assumption is an unstated premise that is required in order to make an argument's conclusion valid.

Go back to the wood-burning argument. Here, you have an observed effect: the townspeople of Shasta burning less wood. You have a possible cause: the mayor's letter. On the LSAT, the arguer will often try to make a direct connection between these two pieces of information—in this case, that the letter *caused* the wood-burning decrease.

However, as you've seen from the above example, you're also assuming the following:

- that the decrease in the burning of wood was not because of an increase in the price of wood
- that the town didn't experience unexpectedly warm temperatures, lessening the demand for wood as a heat source

- that the townspeople actually received and read the letter the mayor sent out
- that…

Once again, you get the point. The author actually made many assumptions when she made the leap of logic from the letter being sent and people burning less wood on one hand, and the conclusion that the letter was successful on the other hand. They all revolve around two basic assumptions: that the letter could have caused the decline in firewood use and that no other factor was the cause of the decline.

## This Is All Really Exciting, But…

You want to get to the answer choices, don't you? Well, we will—soon. But what has been the point of the last several pages? To show you how to read the argument itself in a critical way. This will help you immensely in evaluating the answer choices because you will already understand the author's conclusion and the premises on which it is based, and you'll also have spotted any potential problems with the argument. This means that many times you'll have the answer to the question in mind before you read any answer choices, and you can simply eliminate any that don't match.

The reason we want you to stop and think before going to the answer choices is that the answer choices are not there to help you get a good score on the LSAT. Four of the answer choices are going to be wrong, and their purpose is to distract you from the "best" answer choice. True, many times this "best" choice will merely be the least sketchy of five sketchy answer choices. Nonetheless, the more work you put into analyzing the argument before reading the choices, the better your chance of eliminating the four distracters and choosing the "credited response."

Why do we hammer this into you, anyway? Because you may or may not have had a lot of practice reading critically. You're not simply reading for pleasure, or reading the newspaper or a menu at a restaurant—here, you've got to focus your attention on these short paragraphs. Read LSAT arguments critically, as if you're reading a contract you're about to sign. Don't just casually glance over them so you can quickly get to the answer choices. You'll end up spending more time with the answer choices trying to determine the credited response if you don't have a solid understanding of the author's conclusion and how she got there. The single most important thing to read extremely carefully is the author's conclusion, whenever it is explicitly stated. Take the time to think critically about the argument, to break it down, and to be sure that you can paraphrase what the author is saying and articulate any flaws in his or her reasoning. Doing this will actually save you time by enabling you to evaluate the answer choices more quickly and efficiently.

## WORKING ARGUMENTS: A STEP-BY-STEP PROCESS

We have developed a four-step process for working LSAT arguments. It is a very simple process that will keep you on task and increase your odds of success if you follow it for every argument that you do. Here are the steps.

Step 1: Assess the question
Step 2: Analyze the argument
Step 3: Act
Step 4: Answer using Process of Elimination

Now let's look at these steps in more detail.

**Step 1: Assess the question** Sound familiar? This is one of your mantras. Reading the question first will tip you off about what you need to look for in the argument. Don't waste time reading the argument before you know how you will need to evaluate it for that particular question. If you don't know what your task is, you are unlikely to perform it effectively.

**Analyze**
Some question types don't require you to find the conclusion, premises, and flaws. We'll cover these types later in the chapter.

**Step 2: Analyze the argument** This is what we've been practicing for the last few pages. You've got to read the argument *critically*, looking for the author's conclusion and the evidence used to support it. When the author's conclusion is explicitly stated, mark it with a symbol that you use only for conclusions. If necessary, jot down short, simple paraphrases of the premises and any flaws you found in the argument.

To find flaws, you should keep your eyes open for any shifts in the author's language or gaps in the argument. Remember that the author's conclusion is reached using *only* the information on the page in front of you, so any gaps in the language or in the evidence indicate problems with the argument. You'll always want to be sure that you're reading critically and articulating the parts of the argument (both stated and unstated) in your own words. This will take a few extra seconds, but the investment will more than pay off by saving you loads of time in dealing with the answer choices.

**Step 3: Act** The particular strategy you'll use to answer a given question will be determined by the type of question being asked (one more reason to start by focusing on the question task). Each question task will have different criteria for what constitutes an acceptable answer. You'll want to think about that before going to the choices.

The test writers rely on the fact that the people who are taking the LSAT feel pressured to get through all the questions quickly. Many answer choices will seem appealing if you don't have a clear idea of what you're looking for before you start reading through them. The best way to keep yourself from falling into this trap is to predict what the right answer will say or do before you even look at the choices.

**Step 4: Answer using Process of Elimination** We first mentioned Process of Elimination (POE) in Chapter 1. It's a key to success on every section of the LSAT, especially Arguments and Reading Comprehension.

Process of Elimination

Most people look for the best answer and, in the process, end up falling for answer choices that are designed to look appealing but actually contain artfully concealed flaws. The part that looks good looks *really* good, and the little bit that's wrong blends right into the background if you're not reading carefully and critically. The "best" answer on a tricky question won't necessarily sound very good at all. That's why the question is difficult. But if you're keenly attuned to crossing out those choices with identifiable flaws, you'll be left with one that wasn't appealing, but *didn't have anything wrong with it.* And that's the winner because it's the "best" one of a group of flawed answers. If you can find a reason to cross off a choice, you've just improved your chances of getting the question right. So be aggressive about finding the flaws in answer choices that will allow you to eliminate them. At the same time, don't eliminate choices that you don't understand or that don't have a distinct problem.

## The Eleven Types of Arguments Questions

Almost every question in the Arguments section of the exam will fit into one of the following eleven categories: Main Point, Necessary Assumption, Sufficient Assumption, Weaken, Strengthen, Resolve/Explain, Inference, Reasoning, Flaw, Principle, and Parallel-the-Reasoning. Each of these types of questions has its own unique characteristics, which we'll cover in the following pages. At the end of each question type you'll find a chart summarizing the most important things to remember. The chart will be repeated in full at the end of the chapter for all eleven categories.

## So, Are You Ready?

We're finally going to give you an entire LSAT argument. First, we'll give you the whole argument, and you can approach it by using the process we just outlined. Then, you can compare your results against ours. Finally, after each Argument "lesson," we'll explain some extra techniques that you'll want to absorb. That way, by the end of Lesson 11, you'll know everything you need to answer any Argument question the LSAT might throw at you. This first lesson is about Main Point questions. Good luck!

## LESSON 1: MAIN POINT QUESTIONS

These questions are relatively rare, but because finding the main point is essential to answering most other Arguments questions correctly, it's a good place to start.

### The Argument

1. Editorialist: A growing number of ecologists have begun to recommend lifting the ban on the hunting of leopards, which are not an endangered species, and on the international trade of leopard skins. Why, then, do I continue to support the protection of leopards? For the same reason that I oppose the hunting of people. Admittedly, there are far too many human beings on this planet to qualify us for inclusion on the list of endangered species. Still, I doubt the same ecologists endorsing the resumption of leopard hunting would use that fact to recommend the hunting of human beings.

   Which of the following is the main point of the argument above?

   (A) The ban on leopard hunting should not be lifted.
   (B) Human beings are a species like any other animal and should be placed on the endangered species list.
   (C) Hunting of animals, whether or not they are an endangered species, should not be permitted.
   (D) Hunting of leopards, if they are not an endangered species, should not be regulated.
   (E) Ecologists cannot be trusted when emotional issues such as hunting are involved.

Here's How to Crack It

**Step 1: Assess the question** Did you remember to read the question before you started reading the argument? Here it is again.

> Which of the following is the main point of the argument above?

This question asks for the main point, or conclusion, of the argument. Now analyze the argument with the goal of identifying the author's conclusion.

**Assess**
Always read the question first.

**Hint:** Always mark the conclusion of an argument so that you can quickly refer back to it.

**Step 2: Analyze the argument** Read the argument. Read it slowly enough that you maintain a critical stance and identify the author's conclusion and premises. Here it is again.

> Editorialist: A growing number of ecologists have begun to recommend lifting the ban on the hunting of leopards, which are not an endangered species, and on the international trade of leopard skins. Why, then, do I continue to support the protection of leopards? For the same reason that I oppose the hunting of people. Admittedly, there are far too many human beings on this planet to qualify us for inclusion on the list of endangered species. Still, I doubt the same ecologists endorsing the resumption of leopard hunting would use that fact to recommend the hunting of human beings.

The argument is about hunting leopards. Keep in mind that you need to find only the conclusion and premises when you're working on a Main Point question. Finding assumptions won't help you, so don't waste precious time trying to figure them out. Here's what we found for the author's conclusion and premises.

- Author's conclusion: *Leopards should continue to be protected.*
- Author's premises: *One, because it would be like hunting human beings, and two, the fact that a species is not endangered is not a good enough reason to hunt it.*

If you had trouble identifying the conclusion, try thinking about why the author wrote this argument. The purpose of the argument is to disagree with someone else's conclusion—the ecologists' conclusion that the ban on leopard hunting should be lifted. Therefore, the conclusion is the opposite of the ecologists' conclusion. The purpose of an argument—whether it is intended to interpret facts, solve a problem, or disagree with a position—is intimately connected to the main point.

Remember to use the Why Test to check the author's conclusion if you're not sure. Let's go to Step 3.

**Step 3: Act** Now that you've broken down the argument and have all the pieces clear in your mind, it's time to make sure that you approach the answer choices knowing what it is that you've been asked to find. If you're not sure about exactly what you're supposed to be looking for, you will be much more likely to fall for one of the appealing answer choices designed to distract you from the credited response. Just to be sure you're ready for the next step, we said that the author's main point was that leopards should continue to be protected.

> The credited response to a Main Point question will articulate the author's conclusion.

**Step 4: Answer using Process of Elimination** Okay, now let's look at each of the answer choices. Your goal is to eliminate four of the choices by crossing out anything that doesn't match the paraphrase of the author's main point. If any part of it doesn't fit, the whole thing is wrong and you need to get rid of it.

(A) The ban on leopard hunting should not be lifted.

Does this sound like the author's conclusion? Yes. Keep it.

(B) Human beings are a species like any other animal and should be placed on the endangered species list.

Is this the author's conclusion? No, he or she never mentions anything about putting human beings on the endangered species list. In fact, he or she says that human beings are NOT an endangered species. Cross it off.

(C) Hunting of animals, whether or not they are an endangered species, should not be permitted.

This looks pretty good, except that it's too general. The argument is talking specifically about leopards. Cross it off.

(D) Hunting of leopards, if they are not an endangered species, should not be regulated.

Look carefully at the wording of this answer: it is actually the opposite of the main point. The editorialist argues that it should be regulated, even though leopards are not endangered. Cross it off.

(E) Ecologists cannot be trusted when emotional issues such as hunting are involved.

This choice has the same problem as (D). It doesn't talk about leopards at all, so once again it is not relevant. It's also a bit extreme given the tone of the passage. Cross it off. Well, it looks like you've got (A), the right answer here. Nice job!

## Arguments Technique: Use Process of Elimination

Let's go into a bit more depth with Process of Elimination. Answer choices (B), (C), (D), and (E) above all presented you with specific reasons for crossing them off. Following are ways in which you can analyze answer choices to see if you can eliminate them.

### Make Sure the Answer Is Relevant

LSAT arguments have very specific limits; the author of an argument stays within the argument's scope in reaching his conclusion. Anything else is not relevant. When you read an argument, you must pretend that you know only what is written on the page in front of you. Never assume anything else. Thus, any answer choice that is outside the scope of the argument can be eliminated. You did this for answer choices (B), (D), and (E) in the last example. Many times, answer choices will be so general that they are no longer relevant, like choice (C) in the example. Arguments are usually about specific things—such as leopards—as opposed to just "animals." The ultimate deciding factor about what is or is not within the scope of the argument is the *exact wording* of the conclusion.

**Careful!**
Think of extreme language as a red flag. You should always check it against what was specified in the passage before using it to eliminate an answer choice.

### Watch Out for Extreme Language

Pay attention to the wording of the answer choices. For some question types (most notably Main Point and Inference), extreme, absolute language (*never, must, exactly, cannot, always, only*) tends to be wrong, and choices with extreme language can often be eliminated. You saw this on choice (E) in the last example. Keep in mind, however, that an argument that uses strong language can support an *equally* strong answer choice. You should always note extreme language anywhere—in the passage, the question, or the answer choices—as it will frequently play an important role.

Arguments Technique:
Watch Out for the Word *Conclusion*

You'll notice that we've labeled these first questions "Main Point" questions. Your task on these questions is to determine the author's conclusion. You might be wondering why we don't just call them *conclusion* questions. Well, there is a method to our madness. You'll find that words such as "conclusion" or "concluded" may appear in other types of questions as well. You'll see this when we get to Lesson 7 on Inference questions.

### Beware of Opposites

Make sure that you are not choosing the exact *opposite* of the viewpoint asked for. Many times, this type of answer choice will look good because it's talking about the same subject matter as the correct answer; the trouble is that this answer choice presents an opposite viewpoint. For some question types, such as Weaken, Strengthen, and Main Point, one of the answer choices will almost always be an "opposite."

# Summary: Cracking Main Point Questions

Check out the chart below for some quick tips on Main Point questions. The left column of the chart shows some of the ways in which the LSAT folks will ask you to find the conclusion. The right column is a brief summary of the techniques you should use when approaching Main Point questions.

| Sample Question Phrasings | Act |
|---|---|
| *What is the author's main point?*<br><br>*The main conclusion drawn in the author's argument is that…*<br><br>*The argument is structured to lead to which one of the following conclusions?* | • Identify the conclusion and premises.<br><br>• Use the Why Test, and then match your conclusion against the five answer choices.<br><br>• Be careful not to fall for the opposite.<br><br>• When down to two choices, look for extreme wording and relevance to eliminate one choice. |

Understanding the purpose of an argument can help lead you to the main point.

## LESSON 2: NECESSARY ASSUMPTION QUESTIONS

Assumption questions ask you to pick the choice that fills a gap in the author's reasoning. A *necessary* assumption is something that the argument relies on but doesn't state—something that *needs* to be true in order for the argument to work.

### The Argument

2. Analyst: Television news programs have always discussed important social issues. While in the past such programs were primarily geared toward educating citizens about these issues, today the main focus in television news is on attracting larger audiences. Television viewers tend to prefer news programs that present views in agreement with their own. There can be little doubt, then, that at least some contemporary television news programs harm society by providing incomplete coverage of important social issues.

Which one of the following is an assumption on which the analyst's argument relies?

(A) At least some citizens of earlier eras were better educated about important social issues than are any viewers of contemporary television news programs.
(B) It is to society's advantage that citizens be exposed to some views of important social issues that they may not prefer to see presented in television news programs.
(C) Television news coverage of an important social issue is incomplete unless it devotes equal time to each widely held view about that issue.
(D) The factual accuracy of television news coverage of an important social issue is not the most important criterion to use in assessing its value to society.
(E) Television viewers exhibit the greatest preference for news programs that present only those views of important issues with which they agree.

#### Here's How to Crack It

**If Assumed**

Sometimes a question will ask you, "Which of the following, if assumed, allows the conclusion to be properly drawn?" This is a Sufficient Assumption question, not a Necessary Assumption question.

**Step 1: Assess the question** Here's the question again.

Which one of the following is an assumption on which the analyst's argument relies?

It includes not only the word *assumption*, but also the word *relies.* This sort of language—*relies on*, *depends on*, *requires*—is a sure sign of a Necessary Assumption question.

**Step 2: Analyze the argument** On a Necessary Assumption question, you analyze the argument by finding its conclusion and premises, as before. But there's something else you need to do. If possible, you need to find what's wrong with the argument before you go to the answer choices. Do this by maintaining a skeptical attitude and looking for differences in wording. Here's the argument again.

> Analyst: Television news programs have always discussed important social issues. While in the past such programs were primarily geared toward educating citizens about these issues, today the main focus in television news is on attracting larger audiences. Television viewers tend to prefer news programs that present views in agreement with their own. There can be little doubt, then, that at least some contemporary television news programs harm society by providing incomplete coverage of important social issues.

One thing to look for in any argument like this is a new idea or a judgment call in the conclusion. On the LSAT, you're always looking for whether the conclusion is *properly drawn* from the premises. If an important idea is missing from the premises, then that's a serious problem with the argument. Here's what we came up with.

- Author's conclusion: *Some news programs today harm society by giving incomplete coverage of important social issues.*
- Author's premises: *News programs today are focused on attracting audiences, not educating viewers; viewers tend to prefer news programs that present views that agree with their own.*
- Author's assumption: *Some news programs leave significant views out of their coverage in an effort to attract audiences; harm is done when members of society are exposed primarily to views that agree with their own.*

**Answer Choice Wording**

We've written assumptions in language that matches the tone of the LSAT for the purposes of this book, but you don't have to come up with anything that fancy while you're working under timed conditions. Just locate the potential problems with an argument and leave writing the answer choices to the LSAC

Where did we get our assumptions? By noticing that the key ideas "incomplete coverage" and "harm [to] society" are included in our conclusion but not anywhere else in the argument.

You may be looking at one or the other of the assumptions we found and asking, "Didn't they basically say that?" For example, look at our assumption hinging on the idea of "incomplete coverage." In the premises, we're told that news programs are looking to attract audiences and that audiences tend to prefer to hear views they agree with. Doesn't that tell you for certain that the coverage is going to be incomplete?

Not really. In fact, when you look at it closely, it is a pretty big jump. All we know is that people like to hear their own views covered; does that really mean that they *don't* want to see other views?

When you're looking for the problems in an argument, it's important not to give the argument the benefit of the doubt. Be skeptical, and examine the language of the conclusion very closely.

**Step 3: Act** Once you've found one or more problems with the argument, you're almost ready to go. Realize that an assumption will not only *help* the argument, usually by fixing one of the problems you've identified, but it will also be essential to the argument. Here, you want something that supplies the idea of "incomplete coverage" or "harm [to] society" or, if you get lucky, both.

> The credited response to a Necessary Assumption question will be a statement that is essential for the argument's conclusion to be valid.

**Step 4: Answer using Process of Elimination** Let's take the choices one at a time.

> (A) At least some citizens of earlier eras were better educated about important social issues than are any viewers of contemporary television news programs.

This one seems to go along with the argument more or less, but notice how demanding this choice is. It says that, in the past, there were citizens who were more educated about important social issues than *any* citizens are now. That language is too strong. An assumption is something the argument *needs*, but we don't want to pick a choice that's *more* than what the argument needs. This falls in that category; eliminate it.

> (B) It is to society's advantage that citizens be exposed to some views of important social issues that they may not prefer to see presented in television news programs.

One thing you can say about this choice is that it certainly doesn't have the problem we saw in choice (A). Notice how careful the language here is. We get "to society's advantage" (rather than "essential," say); "some views" (rather than all of them); "may not prefer to see" (instead of "wish to avoid," for example). Choice (B) also seems to go along with the argument. We can associate "society's advantage" with the opposite of "harm" in the conclusion, and the idea of what viewers prefer to see comes right out of the premises. Keep this one for now.

> (C) Television news coverage of an important social issue is incomplete unless it devotes equal time to each widely held view about that issue.

This one sounds good until you realize how demanding it is. Does every news program have to devote absolutely equal time to every widely held view? The argument doesn't need anything quite this strong. Eliminate it.

> (D) The factual accuracy of television news coverage of an important social issue is not the most important criterion to use in assessing its value to society.

Initially you might eliminate this one out of hand because it mentions "factual accuracy," an idea not contained in the argument. You need to restrain yourself for a moment, however. After all, if the argument's primary concern were to point out the factor that is most important in evaluating news coverage, then this answer choice would be relevant, even if factual accuracy were not mentioned as such. In other words, the relevance of the choice is determined by what the argument is trying to do—its *scope.*

To determine the exact scope of the argument, look at the conclusion. Is the argument primarily concerned with saying that completeness is the *most important* factor is assessing news coverage? No. You can now be certain that this choice isn't relevant and eliminate it.

> (E) Television viewers exhibit the greatest preference for news programs that present only those views of important issues with which they agree.

You probably recognize this as a much stronger rendition of one of the argument's premises. The word "only" as it is used here makes this choice so demanding that we should definitely eliminate it. Not only that, but you won't generally find assumptions that are simply one-offs of a premise. The premises are facts already; most of the time, they don't need any further support.

To check out the "Toughest Law Schools to Get Into," visit PrincetonReview.com

You're left with (B), which is the answer here. Notice that choice (B) isn't exactly what we came up with when we analyzed the argument; this is quite common on the LSAT. But we recognized that it related to a part of the conclusion that was problematic (the idea of "harm"), that it connected this idea back to the premises, and that it had the proper strength for this argument. Knowing where the potential problems in an argument are will help you recognize assumptions, even when they don't exactly match the assumptions you expected to find.

## Arguments Technique: How to Spot an Assumption

Finding an assumption can be one of the most difficult things to do on the LSAT. But as we said before, sometimes looking for a language shift between the conclusion and the premises will help you spot it. Let's look at an example of how this works. Consider the following argument:

> Ronald Reagan ate too many jelly beans. Therefore, he was a bad president.

All right. You probably already think you know the assumption here; it's pretty obvious. After all, how do you get from "too many jelly beans" to "bad president"? This argument just doesn't make any sense, and the reason it doesn't make sense is that there's no connection between eating a lot of jelly beans and being a bad president.

But now consider this argument:

> Ronald Reagan was responsible for creating a huge national debt. Therefore, he was a bad president.

Suppose you were a staunch Reagan supporter, and someone came up to you and made this argument. How would you respond? You'd probably say that the debt wasn't his fault, that it was caused by Congress, Jimmy Carter, or the policies of a previous administration. You would attack the premise of the argument rather than its assumption. But why? Well, because the assumption here might seem reasonable to you. Consider the following parts of the argument:

Conclusion: *Ronald Reagan was a bad president.*
Premise: *Ronald Reagan was responsible for creating a huge debt.*

As far as the LSAT is concerned, the assumption of this argument works in basically the same way as the assumption of the first version. Initially, we saw that the link from "ate too many jelly beans" to "bad president" was what the argument was missing. Here, what's missing is the link from "huge national debt" to "bad president." In the first case, the assumption stands out more because it seems ridiculous. It's important to understand, though, that your real-world beliefs about whether or not an assumption is good play no role in analyzing arguments on the LSAT. Even if you consider it reasonable to associate huge national debt with being a bad president, this is still the connection the argument needs to establish in order for its conclusion to be properly drawn. Of course, assumptions that you consider reasonable are more difficult to spot, because unless you pay very close attention, you may not even realize they're there.

It's also important to understand, as you analyze arguments, that there is a *big difference* between an assumption of the argument and its conclusion. The conclusions of the two arguments above are the same: "[Ronald Reagan] was a bad president." The conclusion of an argument is the single, well-defined thing that the author wants us to believe. Once you start thinking about *why* we should believe it, you're moving past the conclusion into the reasoning of the argument. In these two arguments, the premises are different; because assumptions most often connect one or more premises to the conclusion, the assumptions of these two arguments are different, even though their conclusions are the same.

Finally, don't make your life too difficult when you're analyzing an argument to find its assumptions. You don't need to write LSAT answer choices in order to have a good sense of what's wrong with an argument. In the national debt argument above, for example, it's enough to know what the argument does wrong: that it's missing the connection from "huge debt" to "bad president." Knowing that this is the link your answer will need to supply is plenty to get you ready to evaluate the answer choices.

## Arguments Technique: The Negation Test

We said before that a necessary assumption is something the argument *needs* in order for its conclusion to follow from the premises. We've described a number of ways to find necessary assumptions for yourself, but when you're doing Process of Elimination on Necessary Assumption questions, there is something you can do that will tell you for certain whether a particular fact is essential to an argument.

We call it the Negation Test.

**Careful!**
The Negation Test works only for Necessary Assumption questions. Sufficient Assumption questions, which we'll look at next, must be cracked differently.

> Negate the answer choice to see whether the conclusion remains intact. If the conclusion falls apart, then the choice is a valid assumption and thus the credited response.

Because a necessary assumption is required by the argument, all you have to do is suppose the choice you're looking at is *untrue*. If the choice is essential to the argument, then the argument should no longer work without it. It takes a bit of practice, but it's the strongest elimination technique there is for Necessary Assumption questions.

Try it with two choices from the first example in this lesson—the one about television news programs on page 30. If you need to, flip back to review the conclusion and premises of the argument. Then take a look at your answer.

(B) It is to society's advantage that citizens be exposed to some views of important social issues that they may not prefer to see presented in television news programs.

**Hint:**
If it's hard to tell where to throw in a NOT, simply say, "It's not true that…" followed by the answer choice.

To negate a choice, often all you have to do is negate the main verb. In this case, here's how it looks.

It is NOT to society's advantage that citizens be exposed to some views of important social issues that they may not prefer to see presented in television news programs.

What does this mean? It doesn't help society for people to be exposed to views different from their own. Supposing that this is true, how much sense does the argument make? Not much. After all, the whole point was that not getting a range of views is harmful to society.

Notice that the same method can be used to eliminate answers as well as confirm them. Take this other choice from the same question.

(D) The factual accuracy of television news coverage of an important social issue is not the most important criterion to use in assessing its value to society.

Negated, it looks like this

The factual accuracy of television news coverage of an important social issue IS the most important criterion to use in assessing its value to society.

Even if this is true, does that make the conclusion wrong? Not really. Even if accuracy is the most important criterion to use, that doesn't mean that other criteria are meaningless. The argument is concerned with proving that a particular aspect of news coverage is doing harm. It's quite possible that the statement above and the argument's conclusion are both right. In other words, negating this choice has no real effect on the argument, so it can't be a necessary assumption.

Certainly the Negation Test can be difficult to do in some cases. Negating (C) on the same question, for example, is quite a challenge. For this reason, the Negation Test shouldn't be a first-line elimination method for you. It can be quite helpful, however, in a case when you're down to two answer choices that both seem appealing, or as a final check before you settle on your answer. And if you make the effort to practice this technique on Necessary Assumption questions, you'll find that it gets easier to do.

Now let's try another Necessary Assumption question.

## The Argument

3. Car owner: My mechanic believes that my car's wheels must be out of alignment because the fact that the tires are underinflated cannot by itself account for the steering problems I've been having for the past several months. But because my gas mileage has been steady during the same time period, the alignment of my car's wheels must be normal.

Which one of the following is an assumption required by the car owner's argument?

(A) A drop in gas mileage occurs only if a car's wheels are out of alignment.
(B) Underinflated tires can cause a car's gas mileage to drop.
(C) A car's gas mileage varies less under test conditions than it does on the open road.
(D) Misaligned wheels can sometimes cause a change in a car's gas mileage.
(E) Underinflated tires and misaligned wheels cannot both cause steering problems.

### Here's How to Crack It

**Step 1: Assess the question** As always, read the question first. Here it is again.

> Which one of the following is an assumption required by the car owner's argument?

The words *assumption* and *required* tell you that this is a Necessary Assumption question. You know that you'll need to identify the conclusion and the premises and that you'll need to think about the gap in the author's logic.

**Don't Forget!**
Always mark the conclusion on all Necessary Assumption questions.

**Step 2: Analyze the argument** Read the argument. Identify the important components. Here it is again.

> Car owner: My mechanic believes that my car's wheels must be out of alignment because the fact that the tires are underinflated cannot by itself account for the steering problems I've been having for the past several months. But because my gas mileage has been steady during the same time period, the alignment of my car's wheels must be normal.

One common way that you'll see the conclusion phrased on the LSAT is as the opposite of someone else's opinion. (You saw this on the leopard question in the previous section.) You're told that the mechanic believes that the car's wheels are out of alignment. Notice, however, the word *but* at the beginning of the second sentence. This tells you that the author is about to disagree with the mechanic, and you can quickly identify the conclusion as the last line of the argument: "the alignment of my car's wheels must be normal."

What information is given to support this? Well, the author has been having steering problems, underinflated tires by themselves can't be the reason for those problems, and his gas mileage has been holding steady. If you notice that none of these premises mentions wheel alignment, you're on your way to finding the right answer.

- Author's conclusion: *The car's wheels aren't misaligned.*
- Author's premises: *Careful—don't confuse the car owner's premises with the mechanic's premises. The only premise the car owner (author) gives for the impossibility of misalignment is that his or her gas mileage hasn't changed.*
- Author's assumption: *It must link the premises to the conclusion, but you might be having a hard time articulating the idea clearly. Don't worry. That will happen frequently, especially on harder arguments. For now, let's just say it's an idea that relates gas mileage to alignment.*

**Step 3: Act** All you know for sure is that the right answer will have to link the conclusion and the premise together somehow. Use that as your first POE criterion and move to the answer choices.

**Step 4: Answer using Process of Elimination** Here we go.

> (A) A drop in gas mileage occurs only if a car's wheels are out of alignment.

Does this suggest a link between alignment and mileage? Yes, it does. Hold on to it.

> (B) Underinflated tires can cause a car's gas mileage to drop.

Does this suggest a link between alignment and mileage? No, it doesn't. In fact, alignment isn't mentioned at all. This links the car owner's premise with the premise from the mechanic's argument. Cross it off.

> (C) A car's gas mileage varies less under test conditions than it does on the open road.

Test conditions and the open road seem completely irrelevant, and this choice doesn't mention the conclusion at all. Cross it off.

> (D) Misaligned wheels can sometimes cause a change in a car's gas mileage.

This seems a lot like (A). It mentions both the premise and the conclusion. Hold on to it.

> (E) Underinflated tires and misaligned wheels cannot both cause steering problems.

This mentions the main topic of the argument, steering problems, as well as the misaligned wheels from the conclusion. Keep it, just in case.

## You're Down to Three This Time—Now What?

This will happen from time to time. You'll have to do some more thinking. Always reread the conclusion and the question before you compare the answer choices. Here they are again.

> Author's conclusion: *The car's wheels aren't misaligned.*
> Question: *Which one of the following is an assumption required by the car owner's argument?*

Let's start with (E), only because it's unlike the other two. Don't forget about negating answer choices—it's a useful technique. If you negate (E), it will read, "Underinflated tires and misaligned wheels *can* both cause steering problems." Remember that when you negate the correct answer, it should make the argument fall apart. Just because misaligned wheels (and underinflated tires) can both cause steering problems doesn't mean that they are absolutely causing the steering problems in this case. And it doesn't mention the issue of mileage, which is a crucial piece of the car owner's argument. If anything, this choice serves to address the *mechanic's* conclusion, but you want to focus on the *car owner's* conclusion. Cross it off.

How about (A)? Let's look at it more closely.

> (A) A drop in gas mileage occurs only if a car's wheels are out of alignment.

This says that if my mileage drops, then I know for sure that my wheels aren't aligned (because according to the answer choice, misaligned wheels are necessary for a drop in gas mileage to occur). Does this say anything about what I know if I *don't* get a drop in gas mileage? No, it doesn't. Because you care only about what's true if I don't get a drop in gas mileage (because that's the premise in the argument), you can eliminate this choice.

That leaves you with (D).

> (D) Misaligned wheels can sometimes cause a change in a car's gas mileage.

Try negating that one: Misaligned wheels can *never* cause a car's gas mileage to change. If it were true that misaligned wheels could never be the cause of a change in gas mileage, then how could the author cite steady gas mileage as proof that the wheels were aligned? He couldn't. Remember that we originally said the assumption had to relate mileage to alignment; by negating this choice, you effectively say that there is no relationship between the two. Having steady gas mileage, then, would not tell you anything about the alignment of the car's wheels. The negated version of answer choice (D) destroys the argument and is therefore the credited response to the argument.

**Tip:**
The negation of "sometimes" is "never."

# Summary: Cracking Necessary Assumption Questions

We've just covered a ton of information regarding Necessary Assumption questions. Remember that a necessary assumption is something that the argument *needs* in order for its conclusion to be correctly reached. For that reason, any answer you pick on a Necessary Assumption question should, at a bare minimum, help the author's argument. If you negate the right answer on a Necessary Assumption question, what you'll find is that the argument either disintegrates entirely, or the connection between the premises and the conclusion is severed. Finally, watch out for choices that are too strongly worded or overly specific; these types of choices may seem right to you at first, but they frequently go too far or insist upon too much.

**Careful!**
Questions that ask about an assumption that allows the argument to be "properly drawn" are NOT Necessary Assumption questions. They are Sufficient Assumption questions, which we will discuss next.

Below is a chart that summarizes Necessary Assumption questions.

| Sample Question Phrasings | Act |
|---|---|
| *Which of the following is an assumption on which the argument relies?*<br><br>*The argument above assumes which of the following?*<br><br>*The writer's argument depends on which of the following?* | • Identify the conclusion, premises, and assumptions of the author.<br><br>• If you are having trouble finding assumption, look for a gap between two different ideas in the argument.<br><br>• The assumption will always at least mildly strengthen the author's conclusion and is NECESSARY for the conclusion to follow from the information provided.<br><br>• When down to two choices, negate each statement to see if the argument falls apart. If it does, that's your answer. |

## LESSON 3: SUFFICIENT ASSUMPTION QUESTIONS

Sufficient Assumption questions have a lot in common with the Necessary Assumption questions you just looked at it. Both ask you to identify the missing gap in the author's reasoning.

Sufficient Assumption questions, however, differ in that they aren't asking you for an assumption that is *required* by the argument; rather, they simply are asking you for an assumption, that, if true, would allow for the conclusion to follow.

Because of this, Sufficient Assumption questions will often have credited answers that are stronger, broader, or more far-reaching than credited responses on Necessary Assumption questions. Let's revisit Ronald Reagan to see why.

> Ronald Reagan ate too many jelly beans. Therefore, he was a bad president.

Now, when we originally analyzed this argument, we identified the huge assumption that the argument makes: namely, that eating a certain quantity of jelly beans reflects in some way upon one's skill at being leader of the free world.

This is a necessary assumption; if eating jelly beans didn't reflect at least *somewhat* upon Reagan's ability to be president, then this argument has no hope of proving its conclusion.

But what if the LSAT was willing to grant to you a premise that said that the number of jelly beans one eats is the *only* indicator of one's ability to preside? Would that do it for the argument? We don't *need* jelly beans to be the only factor, but if they were, would the conclusion follow logically? You bet it would.

Try the Negation Test though. If eating jelly beans wasn't the only indicator of Ronald Reagan's presidential prowess, would the argument fall to pieces? Not necessarily—you needed to know only that jelly beans have something to do with his abilities as a president.

This is what separates Sufficient Assumption questions from Necessary Assumption questions. The credited responses can be more extreme, and the Negation Test can't help us.

Let's look at an example closer to what you'll see on the LSAT.

## The Argument

4. Politician: The interstate highway system in Case County connects its three cities. The interstate connecting Bryantsville with Carptown has three more lanes than the interstate connecting Bryantsville with Alephtown. So clearly, Bryantsville has stronger economic ties to Carptown than it does to Alephtown.

The politician's argument follows logically if which one of the following is assumed?

(A) The roads connecting Bryantsville with Alephtown and Carptown are more developed than the roads connecting Bryantsville to any other town.
(B) Bryantsville doesn't have stronger economic ties to some city other than Carptown.
(C) Some other city doesn't have its strongest economic ties with Bryantsville.
(D) The interstate system in Case County is one of the best in the world.
(E) The number of lanes on an interstate connecting two cities is directly proportional to the degree of economic development between them.

### Here's How to Crack It

**Step 1: Assess the question** What makes this a Sufficient Assumption question? Here it is.

The politician's argument follows logically if which one of the following is assumed?

The word *assumed* can pretty reliably tell you that you're looking at an assumption question of some sort. Notice, however, that the test writers aren't asking you for an assumption on which the argument relies or depends, as they did with Necessary Assumption questions. Rather, they're giving you a hypothetical: If you plug this answer choice into the argument as a missing premise, would it be enough to get you to the conclusion?

**Step 2: Analyze the argument** Just as you did with Necessary Assumption questions, you'll start off by looking for the argument's conclusion and premises. Here's the argument one more time.

> Politician: The interstate highway system in Case County connects its three cities. The interstate connecting Bryantsville with Carptown has three more lanes than the interstate connecting Bryantsville with Alephtown. So clearly, Bryantsville has stronger economic ties to Carptown than it does to Alephtown.

And here's what our analysis reveals.

- Author's conclusion: *Bryantsville has stronger economic ties to Carptown than to Alephtown.*
- Author's premises: *Bryantsville has three more interstate lanes connecting it to Carptown than connect it to Alephtown.*
- Author's assumption: *There is some connection between the number of lanes connecting one town to another and the economic ties between them.*

**Step 3: Act** The good thing about Sufficient Assumption questions is that the correct responses don't introduce new information. Instead, they make the connection between the premises and the conclusion as strong as possible. Go ahead; make a wish for the answer choice that would do the best job of sealing the deal on the conclusion, and you're likely to find something similar in the answer choices.

In this case, there is a language shift between the number of lanes (discussed in the premises) and the strength of economic ties (discussed in the conclusion). You'd love to see an answer choice telling you that you can judge the strength of economic ties between two cities by the amount of lanes on the interstate between them. Keep your wish in mind as you go to the answer choices.

> The credited response to a Sufficient Assumption question will make an explicit connection between the premises and the conclusion—strong enough to prove the conclusion.

**Step 4: Answer using Process of Elimination** Now go to the answer choices, keeping in mind that your correct answer choice must prove the conclusion and will not bring in new information. Let's take a look.

(A) The roads connecting Bryantsville with Alephtown and Carptown are more developed than the roads connecting Bryantsville to any other town.

This would not tell us anything about the economic ties between the two cities. Also, this answer choice requires additional information about the roads connecting Bryantsville to towns other than Alephtown and Carptown, so this is a no-go.

(B) Bryantsville doesn't have stronger economic ties to some city other than Carptown.

This is not relevant to the argument, whose scope is limited to the comparative economic ties of Bryantsville with Carptown and Bryantsville with Alephtown.

(C) Some other city doesn't have its strongest economic ties with Bryantsville.

Like choice (B), this is not relevant to the argument. It brings in new information you simply don't care about.

(D) The interstate system in Case County is one of the best in the world.

Again, this does not tell you anything about how the roads relate to economic ties.

(E) The number of lanes on an interstate connecting two cities is directly proportional to the degree of economic development between them.

Aha! This is exactly what you need. If you add this to the premises, the conclusion clearly follows directly from the premises. It is the missing link, shoring up the gap between the language of the premises and the language of the conclusion.

# Summary: Cracking Sufficient Assumption Questions

Sufficient Assumption questions always bring up ideas in the conclusion that are not discussed in the premises. The credited response will make an explicit connection between the two, positively sealing the deal on the conclusion. On more difficult Sufficient Assumption questions, you may see conditional statements or answer choices that seem very similar. Focus on proving the conclusion and making sure the answer choice goes in the right direction, eliminating answer choices that bring in new information that doesn't get you any closer to the conclusion. Look for the strongest answer.

| Sample Question Phrasings | Act |
|---|---|
| *Which one of the following, if assumed, would enable the conclusion to be properly drawn?*<br><br>*The conclusion follows logically if which one of the following is assumed?* | • Identify the conclusion, premises, and assumptions of the author.<br>• Look for language in the conclusion that is not accounted for in the premise.<br>• Paraphrase an answer that would strongly connect the premises to the conclusion and shore up the language gap.<br>• Eliminate answer choices that bring in new information. |

# LESSON 4: WEAKEN QUESTIONS

Weaken questions ask you to identify a fact that would work against the argument. Sometimes the answer you pick will directly contradict the conclusion; at other times, it will merely sever the connection between the premises and the conclusion, destroying the argument's reasoning. Either way, the right answer will exploit a gap in the argument.

## The Argument

5. Goiter is a disease of the thyroid gland that can be caused by an iodine deficiency. Although goiter was once relatively common in the United States, especially among the poor, it has become rare, due in part to the wide use of iodized table salt. Thus, although health professionals often counsel patients to avoid salt, it is clear that residents of the United States must consume at least some table salt in order to assure good health.

   Which one of the following, if true, would most seriously undermine the argument?

   (A) Excess salt consumption is a contributing factor in hypertension, which can lead to heart attack and stroke.
   (B) Factors other than the prevention of goiter are also crucial to maintaining good health.
   (C) Historically, goiter due to iodine deficiency was found only in people who consumed low quantities of iodine-rich foods such as fish and dairy products, which are now as easily available to all United States residents as iodized salt.
   (D) Goiter was only widespread in the United States before it was known that an iodine deficiency was responsible for the disorder.
   (E) It is nearly impossible for residents of the United States to avoid consuming at least some iodized salt, because it is almost universally used in processed, packaged, and prepared foods.

### Here's How to Crack It

**Step 1: Assess the question** Always go to the question first. Here it is.

> Which one of the following, if true, would most seriously undermine the argument?

The word *weaken* or one of its synonyms—*undermine, call into question, cast doubt upon*—is a clear indication of the kind of question you're facing here.

**Step 2: Analyze the argument** As usual, start by finding and marking the conclusion and the premises. And because the right answer on a Weaken question will often attack a conspicuous problem with the argument's reasoning, you also need to look for those flaws before you proceed. Here's the argument again.

> Goiter is a disease of the thyroid gland that can be caused by an iodine deficiency. Although goiter was once relatively common in the United States, especially among the poor, it has become rare due in part to the wide use of iodized table salt. Thus, although health professionals often counsel patients to avoid salt, it is clear that residents of the United States must consume at least some table salt in order to assure good health.

And here's what we came up with from our analysis.

- Author's conclusion: *U.S. residents must consume at least some salt in order to maintain good health.*
- Author's premises: *Goiter can be caused by an iodine deficiency; the wide use of iodized table salt has helped to virtually eliminate goiter in the United States.*
- Author's assumption: *Salt is the only possible way for U.S. residents to avoid iodine deficiency; preventing goiter is essential for maintaining good health.*

This second assumption—that avoiding goiter is necessary for maintaining good health—might fall under the heading of a "commonsense" assumption, to borrow a word from the directions on this section. That is, because goiter is described in the argument as "a disease," the link between that and health seems pretty solid. Your job when you work these questions is to identify *possible* problems, not to write the answer choices. When you notice a difference in language or a questionable interpretation of the facts, all you need to do is note it and realize that it might be significant.

**Step 3: Act** On a Weaken question, you won't usually be able to predict the exact content of the right answer. You know what's wrong with the argument, and the chances are that the right answer will exploit that flaw somehow. In this case, you anticipate that the answer choice you want will tell you how a U.S. resident might avoid goiter without having to consume any table salt.

> Remember that the premises must be accepted as true. The credited response to a Weaken question will give a reason why the author's conclusion might not be true, despite the true premises offered in support of the conclusion.

**Step 4: Answer using Process of Elimination** Keep your eyes on the prize; remember that what you want are things that work against the conclusion.

> (A) Excess salt consumption is a contributing factor in hypertension, which can lead to heart attack and stroke.

Broadly speaking, this works against the conclusion by showing a way salt consumption might be inimical to good health. Keep it for now.

> (B) Factors other than the prevention of goiter are also crucial to maintaining good health.

This does pertain to the new idea "good health" in the conclusion, and it does seem to be going against the argument in some way. But is it really an effective attack? Check the conclusion. It says that consuming table salt (to prevent goiter) is something that you have to do, but it never claims this is the *only* thing you have to do. The only real impact this choice has is to confirm that avoiding goiter really is necessary to good health. This certainly doesn't weaken, so eliminate it.

**POE Hint:**
Answer choices for question types that contain the words "if true" in the question stem sometimes bring in new information. If the new information is relevant, the fact that it's "new" is not a reason to eliminate it.

> (C) Historically, goiter due to iodine deficiency was found only in people who consumed low quantities of iodine-rich foods such as fish and dairy products, which are now as easily available to all United States residents as iodized salt.

You might initially be turned off by the mention of history, but what is this choice really telling us? That there's something else that is evidently effective at preventing goiter, and that this thing is just as widely available in the United States now as iodized salt is. That works against the conclusion, so keep it.

> (D) Goiter was only widespread in the United States before it was known that an iodine deficiency was responsible for the disorder.

This is nice to know, but it's difficult to see what effect this has on our conclusion about salt. Eliminate it.

> (E) It is nearly impossible for residents of the United States to avoid consuming at least some iodized salt, because it is almost universally used in processed, packaged, and prepared foods.

Even if this is true, it doesn't work against our conclusion. Whether it's possible to avoid iodized salt or not really has nothing to do with the question of whether we *need* to consume iodized salt to remain healthy. Eliminate this one.

You have two choices left, a circumstance you'll frequently encounter on the LSAT. How do you make up your mind?

## Arguments Technique: Look for Direct Impact

On Weaken questions, your task is to find the strongest attack on the conclusion. There might be more than one answer that seems to be working against the overall reasoning, so you need to go back, make sure you understand the conclusion fully, and then look for the one that has the most direct impact on it.

Things that can be important here are quantity words and the overall strength of language involved. Generally speaking, because you want a clear attack, you'll often see strong wording in the right answer. More important, you want to make sure that the answer we pick hits the conclusion squarely and doesn't just strike a glancing blow somewhere off to the side. Try comparing the impact of your two remaining choices in the previous example.

As a reminder, here's the argument's conclusion.

> Residents of the United States must consume at least some table salt in order to assure good health.

And here's choice (A).

> Excess salt consumption is a contributing factor in hypertension, which can lead to heart attack and stroke.

Does this really hurt the conclusion? Not once you focus your attention on the strength of language involved. The argument states only the relatively minimal conclusion that you need to consume "at least some table salt." Choice (A) talks about "excessive salt consumption." Are they really the same thing? No.

By contrast, here's choice (C).

> Historically, goiter due to iodine deficiency was found only in people who consumed low quantities of iodine-rich foods such as fish and dairy products, which are now as easily available to all United States residents as iodized salt.

Notice the strength of "only" here. It seems innocuous, but it's plenty to let us know that the lack of these iodine-rich foods was the real culprit in causing goiter related to iodine deficiencies. Now, though, these foods are "as easily available to all United States residents as iodized salt." That is, there's no benefit table salt offers—either in terms of efficacy or availability—that isn't also offered by these other foods. This is a direct attack and, thus, is the choice you want to pick.

When more than one answer choice seems to do the job, make sure you go back to the conclusion and look for the choice that attacks it most directly.

## Arguments Technique: Common Flaw Types

There are a few classic flaw types that show up repeatedly on the LSAT. It's helpful to become familiar with these so that you can more easily recognize the assumptions that are built into them.

### Causal Arguments

"Causal" is shorthand for cause and effect. A causal argument links an observed effect with a possible cause for that effect. A causal argument also assumes that there was no other cause for the observed effect.

Take a look at this simple causal argument

> Every time I walk my dog, it rains. Therefore, walking my dog must be the cause of the rain.

Causal Assumptions

- The stated possible cause is the ONLY cause.
- The causal relationship is NOT reversed.
- The two items are not merely correlated

Absurd, right? However, this is classic causality. You see the observed effect (it's raining), you see a possible cause (walking the dog), and then the author connects the two by saying that walking his dog caused the rain, thereby implying that nothing else caused it. So why are causal assumptions so popular on the LSAT? Because people often confuse *correlation* with *causality*. If you use shorthand for the possible cause (A) and the effect (B), you can see what the common assumptions are when working with a causal argument.

1. Something caused B—that is, B didn't occur by chance.
2. Nothing other than A could have caused B.
3. B did not cause A.

Of course, causal arguments on the LSAT won't be that absurd, but they'll have the same basic structure. The great thing about being able to identify causal arguments is that once you know where their potential weaknesses are, it becomes much easier to identify the credited response for both Weaken, Strengthen questions.

- On Necessary and Sufficient Assumption questions, the credited response will be a paraphrase of the causal assumption you've identified.
- For Weaken questions, the credited response will suggest an alternate cause for the observed effect.
- For Strengthen questions, the credited response will eliminate a possible alternate cause or give more evidence linking the stated possible cause with the stated effect.

## Sampling Arguments

Another popular type of Argument on the LSAT is the *sampling* or *statistical* argument. This assumes that a given statistic or sample is sufficient to justify a given conclusion or that an individual is representative of a group. Here's an example.

> In a group of 50 college students chosen from among those who receive athletic scholarships, more than 80 percent said in a recent survey that they read magazines daily. So it follows that advertisers who wish to reach a college-age audience should place ads in magazines.

What is being assumed here? That the students who were chosen are a representative sample of the college-age population. In this case, the students who are used as evidence are (a) college students and (b) recipients of athletic scholarships. That's a small subset of the population. The population the advertisers wish to reach is a "college-age" audience, a much broader group. In this case, there may be two ways in which the sample fails to represent the larger group. Those surveyed are college students while the target audience is "college-age." Can you assume that college students are representative of everyone who is college-age? If not, the argument has a problem. Further, even if you could accept college students as representative of college-age people in general, you would still have to believe that those college students who receive athletic scholarships are representative of all college students.

Sampling Assumptions

- A given statistic or sample is representative of the whole.
- The sampling was conducted correctly.

Whenever you see something about a group being used as evidence to conclude something about a larger population, remember that the argument's potential weakness is that the sample is skewed.

## Arguments by Analogy

A third type of common Argument type on the LSAT is argument *by analogy*. In this case the author assumes that a given group, idea, or action is logically similar to another group, idea, or action. Read the argument below.

Analogy Assumption

One group, idea, or action is the same as another, with respect to the terms of the argument.

> Overcrowding of rats in laboratory experiments has been shown to lead to aberrant behavior. So it follows that if people are placed in overcrowded situations, they will begin to exhibit aberrant behavior as well.

What is the potential weakness here? That, with respect to the conditions of the argument—here, overcrowding and aberrant behavior—people and rats might not be *analogous*. To weaken such an argument, you would need to find a relevant way in which the two things being compared are dissimilar.

## The Argument

6. A study was conducted to determine what impact, if any, last year's aggressive shark-fishing campaign had on the local seal population. Since the campaign began, the seal population has increased by 25 percent. Thus, the removal of large numbers of sharks from the ecosystem allowed the population of seals to increase.

   Which of the following, if true, most seriously weakens the argument?

   (A) A previously unidentified virus was responsible for the deaths of a large number of sharks in the same area in the last year.
   (B) Sharks prey on many species of fish as well as seals.
   (C) Excess bait used to lure the sharks provided the seals with a plentiful source of nutrition.
   (D) The shark-fishing campaign included many different shark species.
   (E) Reducing the shark population has a number of negative side effects on the ecosystem as a whole.

### Here's How to Crack It

**Step 1: Assess the question** This question might be familiar. Here it is again.

> Which of the following, if true, most seriously weakens the argument?

Clearly, you're out to weaken the argument.

**Step 2: Analyze the argument** Read the argument carefully. Identify the conclusion, the premises the author offers as evidence, and any assumptions he or she makes. Here's the body of the argument.

> A study was conducted to determine what impact, if any, last year's aggressive shark-fishing campaign had on the local seal population. Since the campaign began, the seal population has increased by 25 percent. Thus, the removal of large numbers of sharks from the ecosystem allowed the population of seals to increase.

Did you recognize this as a causal argument? The conclusion suggests that the decrease in the shark population caused the increase in the seal population. What evidence did the author use to back this up? Nothing more than the increase in population itself since the time the fishing began. This is a classic causal argument. The author wants you to believe that just because two things happened at the same time, one of them must have caused the other.

What are the automatic assumptions that an author makes in a causal argument? One is that the cause-and-effect relationship isn't reversed. In this case, that isn't very helpful. How could an increase in the seal population cause the shark population to go down? The second assumption is that nothing else caused the observed effect. In this case, that means the author is assuming that nothing else besides the decrease in the shark population caused the increase in the seal population.

Let's summarize:

- Author's conclusion: *Fewer sharks caused more seals.*
- Author's premises: *The seal population increased at the same time that the shark population decreased.*
- Author's assumption: *Nothing else caused the seal population to increase.*

**Step 3: Act** You're looking for an alternate cause, and there could be many of them. In fact, it's highly unlikely that you'll be able to predict the "right" one so you shouldn't even bother with predictions. In general, you're looking for a choice that suggests another reason the seal population increased.

**Step 4: Answer using Process of Elimination** Be careful here. Because you're looking for an alternate cause, the right answer might seem out of scope because it introduces new information that doesn't necessarily refer to something in the body of the argument. Let's look at them one by one.

> (A) A previously unidentified virus was responsible for the deaths of a large number of sharks in the same area in the last year.

This seems to give an alternate cause for the decrease in the number of sharks, not the increase in the number of seals. It's not quite what you're looking for, but leave it in for now.

> (B) Sharks prey on many species of fish as well as seals.

This is completely out of the scope of our argument, and it doesn't give a reason the seal population may have increased other than the removal of the sharks. Cross it out.

(C) Excess bait used to lure the sharks provided the seals with a plentiful source of nutrition.

This is what you need to be careful of. The choice seems irrelevant at first glance, but it does give another reason the seal population went up. If you accept this information as true, then you can conclude that it wasn't *necessarily* the absence of the sharks that caused the increase in the seal population. It could have been that the seals were getting more food. Weakening an argument doesn't require destroying it; casting doubt by providing an alternate explanation is all that's required of the credited response. This effectively weakens the argument.

(D) The shark-fishing campaign included many different shark species.

This is out of the scope of your argument. Get rid of it.

(E) Reducing the shark population has a number of negative side effects on the ecosystem as a whole.

This weakens the idea of the shark-fishing campaign in general, but that's not what our argument is about. Your argument is about the link between the removal of sharks and the seal population. Get rid of it.

You did leave (A) at first, but compared with (C), it's a bad answer because it provides an alternate cause for the premise, not for the conclusion.

# Summary: Cracking Weaken Questions

Remember these two key ideas when answering Weaken questions: The correct answer will probably attack one of the author's assumptions, and you should treat each answer choice as hypothetically true, looking for its direct negative impact on the conclusion. On more difficult Weaken questions, there will often be an appealing answer that, with just a little interpretation, looks right. The key is to avoid making any new assumptions when you try to determine the impact of an answer. Look for the *most direct* impact.

| Sample Question Phrasings | Act |
|---|---|
| *Which one of the following, if true, would most undermine the author's conclusion?*<br><br>*Which of the following statements, if true, would most call into question the results achieved by the scientists?* | • Identify the conclusion, premises, and assumptions of the author.<br><br>• Read critically, looking for instances in which the author made large leaps in logic.<br><br>• Then, when you go to the answer choices, look for a choice that has the most negative impact on that leap in logic.<br><br>• Assume all choices to be hypothetically true. |

## LESSON 5: STRENGTHEN QUESTIONS

Strengthen questions are the flipside of Weaken questions. Now what you're asked to do is pick a new fact that confirms the conclusion, or at the very least, helps the conclusion seem more likely. If there are problems with the argument, the answer here will most often address them.

## The Argument

_______________

7. In 1940 archaeologists in Costa Rica found a number of huge, human-made stone spheres of apparently ancient origin, but since then little has been learned about them. A primary reason for this is that, after 1940, the spheres became valued as decorations or status symbols, and most have since been moved. This is why the discovery of several spheres in a newly excavated burial site is so important. The same site included gold jewelry in a style that is not known to have existed earlier than 1000 A.D., leading some archaeologists to conclude that the stone spheres were still being made as recently as a thousand years ago.

   Which one of the following facts, if known, would most strongly support the conclusion of the archaeologists described in the argument?

   (A) Gold jewelry continued to be made in the style found at the burial site until at least 1600 A.D.

   (B) Although some accounts from the 1940s claim that lines of spheres were found pointing toward magnetic north, indicating that the spheres might have had a navigational purpose, all such arrangements were broken up by looters before these observations could be verified.

   (C) Archaeological evidence indicates that the spheres were in place before the burial structure in which they were found was erected around them.

   (D) The removal of important artifacts from archaeological sites is a common problem throughout the world and results in the loss of significant historical knowledge.

   (E) Other burial sites similar to the one newly excavated have been definitively dated to within the past thousand years and include depressions that indicate something heavy once stood there but has since been moved.

### Here's How to Crack It

**Step 1: Assess the question** As always, begin with the task at hand. Here it is.

> Which one of the following facts, if known, would most strongly support the conclusion of the archaeologists described in the argument?

Note the use of the word *support* here. This word and the word *strengthen* are the two most frequently seen clues that you're looking at in a Strengthen question. As you'll see later, however, it's important to make sure what's supporting what on a question like this. You're asked to pick the *answer* that supports the *argument*. This is the pattern you see in Strengthen questions.

**Step 2: Analyze the argument** Once you've identified the question, you know how much analysis you need to do. As with Weaken and Assumption questions, start off by finding the conclusion and the premises on which it is based. Then look for problems. Here's the argument for this question.

> In 1940 archaeologists in Costa Rica found a number of huge, human-made stone spheres of apparently ancient origin, but since then little has been learned about them. A primary reason for this is that, after 1940, the spheres became valued as decorations or status symbols, and most have since been moved. This is why the discovery of several spheres in a newly excavated burial site is so important. The same site included gold jewelry in a style that is not known to have existed earlier than 1000 A.D., leading some archaeologists to conclude that the stone spheres were still being made as recently as a thousand years ago.

And here's a quick analysis.

- Author's conclusion: *The stone spheres were still being made as recently as a thousand years ago.*
- Author's premises: *Spheres were found in a newly excavated burial site that also included jewelry of a type not known to have existed before a thousand years ago.*
- Author's assumption: *The age of the jewelry is a reliable indicator of the age of the stone spheres; current knowledge of when this type of jewelry was first made is accurate.*

**Step 3: Act** Having found some potential problems with the argument, you're halfway home. Chances are that you'll find an answer that fixes one or more of these problems. Failing that, you'll need to keep in mind that you're broadly looking for choices that go along with the author's conclusion. You're hoping for something that strengthens the association between the spheres and the jewelry, or else tells you that the jewelry really was made when the archaeologists think it was.

The credited response to a Strengthen question will provide information in support of the conclusion, or it will weaken an alternate interpretation of the premises.

**Step 4: Answer using Process of Elimination** Remember that you want something that helps the conclusion here.

(A) Gold jewelry continued to be made in the style found at the burial site until at least 1600 A.D.

All this choice tells you is when, at the latest, the jewelry might have been made. This doesn't really provide supporting information, because it's the *beginning* of the time when this jewelry was made that's being used to establish the age of the spheres. Eliminate this one.

(B) Although some accounts from the 1940s claim that lines of spheres were found pointing toward magnetic north, indicating that the spheres might have had a navigational purpose, all such arrangements were broken up by looters before these observations could be verified.

At best, what this does is support the explanation of why it has been difficult to determine when or why the spheres were made. This explanation isn't in need of any further support, however. It isn't essential to the argument, for one thing; for another, it's stated as evidence and thus is already established as fact. Eliminate this one.

(C) Archaeological evidence indicates that the spheres were in place before the burial structure in which they were found was erected around them.

**Careful!**

Watch out for Weaken answers on Strengthen questions, and vice versa.

Careful here! This one tells you that the spheres were in place before the burial structure was built. This suggests, at least, that the spheres might have been in place long before the burial, which would weaken the argument.

(D) The removal of important artifacts from archaeological sites is a common problem throughout the world and results in the loss of significant historical knowledge.

This is a very sad story, but it doesn't appear to have anything to do with dating the spheres, which after all is the point of our argument. Eliminate this one.

(E) Other burial sites similar to the one newly excavated have been definitively dated to within the past thousand years and include depressions that indicate something heavy once stood there but has since been moved.

This one sounds decent, doesn't it? There are similar cases where the date is certain and there are indications, at least, that spheres might have been there. Does this indicate for certain that the conclusion is correct? No. It's still possible that the spheres predate the burial sites. Is this exactly what you were looking for in the answer? No. There's no mention of the jewelry at all.

On the other hand, this choice does at least help the conclusion, even if it doesn't make it rock-solid. Because it presents the strongest and most direct support provided by any of the answer choices, this is the one to pick.

## Principle Strengthen

Another type of Strengthen question asks you to find a "Principle" to "justify" the argument. This time, instead of a specific fact or piece of evidence, the correct answer will be a general rule that will strengthen the argument as a whole. The answer may help the conclusion in an unexpected or rather extreme way, so don't shy away from answers that are strongly worded.

## The Argument

8. Because of his reckless spending, Scott is deeply in debt. Unless he can obtain five thousand dollars, he will be forced to declare bankruptcy this year. Even if he avoids bankruptcy this year, Scott will not be able to avoid it in future years unless he moderates his spending. Scott's cousin Juana has five thousand dollars she could give him without causing herself undue hardship. Nevertheless, Juana believes that she is not obligated to give her cousin Scott the money he needs to avoid bankruptcy.

   Which one of the following principles, if established, would most help to justify Juana's belief?

   (A) One person is not obligated to help another if that help would cause undue hardship to the person giving it.

   (B) One person is not obligated to help another unless there is no other foreseeable means by which the person requiring help could receive it.

   (C) One person is obligated to help another if there is reason to believe that receiving help now will prevent that person from requiring further help later.

(D) One person is obligated to help another only if the person's need for help is solely the result of the hostile actions of others.

(E) One person is obligated to help another even if the long-term efficacy of that help depends in part upon a change in the behavior of the person receiving it.

## Here's How to Crack It

**Assess**

There are two kinds of Principle questions. Some ask you to "justify," or strengthen the conclusion. Some ask for a principle that "conforms," or matches information (see Lesson 10). When the question asks you to justify a conclusion, be sure to find the conclusion and premises.

**Step 1: Assess the question** As always, look at the question first.

> Which one of the following principles, if established, would most help to justify Juana's belief?

Now you're looking to "justify"—basically, to strengthen—Juana's conclusion. Notice how the question also includes the proviso "if established," just as a Strengthen question would include "if true." These are very similar to Strengthen questions, except now your choices are going to be generally worded rules rather than specific facts.

**Step 2: Analyze the argument** Just as you would on a Strengthen question, analyze the argument by finding the conclusion (the judgment we're looking to justify) and the premises (the circumstances involved). You'll also want to see if you can find a conspicuous gap in the reasoning. Take a look at the argument.

> Because of his reckless spending, Scott is deeply in debt. Unless he can obtain five thousand dollars, he will be forced to declare bankruptcy this year. Even if he avoids bankruptcy this year, Scott will not be able to avoid it in future years unless he moderates his spending. Scott's cousin Juana has five thousand dollars she could give him without causing herself undue hardship. Nevertheless, Juana believes that she is not obligated to give her cousin Scott the money he needs to avoid bankruptcy.

Here's how to break it down:

Author's conclusion: *Juana is not obligated to give Scott the money he needs to avoid bankruptcy.*

Author's premises: *Scott is in financial trouble because of his reckless spending; if he receives the money needed to avoid bankruptcy this year, he'll be in the same trouble again unless he changes his ways.*

Author's assumption: *The fact that Scott brought the trouble on himself and/or the fact that there's a reasonable chance he will do so again means that Juana doesn't have to help him get out of trouble.*

Admittedly, the assumption stated above is a bit clunky. As with a Strengthen question, you want to identify the gaps on a Principle question like this one by understanding the premises and comparing them to the conclusion, but you may not be able to predict exactly how the right answer will fill those gaps.

**Step 3: Act** Broadly speaking, you're looking for an answer that supports Juana's decision that she isn't obligated to help Scott. The right answer will probably do this by focusing on one of the key premises: that it's his own fault that he's in trouble or that even if he's let off the hook this time, he has to make a change in his behavior to keep it from happening again.

**Step 4: Answer using Process of Elimination** All you can really do here is take each answer choice back to the argument and see whether it supports Juana's conclusion. The stronger the support, the better the answer choice, so don't shy away from a choice because it's strongly worded. In fact, strongly worded choices are often better in situations like this.

(A) One person is not obligated to help another if that help would cause undue hardship to the person giving it.

You're actually told that Juana could help Scott without causing herself undue hardship. Because this principle definitely doesn't apply to Juana's situation, you have to eliminate it.

(B) One person is not obligated to help another unless there is no other foreseeable means by which the person requiring help could receive it.

Although you're told that Juana could help, you don't know that Juana is the *only* potential source of help. At the same time, you don't know that Juana *isn't* the only potential source of help. In other words, you don't have enough information to know how you should apply this principle to the situation. Because its impact is uncertain, eliminate it.

(C) One person is obligated to help another if there is reason to believe that receiving help now will prevent that person from requiring further help later.

There are a host of problems with this choice. A big one is that you don't know how to apply this principle to our situation, because we don't know anything about what kind of further help Scott might need if he doesn't get the money now. Worse, there's absolutely no way that this principle could support the conclusion that Juana isn't obligated to help, because all it talks about is when she is obligated. Definitely eliminate this one.

(D) One person is obligated to help another only if the person's need for help is solely the result of the hostile actions of others.

Watch out! Your inclination here is probably to eliminate this choice because it includes "the hostile actions of others," which are not mentioned anywhere in the argument. This is one way a Principle question that asks you to justify can be tricky. Check out how this choice works.

### Understanding Principle Strengthen Questions

In Principle Strengthen questions, a principle that "justifies" the conclusion may legitimately help the conclusion using a method that's a little different from the one in the original argument. Make sure you know what kind of Principle question you are dealing with: Principle Strengthen question or Principle Match (page 96), which requires a somewhat different method.

It tells you that the only way Juana could ever be obligated to help Scott is if his trouble comes solely from others' hostile actions. You know that Scott doesn't fit this requirement; his trouble is at least in part the result of his own actions. Because he doesn't fit the minimum requirement for Juana being obligated to help him, you can then conclude for certain that Juana isn't obligated. In other words, this principle would provide full, unshakable support for Juana's belief. That makes it the answer you want.

You should consider (E) before you pick (D), however.

> (E) One person is obligated to help another even if the long-term efficacy of that help depends in part upon a change in the behavior of the person receiving it.

This one's pretty easy to eliminate. If you apply it to Juana's situation, it would tell you that she is obligated to help Scott. This is the opposite of the conclusion you wanted to support, so it's definitely not the right answer.

---

## What If I Can't Find an Assumption?

We've been talking quite a bit about what an important role the assumptions play in weakening or strengthening arguments on the LSAT. You may be asking yourself, "What am I supposed to do if I can't find an assumption?" Well, there's still hope. Finding assumptions is one of the trickier skills for many students to develop. Here are two ideas to keep in mind.

First, look for any shifts in the author's language. Any time the author makes a conclusion, evaluate that conclusion *only* on the basis of the evidence we're given in support of that conclusion. If there are any changes in language between the premises and the conclusion, these changes clue you into assumptions. This shift can be blatant, as when something that was never mentioned before suddenly shows up in the conclusion. Or it can be more subtle, such as if the author makes a statement that is more strongly qualified than the evidence. For instance, if you had evidence about what "almost always" is the case and concluded something that "will" happen, that would require a leap in logic.

Remember also that arguments have multiple assumptions. Even if you identify an assumption correctly, it might not be the "right" one (meaning it might not be the one the credited response hinges on).

What if you can't articulate an assumption, or you find the "wrong" one? Don't worry; there's *still* hope. As we've been saying, you should approach the answer choices armed with an assumption or at least an understanding of the gap between the conclusion and premises. This is because it's not necessary for you to be able to *generate* the assumption to find the best answer. You can also be prepared to *recognize* an assumption (or an answer that will impact it, in the case of Weaken and Strengthen questions). Sure, you might find that you can get through POE more quickly if you have an assumption neatly paraphrased in your head, but if you've at least identified any gaps in the argument, you'll be able to evaluate the answer choices and recognize the one that has the proper impact.

## Arguments Technique: What to Do When You're Down to Two

As you do more LSAT arguments, you may find yourself falling into a predictable pattern in which you find it easy to eliminate three of the answer choices but then have no clear idea of which one of the two remaining choices is correct. There's the first problem. You should know that it isn't your job to determine which is the *correct* answer. The trickiest incorrect answers on LSAT arguments are usually mostly right—they contain just a word or two that makes them wrong.

Very often these wrong answers will even sound better than the "credited response." The writers of the LSAT are experts at writing answers that are *almost* all correct, so if you spot anything that makes the choice wrong, eliminate it.

Now, what do you do when you get down to two choices? Well, you focus on finding something that makes one of them incorrect. There must be something appealing about each of them, or you would have eliminated one of them by now.

Here are a few steps to follow when you are down to two choices.

1. Identify how the answer choices are different.
2. Go back to the argument and reread, keeping the difference in mind. Use the difference that you've spotted to help you read the argument from a new, critical perspective. Try to find something in the language of the argument that points out a problem with one of the remaining two choices. Focus on the statement of the conclusion; this is very often what makes the final decision, especially if you didn't read it closely enough the first time.
3. Eliminate the choice with the flaw. Now that you've found the problem, cross off that choice and move on.

This process will work on any type of Argument question—and, for that matter, on Games and Reading Comprehension. Be critical and methodical, and you'll get results.

# Summary: Cracking Strengthen Questions

With Strengthen questions, you once again looked for what impact each of the answer choices had on the argument—only this time, a favorable impact. Focus on finding the flaws that allow you to eliminate the attractive wrong answers and leave you with the only choice that has a direct impact on the argument. Look at the chart below.

**Careful!**
Not all questions that use the word support are Strengthen questions. Strengthen questions ask you to support the argument's conclusion, but Inference questions ask you use the passage to support an answer choice.

| Sample Question Phrasings | Act |
|---|---|
| *Which one of the following statements, if true, would most support the author's conclusion?*<br><br>*Which of the following statements, if true, would strengthen the author's argument?*<br><br>*Which of the following principles, if established, justifies the actions taken by Mia in the argument above?* | • Identify the conclusion, premises, and assumptions of the author.<br>• Read critically, looking for where the author made large leaps in logic.<br>• Then, when you go to the answer choices, look for a choice that has the most positive impact on that gap.<br>• Assume all choices to be hypothetically true. |

# LESSON 6: RESOLVE/EXPLAIN QUESTIONS

So far, you've been working with arguments in which the author has presented evidence to support a conclusion. And with the exception of Main Point questions, you've been paying attention to any gaps in the argument that might help you to pinpoint the assumptions the author has made. The process for analyzing the argument (Step 2) has been almost identical for Main Point, Assumption, Weaken, and Strengthen question types.

Step 2 is a bit different in answering Resolve/Explain questions. That's because the "argument" attached to these questions is more like a passage. With these types of questions, the author will present a couple of pieces of information that don't seem to fit together. Your task will be to find the answer choice that will do the best job of *resolving* the apparent discrepancy between these two pieces of information and that will *explain* how both pieces of information could be true at once. The other steps remain the same; you just don't have the same pieces to break down that you've seen so far.

Look at a typical passage that would be used in asking a Resolve/Explain question.

> The ancient Dirdirs used water power for various purposes in the outlying cities and towns in their empire. However, they did not use this technology in their capital city of Avallone.

Your goal will be to spot an answer choice that resolves or explains the discrepancy or paradox.

Notice that there's no evidence provided to support a particular claim, just two pieces of information that don't really seem to fit with each other. Here you've got this ancient culture that has this certain type of technology but doesn't use it in the capital city. That's the discrepancy or paradox, right? Good. Your goal then will be to spot an answer choice that in some way resolves or explains that discrepancy or paradox. You might be able to think up a few reasons the Dirdirs had this technology and didn't use it, such as the following:

- There were no rivers or other bodies of water in or near Avallone.
- It was cheaper or more efficient to use another source of power in the capital, such as abundant labor.
- There was not enough space for the equipment in Avallone.

That's good for a start. You could actually come up with a multitude of theoretical reasons they didn't use this technology (the actual historical reason has something to do with the fact that it would have caused social unrest because this technology would have put too many people out of work), but the nice thing is that you don't have to! All you have to do is identify the discrepancy and be able to recognize the answer choice that allows both parts of the discrepancy to be true. That'll save you a lot of work and keep you from generating ideas that are far away from what the test writers were thinking when they wrote the question. Now you will put this idea to work on a full question.

## The Argument

9. A psychologist once performed the following experiment. Subjects were divided into two groups: excellent chess players and beginning chess players. Each group was exposed to a position arising from an actual game. Not surprisingly, when asked to reconstruct the position from memory an hour later, the expert chess players did much better than the beginners. On a board where the pieces were placed in a position at random, however, the expert players were no better able to reconstruct the position from memory than were the beginners.

   Which of the following best explains the result of the psychologist's experiment above?

   (A) Memory is an important part of chess-playing ability.
   (B) The beginning chess players as well as the experts were less able to memorize the random position than the "actual" position.
   (C) The ability to memorize varies with experience and ability.
   (D) Memory is a skill that can be improved with practice.
   (E) Being able to infer the causes of a situation plays an important role in memorization.

### Here's How to Crack It

**Step 1: Assess the question** Here it is again.

> Which of the following, if true, best explains the result of the psychologist's experiment above?

This question is once again tipping your hand—it's telling you that there is something you need to *explain*. That means that somewhere in the "argument" is a *discrepancy* or *paradox*, and you're going to have to find an answer choice that resolves these seemingly opposing facts.

**Step 2: Analyze the argument** Read through the argument, looking for any situations or facts that seem contrary to one another. Here it is again.

> A psychologist once performed the following experiment. Subjects were divided into two groups: excellent chess players and beginning chess players. Each group was exposed to a position arising from an actual game. Not surprisingly, when asked to reconstruct the position from memory an hour later, the expert chess players did much better than the beginners. On a board where the pieces were placed in a position at random, however, the expert players were no better able to reconstruct the position from memory than were the beginners.

**Analyze**
There's no need to find the conclusion and premises on Resolve/Explain questions.

What is the apparent paradox? On the one hand, when the pieces were arranged in a position that was part of a real game, the experts were much better at reconstructing the board. But in another scenario, where the pieces were randomly arranged, the beginners were just as good as the experts. How come the experts lost their edge when the pieces were randomly arranged?

In Resolve/Explain questions, all the answer choices are hypothetically true.

**Step 3: Act** Remember that there are probably a number of specific theories we could come up with to explain this discrepancy, and if one possible explanation jumps into your head, that's fine—it may turn out to be an answer choice. But fundamentally, you just need to be aware of the *discrepancy* and see what impact, if any, each of the answer choices will have on it.

> The credited response to a Resolve/Explain question will be a hypothetically true statement that explains how all aspects of the paradox or discrepancy can be true.

**Step 4: Answer using Process of Elimination** Just as with Weaken and Strengthen answer choices, you first have to accept each of the answer choices here as facts, and then apply them to the argument. One of these facts, when added to the argument, will resolve the apparent paradox, or explain the supposed discrepancy.

Let's see which one of the following choices does this.

(A) Memory is an important part of chess-playing ability.

That's right; it is. That's why the expert players were able to memorize the first situation better than the beginners were. However, it doesn't explain the second situation. The correct answer will have to help both parts of the argument make sense. Cross it out.

(B) The beginning chess players as well as the experts were less able to memorize the random position than the "actual" position.

This is interesting information, but it doesn't explain why the experts did just as poorly as the beginners did. Get rid of it.

(C) The ability to memorize varies with experience and ability.

This is like answer choice (A) in that it explains the first situation well, but it fails to provide an explanation for the second situation—where the experts did just as poorly as the beginners. Toss it.

(D) Memory is a skill that can be improved with practice.

Again, this is like answer choices (A) and (C). Certainly the experts have practiced more, which is why they're experts to begin with. However, it still doesn't provide an explanation for the second scenario. Cross it out.

(E) Being able to infer the causes of a situation plays an important role in memorization.

Aha! There is a link between memory and familiarity, i.e., "inferring the cause of a situation." The expert chess players were able to make sense of the position of the pieces in the first scenario, so they could memorize it more easily. However, there was nothing to help make sense of the second scenario. This is why, when presented with a random pattern of chess pieces, the experts didn't do any better than the beginners did.

## Arguments Technique: Using Process of Elimination with Resolve/Explain Questions

In using Process of Elimination (POE) with Resolve/Explain questions, it is important to remember that the correct answer will be some explanation that will allow *both* of the facts from the argument to be true. In the Dirdir argument, the two facts were (a) they had water power and (b) they did not use this technology in their capital city. In the chess argument, the facts were (a) the experts did better than the beginners at memorizing the positions of chess pieces from a previously played position and (b) the experts did not do any better at memorizing a set of pieces randomly placed on the board. The correct answer in each case allowed each of these facts to be true independently of the other and allowed both to make sense together.

Additionally, note that the phrasing of most Resolve/Explain questions contains the clause "if true." Your methodology should be exactly the same here as it is with Weaken and Strengthen questions—you assume each of the five answer choices to be hypothetically true and look for the impact of each one on the argument. In the case of Resolve/Explain questions, the impact will relate to whether or not or how well the choice resolves an apparent discrepancy.

# Summary: Cracking Resolve/Explain Questions

With Resolve/Explain questions, the only thing you must find before going to the answer choices is the apparent discrepancy or paradox. Remember that you have to work under the belief that the answers are true, regardless of how unreasonable they may seem. Evaluate what impact the answer choice would have on the argument *if it were true*. Finally, look to see which one of the answer choices allows both of the facts or sides of the argument to be true at the same time. Only one of them will do this.

| Sample Question Phrasings | Act |
|---|---|
| *Which one of the following provides the best resolution to the apparent paradox described by the committee member?*<br><br>*Which of the following statements, if true, would explain the discrepancy found by the scientists?* | • Identify the apparent discrepancy or paradox.<br><br>• Go to the answer choices and look for a piece of information that, when added to the argument, allows both facts from the argument to be true.<br><br>• Assume all choices to be hypothetically true. |

## LESSON 7: INFERENCE QUESTIONS

Like the arguments attached to Resolve/Explain questions, most Inference arguments are not written in the familiar *conclusion supported by premises* format. Instead, they will be passages that may or may not seem to be headed somewhere. And the test writers will ask you to find a piece of information that either must be true, based on the information provided in the argument, or will be best supported by the argument. That something can come from anywhere in the argument and doesn't have to come from anything important.

Here are a few tips right off the bat. You can't go beyond the boundaries of the argument, you don't have to find the conclusion, and you have to pay very close attention to any qualifying language (e.g., *most, always, each, few, might*) that is used. Ready to put this information to work? Then let's get to it.

### The Argument

10. Whenever Mega Motors develops a new car model, exactly 20 percent of the development budget is allocated to design costs. The larger the model, the higher the development budget for that model tends to be. For example, every new luxury car model developed by Mega Motors receives a development budget that is at least 50 percent higher than the development budget for any new compact car model that Mega Motors develops.

    If the statements above are true, then which one of the following must also be true?

    (A) If two new car models developed by Mega Motors receive development budgets that differ by 50 percent or more, then one of the new models must be a compact car, while the other must be a luxury car.

    (B) If any new car model developed by Mega Motors receives a development budget that is larger than the average development budget, then that car model must be of above-average size.

    (C) If Mega Motors develops two new compact car models and one new luxury car model in a given year, then the design costs allocated to the luxury car model must exceed those allocated to the two compact car models combined.

    (D) If Mega Motors develops a new midsize car model, then the development budget for that model must be greater than the development budget for any new compact car model but less than the development budget for any new luxury car model.

    (E) If Mega Motors develops both a new luxury car model and a new compact car model in the same year, then Mega Motors allocates more for the design costs of the luxury car than for the design costs of the compact car.

### Here's How to Crack It

**Step 1: Assess the question** Inference questions can be worded in several ways. Here's a common one.

> If the statements above are true, then which one of the following must also be true?

You're looking for something that's an absolutely 100 percent airtight logical consequence of the material presented in the argument, which as you can see in this case is more like a short descriptive passage.

**Step 2: Analyze the argument** Sometimes on Inference questions there isn't a lot of analysis you can do. Most often, these passages are not arguments, although they may take the form of a collection of premises that seem to be leading toward a conclusion. Sometimes there are parts of the passage on an Inference question that appear to be begging to be put together. Look at the passage again.

**Analyze**
Do not look for the conclusion and premises on Inference questions.

> Whenever Mega Motors develops a new car model, exactly 20 percent of the development budget is allocated to design costs. The larger the model, the higher the development budget for that model tends to be. For example, every new luxury car model developed by Mega Motors receives a development budget that is at least 50 percent higher than the development budget for any new compact car model that Mega Motors develops.

If you focus on the most strongly worded facts in this passage, you realize that we're looking at two things that definitely can be combined. Here they are, paraphrased.

- Fact 1: *20 percent of every car's development budget is spent on design costs.*
- Fact 2: *Every luxury car's development budget is at least 50 percent greater than the development budget of any compact car.*

When you notice something like this on an Inference question, it always pays to go ahead and combine the facts for yourself during the analysis step. It usually isn't too complicated.

- Conclusion: *The design costs for every luxury car are at least 50 percent greater than those for any compact car.*

**Step 3: Act** The conclusion above is very likely to figure into the right answer somehow, which is why you should bother to do it in the first place. In addition to this, you need to make sure you understand the passage well before moving on.

> The credited response to an Inference question is the statement best supported by the passage.

**Step 4: Answer using Process of Elimination** When looking for something like the conclusion on the previous page, look at the choices with an open mind. Combining facts is only one way to make inferences on the LSAT. Sometimes the test writers will make an inference by just taking a small logical step away from something said in the passage. Take each choice on its own merits.

(A) If two new car models developed by Mega Motors receive development budgets that differ by 50 percent or more, then one of the new models must be a compact car, while the other must be a luxury car.

The original passage tells you that every luxury car gets 50 percent more money than any compact car. This choice is trying to get you to go back in the other direction: Whenever there's a 50 percent difference, the two cars involved must be a luxury car and a compact car. But you certainly don't have complete information about all the models that Mega Motors might produce, or even how big the budget variation within each model size is. You simply can't make this inference; you don't have enough information, so eliminate the choice.

(B) If any new car model developed by Mega Motors receives a development budget that is larger than the average development budget, then that car model must be of above-average size.

This seems to go along with the passage's statement that the bigger the model, the bigger the budget tends to be. But check the difference in strength: In the passage, the verb *tends* leaves some substantial wiggle room. In this choice, however, the word *must* indicates a solid correlation. This choice is more specific and more demanding than our original. You should eliminate it.

(C) If Mega Motors develops two new compact car models and one new luxury car model in a given year, then the design costs allocated to the luxury car model must exceed those allocated to the two compact car models combined.

Careful! You're told that the luxury car gets at least 50 percent more money—not *twice* as much, which would be 100 percent more. This is definitely not a solid inference, so you should eliminate it.

(D) If Mega Motors develops a new midsize car model, then the development budget for that model must be greater than the development budget for any new compact car model but less than the development budget for any new luxury car model.

This brings up a new model size, which you know nothing about, and then tries to make some specific demands about the size of the model's budget. Do you have enough information to conclude this? Not at all, so eliminate it.

(E) If Mega Motors develops both a new luxury car model and a new compact car model in the same year, then Mega Motors allocates more for the design costs of the luxury car than for the design costs of the compact car.

Here, at last, is the conclusion we came up with in the first place. Notice that it doesn't take the same exact form as the prediction—that the luxury car gets at least 50 percent more design costs—but this choice is certainly a safe logical step away from our conclusion. This is the choice you want.

---

## Arguments Technique: Look for Extreme Language

Do you remember the Process of Elimination techniques used to cross off wrong answer choices in Main Point questions in Lesson 1? They included relevance, opposites, and extreme language. Relevance is still certainly an issue with Inference questions because if there is something in an answer choice that wasn't mentioned in the argument, there's no way you could have inferred it from the information presented. However, when it comes to Inference questions, extreme wording (as you saw in the previous example) plays a key role. It is much easier to say that something is *usually* true than to say that something is *always* true. You have to spend a lot more time backing up the second phrase. Take a look at another example.

1. Most literature professors are skilled readers.
2. All literature professors are skilled readers.

It's much easier to prove that something is usually true than it is to prove that something is always true.

There's only one difference between these two sentences: One has the word *most;* the other has the word *all.* Yet there is a vast difference between these two statements. Certainly, anyone who has reached such a high position has done more than her fair share of reading. Very rigorous standards must be met and outstanding academic performance must be demonstrated. This requires a ton of reading. It's reasonable to think that if someone's doing that much reading, he or she is probably a skilled reader. But if you were asked which of those statements *must be true,* you would have to eliminate the second statement. It would be incredibly difficult to prove that *all* literature professors are skilled readers. It would take only *one* person who never really liked to read, but was driven to this level of success for other reasons, to disprove the second statement. It would be much easier to prove the first statement because it leaves a lot more room for a few exceptions to the general rule. Both statements involve strong wording, but the second is *too* strong.

Take a look at the following chart:

| Safely Vague | | Dangerously Extreme | |
|---|---|---|---|
| might | possible | always | not |
| could | usually | never | positively |
| may | sometimes | at no time | absolutely |
| can | at least once | must | unequivocally |
| some | frequently | will | every |
| | | all | |

The sample Inference question you just worked through asked you to find the answer choice that could be "properly inferred," in other words, the one that *must be true* based on the information in the argument. Other Inference questions will require a slightly different task. Rather than finding the answer that must be true, you will be asked to find the one that would be best supported by the information in the argument. This may seem like a subtle difference, but it is important to pay attention to nuances in language such as this on the LSAT. Let's take a look at how these work.

## The Argument

11. Chinchillas raised in captivity who have not yet learned to feed on their own often stop squawking from hunger when the bottle used to feed them is brought into their view. Bringing in bottles of other sizes or colors has no similar effect.

    Which one of the following is most strongly supported by the information above?

    (A) Chinchillas raised in captivity learn to recognize the bottle used to feed them before they recognize any other objects.
    (B) Chinchillas more easily learn to recognize the bottle used to feed them than any bottles of other sizes or colors.
    (C) Chinchillas raised in captivity are able to connect the presence of their feeding bottle with a release from hunger.
    (D) The best way to stop chinchillas raised in captivity from squawking is to bring their feeding bottle into their visual field.
    (E) Chinchillas raised in captivity will feed only from the bottle that has been used to feed them in the past.

### Here's How to Crack It

**Step 1: Assess the question** Make sure that you're clear about your task. This question asks us to find the answer that is "most strongly supported" by the information in the passage. You don't have to be able to show that the answer *must be true* according to the information we have from the author. You still need evidence from the author's language, but it doesn't *have to be* true.

**Step 2: Analyze the argument** You still need to read the argument carefully. This step will be the same as it was with your first Inference question. Pay close attention to qualifying language, underlining key words and jotting down any notes you need to keep things straight. Here's the passage again.

> Chinchillas raised in captivity who have not yet learned to feed on their own often stop squawking from hunger when the bottle used to feed them is brought into their view. Bringing in bottles of other sizes or colors has no similar effect.

You're told that for a particular group one action causes a given response, but other similar actions don't yield the same response.

**Step 3: Act** Remember that on Inference questions, you can't predict with any assurance what the test writers will look for. Head right to the answer choices and start Step 4.

**Step 4: Answer using Process of Elimination** Check out each answer choice in turn and see which ones you can eliminate. Be on the lookout for answers that fall outside of the scope of the information that you've been given or are inconsistent with what you were told, answers that include extreme language, and answers that make unwarranted comparisons. If any part of an answer choice isn't supported, get rid of it. Here we go.

> (A) Chinchillas raised in captivity learn to recognize the bottle used to feed them before they recognize any other objects.

You have pretty good evidence that these chinchillas learn to recognize the bottle used to feed them, but do you have support for the idea that they recognize that bottle "before they recognize *any* other objects"? That's more than the passage can support, so get rid of it.

> (B) Chinchillas more easily learn to recognize the bottle used to feed them than any bottles of other sizes or colors.

Again, you have evidence that chinchillas learn to recognize at least some bottles, but can you say that they learn to recognize some "more easily" than any others? You don't have any evidence about how easy it is for them to learn recognition, so that's an unwarranted comparison. Cross it off.

(C) Chinchillas raised in captivity are able to connect the presence of their feeding bottle with a release from hunger.

The language in this one seems reasonable. When the hungry chinchillas see their feeding bottle, they temporarily stop squawking. It seems to support the idea that they make some connection between seeing this bottle and not being hungry anymore. This might be a bit of a stretch to prove beyond the shadow of a doubt from the argument, but because you have to find only the answer choice that is most strongly supported, so keep it for now.

(D) The best way to stop chinchillas raised in captivity from squawking is to bring their feeding bottle into their visual field.

You know that bringing the feeding bottle into sight leads to a temporary stop in the chinchillas' squawking, but is there any evidence to suggest that this is the "best" way to stop them from squawking? There could be a number of other ways to stop them from squawking, but you're not given any information about them, so you can't say that this is *the best* way to do it. Get rid of it.

(E) Chinchillas raised in captivity will feed only from the bottle that has been used to feed them in the past.

In this answer choice you have another one of those really strong words only his is another choice that goes further than the information you have to support it. You not given any information, one way or the other, about what sources these chinchillas will feed from. This one should be crossed off, too.

There you have it. You found (C), which is the credited response. Notice that you can't say *for sure* that the chinchilla can connect the presence of the feeding bottle with a release from hunger. Although there could be other explanations, this is a reasonable inference.

Basically, when you have this kind of weaker inference, you have a little bit more latitude. You still need evidence from the passage to support the choice, but you don't have to be able to show that an answer *must be true*.

## Arguments Technique: Watch Out for the Word *Support*

The word *support* shows up in two different types of Arguments questions and you'll need to be able to keep them straight if you hope to approach the questions effectively. Take a look at a couple of sample questions.

> Which one of the following, if true, provides the most support for the argument?

> The passage provides the most support for which one of the following?

If you're not careful, you might mistakenly think that these two questions ask you to perform the same task. After all, they both talk about support, right? Actually, you have two different tasks here, and if you get them mixed up you're going to have a difficult time with POE. Examine the first question more closely. Here it is again.

> Which one of the following, if true, provides the most support for the argument?

**Read Carefully!**

"The statements above, if true, provide the most support for which one of the following?" Notice that "if true" refers to "the statements above." Because these statements are being used to support one of the answer choices, this is an *Inference* question, not a *Strengthen* question.

This should look familiar. Care to guess what your task is here? If you identified this as a Strengthen question, bravo! There are two indicators that will help you to properly identify it. First, notice the phrase "if true," referring to "the following," and recall that it is the answers on Strengthen questions that are hypothetically true. Second, notice that you are being asked to find the answer choice that *provides the most support for* the argument. In other words, you're being asked to evaluate the impact that each answer choice has on the author's conclusion. Sound familiar? We hope so.

Here's the second question again.

> The passage provides the most support for which one of the following?

Notice the difference here. Aside from the obvious lack of the words *if true*, this question also asks for the support to happen, but *in the other direction*. Here you are asked to find the answer choice that *is best supported by* the passage. That's what you were just doing in the question you worked on a minute ago, so this is an Inference question.

Here, eliminate answers that aren't relevant because the passage doesn't offer enough evidence to support them, a pretty different mode of elimination from that used with Strengthen questions. The words *if true*, when referring to the choices, indicate hypotheticals in the answers, so it won't be an Inference question.

Two things to look for: If the *answer choices* are being used to support the *argument*, you have a Strengthen question. If the *passage* is being used to support one of the *answer choices*, you have an Inference question.

## Arguments Technique: Look for Conditional Statements and Find the Contrapositive

Do you know what an "if…then" statement is? If you've taken any classes in logic, you might know it as a "conditional statement." Actually, it's very simple. Read this sentence.

> If you hit a glass with a hammer, the glass will break.

When you run across a statement such as this, you can diagram it. A common way to diagram conditional statements is to use a symbol for each element in the statement—here we'll use "H" for hitting the glass with a hammer and "B" for breaking—and use an arrow to connect them, showing that the action leads directly to the effect. So H → B would represent the original statement.

This statement would seem reasonable to most people because it's what you would expect to happen in the real world. On the LSAT, you have to take this statement as true if it were part of an argument because, as we stated earlier, you have to accept all of the evidence presented in arguments at face value. This is true even when they aren't things that necessarily make reasonable sense.

With Inference questions, you are often asked to identify another statement—in the form of an answer choice—that also *must be true* if the statements in the argument are accepted as true.

Here's the original statement.

> If you hit a glass with a hammer, the glass will break.

You can come up with a few other statements that you think would also have to be true.

For example, you could say

> If the glass is broken, it was hit with a hammer.

### Conditional Statements: Sufficient and Necessary

Once you diagram a conditional statement, use the terms *sufficient* and *necessary* to describe the function of each side of the diagram.

The left side is the sufficient side because it is enough, on its own, to know something else (the right side).

The right side is the necessary side because it is a requirement of something else (the left side).

You can use these terms to take apart and diagram difficult sentences containing conditional language by asking yourself, "Which factor is enough to know something else?" or "Which factor seems to be a requirement of something else?"

You would symbolize this as B → H. That seems like a reasonable outcome, but can you say that it *must be true* given our original statement?

Not *necessarily*. The glass could have been thrown out the window, stepped on by a giraffe, shot up with a Red Rider BB gun, and so on. If this were an answer choice on an Inference question in which the argument contained our original statement, what would you do? Hopefully, you would cross it out because it doesn't have to be true. You could also suppose that

If you don't hit a glass with a hammer, the glass won't break.

In this case, your symbolization would become ~H → ~B. Once again this seems reasonable in many cases, but does it *have to be true*? Again, not necessarily. It could have been thrown out the window, run over by a car, shattered by an opera singer's high C note, and so on. If this were an answer choice on an Inference question in which the argument contained our original statement, what would you do? Hopefully, you would cross it out too because just like the last one, it doesn't have to be true.

How about this statement.

If the glass isn't broken, it wasn't hit with a hammer.

This would be symbolized as ~B → ~H. This *must* be true. It makes sense if you think about it because you know for sure that if you hit the glass with a hammer, you're definitely going to break the glass. So if you come across an unbroken glass, there's no way it could have been hit with a hammer, at least not if you accept the truth of the original statement the way we have to on the LSAT. The only way that you could argue the truth of the above statement is by arguing the truth of the original. And while you can do that in real life, you can't do it on the LSAT.

This statement, which must always be true given that the original statement is true, is known as the *contrapositive*.

To create the contrapositive of a statement, take the original statement (or its symbolization, which is easier to work with) and perform the following two steps: Flip the order of the statements and then negate each of them.

Here's how it works with our original.

H → B

Flip the order of the statements and negate each of them to get the contrapositive.

~B → ~H

Now, what do you do if you have to negate something that's already negative? Let's take a look at an example.

> If Pablo attends the dance, Christina won't attend the dance.

You can symbolize this as follows:

P → ~C

How do you negate ~C? Well, two negatives make a positive. When you negate a statement like "Christina won't attend the dance," it becomes "Christina will attend the dance." The contrapositive of your original statement is

C → ~P

With these examples, which are tied to real life and make reasonable sense, it might seem like it's more work to learn how to apply this process than it would be to just reason out what the only other true statement would be. And it would be pretty reasonable to do that if you understand the way conditionals and contrapositives work and if the original statement makes sense. If only the LSAT were always that straightforward.

Instead, what will often happen is the original statement will be some abstract and complicated notion that's hard to get a handle on. For instance, you might see a conditional statement such as "Copper will not be added to the alloy only if aluminum is also not added to the alloy." Not nearly as intuitive, is it? Add to that the pressure of taking a timed, standardized exam and you'll wish you had memorized the simple steps above.

These steps always work so it's worth having them at your disposal. We're telling you all this because sometimes arguments contain "if...then" statements like the ones above. Usually the LSAT writers then ask an Inference question that requires you to find the answer that *must be true*. A couple of the answer choices will seem like reasonable things to believe. Another one or two may be variations on the original conditional statement, but won't be valid contrapositives.

It's possible that the credited response may just actually be the contrapositive—that depends on how complicated the argument is and how many pieces of information the passage contains—but regardless, knowing how to derive the contrapositive will help you eliminate wrong choices. Having both the original and contrapositive statements makes it easier to see the difference between what is *definitely* true and what merely *could* be true.

## Arguments Technique: Look for Little Things That Mean a Lot

Another key to cracking Inference questions is to pay close attention to detail. Inferences are often made around seemingly innocuous words or phrases. For instance, any time you see a term of quantity, comparison, or frequency, odds are it contains an inference.

Statement: *Most people like Picasso.*

Inference: *Some people do not like Picasso.*

Statement: *Unlike her jacket, mine is real leather.*

Inference: *Her jacket is not real leather.*

Statement: *Russ almost never shows up on time.*

Inference: *Russ rarely (or occasionally) does show up on time.*

Keep an eye out for details, and you'll stand a better chance of getting Inference questions right.

# Summary: Cracking Inference Questions

With Inference questions, read the argument closely and pay close attention to details such as qualifying language. Once you're at the answer choices, your goal is to eliminate the four answer choices that *don't have to be true* or are not *wholly supported* by evidence provided in the argument. You're also going to look out for relevance and, especially, issues of extreme language.

The way that Inference questions are phrased can be very tricky. See the "Sample Question Phrasings" column in the chart below for some examples.

| Sample Question Phrasings | Act |
|---|---|
| *Which one of the following statements can be validly inferred from the information above?*<br><br>*If the statements above are true, then which of the following must also be true?*<br><br>*Which one of the following conclusions can be validly drawn from the passage above?**<br><br>*Which one of the following conclusions is best supported by the passage above?** | • Read carefully, paying close attention to qualifying language, and then go to the answer choices.<br><br>• Once there, cross off any answer choices that are not *directly* supported by evidence in the passage.<br><br>• Look for relevance and extreme language to eliminate answer choices.<br><br>• Use the contrapositive if there are "if…then" statements contained in the passage and in the answer choices. |

*Even though the stems in these questions contain the term "conclusions," they are not Main Point questions. Main Point questions ask you to find the conclusion, whereas Inference questions ask you for a conclusion, one of many that could possibly be derived from the passage. They are *Inference* questions, not *Main Point* questions. For contrast, review the sample Main Point question phrasings on page 29.

## LESSON 8: REASONING QUESTIONS

So far, the questions you've seen in the Arguments section have been concerned with the literal contents: What's the conclusion, how do you attack or support it, or what does it assume? What piece of information will resolve two seemingly inconsistent pieces of information, or what else do you know to be true if the statements in the argument are true? Now you're going to look at some questions that deal with the arguments on a more abstract or descriptive level.

The first of these is the Reasoning question task, which asks you to determine not what the argument is about, but how the argument is made. This sounds quite straightforward, doesn't it? Well, sometimes it will be, but sometimes it will be rather difficult because of very attractive incorrect answers and deliberately impenetrable vocabulary. The answers to Reasoning questions will fall into one of two categories: general answers that don't actually mention the subject matter of the argument, and specific answers that do address the subject matter of the argument. Occasionally, the answer choices will be a mix of both.

So how do you approach questions such as these? Well, first you have to be able to identify the task. Then your goal is to describe what's happening in the argument—in other words, how the author arrived at his or her conclusion. Give one a try.

### The Argument

12. Fortunately for the development of astronomy, observations of Mars were not exact in Kepler's time. If they had been, Kepler might not have "discovered" that the planets move in elliptical rather than circular orbits, and he would not have formulated his three laws of planetary motion. There are those who complain that the science of economics is inexact and that economic theories neglect certain details. That is their merit. Theories in economics, like those in astronomy, must be allowed some imprecision.

    In the passage above, the author reaches his or her conclusion by

    (A) finding an exception to a general rule
    (B) drawing an analogy
    (C) appealing to an authority
    (D) attributing an unknown cause to a known effect
    (E) using the word "theory" ambiguously

## Here's How to Crack It

**Step 1: Assess the question** You've read the question, but here it is again.

> In the passage above, the author reaches his conclusion by

This asks you to describe the author's method of reasoning. Read the argument and see how he or she gets from the evidence to his main point.

**Step 2: Analyze the argument** Read the argument closely, paying attention to the author's reasoning. To do this, you'll have to identify the conclusion and the premises because this will allow you to understand the structure of the argument—in other words, how the author used the evidence to support his or her conclusion. Here it is again.

> Fortunately for the development of astronomy, observations of Mars were not exact in Kepler's time. If they had been, Kepler might not have "discovered" that the planets move in elliptical rather than circular orbits, and he would not have formulated his three laws of planetary motion. There are those who complain that the science of economics is inexact and that economic theories neglect certain details. That is their merit. Theories in economics, like those in astronomy, must be allowed some imprecision.

**Analyze**
Find the conclusion and premises on Reasoning questions.

Make sure that you understand the pieces.

Author's conclusion: *Economic theories must be allowed some imprecision.*
Author's premises: *Look at Kepler's laws of planetary motion; their discovery was made possible by the imprecision in the observations of Mars in Kepler's time. And people complain about the inexact nature of economics.*

Notice that you didn't have to worry about identifying any assumptions for this type of question.

**Step 3: Act** Your goal here is simply to describe how the author made his argument. In this case, it looks as if the entire thing about Kepler is an analogy used to say that it's actually a good thing that economic theories are imprecise. This author made his argument by analogy, one of our common types of arguments.

> The credited response to a Reasoning question will describe how the author constructed the argument.

**Step 4: Answer using Process of Elimination** Now you're going to approach the answer choices. You can eliminate any answer choices that don't have to do with the author making an analogy. Check them out:

(A) finding an exception to a general rule

The author doesn't make an exception to any rule, so cross it off.

(B) drawing an analogy

Looks pretty good. Keep it.

(C) appealing to an authority

Who does the term authority apply to in the argument? The author doesn't look to any authority to justify his conclusion. Get rid of it.

(D) attributing an unknown cause to a known effect

Sounds impressive, but this argument isn't about cause and effect. It's about making an analogy. Eliminate it.

(E) using the word "theory" ambiguously

How is the word *theory* used ambiguously? It's used the same way in reference to both astronomy and economics. Cross it off.

---

That one was pretty straightforward. You were able to recognize the credited response pretty easily because you understood the author's reasoning—using an analogy—before you approached the answer choices. Note how abstract the answers were. They didn't mention any of the specifics (e.g., astronomy, theories, Kepler, and so on) but took a much broader view.

## Arguments Technique: Using Process of Elimination with Reasoning Questions

You may have noticed that when we discussed some of the answer choices, we took each word or phrase from the answer choice and asked, "Does this correspond to anything that actually occurred in the argument?" Most of the time, the answer to this question was no. The answer choices might sound abstract and technical, but unless you can go back to the argument and say, "Ah, yes, this is where the author gives the example and this is where he or she gives the counterexample," then an answer choice that mentions "examples" and "counterexamples" will be wrong. This technique is the key to dealing with Reasoning questions; it should allow you to eliminate two or three answer choices every time. One other nice advantage of this technique is that it works even if you can't articulate the author's reasoning in your own words.

**Hint:**
On Reasoning questions, try to match each piece of the answer choice to a piece of the argument.

Look through the answers on Reasoning questions slowly and make sure to match each piece of the answer choice to a piece of the argument. When you come across something in an answer choice that doesn't correspond to anything in the argument, get rid of that choice. If it's even a little wrong, it's all wrong.

# Summary: Cracking Reasoning Questions

In Reasoning questions, you'll want to come up with your own description of how the argument unfolds. If you're able to come up with a terse, exact description of the argument, you can usually match it with one of the answer choices. Even if you can't come up with a good description, you can eliminate any answers that have elements that don't correspond with what actually happens in the author's argument. The vocabulary in the answer choices will probably be more esoteric than that which you used, but as long as the meaning is the same, you're fine.

| Sample Question Phrasings | Act |
|---|---|
| *The argument proceeds by…*<br><br>*Leah responds to Kevin by doing which of the following?*<br><br>*The method the activist uses to object to the developer's argument is to…*<br><br>*Dr. Jacobs does which of the following?*<br><br>*Which one of the following most accurately describes the role played in the argument by the claim that...* | • Read the argument carefully and then describe what is happening in your own words, focusing on the author's conclusion and premises.<br><br>• Take this description and rigorously apply it to all the answer choices.<br><br>• Once you're at the answer choices, use the technique of comparing the actions described in the answer choices against those that actually occur in the argument.<br><br>• Cross out anything that doesn't appear in the argument. |

## LESSON 9: FLAW QUESTIONS

Flaw questions are similar to Reasoning questions, but they're dissimilar enough that they call for a slightly different approach. On recent LSATs, Flaw questions have been far more common than have Reasoning questions. So what's the difference? Well, while a Reasoning question asks you to identify what the argument does or how it's argued, a Flaw question asks you what the argument does *wrong*. And as we mentioned before, if you find a problematic assumption in an argument, you've probably found its flaw. The approach to Flaw and Reasoning questions is the same, but with one important distinction: During Step 2, you'll want to break down the argument into its parts and locate the assumption. After you've spotted the assumption, you just need to state what's wrong with the argument. Look at the Kepler argument again.

### The Argument

13. Fortunately for the development of astronomy, observations of Mars were not exact in Kepler's time. If they had been, Kepler might not have "discovered" that the planets move in elliptical rather than circular orbits, and he would not have formulated his three laws of planetary motion. There are those who complain that the science of economics is inexact and that economic theories neglect certain details. That is their merit. Theories in economics, like those in astronomy, must be allowed some imprecision.

Which one of the following most accurately describes a flaw in the argument?

(A) It fails to cite other authorities.
(B) It fails to consider nonscientific theories.
(C) It neglects the possibility that there may have been other reasons for Kepler's success.
(D) It presupposes the truth of the very position it is trying to prove.
(E) It ignores the differences between the sort of imprecision allowed in astronomy and that allowed in economics.

### Here's How to Crack It

**Step 1: Assess the question** You've already read the question, but here it is again.

> Which one of the following most accurately describes a flaw in the argument?

Now, you're expected to describe why the above argument is bad. Remember that this is different from "weakening" an argument, in which you'd hypothesize that the five answer choices were true. All you're looking for here is to describe the way in which the argument is bad, not add something that would make it worse.

**Step 2: Analyze the argument** Okay, so start by breaking it down into its parts.

Author's conclusion: *Economic theories must be allowed some imprecision.*
Author's premises: *Look at Kepler's laws of planetary motion; their discovery was made possible by the imprecision in the observations of Mars in Kepler's time. And people complain about the inexact nature of economics.*
Author's assumption: *With respect to the terms of the argument, theories of astronomy are analogous to theories of economics.*

**Step 3: Act** The correct answer to a Flaw question often draws attention to an assumption. If an assumption is that astronomy and economics are in some way similar, the *flaw* is the failure of the argument to demonstrate that similarity. The correct answer should draw attention to the fact that the two fields are not necessarily similar.

> The credited response to a Flaw question will describe how the premises don't necessarily lead to the conclusion, often drawing attention to a key assumption.

**Step 4: Answer using Process of Elimination** Now we're going to attack the answer choices. Let's see if we can find an answer choice that has something to do with the author making an analogy.

> (A) It fails to cite other authorities.

This is almost never the correct answer in a Flaw question. Although it may be true that the author doesn't cite other authorities, this isn't what makes the argument's logic problematic. Usually, the argument is wrong somehow internally, not because the author didn't bring in some expert. Cross it off.

(B) It fails to consider nonscientific theories.

True, but once again, so what? The author doesn't talk about nonscientific theories, but that omission has no bearing on whether the analogy is valid. Get rid of it.

(C) It neglects the possibility that there may have been other reasons for Kepler's success.

Aha. This means that Kepler might have been great for other reasons. However, you're not trying to weaken causality here; we just need to show how the analogy is weak. Cross it off.

(D) It presupposes the truth of the very position it is trying to prove.

An answer choice like this one can be a correct answer to a Flaw question, but only when the argument is circular—when the conclusion just restates one of the premises. That's not the case here; the author is drawing an analogy. Cross it off.

(E) It ignores the differences between the sort of imprecision allowed in astronomy and that allowed in economics.

This is true: The author doesn't prove that these two fields can be legitimately compared in terms of imprecision, so it's possible there are differences between them that the author has overlooked. Therefore, the analogy between astronomy and economics isn't very good, and you'd have to pick this one as your answer.

---

You know that Flaw questions deal with gaps or assumptions in an argument. You also know that they're pretty similar to Reasoning questions and that they can exhibit similar "traps" (such as overly wordy or confusing answers). Finally, you can use similar POE techniques on Flaw questions, such as trying to match each word or phrase in the answer choices with something in the argument.

Try another one.

### Arguments Technique: Using Process of Elimination with Flaw Questions

One thing you might have noticed that we did when discussing some of the answer choices was again to take each word or phrase from the answer choice and ask, "Does this correspond to anything that actually occurred in the argument?" Most of the time, the answer is no. The answer choices might sound impressive ("the author assumes what he sets out to prove," "the author appeals to authority," and so on), but unless you can go back to the argument and say, "Ah, yes, *this* is where the author gives evidence" or "*this* is where the author makes a prediction," then an answer choice that mentions "examples" or "predictions" will be wrong. This technique is HUGE. It will eliminate two or three answer choices every time.

Therefore, take answer choices on Flaw questions very slowly, and make sure to match each piece of the answer choice to a piece of the argument. Once you come across something in an answer choice that doesn't correspond to anything in the argument, you can get rid of that answer choice. Once it's a little wrong, it's all wrong.

This process will allow you to eliminate two or three answer choices in most cases, but what about the ones that remain? You'll find that some of the answer choices on Flaw questions will be consistent with the argument but won't represent a flaw in the author's reasoning. Once you've eliminated any answer choices on Flaw questions that are not consistent with what actually happened in the argument, then go back to check the rest to see if they represent a logical flaw in the structure of the author's argument.

## The Argument

14. Expert musicologists believe that Beethoven wrote his last piano sonata in 1824, three years before his death. However, the manuscript of a piano sonata was recently discovered that bears Beethoven's name and dates from 1825. Clearly, the experts are mistaken because not every piece that Beethoven wrote was cataloged in his lifetime, and it is known that Beethoven continued to compose until just weeks before his death.

    The reasoning in the argument is most vulnerable to which of the following criticisms?

    (A) A given position that is widely believed to be true is taken to show that the position in question must, in fact, be true.
    (B) That either of two things could have occurred independently is taken to show that those two things could not have occurred simultaneously.
    (C) Establishing that a certain event occurred is confused with having established the cause of that event.
    (D) A claim that has a very general application is based entirely on evidence from a narrowly restricted range of cases.
    (E) An inconsistency that, as presented, has more than one possible resolution is treated as though only one resolution is possible.

### Here's How to Crack It

**Step 1: Assess the question** Here's the question again.

> The reasoning in the argument is most vulnerable to which of the following criticisms?

This is a classic Flaw question. You're asked to describe what's wrong with the author's reasoning.

**Step 2: Analyze the argument** Again, you're reading for the conclusion and the premises, and you should think about assumptions the author makes. Here's the argument again.

> Expert musicologists believe that Beethoven wrote his last piano sonata in 1824, three years before his death. However, the manuscript of a piano sonata was recently discovered that bears Beethoven's name and dates from 1825. Clearly, the experts are mistaken because not every piece that Beethoven wrote was cataloged in his lifetime, and it is known that Beethoven continued to compose until just weeks before his death.

Thus, the conclusion is that the experts are mistaken: Beethoven wrote a piano sonata after 1824. How does the author justify this? By showing that a sonata with Beethoven's name on it was written in 1825 and giving reasons that support the idea that Beethoven wrote it.

Any idea what's wrong here? If you noticed that the author didn't prove that Beethoven actually wrote the sonata that was written in 1825, then you're on the right track. Let's summarize.

Author's conclusion: *The experts are wrong about when Beethoven wrote his last piano sonata.*
Author's premises: *There's a sonata with Beethoven's name on it dated 1825, and it's possible the experts didn't know about it, and Beethoven could have written it.*
Author's assumption: *Beethoven actually wrote the 1825 sonata.*

**Step 3: Act** Remember that this is a Flaw question, so we need to describe what's wrong. You may come up with something like, "Just because he could have written it doesn't mean he did write it." Keep this in mind as you look through the answer choices.

**Step 4: Answer using Process of Elimination**

(A) A given position that is widely believed to be true is taken to show that the position in question must, in fact, be true.

This doesn't seem to match what you're looking for. The "widely held belief" (that of the experts) is what the argument is trying to disprove, not prove. Cross it out.

(B) That either of two things could have occurred independently is taken to show that those two things could not have occurred simultaneously.

The argument didn't talk about two things that could have occurred independently. Cross it out.

(C) Establishing that a certain event occurred is confused with having established the cause of that event.

Maybe. What's the "certain event"? The writing of the 1825 sonata. What's the cause of that event that it's being confused with? Beethoven writing it. Does it fit with the idea of "Just because he could have written it doesn't mean he did write it"? Sort of. It's not great, but it's the best so far. Keep it.

(D) A claim that has a very general application is based entirely on evidence from a narrowly restricted range of cases.

The claim in the argument is very specific: that Beethoven wrote piano sonatas after 1824. And it wasn't based on a narrow range of test cases, it was based on a single counterexample to the experts' belief. This doesn't match. Cross it off.

> (E) An inconsistency that, as presented, has more than one possible resolution is treated as though only one resolution is possible.

What's the inconsistency? The experts' belief versus the newly discovered manuscript. Could it have more than one possible resolution? Yes, the experts could be wrong, or the manuscript could be a fake. Is it treated as though there could be only one solution? Yes, the author concludes that the experts are wrong. Does this fit with the idea of "Just because he could have written it doesn't mean he did write it"? Yes, very closely.

So, although (C) had some good things going for it, you could easily match each general term in (E) (e.g., "inconsistency" and "one possible resolution") to a specific concept in the argument itself. With (C), the fit wasn't as close (i.e., is the "cause" of an "event" the same thing as someone writing a sonata?). (E) is a better answer.

# Summary: Cracking Flaw Questions

The key to cracking Flaw questions is finding what's wrong with the argument before you go to the answer choices. Just remember that these questions are different from Weaken questions, in which new information is brought in to attack the argument, and are different from Reasoning questions, in which finding the key assumption won't be nearly as useful.

| Sample Question Phrasings | Act |
|---|---|
| *Which of the following indicates a flaw in the author's reasoning?*<br><br>*The reasoning in the argument is most vulnerable to criticism on the grounds that the argument…*<br><br>*The argument above relies on which of the following questionable techniques?* | • Break down the argument into its parts; the flaw is usually related to the assumption.<br><br>• State in your own words what the problem with the argument is.<br><br>• With each answer, try to match the actions described in the answer choices with those of the argument itself. Look for the choice that has the same problem you found.<br><br>• Eliminate the answers that don't match; look for the answer that addresses the assumption. |

# LESSON 10: PRINCIPLE MATCH QUESTIONS

You're nearing the home stretch. The last two question types we will cover are Principle Match and Parallel-the-Reasoning.

We've already covered questions that ask you to find a Principle that strengthens or justifies the conclusion. Principle Match questions, on the other hand, ask for a generalization or rule that "conforms," or is consistent with the argument's method. The analysis you need to do will be similar to Reasoning questions, but the answers may be broader than you might expect.

While many Principle questions are reasonable, some can get nasty, and it's hard to tell which is which until you're in the middle of them. Therefore, you might consider holding off on Principle Match questions until you've worked most other types.

Let's look at how one works.

## The Argument

15. The development of secured-funds transfer via the Internet has played an important role in legitimizing those who support the new era of Internet commerce. People can now have access to a huge variety of goods without ever leaving their homes. This allows people to cut transportation time and fuel costs, and avoid the frustration of arriving at a store only to find that the item they want is out of stock. It is not surprising, then, that the proponents of Internet commerce have conveniently overlooked the dangers inherent in this activity before the technology has come far enough to eliminate potential identity theft and fraud, dangers that could be serious enough to dissuade consumers from embracing the technology.

The reasoning above would most closely conform to which one of the following principles?

(A) People have a tendency to ignore possible negative consequences of actions that support their own goals.
(B) Technology often has some negative impact on society, even when the technology is largely beneficial.
(C) Even solutions that are well intentioned can, at times, do more harm than good.
(D) A negative result of an action may be outweighed by its potential positive results.
(E) Many technological advances have unanticipated consequences that turn out to be detrimental.

### Here's How to Crack It

**Step 1: Assess the question** First, as always, you have to identify our task. Here it is again.

> The reasoning above would most closely conform to which one of the following principles?

You are asked to find a principle among the answers with which the argument would be consistent. The choices will be generally worded statements, and what you need to do is pick the one to which the argument "conforms," or fits. If this sounds like a Reasoning question to you, then you're on the right track.

**Assess**
Be sure to assess where the general principle will be found. Some principles are in the answer ("the following principle"), but some principles are in the passage ("the principle above").

**Step 2: Analyze the argument** You need to have a clear understanding of what's happening in the argument. Basically, you are presented with some pretty good reasons for supporting the spread of Internet commerce: It saves time, money, and frustration. But then you're told that the people who support Internet commerce tend to overlook some of the drawbacks of using such technology; you might wonder why they would still support it given its potential danger.

**Analyze**
There is no need to find conclusion and premises on a Principle Match question!

**Step 3: Act** Because you're going to be asked to identify the principle with which the argument would fit best, you'll want to be able to state in basic terms what's going on. For this example, you might come up with something like: Proponents of a cause sometimes overlook the drawbacks when there is good evidence to support their case. See if you can find a match in the answers.

**Step 4: Answer using Process of Elimination** As you evaluate the answer choices, you'll want to cross off any that are not consistent with the basic premise you just came up with or with the information presented in the argument.

> (A) People have a tendency to ignore possibie negative consequences of actions that support their own goals.

This sounds like a pretty close match to what you are looking for; it says that possible drawbacks don't dissuade people from promoting their cause. Hold on to it.

> (B) Technology often has some negative impact on society, even when the technology is largely beneficial.

Although this may be true, it leaves out some important elements mentioned in the argument. It never talks about why people would still support technology that has some negative impact. Get rid of it.

> (C) Even solutions that are well intentioned can, at times, do more harm than good.

Again, this addresses some possible harm, but, like (B), it doesn't help you to understand why the proponents in the argument would overlook the dangers involved. Cross it off.

(D) A negative result of an action may be outweighed by its potential positive results.

Once again, you have a statement that seems reasonable but doesn't match the argument. The fact that the positives outweigh the negatives doesn't get at the particular agenda of the proponents in the argument. You have to find an answer choice that suggests why it's "not surprising" that the proponents would overlook the negative. Get rid of it.

(E) Many technological advances have unanticipated consequences that turn out to be detrimental.

That's all fine and good. And you probably know from your own experience that this is often the case. But again, this answer falls short in addressing the element of why the proponents act in the way they do. Eliminate it.

Now you're left with (A), the correct answer. Notice that once you understood why the people mentioned in the argument acted the way they did, you were able to eliminate any answer that didn't match up with your paraphrase.

---

This question illustrates how there can be a pretty big difference between a Principle Match question that asks you to find a principle that conforms to the reasoning and a Principle Strengthen question that asks you to justify the reasoning. (See page 59 for Principle Strengthen questions.) Of course, the answer on both will go along with the conclusion of the argument. But a principle to which the argument "conforms" will match the argument's method.

## Arguments Technique: Using Process of Elimination with Principle Match Questions

As we saw from this example, you are looking for a principle among the answer choices that will match the conditions or actions stated in the argument. If the principle were contained in the argument, you might be asked to find an answer choice that would conform to that principle. But your task would stay the same: Eliminate any answers that don't match up with your paraphrase.

The important thing to remember: You're looking for an answer choice that matches the decision or action in the argument. The principle will be more general, but will match the whole.

The credited response to a Principle Match question will either match or validate a decision or action, and may be broader than the given argument.

# Summary: Cracking Principle Match Questions

Refer to the chart below on how to approach Principle Match questions.

| Sample Question Phrasings | Act |
|---|---|
| *The reasoning above most closely conforms to which of the following principles?*<br><br>*Which of the following examples conforms most closely to the principle given in the argument above?* | • Make sure you know in which direction the argument flows. Are you being asked to find a principle that conforms to a situation, or a situation that conforms to a principle?<br><br>• Once you're sure, look for an answer that most closely matches the general principle underlying the argument. |

## LESSON 11: PARALLEL-THE-REASONING QUESTIONS

We're finally at the end. And there is a reason we saved Parallel-the-Reasoning questions for last—because you should probably avoid them until you've worked all the other questions you can tackle. These questions are not necessarily more difficult, but they are certainly more time consuming on average than most other question types. Don't forget that all of the questions are worth one point each; why spend more time for the same reward?

**Hint:**
Save Parallel-the-Reasoning questions for last or skip them altogether.

The reason that these take so long is that you have to perform Step 2 (Analyze the argument) for six arguments rather than just one! Each answer choice is another argument. Many arguments attached to Parallel-the-Reasoning questions can be diagrammed in some fashion. Your job is then to find the answer choice that has the same diagram.

There are two major types of Parallel-the-Reasoning questions. One type asks you to simply parallel (match) the reasoning, which means the argument and the credited response are not logically flawed. The other type asks you to parallel the "flaw" or "error," which means the argument and the answer will contain the same reasoning error. Use this to guide your process of elimination: Cross off flawed answers on a Parallel-the-Reasoning, and cross off logically correct answers on a Parallel-the-Flaw.

Let's do a more diagrammable Parallel-the-Flaw first.

## The Argument

16. A full moon is known to cause strange behavior in people. People are behaving strangely today, so there is probably a full moon.

    Which of the following most closely parallels the flawed pattern of reasoning used in the argument above?

    (A) Abnormal sunspot activity causes animals to act strangely. We are experiencing abnormal sunspot activity today, so animals are probably acting strangely.

    (B) Studies have shown that the use of turn signals reduces the likelihood of highway accidents. There has been a decrease in highway accidents, so people are most likely using their turn signals.

    (C) The law of gravity has worked for as long as mankind has been able to observe it. It's working today, and it will probably continue to work tomorrow.

    (D) Increased stress has been shown to decrease the effectiveness of a person's immune system. So it follows that someone who does not have a diminished immune system is not likely to be experiencing an increased level of stress.

    (E) People with an ear for music often have an equal facility for learning languages. Bill doesn't have an ear for music, so he probably doesn't have a facility for learning languages.

### Here's How to Crack It

**Step 1: Assess the question** Good, you've read the question. Here it is again.

> Which of the following most closely parallels the flawed pattern of reasoning used in the argument above?

Okay, so it's a Parallel-the-Reasoning argument, and you know that you have to try to diagram the argument, if possible, and match that diagram against the diagrams for each of the answer choices. You also know that the reasoning itself is bad because the question tips us off to that.

**Careful!**
Some Parallel-the-Reasoning questions are not about flawed arguments. Read the question carefully.

**Step 2: Analyze the argument** As always, read it through carefully. Here it is again.

> A full moon is known to cause strange behavior in people. People are behaving strangely today, so there is probably a full moon.

This looks eminently diagrammable. It also sounds like an invalid contrapositive, doesn't it? Let's see.

**Step 3: Act** Here's what we get when we diagram.

A full moon is known to cause strange behavior in people (A → B); people are behaving strangely today, so there is probably a full moon (B → A). This looks familiar from our earlier discussion about the contrapositive, but it's not correct.

The arguer didn't properly create a contrapositive in the second sentence. The elements are flipped but not negated. Now all we have to do is eliminate any answer choice that doesn't exhibit the same flawed logic (flipping a conditional, but not negating it).

> The credited response to a Parallel-the-Reasoning question will be a new argument that matches the key features and structure of the original argument.

**Step 4: Answer using Process of Elimination** Now you're going to carry your diagram to the answer choices and eliminate anything that doesn't match.

> (A) Abnormal sunspot activity causes animals to act strangely. We are experiencing abnormal sunspot activity today, so animals are probably acting strangely.

Diagram it: Abnormal sunspot activity causes animals to act strangely (A → B); we are experiencing abnormal sunspot activity today, so animals are probably acting strangely (A → B again). This doesn't match the argument, so it isn't the answer. Cross it off.

> (B) Studies have shown that the use of turn signals reduces the likelihood of highway accidents. There has been a decrease in highway accidents, so people are most likely using their turn signals.

Diagram it: Using turn signals reduces the likelihood of accidents (A → B). There has been a decrease in highway accidents, so people are probably using their turn signals (B → A). Bingo! This is the same type of flawed reasoning, another conditional that has been flipped without being negated. Hold on to it.

> (C) The law of gravity has worked for as long as mankind has been able to observe it. It's working today, and it will probably continue to work tomorrow.

Can we even diagram this? It looks like the entire thing is merely saying that the law of gravity has worked in the past, it's working today, and it'll work tomorrow. So it's just (A → B → C) and nothing else. Eliminate it.

> (D) Increased stress has been shown to decrease the effectiveness of a person's immune system. So it follows that someone who does not have a diminished immune system is not likely to be experiencing an increased level of stress.

This is (A → B) and then in the second sentence (~B → ~A). This is actually a valid contrapositive, fixing the flaw in the original argument. This can be appealing because it fixes the flawed logic, so be careful *not* to fix the flaw in a "Parallel-the-Flaw" question. Find the *same* flaw. Get rid of this one.

> (E) People with an ear for music often have an equal facility for learning languages. Bill doesn't have an ear for music, so he probably doesn't have a facility for learning languages.

You have (A → B) in the first sentence, and then (~A → ~B) in the second sentence. Here, the original was negated without being flipped. It's flawed, but not flawed in the *same* way as the original. It's out.

Nice job! You got the right answer simply by diagramming the statement in the argument, and then diagramming each of the answer choices until we found the one that matched our original diagram. However, you probably noticed that it took a long time to do this question. Many times, Parallel-the-Reasoning questions are even longer than this one and could take you three minutes to do. If you spend your time doing these questions, you might get through only half of an Arguments section! Therefore, be sure to save these for the end.

## The Argument

17. All known samples of the fossil trichiobite have been found in Northern Canada. Therefore, because Frank studies only trichiobite fossils, he is unlikely to ever study a fossil that did not come from Northern Canada.

    Which of the following is most similar in its reasoning to the argument above?

    (A) Many cacti grow on Isla Hill in Genovesa. Since the iguanas of Genovesa eat nothing but prickly-pear cacti from Genovesa, the iguanas will probably never eat many cacti that grow somewhere other than Isla Hill.

    (B) Every prickly-pear cactus ever seen in Genovesa grows on Isla Hill. The prickly-pear cacti are eaten only by the iguanas in Genovesa, and hence the iguanas may never eat a cactus that grows somewhere other than Isla Hill.

    (C) Prickly-pear cacti are the only plants that grow on Isla Hill in Genovasa. The diet of the iguanas in Genovesa consists of nothing but prickly-pear cacti. Therefore, the iguanas are unlikely ever to eat a cactus that grows somewhere other than Isla Hill.

    (D) The only prickly-pear cacti yet discovered in Genovesa grow on Isla Hill. The diet of the iguanas in Genovesa consists entirely of prickly-pear cacti, so the iguanas will probably never eat a cactus that grows somewhere other than Isla hill.

    (E) Each prickly-pear cactus in Genovesa grows on Isla Hill. No iguana in Genovesa is known to eat anything besides prickly-pear cacti from Genovesa. It follows that no iguana in Genovesa will eat anything that grows somewhere other than Isla Hill.

**Step 1: Assess the question** Read the question first, as always. Here it is.

> Which of the following is most similar in its reasoning to the argument above?

This question is asking us to parallel the reasoning, with no mention of any flaws. You'll have to diagram or summarize the argument as best you can, diagram each answer, and see if they match.

**Step 2: Analyze the argument** Read it carefully, keeping a sharp eye out for "all," "only," "some," or "most" wording, as well as conditional statements.

> All known samples of the fossil trichiobite have been found in Northern Canada. Therefore, because Frank studies only trichiobite fossils, he is unlikely to ever to study a fossil that did not come from Northern Canada.

This looks somewhat less diagrammable, but it still has a clear logical pattern we can map out.

**Step 3: Act** Here's what we can diagram out.

All *known* trichiobite fossils are from Northern Canada (*known* A are B). Notice this doesn't say "all." It's just the fossils we know about. But no one's found one that's *not* from Northern Canada yet.

Frank studies only trichiobite fossils (C → A). The "only" in this sentence makes it a clear conditional.

Therefore, he is *unlikely* to study a fossil that did not come from Northern Canada. (*unlikely* to have C and not B).

Not as simple to diagram, but let's sum it up anyway.

> Known A are B.
>
> C → A.
>
> Therefore, it's unlikely to have C and not B.

Now we need to find an answer that follows the same pattern, and has the same features (known, only, unlikely) in the same order.

**Step 4: Answer using Process of Elimination** Now map out your answers and eliminate answers that don't match.

> (A) Many cacti grow on Isla Hill in Genovesa. Since the iguanas of Genovesa eat nothing but prickly-pear cacti from Genovesa, the iguanas will probably never eat many cacti that grow somewhere other than Isla Hill.

Look at the first sentence. Already it doesn't match. This doesn't say anything about what we know or don't know about where they come from. Cross it off!

(B) Every prickly-pear cactus ever seen in Genovesa grows on Isla Hill. The prickly-pear cacti are eaten only by the iguanas in Genovesa, and hence the iguanas may never eat a cactus that grows somewhere other than Isla Hill.

The first premise seems to match! All the known prickly-pear cacti are from Isla Hill. (Known A are B). Check. But diagram out the second sentence: If a prickly-pear is eaten, it's eaten by an iguana. (A → C). Wrong direction, so it doesn't match. Eliminate it.

(C) Prickly-pear cacti are the only plants that grow on Isla Hill in Genovasa. The diet of the iguanas in Genovesa consists of nothing but prickly-pear cacti. Therefore, the iguanas are unlikely ever to eat a cactus that grows somewhere other than Isla Hill.

Check out the first premise. It's a clear conditional (B → A). Not only is it in the wrong direction, but it also doesn't say anything about the *known* prickly pears. Doesn't match. Get rid of it.

(D) The only prickly-pear cacti yet discovered in Genovesa grow on Isla Hill. The diet of the iguanas in Genovesa consists entirely of prickly-pear cacti, so the iguanas will probably never eat a cactus that grows somewhere other than Isla hill.

Diagram the first sentence. "Yet discovered" means the same thing as "known," so (known A are B). Match. If an iguana eats it, it's a prickly pear, so (C → A). So far so good! iguanas probably don't eat anything not from Isla hill (unlikely C and not B). Bingo! Let's keep it.

(E) Each prickly-pear cactus in Genovesa grows on Isla Hill. No iguana in Genovesa is known to eat anything beside prickly-pear cacti from Genovesa. It follows that no iguana in Genovesa will eat anything that grows somewhere other than Isla Hill.

The features we want ("known" and so on) are there, but in the wrong order. Look at the first sentence: All prickly pears are from Isla Hill, which makes it a clear conditional (A → B) and therefore doesn't match.

Wow. Good work! But notice again how long it took to map out each and every answer choice, which means you might want to skip this one altogether, or save it for the very end. Notice, also, how similar the answers were; they all had the same conclusion. You can save a little time and headache by crossing out an answer as soon as you find a part that doesn't match.

**Hint:** Whenever possible, diagram Parallel-the-Reasoning arguments.

## Arguments Technique: Using Process of Elimination with Parallel-the-Reasoning Questions

It's pretty straightforward—if you are able to diagram the argument, then you must go to the answer choices and diagram those as well. Write it out and then you've got proof that the choice either matches or doesn't match the argument.

Sometimes you can't diagram Parallel-the-Reasoning questions. In these instances, try to describe the reasoning in the argument in general terms. Look for patterns that can be easily summed up (e.g., we have two things that appear to be similar, then we note a difference, or one thing is attributed to be the cause of another). Try to find an answer that could be summed up in the same way. Start by matching up conclusions; then work backwards through the argument to match up each piece. If you find any part of an answer choice that you can't match up with part of the original argument, eliminate it.

# Summary: Cracking Parallel-the-Reasoning Questions

Refer to the chart below on how to approach Parallel-the-Reasoning questions.

| Sample Question Phrasings | Act |
|---|---|
| *Which one of the following is most similar in reasoning to the argument above?*<br><br>*The flawed pattern of reasoning exhibited by the argument above is most similar to that in which of the following?* | • Parallel-the-Reasoning questions will either contain flawed or valid reasoning, and the question will tip you off.<br><br>• Try to diagram the argument and then diagram each of the answer choices, comparing each one to the diagram you came up with for the argument itself.<br><br>• If the argument is flawed, be careful not to choose an answer that fixes it.<br><br>• Save Parallel-the-Reasoning questions for LAST. |

## CRACKING ARGUMENTS: PUTTING IT ALL TOGETHER

Now you've learned how to approach every type of question they will throw at you in an Arguments section.

How do you integrate this knowledge into working a whole Arguments section?

### Pace Yourself

You know that you have only 35 minutes to tackle an entire Arguments section. But you're also faced with the fact that to get the credited response, you have to invest a significant amount of time in each argument. Hopefully, you've seen that these questions are doable—with the right approach—but that you might fall for traps or miss key words if you rush through them too quickly.

**Hint**
Check out the pacing chart on page 308.

The bottom line on effective pacing is this: *Don't rush!* There are questions in which you'll be able to analyze the argument easily, predict the answer accurately, and find the answer you predicted quickly. Keep moving through these questions. But there will be others in which the argument takes a little extra time to analyze, or in which two or more of the answer choices seem like they have a shot—or, alternatively, in which none of the answer choices is what you were hoping for. In these cases, it's important to slow down. Take more time to understand the question, the argument, and the answer choices when you're struggling. This isn't wasted time; it's the real work of LSAT Arguments.

Of course, along with spending time where you need to spend it, you'll also want to keep an overall sense of what target you need to hit. You can arrive at a rough pacing target for Arguments by looking at the percentage you get right on the section and dividing that number by 3; round up to get a sense of what number of questions you're aiming for. For example, if you're getting 60 percent right on Arguments sections, then you'll want to shoot for 20 questions on each Arguments section. You might not hit this number exactly, but if you're significantly short of that number, then chances are you'll need to work faster to improve; if, on the other hand, you're getting 60 percent right but more or less finishing the section, then the only way you're going to be able to improve is to work on your accuracy; that will most likely necessitate slowing down.

## Choose Wisely

You know that you have to invest a certain amount of time into each type of Arguments question to get the credited response. But you also know that some types of Arguments take less time than others. For instance, compare the amount of time that a Main Point question takes to the amount of time that a Parallel-the-Reasoning question takes. You have a choice in how to spend your time with each question. Does it make sense to tackle a bunch of time-consuming questions when there are others that take much less time to do but give you the same number of points? As you do more practice problems and evaluate your performance on them, you should get a pretty clear sense of where your strengths and weaknesses lie. You'll benefit by making charts of your performance on each section, broken down by question type, so that you can see your progress. (See Chapter 6 for additional study tips and information on evaluating your progress.) To help you plan your approach, here's a chart of the proportion of questions of each type that have shown up on recently administered LSATs.

| | Approximate Number Per Section | Approximate % of Total Arguments |
|---|---|---|
| Main Point | 2 | 7% |
| Necessary Assumption | 3 | 7% |
| Sufficient Assumption | 3 | 7% |
| Weaken | 3–4 | 13% |
| Strengthen | 2 | 8% |
| Resolve/Explain | 1–2 | 5% |
| Inference | 4 | 14% |
| Reasoning | 2 | 6% |
| Flaw | 3–4 | 13% |
| Principle | 2–3 | 10% |
| Parallel-the-Reasoning | 2 | 7% |
| Other | 1 | 3% |

The bottom line is this: Do the questions that take you the least amount of time and that you're most comfortable with first. Open your test booklet, and just take a look at what's on the page. Go after the ones that look short, sweet, and to the point, and leave the longer ones for later. Give priority to the tasks that you know play to your strengths. Likewise, if you come to an argument that really stumps you, don't worry about it—just put a mark next to it and move on. You can always come back once you've gone through all of the other arguments in the section.

**For Additional Practice**
Real LSATs provide the best source of practice material. However, if you want to work on tougher LSAT questions, pick up a copy of our *LSAT Workout*. And don't forget about the online tools that we provide for you.

## Finally...

Practice, practice, practice. There are a number of different tasks that you'll be asked to perform in the Arguments section. As we've seen, each task will vary slightly in how you approach the argument and what you need to get out of it. There's no substitute for experience here. Use those previously administered LSATs that you've ordered from LSAC to get plenty of practice.

And remember that it's not enough to just work all the Arguments questions under the sun. You'll have to go back and carefully evaluate your work. Figure out *why* you missed a question rather than simply looking at the right answer to learn why that one works. Did you miss the question because you didn't understand the argument? Did you miss a key word? Did you fall for an attractive distractor? Was the credited response one that didn't look very good but didn't have any flaw? Did you misinterpret the task presented by the question?

This kind of detailed evaluation will take time, but it is well worth it. Do it for Arguments. Do it for Games. Do it for Reading Comprehension. There are many places where errors can creep into the process. You'll be able to improve only if you know what your tendencies are and how you can go about changing those tendencies that negatively impact your performance.

Now you know what you need to do, so keep up the effort and you'll see the results.

# YOU AND YOUR CHART

The chart on the following pages will help you on the Arguments section. You should probably retype the chart yourself (it will help you to better remember all the information in it), and then print out a copy for yourself. Put it in a prominent place. Make another copy and carry it along with you so you can refer to it while you're working practice problems. You should know this chart like the back of your hand by the time you take the real LSAT.

| Question Type | Sample Question Phrasings | Act |
|---|---|---|
| **Main Point** | *What is the author's main point?*<br><br>*The main conclusion drawn in the author's argument is that...*<br><br>*The argument is structured to lead to which one of the following conclusions?* | • Identify the conclusion and premises.<br><br>• Use the Why Test and then match your conclusion against the five answer choices.<br><br>• Be careful not to fall for the opposite.<br><br>• When down to two choices, look for extreme wording and relevance to eliminate one choice. |
| **Necessary Assumption** | *Which of the following is an assumption on which the argument relies?*<br><br>*The argument above assumes which of the following?*<br><br>*The writer's argument depends upon assuming which of the following?* | • Identify the conclusion, premises, and assumptions of the author.<br><br>• If you're having trouble finding the assumption, look for a gap between two different ideas in the argument.<br><br>• The assumption will always at least mildly strengthen the author's conclusion and is NECESSARY for the conclusion to follow from the information provided.<br><br>• When down to two choices, negate each statement to see if the argument falls apart. If it does, that's your answer. |

| Question Type | Sample Question Phrasings | Act |
|---|---|---|
| Sufficient Assumption | *Which one of the following, if assumed, would enable the conclusion to be properly drawn?*<br><br>*The conclusion follows logically if which one of the following is assumed?* | • Identify the conclusion, premises, and assumptions of the author.<br>• Look for language in the conclusion that is not accounted for in the premise.<br>• Paraphrase an answer that would strongly connect the premises to the conclusion and shore up the language gap.<br>• Eliminate answer choices that bring in new information. |
| Weaken | *Which one of the following, if true, would most undermine the author's conclusion?*<br><br>*Which of the following statements, if true, would most call into question the results achieved by the scientists?* | • Identify the conclusion, premises, and assumptions of the author.<br>• Read critically, looking for instances in which the author made large leaps in logic.<br>• Then, when you go to the answer choices, look for a choice that has the most negative impact on that leap in logic.<br>• Assume all choices to be hypothetically true. |

| Question Type | Sample Question Phrasings | Act |
|---|---|---|
| Strengthen | *Which one of the following statements, if true, would most support the author's conclusion?*<br><br>*Which one of the following statements, if true, would strengthen the author's argument?*<br><br>*Which of the following principles, if established, justifies the conclusion drawn in the argument above?* | • Identify the conclusion, premises, and assumptions of the author.<br><br>• Read critically, looking for where the author made large leaps in logic.<br><br>• Then, when you go to the answer choices, look for a choice that has the most positive impact on that gap.<br><br>• Assume all choices to be hypothetically true. |
| Resolve/ Explain | *Which one of the following provides the best resolution to the apparent paradox described by the committee member?*<br><br>*Which one of the following statements, if true, would explain the discrepancy found by the scientists?* | • Identify the apparent discrepancy or paradox.<br><br>• Go to the answer choices and look for a piece of information that, when added to the argument, allows both facts from the argument to be true.<br><br>• Assume all choices to be hypothetically true. |
| Inference | *Which one of the following statements can be validly inferred from the information above?*<br><br>*If the statements above are true, then which of the following must also be true?*<br><br>*Which one of the following conclusions can be validly drawn from the passage above?*<br><br>*Which one of the following conclusions is best supported by the passage above?* | • Read carefully, paying close attention to qualifying language, and then go to the answer choices.<br><br>• Once there, cross off any answer choices that are not directly supported by evidence in the passage.<br><br>• Look for relevance and extreme language to eliminate answer choices.<br><br>• Use the contrapositive if there are "if...then" statements contained in the passage and in the answer choices. |

| Question Type | Sample Question Phrasings | Act |
|---|---|---|
| Reasoning | *The argument proceeds by...*<br><br>*Leah responds to Kevin by doing which one of the following?*<br><br>*The method the activist uses to object to the developer's argument is to...*<br><br>*Dr. Jacobs does which of the following?* | • Read the arguments carefully and then describe what is happening in your own words, focusing on the author's conclusion and premises.<br><br>• Take this description and rigorously apply it to all the answer choices.<br><br>• Once you're at the answer choices, use the technique of comparing the actions described in the answer choices against those that actually occur in the arguments.<br><br>• Cross out anything that didn't appear in the argument. |
| Flaw | *Which of the following indicates a flaw in the author's reasoning?*<br><br>*A criticism of the arguments would most likely emphasize that it...*<br><br>*The reasoning in the argument is most vulnerable to criticism on the grounds that the argument...*<br><br>*The argument above relies on which of the following questionable techniques?* | • Break down the argument into its parts; the flaw is usually related to an assumption.<br><br>• State in your own words what the problem with the argument is.<br><br>• With each answer, try to match the actions described in the answer choices with those of the argument itself. Look for the choice that has the same problem you found.<br><br>• Eliminate the answers that don't match; look for the answer that addresses the assumption. |

| Question Type | Sample Question Phrasings | Act |
|---|---|---|
| **Principle Match** | *The reasoning above most closely conforms to which of the following principles?*<br><br>*Which one of the following examples conforms most closely to the principle given in the argument above?* | • Make sure you know in which direction the argument flows. Are you being asked to find a principle that conforms to a situation, or a situation that conforms to a principle?<br><br>• Once you're sure, look for an answer that most closely matches the general principle underlying the argument. |
| **Parallel-the-Reasoning** | *Which one of the following is most similar in reasoning to the argument above?*<br><br>*The flawed pattern of reasoning exhibited by the arguments above is most similar to that in which of the following?* | • Parallel-the-Reasoning questions will contain either flawed or valid reasoning, and the question will tip you off.<br><br>• Try to diagram the arguments and then diagram each of the answer choices, comparing each one to the diagram you came up with for the argument itself.<br><br>• If the argument is flawed, be careful not to choose an answer that fixes it.<br><br>• Save Parallel-the-Reasoning questions for LAST. |

## APPLY WHAT YOU'VE LEARNED

Now it's time to put everything you've learned in this chapter to work on the following 13 arguments. The goal of this drill is to see how well you've mastered the four steps and how accurately you can work, not to see how fast you can get through these arguments.

If you want, you can measure the time it takes you to do all 13 questions. By measure, we mean set your timer to count up, and then turn it away so that you can't see the clock as you work on the questions. Put the timer in a drawer or in another room if necessary. When you're done, stop the clock and note how long it took you to complete them and then see how accurate you were. You should be learning to balance speed and accuracy throughout your preparation for the LSAT, but when in doubt, slow down and work for accuracy.

# Arguments Practice Drill

1. Biologist: A recent study investigated individuals' use of over-the-counter pain medicines and discovered a disturbing trend: Many people use these medications instead of seeking medical help for potentially serious conditions. Among those who used over-the-counter pain medications most frequently, the rate of disorders such as heart disease, cancer, and liver disease was nearly twice as high as it is in the overall population, even though these individuals were actually more likely to have adequate health insurance than the overall population.

Which one of the following statements, if true, most seriously weakens the biologist's argument?

(A) Overuse of some over-the-counter pain medications is known to be a contributing factor in the development of liver disease.

(B) At least some patients who have adequate health insurance consult physicians whenever they experience pain that others without health insurance would treat with over-the-counter pain medications.

(C) Many physicians recommend the daily use of over-the-counter pain medications to patients who have been diagnosed with heart disease or certain types of cancer.

(D) Among those who use over-the-counter pain medications either infrequently or never, the rate of most serious medical conditions is no lower than it is in the overall population.

(E) Many patients with adequate health insurance are hesitant to seek medical help for conditions that are serious enough to require specialized care, which is often only partially covered only by their insurers.

2. Over recent decades, average ocean temperatures on Earth have steadily risen, causing the destruction of much marine habitat. It has been established that the emission of greenhouse gases such as carbon dioxide into the atmosphere can increase average ocean temperatures, and over the past century the emission of carbon dioxide by human industry has increased dramatically. Although many scientists believe that these emissions are responsible for the increase in average ocean temperatures, geological evidence shows that both carbon dioxide levels in the atmosphere and average ocean temperatures have fluctuated widely in the past with no human intervention.

Which one of the following most accurately expresses the main conclusion of the argument?

(A) Human industry is not responsible for the rise in average ocean temperatures over recent decades.

(B) The effect of increased levels of carbon dioxide in the atmosphere is not reflected in increased average ocean temperatures until several decades after the increase in carbon dioxide levels has begun.

(C) Although the emission of carbon dioxide into the atmosphere can increase average ocean temperatures, there is no evidence that such emissions by human industry are responsible for the increase in average ocean temperatures over recent decades.

(D) There is evidence of significant natural fluctuations in atmospheric carbon dioxide levels and average ocean temperatures in Earth's distant past.

(E) There is evidence that the beliefs of many scientists concerning the cause of recent increases in average ocean temperatures on Earth may not be correct.

3. Editorial: The insurance industry claims that legal costs associated with frivolous lawsuits and outrageous awards are responsible for the skyrocketing price of insurance, but this explanation cannot be correct. Although it is true that legal costs incurred by insurance companies have increased at an accelerating rate over the past several years, these costs have increased at only a fraction of the rate at which the prices that insurance companies charge have increased.

Which one of the following, if true, lends the greatest support to the editorial's argument?

(A) Prices charged by insurance companies do not take into account likely future increases in the legal costs incurred by those companies.
(B) Because insurers are publicly traded companies that must meet profit goals, many increases in cost are followed by an increase in prices that exceeds the amount of the cost increase by a fixed amount.
(C) The bond market, which has yielded historically low returns in recent years, has no significant effect on the prices that insurance companies charge.
(D) The increase in awards is due to the increased incidence of catastrophic losses in the most populous cities, where operating costs are highest.
(E) The legal costs of companies outside the insurance industry have increased at a rate that is comparable to the rate at which legal costs to insurers have increased.

4. Restaurant manager: The restaurant next door has a larger dining room, more appealing décor, and a more extensive wine list than our restaurant does. It is also more popular than our restaurant, but our customers do not care how large our dining room is or how appealing our décor is. Therefore, if we increase the size of our wine list, our restaurant will definitely become more popular.

Each of the following is an assumption on which the restaurant manager's argument relies EXCEPT

(A) Factors not considered important by those who are currently the customers of the manager's restaurant will not prevent the restaurant's overall popularity from increasing.
(B) The popularity of the manager's restaurant depends at least in part upon the size of the restaurant's wine list.
(C) The restaurant next door does not serve food that is far more popular with most potential customers than is the food that the manager's restaurant serves.
(D) The popularity of the restaurant next door is due to its overall superior quality of service.
(E) Customers who would be appealed to by increasing the size of the wine list in the manager's restaurant do not demand the finest décor in restaurants they choose to patronize.

5. Juan: The candidates in this election are not making enough of an effort to address the issues. The majority of advertising during the campaign has been used to attack the other candidates, not to clarify positions on the most pressing problems facing the community.

Michiko: Your judgment could not be less accurate. A recent survey has shown that more than 80 percent of likely voters in this election are correctly able to identify the candidates' positions on the five issues that they consider most important.

Michiko responds to Juan by

(A) identifying a contradiction between Juan's evidence and the conclusion he draws from it
(B) dismissing the relevance of advertising to Juan's conclusion about the electorate's knowledge
(C) attacking Juan's qualifications to criticize candidates for public office
(D) introducing an alternative criterion for evaluating the adequacy of the candidates' efforts
(E) calling into question the accuracy of Juan's evidence

6. Classical mechanics predicts that the same experiment conducted by different investigators must yield similar results. Yet at the subatomic level, even simple experiments conducted by different investigators may yield contradictory results. Because quantum mechanics predicts that the contradictory results of these experiments are not only possible but also inevitable, quantum mechanics provides the only correct explanation of the behavior of matter at the subatomic level.

The reasoning in the argument above is questionable because it

(A) applies a standard for accepting the correctness of a single theory that may be equally well satisfied by some other competing theory
(B) fails to establish that the contradictory results mentioned in the argument are the result of error on the part of investigators
(C) relies upon the ambiguous use of a key term
(D) confuses an experimental result that may be possible with one that is observed in all cases
(E) presupposes without warrant that no reputable scientist considers classical mechanics to provide a correct explanation of subatomic phenomena

7. Editor: Our newspaper's coverage of the ballot initiative has been called irresponsible, but this criticism is unwarranted. To be responsible, press coverage of an issue must provide equal time to all significant alternative views of that issue, and there are a large number of alternative views on the ballot initiative. Because our newspaper did not have space available to accommodate all of them, we decided not to include any coverage of the ballot initiative.

Which one of the following identifies a flaw in the editor's reasoning?

(A) The fact that the newspaper's coverage of the ballot initiative is not irresponsible is taken as evidence that the coverage is adequate.
(B) The fact that the newspaper's coverage of the ballot initiative meets one condition necessary for it to be responsible is taken as evidence that the coverage is not irresponsible.
(C) The fact that a single requirement exists for evaluating whether the newspaper's coverage of the ballot initiative is responsible is taken as evidence that all responsible coverage must include the same views of the ballot initiative.
(D) The fact that alternative views on a controversial issue must be provided in the newspaper's coverage of the ballot initiative is taken as evidence that the ballot initiative itself is controversial.
(E) The fact that the newspaper elected not to provide any coverage of the ballot initiative is taken as evidence that the coverage was therefore not responsible.

8. Psychological studies have shown that a person's memory of an event can be influenced by things he or she is told about the event after the fact. Hence, an eyewitness's memory of a crime's important details may not be entirely accurate. For example, an eyewitness who is told that the perpetrator of a crime was wearing sunglasses may subsequently report that he or she remembers seeing the perpetrator wearing sunglasses, whether or not that is actually true. It seems inevitable that our legal system's reliance on eyewitness testimony must lead to the conviction of innocent defendants in at least some cases.

The statement that an eyewitness's memory of a crime's important details may not be accurate plays which one of the following roles in the argument?

(A) It is a premise offered to support the conclusion that a person's memory of an event can be influenced by things that he or she is told about the event after the fact.
(B) It is a conclusion supported by the claim that the legal system's reliance on eyewitness testimony must lead to the conviction of innocent defendants in at least some cases.
(C) It is a generalization employed to illustrate the claim that eyewitness testimony concerning a perpetrator's appearance may not be exactly accurate.
(D) It is a subsidiary conclusion on which the argument's main conclusion is based.
(E) It is the main conclusion that the argument sets out to establish.

9. A habitat's carrying capacity for a particular species is defined as the largest number of individuals of that species that the environment can support for an extended period of time. Each species has its own set of resource requirements, and the carrying capacity of a given habitat for a species is determined by which one of these key resources is scarcest relative to the animal's requirements, and how much of that resource is available. In a particular area of wetland habitat that supports snowy egrets, it is observed over a period of several years that many nesting sites suitable for snowy egrets remain unused.

If the statements above are true, then which one of the following must also be true about the wetland habitat described in the passage above?

(A) The habitat's carrying capacity for snowy egrets is greater than its current population of that species.
(B) Suitable food sources are scarcer, relative to the snowy egrets' need for them, than are suitable nesting sites in the habitat.
(C) At least one resource that snowy egrets require is not present in the habitat.
(D) The number of suitable nesting sites that are available but remain unused is determined by the abundance of some other resource in the habitat.
(E) Efforts to increase the snowy egret population in the habitat through the careful introduction of additional individuals and key resources are unlikely to be successful.

10. A company wishing to measure employee satisfaction after a series of layoffs and cutbacks conducted an internal survey. The responses to the survey were anonymous, and analysis of them was conducted by the company's research department. Despite widespread rumors of employee dissatisfaction, however, the research department was astonished to discover that employees' satisfaction with their jobs was, on average, higher than it had been at any time in the past when similar surveys had been conducted.

Each of the following helps to explain the unanticipated results of the survey EXCEPT:

(A) The number of employees who said they were mildly or strongly dissatisfied with their jobs was greater than it had been in any similar survey conducted in the past.
(B) The employees chosen to be laid off were generally those whose dissatisfaction with their jobs was highest.
(C) Past employee satisfaction surveys were conducted only at times when there were widespread indicators of employee dissatisfaction within the company.
(D) Several of the survey's questions required free-response answers that made it possible to determine the identity of respondents.
(E) Those who retain their jobs after a series of layoffs routinely express increased job satisfaction once it becomes clear that their jobs are not being eliminated, even if they are dissatisfied with those jobs.

11. Registrar: Each student who registers for a course does so either early or late. If a nonmajor registers early for this course, then he or she is assured of a space in this course unless the number of majors who register early for the course is equal to or greater than the number of spaces allocated to the course. If a nonmajor registers late for this course, then he or she is assured of a space in this course only if the number of nonmajors who registered early for the course combined with the number of majors who registered for the course either early or late is less than the number of spaces allocated to the course.

Which one of the following predictions is best supported by the registrar's statements?

(A) Kim, a nonmajor, registered late for this course. Because the total number of nonmajors who registered early for this course and majors who registered for the course either early or late is less than the number of spaces allocated to the course, Kim is assured of a space in this course.
(B) Joe, a major, registered late for this course. Because the total number of majors and nonmajors who registered early for the course is less than the number of spaces allocated to the course, Joe is assured of a space in this course.
(C) Wendy, a nonmajor, registered early for this course. Because the number of majors who registered early for the course does not exceed the number of spaces allocated to the course, Wendy is assured of a space in this course.
(D) Dorothy, a nonmajor, registered late for this course. Because the total number of majors who registered for the course either early or late exceeds the number of spaces allocated to the course, Dorothy is not assured of a space in this course.
(E) Philip, a major, registered late for this course. Because the total number of majors and nonmajors who registered early for the course is exactly equal to the number of spaces allocated to the course, Philip is not assured of a space in this course.

12. Attorney: The highway patrol claims that the reason it stopped Mr. Smith was that he was traveling at a dangerous rate of speed. No one disputes that Mr. Smith was speeding, but the highway patrol's explanation of its reasons for stopping him cannot be complete. After all, many drivers near Mr. Smith were traveling at the same speed he was, and yet the highway patrol did not stop them.

The reasoning in the attorney's argument conforms most closely to which one of the following principles?

(A) Any action by law enforcement officials that involves unequal treatment of citizens is unjustified.
(B) An action by law enforcement officials is justified only when their stated reason for that action is complete.
(C) An action by law enforcement officials cannot be entirely explained by any reason that applies equally to some situation in which no action taken.
(D) Action by law enforcement officials can be justified only by a desire to protect citizens from danger.
(E) The explanation of any action by law enforcement officials must include a complete explanation of why all other potentially appropriate actions were not taken.

13. The industrial production of integrated circuits requires a sterile environment. Otherwise, environmental contaminants are deposited along with the circuit materials, which often leads to the malfunction of the circuit. This is why producers of integrated circuits who make use of robots in the manufacturing process do not use conventional petroleum-based lubricants when lubricating those robots' moving parts.

Which one of the following can most properly be concluded from the statements in the passage above?

(A) The robots used in manufacturing integrated circuits are a major source of environmental contaminants during their industrial production.
(B) The nonmoving parts of robots used during the industrial production of integrated circuits are not a potential source of environmental contamination.
(C) The evaporation of conventional petroleum-based lubricants during the normal operation of robots used to manufacture integrated circuits can produce an environment that is not sterile.
(D) The deposition of any amount of environmental contaminant along with the materials in an integrated circuit will lead to the malfunction of that circuit.
(E) Some lubricant that is less likely than are conventional petroleum-based lubricants to compromise a sterile environment is suitable for lubrication of the moving parts of some robots.

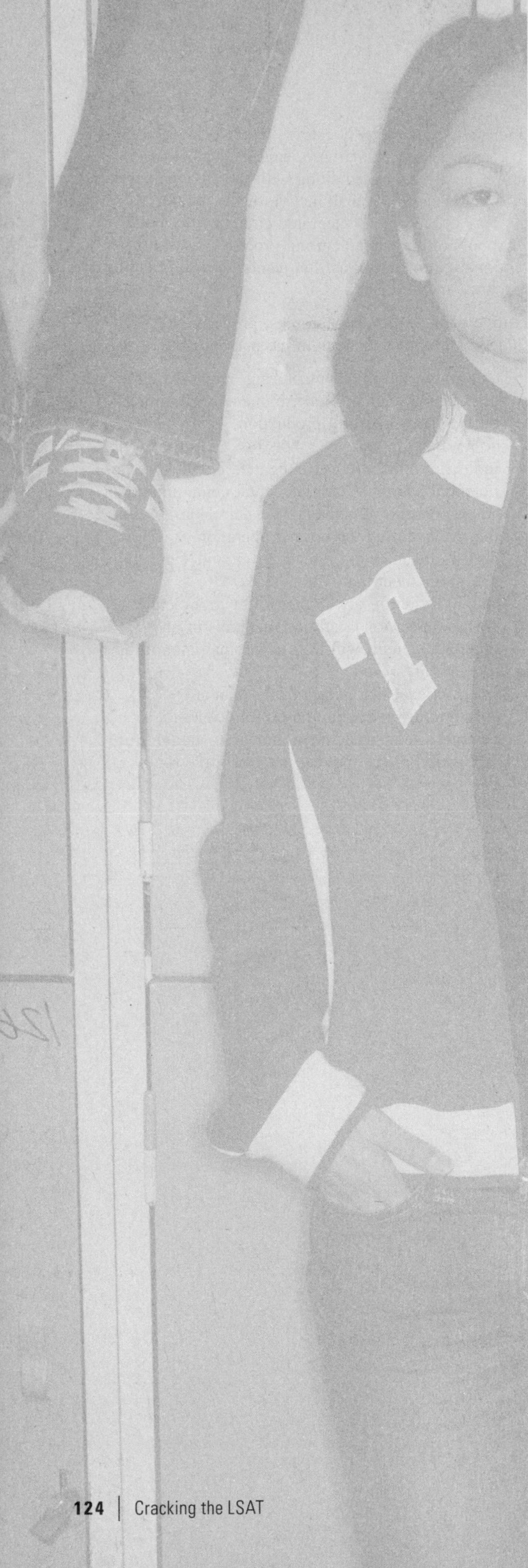

# Summary

- Arguments make up half of the questions on the LSAT. You must work hard to improve in this section if you want to reach your potential on test day.
- Always understand the question task before you read the argument. Some questions require you to find the conclusion and the premises; others require a different analysis. Knowing the question types and what makes the credited response correct for that question type will help you get through the section with speed and accuracy.
- Start thinking about your pacing plan. Know how many arguments you will be attempting on test day.
- As you practice, look for similarities among arguments. You'll find that many arguments follow recognizable patterns; understanding these patterns will help you analyze the argument, eliminate wrong answers, and select the credited response.

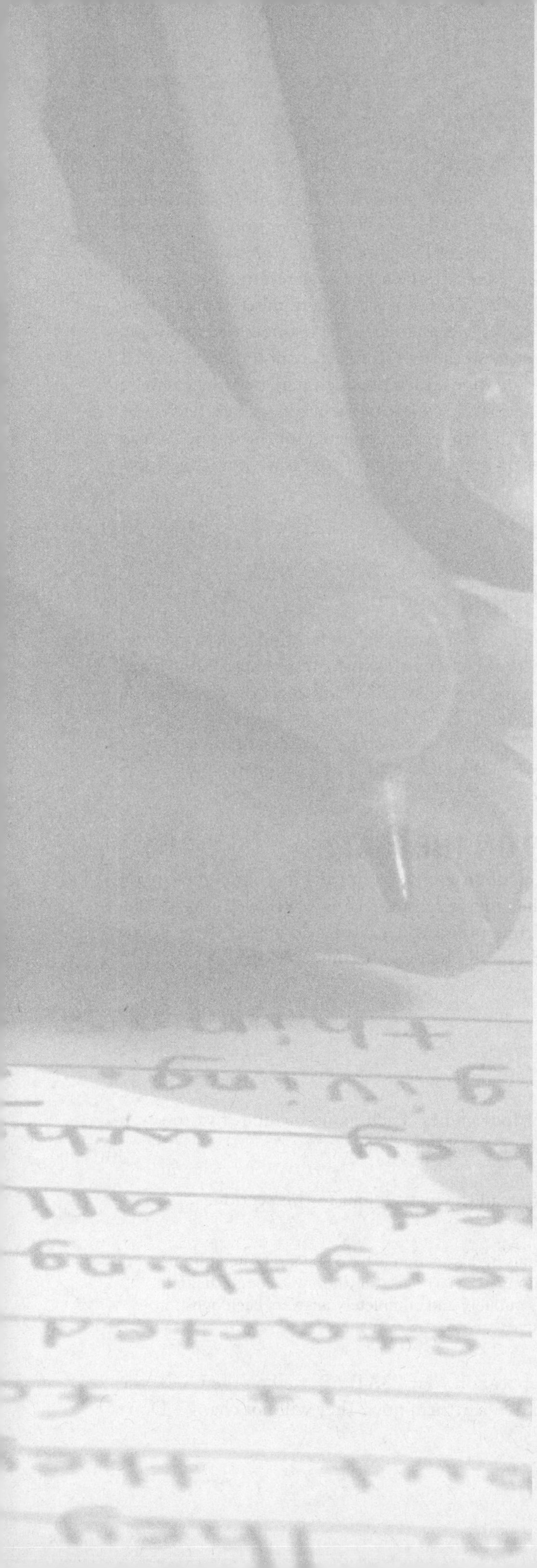

# Chapter 3
# Games

Of all the sections on the LSAT, Analytical Reasoning is the section that initially seems the most intimidating, but we have some good news for you: It's the section where solid technique and plenty of practice pay off the most. If you learn the techniques in this chapter and apply them consistently as you practice, you'll see that these questions follow set patterns, and that all they require is a consistent, careful approach. In fact, you may eventually come to find these questions a little bit—dare we say it?—fun. Don't worry, though; we won't tell your friends.

## WHAT IS A GAME?

The folks who write the test call this section the "Analytical Reasoning" section, but really the questions are just puzzles, so we call it the "Games" section. You are presented with the basic format and structure of the game in the *setup*, an initial paragraph that also provides the *elements*; you will be asked to determine the relationships between these elements. Following the setup will be a number of conditions, or *clues*, which put restrictions on how the elements can be manipulated and sometimes give you valuable information about the overall structure of the game, as well. Finally, you will have a number of questions, each of which may introduce new restrictions or even occasionally change or replace one of the original clues. Each question is independent of the others, although work completed for one question may help in eliminating answer choices on another question. You'll see how this works later on.

## WHAT DOES THIS SECTION TEST?

Games test how well you can organize an incomplete set of spatial relations to extract information efficiently.

Games test how well you can organize information, understand spatial relationships, and make deductions from those relationships when presented with limitations on the arrangements allowed by the rules. They also reward you for being able to extract this information efficiently.

## WHY IS THIS SECTION ON THE LSAT?

Games are designed to predict your ability to perform the kind of detailed analyses required of law students. What they really test is how well you answer the games on the LSAT under strict time pressure. You won't do any of these in law school. And you certainly won't do these when you become a lawyer.

## THE SECTION ITSELF

The Games section is made up of four games. Each game includes five to seven questions. The section normally has 22 to 24 questions.

Before we begin, take a moment to read the instructions to this section.

> Directions: Each group of questions in this section is based on a set of conditions. In answering some of the questions, it may be useful to draw a rough diagram. Choose the response that most accurately and completely answers each question and blacken the corresponding space on your answer sheet.

These are the directions that will appear on your LSAT. As usual on the LSAT, the official directions are of little help. Review them now. They will not change. Don't waste time reading them in the test room.

## THE GOOD NEWS

The good news is that with some rigorous practice diagramming games, you can radically improve your LSAT score. Many students have walked into The Princeton Review classes getting only a few Games questions right, but they walk out scoring 75 percent or higher on this section. You can do the same, as long as you follow our step-by-step process and practice, practice, practice.

## GAMES: GENERAL STRATEGIES

Following is a list of general strategies that you should use when you are working the Games section. Make sure you take these strategies to heart.

### Slow and Steady Wins the Race

More than any other type of question on the LSAT, Games questions require a methodical approach. Trying to rush through the section to make sure you'll finish every question will not help your score. You will achieve the highest level of accuracy by using an approach that increases efficiency—not necessarily pace—without sacrificing your ability to be accurate. If you find you can't finish a Games section in the allotted time, don't fret—very few test takers can. Through consistent practice, you will be able to move more quickly through the section without having to work so fast that you start to make careless errors.

Your mantra: *I will not rush through the games just so that I can finish. I will work to improve efficiency and accuracy, thereby improving my score.*

### Survey the Field

Every correct answer on the LSAT is worth an equal number of points. Since time is of the essence on games, spend your time on easier questions. Remember: The LSAT games and the questions attached to them are not necessarily arranged in order of difficulty. Therefore, you should always try to estimate the difficulty of a game before you work it; if it looks difficult, move on. We'll spend time later outlining what characteristics make a game more or less attractive.

Your mantra: *I will assess the difficulty of games before I begin working on them.*

### Just Do Something

Keep working, keep moving forward, and don't ever just stare at a game in search of divine inspiration. The only way to deal with a difficult game is to *work* through it, not *think* through it.

Your mantra: *I will keep moving forward.*

## Transfer Your Answers After Each Game

As soon as you've finished working on all the questions on a particular game, transfer those answers to your answer sheet. This method has a number of advantages: It is the most efficient approach, it helps prevent careless errors, and it gives your brain a much needed change of task before you dive into the next game. When there are five minutes remaining in the section, fill in answers for all the remaining questions. Then you can go back and work on the remaining questions you have time for, changing the bubbles one at a time as you go.

Your mantra: *I will transfer my answers in a group after each game until five minutes are left.*

## Take Short Breaks

After you've completed each game, take a short break. Not a nap, just ten seconds to take three deep breaths and ready yourself for the next game. Transfer your answers from that game, and then start the next game. You've cleared your mind, and you're ready to push on.

Your mantra: *I will use ten seconds after each game I complete to take some deep breaths and refocus.*

Here Are Your Games Mantras:

*I will not rush through the games just so that I can finish. I will work to improve efficiency and accuracy, thereby improving my score.*

*I will assess the difficulty of games before I begin working on them.*

*I will keep moving forward.*

*I will transfer my answers in a group after each game until five minutes are left.*

*I will use ten seconds after each game I complete to take some deep breaths and refocus.*

# GAMES: SPECIFIC STRATEGIES

The directions for the Games section misleadingly state that "it may be useful to draw a rough diagram" when working the section. That's like saying it may be useful to train before running your first marathon.

## Make It Visual

Games are a visual exercise. Games test your ability to determine how various elements can be arranged in space. Therefore, words don't help you; images do. Your goal will be to translate all the words that you are given in the setup and the clues, and sometimes in the questions themselves, into visual symbols. Once you've done this, you won't need to (or want to) refer to that confusing verbal mess again.

The LSAT writers are banking on the fact that most test takers will try to organize all this information in their heads in their rush to finish. That's a recipe for disaster. Accuracy is crucial on this section, and the only way to ensure accuracy is to work with the information on the page by translating it and drawing it out.

## Be Consistent

There are various ways you can symbolize and diagram the information that is presented to you in a game. We're going to show you what we've found to be the best and most efficient way to diagram and symbolize. Whatever method you choose, be consistent with your symbols and your diagram. When the pressure is on, you don't want to misinterpret a symbol you've drawn.

## Be Careful

You should be confident and aggressive on games, but there is a fine line between aggressiveness and carelessness; don't put yourself on the wrong side of it. This is the only section of the LSAT in which you can be sure an answer is right. Do the work required to take advantage of that.

## Be Flexible

The four games that you will see on the real LSAT may look slightly different from the games you have practiced on. Once you understand how games work and can recognize the basic structures the test writers use to build them, you can see how consistent they really are. Just stay calm and take a step back to evaluate the information. The details will change, but the basic ingredients won't. Focus on the big picture. Focus on the similarities to other games you've already done. And get to work.

Don't simply stare at a game that seems confusing. Focus on the underlying similarities to games you've already seen, and get to work applying the process.

## GAMES: A STEP-BY-STEP PROCESS

Just as we did in the Arguments section, The Princeton Review has boiled down the Games section into a step-by-step process. You will follow this process for every game that you do. Learn these steps, practice them rigorously, apply them consistently, and you'll improve your score. Sound good? Then let's get to it!

**Step 1: Diagram and inventory** Your first step will be to determine the appropriate diagram for the game by evaluating both the setup and the clues. You will be given enough information to understand the basic structure of the game. Your diagram is the fixed gameboard onto which you will place the game pieces—your elements. You will want to make an inventory of the elements next to the diagram, so that you'll have everything in one place and will be able to keep track of it easily. Don't rush through this step, because this is the core of your process. People often want to start scribbling a diagram as soon as something pops out at them from the setup. Take the time to evaluate both the setup and the clues, and you'll be well equipped for the rest of the process.

**Remember!**
The elements are the mobile pieces in a game; don't forget to list them in an inventory near your diagram.

**Step 2: Symbolize the clues and double-check** After you've drawn your diagram, symbolize the clues listed below the setup. Once again, we'll convert the written clues into visual symbols. The clues should be symbolized in a way that is consistent with the diagram you have set up. The goal is to transform the clues into pieces that will fit into your diagram visually. Remember the three C's: Keep your symbols *clear*, *concise*, and *consistent*.

Never forget how important it is to correctly symbolize everything. Invest the few seconds it will take to be sure that your symbols match the information given in the clues. Be sure to go back over the information presented in the setup as well because some games may have longer, more complicated setups than others. A foolproof way to accomplish this is to *work against the grain*: Articulate what each of your symbols means and then carry that back up to the clues you were given. When you find a match, check off that clue. Once you're sure everything is all accounted for, you're finished. It's that simple.

**Hint:**
Repeated elements often provide the opportunity for deductions. If an element is listed in two or more clues, try to combine information to arrive at a new fact.

**Step 3: Make deductions and size up the game** Now that you're sure you've got everything properly symbolized, it's time to make sure that you've made any *deductions* that you can from the information that was given. Look for overlap between the clues and the diagram and among the clues that share elements, and see if there's anything else that you know *for sure*. It isn't enough to suspect that something has to be true; a deduction is something you're certain of. Add your deductions to the information you already have. You'll notice that many deductions give you concrete limitations about where elements are restricted—where they *can't* go—rather than where they *must* go. Does putting two clues together give you a third piece of definite information? Consider each clue individually to see what it says about the elements. Is there anything you could fill in based on that clue?

While you're looking for these deductions, you'll find that you're also learning how the game is going to work. Keep your eyes open for anything that seems as if it will have a particularly large impact on the outcome of the game. The most restricted places and the most restrictive clues tend to have the most impact when you start working the questions. The more you know about how the game will work, the more efficient you'll be at working through the questions.

**Step 4: Assess the question** Not all games questions are on the same level of difficulty. Always look for what we call "Grab-a-Rule" questions to do first. These are questions that give you full arrangements of the elements in each answer, and ask you which one doesn't break the rules. Next, look for Specific questions that further limit the initial conditions of the game and provide you with more information. Once you've done these Specific questions, you'll be better able to work General or Complex questions on a second pass through the game. You should also make a point of either circling or underlining what each question asks you for. This will help you to determine the best approach to the question and the type of answer you'll need.

**Step 5: Act** Each question task requires its own strategy. Making sure that you use the proper strategy means saving time on a given question without sacrificing accuracy. Plus, by approaching the questions in an efficient order, you'll find that the work you've done on earlier questions will often help you to find the right answer on a later question.

**Step 6: Answer using Process of Elimination** Different questions require POE to different degrees. Sometimes you'll be able to go straight to the right answer from your deductions, but often you'll need to work questions by finding the four wrong answers. As a last resort, you may need to test answer choices one at a time to find the right one.

## READY FOR SOME GAMES?

Now let's see how the six steps work on a real game. Give yourself as much time as you need to apply the method to the following game. Focus on using the proper technique (feel free to have the steps written out next to you) and pay no attention to time—that will come later. Work the game using only the space available on the page. On the day of the test, you won't have any scratch paper, so you'll have to get accustomed to writing small and keeping things neat. Do the best you can, and then compare what you did to our explanation. After each game, we'll give you some extra techniques for approaching this section of the LSAT. You should work through each exercise fully before going on to the next game.

Don't worry about time yet. Just focus on the process. Your speed will increase naturally with practice.

## GAME #1: DAYS AND ENTREES

A restaurant must choose its main dinner entree for each night of one week, beginning on Sunday and ending on Saturday. The possible entrees are beef, lamb, manicotti, pork, spaghetti, trout, and veal, each of which will be used on a different night. The following conditions must be met when determining the menu:

The lamb must be served either the night before or the night after the spaghetti is served.

The beef must be served either the night before or the night after either the pork or the trout is served.

The manicotti cannot be served the night before or the night after the veal is served.

The veal must be served on Monday.

1. Which one of the following is a possible menu in order from Sunday to Saturday?

   (A) Pork, veal, trout, lamb, beef, spaghetti, manicotti
   (B) Trout, veal, manicotti, beef, lamb, spaghetti, pork
   (C) Spaghetti, veal, lamb, trout, manicotti, beef, pork
   (D) Trout, veal, beef, pork, manicotti, lamb, spaghetti
   (E) Manicotti, veal, beef, trout, lamb, spaghetti, pork

2. If lamb is served on Saturday, which one of the following must be true?

(A) The spaghetti is served on Thursday.
(B) The beef is served on Tuesday.
(C) The manicotti is served on Thursday.
(D) The pork is served on Wednesday.
(E) The trout is served on Sunday.

3. If the trout is served on Thursday, the pork must be served on

(A) Sunday
(B) Tuesday
(C) Wednesday
(D) Friday
(E) Saturday

4. Which one of the following is a night on which the manicotti could be served?

(A) Sunday
(B) Tuesday
(C) Wednesday
(D) Friday
(E) Saturday

5. If beef is served on Saturday, which one of the following must be true?

(A) The trout is served on Friday.
(B) The pork is served on Thursday.
(C) The spaghetti is served on Wednesday.
(D) The lamb is served on Tuesday.
(E) The manicotti is served on Thursday.

**CRACK THIS GAME STARTING ON THE NEXT PAGE.**

**Hint:**
If a game asks you to put the elements in order, the ordered collection (days of the week, times, positions from left to right) will usually serve as the core of your diagram.

## Cracking Game #1

**Step 1: Diagram and inventory** What we have here are seven days of the week and seven entrees. We learned this from the first paragraph, which is called the *setup*. We recommend using a table in this situation to organize the information. In this case, we need to decide what goes on top of the table—the days of the week or the entrees. We want the things that won't change (our core) across the top of our diagram. Notice that the clues give us information about how the entrees can be organized in relation to one another. We are assigning elements (entrees) to places (days), so the days go on top of the grid. We can list the elements (the entrees) off to the side so it's easy to keep track of them.

Also, we have what is called a *one-to-one correspondence* in this game—there are seven places (days) and seven elements (entrees) that correspond to each of the places. In addition, we're told that each will be used, so we have to use all of them; one-to-one correspondence isn't just a matter of the number of each, but also whether all are used, or any can be reused. This is a good thing because it will limit the number of possible places to which the elements can be assigned. We have to use each element once and because we have only seven nights, we can't repeat any of the elements. That answers two questions you'll want to ask for each game you work: "Can we leave out any elements?" and "Can there be any repeats?". If the answer to either of these is yes, the game becomes more complicated.

In general, factors with a natural order (such as days of the week, rooms numbered 1 through 4, and so on) will act as the core of the diagram. For most diagrams, put what doesn't change on top of the diagram.

Take a look at our diagram for this game.

**Tip!**
Take advantage of the space at the bottom of each page. Practice drawing diagrams as large as possible in the space provided.

| BLMPSTV | Su | M | Tu | W | Th | F | Sa |
|---|---|---|---|---|---|---|---|
| | | | | | | | |

**Step 2: Symbolize the clues and double-check** Now that we've drawn a diagram, it's important that we symbolize the clues so that they fit into our diagram. We want to get rid of the words and transform the clues into visual puzzle pieces that fit into the framework that we've already drawn. Let's take a look at the first clue.

> The lamb must be served either the night before or the night after the spaghetti is served.

1. 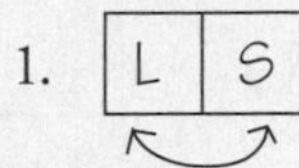


As you can see, we created a shorthand for each of the entrees, denoting them by their first letter (L = lamb and S = spaghetti). We then put these two letters next to each other to show that they must be *consecutive*. We then put a box around the two letters to show that this is a "block" of information that is fixed. Finally, we put the double-pointed arrow underneath the block to show that the order can be either "LS" or "SL."

The great thing about this piece of information is that it will occupy two of the seven possible spaces. Blocks are concrete, restrictive clues that limit the possible arrangements and will make your job easier, so look for them when you are reading over the clues and deciding whether to do a particular game.

> The beef must be served either the night before or the night after either the pork or the trout is served.

2. 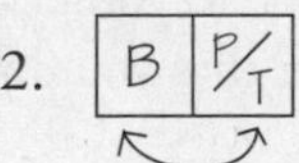


This is also good information, but not quite as good as the "LS" block. We do know that B (beef) must be next to either P (pork) or T (trout), so we indicated that by having P and T share a box next to B. Note the double arrow again, indicating that it could either be "BT" or "TB" if T is next to B, or "BP" or "PB" if P is next to B. The good thing here is that B *must* be next to one or the other of these elements.

> The manicotti cannot be served the night before or the night after the veal is served.

3. 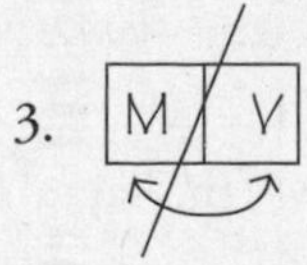


Draw exact symbols for the information given to you. Remember the three C's for symbols: *clear*, *concise*, and *consistent*.

**Tip**
Keep the game organized on your paper: Number your clues as symbolize them.

**Careful!**
Avoid algebraic expressions for clues. Remember that we want to draw a picture of the clue.

As you can see, this clue is telling us what we *can't* have. Here, we can't have the M (manicotti) next to the V (veal). So we drew another block, again with the double arrow underneath, and then we drew a slash through the block itself to indicate that this can never be true. We've just drawn our first *antiblock clue*.

The veal must be served on Monday.

| BLMPSTV | Su | M | Tu | W | Th | F | Sa |
|---|---|---|---|---|---|---|---|
| Clue Shelf | | (V) | | | | | |
| | | | | | | | |

**Tip!**
Make the first row in your diagram a clue shelf. You can symbolize some clues directly in the diagram on a clue shelf. You'll also record deductions there.

As you can see, this piece of information is so definitive that we were able to put it directly into the diagram. Filling in such concrete information right away will save time and your diagram will be better for it. Additionally, we circled the letter to remind ourselves to fill it in as a constant each time we work out a new question in the chart.

As we mentioned, this is the time to compare your symbols to the clues and make sure nothing got mixed up in the translation from verbal to visual. This may seem like a waste of time, but it is essential to your approach. A mistake at this stage can be extremely costly. It is imperative that you double-check your work.

**Step 3: Make deductions and size up the game** By now you should have a list of clues that looks something like this

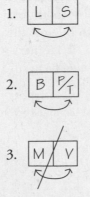

1. 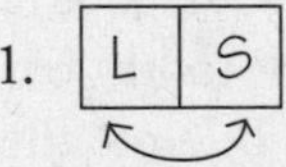


2. B P/T

3. M V

4. V = M (In diagram)

Making a list of the clues—with the number of the clue in front—is a great way to make sure you have accounted for all the clues in the game.

Now, let's take a look at the clues we've drawn to see what kinds of deductions we might make. The first thing we notice, perhaps, is that V is fixed on Monday. What else do we know about V? That M cannot be next to it. Therefore, we know that M cannot be Sunday or Tuesday because V is always on Monday. Look at the diagram below to see how we indicated this.

| BLMPSTV | Su | M | Tu | W | Th | F | Sa |
|---|---|---|---|---|---|---|---|
| Clue Shelf | ~~M~~ | (V) | ~~M~~ | | | | |
| | | | | | | | |

Now, what is our next most definitive piece of information? It is the fact that L and S must always be next to each other. This is good information because there is one place that neither L nor S can go because they must be next to each other—that place is Sunday. Why? Because there's no consecutive space next to Sunday for the second letter to go in. We are only dealing with this one week (Saturday and Sunday are not consecutive), and V is in Monday. Therefore, *neither* L nor S can go in Sunday.

Next, let's go to our B block. We know that one other entree (either P or T) must go next to B. Therefore, B needs a space next to it just like L and S do. Thus, B can't go in Sunday either, for the same reason that L and S can't. Now let's look at the work we did.

| BLMPSTV | Su | M | Tu | W | Th | F | Sa |
|---|---|---|---|---|---|---|---|
| Clue Shelf | ~~M~~ ~~L~~ ~~S~~ ~~B~~ | (V) | ~~M~~ | | | | |
| | | | | | | | |

Pay close attention to slots that are very restricted.

It looks as if Sunday is a very restricted day, right? Four of our seven letters can't go there. If you count V also (which you should), it's actually five out of seven letters that can't go in Sunday. Now, what can go in Sunday? Only P or T. Let's add that information to our diagram.

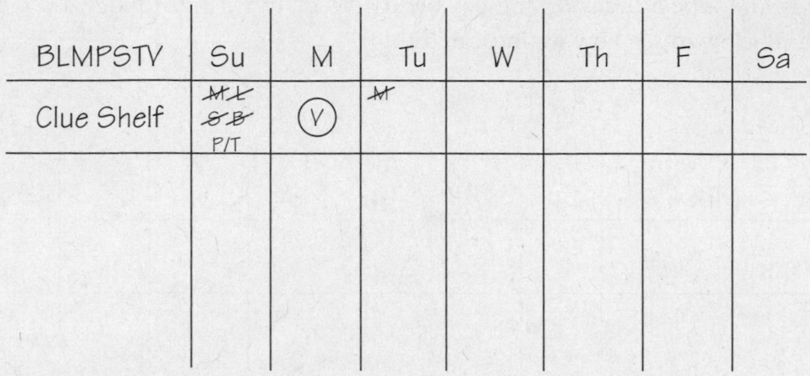

| BLMPSTV | Su | M | Tu | W | Th | F | Sa |
|---|---|---|---|---|---|---|---|
| Clue Shelf | ~~M~~ ~~L~~ ~~S~~ ~~B~~ P/T | (V) | ~~M~~ | | | | |
| | | | | | | | |

**Remember!** Wherever possible, symbolize clues directly in your diagram.

Clearly, we've done some good work with the left side of our diagram. We looked at each of the clues against the diagram itself, and came up with some solid restrictions to indicate on our diagram. We know that both blocks will need to go to the right of Monday. That leaves one more space to be filled after we place the blocks, which will have to be occupied by M (manicotti). Having both blocks—each with two elements—fit in five spaces leaves us with only a few possibilities. Can you see any other restrictions this places on M?

As it turns out, we can deduce the following:

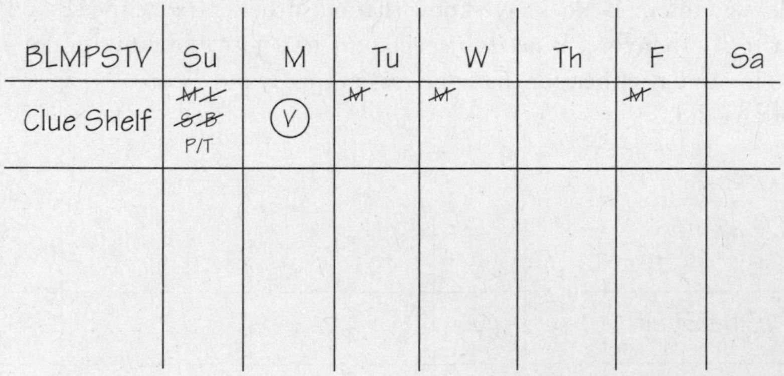

| BLMPSTV | Su | M | Tu | W | Th | F | Sa |
|---|---|---|---|---|---|---|---|
| Clue Shelf | ~~M~~ ~~L~~ ~~S~~ ~~B~~ P/T | (V) | ~~M~~ | ~~M~~ | | ~~M~~ | |
| | | | | | | | |

How did we get to these deductions about M? Following is an illustration of what the possibilities are when you've got two blocks of two spaces each that need to go into a total of only five consecutive slots.

Take a look at what happens.

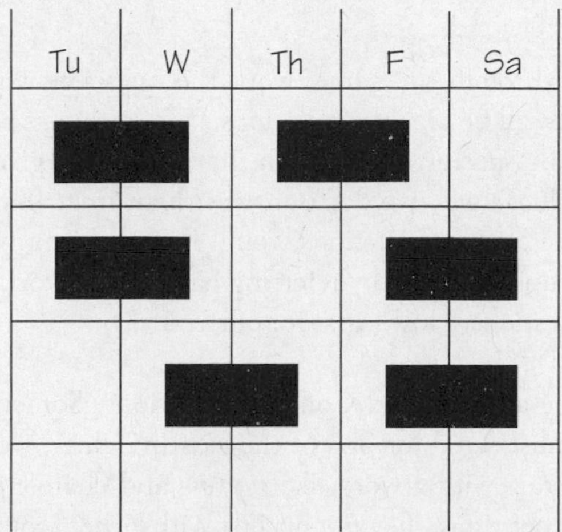


As you can see, the second and fourth spaces are always going to be needed for half of one of the blocks. In our diagram, we're playing with five spaces—Tuesday, Wednesday, Thursday, Friday, and Saturday. Therefore, M cannot go in either the second (Wednesday) or the fourth (Friday) space because we have two blocks that we must place in those five spaces. Make sense? M is one of the most restricted elements left, so if we can place M—which can now only go on Thursday or Saturday—we'll know exactly where our blocks can and can't go!

At this point, we've come up with all the deductions we can and have a pretty good sense of the way this game is going to work. Things will hinge on the most restricted places (like Sunday), and the placement of restricted elements (like M and the two blocks). All the information that we've put in the diagram so far will be true for the whole game, so we'll draw a line under it to separate it off and remind ourselves to pay attention to those limitations as we work each new question. We'll call this row of restrictions that apply to the whole game our *clue shelf.*

**Tip:**
Leave your clue shelf at the top of your diagram and don't work questions in it. Generally, if a line of your diagram tells you what *must* be true, keep it separate from what *could* be true.

**Steps 4 and 5: Assess the question and Act** There are basically four types of questions that you will encounter on games—Grab-a-Rule, Specific, General, Complex.

Grab-a-Rule questions are technically a type of General question, but these should be tackled first because they are quick questions that will help you comprehend the game itself. But be careful—not all games have Grab-a-Rule questions, so if you don't see this type of straightforward question, fear not. Just keep moving and look for the next type of question on the list—Specific questions.

Our favorite kind—the kind you'll want to search out and do after Grab-a-Rule questions, or first if there aren't any Grab-a-Rules—we'll call Specific questions. You'll be able to identify them because they often start with the word *if* and ask you to find the answer choice that *must be true, must be false, could be true,* or *could be false.* These questions give you an extra piece of information that will further limit the possibilities on your diagram—for that question only, of course. The more concrete the information given by a Specific question, the easier the question will be to do.

On your next pass through the game, work the questions you skipped the first time. Some of these will be General questions. These usually begin with the word *which* and differ from Specific questions in that they don't give you any extra limiting information. That's why we don't answer them first. If you save these until after you've done the Specific questions, you'll find that you will be able to eliminate many answer choices simply by referring back to the work that you've already done on Specific questions. How's that for efficiency?

Finally, there are the aptly named Complex questions. Sometimes these will ask what new rule, if substituted for one of the existing clues, would have the same effect. Others will start with a word like *suppose* and change or remove an established condition. Other times they might start with either *if* or *which* but will have a complicated task like figuring out which of the answer choices, if it were true, would completely determine the outcome of the game. These questions are often among the most difficult. You'll see later why you should do them last, if it's not clear already.

**Step 6: Answer using Process of Elimination** You won't always have to work with the answer choices one at a time. Often, you can deduce the answer and go directly to it. This is the most efficient approach.

But when you can't do that, POE is the way to go. You'll have to use different methods in different situations, but the point is that it's often faster to find four wrong answers than it is to find the right answer.

Take a look at the following question:

---

1. Which one of the following is a possible menu in order from Sunday to Saturday?

    (A) Pork, veal, trout, lamb, beef, spaghetti, manicotti
    (B) Trout, veal, manicotti, beef, lamb, spaghetti, pork
    (C) Spaghetti, veal, lamb, trout, manicotti, beef, pork
    (D) Trout, veal, beef, pork, manicotti, lamb, spaghetti
    (E) Manicotti, veal, beef, trout, lamb, spaghetti, pork

### Here's How to Crack It

We call this type a Grab-a-Rule question because all you have to do is apply each rule—or clue—to the answer choices and eliminate any choice that violates it. It gives you five complete lists and asks you to pick the one that follows the rules. These tend to be straightforward, quick questions that will give you valuable insight into how a game works (if you missed anything during the deductions step).

You should do Grab-a-Rule questions first. They sound almost too good to be true, and, as you know, there's a catch: Not all games have one. But if they do, it's the first question and you should work on it right away.

Our first rule tells us that L and S have to be together; that eliminates (A) and (C).

Our second rule tells us that B has to be next to either P or T; that eliminates (B).

Our third rule tells us that M can't be next to V; that eliminates (E).

Choice (D) is the only one left; it must be the answer.

Note: Your process here is to take the clues and apply them to the choices, *not* the other way around. Taking each choice and applying it to each of the clues is very cumbersome. It will take more time and could lead to careless errors. Trust us.

**Hint:**
For a Grab-a-Rule question, take one rule at a time, scanning the answer choices and eliminating those that don't follow the rule. When there's only one choice left, pick it and move on.

---

Let's tackle the next one.

---

2. If lamb is served on Saturday, which one of the following must be true?

   (A) The spaghetti is served on Thursday.
   (B) The beef is served on Tuesday.
   (C) The manicotti is served on Thursday.
   (D) The pork is served on Wednesday.
   (E) The trout is served on Sunday.

### Here's How to Crack It

First, include the extra information from this question into a row of your diagram. Next, determine what other restrictions will allow you to fill in more information by looking for any overlap with your clues. Continue to work on your diagram until you can't fill in any more information. If you find yourself in a situation where slots have been limited to only two options, it's worth filling them in. If there are more than two options, don't bother writing them down, or it will get messy fast.

Fill in all of the information you can BEFORE looking at the answer choices.

**Tip:**
Write the number of the question next to your work in the diagram. Circling the question number helps keep it distinct from the numbers on your clue list.

| BLMPSTV | Su | M | Tu | W | Th | F | Sa |
|---|---|---|---|---|---|---|---|
| Clue Shelf | ~~M L~~ ~~S B~~ P/T | (V) | ~~M~~ | ~~M~~ | M | ~~M~~ | M |
| (2) | P/T | (V) | | | M | S | L |
| | | | | | | | |

As you can see, putting L into the Saturday slot forces the S into the Friday slot because they need to be together. And because M can go on only Saturday or Thursday, we know that M is now in the Thursday slot. L in Saturday, S in Friday, and M in Thursday: These three things MUST be true. We don't know for sure where B, P, or T is, so we won't try to write down all the possible options for them. Remember that our task is to find the answer choice that *must be true*, so odds are we won't need to know anything about elements that we can't place concretely anyway. We'll just head to the answer choices and see if we can find an answer. We can—it's answer choice (C).

On to our next Specific question.

**Hint:**
When working a Specific question, follow this process: Symbolize the new information. Then, deduce everything you can from it. In many cases, this will take you directly to the answer. If it doesn't, then you should begin POE.

3. If the trout is served on Thursday, the pork must be served on

(A) Sunday
(B) Tuesday
(C) Wednesday
(D) Friday
(E) Saturday

### Here's How to Crack It

Wait! Don't erase the information from the last question. The work you do for the Specific questions will help you with POE when you get to the General questions. Just leave that information for now, draw a line, and start another row of information. It's useful to write the number of the question next to the row that you're working on in case you need to come back to it later for some reason.

We have another Specific question, which will give us a new set of possibilities for entree orders, so we'll fill in new information for this question first and then look for any other ramifications until we've gotten all the concrete information written down.

| BLMPSTV | Su | M | Tu | W | Th | F | Sa |
|---|---|---|---|---|---|---|---|
| Clue Shelf | ~~M~~ ~~L~~ ~~S~~ ~~B~~ P/T | (V) | ~~M~~ | ~~M~~ | M | ~~M~~ | M |
| (2) | P/T | (V) | | | M | [S | L] |
| (3) | P | (V) | [S/L | L/S] | [T | B] | M |
| | | | | | | | |

This question tells us to put T into Thursday. This forces M into Saturday. Putting T into Thursday also forces P into Sunday, because Sunday can be only P or T. Finally, there are only three spaces left, and only two (Tuesday and Wednesday) are consecutive. Thus, the S/L block must go into Tuesday and Wednesday. Notice that we couldn't be sure of their order, but there were only two possibilities, so it was worth writing down what we knew. We indicated the possibility with a slash. Now, we've got only B left, and the only place it can go is Friday. What's the question again? P must be where? Sunday, of course. (A) is our answer.

---

You might be wondering why we filled in all that information. After all, our initial deduction, combined with the information about T, was enough to go directly to the answer. Keep in mind that the work we do here can often be used in later general questions, and the more complete your diagrams are, the more useful they'll be. It often turns out that whatever time you seem to save yourself on the first pass through the questions, you give back on the second pass. If you see another deduction, go ahead and write it down.

We'll skip number 4 and move on to our final Specific question.

---

5. If beef is served on Saturday, which one of the following must be true?

   (A) The trout is served on Friday.
   (B) The pork is served on Thursday.
   (C) The spaghetti is served on Wednesday.
   (D) The lamb is served on Tuesday.
   (E) The manicotti is served on Thursday.

### Here's How to Crack It

Use the same process. Fill in the information the question gives you plus any other concrete information that you can.

Here's what we've found.

| BLMPSTV | Su | M | Tu | W | Th | F | Sa |
|---|---|---|---|---|---|---|---|
| Clue Shelf | ~~M L~~ ~~S B~~ P/T | (V) | ~~M~~ | ~~M~~ | M | ~~M~~ | M |
| (2) | P/T | (V) | | | M | S | L |
| (3) | P | (V) | S/L | L/S | T | B | M |
| (5) | P/T | (V) | S/L | L/S | M | P/T | B |

We're told that B is on Saturday. That leaves only Thursday for M, and P or T must be in the Friday slot next to B. This once again pushes the S/L block into Tuesday and Wednesday. That's all we can fill in so we'll head to the answers. We can eliminate any that *could be false.* Let's see how it works.

Choice (A) could be false because P could be in Friday. Cross it off.

Choice (B) *must* be false according to our diagram. Cross it off.

Choice (C) could be false because L could also be in Wednesday. Cross it off.

Choice (D) could be false because S could also be in Tuesday. Cross it off.

Choice (E) must be true from our diagram. Keep it.

It's much easier to get through the answer choices once you have that diagram filled in, isn't it? The investment is worth it.

Here's our last question.

---

4. Which one of the following is a night on which the manicotti could be served?

(A) Sunday
(B) Tuesday
(C) Wednesday
(D) Friday
(E) Saturday

### Here's How to Crack It

Well, we deduced that M can go in only one of two places—Thursday or Saturday. Even if we hadn't come up with that deduction, we could check back to our previous work to see where M has been placed throughout the game—we'd see that M has worked on both Thursday and Saturday. Only Saturday is listed in the choices, so (E) is our answer.

---

Now, what did we just do? Once again, here's the step-by-step approach to all games.

| | |
|---|---|
| Prepare the Game | Step 1: Diagram and inventory<br>Step 2: Symbolize the clues and double-check<br>Step 3: Make deductions and size up the game |
| Work the Questions | Step 4: Assess the question<br>Step 5: Act<br>Step 6: Use Process of Elimination |

## Games Technique: Use Good Symbolization

Good symbolization is a major step toward getting all the questions in a particular game correct. Success with symbolization comes from familiarity and practice. There are a number of common types of clues that you'll see repeatedly on the LSAT; once you become familiar with them, most of the process becomes mechanical. While you're practicing your symbolization, keep in mind the three C's: *clear*, *concise*, and *consistent*.

*Clear:* Your symbols should make quick and apparent sense. If you find yourself having to interpret a clue as you use it in the game, it's not working.

*Concise:* Keep symbols as short and simple as possible. Part of the reason for having them is to eliminate the wasted energy of reading those long-winded, confusing clues each time you refer to them in working the questions.

*Consistent:* As we mentioned above, you should start to recognize distinct types of LSAT clues that you'll symbolize in the same manner each time they show up in a game. But you should also be sure that your clues are consistent with one another within a game and that they are consistent with the way that you drew your diagram. They should all fit together.

Let's take a look at good symbols for some common types of clues.

Anna sits to the east of Bob and to the west of Carol.

This clue is giving you two pieces of information about A. It is always best to consolidate these pieces of information into one symbol, but be careful! Make sure you are consistent throughout the game about which way is east and which way is west—under time pressure, these basic pieces of knowledge can get twisted around.

B – A – C

As you can see, we've put A in between B and C. "To the east" here means to the right, so the first thing we did was to put A to the right of B. Then, we read that Anna sits "to the west," or to the left, of Carol, so we can place A to the left of C. We didn't put this in a box because we don't know whether these people are sitting right next to one another—all we know is "to the right" and "to the left." Therefore, we used a line to show that there might be one or more elements in between them or that they could end up right next to one another. We'll call these *range* clues because they tell us only the range of places that one element can occupy in relation to another element. You can think of the line as a rubber band; sometimes the elements will be pulled apart from one another and one or more other elements will be placed in between them, and other times they will pull right up next to one another.

Because we were able to link these two range clues into one larger clue, we actually know more than if we had symbolized them separately. For instance, we know that A must always be placed in between the other two elements. And we know that B must always have *at least* two other elements to its right. Combining clues is a powerful way to generate new information about a game.

---

The two philosophers never sit together.

**Hint:**
Combine clues, when possible, into a single symbol. This is particularly useful on ordering games.

This is very similar to a clue we had in the menu-planning game we just did. Remember the manicotti-veal antiblock? It didn't give us information about how two elements *must be* positioned with relation to each other, but rather how they *cannot be*. Here we know that there are two P's and that these two P's can never be together. It's another basic antiblock.

P/P

If the game ever gives us the placement of one of the philosophers, we know now that the other philosopher can't go immediately to the right or left of the first one. We also know that there are only two philosophers from the concrete language used in the clue. If we weren't sure how many philosophers there were in the game, we would want to be sure to note that fact in addition to our antiblock clue.

---

In a five-story building, J lives two floors above W.

A clue's symbol makes sense only in the context of a diagram. So for our example, we're going to draw a rough little diagram similar to what you would have already constructed had you come across this clue in an actual game.

5
4
3
2
1

Remember one of our C's: *consistent.* We want our symbol to look like what happens in our diagram. That's why the clue should be vertical too. But be careful here—if J lives two floors above W, there is only one floor that actually separates them. Take a look at our symbol.

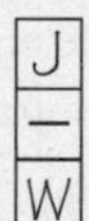


As you can see, the wording is meant to lead you astray: There is a big difference between 'J lives two floors above W' and 'There are two floors between J and W.' If you weren't vigilant and had inserted an extra floor, your game would have swiftly degenerated into confusion.

Reread each clue to see if your visual matches the exact text of the clue.

---

The three boys all sit in consecutive seats, with one girl immediately before them and one girl immediately after.

This clue gives you several pieces of information. First, there are exactly three boys. Second, there are at least two girls. Third, the three boys all sit together. Fourth, one girl sits on either end of the line of boys. Let's put it all together.

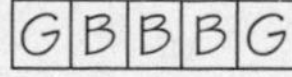

Notice that we didn't write "G3BG." Instead, we wrote out three separate B's. The same goes for symbolizing the elements when you know how many of each type you have. If a clue tells you that you have five engines, for example, write "EEEEE" and not "5E." And if later you are given further characteristics about the boys and girls, such as what color hats they might be wearing, you will be able to note these characteristics as another layer below the first symbol.

---

A, B, and C are saxophonists; D, E, and F are percussionists.

In this case, we are given elements that fall into two categories: saxophonists and percussionists. We must have a way to keep these straight as we work the game. Probably the simplest way to accomplish this is by symbolizing one group with uppercase letters and the other with lowercase letters. We'll end up with the following symbols:

S: A B C
p: d e f

There are games that have more than two types of elements, or elements that can have more than one characteristic associated with them. In these cases, you should use subscripts to distinguish the elements. For instance, if we had those same saxophonists and percussionists, but we were also told that A and f were leads and C and e were backups, we would need some way to keep all of this straight. Furthermore, we might have to assign these elements to either the marching band or the orchestra, if these are the groups available in the game. We would need to make sure that we could tell what characteristics each element had so that we could assign them accordingly. Here's how we would symbolize the leads (L) and backups (B).

S: $A_L$ B $C_B$
p: d $e_B$ $f_L$

You'll have to make an effort to keep things neat, but now you'll be able to work with the elements effectively.

---

There is at least one fire drill per week.

How would you do this one? This doesn't give us very concrete information because we still don't know exactly how many fire drills there will be each week. But it is an important piece of information because we know for sure that we have to include a fire drill in each valid arrangement for the game. It's a pretty simple piece of information, so our symbol will also be pretty simple. Don't succumb to the urge to just keep it in your head; yes, it's simple, but no, that doesn't give you license to skip the visualization. Here's a good way to symbolize it.

$F^{1+}$

We used the plus sign to indicate *at least*, which will remind us that we can have more than one of these, according to the rules. A corollary clue type is one that tells you that an element will be used *at most* a certain number of times; in that case we would use a minus sign as the superscript.

Here's a summary chart of how we symbolized each clue.

| Clue | Symbol | Clue Pattern |
|---|---|---|
| Anna sits to the east of Bob and to the west of Carol. | B— A— C | Range Clue |
| The two philosophers never sit together. | [P/P] (crossed out) | Antiblock Clue |
| In a five-story building, J lives two floors above W. | [J] / [–] / [W] | Block Clue |
| The three boys all sit in consecutive seats, with one girl immediately before them and one girl immediately after. | [G\|B\|B\|B\|G] | Block Clue |
| A, B, and C are saxophonists; D, E, and F are percussionists. | S: A B C<br>p: d e f | Inventory Clue |
| There is at least one fire drill per week. | $F^{1+}$ | Distribution Clue |

## Games Technique: When Words Are Better than Pictures

Ideally, you will symbolize every clue. Some clues, however, have no clear and concise visual equivalent, especially negative clues that do not refer to any specific element. For example, consider the following clues.

> No more than three books of any given subject are put on the shelf.
>
> Players cannot score more than three points in the first round.

A visualization of these would end up being obtuse and potentially confusing. Now we need another method. Remember that we want to keep all the information in one place and not have to refer to the written information provided. Just jot down the essence of the clue in a few words among the rest of your clues. That way you can't forget about it and you won't have to wade through the original, confusing clue. Now let's try another game.

## GAME #2: FLIGHTS

On Saturday, eight flights—J, K, L, M, N, O, P, and R—are scheduled to depart from a small airport in Darbyfield. For safety reasons, no two flights depart at the same time, and each flight departs exactly once. The flights depart according to the following conditions:

Flight R departs at some time after flight L.

Flight K departs at some time after flight P, but before flight R.

Flight L departs at some time before flights O and J.

Flight M departs at some time before flight K, and flight N departs at some time after flight R.

Flight J is the seventh flight to depart.

1. Which of the following could be the order, for first to last, in which the flights depart?

(A) L, P, M, K, R, N, J, O
(B) P, K, R, N, L, O, J, M
(C) M, L, P, K, R, O, N, J
(D) M, K, P, L, O, R, J, N
(E) P, M, K, R, L, N, J, O

2. Each of the following could be the fourth flight to depart EXCEPT

(A) K
(B) R
(C) O
(D) P
(E) M

3. If L is the fourth flight to depart, each of the following could be false EXCEPT

(A) M is the second flight to depart.
(B) O is the eighth flight to depart.
(C) N is the sixth flight to depart.
(D) K is the third flight to depart.
(E) P is the second flight to depart.

4. If flight N departs before flight O, which of the following could be true?

(A) Flight R departs sixth.
(B) Flight K departs third.
(C) Flight O departs earlier than flight J.
(D) Flight K departs fifth.
(E) Flight M departs fourth.

5. Which of the following must be true?

(A) Flight M departs before flight L.
(B) Flight P departs before flight O.
(C) Flight L departs before flight N.
(D) Flight K departs before flight O.
(E) Flight L departs before flight K.

**CRACK THIS GAME STARTING ON THE NEXT PAGE.**

**Tip!**
If most of the questions are on the second page of a game, start drawing the diagram on the second page so your workspace is more compact.

## Cracking Game #2

**Step 1: Diagram and inventory** Here we have another game with a one-to-one correspondence in the inventory: There are eight flights, and they take off in order from first to last. That means we can build a diagram similar to the one we used in the first game, with the order first through last forming the core of the diagram along the top. We can list the elements (the flights) off to the side so it's easy to keep track of them.

| JKLMNOPR | 1 | 2 | 3 | 4 | 5 | 6 | 7 | 8 |
|---|---|---|---|---|---|---|---|---|
| | | | | | | | | |

**Step 2: Symbolize the clues and double-check** The rules in this game are a little different from the ones we saw in the first game. Take another look at the first clue, "Flight R departs at some time after flight L." Notice that it doesn't say whether R comes immediately after L or a long time after L. All it tells us is that R is sometime after L. We'll call clues like this "range clues," and we can symbolize them like this

1. L – R

That band between L and R means that R could be the very next one after L, or it could be much later, as long as L comes earlier in the diagram than R. Remember to treat the band like a stretchy rubber band: It can scrunch up to nothing or stretch across the whole diagram.

When we get to the next clue, we see that it is giving us similar information, but this time, it tells us about three elements, not just two. No problem: We can still symbolize them all in one rule.

2. P – K – R

You can probably already see how important double-checking will be on clues like this. It's very easy to get the order mixed up, so be extra careful here!

The next clue is also about three elements, but this time we don't know exactly what order they are in. We know only that L must come before O and that it must come before J. It would be possible to write this as two separate rules, but let's put it all together into one rule that shows L before both O and J, so that our clues are as concise as possible.

```
    L – O
3.   \
      J
```

Notice that we haven't decided whether O comes before J or vice versa, only that they both are after L.

One more range clue to go:

```
4. M – K
   R – N
```

And finally a familiar-looking clue that we can put right into our diagram, just like in the first game.

| JKLMNOPR | 1 | 2 | 3 | 4 | 5 | 6 | 7 | 8 |
|---|---|---|---|---|---|---|---|---|
| | | | | | | | J | |

Make sure to double-check those clues, and we're on to the deductions.

**Step 3: Make deductions and size up the game** By now you have a list of clues that should look something like this

```
 1. L – R
 2. P – K – R
 3. L – O
     \
      J
 4. M – K
      R – N
5. J = 7 (in diagram)
```

Do you see how R shows up in both of the first two clues? Let's link them together into one clue, so we can get all of our information in one place.

```
         L
          \
P – K – R
```

In fact, let's go ahead and link together as many of the clues we can. We should end up with something like this

```
          J
         /
        L – O
         \
P – K – R – N
  /
 M
```

In games that give you lots of range clues, it is very common to be able to link them up into a big tree, like we've done here. Linking range clues like this can be a great time-saver when you get to the questions, so make sure to do it whenever you get the chance.

Once you've got your tree made, there are lots of useful deductions you can still get out of it. For instance, which elements are allowed to go in spot number 1? Only P, M, and L. All the others must have at least one element come earlier in the diagram. Let's put that into the diagram!

| JKLMNOPR | 1 | 2 | 3 | 4 | 5 | 6 | 7 | 8 |
|---|---|---|---|---|---|---|---|---|
| | P/M/L | | | | | | J | |

Now that we know our options for slot 1, let's check slot 8, since the two end slots are the most heavily restricted. What are the only elements that don't have to come before something? Only O and N (remember: J is already in spot 7). That means that either O or N must be last.

| JKLMNOPR | 1 | 2 | 3 | 4 | 5 | 6 | 7 | 8 |
|---|---|---|---|---|---|---|---|---|
| | P/M/L | | | | | | J | O/N |

We could make more deductions about which spaces are off-limits to the various elements, but there will be so many that our diagram will get messy fast. Since spots 1 and 8 are the most restricted, it's good to get whatever information we can about them, but beyond that, we might start to put in a lot of work without getting much concrete information in exchange. Time to move on to the questions.

**Steps 4 and 5: Assess the question and Act** See a Grab-a-Rule question? Yes! Do it even before the Specific questions.

### Step 6: Answer using Process of Elimination

1. Which of the following could be the order, for first to last, in which the flights depart?

(A) L, P, M, K, R, N, J, O
(B) P, K, R, N, L, O, J, M
(C) M, L, P, K, R, O, N, J
(D) M, K, P, L, O, R, J, N
(E) P, M, K, R, L, N, J, O

#### Here's How to Crack it

Remember to grab rules one by one, starting with any deductions that are already in your diagram.

J must be 7th, so there goes (C).

Only O or N can be last, so we can say goodbye to (B).

L must be before R, so (E) is out.

K must be between P and R, so we can eliminate (D).

Choice (A) is the only one that's left, so it must be our answer.

Time to move on to the Specific questions, so let's go to number 3.

3. If L is the fourth flight to depart, each of the following could be false EXCEPT

(A) M is the second flight to depart.
(B) O is the eighth flight to depart.
(C) N is the sixth flight to depart.
(D) K is the third flight to depart.
(E) P is the second flight to depart.

### Here's How to Crack it

Note the strange question ending: "could be false EXCEPT." That means the four wrong answers could be false. Thus the credited response can't be false. But when something can't be false, that just means it must be true. Cross out "could be false EXCEPT" and write in "must be true" instead.

Now, on to business: Plug In the new information and deduce.

| JKLMNOPR | 1 | 2 | 3 | 4 | 5 | 6 | 7 | 8 |
|---|---|---|---|---|---|---|---|---|
| Clue shelf | P/M/L | | | | | | J | O/N |
| ③ | P/M | | | L | | | J | O/N |

We know that L comes before O, J, R, and N (since N has to follow R). We don't know exactly where they'll go, but we do know that O, R, and N must occupy spots 5, 6, and 8 in some way. We also know that R can't be last, and that, in this case, N can't be 5, since R has to come before N, but after L. Still, nothing much must be true, so we'd better keep deducing.

| JKLMNOPR | 1 | 2 | 3 | 4 | 5 | 6 | 7 | 8 |
|---|---|---|---|---|---|---|---|---|
| Clue shelf | P/M/L | | | | | | J | O/N |
| ③ | P/M | | | L | O/R | O/R/N | J | O/N |

The only spots we still haven't accounted for are 2 and 3. Since the only letters available still are P, M, and K, let's see what we know about them. We know that K can't be first or second, since both P and M need to come before it. That means K must be third! We don't know what order P and M go in, so we end up with the following

| JKLMNOPR | 1 | 2 | 3 | 4 | 5 | 6 | 7 | 8 |
|---|---|---|---|---|---|---|---|---|
| Clue shelf | P/M/L | | | | | | J | O/N |
| ③ | P/M | P/M | K | L | O/R | O/R/N | J | O/N |

All that must be true is that K is third. Pick answer choice D.

---

Now you can move on to the next Specific question.

---

4. If flight N departs before flight O, which of the following could be true?

   (A) Flight R departs sixth.
   (B) Flight K departs third.
   (C) Flight O departs earlier than flight J.
   (D) Flight K departs fifth.
   (E) Flight M departs fourth.

### Here's How to Crack it

The question tells us that N comes before O. What else do we know about N and O? That one of them must be last. That means O is last. Let's write it in and see if we can make any more deductions.

| JKLMNOPR | 1 | 2 | 3 | 4 | 5 | 6 | 7 | 8 |
|---|---|---|---|---|---|---|---|---|
| Clue shelf | P/M/L | | | | | | J | O/N |
| ③ | P/M | P/M | K | L | O/R | O/R/N | J | O/N |
| ④ | | | | | | | J | O |

See any more deductions? No? There are a few out there, but let's take it from here just to see what we can do in a situation where you might not see everything that it is possible to deduce. This question asks what could be true, which means that if we start trying answer choices, there will be only one that doesn't force us to violate a rule. Let's just start plugging them in one by one until we find the only one that works. (A) says R is sixth. If we plug it in and deduce, we don't have any place for N to go. (A) forces us to break a rule, so it couldn't be true. Cross it out and try (B).

| JKLMNOPR | 1 | 2 | 3 | 4 | 5 | 6 | 7 | 8 |
|---|---|---|---|---|---|---|---|---|
| Clue shelf | P/M/L | | | | | | J | O/N |
| ③ | P/M | P/M | K | L | O/R | O/R/N | J | O/N |
| ~~④ (A)~~ | | | | | | | ~~J~~ | ~~O~~ |

Choice (B) says K is third. Let's give it a try. K needs P and M before it—no problem. That leaves L, R, and N. L needs to be before R, which is before N—a perfect fit in spots 4, 5, and 6. (B) doesn't break any rules, so it's our answer. Time to move on.

| JKLMNOPR | 1 | 2 | 3 | 4 | 5 | 6 | 7 | 8 |
|---|---|---|---|---|---|---|---|---|
| Clue shelf | P/M/L | | | | | | J | O/N |
| ③ | P/M | P/M | K | L | O/R | O/R/N | J | O/N |
| ~~④ (A)~~ | | | | | | | ~~J~~ | ~~O~~ |
| ④ (B) | P/M | P/M | K | L | R | N | J | O |

Now for the general questions.

2. Each of the following could be the fourth flight to depart EXCEPT

(A) K
(B) R
(C) O
(D) P
(E) M

This question asks us to find out which flights can be fourth and which one can't. Now's the time to check back in with our range clue tree.

```
            J
           /
          L—O
           \
    P—K—R—N
     /
    M
```

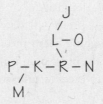

To find the element that can't go fourth, we need to find the element that must come either earlier or later.

Answer choice (A), K, must have at least two elements (P and M) before it so the earliest it could go would be 3. It must have at least two after it (R and N) so the latest it could go is 6. Since K could be anywhere between 3 and 6, it could be fourth. Eliminate (A).

We'll have to repeat this process until we find the only one that can't go fourth.

Answer choice (B), R, needs four to come before it (P, M, K, and L) so the earliest we'll see R is fifth. Choice (B) is our answer.

We have our answer now, but for the sake of practice, try proving that O, P, and M could all be fourth. Count the number of elements that must come earlier than each one and the number that must come later. You'll see that P could be anywhere from 1–5; M could be anywhere from 1–5, and O could go anywhere from 2–8, except for 7 (which is always J in this game).

One question to go!

5. Which of the following must be true?

(A) Flight M departs before flight L.
(B) Flight P departs before flight O.
(C) Flight L departs before flight N.
(D) Flight K departs before flight O.
(E) Flight L departs before flight K.

### Here's How to Crack it

This is another question that lets us use our range clue tree.

Nothing in the tree says M is before L. Eliminate (A).

Nothing in the tree says P is before O. Eliminate (B).

L always comes before R, which is before N, so (C) must be true, and we're home free.

## Games Technique: Making Deductions

Since we've worked through two games now, you should recognize how important it is to make deductions before you start to work the questions. Think of them as unwritten clues. You can't make good deductions by briefly glancing at your diagram and clues while hurrying to get to the questions. You have to look carefully at the diagram and your symbols. Some people think that making deductions is the result of some kind of epiphany—that you either see them or you don't. Actually, finding deductions is the result of a purely mechanical process. Once you understand the process and have had some time to practice it on a number of different games, you'll be able to ferret out those critical extra pieces of information that will save you valuable time down the road. Here's an overview of the process.

The number one way to find deductions: Look for repeated elements.

- Look for elements, or for areas of your diagram, that are mentioned in more than one clue. Sometimes, particularly in ordering games, you'll be able to combine more than one range clue or block into a single symbol, and that provides you with new information. Still other times—as in our first game with the veal and manicotti—you can apply a clue to some definite information in your diagram and get more definite information as a result.
- Check the fit of your clues into your diagram. Sometimes combined clues can get very large, and they may fit into your diagram in only one or two ways. Even if a clue isn't particularly large, you should still be able to get some information this way: For a range clue, often you can find places where the elements involved can't go; for a block clue, you will sometimes find that the number of places it can actually fit is very restricted.
- Look for sweeping or powerful clues. These are clues that affect many elements and many areas of your diagram. Such clues are fairly rare—we actually haven't seen one yet in this chapter—but when they're present, pay close attention to them. They often work like super-antiblocks—clues that tell you whole element types can't appear next to one another in your diagram. Because they apply so broadly, they're often the source of fruitful deductions.
- Deductions that start with *if* are bad; deductions that start with *either* are good. In other words, you don't want to find yourself following lines of reasoning like this: "Well, if F goes there, then that means G has to go here, and then…." Those can be useful in limited cases, but remember that you're looking for things you can write down that are true all the time. The good twin of this kind of deduction is the one that goes something like this: "Either F is here, or else F is there; there are no other choices." That deduction, because it's so well defined and concrete, is going to be extremely useful.

Finally, it's important to keep deductions in perspective. Remember that the reason you're looking for them is to make your life *easier*, not harder. Deductions save you time by giving you more information to use on every question, but you give that advantage back if you spend a long time staring unproductively at a game, hoping to find a deduction.

When you're looking for links, go through the checklist. When you're done, move decisively to the questions. It's okay if you don't find any deductions, or if you find just one or two small ones; games don't always have big deductions. And realize that it's not the end of the world if you're working a game that does have big deductions and you somehow miss them. The first few questions may take a little longer, but they'll still be workable, and you can learn about the game as you go. Sometimes the only way to find big deductions on a game is to stumble across them, and the only way to do that is to actually get into the game and start working with it. As long as you keep moving forward, you'll be all right. If you sit and stare, you'll get yourself in trouble.

The first two games on which we worked used one of the most common diagrams found on the LSAT: a straight grid diagram with the core across the top or on one side, to which we add rows or columns as we work the questions. But sometimes, as in Game #3 on the next page, the setup will describe a spatial relationship that doesn't fit into that pattern. If that happens, just be flexible and use the information given to create a visual framework that matches the description in the setup. You'll still assign elements to places according to the rules; you'll just put them into a different structure. Remember to work on the limited space of the page—so that you won't be in for an unpleasant surprise when you get to the real thing. We're still working on cementing the games process, so don't be concerned about time right now. Be methodical and refer to the earlier parts of the chapter as necessary. After you've finished, compare your results to ours.

## GAME #3: OFFICES AND FURNISHINGS

There are exactly ten offices arranged on either side of a hallway. The offices with windows facing north are on one side of the hallway and are numbered 1, 2, 3, 4, and 5, respectively, from the west end of the building to the east. The offices with windows facing south are on the other side of the hallway and are numbered 6, 7, 8, 9, and 10, respectively, also from west to east. The offices on the north side are directly across from the offices on the south side, facing each other in the following pairs: 1 and 6, 2 and 7, 3 and 8, 4 and 9, and 5 and 10. Each office has been furnished in exactly one of the following styles: Bauhaus, Moderne, or Pop, according to the following conditions:

None of the offices is furnished in the same style as the office that is located directly across the hallway from it.

None of the offices is furnished in the same style as any office adjacent to it.

Bauhaus furnishings are found in exactly one office on each side of the hallway.

Bauhaus furnishings are found in office number 3.

Moderne furnishings are found in office number 7.

1. Which one of the following could be an accurate list of the styles of furnishings found in offices 6, 7, 8, 9, and 10, respectively?

(A) Pop, Moderne, Pop, Moderne, Pop
(B) Pop, Moderne, Pop, Bauhaus, Moderne
(C) Bauhaus, Pop, Moderne, Pop, Moderne
(D) Bauhaus, Moderne, Pop, Moderne, Bauhaus
(E) Pop, Moderne, Bauhaus, Pop, Moderne

2. If Pop furnishings are found in exactly five of the offices along the hallway, then which one of the following statements must be true?

(A) Moderne furnishings are found in office 6.
(B) Moderne furnishings are found in office 4.
(C) Pop furnishings are found in office 5.
(D) Moderne furnishings are found in office 10.
(E) Bauhaus furnishings are found in office 9.

3. Which one of the following statements must be false?

(A) Pop furnishings are found in office 10.
(B) Pop furnishings are found in office 1.
(C) Moderne furnishings are found in office 9.
(D) Bauhaus furnishings are found in office 9.
(E) Bauhaus furnishings are found in office 10.

4. If office 4 is furnished in Pop, then each of the following statements could be false EXCEPT

(A) Pop furnishings are found in office 10.
(B) Pop furnishings are found in office 6.
(C) Bauhaus furnishings are found in office 6.
(D) Moderne furnishings are found in office 5.
(E) Moderne furnishings are found in office 9.

5. Which of the following, if substituted for the condition that Bauhaus furnishings are found in office 3, would have the same effect on determining the style of furnishings found in each office?

(A) Pop furnishings are found in office 8.
(B) Moderne furnishings are found in office 10.
(C) Moderne furnishings are found in office 1.
(D) If Bauhaus furnishings are not found in office 3, then Moderne furnishings are not found in office 7.
(E) Bauhaus furnishings cannot be found in an office adjacent to an office in which Moderne furnishings are found.

**CRACK THIS GAME STARTING ON THE NEXT PAGE.**

## Cracking Game #3

**Step 1: Diagram and inventory** Each of our first two games was arranged in a grid, one with one level of information and the other with two. Each had a one-to-one correspondence between elements and slots. With this game, things get a little bit more complicated. No worries, though. All we have to do is follow the process and we'll be able to approach it effectively. The setup tells us that this game has a particular spatial arrangement of the slots we'll assign elements to, but the process of assigning elements to spaces is still the same. So what will our diagram look like? Just take a cue from the setup and make it look the way it's described. We ended up with this arrangement.

Don't forget to list the elements next to the diagram so that you'll have everything within easy reach. It's a pretty straightforward diagram. But it would be difficult to add rows in the way that we have with our previous games.

Instead, we'll use this as a template and then create another simple diagram—after all, it's only a few lines—to work each of the questions. We'll fill in the template with all of the concrete information that we have, effectively like a clue shelf. And then each of the new little diagrams that we create to work on the questions will just be a quick sketch that we can use right now as a framework to place our elements according to the restrictions of the question. And we still won't erase our previous work, for the same reason as before. If it's not clear right now, then you'll see what we mean in a moment.

Notice that we have only three elements to be distributed among ten offices. That means that we'll have to repeat them. And based on how restrictive the clues are about the placement of elements of the same type in adjacent slots, we'll have to use all of the elements. Make a note of that.

**Step 2: Symbolize the clues and double-check** Let's get right to it and make the restrictions visual.

> None of the offices is furnished in the same style as the office that is located directly across the hallway from it.

This clue tells us how elements cannot be arranged with respect to one another, so this is an antiblock clue, but it's broader than what we're used to. The antiblock clues we've seen so far have listed specific elements that can't be next to one another, but here it applies to all of the elements. No big deal. General clues—those that apply to all elements, all spaces, or even one entire type of element—are often the most powerful clues in a game. In this game, we have only three types of elements, so it would be easy enough to jot down the three possibilities as individual antiblocks. Because "facing" here is vertical, they would look like this

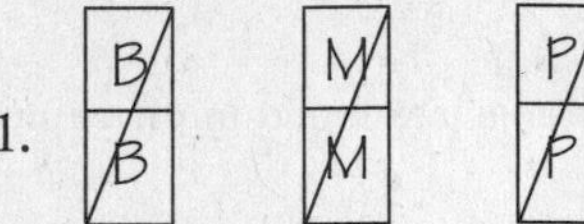


None of the offices is furnished in the same style as any office adjacent to it.

We have another antiblock clue that applies to all of the elements. Adjacent means "right next to" so it's basically the same as our first clue, but horizontal. Like this

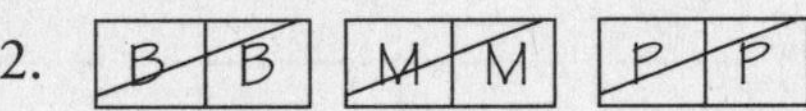


Bauhaus furnishings are found in exactly one office on each side of the hallway.

This is very specific about how many times we'll place B, but vague as to exactly where it will go within each row. So we'll jot down what we know. We'll use B exactly two times, so let's put two B's down in our list of elements. And we'll make a note over to the side of our diagram to show that we must use B once in each row. We also know that we have eight slots to fill with M and P, so we'll have to use each more than once. Our symbol for "more than once" is a superscript 1+ next to each element in our list next to the diagram.

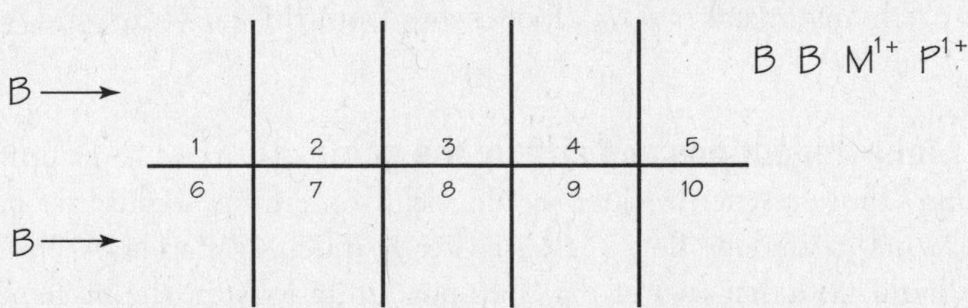


Bauhaus furnishings are found in office number 3.

Aha! More about B. This time we are able to definitively place one of the B's, so we'll go ahead and put it right into our diagram. We'll circle it the same way we did the permanently placed element in the first game, so that we never forget to place it in the same space for each question we work through. Keep in mind that we have only one more B to use and it will have to go in the other row.

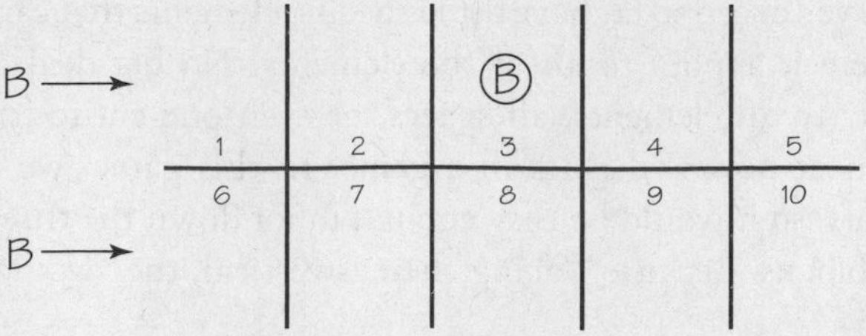


Moderne furnishings are found in office number 7.

Another wonderfully restrictive clue. We can go ahead and drop that right into the diagram as well.

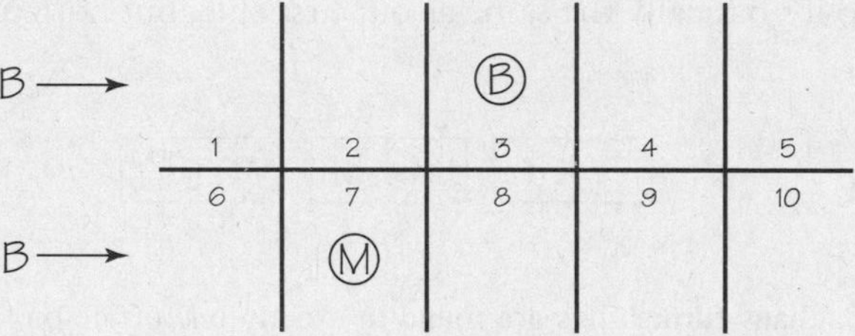


These are some pretty restrictive clues to work with. That should help to compensate for the fact that we don't have a one-to-one correspondence between elements and slots. Plus, we have only three possibilities (and in some cases fewer) for each space.

The final thing we need to do before going on to Step 3? That's right: double-check. This is especially important here because it seems we're going to be able to put together some additional information based on these fairly restrictive clues. If we don't catch any mistakes now, all our work from this point forward will be in vain.

**Step 3: Make deductions and size up the game** Can we come up with any deductions? Those restrictive clues should yield something because we have only three elements in any one slot. There isn't really much overlap between the clues, but we should note that two of the clues put limitations on the placement of B. Let's start by looking for any further limitations that result from having B in office 3. We know that we can't have another B across from or next to 3, so we can show that we can't have B in 8, 2, or 4.

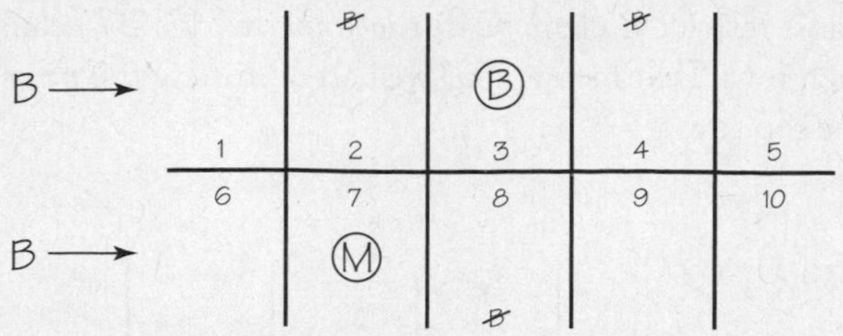

And we'll have similar results from the fact that M is placed in 7. That will eliminate the possibility of having another M in 2, 6, or 8.

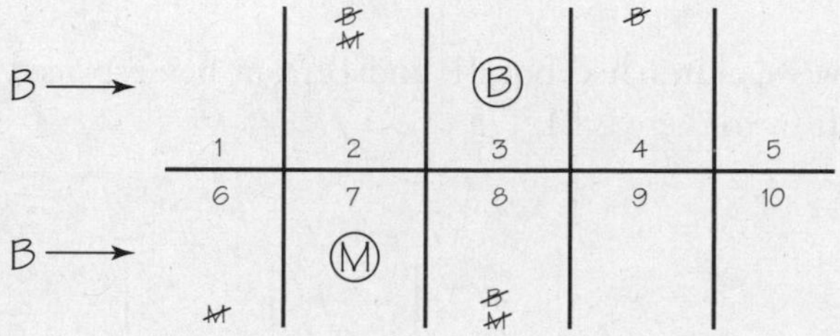

We now have two slots that can have neither B nor M, leaving only one element to place in 2 and 8. Let's put P in both of those offices.

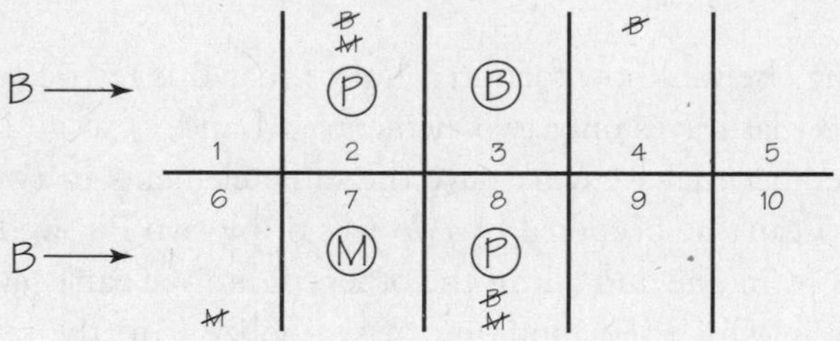

Placing P in 2 and 8 gives us further restrictions. After each new restriction, we can look for further impact. We can now eliminate the possibility of having P in either 1 or 9.

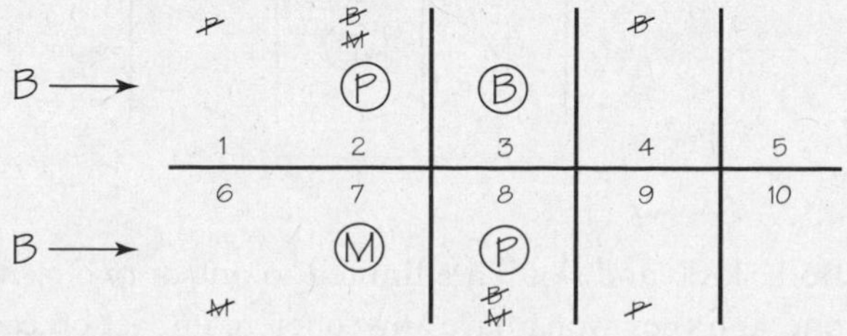

Which is the most restricted element in the top row? It's B because we can use it only once in each row. That means that we can eliminate the possibility of having another B in the top row.

| | | | | | |
|---|---|---|---|---|---|
| | ~~P~~ ~~B~~ | ~~B~~ ~~M~~ | | ~~B~~ | ~~B~~ |
| B ⟶ | | (P) | (B) | | |
| | 1 | 2 | 3 | 4 | 5 |
| | 6 | 7 | 8 | 9 | 10 |
| B ⟶ | | (M) | (P) | | |
| | ~~M~~ | | ~~B~~ ~~M~~ | ~~P~~ | |

And now that we've eliminated both P and B from being placed in office 1, the only element left to go there is M.

| | | | | | |
|---|---|---|---|---|---|
| | ~~P~~ ~~B~~ | ~~B~~ ~~M~~ | | ~~B~~ | ~~B~~ |
| B ⟶ | (M) | (P) | (B) | | |
| | 1 | 2 | 3 | 4 | 5 |
| | 6 | 7 | 8 | 9 | 10 |
| B ⟶ | | (M) | (P) | | |
| | ~~M~~ | | ~~B~~ ~~M~~ | ~~P~~ | |

Is there anything else we know for sure? Notice that B is restricted from being in either 4 or 5, so that leaves only two elements (M and P) to go in each of those slots. And remember that we can't have the same elements in two adjacent slots. Because 4 and 5 can't be occupied by two M's or by two P's, we know that we'll have to have an M in one and a P in the other, right? We can't say for sure which element will be in which slot, but we can symbolize it in the same way we did before, using a slash between them.

| | | | | | |
|---|---|---|---|---|---|
| | (M) | (P) | (B) | M/P | P/M |
| | 1 | 2 | 3 | 4 | 5 |
| | 6 | 7 | 8 | 9 | 10 |
| B ⟶ | | (M) | (P) | | |
| | ~~M~~ | | | ~~P~~ | |

Anything else? Both slot 6 and slot 9 are limited to one of two elements, but we're not sure which one, and they won't have any concrete impact on each other. We've reached a point at which we can come up with a few speculative deductions. For instance, if B were in 6, we would know that we can't use any more B's in the bottom row and so we'd place M in office 9. But that's a big if. Once you've gotten to the point where you can't write down any more concrete information, it's time to move on. You could spend all day running through the permutations, but that wouldn't be a good use of your limited time. The questions will give us more concrete information to work with, so let's get to them. We've got many restrictions already, so we should be able to do some efficient POE in answering the questions.

**Steps 4 and 5: Assess the question and act** You know what to do—head straight for the Specific questions.

**Step 6: Use Process of Elimination** Now it's time to let our investment in Step 3 pay off. Let's get right to it. Question 2 is our first Specific question.

2. If Pop furnishings are found in exactly five of the offices along the hallway, then which one of the following statements must be true?

   (A) Moderne furnishings are found in office 6.
   (B) Moderne furnishings are found in office 4.
   (C) Pop furnishings are found in office 5.
   (D) Moderne furnishings are found in office 10.
   (E) Bauhaus furnishings are found in office 9.

What's the first thing we do? Put any new information the question gives us into the diagram. Until now, we've been working in our original template. Now that we'll be filling in information that won't be true for the whole game, it's time to draw a simple diagram for each question. Just draw a basic outline and carry along the elements we placed from our template.

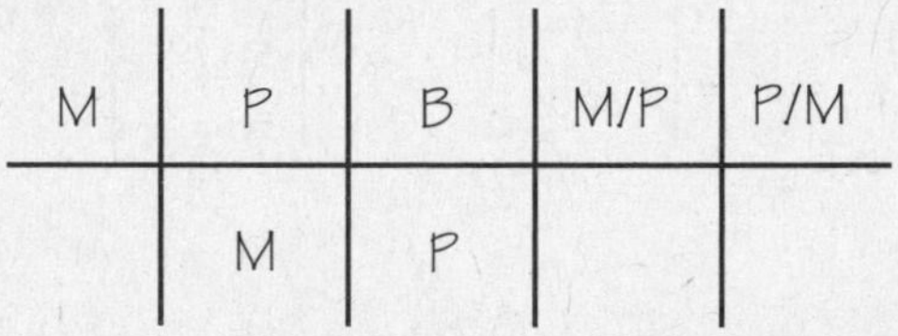

| M | P | B | M/P | P/M |
|---|---|---|---|---|
| | M | P | | |

We'll redraw one of these for each question. We can start by filling in the new information we were given in question 2: P occupies five slots. How can we make that happen? Well, we can already see 3 P's from our template—one in office 2, one in office 8, and one in either office 4 or 5. Where can we put the last two? We know that we can't have one in office 9, so that only leaves 6 and 10. Once we put a P in 10, we know that we can't have one in 5, so that pushes P into 4 and M into 5. Now we have only one open slot. We know we can't use P, so that leaves M or B. Can we tell which one it'll have to be? Remember that we have to use B twice, so we'll have to put B in office 9. That's it. Our diagram's all filled in.

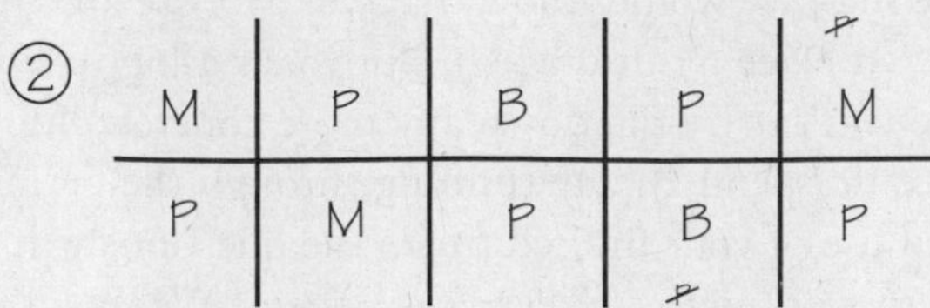


Choice (E) is the only one that matches our diagram. Circle it, and move on.

Our next Specific question is number 4.

4. If office 4 is furnished in Pop, then each of the following statements could be false EXCEPT

   (A) Pop furnishings are found in office 10.
   (B) Pop furnishings are found in office 6.
   (C) Bauhaus furnishings are found in office 6.
   (D) Moderne furnishings are found in office 5.
   (E) Moderne furnishings are found in office 9.

We have an EXCEPT question here, so our answer will be the one that's not like the others. But first we have to draw another sketch and fill in the information we're given in the question.

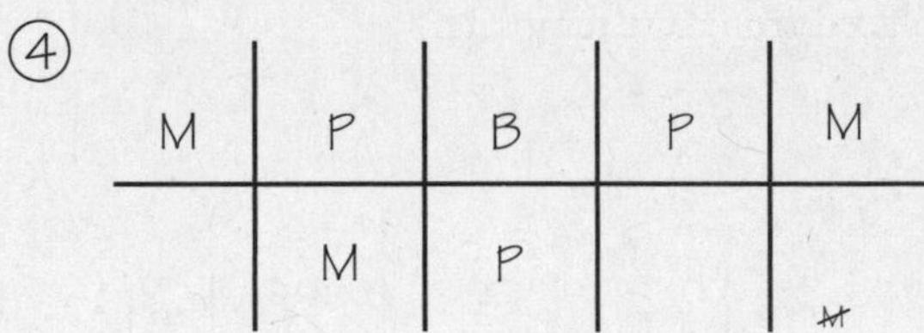


Once we put P in 4, we know that M will have to be in 5. That means no M in 10. Can we put down anything else that we know for sure? We know that we'll have to use our second B in the bottom row, but we don't know exactly where at this point. That looks like about all we can do. Let's see what we can eliminate.

Answer choice (A) could be false because we could put B in 10. Cross it off.

Answer choice (B) could be false because we could put B in 6. Eliminate it.

Answer choice (C) could be false because we could put P in 6. Eliminate it.

Answer choice (D) has to be true from our diagram for this question. That's the answer we want.

In case you're curious, choice (E) could be false because, once again, we could also fill 9 with B. Eliminate it and we're done. Notice that we don't really have to look at (E) here; we found our answer in (D). We trust our work and we should pick the correct answer as soon as we find it, and then move on.

---

We're done with all of the Specific questions, so we'll move on to General questions. Question 1 is a General question that hits the elements in the bottom row. This isn't a Grab-a-Rule question as we're used to seeing it—these are only partial lists—but we can start our POE the same way. Eliminate choices that violate rules or that don't match the deductions we've made.

---

1. Which one of the following could be an accurate list of the styles of furnishings found in offices 6, 7, 8, 9, and 10, respectively?

(A) Pop, Moderne, Pop, Moderne, Pop
(B) Pop, Moderne, Pop, Bauhaus, Moderne
(C) Bauhaus, Pop, Moderne, Pop, Moderne
(D) Bauhaus, Moderne, Pop, Moderne, Bauhaus
(E) Pop, Moderne, Bauhaus, Pop, Moderne

Since we have so many deductions, it's easiest to start with those.

We know from our template that slots 7 and 8 have to be occupied by M and P, respectively. That eliminates answer choices (C) and (E).

What else do we know about the bottom row? You might have spent some time trying to get rid of the remaining choices if you forgot about the restriction on B. It's a big-picture clue that's easy to lose sight of. If you find yourself struggling on a Grab-a-Rule question, look back to see if there are any of those big-picture clues that you forgot to apply. Let's see if we can find violations of the rule that we have to use B once—and once only—in the bottom row. That rule gets rid of (A), which has no B at all, and (D), which has two B's. That leaves only (B), so we've got our answer.

---

Let's move on to our next General question.

**Remember!**
The goal on all games questions is to find either the one right answer or the four wrong answers, but not both. Your goal in all cases is to work carefully and accurately. Trust your work.

3. Which one of the following statements must be false?

(A) Pop furnishings are found in office 10.
(B) Pop furnishings are found in office 1.
(C) Moderne furnishings are found in office 9.
(D) Bauhaus furnishings are found in office 9.
(E) Bauhaus furnishings are found in office 10.

Here we have to find the choice that must be false. You'll remember that we can eliminate any choice if it could be true, even one time. Let's see what we can do. Don't forget to use the good work you've done on the Specific questions to help with POE whenever possible.

We can use our work from question 2 to eliminate both (A) and (D). And we saw the possibility of both (C) and (E) in question 4, so we can get rid of those, too. If you were unsure about them, you could always draw another quick diagram and try them out. Answer choice (B) violates one of our deductions, so that's our answer. If we didn't already have that deduction, we would still get the answer by testing P in office 1 and seeing that we couldn't fill out a full arrangement that follows the rules.

We have only one question left.

5. Which of the following, if substituted for the condition that Bauhaus furnishings are found in office 3, would have the same effect on determining the style of furnishings found in each office?

(A) Pop furnishings are found in office 8.
(B) Moderne furnishings are found in office 10.
(C) Moderne furnishings are found in office 1.
(D) If Bauhaus furnishings are not found in office 3, then Moderne furnishings are not found in office 7.
(E) Bauhaus furnishings cannot be found in an office adjacent to an office in which Moderne furnishings are found.

This is one of those complex questions that asks us to replace a clue with another clue that would have exactly the same effect. Thus our correct answer must, based on the other clues, allow us to deduce that Bauhaus furnishings are found in office 3 without adding any deductions that we didn't already have. When doing these questions, then, use your previous work and deductions. If an answer, for example, makes something certainly true that could only be true by the previous set of rules (or contradicts something that had to be true), you can eliminate it. Let's see how it goes.

In answer choice (A), Pop is found in office 8. In this situation we could still find either Bauhaus or Moderne furnishings in office 3, so this clue gives us less information than the original clue, and we can eliminate (A).

In answer choice (B), M is in office 10, which would allow any of the three furnishings to be in office 3. This would also add a limitation to office 10 that was not present in the original, so we can eliminate (B).

Answer choice (C), like answer choice (A), is a deduction we could make from the original set of clues that does not work in reverse. Placing M in office 1 would allow any of the three furnishings to be found in office 3, so eliminate (C).

Answer choice (D) is a conditional statement like the ones we discussed in the Arguments chapter. The contrapositive of (D) would state Moderne furnishings in office 7 guarantee Bauhaus furnishings in office 3. Adding this clue to the clue that tells us that Moderne furnishings are found in office 7, which forces Bauhaus furnishings to be found in office 3. Since (D) provides the same deductions without any additional limitations, it is the one we are looking for.

At this point, you would pick choice (D) and move on. But let's see why choice (E) is incorrect. This antiblock clue would require Bauhaus furnishings to be adjacent to Pop furnishings, which would still allow either Pop or Bauhaus to be in office 3. Answer choice (E) is incorrect since these deductions do not match the original.

---

Okay, that wasn't so bad. We just followed the structure they gave us and got to work. You might think that redrawing the diagram for each question is too time-consuming, but if you keep it simple, you can create one quickly and then have a concrete space in which to work through the question. And you'll notice that making a new diagram for each question allowed us to use POE on the later questions quickly and painlessly. Our investment paid off.

Hint:
If a game asks you to arrange elements *spatially*, draw a picture of the space, and use that as your diagram. Keep your pictures small so you can redraw the template for every question.

## Games Technique: Draw the Right Diagram

How can you tell when to use one of these template diagrams? The setup will let you know that you have a spatial arrangement that is not linear. Let's try it with another setup.

> Eight dishes—artichoke, beef, celery, danish, eggplant, fennel, grapes, and halibut—are being placed around a circular table.

This is similar to what you just did, but here we are dealing with a circular diagram. The simplest way to deal with a circular diagram is to draw intersecting lines. Draw as many lines as you need so you have the appropriate number of spaces around the circle. Place each element at the end of a line. The basic idea is the same: Match what the setup tells you about the spatial arrangement. Remember to redraw the basic structure for each question you do. Don't erase!

Occasionally, the LSAT folks will surprise you with their generosity and will actually tell you how to draw the diagram. By all means, use their description. Copy it as many times as you need to. Draw it a bit more simply if necessary.

Make sure you've got this question strategy down COLD. Put it next to your Arguments chart on your refrigerator.

## Games Technique: POE with "Could" and "Must"

In the previous game, we saw a variety of different question phrasings. In the end, though, it turns out that all of the variations of must/could, true/false, and EXCEPT/NOT require only two POE strategies. Understanding what the questions actually mean can show you why.

If a question asks what could be true, there needs to be only one situation when the right answer can happen. What, then, do we know about the other four choices? Well, if the right answer can happen, then the four wrong answers can't. That is, the wrong answers on a could-be-true question are things that must be false.

Think about a must-be-false question now. What do we know about the other choices? Well, since the right answer is something that can never happen, the wrong answers are things that can. It shouldn't surprise you, then, that the wrong answers on a must-be-false question are things that could be true.

What happens if we add an "EXCEPT" or a "NOT" to one of these questions? These words, on the LSAT, can be interpreted as meaning "find four." So when a question asks you "…each of the following could be true EXCEPT," what they're asking you to find is four choices that could be true; the remaining one is the answer you want to pick. What do we know about this choice? That's right: It must be false.

What we're seeing here is that *could be true/must be false* form a pair. Adding an "EXCEPT" or a "NOT" just changes one into the other.

Now think about an answer choice that must be true. This means it has to be true all the time, no matter what. When the right answer must be true, what we know is that the other four don't have to be true all the time—that is, they could be false. Not surprisingly, could-be-false questions turn out to be the flipside of this; on a could-be-false question, the other four answers must be true. And as before, adding "EXCEPT" or "NOT" turns one of these types of questions into the other.

The good news is that each pair of questions has a POE strategy that will work for them both, but you have to be careful to keep your eye on the ball. It's easy to forget what you're doing in the midst of actually doing it. It's also extremely important to understand that the only way you can be sure something happens all the time—or that it can never happen—is to deduce that fact. When you generate an example, you're looking at what could happen, not what must happen.

The upshot of all this is best summarized in the gray box. If you put these ideas in your own words and use them assiduously whenever you work games, they will become more intuitive, but you'll have to focus and work carefully for some of the more complicated variations.

POE Guide: Knowing Right from Wrong with "Could" and "Must"

**Could Be True/Must Be False**

POE strategy: Try to make the choice true; make an example.

For *could be true* and *must be false* EXCEPT
- If you can make the choice true, pick it.
- If you can't, eliminate it.

For *must be false* and *could be true* EXCEPT
- If you can make the choice true, eliminate it.
- If you can't, pick it.

**Must Be True/Could Be False**

POE strategy: Try to make the choice false; make a counterexample.

For *must be true* and *could be false* EXCEPT
- If you can make the choice false, eliminate it.
- If you can't, pick it.

For *could be false* and *must be true* EXCEPT
- If you can make the choice false, pick it.
- If you can't, eliminate it.

Generally speaking, to turn an unfamiliar question into its more familiar counterpart, change "could" to "must" (or vice versa), and "false" to "true" (or vice versa). Thus, if you're unsure what to do on a must-be-false question, flip it around to see that it most closely resembles a could-be-true question. The POE strategy is the same; the only difference is that you eliminate the choices that could be true, rather than picking them.

**Hint:**
A grouping game asks you to put the elements into collections of some sort; grouping games usually include clues that can easily be translated as blocks or antiblocks.

So far, the games we've seen have asked us to put things in order to arrange them in space. There is one last basic games task we haven't seen yet: *grouping*. Grouping games are often fairly easy to identify from the setup: putting people on committees, assigning commuters to cars, picking players for teams, and so on. Sometimes they can be more difficult to recognize, but in those cases you can get help from the clues. In a grouping game, the clues most often talk about elements that have to go together, or those that can't go together.

A key thing to keep track of in grouping games is how many elements each group contains. Any time you can fill up a group as you work, you'll discover that making further deductions becomes much easier—but of course you need to know how big the groups are before you can tell when one of them is full. Sometimes group sizes will be given to you directly, but sometimes you will have to deduce them. These kinds of *distribution* deductions can be time-consuming to make, but they're extremely helpful. Try Game #4, a grouping game, but remember: Try to determine the group sizes before you move on to the questions.

## GAME #4: THREE BUSES

Five girls—Fiorenza, Gladys, Helene, Jocelyn, and Kaitlin—and four boys—Abe, Bruce, Clive, and Doug—ride to school each day in three separate buses.

Abe and Fiorenza always ride together.
Gladys and Helene always ride together.
Jocelyn and Kaitlin never ride together.
Doug always rides in the bus with the fewest children.
Boys cannot outnumber girls in any bus.
The maximum number of children in any bus is four.

1. The bus in which Doug rides can hold how many children?

(A) 1
(B) 2
(C) 3
(D) 4
(E) 5

2. Bruce can ride with each of the following EXCEPT

(A) Abe
(B) Clive
(C) Doug
(D) Fiorenza
(E) Helene

3. If Bruce and Clive ride in the same bus, which one of the following must also be in the bus?

(A) Abe
(B) Fiorenza
(C) Gladys
(D) Jocelyn
(E) Kaitlin

4. Which of the following could be a list of all the passengers in one bus?

(A) Doug, Gladys
(B) Fiorenza, Abe, Bruce
(C) Jocelyn, Kaitlin, Clive, Bruce
(D) Fiorenza, Gladys, Bruce, Clive
(E) Abe, Bruce, Fiorenza, Jocelyn

5. Abe can NEVER ride with which one of the following?

(A) Bruce
(B) Clive
(C) Gladys
(D) Jocelyn
(E) Kaitlin

6. If Bruce rides with Fiorenza, Gladys must ride with which one of the following?

(A) Clive
(B) Doug
(C) Fiorenza
(D) Jocelyn
(E) Kaitlin

**CRACK THIS GAME STARTING ON THE NEXT PAGE.**

## Cracking Game #4

**Step 1: Diagram and inventory** We've got a total of nine children to distribute in three buses. Our diagram will consist of three columns—the only thing missing will be the exact number of children to be placed in each bus. We know that we'll need to use all of the elements and that we can't have any repeats. We also see that the buses are not named—that is, there does not appear to be any difference between the groups. You can number them if you wish, but there's no real need to. Don't forget to distinguish between the two types (girls and boys).

**Hint:**
First draw the diagram, and then worry about distribution.

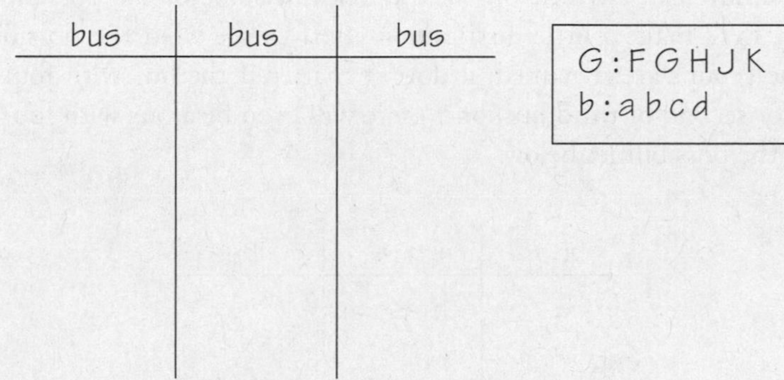


**Step 2: Symbolize the clues and double-check** We've got several clues here; some should look familiar, and some will be new. You should be comfortable by now with how the blocks and antiblocks work. We'll see how the others—known as distribution clues—work as we move through the rest of this game. Distribution clues give you information about how the elements will be distributed among the slots. In some cases, they may lead to only one possible distribution, and in others, they may merely limit the options, leaving a couple of different possible distributions. Let's get to work and see how it plays out.

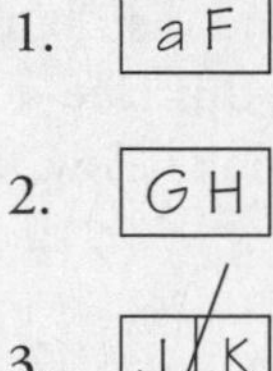


The first three clues are all pretty straightforward. We've already worked with similar clues and the symbols are becoming second nature. Now let's briefly symbolize our distribution clues to make sure we have a clear handle on how they work.

4. d = fewest
5. $b \leq G$
6. Maximum 4 per group

We are able to symbolize the information, but it may not seem very useful at this point. Don't forget to double-check before moving on to the next step.

Spend a few minutes trying to narrow down the possible distributions—it's worth it!

**Step 3: Make deductions and size up the game** Now let's see if we can come up with any deductions. We'll use our standard methods because we're not sure of the distribution at this point. We'll also pay special attention to the distribution clues to see if we can narrow down the possible ways that the elements can be arranged in terms of the number of elements (children) in each group (bus). If we can figure that out, the questions should be a lot easier.

Which of the distribution clues is most limiting? The fact that there can't be more than four children in any one bus will knock out some of the possibilities right off the bat. Let's make a little distribution chart to see what the possibilities are. Because the groups aren't named, it doesn't matter if the bus with four children is the first or second or third bus, or if there will even be a bus with four children. Check out the possibilities below.

| bus | bus | bus |
|---|---|---|
| 3 | 3 | 3 |
| 4 | 3 | 2 |
| 4 | 4 | 1 |

As you can see above, limiting the maximum number of elements to four per group narrows the possibilities to three separate distributions: 3-3-3, 4-3-2, and 4-4-1. Let's take a look at our second distribution clue, the fact that boys cannot outnumber girls in any bus. Does this clue do anything to limit the number of distributions? It sure does. Take a look below.

| 1 | 2 | 3 |
|---|---|---|
| ~~3~~ | ~~3~~ | ~~3~~ |
| ④ | ③ | ② |
| 4 | 4 | 1 |

If boys cannot outnumber girls in any bus, and there are four boys, that means that the 3-3-3 distribution cannot be valid for this game. Why not? Because if the distribution is 3-3-3, then in one of the buses, there must be two boys and one girl, which we can't have. Another limitation. Now what about the final clue, that Doug must ride in the bus with the fewest children? Take a look below.

| bus | bus | bus |
|---|---|---|
| ~~3~~ | ~~3~~ | ~~3~~ |
| 4 | 3 | 2 |
| ~~4~~ | ~~4~~ | ~~1~~ |

If Doug must ride in the bus with the smallest number of children, then the 4-4-1 distribution isn't possible in this game either. Doug would have to go alone. Doug is a boy, and we know that boys cannot outnumber girls in any bus, so he can't be the only rider. Therefore, after eliminating distributions that violate the rules, we're left with a diagram that will look like this

| bus (4) | bus (3) | bus (2) |
|---|---|---|
| _ _ _ _ | _ _ _ | _ d |

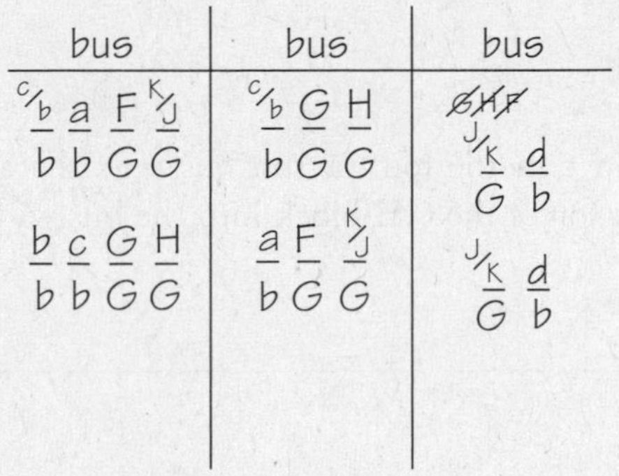

**Hint:**
When a clue mentions numbers—the number of elements in a group, for example, or the number of times an element can be used—be on the lookout for distribution deductions. You may have to try several possibilities in order to learn that only certain distributions are possible.

Any other deductions? Using the diagram above, go back to your relationship clues. Is there any more overlap that provides further limitations? Check this out.

| bus | bus | bus |
|---|---|---|
| C/b a F K/J<br>b b G G | C/b G H<br>b G G | ~~C/H/F~~<br>J/K d<br>G b |
| b c G H<br>b b G G | a F K/J<br>b G G | J/K d<br>G b |

Yes, we've spent some precious minutes figuring out all this stuff. However, we now know the exact distribution of the children, how many of each gender are in every bus, the definitive placement of one child, and several other limiting factors—such as the fact that neither the GH block nor the aF block can go in d's bus, leaving d to go with either J or K only.

We've really narrowed things down to the only two possible scenarios based on the two places where GH can fit. Remember that we'll keep an eye on the most restricted spots first as we deal with the questions.

**Steps 4 and 5: Assess the question and Act** We don't have a Grab-a-Rule question, so let's start with any Specific questions.

### Step 6: Use Process of Elimination

---

3. If Bruce and Clive ride in the same bus, which one of the following must also be in the bus?

   (A) Abe
   (B) Fiorenza
   (C) Gladys
   (D) Jocelyn
   (E) Kaitlin

#### Here's How to Crack It

Because boys cannot outnumber girls, we know where b and c have to go if they're together, right? Let's check it out.

| | bus | bus | bus |
|---|---|---|---|
| Clue Shelf | b b G G | b G G | $\frac{J/K}{G}$ $\frac{d}{b}$ |
| ③ | b c G H | a F _ | _ d |
| | | | |

As you can see, b and c in the four-person bus puts the aF block in the three-person bus. This then forces the GH block into the bus with b and c. Looks like (C) is our answer.

---

Now try this problem.

---

6. If Bruce rides with Fiorenza, Gladys must ride with which one of the following?

(A) Clive
(B) Doug
(C) Fiorenza
(D) Jocelyn
(E) Kaitlin

### Here's How to Crack It

Well, you know that a always comes with F, so you've once again got two boys (a and b) to place. Take a look at the diagram below.

| | bus | bus | bus |
|---|---|---|---|
| Clue Shelf | _ _ _ _ b b G G | _ _ _ b G G | J/K over G; d over b |
| ⑥ | b a F J/K | c G H | J/K d |

We've got b, a, and F in the four-person bus, which means that the GH block must go in the three-person bus. A boy must also go in there, and the only one left is c. It's our answer—choice (A).

---

The final four questions in this game are General. However, you were able to deduce so much that they probably won't present too much of a problem. Let's do this one first.

---

4. Which of the following could be a list of all the passengers in one bus?

(A) Doug, Gladys
(B) Fiorenza, Abe, Bruce
(C) Jocelyn, Kaitlin, Clive, Bruce
(D) Fiorenza, Gladys, Bruce, Clive
(E) Abe, Bruce, Fiorenza, Jocelyn

### Here's How to Crack It

This isn't quite a Grab-a-Rule question because it doesn't address all the elements in each answer choice. But we can probably eliminate at least a few answers by applying the clues to the answer choices and crossing off any violations. If more than one choice remains, we can see if there might be any violations in possible arrangements of the groups that are not shown in the answers, given what we know from this one group. The G/H block eliminates (A) and (D), the boys not being able to outnumber the girls eliminates (B), and the J/K antiblock eliminates (C). We're left with (E).

Let's move on to another question.

1. The bus in which Doug rides can hold how many children?

   (A) 1
   (B) 2
   (C) 3
   (D) 4
   (E) 5

### Here's How to Crack It

We've answered this one already because we made the proper deductions. The bus can hold two children, answer (B).

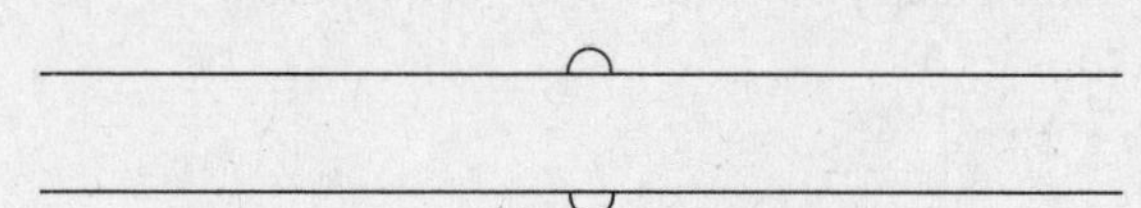

2. Bruce can ride with each of the following EXCEPT

   (A) Abe
   (B) Clive
   (C) Doug
   (D) Fiorenza
   (E) Helene

### Here's How to Crack It

Look at your diagram and your previous work. Is there anywhere b can't go? It can't go in d's bus, so (C) is our answer. Also note that you had b with a, c, F, and H in previous questions, so we can cross off (A), (B), (D), and (E).

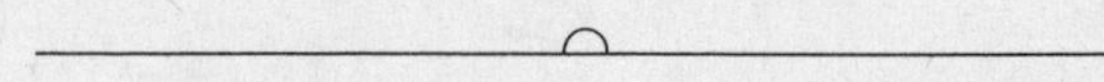

Let's finish off the last question.

5. Abe can NEVER ride with which one of the following?

 (A) Bruce
 (B) Clive
 (C) Gladys
 (D) Jocelyn
 (E) Kaitlin

### Here's How to Crack It

We can approach this in several ways; using our previous work is one way. We've had a with b in the past, so (A) is gone. And because J and K are interchangeable, neither (D) nor (E) can be the answer either. That leaves us to try either c or G to see whether it's possible to group either one with a. If we look at the work we did for question 6, we see that it would be possible to switch c and b, putting both a and c in the same group and allowing us to eliminate (B). Therefore, our answer must be (C), Gladys, because you can't have a situation in which both blocks are in the same bus. Try it if you need to. Now you're done.

## IN AND OUT GAMES

The first two games we worked were relatively straightforward *ordering* games. The basic task in these was to arrange the elements in a single line. Game #3 was similar, with the slight difference that the task was to arrange elements in a *two-dimensional* grid. These two kinds of tasks are very important and are often seen in LSAT games, but they aren't the only games tasks around.

In Game #5, the task is to pick some, but not all, of the elements. Those selected will be "In" the collection; those not selected will be "Out." In games with an In/Out task, it ends up being just as important to keep track of the "Out" elements—those not chosen—as it is to keep track of the ones that are "In." Remember that we always want to have a place in our diagram to put all the elements in a game.

**Remember!**
Conditional clues tell you what happens if a particular condition is met; we symbolize them with arrows because they can be read only from left to right. DON'T GO AGAINST THE ARROW.

## Games Technique: Conditional Clues

We have already seen how important conditional clues are on the Arguments section. Not surprisingly, they are also extremely important to the Games section of the LSAT. These are also the most frequently misinterpreted and misunderstood clues; everyone who takes the LSAT should exercise extra care when working with them.

We have previously introduced the arrow as a symbol for conditional clues on arguments; we'll use them in games as well. Suppose we're symbolizing the following clue:

If X is chosen, then Y is not chosen.

As indicated above, the central task on an In/Out game is to decide which elements are chosen and which are not. As we'll see in a moment, we diagram these by having two columns—one marked "In," the other marked "Out"—to keep track of our elements. When we see clues like the previous one, we use a little shorthand, since they're so common. To show that an element is In, we leave it alone; to show that it's Out, we negate it with a slash. Thus the clue above would have a symbol that looks like this

$$X \rightarrow \not{Y}$$

Whenever we're given a conditional clue, we should also represent its contrapositive. The way we make the contrapositive is flip and negate: We exchange the order of the statements around the arrow, and we negate each one. As usual, the negative of a negative becomes a positive. The contrapositive of the clue we symbolized above is as follows:

$$Y \rightarrow \not{X}$$

The *contrapositive* of a conditional clue is formed by flipping the order of the statements around the arrow and negating each one; this is the only certain deduction that can be made from a conditional clue. When you symbolize a conditional clue, symbolize its contrapositive right away.

It's important to understand what we can conclude—and, just as important, what we can't conclude—from this pair of conditional statements. Generally speaking, we use an arrow to symbolize these clues because we can draw conclusions only in one direction. It's best to think of using these clues as a two-stage process: First, we examine the statement on the left-hand side of the arrow. If it doesn't apply, there's nothing more we can do; the rule might as well not exist. If that statement does apply, then we can move on to stage two: Follow the arrow to the right-hand side, which shows the conclusion we're allowed to draw.

Here's a summary of this process for the clue on the previous page.

$$X \rightarrow \not{Y}$$
$$Y \rightarrow \not{X}$$

| If we know... | ...then we can conclude |
|---|---|
| X is In | Y is Out |
| Y is In | X is Out |
| X is Out | nothing |
| Y is Out | nothing |

Possible arrangements that satisfy this rule include

| IN | OUT |
|---|---|
| X | Y |
| Y | X |
| | X Y * |

The only arrangement that this rule forbids is the following:

| IN | OUT |
|---|---|
| X Y | |

The arrangement marked with the * above is usually the one that gives test takers trouble; for this reason, you'll often encounter it. Note that we can conclude nothing from this rule if we know that X is Out; similarly, we can conclude nothing if Y is Out. Thus, this rule has nothing to say about the situation when both X and Y are Out.

Interpreting your symbols correctly is a big part of being able to work with conditional clues. You must be careful to follow the symbols, rather than relying on what you think "should" be true.

Once you can use the symbols correctly, the next challenge is correctly rendering the text of the clue into a correct symbol. There are three major patterns in which games clues appear. They're summarized below; every one of the phrasings in this box lead to the symbol we discussed. Examine the rule for each closely, and make sure you can successfully arrive at the diagram for each of the example phrasings given.

$$X \rightarrow \not{Y}$$
$$Y \rightarrow \not{X}$$

**If...then and its relatives:**

If X is In, Y is Out.
Y is Out if X is In.
Whenever X is In, Y must be Out.
(also sometimes used: "all," "any," "every")

Rule: The statement following the key word ("if," "all," and so on) goes to the left of the arrow. The translation here is fairly intuitive.

**Only if:**
X will be In only if Y is Out.
Y will be In only if X is Out.
Only if Y is Out will X be In.
(also sometimes used: "only," "only when")

Rule: Draw an arrow pointing to the right through the word "only." The thing on the point of the arrow should also be on the point of the arrow in your diagram. Be careful with these; it is easy to reverse them by mistake.

**Unless:**
X will not be In unless Y is Out.
Y will not be In unless X is Out.

Rule: Cross out "unless" and write "if not," and then symbolize the clue as you would an ordinary "if…then." The word "unless" is the most frequently misinterpreted one on the LSAT; be extremely careful here.

## Games Technique: Conditionals with "And" or "Or"

On the LSAT, the word "and" means just what you think it does. "Or," on the other hand, means one or the other, and it also implicitly includes the possibility "or both." Take a look at the following clue:

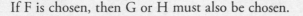

If F is chosen, then G or H must also be chosen.

What does this mean? Well, whenever F is In, we know that at least one of G or H is In, and possibly both of them are. The only possibility this excludes is having both G and H Out.

How do we symbolize this? Since "and" and "or" arise so often on the test, we will simply incorporate them into our symbols.

$$F \rightarrow G \text{ or } H$$

As always, we need to draw a symbol for the contrapositive of this clue. Remember the rationale behind the contrapositive: We look for a case when the thing on the right-hand side of the arrow is untrue, and that tells us that the thing on the left-hand side must also be untrue.

What does it mean for the statement "G or H" to be untrue? Well, the only way we can be sure that neither G nor H is In would be to have them both Out. Put another way, the contrary of the statement "G is In or H is In (or both)" is "G is Out and H is Out." Negating our "or" statement turns it into an "and" statement. Thus the contrapositive here is as follows:

$$\not{G} \text{ and } \not{H} \rightarrow \not{F}$$

This is how we negate the "or" statement. Not surprisingly, negating an "and" statement changes it into—you guessed it—an "or." After all, if we flip and negate the symbol we've drawn above, we should get our original symbol back. In order to do that, we would turn the statement "not G and not H" into the statement "G or H."

Remember that when you're working with a statement involving "and" or "or," you have to negate every part of the statement. When you negate an "and," it turns into an "or"; when you negate an "or," it turns into an "and."

The table below provides some practice with these crucial skills and concepts involving conditional statements. We've left you some blank space so you can try them on your own first. Make sure you can successfully translate every one of these statements and correctly generate their contrapositives before you move on.

| CLUE | YOUR SYMBOL | YOUR CONTRAPOSITIVE | OUR SYMBOL | OUR CONTRAPOSITIVE |
|---|---|---|---|---|
| If Jack attends, Mark must attend. | | | J → M | ~M → ~J |
| Ann will work only if Kate works. | | | ~K → ~A | A → K |
| Bob cannot work unless Gary is working. | | | ~G → ~B | B → G |
| If Will goes to the party, Cam won't go. | | | W → ~C | C → ~W |
| Doug will not drive unless May also drives. | | | ~M → ~D | D → M |
| If Harry is invited, both Charles and Linda must be invited. | | | H → C and L | ~C or ~L → ~H |

Now that you've practiced this, let's take a look at Game #5: Hats and Scarves.

## GAME #5: HATS AND SCARVES

A store is creating a window display featuring four hats and three scarves. The only hats being considered are A, B, C, D, E, and F, and the only scarves being considered are J, K, L, M, and N.

If A is displayed, then neither B nor L can be displayed.
B is displayed only if D is displayed.
C cannot be displayed unless J is displayed.
D can be displayed only if K is displayed.
If L is displayed, then M must be displayed.
F cannot be displayed unless D is not displayed.

1. Which one of the following is a possible display of hats in the window?

(A) A, B, C, F
(B) A, C, D, E
(C) A, D, E, F
(D) B, C, D, F
(E) B, C, E, F

2. If F is displayed, which one of the following must be true?

(A) A is not displayed.
(B) B is not displayed.
(C) K is not displayed.
(D) L is displayed.
(E) M is displayed.

3. If both B and E are displayed, then which one of the following CANNOT be a partial list of items displayed?

(A) C, D, E
(B) C, J, M
(C) C, D, F
(D) C, J, K
(E) D, K, M

4. Each of the following could be displayed together EXCEPT

(A) B and K
(B) B and F
(C) B and M
(D) E and F
(E) E, J, and M

5. If B is displayed, which one of the following is a list of items that could also be displayed?

(A) A, M, N
(B) C, E, F
(C) C, L, M
(D) E, F, M
(E) E, J, M

**CRACK THIS GAME STARTING ON THE NEXT PAGE.**

## Cracking Game #5

When elements are either "In or Out" or "selected or not selected," draw a two-column diagram.

**Step 1: Diagram and inventory** Well, we've got a lot going on here—first of all, we've got two sets of elements (hats ABCDEF and scarves jklmn). Next, we know that not all of the elements will be used because only four out of the six hats are being displayed, and only three out of the five scarves are being displayed. Remember: We want to have a place in our diagram for all the elements, so we have an "Out" column to hold them.

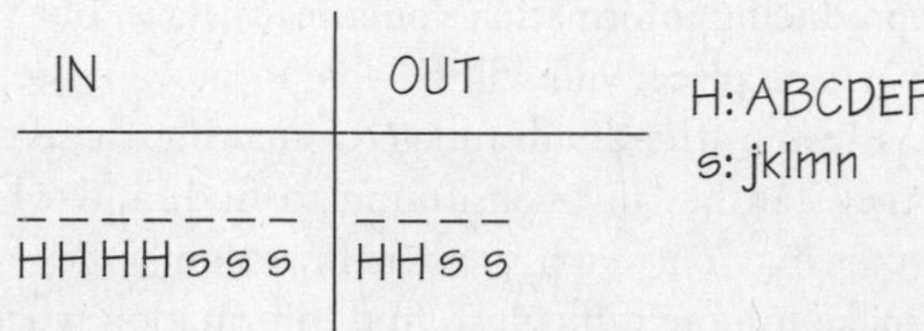


As you can see, we created an "In" column and an "Out" column. We've also reserved spaces in each column because we know precisely how many hats and scarves go on each side. Reserving spaces like this is an extremely useful addition to any diagram. Now let's look at the clues.

Go slowly with "if....then" clues and making contrapositives.

**Step 2: Symbolize the clues and double-check** We've got a whole mess of conditional clues here. Remember that every time you have a conditional clue, you also can deduce the contrapositive. Symbolize the contrapositive as soon as you've symbolized the clue. Here's what we have so far.

1. $\begin{cases} A \rightarrow \not{B} \text{ and } \not{l} \\ B \text{ or } l \rightarrow \not{A} \end{cases}$
2. $\begin{cases} B \rightarrow D \\ \not{D} \rightarrow \not{B} \end{cases}$
3. $\begin{cases} \not{j} \rightarrow \not{C} \\ C \rightarrow j \end{cases}$
4. $\begin{cases} D \rightarrow k \\ \not{k} \rightarrow \not{D} \end{cases}$
5. $\begin{cases} l \rightarrow m \\ \not{m} \rightarrow \not{l} \end{cases}$
6. $\begin{cases} D \rightarrow \not{F} \\ F \rightarrow \not{D} \end{cases}$

It's crucial to double-check carefully when you're symbolizing conditional clues, and check your contrapositives closely as well. Forgetting even one negation can cause a great deal of mischief. If your symbols don't match the ones above, be sure to go back and review the previous section on symbolizing conditional clues.

**Step 3: Make deductions and size up the game** When a game involves conditional clues, you have a decision to make. Take a look at the second and fourth clues, for example. The second clue tells us that if B is In, D must also be; the fourth clue tells us that if D is In, then k must also be. In a case like this, it's possible to combine the clues together into a single "chain" leading from B In, to D In, and then finally to k In; similarly, this chain has a contrapositive—k Out means that D is Out, which means that B is Out—which we form as usual by flipping the order of all the statements and negating each of them.

This is only one example of several such chains that can be made on this game, which is why you have a choice to make. In the end, by writing out the chain you're primarily reproducing information you already have, but you do benefit by putting it together in one place; you will be able to move more quickly through some questions as a result. The disadvantage of making these chain deductions is twofold: First, they can be time-consuming to find, and when the clues are complicated, that cost may outweigh the benefit; second, they clutter your page and may actually make it more difficult to find information when you're working questions, rather than easier.

The choice, in the end, is up to you. A good rule of thumb is that chain deductions are most useful on games that include a small number of relatively straightforward conditional clues. If there are a large number of conditionals, and if some of them are complicated, it's usually best to keep your clue list as uncluttered as possible.

For the purposes of this game, we will not use the chain deductions. We will, however, make some deductions that are rather sophisticated but are useful on many games—In/Out games in particular. We call them placeholder deductions.

We've already managed to reserve spaces in our diagram for hats and scarves, but we can do even more than this. Within this separation, we see that a few of our clues tell us things about the relationship of some hats to other hats. These kinds of clues can give us either/or deductions, which are some of the strongest deduction types available.

Consider the very last clue. It tells us that, whenever D is In, F has to be Out; its contrapositive, of course, assures us that whenever F is In, D has to be Out. This means that, no matter what, at least one of D or F is Out. Since D and F are both hats, we can improve our diagram by reserving one of the H spaces on the "Out" side for either D or F. This has the effect of shrinking our "Out" column by one space, which as we'll see in a moment is quite useful.

Can we conclude that the other one of D or F is In? Not from this clue alone. Remember that this clue tells us only what has to happen when one of them is In; it's important not to read too much into conditional clues. This one, by itself, reserves only one space in our diagram.

However, there is another nice placeholder deduction available: Look at the first clue. This tells us that, whenever A is In, both B and l have to be Out. Now, l is a scarf, so this part of the clue won't allow us to reserve a space in the diagram as we've constructed it, but the fact that A In causes B to go Out—and that B In forces A to go Out—is very useful. As we did before, we can reserve a space in the "Out" column for one of A or B; they're both hats, which means that both of our "Out" spaces for hats are now reserved.

What does this mean for the rest of the hats? Well, for one thing, C and E don't appear in our placeholders. That means that there will never be space for them in our "Out" column, which in turn means that both of them always have to be In. You've just seen the big reason that we keep track of "Out" elements: When there's no more space available on the "Out" side, we can find elements that have to be In.

C is always In, which means by the third clue that j is always In. E, as we said above, is always In, and that leaves only two spaces available on the "In" side. In this case, we can go ahead and reserve those spaces for B/A and F/D, but it's important to reiterate that we were able to make this deduction only because of space constraints; the conditional clues by themselves aren't enough to give us this information.

Here, then, is the clue shelf for this game.

| IN | | | | | | | OUT | | | |
|---|---|---|---|---|---|---|---|---|---|---|
| C | E | B/A | F/D | j | __ | __ | A/B | D/F | __ | __ |
| H | H | H | H | s | s | s | H | H | s | s |

We note now that B and D are linked by the second clue, so information about one of them may give us further information about the other, and D may in turn give us information about k, or vice-versa. As you see, these chain deductions don't really give us anything definite we can put into our diagram. This is why placeholder deductions are, in the end, more useful than chain deductions. In general, when you have a conditional in which one element forces another onto the other side of your In/Out diagram, you should try to reserve a space.

If you feel that these deductions are difficult or complex, don't fret. They are more sophisticated than the straight-line deductions we've been making so far. Chances are that, if you worked this game all the way through before reading this explanation, you were able to work all the questions successfully without them. This is the beauty of games, in fact: There is never just one way to get through them. Some ways, however, are faster than others, and in the end, speed is the reason to make deductions, get better at them, and gain some experience at spotting them. There are very few games in which the deductions are essential; in virtually every game, however, they are extremely useful.

**Steps 4–6: Assess the question, Act, and Use POE as appropriate** We'll use the deductions as represented above to work the questions, with specific questions on the first pass as always. Here's the first one.

2. If F is displayed, which one of the following must be true?

    (A) A is not displayed.
    (B) B is not displayed.
    (C) K is not displayed.
    (D) L is displayed.
    (E) M is displayed.

### Here's How to Crack It

F In means that D must be Out; D Out means that B must be Out; B Out means that A must be In (according to our placeholder); A In means that l must be Out. Here's our diagram.

| | IN | OUT |
|---|---|---|
| Clue Shelf | C E B/A F/D j __ __<br>H H H H s s s | A/B D/F __ __<br>H H s s |
| ② | C E A F j __ __<br>H H H H s s s | B D l __<br>H H s s |

The only choice that's consistent with what we know is (B).

Let's move on to the next Specific question.

3. If both B and E are displayed, then which one of the following CANNOT be a partial list of items displayed?

    (A) C, D, E
    (B) C, J, M
    (C) C, D, F
    (D) C, J, K
    (E) D, K, M

### Here's How to Crack It

We already know that E has to be In. B In means that D must be In; B and D In means that A and F must be Out. D In also means that k must be In. Now we have only one space left in the "In" column, and notice that l, if we put it In, would force us to put m In as well. Since there's no space for that, we know l must be Out. The remaining elements—m and n—can go in the remaining two spaces in either arrangement. (Note that the clue involving l and m is satisfied either way.) Here's the full diagram.

| | IN | OUT |
|---|---|---|
| Clue Shelf | C E B/A F/D j _ _<br>H H H H s s s | A/B D/F _ _<br>H H s s |
| ② | C E A F j _ _<br>H H H H s s s | B D l _<br>H H s s |
| ③ | C E B D j k m/n<br>H H H H s s s | A F l n/m<br>H H s s |

A little examination reveals that only (C) includes an element that has to be Out—namely, F. That makes it our answer.

One more Specific question to go.

5. If B is displayed, which one of the following is a list of items that could also be displayed?

(A) A, M, N
(B) C, E, F
(C) C, L, M
(D) E, F, M
(E) E, J, M

### Here's How to Crack It

You may have noticed that the condition in this specific question is, in effect, the same as the condition in question 3; the only difference is that question 3 told us something about E that has to be true all the time. As a result, we can simply use the same diagram.

Every answer choice here includes at least one element that we know has to be Out, except for (E). That's the answer we want.

Now for our second pass through the game.

---

1. Which one of the following is a possible display of hats in the window?

(A) A, B, C, F
(B) A, C, D, E
(C) A, D, E, F
(D) B, C, D, F
(E) B, C, E, F

### Here's How to Crack It

This isn't quite a Grab-a-Rule question, since it lists only the hats. On the other hand, the hats are what we know most about. From our deductions we know that C and E both have to be In; that eliminates answer choices (A), (C), and (D) right away. You may have to check a few things until you find that (E) violates the second rule by including B but not D. However you get there, (B) is the choice we want.

---

And the last question.

---

4. Each of the following could be displayed together EXCEPT

(A) B and K
(B) B and F
(C) B and M
(D) E and F
(E) E, J, and M

### Here's How to Crack It

There are lots of ways to go here when you're doing POE. Chances are that you're accustomed enough to the B-D connection by now that you see the problem with answer choice (B) right away: Whenever B is In, D has to be as well, and there's only space for those two in addition to C and E, so B and F can never be In together.

Prior work will do the trick if you don't see (B) right away. Our work on question 3 shows that (A), (C), and (E) are possible. Our work on question 2 shows that (D) is possible. Only (B) is left.

---

## Games Technique: Smart POE

In Game #5, we showed how having a good set of deductions can simplify a game and improve speed. Another factor in how quickly you're able to work games is having a smart approach to the questions, and especially to the answer choices. We've already discussed the general theory of POE with the most common question types—"must be true," "could be true," and so forth. As you're gaining experience with games, though, you've no doubt seen other types of questions, and you've also probably noticed that some methods of getting to the answer turn out to be faster than others.

For many questions, it's hard to know in advance which method will turn out being the fastest, and there are often several to choose from. But there are some methods that are more time-efficient than others on average. Here, in rough order of decreasing speed, are the strongest POE techniques for Games.

**1. Deductions** When you work a game, you should always look for deductions. When you work a Specific question, the first thing you should do is represent the new information given and deduce everything you can from it. Why? Because deductions give you the best chance of getting to the answer quickly. Of course you must be efficient when you're making deductions—don't just stare; keep your pencil moving—but the deductions you find will always be your best ammunition. In many cases, your deductions will allow you to find the correct answer directly, and in many others they will allow you to eliminate four, which is just as good. If they don't, a good set of deductions will usually eliminate a few answer choices and help you narrow the field significantly.

**2. Prior Work** A big benefit of working Specific questions on the first pass through the game is that, when you get to the General questions, you already have a set of examples and counterexamples handy. Often you can use this information to find the answer to a General question without having any real idea why it's the answer. This is not only a satisfying feeling, but a very time-efficient practice. The one caution about using prior work is that, generally, you cannot use information from one Specific question to help you answer another. There are certain special circumstances where this can be made to work, but it should be done with extreme caution. On General questions, however, this is an extremely powerful technique.

**3. Grabbing Rules** When the answer choices contain a lot of information, often you can narrow the field significantly by eliminating blatant rule violations. In a pure Grab-a-Rule question, in which the answer choices are all complete listings, this is the only technique you need in order to find the answer. Even in less extreme circumstances—in which the answer choices are partial lists, or even in many specific questions—you'll be able to find choices that contain outright violations of the rules. Spotting them may be a matter of going through your clue list only once and looking for these violations in the remaining choices.

## POE Guide: Methods

For most Games questions you can either deduce the correct answer (on Specific questions), use rules to eliminate wrong answers (on Grab-a-Rule questions), or look at previous work to prove answers wrong or right (especially on General questions). Unfortunately, every once in a while you will encounter a question where, even after applying these three techniques, you still have more than one answer choice left. In these cases, you need to know what kind of answer you want, which is covered in the gray box on page 175, but you also need to have a method for making choices true or false.

If an answer choice could be true, that just means that if you plugged it into the diagram, it wouldn't force you to break any rules. So when all else fails on a could be true or must be false question, you can always Plug In The Answers.

Having a consistent method is particularly helpful when you get stuck on a *must-be-true* question, since most of these are answered by deductions (on general questions) or by deducing from the information in the question (on specific questions).

When an answer choice must be true, that means that it could never be false. If you can find one instance—any instance—for which the answer choice isn't true, it's an answer choice that could be false. So, if you get stuck on a *must-be-true* question, you can make up any scenario, and chances are that several of the answers won't be true in that scenario: Those are answers that could be false. If one scenario won't eliminate all four that could be false, rearrange your scenario to see what else you can get rid of. It usually takes only two or three scenarios to get rid of all the wrong answers.

**For *could-be-true* and *must-be-false* questions:**

- Find the answer or answers that must be false by plugging in the answers and deducing.
- If the answer must be false, it will force you to break a rule.

**For *must-be-true* and *could-be-false* questions:**

- Find the answers that *could be false* by making up any possible scenario you want, within the constraints of the question.
- If an answer is false in that scenario, it must be false.
- On a *must-be-true* question you may have to make up a new scenario or two to eliminate the remaining answers.

## Games Technique: Identify the Interchangeable Elements

In Game #3: Three Buses, we mention that J and K are interchangeable, but what are interchangeable elements? Interchangeable elements are collections—usually pairs—of elements that have exactly the same restrictions (or no restrictions at all). In Game #5, J and K are interchangeable because they are both girls and the only limitation on either is mutual: They cannot be in the same group. This means that unless a question gives us additional information about one or both of the elements, there is no reason we couldn't switch J and K without affecting any other elements.

Interchangeable elements are important to identify because they often allow you to eliminate wrong answers and thus are useful for POE. As we just saw in question number 5, we were able to eliminate answers (D) and (E) because J and K are interchangeable. Unless we're given information about the elements in the question, we will always be able to swap their positions in our diagram.

## Games Technique: Identify the Difficulty of Each Game

To be successful in a Games section, it is important to be able to predict the relative difficulty of the games before you get started. How can you tell? There are several things to look for after you've read through the setup and the clues.

Being able to predict the relative difficulty of Games before you start working on them will have a significant impact on your games performance.

Start with the relationship between the elements and the places to which they'll be assigned. In an ordering game, you want a one-to-one correlation between elements and slots. In a grouping game, by definition, there will be more than one element in each group. In this case, you want to know if there is a set number of elements per group. If there are multiple distributions, the game is more complicated than if everything is determined from the outset. Pure In/Out games usually do not have big deductions, but if they have several complex conditional clues, they may be very time consuming.

Then, you'll want to ask two important questions: Can we leave out any elements? Can there be any repeats? If the answer to either or both of those questions is yes, the game will be more complicated. Remember that whenever elements can be left out, we need to add an "Out" column so that we'll have a place to put them.

Next, you'll evaluate the clues. The more restrictive and concrete they are, the better, because you'll have more limitations on the game to help in placing the elements. For instance, consider this clue.

> Wednesday must be staffed by a member of the Quality committee.

This clue is much more useful than the following one:

> The juggler will perform at least once, but no more than three times during the week.

Finally, briefly scan the questions. The more Specific questions with straightforward tasks, the better. The more complicated questions there are, the more time you'll end up spending with the questions and answer choices to find the correct response.

We've presented these things to look for in order of importance; the characteristics near the top of this list are much more important predictors of a game's level of difficulty than the ones near the bottom. Thus, a game that has great questions, but allows you to use elements more than once and doesn't have a set distribution, is still a bad choice to do early in the section.

The process of evaluating a game shouldn't take more than 15 or 20 seconds once you've had some practice. Spend enough time with the setup and clues so that you have a good grasp of the concepts mentioned above, but spending too much time sweating all the minor details will defeat the purpose of making you a more efficient "game player."

You should evaluate the level of difficulty even if you are planning to work through all four games. You always want to start with an easier game so that you can get into the groove. Let's try another one.

Now we think you're ready to handle something a bit more complex, so check out Game #6. Remember that not all games will use each element only once. Sometimes you will not know how many times a given element might be used. However, your process remains exactly the same for these games as it is for all other games.

## GAME #6: BIRDS AND MAMMALS

A zoomaster is deciding which birds and mammals will go in five consecutive cages, numbered 1 through 5, left to right. Each cage will contain one of three species of birds—egret, finch, or parrot—and one of three species of mammals—antelope, giraffe, or otter. The zoomaster must abide by the following conditions:

- If finches are in a given cage, antelopes must also be placed in that cage.
- If otters are in a given cage, egrets cannot be in that same cage.
- In at least one cage, parrots and antelopes are together.
- Parrots are never in consecutively numbered cages.
- If egrets and finches are both exhibited, the egrets must always be in lower-numbered cages than the finches.
- The second cage contains otters.

1. Which one of the following must be true?

   (A) Egrets are exhibited in the first cage.
   (B) Parrots are exhibited in the second cage.
   (C) Parrots are exhibited in the third cage.
   (D) Antelopes are exhibited in the fourth cage.
   (E) Antelopes are exhibited in the fifth cage.

2. Each of the following is a possible line-up of mammals in the five cages EXCEPT

   (A) antelope, otter, antelope, giraffe, otter
   (B) antelope, otter, giraffe, antelope, antelope
   (C) antelope, otter, antelope, antelope, antelope
   (D) giraffe, otter, giraffe, giraffe, antelope
   (E) giraffe, otter, antelope, antelope, antelope

3. Which one of the following is not possible when both egrets and finches are exhibited?

   (A) Antelopes are exhibited in two consecutive cages.
   (B) Finches are exhibited in two consecutive cages.
   (C) Giraffes are not exhibited.
   (D) Otters are exhibited in the third cage.
   (E) Parrots are exhibited in two different cages.

4. If egrets are exhibited in the fifth cage, which one of the following must be true?

   (A) Antelopes are exhibited in the third cage.
   (B) Egrets are exhibited twice.
   (C) Finches are exhibited twice.
   (D) Giraffes are not exhibited in consecutively numbered cages.
   (E) If giraffes are exhibited, then they are exhibited in the fifth cage.

5. If egrets are exhibited exactly twice, each of the following must be true EXCEPT

   (A) Antelopes are exhibited in the fourth cage.
   (B) Antelopes are exhibited in the fifth cage.
   (C) Egrets and finches are exhibited in consecutively numbered cages.
   (D) If antelopes are exhibited in as many cages as possible, then they are exhibited four times.
   (E) Giraffes cannot be exhibited in consecutively numbered cages.

6. If finches are exhibited exactly twice, it is possible to determine the types of mammals and birds for how many of the 10 slots?

   (A) 7
   (B) 6
   (C) 5
   (D) 4
   (E) 3

**CRACK THIS GAME STARTING ON THE NEXT PAGE.**

## Cracking Game #6

**Step 1: Diagram and inventory** Well, the diagram is pretty well laid out for you. Five cages, with a bird and a mammal in each cage. Here's what we developed.

| | 1 | 2 | 3 | 4 | 5 |
|---|---|---|---|---|---|
| B | | | | | |
| m | | | | | |

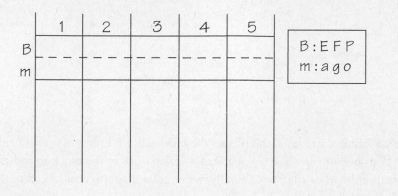

B:EFP
m:ago

Now let's examine the clues.

**Step 2: Symbolize the clues and double-check** We have many different types of clues here. Clues 1, 2, and 5 are conditional; clue 3 is a block; clue 4 is an antiblock; and clue 6 definitively places something into our diagram. Let's look at clues 1 and 2 more carefully. These are worded as conditionals, but are they really? Clue 2 says that o means we can't have E; likewise, E means we can't have o. In other words, this is simply an antiblock.

**Careful!**
Remember to number your clues, particularly if you are not symbolizing them in order.

2. [E / o] (crossed out)

Now let's look at clue 1. This is more or less a block, but there's an important difference: F forces us to use a, but does a force us to use F? No. These block variants are very common in games where elements can be reused. The symbol below captures the meaning of the clue efficiently.

1. F→ [F / a]   ~~a~~ → ~~F~~
2. [E / o] (crossed out)

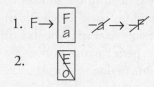

Finally, clue 5 is basically a range clue with a stipulation. Instead of symbolizing it as a full conditional, make it more intuitive by symbolizing it in the following way:

5. E — F (if both)

You'll notice that our clue symbolizing egrets in lower-numbered cages is represented as a range clue with E to the left of F because lower-numbered cages are to the left of higher-numbered cages in our horizontal diagram.

Looks okay, right? Of course, we've added the contrapositives for each conditional clue. Here are the other two clues.

3. P / a (1+)

4. ~~P P~~

There's a small wrinkle to the block: the fact that we know that there might be more than one of them. So we've added a little "+" after the block to indicate that there might be more than one. Finally, we've got a diagram that has an o placed in the mammal slot for cage 2.

**Remember!**
Always keep track of the rules for using elements: Can they be used more than once? Do all of them have to be used?

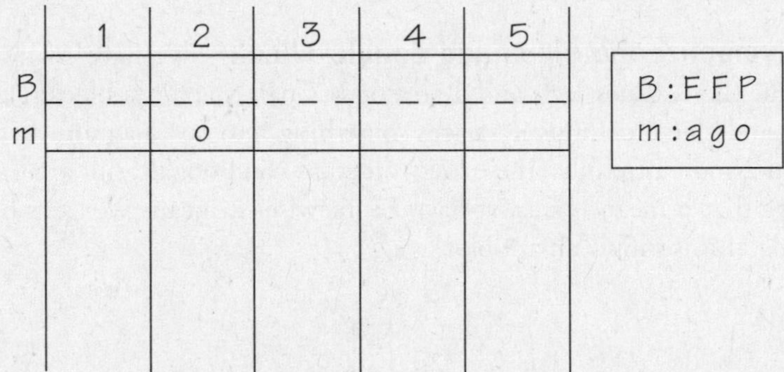


Have you reread the clues to make sure you've used symbols correctly? The more complex the game, the greater the opportunity to make an error in using symbols. If you'd gotten one thing even slightly wrong, everything could fall apart. If you're lucky, you'll notice the error while doing the first question, but you might find what appear to be valid answers for the first couple of questions and realize the problem only when the second or third question just doesn't work. At that point, you'd have to fix the error and go back to rework those first questions. What a nightmare. It causes you not only to waste valuable time, but also to become frustrated, which can affect your performance on the next game or the next section. Avoid this by investing the time to double-check.

**Step 3: Make deductions and size up the game** As for deductions, there's a major one that you can find. Start by identifying elements that aren't able to go in certain cages, and also remember that there are only three possibilities for any given slot. Start by looking at the most restricted elements or places.

Here's what we found.

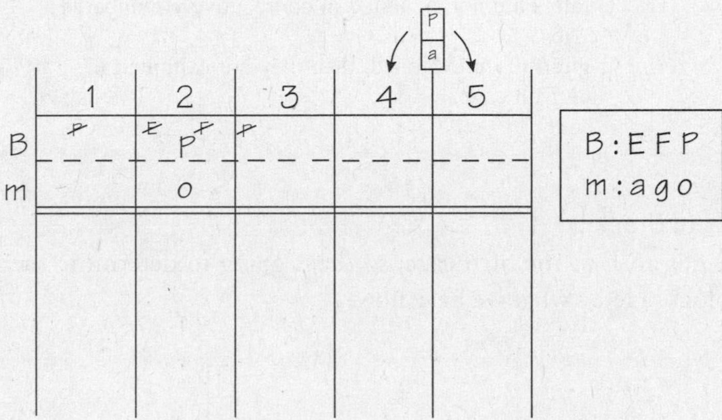


We were able to place P definitively along with o in cage 2 because neither F nor E can go with o—because if you have o, you can't have E, and if you have F, you need to have a with it. In fact, if you have o in a column, you'll never be able to have F with it, so we can add another deduction to our list: an Fo antiblock.

Also, as a result of placing P definitively in slot 2, we know that P can be in neither slot 1 nor slot 3. That leaves only two slots for any other P to go in. And remember that we always have to place at least one Pa block. So that block will have to go in either slot 4 or slot 5, but not both. Let's make a note of that over the columns.

Let's step back and survey the big picture. In almost all games that contain two sets of elements, one set will be more restricted than the other. You will have more information on that set of elements, and when answering questions, that set of elements is the set you should focus on first. In this game, there are more restrictions and information about birds than there are about mammals. Additionally, note the fact that you have a block you must place every time—the Pa block. Where can this block go? It can't go in cage 1, 2, or 3 anymore. Placing the Pa block is a major key to answering each question, then. Let's see what we can do with the questions.

**Steps 4 and 5: Assess the question and Act** We've got some Specific questions, so let's start with those.

## Step 6: Use Process of Elimination

4. If egrets are exhibited in the fifth cage, which one of the following must be true?

    (A) Antelopes are exhibited in the third cage.
    (B) Egrets are exhibited twice.
    (C) Finches are exhibited twice.
    (D) Giraffes are not exhibited in consecutively numbered cages.
    (E) If giraffes are exhibited, then they are exhibited in the fifth cage.

### Here's How to Crack It

Fill in everything you can, and then head to the answer choices.

Well, we've got an E in the fifth cage, so that's going to determine the placement of our Pa block. Here's what we have now.

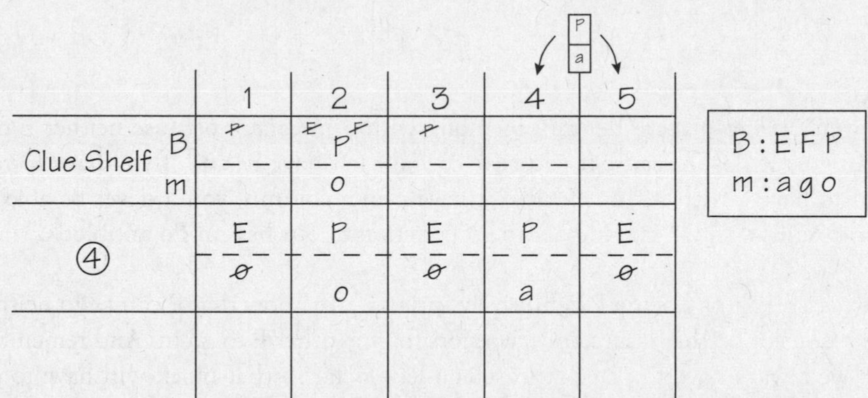


As you can see, putting E into the fifth slot forces our Pa block into cage 4. The other piece of information we want to focus on is the following clue: "If egrets and finches are both exhibited, the egrets must always be in lower-numbered cages than the finches." Because we have an egret in cage 5, no finches can be exhibited because if you put a finch in a lower-numbered cage than an egret, it would violate this clue. Hey, wait a minute! Can we have an arrangement with no finches? Well, you'll notice that it was never mandated by the setup that we use all the elements, so it is a possibility. Hence, we have egrets in cages 1, 3, and 5. We've wound up filling in seven out of our ten spaces. When we check the answer choices, the only thing that must be true is (D), the fact that giraffes can't be exhibited in consecutively numbered cages because we have an o in cage 2 and an a in cage 4. Thus, that's our answer.

Here's the next Specific question.

5. If egrets are exhibited exactly twice, each of the following must be true EXCEPT

(A) Antelopes are exhibited in the fourth cage.
(B) Antelopes are exhibited in the fifth cage.
(C) Egrets and finches are exhibited in consecutively numbered cages.
(D) If antelopes are exhibited in as many cages as possible, then they are exhibited four times.
(E) Giraffes cannot be exhibited in consecutively numbered cages.

### Here's How to Crack It

You now know from the question the exact number of times each type of bird is exhibited—you've probably already figured out that P is always exhibited twice because you need a Pa block and Po is in cage 2. This question tells us that E is exhibited twice also, so you know that there is one F. And because we're using both E and F, we'll have to be sure that both Es come before the F. Here's our diagram.

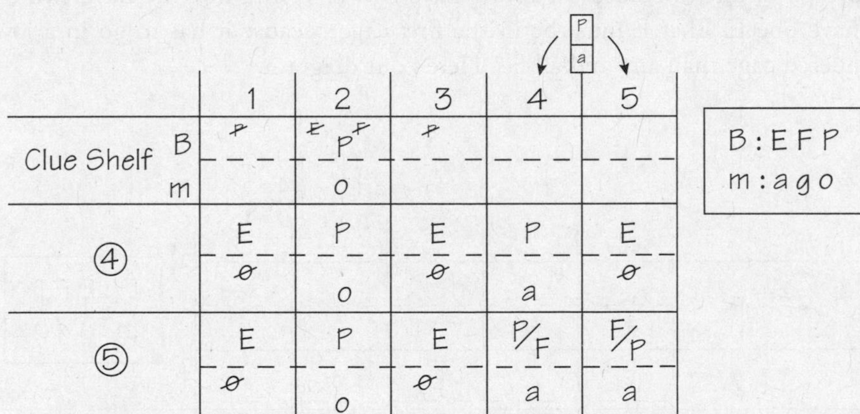


Now, we have the E's definitively in cages 1 and 3. This means that P and F must be in cages 4 and 5—you don't know exactly where each one goes. Either way, however, an a must be in both cage 4 and cage 5 because a must always go with F and we already know the other spot is our Pa block. This means that the mammal slots for cages 1 and 3 must be either giraffes or antelopes. Thus, (A), (B), (D), and (E) must all be true. Only (C) can be false, so it's our answer.

6. If finches are exhibited exactly twice, it is possible to determine the types of mammals and birds for how many of the 10 slots?

(A) 7
(B) 6
(C) 5
(D) 4
(E) 3

## Here's How to Crack It

Question 6 starts with the word *if,* but it's not one with a straightforward task such as finding what must be true or what could be false. This may seem confusing, but it's no harder than the others. If the task seems too complicated, it might be worth coming back to, but there's no need to fear such a question. Whenever you answer it, it's just a matter of breaking up the question into bite-sized pieces to expose what it's asking.

As with the last question, the information provided tells us the exact number of each type of bird. Because we always have two of P, and now we have two of F, we have one E. That E must be in the first cage because it has to go in a lower-numbered cage than any and all F's. Here's our diagram.

P/a (block over 4 and 5)

| | | 1 | 2 | 3 | 4 | 5 |
|---|---|---|---|---|---|---|
| Clue Shelf | B | ~~P~~ | ~~E~~ ~~F~~ P | ~~P~~ | | |
| | m | | o | | | |
| ④ | B | E | P | E | P | E |
| | m | ~~o~~ | o | ~~o~~ | a | ~~o~~ |
| ⑤ | B | E | P | E | P/F | F/P |
| | m | ~~o~~ | o | ~~o~~ | a | a |
| ⑥ | B | E | P | F | P/F | F/P |
| | m | ~~o~~ | o | a | a | a |

B : E F P
m : a g o

We've wound up being able to place only three birds definitively, but because cages 4 and 5 contain either an F or a P, we know that the mammal exhibited must be an a. Now we've got four mammals definitively placed as well, giving us seven total. Our answer here is (A).

Now we're on to the General questions. Let's take a look at number 1.

1. Which one of the following must be true?

(A) Egrets are exhibited in the first cage.
(B) Parrots are exhibited in the second cage.
(C) Parrots are exhibited in the third cage.
(D) Antelopes are exhibited in the fourth cage.
(E) Antelopes are exhibited in the fifth cage.

### Here's How to Crack It

We've done a lot of work on this game, so chances are that our previous work will allow us to eliminate some answer choices by showing us that they could be false. In the questions we've worked through so far, E was in slot 1, but that doesn't necessarily mean it must be true every time, so let's leave answer choice (A) in for the moment. We know for sure that (B) must be true (it's our deduction), so it's our answer. If you're confident with that, you can move on. If you'd feel better checking the last three answers, it will take only a few seconds.

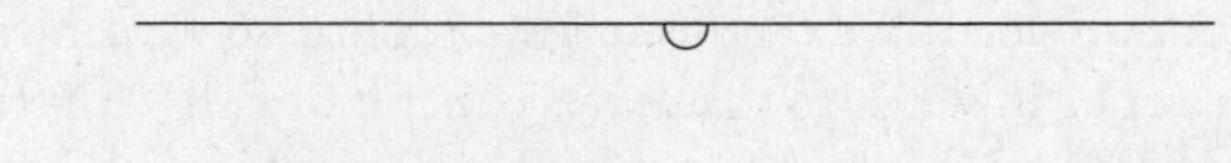

2. Each of the following is a possible line-up of mammals in the five cages EXCEPT

(A) antelope, otter, antelope, giraffe, otter
(B) antelope, otter, giraffe, antelope, antelope
(C) antelope, otter, antelope, antelope, antelope
(D) giraffe, otter, giraffe, giraffe, antelope
(E) giraffe, otter, antelope, antelope, antelope

### Here's How to Crack It

On this question, you're looking for the one line-up that can't work. You can still use the Grab-a-Rule technique of applying the clues to the answer choices, but here a violation of the rule means you want to keep the answer rather than eliminate it. Your two best clues are, of course, (1) an otter must be in cage 2, and (2) there is a Pa block in either cage 4 or cage 5. The Pa block in cage 4 or cage 5 means that line-up (A) can't work because it doesn't have a in either slot 4 or slot 5, so it's our answer.

Here's the next question.

---

3. Which one of the following is not possible when both egrets and finches are exhibited?

   (A) Antelopes are exhibited in two consecutive cages.
   (B) Finches are exhibited in two consecutive cages.
   (C) Giraffes are not exhibited.
   (D) Otters are exhibited in the third cage.
   (E) Parrots are exhibited in two different cages.

## Here's How to Crack It

We're asked to find the one that's not possible, so really our task is to find the one that must be false. We've learned that we'll eliminate any answer that could be true. Take a look at previous scenarios in which you've had both egrets and finches exhibited. Then, run through the answer choices to see if you've already drawn any of them. You've had the possibility of (A), (C), and (E) in question 5. Now we have to try the last two. Let's see if we can make (B) work.

If we have F in two consecutive slots, they would have to be slots 3 and 4, forcing the Pa block into slot 5. Because we have to include E according to the question, we'll have to put it into slot 1. We can make it work once, so we can cross out (B). We know that P can't be in slot 3, so that leaves either E or F. If we have E in 3, we know that we can't use o. Likewise, if we have F in 3, we know that we must use a—which is the same as saying that we can't use o. So it looks as if we can't use o in 3 no matter what. That's another deduction that we can put into our clue shelf. And we can circle (D). Nice work.

---

## Games Technique: Be Flexible in Your Approach

The previous game was a good example of a fact of life on the LSAT: Although some of the games you encounter will be straightforward, many will require you to adapt your techniques to an unusual situation. For example, in the previous game, the clue involving F combined the characteristics of a block clue with those of a conditional clue; the clue involving E and F combined the characteristics of a range clue with those of a conditional.

The methods we've taught you for handling Games are extremely flexible, and there are lots of ways to mix and match to come up with symbols that fit the circumstances. This is important because the people who write the LSAT also like to mix and match. They may combine ordering and grouping in a single game, or ordering and In/Out; they may add slight wrinkles to familiar clue types.

When you encounter these variations on the day of the LSAT, you should focus not on how these variations are different from the things you've seen before, but on how they're similar—how they fit patterns you already know. Often, familiar symbols can be adapted—sometimes with nothing more than a brief comment off to the side—to represent the clue effectively. The only important things about your symbol are whether you can understand it and whether it faithfully represents the information in the clue. Don't worry about whether it's the "perfect" symbol. Folks who have a lot of experience with the LSAT may come up with very different symbols for an unusual clue; each may have compelling arguments for why his or her symbol is best. In the end, the only thing you need to think about is whether it gets the job done. Be flexible, remain calm, and focus on what's familiar in a game. Once you've found a framework for a diagram, adapt it to the situation at hand; don't try to reinvent the wheel on test day.

You will be able to use a table diagram with many types of games. However, at times you'll need to use a grid or chart, because you have two items of information about each element. Not to worry—it's very approachable. In Game #7, you will need a grid, because you want to know not only what floor each tenant is on, but also what kind of apartment he or she lives in.

## GAME #7: TENANTS AND APARTMENTS

Eight tenants—J, K, L, M, N, O, P, and Q—live in a five-story building. On each floor, there is one studio apartment and one one-bedroom apartment. From the ground floor up, the floors are numbered one through five. The following is known about the tenants' living arrangements:

No tenant shares an apartment with any other tenant.
No one lives in the fifth-floor studio.
No one lives in the third-floor one-bedroom.
M lives in the second-floor studio.
P lives in the fourth-floor studio.
Both M and O live on a higher floor than Q.
K, N, and Q live in one-bedroom apartments.

1. If K lives on a lower floor than P, then who must live in the second-floor one-bedroom?

(A) J
(B) K
(C) L
(D) N
(E) Q

2. What is the number of tenants any one of whom could be the one who lives in the fifth-floor one-bedroom?

(A) 1
(B) 2
(C) 3
(D) 4
(E) 5

3. If J lives on a lower floor than L, then which of the following statements must be false?

   (A) J lives in the second-floor one-bedroom.
   (B) K lives in the fourth-floor one-bedroom.
   (C) L lives in the third-floor studio.
   (D) N lives in the fourth-floor one-bedroom.
   (E) O lives in the fifth-floor one-bedroom.

4. If P lives on the floor above O, and O lives on the floor above N, then what is the maximum number of possible living arrangements for all eight tenants?

   (A) 1
   (B) 2
   (C) 3
   (D) 4
   (E) 5

5. Suppose that M moves from the second-floor studio into the second-floor one-bedroom, but all the other conditions remain the same. Which of the following statements could be false?

   (A) J lives on a floor below K.
   (B) K lives on a floor below N.
   (C) L lives on a floor below K.
   (D) O lives on a floor below N.
   (E) O lives on a floor below K.

**CRACK THIS GAME STARTING ON THE NEXT PAGE.**

We have a grid here—and we'll use two columns for each question.

## Cracking Game #7

**Step 1: Diagram and inventory** This looks a bit more complex than what we've seen so far. Notice here that there are more spaces (10) than elements (8). However, the clues tell us that there are two unoccupied spaces, so we will end up using all of our elements, without repeating any of them; we have another one-to-one ratio of elements to slots. In this game we have two types of apartments: studios and one-bedrooms. Here's how we drew our diagram.

| | S | 1B | S | 1B | S | 1B |
|---|---|---|---|---|---|---|
| 5 | | | | | | |
| 4 | | | | | | |
| 3 | | | | | | |
| 2 | | | | | | |
| 1 | | | | | | |

**Hint:**
If an ordering game asks you to put more than one thing at a particular time or position, stack your boxes into tiers or use a chart.

First, we drew a vertical grid because it will mimic an apartment building. The clues include words such as *above* and *below* when referring to the relationship between the elements, so a vertical diagram will keep us organized. Second, notice the fact that we really had to make two columns in the diagram for each arrangement—a studio apartment column and a one-bedroom column. We indicated the difference between the columns by making dashed lines. We used solid lines to separate the work we do for each new question. Now let's look at the clues.

**Step 2: Symbolize the clues and double-check** The first clue tells us that we'll put one element in each slot. We can jot down a note like "one per slot." The next four clues are all things we can put directly into our diagram.

> No one lives in the fifth-floor studio.
> No one lives in the third-floor one-bedroom.
> M lives in the second-floor studio.
> P lives in the fourth-floor studio.

We'll get to these clues in a minute. The fifth clue is this

> Both M and O live on a higher floor than Q.

This clue is giving us two pieces of information, that both M and O live on a higher floor than Q.

Here are our symbols for this clue.

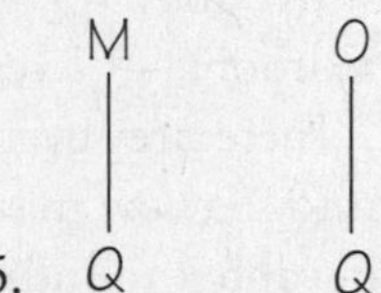


As you can see, all we did was show how M and O are both "above" Q. We used a line because we don't know how far above Q each one is. This is another range clue. Here's the sixth and final clue.

K, N, and Q live in one-bedroom apartments.

Now we know that K, N, and Q all have to be in the one-bedroom column. We made a quick notation of that clue.

6. K,N,Q = 1B

However, we'll probably wind up integrating this information directly into the diagram before we go to the questions. Now, here are the first four clues again—and then our diagram that shows how we added the information.

No one lives in the fifth-floor studio.
No one lives in the third-floor one-bedroom.
M lives in the second-floor studio.
P lives in the fourth-floor studio.

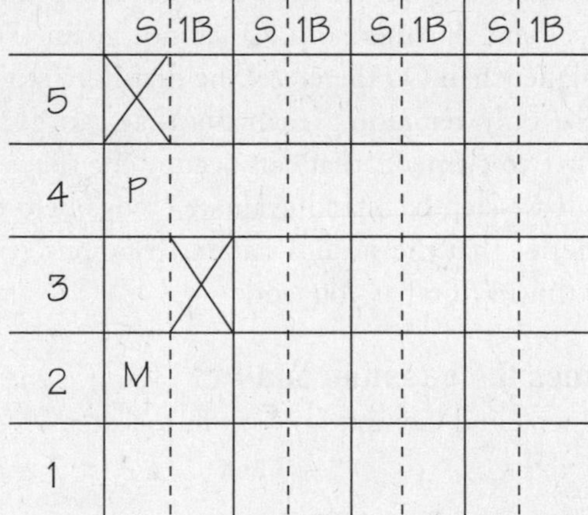


We've put Xs through the two empty apartments and then put the P and the M directly into the diagram. Now, once we double-check, we're ready for Step 3.

**Step 3: Make deductions and size up the game** As for deductions, if M lives on the second floor and must live above Q, then Q must live on the first floor. Because Q must live in a one-bedroom, Q lives in the first-floor one-bedroom. That's our first major deduction. There are several more deductions that we can make. Take a look at the diagram to see how many other deductions we were able to make. Remember also that we wanted to indicate that K, N, and Q all had to be in one-bedrooms, but because we have no way of knowing which one each will be in, we'll note the places where they *cannot* be. Here is our diagram.

| | Clue S | Shelf 1B | S | 1B | S | 1B | S | 1B |
|---|---|---|---|---|---|---|---|---|
| 5 | X | | | | | | | |
| 4 | P | | | | | | | |
| 3 | ~~N~~ ~~K~~ | X | | | | | | |
| 2 | M | | | | | | | |
| 1 | ~~O~~ ~~N~~ ~~K~~ J/L | Q | | | | | | |

There are only two studios that remain open. Both are limited because neither N nor K can go into them. Furthermore, O cannot go in the first-floor studio, because O must be higher than Q. Therefore, the first-floor studio is an extremely limited space, and the only remaining elements that can go into it are J or L. Because there are only two elements that can occupy the space, it's worth writing this in our diagram. If we step back and evaluate things before diving right into the questions, we'll notice that the studios are much more restricted than are the one-bedrooms. Keep this in mind as you work.

**Steps 4 and 5: Assess the question and Act** Go for the Specific questions first and leave the General and Complex questions for later.

## Step 6: Use Process of Elimination

Here's our first Specific question.

1. If K lives on a lower floor than P, then who must live in the second-floor one-bedroom?

   (A) J
   (B) K
   (C) L
   (D) N
   (E) Q

### Here's How to Crack It

This question provides us with new information about the relationship between K and P. It tells us that K must live on a lower floor than P, and there is only one open slot below P for K to fill. Now, take a look at our diagram.

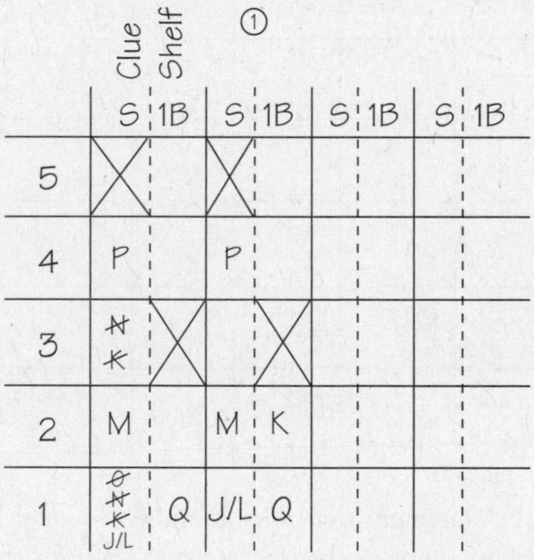

| | Clue S | Shelf 1B | ① S | ① 1B | S | 1B | S | 1B |
|---|---|---|---|---|---|---|---|---|
| 5 | X | | X | | | | | |
| 4 | P | | P | | | | | |
| 3 | ~~N~~ ~~K~~ | X | | X | | | | |
| 2 | M | | M | K | | | | |
| 1 | ~~Q~~ ~~N~~ ~~K~~ J/L | Q | J/L | Q | | | | |

That's right! K is forced into the second-floor one-bedroom, and hence it's our answer. Circle (B).

Let's work on the next Specific question.

3. If J lives on a lower floor than L, then which of the following statements must be false?

   (A) J lives in the second-floor one-bedroom.
   (B) K lives in the fourth-floor one-bedroom.
   (C) L lives in the third-floor studio.
   (D) N lives in the fourth-floor one-bedroom.
   (E) O lives in the fifth-floor one-bedroom.

### Here's How to Crack It

Well, this settles the question about who will occupy the first-floor studio, doesn't it? If J is lower than L, that means that J must live in the first-floor studio and L must be somewhere above the first floor. Take a look at our diagram.

| | Clue Shelf | | ① | | ③ | | | |
|---|---|---|---|---|---|---|---|---|
| | S | 1B | S | 1B | S | 1B | S | 1B |
| 5 | X | | X | | X | | | |
| 4 | P | | P | | P | | | |
| 3 | ~~N~~ ~~K~~ | X | | X | ~~N~~ ~~K~~ | X | | |
| 2 | M | | M | K | M | | | |
| 1 | ~~O~~ ~~N~~ ~~K~~ J/L | Q | J/L | Q | J | Q | | |

Our task is to find the statement that must be false. So we'll head to the answer choices and cross out any choices that can be true. You do this by reading each choice and looking at your diagram. Let's do that. (A) cannot be true because we've already definitively placed J on the first floor L; (A) is therefore our answer. (B), (C), (D), and (E) can all be true because those spaces are still open on the diagram.

Let's move on.

4. If P lives on the floor above O, and O lives on the floor above N, then what is the maximum number of possible living arrangements for all eight tenants?

   (A) 1
   (B) 2
   (C) 3
   (D) 4
   (E) 5

## Here's How to Crack It

This question contains two very good pieces of information. Let's put the information in first and then talk about exactly what our task is.

| | Clue Shelf | | ① | | ③ | | ④ | |
|---|---|---|---|---|---|---|---|---|
| | S | 1B | S | 1B | S | 1B | S | 1B |
| 5 | X | | X | | X | | X | |
| 4 | P | | P | | P | | P | |
| 3 | N K (crossed out) | X | | X | N K (crossed out) | X | O | X |
| 2 | M | | M | K | M | | M | N |
| 1 | O N K (crossed out) J/L | Q | J/L | Q | J | Q | J/L | Q |

Good, we were able to definitively place two other elements. However, the question asks us about how many different ways the full diagram can look. The manner in which the question is phrased ("the maximum number of possible living arrangements for all eight tenants") might be confusing. If so, translate it to say something like, "How many ways can we make the diagram work?" Then write out the possibilities in your diagram. The only open spaces are the first-floor studio, fourth-floor one-bedroom, and the fifth-floor one-bedroom. Additionally, the first-floor studio can be only one of two possible elements—J or L. So, break it down as we do on the next page.

WHEN *J* IS IN 1S:

| 1S | 41B | 51B |
|---|---|---|
| J | K | L |

OR

| 1S | 41B | 51B |
|---|---|---|
| J | L | K |

WHEN *L* IS IN 1S:

| 1S | 41B | 51B |
|---|---|---|
| L | J | K |

OR

| 1S | 41B | 51B |
|---|---|---|
| L | K | J |

Now we have two possibilities for each of the two scenarios—when J is in the first-floor studio, and when L is in the first-floor studio. Hence, a total of four possibilities, so the answer is (D). Let's move on.

---

The final two questions of this game are Complex questions. Let's leave the one that changes the rules for the end.

---

2. What is the number of tenants any one of whom could be the one who lives in the fifth-floor one-bedroom?

(A) 1
(B) 2
(C) 3
(D) 4
(E) 5

### Here's How to Crack It

This is an overly complex way of asking how many different people can be in the fifth-floor one-bedroom. You know it can't be P, M, or Q. Now check your previous work and see whom we've placed there before: On question 4, we put K, J, and L there. This leaves us with O and N. Can we put them there without breaking any rules? Try, and you'll find we can, making. the correct answer (E).

---

Now let's knock out the last question, the Rule-Changer question. You can use your original diagram for this question, but you must review all the clues before you can start filling anything in. Not all LSAT games have Rule-Changer questions, but if a game has one, it will appear last. You should do it last, too, to prevent confusion with other questions.

It's important to understand how these are different from Specific questions: A Specific question adds a rule to the ones already given. A Rule-Changer question removes or replaces a rule that was given. In effect, it creates a slightly different game. Be sure that all the initial deductions you make still hold. Sometimes a Rule-Changer question takes them away!

---

5. Suppose that M moves from the second-floor studio into the second-floor one-bedroom, but all the other conditions remain the same. Which of the following statements could be false?

    (A) J lives on a floor below K.
    (B) K lives on a floor below N.
    (C) L lives on a floor below K.
    (D) O lives on a floor below N.
    (E) O lives on a floor below K.

### Here's How to Crack It

Well, we have to shift M over to the second-floor one-bedroom. Do that, and then make sure this doesn't disturb any of your original deductions. Does it?

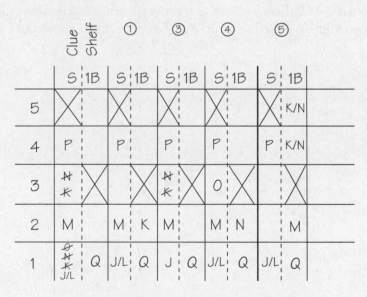

| | Clue Shelf | | ① | | ③ | | ④ | | ⑤ | |
|---|---|---|---|---|---|---|---|---|---|---|
| | S | 1B | S | 1B | S | 1B | S | 1B | S | 1B |
| 5 | X | | X | | X | | X | | X | K/N |
| 4 | P | | P | | P | | P | | P | K/N |
| 3 | ~~N~~ ~~K~~ | X | | X | ~~N~~ ~~K~~ | X | O | X | | X |
| 2 | M | | M | K | M | | M | N | | M |
| 1 | ~~O~~ ~~N~~ ~~K~~ J/L | Q | J/L | Q | J | Q | J/L | Q | J/L | Q |

Fortunately, it doesn't. In fact, it further limits the diagram (as we've indicated) because now K and N have only two places to go. Now let's approach the answer choices, and we'll do that by eliminating anything that must be true to isolate the one that could be false. (A) must be true because K, N, P, and an empty apartment take up the entire fourth and fifth floors. Cross it out. (B) does not have to be true—K could also live above N. Therefore, it "could be false" and it's our answer. (C), (D), and (E) all must be true, if you feel like checking. That's another game under our belts.

**Want Harder Games?**
For practice with devilishly difficult games, try the ones in our *LSAT Workout* or *LSAT Logic Games Workout.*

---

No matter how many games you see, there may be some that initially look innocuous but turn out to be harder than you expect. Don't let these make you anxious, though. With a bit of experience, you should have no trouble identifying a tricky game.

There are things you can look for that may suggest difficulty: Uncertainty about the diagram is a big one. Still, you may have a diagram solidly in mind and encounter problems once you begin working the questions. If this happens to you on the LSAT, don't panic—and, especially, don't abandon ship. Many games start slowly, but if you keep going, you realize that not all of the questions are equally tough. Remember that there is always more you can do, even if it's just generating an example to eliminate that next answer choice. Games become better only when you work with them one step at a time and remain calm. Don't just stare, and don't give up! Keeping that in mind, let's move on to Game #8: Ad Campaign.

## GAME #8: AD CAMPAIGN

During an ad campaign, a local retailer advertises exactly five products—F, G, H, J, and K—by placing three ads—one in print, one on the radio, and one on television. Each ad features at least two products, and each product is featured in at least one ad. The products are advertised in accordance with the following conditions:

No product that is featured in the radio ad is also featured in the print ad.

Exactly one product that is featured in the television ad must be featured in the radio ad.

H is featured in every ad which features G, but in no ad which features F.

F and J are not featured in the same ad.

1. Which one of the following could be a complete and accurate list of products featured in the radio ad?

(A) F, G
(B) F, J
(C) G, J
(D) H, K
(E) J, K

2. The largest number of products that could appear in the television ad is

(A) 1
(B) 2
(C) 3
(D) 4
(E) 5

3. If G is featured in exactly two ads, then which one of the following could be false?

   (A) H is featured in more ads than is F.
   (B) K is featured in more ads than is F.
   (C) F and J are featured in the same number of ads.
   (D) G and K are featured in the same number of ads.
   (E) H and K are featured in the same number of ads.

4. Which one of the following is a complete and accurate list of the products, any one of which could be the product that is featured in both the radio ad and the television ad?

   (A) K
   (B) H, K
   (C) J, K
   (D) F, H, K
   (E) H, J, K

5. If H and J are not featured in the same ad, then for how many of the products can it be completely determined in which ads they are featured?

   (A) 1
   (B) 2
   (C) 3
   (D) 4
   (E) 5

6. If there are exactly two products that are each featured in only one ad, then which one of the following must be true?

   (A) F is featured in the print ad.
   (B) G is featured in the television ad.
   (C) H is featured in the radio ad.
   (D) J is featured in the print ad.
   (E) K is featured in the television ad.

**CRACK THIS GAME STARTING ON THE NEXT PAGE.**

## Cracking Game #8

**Step 1: Diagram and inventory** It seems clear that we're dealing with a grouping game, but we have to decide which things will be our elements and which will be our groups. Check the clues: The first two talk about ads in relation to ads, pushing us in the direction of using the ads as our elements. That way, one of these clues is an antiblock, and the other is a block. But the last two clues talk about products in relation to products, which would push us in the direction of making them our elements. Uh-oh.

**Remember!**
To diagram the game, look for what remains the same. If it isn't clear what stays the same, be sure to inspect the clues for ideas.

It probably seems more intuitive to you to assign products to ads—that is, to make the products your elements. You're encouraged to do this by the fact that our most definite information about numbers is that each ad features at least two products, which would make it easier to have them be the groups. We'll have to be a little creative about how we symbolize some of the clues, however.

As a side note, this is something that has been seen on several LSATs over the past few years: grouping games in which some clues push one method of setting it up while other clues push the other way. The good news is that such games aren't impossible either way you set them up; the bad news is that they're often fairly difficult no matter which way you choose.

Here's what we'll be using.

$F^+ G^+ H^+ J^+ K^+$

| p | r | t |
|---|---|---|
| $- -_+$ | $- -_+$ | $- -_+$ |

**Step 2: Symbolize the clues and double-check** We've already taken care of the numbers in our diagram and inventory. The diagram is the appropriate place to take care of the first two clues as well. We want to make a note that groups p and r have no elements in common, and that groups r and t have exactly one. We'll use an asterisk as a convenient notation to help us keep track of the repeated element there. Here's what we have so far based on the info in the first two clues.

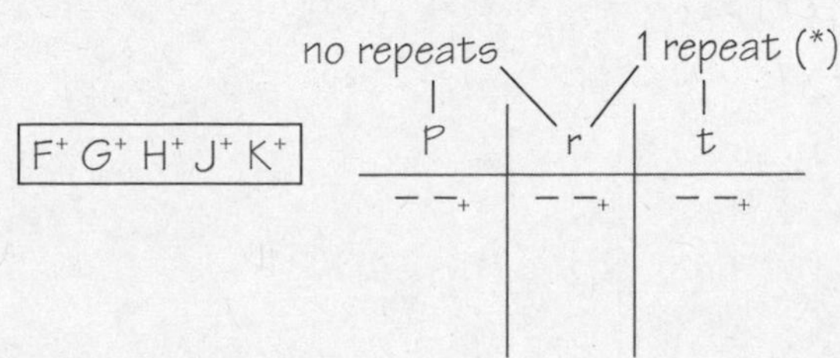

We have two bits of information about H in the third clue—more like two clues, actually. The first part is conditional: Anytime we have G, H has to be there as well; of course, this has a contrapositive. The second part is a straight antiblock, as is the game's final clue. Here are symbols for all of the element-specific clues.

3. G → [GH]; ~~H~~ → ~~G~~; [~~FH~~]

4. [~~FJ~~]

As always, be sure to double-check your symbols.

**Step 3: Make deductions and size up the game** One deduction might have jumped off the page at you when we were symbolizing the H clue above: F can't go with G. This is a straight combination of our FH-antiblock with the contrapositive of our conditional clue.

When you look at F, you realize it's very restricted. It can't go with G, H, or J, leaving K as the only other element with which F could appear. This is another conditional similar to the one we made with G and H above.

[~~FG~~]

F → [FK]

~~K~~ → ~~F~~

There are other deductions in this game that you might have gotten at this stage. If so, good job! Because they're rather situational, we're going to cover these questions as if the deductions above—which all come from putting clues together—were the only ones you had. One thing that's worthwhile noting is how restricted F is; because it will be relatively difficult to place, we'll probably want to look for where it goes early on in each question.

**Steps 4 and 5: Assess the question and Act** Because question 1 isn't a complete Grab-a-Rule question, we'll move to the first Specific question: number 3.

## Step 6: Use Process of Elimination

3. If G is featured in exactly two ads, then which one of the following could be false?

(A) H is featured in more ads than is F.
(B) K is featured in more ads than is F.
(C) F and J are featured in the same number of ads.
(D) G and K are featured in the same number of ads.
(E) H and K are featured in the same number of ads.

### Here's How to Crack It

No element can be in both p and r, so if G is going to be used twice, it must be in p and t, since r and t have only one element in common. H, of course, goes with it. We can make a number of element-specific deductions to arrive at the following diagram:

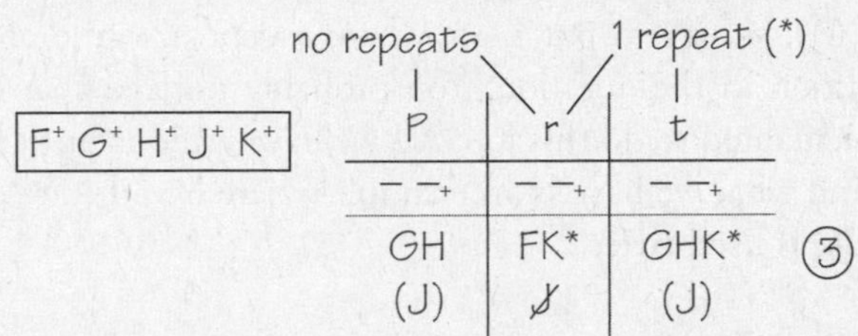


Because H was in the other two groups, F had to go in r, which meant K had to go there as well. Nothing else can go with F, so that meant K had to be the element repeated in r and t. K can't go in p (it's already in r), so the only open question is where J can go. It can't go in r (thanks to F), but it will work in any combination of p and t. The only choice that we don't see reflected in our diagram is (C). Time to think about what question to do next.

Question 5 provides us with new information, but take a look at what it wants us to do with it. We will want to be familiar with this game before we try this one, because the answer choices won't help us very much here. Best to leave complex tasks like this one for later.

Question 6 doesn't look like much more fun, but it's the last of the Specific questions, and at least the answer choices are concrete. Let's do that one next.

6. If there are exactly two products that are each featured in only one ad, then which one of the following must be true?

(A) F is featured in the print ad.
(B) G is featured in the television ad.
(C) H is featured in the radio ad.
(D) J is featured in the print ad.
(E) K is featured in the television ad.

### Here's How to Crack It

It's tough to work this one from straight deductions, because the new condition is so vague. You can try it, but it's almost certainly faster to go to the choices and start eliminating. We have to be careful, however. Because this is a must-be-true question, we can't confirm an answer by just plugging it in. All that would tell us is whether the choice *could* be true. Instead, the smarter strategy is to make a counterexample of the choice—to find out, in other words, whether it *could be false.*

To do this with (A), we try to put F anywhere except p, while of course staying true to the condition in the question. You probably noticed that our work from number 3 can be adapted to do this job. All we have to do is put J in one of p or t (but not both), and what we have is an example where F and J are each used once, and everybody else is used twice.

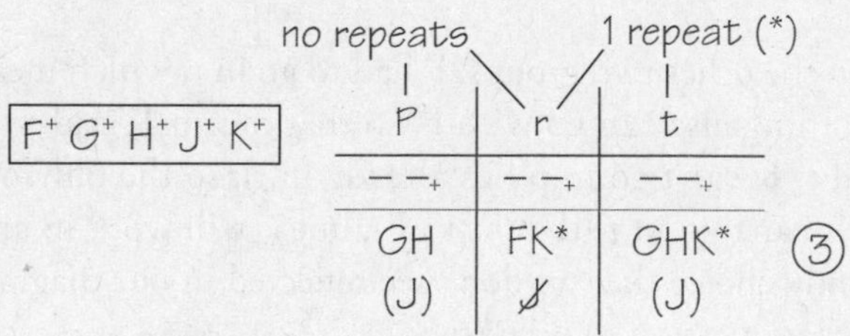


This shows us that F doesn't have to be in p, so we can eliminate choice (A).

The nice thing about POE on a must-be-true question is that our examples can often be used to eliminate more than one answer. In this case, H does not appear in r, so we can eliminate choice (C); and J doesn't have to appear in p (it could be in t instead), so we can eliminate choice (D). Our one example got rid of three answer choices.

To work on (B), we have to try to keep G out of group t. We can easily adapt our example from question 3 by removing G from group t and using J in both p and t. This option follows all the rules, follows the new condition in the question (now it's F and G that are each used once, while everyone else is used twice), and shows that G doesn't have to be in group t. We eliminate (B) and—at long last—get to pick the answer to this question: (E). K must be in t, no matter how we rearrange the elements.

What we have left now are General questions and the Complex question we decided to leave for later. We'll start with number 1.

1. Which one of the following could be a complete and accurate list of products featured in the radio ad?

(A) F, G
(B) F, J
(C) G, J
(D) H, K
(E) J, K

### Here's How to Crack It

We can go far just by grabbing rules. (A), (B), and (C) all have relatively obvious problems: (A) and (C) are missing H; (B) has F and J together. We try (D) and discover that it, too, has a big problem. With H and K in r, take a look at what happens in p. Because these two groups have no members in common, H and K can't go there. Because of the contrapositives we have for each of these elements, G and F can't go there either. There's no way we can get two elements into group P, so we eliminate (D). Choice (E) is the only one left and is the answer we want.

Let's try number 2 next.

2. The largest number of products that could appear in the television ad is

(A) 1
(B) 2
(C) 3
(D) 4
(E) 5

## Here's How to Crack It

We're glad that we waited for this one. Had we worked it second, it would have seemed difficult; now, it's more straightforward. Our example from number 3 showed an instance in which 4 of the 5 elements (G, H, J, K) are all in group t. The only remaining possible answer, then, is 5, but the fifth element is F—no way could we put that in group t with the others. Thus, the choice we want here is (D).

---

On to the next General question:

---

4. Which one of the following is a complete and accurate list of the products, any one of which could be the product that is featured in both the radio ad and the television ad?

(A) K
(B) H, K
(C) J, K
(D) F, H, K
(E) H, J, K

## Here's How to Crack It

**Hint:**
For list questions, eliminate using your deductions and/or your prior work; then look for the differences in the remaining choices.

We've been so efficient with our prior work (number 3) that we only have a little bit of work to do here. We've already seen K as the repeater, but it's in all of the answer choices. A moment's thought helps us eliminate F (or G, for that matter) as possible repeaters; after all, if we use F in r and t, then we have to use K in both places as well, which isn't allowed. Choice (D) is gone.

Under time pressure you might be tempted to just pick (E) and run, and if time is about to be called, you don't really have a choice. In any other situation, it's better to put in a little extra work to make sure. We have to find out whether it's possible for H and J to be the repeaters. Here's a sample of what you might come up with.

no repeats (p) — 1 repeat (*) (r, t)

$F^+ G^+ H^+ J^+ K^+$

| p | r | t | |
|---|---|---|---|
| – –₊ | – –₊ | – –₊ | |
| GH | FK* | GHK* | ③ |
| (J) | ~~J~~ | (J) | |
| FK | JGH* | KH* | ④ |
| FK | GHJ* | KJ* | |

(E) is definitely the answer here.

---

And now we're left with the one we skipped in the first place.

5. If H and J are not featured in the same ad, then for how many of the products can it be completely determined in which ads they are featured?

(A) 1
(B) 2
(C) 3
(D) 4
(E) 5

### Here's How to Crack It

Be careful here. If you miss one deduction, you miss the question. At this stage of the game, you probably notice that this new condition makes J just like F—now K is the only other element it can go with. This means K has to be our repeater, leading us to the following:

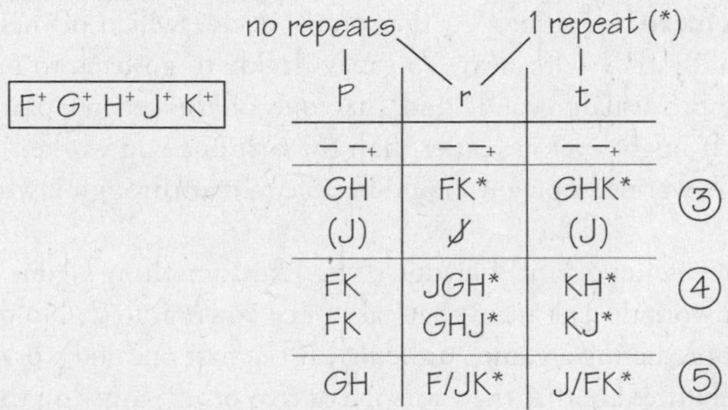


We know the exact whereabouts of every product but F and J, so the answer here is (C).

## Games Technique: Order Your Games

We talked about how to predict the relative difficulty of the games earlier in this chapter. Now let's make sure we're clear on how to put that knowledge to use.

Approaching the games in a "workable" order is the most powerful tool you have for doing well on this section. Even if you're working all four games, it still makes sense to leave the one that looks worst for last. The easiest and quickest way to order your section is, when you open it up, to read the setup and the clues for each of the first two games. Don't work with your pencil; just evaluate each to see whether you know how to diagram them and whether the clues look familiar and straightforward, or intricate and complicated. You should be able to tell how many wrinkles they've put into each game. Generally speaking, the fewer wrinkles there are, the easier the game is.

You'll probably find you have a preference for one over the other. At that stage, it's smart to dive right into it. In the rare case in which both games look awful, you can turn the page and look at the other two, but you don't want to spend a ton of time previewing. Get down to work as soon as possible.

Once you've finished your first game, bubble in your answers and then turn over to evaluate the next two games. At that point, decide which of the three remaining games you'd rather work next. You may decide to go back to one of the first ones you saw, but usually you'll find that one of the second pair looks pretty approachable. It might even be easier than the first one you worked, which is fine. Now that you're warmed up, you should be able to tear through it with confidence.

Selecting games is important, but don't feel like something's gone wrong if the first game you work doesn't seem that easy once you're into it. No one is 100 percent reliable at predicting a game's difficulty. If the first one you work on takes you a little while, chances are that there are one or two other games on the section that will take you less time. Remain calm, keep working, and look for an easy game to do next so you can make up time.

## Games Technique: Practice on Your Own

- Do everything in pencil, and don't erase your work.
- Work and write small—you will not be given much space to draw your diagram.
- If a particular symbol isn't working, or is even causing mistakes, stop using it. Try something else.
- Do games over and over. If you had trouble with one, go back to it later, and try it again until you get it.
- Practice games only when you are able to give them your full attention.
- Very important: Rework all the games you do (including the games in this chapter) at least once.
- Always keep in mind which types of games you're able to do most quickly. Look for those games and do them first on the real LSAT.

## APPLY WHAT YOU'VE LEARNED

Now it's time to put everything you've learned in this chapter to work on the following five games. The goal of this drill is to see how well you've mastered the six steps and how accurately you can work, not to see how fast you can get through these games. Remember: If you finish a section but acquire only half the number of points possible, you may as well have done only two games. Work carefully and thoroughly on these until you're sure you have them right.

If you want, you can measure the time it takes you to do each game. By measure, we mean set your timer to count up, and then turn it away so that you can't see the clock as you work on the game. Put the timer in a drawer or in another room if necessary. When you're done, stop the clock and note how long it took you to complete the game and then see how accurate you were. This will help you figure out approximately how long it takes you to do a game accurately, and by extension, how many games you can reasonably expect to get through on a given section. Take note, too, of the difficulty level of each game—if you found a game particularly challenging, it's only natural that it would have taken longer to work on.

# Games Practice Drill

## Game 1

In one day, a software maker updates exactly six files—G, H, J, K, L, and M—one at a time, not necessarily in that order. Each updated file is assigned a priority for distribution to users of the software. One of these files receives top priority, two of them receive standard priority, and the rest receive rush priority. The order in which the software maker updates the files and the priorities they receive are subject to the following conditions:

No two files that are updated consecutively receive the same priority.

File H is updated later than is the file that receives top priority but earlier than file K, which receives rush priority.

Files G and M are not updated consecutively.

File G receives top priority, and file H receives standard priority.

The fourth file updated receives rush priority.

1. Which one of the following must be true of the order in which the files are updated?

(A) File G is updated later than is file H.
(B) File H is updated later than is file J.
(C) File K is updated later than is file G.
(D) File K is updated later than is file M.
(E) File M is updated later than is file G.

2. If M is the third file updated, then each of the following must be true EXCEPT

(A) G is the first file updated.
(B) H is the fifth file updated.
(C) L is the second file updated.
(D) The third file updated receives standard priority.
(E) The sixth file updated receives rush priority.

3. Which one of the following must be false?

(A) G is the third file updated.
(B) H is the third file updated.
(C) J is the fifth file updated.
(D) L is the third file updated.
(E) M is the second file updated.

4. If the file that receives top priority is updated immediately before a file that receives standard priority, then it CANNOT be true that

(A) G is the second file updated
(B) H is the fifth file updated
(C) J is the first file updated
(D) K is the fourth file updated
(E) M is the third file updated

5. If file J is updated immediately before file L is updated, then which one of the following must be true?

(A) G is the third file updated.
(B) J is the second file updated.
(C) K is the fourth file updated.
(D) L is the sixth file updated.
(E) M is the second file updated.

6. Each of the following could be false EXCEPT

(A) Either the first or the second file updated receives rush priority.
(B) Either the first or the second file updated receives standard priority.
(C) Either the second or the third file updated receives standard priority.
(D) Either the second or the third file updated receives top priority.
(E) Either the fifth or the sixth file updated receives top priority.

## Game 2

A company's board of directors consists of exactly seven members: three founding members—Garcia, Hayes, and Jackson—and four recent members—Stone, Tan, Uqbar, and Vellini. The board evaluates three proposals—K, M, and O—with three board members evaluating K, four board members evaluating M, and four board members evaluating O. Each board member evaluates either one or two of the proposals, and each proposal is evaluated by at least one founding member. The assignment of proposals to board members is subject to the following restrictions:

Exactly twice as many founding members evaluate M as evaluate O.

If exactly two founding members evaluate K, then Garcia does not evaluate any proposal that is evaluated by either Hayes or Jackson.

If Stone evaluates a proposal, then Uqbar does not also evaluate that proposal.

Any proposal evaluated by Tan must also be evaluated by Garcia.

1. Which one of the following could be a complete and accurate list of the board members who evaluate proposal K?

(A) Garcia, Hayes, Jackson
(B) Garcia, Jackson, Tan
(C) Hayes, Jackson, Tan
(D) Hayes, Jackson, Vellini
(E) Hayes, Stone, Uqbar

2. If Vellini does not evaluate proposal M, then which one of the following must be true?

(A) Garcia evaluates exactly one proposal.
(B) Hayes evaluates exactly two proposals.
(C) Jackson evaluates exactly one proposal.
(D) Stone evaluates exactly two proposals.
(E) Vellini evaluates exactly one proposal.

3. Which one of the following statements must be true?

(A) Garcia evaluates proposal M.
(B) Jackson evaluates proposal K.
(C) Tan evaluates proposal M.
(D) Uqbar evaluates proposal M.
(E) Vellini evaluates proposal O.

4. If Garcia evaluates at least one proposal that is evaluated by Jackson but does not evaluate any proposal that is evaluated by Hayes, then how many different assignments of proposals to board members are possible?

(A) 3
(B) 4
(C) 5
(D) 6
(E) 7

5. If Jackson evaluates proposal K but does not evaluate any other proposal, then which one of the following could be true?

(A) Garcia evaluates exactly one proposal.
(B) Hayes evaluates exactly two proposals.
(C) Stone evaluates exactly one proposal.
(D) Tan evaluates exactly one proposal.
(E) Vellini evaluates exactly one proposal.

6. Which one of the following CANNOT be true?

(A) Both Garcia and Hayes evaluate proposal M.
(B) Both Garcia and Stone evaluate proposal O.
(C) Both Garcia and Uqbar evaluate proposal K.
(D) Both Hayes and Jackson evaluate proposal M.
(E) Both Tan and Vellini evaluate proposal M.

## Game 3

The four participants in a chess tournament will be selected from a group of six players—S, T, V, W, X, and Z. The participants will be seeded in rank order from first through fourth, with first considered the highest seed and fourth considered the lowest seed. The seeding of the tournament is made according to the following considerations:

Player V cannot be seeded lower than any of players S, T, or X.

Player T cannot be seeded lower than player X.

Player X cannot be seeded lower than player S.

If player W participates in the tournament, then player X must be the tournament's second seed.

If player Z participates in the tournament, then player T also participates, with player Z seeded higher than player T.

1. Which one of the following could be a complete and accurate list of the players participating in the tournament and their seeds?

(A) First: V; second: T; third: X; fourth: W
(B) First: V; second: X; third: Z; fourth: W
(C) First: V; second: Z; third: T; fourth: S
(D) First: Z; second: T; third: V; fourth: S
(E) First: Z; second: X; third: W; fourth: T

2. Which one of the following is a complete and accurate list of the players, any one of who could be seeded first?

(A) V, Z
(B) T, V, Z
(C) V, W, Z
(D) T, V, X, Z
(E) V, W, X, Z

3. If T is the second-seeded player in the tournament, then which one of the following could be true?

(A) W is the third-seeded player in the tournament.
(B) X is the fourth-seeded player in the tournament.
(C) S does not participate in the tournament.
(D) X does not participate in the tournament.
(E) Z does not participate in the tournament.

4. Which one of the following is a pair of players, at least one of whom must participate in the tournament?

(A) S and W
(B) T and Z
(C) V and W
(D) X and W
(E) X and Z

5. If X participates in the tournament but S does not, then which one of the following must be true?

(A) T is the third-seeded player.
(B) V is the first-seeded player.
(C) W is the third-seeded player.
(D) X is the third-seeded player.
(E) Z is the first-seeded player.

6. Which one of the following, if substituted for the condition that player T cannot be seeded lower than player X, would have the same effect on determining the seeding of the tournament?

(A) Player T cannot be seeded fourth.
(B) The only players eligible to be seeded higher than player X are players V, T, and Z.
(C) Player T must be selected, and cannot be seeded lower than player X.
(D) The only players eligible to be seeded higher than player T are players V, S, W, and Z.
(E) Players S and X cannot be seeded first or second.

## Game 4

A professional wrestling organization will hold two matches: a qualifying fight and a title bout. One of the matches will be a cage match between two wrestlers and the other will be a battle royal, in which more than two wrestlers compete. The wrestlers' participation in the matches is consistent with the following conditions:

If the qualifying fight is the battle royal, exactly three wrestlers participate in it.
If the title bout is the battle royal, exactly four wrestlers participate in it.
The only wrestlers eligible to participate in the qualifying fight are Bruiser, Elephant, Iron Man, and Snake.
The only wrestlers eligible to participate in the title bout are Bruiser, Crusher, Destroyer, and Elephant.
At least one wrestler participates in both matches.
Destroyer participates in the title bout.

1. Which one of the following could be a complete and accurate list of wrestlers participating in the two matches?

(A) Qualifying Fight: Bruiser, Elephant, Iron Man, Snake
Title Bout: Destroyer, Elephant
(B) Qualifying Fight: Bruiser, Elephant, Iron Man
Title Bout: Destroyer, Elephant
(C) Qualifying Fight: Elephant, Iron Man, Snake
Title Bout: Bruiser, Destroyer, Elephant
(D) Qualifying Fight: Bruiser, Elephant, Snake
Title Bout: Bruiser, Crusher
(E) Qualifying Fight: Elephant, Iron Man, Snake
Title Bout: Bruiser, Destroyer

2. If a total of exactly five different wrestlers participate in the two matches, which of the following must be false?

(A) Snake and Iron Man participate in the qualifying fight.
(B) Snake participates in the cage match.
(C) Elephant participates in exactly one of the matches.
(D) Iron Man does not participate in either match.
(E) Elephant participates in both matches.

3. If Crusher does not participate in the title bout, then which one of the following could be false?

   (A) The qualifying fight is the battle royal.
   (B) Exactly one wrestler participates in both matches.
   (C) Iron Man, Snake, or both participate in the qualifying fight.
   (D) If Bruiser participates in the title bout, Elephant does not.
   (E) Both Destroyer and Elephant participate in the cage match.

4. Each of the following must be false EXCEPT

   (A) Both Iron Man and Snake participate in the cage match.
   (B) Both Crusher and Destroyer participate in the cage match.
   (C) Neither Bruiser nor Elephant participates in the cage match.
   (D) Neither Iron Man nor Snake participates in the qualifying fight.
   (E) Neither Bruiser nor Elephant participates in the title bout.

5. If the qualifying fight is the cage match, each of the following could be true EXCEPT

   (A) Bruiser and Elephant participate in exactly the same matches as each other.
   (B) Bruiser participates in the title bout, but not in the qualifying fight.
   (C) Neither Snake nor Bruiser participates in the qualifying fight.
   (D) Elephant and Bruiser each participate in exactly one match.
   (E) Iron Man participates in the cage match.

## Game 5

Two panels of presenters, panel 1 and panel 2, will be selected from among eight friends that attend a science - fiction convention together, and no other people. Four of the friends—Leticia, Nora, Oswald, and Sasha—have dressed up as goblins. The other four—Alfredo, Carl, Dusty, and Fatima—have dressed up as elves. Panel 1 includes exactly four people and panel two includes exactly three people. Each panel must include at least one person dressed as a goblin and at least one person dressed as an elf. None of the friends is on both panels. The panels' composition conforms to the following conditions:

Dusty and Leticia cannot be on the same panel.
Dusty and Oswald cannot be on the same panel.
Any panel that includes Alfredo must also include Oswald.
If Fatima is on panel 2, Leticia is on panel 1.
Neither panel includes both Sasha and Nora.

1. Which of the following could be the list of friends on the two panels?

(A) Panel 1: Carl, Dusty, Nora, Sasha
Panel 2: Fatima, Alfredo, Oswald
(B) Panel 1: Alfredo, Dusty, Carl, Oswald
Panel 2: Fatima, Sasha, Leticia
(C) Panel 1: Carl, Dusty, Fatima, Sasha
Panel 2: Alfred, Nora, Oswald
(D) Panel 1: Alfredo, Carl, Fatima, Leticia
Panel 2: Sasha, Nora, Oswald
(E) Panel 1: Fatima, Dusty, Leticia, Sasha
Panel 2: Carl, Nora, Oswald

2. Which of the following friends must be included in one of the panels?

(A) Alfredo
(B) Sasha
(C) Carl
(D) Oswald
(E) Dusty

3. If Dusty is on panel 1, each of the following could be true EXCEPT

(A) Nora is on panel 1.
(B) Sasha is not on either panel l.
(C) Carl is on panel 1.
(D) Leticia is on panel 2.
(E) Oswald is on panel 1.

4. If Fatima and Oswald are on the same panel as each other, which of the following must be on team 1?

(A) Nora
(B) Dusty
(C) Fatima
(D) Alfredo
(E) Carl

5. Each of the following is a pair of friends that could be on panel 2 together EXCEPT

(A) Fatima and Sasha
(B) Carl and Leticia
(C) Alfredo and Fatima
(D) Carl and Dusty
(E) Fatima and Dusty

6. If Nora is not on either panel, which of the following is a pair of friends that must serve on the same panel as each other?

(A) Oswald and Leticia
(B) Dusty and Carl
(C) Carl and Sasha
(D) Leticia and Sasha
(E) Oswald and Fatima

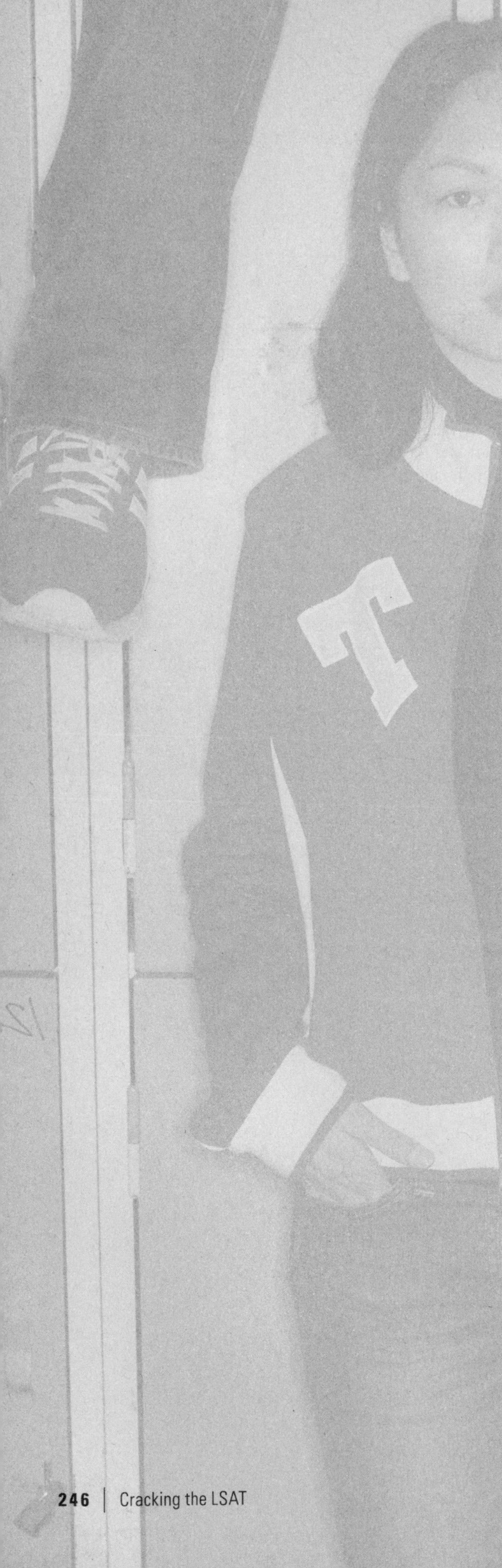

# Summary

Here's a list of the major ideas and strategies for the Games section.

- Pacing and Selection
  - If you're getting fewer than 12 questions right on the Games section, focus on two games; if you're getting fewer than 18 questions right, focus on three games.
  - Look for games with familiar clues, a one-to-one correspondence, and concrete questions; avoid games with difficult diagrams, vague clues, and Complex questions.
- Step 1: Diagram and Inventory
  - The elements are the mobile pieces in a game; don't forget to list them in an inventory near your diagram.
  - When elements come with two types of fixed characteristics, use uppercase and lowercase letters to distinguish them; if uppercase and lowercase are not appropriate, use subscripts.
  - Always keep track of the rules for using elements: Can they be used more than once? Do all of them have to be used?
  - To diagram the game, look for what stays the same. If it isn't clear what stays the same, be sure to inspect the clues for ideas.
  - If the game asks you to put the elements in order, the ordered collection (days of the week, times, positions from right to left) will usually serve as the core of your diagram.
  - If an ordering game asks you to put more than one thing at each time/position, stack your boxes into tiers or use a chart.
  - If a game asks you to arrange elements spatially, draw a picture of the space and use that as your diagram. Keep your pictures small so you don't have to erase.
  - A grouping game asks you to put the elements into collections of some sort; grouping games usually include clues that can be easily translated as blocks or antiblocks.

- An In/Out game asks you to choose some of the elements but not others; these are similar to grouping games, but the "Out" column may not obey the same rules as the "In" column.
- Hybrid games may combine two or more of the tasks described; construct the diagram for a hybrid game by fusing together the diagrams appropriate for each task. If one task is more important than another, make that one the core of your diagram.

o Step 2: Symbolize the Clues and Double-Check

- Remember the three C's: clear, concise, and consistent. Symbols should be visual (if possible), easily understood, and should match your diagram.
- Range clues talk about the order in which elements must appear, but they don't indicate a fixed amount of space that must appear between the elements.
- Block clues indicate a fixed relationship. In ordering games, they show the precise position of elements relative to one another; in other games, they indicate elements that must appear in the same area of the diagram.
- Antiblock clues are the opposite of blocks; they show elements that can't appear together.
- Conditional clues tell you what happens if a particular condition is met; we symbolize them with arrows because they can be read only from left to right. DON'T GO AGAINST THE ARROW.
- The contrapositive of a conditional clue is formed by flipping the order of the statements around the arrow and negating each one; this is the only certain deduction that can be made from a conditional clue. When you symbolize a conditional clue, symbolize its contrapositive right away.
- Conditional clues most often include the words "if," "only," or "unless." Each of these must be translated into symbols in slightly different ways; make sure you know these methods.

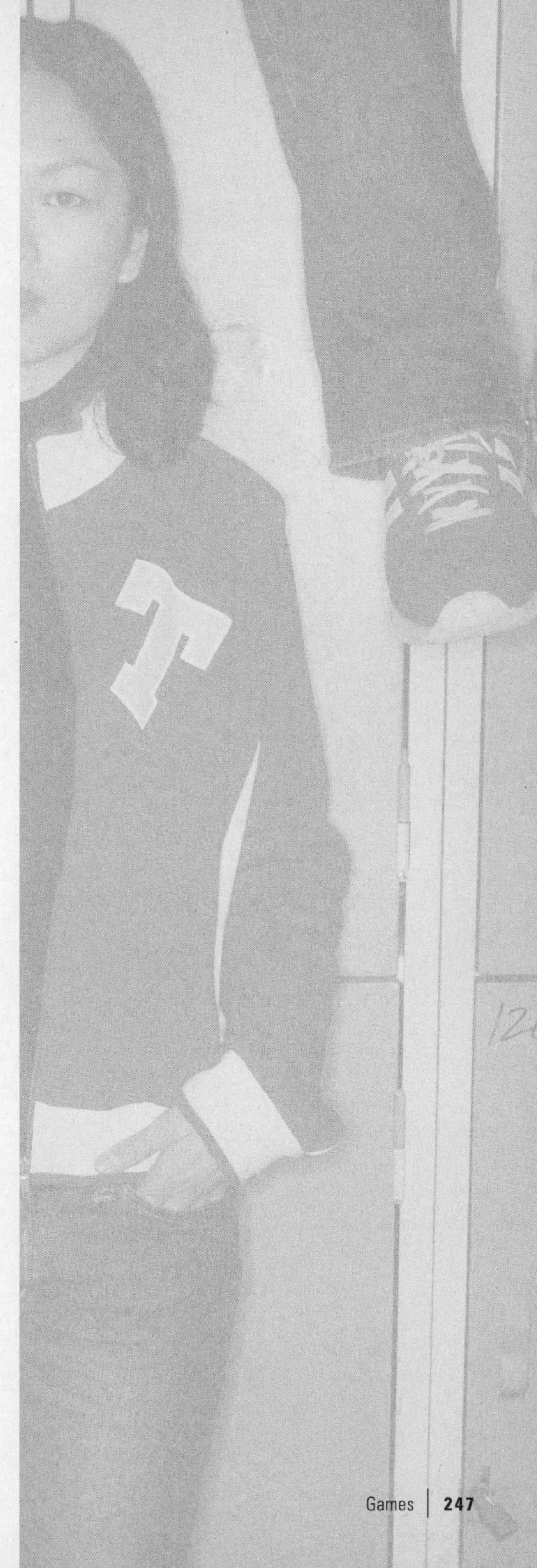

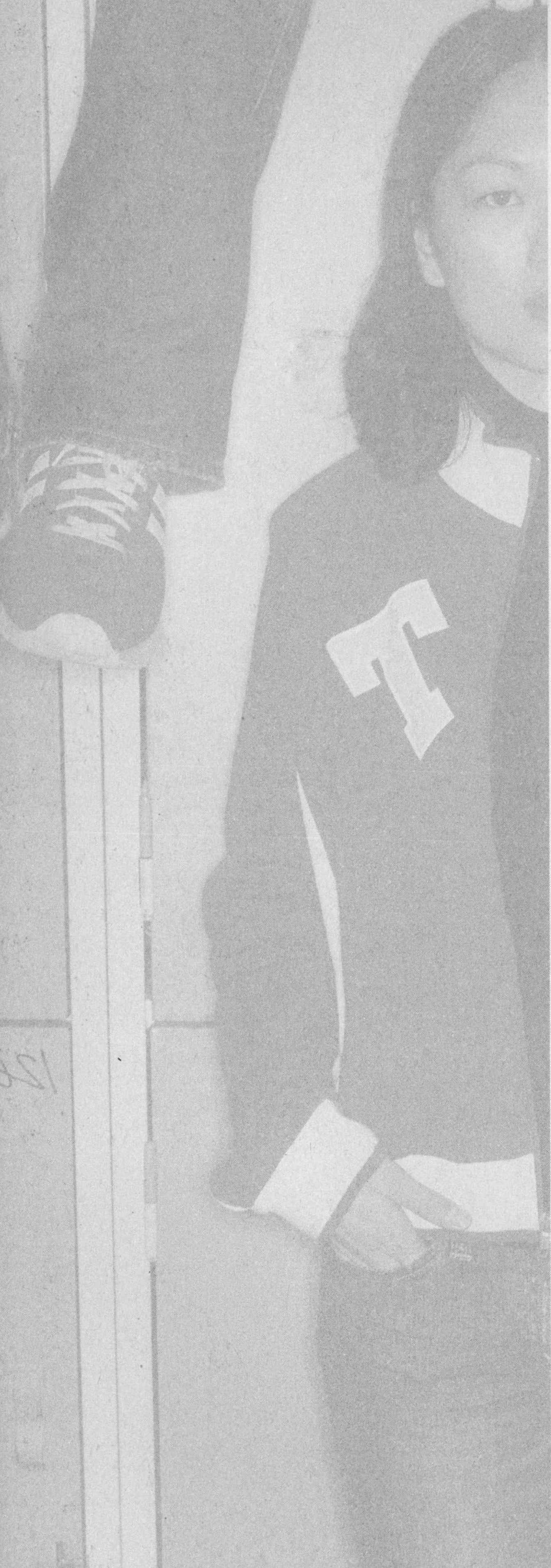

- Wherever possible, symbolize clues directly on or above your diagram.
- Double-check by going against the grain: Look at each clue, express its meaning in your own words, and look for a listed clue that means the same thing; once you find it, check the clue off in the original list. Before you move on, make sure all of the clues are checked.

o Step 3: Make Deductions and Size Up the Game
  - Deductions improve efficiency by saving you time on the questions; look for them, but don't get bogged down.
  - Repeated elements often provide the opportunity for deductions: If an element is mentioned in two or more clues, try to combine the information to arrive at a new fact.
  - Combine clues, when possible, into a single symbol. This is particularly useful on ordering games.
  - Large clues, such as blocks or range clues containing multiple elements, are often a good source of deductions. There may be only a few ways you can fit a large clue into your diagram.
  - General clues—clues that pertain to many elements and to many places in the diagram—often yield deductions when they are applied to specific items of information within the diagram.
  - When a clue mentions numbers—the number of elements in a group, for example, or the number a times an element can be used—be on the lookout for distribution deductions. You may have to try several possibilities to learn that only certain distributions are possible.
  - Before you move to the questions, ask yourself "What's the most restricted part of this game? What's the least restricted? What's likely to be the most useful clue?"

- Step 4: Assess the Question
    - A Grab-a-Rule question has answer choices that are complete listings of where the elements go. If a game has this type of question, it will appear first; you should work it first.
    - A Specific question adds information to the rules initially given for the game; this new rule applies only to that question. Work Specific questions on your first pass through the game, except for those you identify as Complex.
    - A General question asks you to deal with the game as - is, without offering further information. Work these on your second pass through the game.
    - A Complex question has a vague, open-ended, or difficult task. Work through these on your second pass through the game.
    - A Rule-Changer question removes or replaces a clue initially given for the game. If a game has this type of question, it will appear last; you should work it last. If you relied on the changed rule in making your initial deductions, you will have to go back and review them to see which ones still apply.

- Step 5: Act
    - On a Specific question, follow this process: Symbolize the new information; often this can be done right in a new line of your diagram. Then deduce everything you can from it. In many cases, this will get you directly to the answer. If it doesn't, then you should begin POE.
    - If a General question asks you about something in your initial deductions, you may be able to answer it right away. Most often, you'll have to use POE.

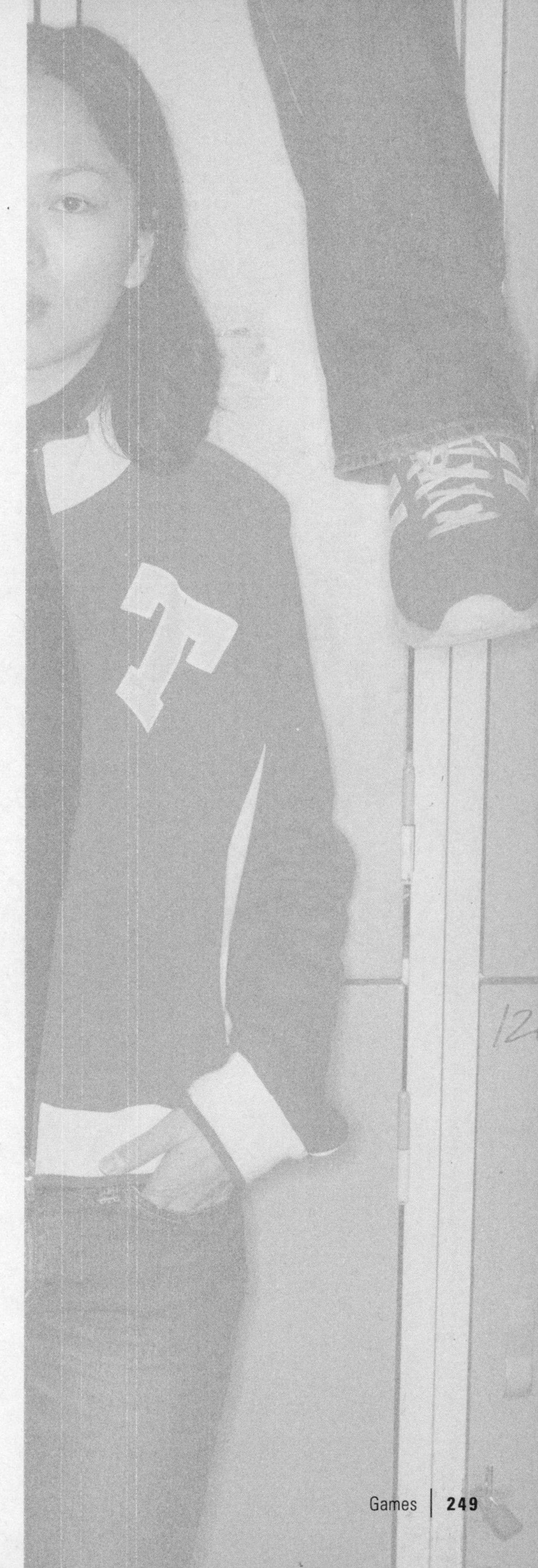

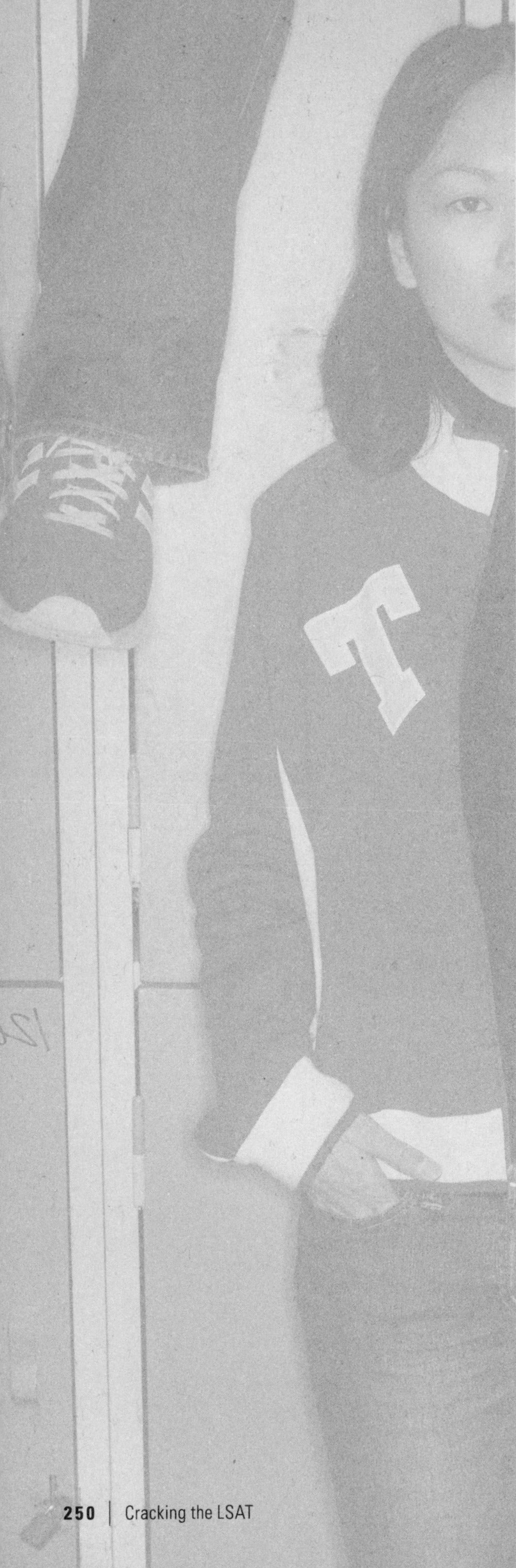

- Step 6: Using POE
  - For a Grab-a-Rule question, begin by eliminating anything that obviously doesn't fit your deductions. Then take one rule at a time, scanning the answer choices and eliminating those that don't follow the rule. When there's only one left, pick it and move.
  - For General questions, use your prior work to find examples and counterexamples to help you with POE. This can save you a great deal of time and effort.
  - For could-be-true and must-be-false questions, try to make the choice you're working on true.
  - For must-be-true and could-be-false questions, try to make the choice you're working on false.
  - For listing questions, eliminate using your deductions and/or your prior work; then look for differences in the remaining choices.
  - For max/min, count the ways, or completely determined questions, make your deductions carefully. You may be able to use your prior work to help with POE, but remember that prior work tells you only what could be true, not what must be true.
  - Remember that the goal on all games questions is to find either the one right answer or the four wrong answers, but not both. Your goal is to work carefully and accurately. Trust your work.

# Chapter 4
# Reading Comprehension

The Reading Comprehension section, as you might suspect, consists of long, fairly complex passages, each accompanied by a series of questions about that passage. The passages span quite a range in subject matter, but typically there's one from each of the following areas: arts/humanities, social sciences, natural sciences, and law. You do not need any prior knowledge of any of these areas to be able to answer the questions.

LSAC's latest twist to the Reading Comprehension section is the inclusion of dual passages (or comparative reading). In this chapter, we will walk through the basics of taking apart Reading Comprehension passages and answering each type of Reading Comprehension question, with a special focus on the skills and techniques specific to the newer comparative question types.

## WHAT IS READING COMPREHENSION?

You may be wondering where these passages come from. Does LSAC write them, or do they come from some other published source? Actually, it's a little bit of both. Most of the time, the LSAT writers will take material from a book or journal and then adapt it to make it suitable for testing purposes. What does "adapt" mean? Because you're not supposed to need outside information to be able to understand the passage, the test writers must remove any material that would require a deeper understanding of the subject beyond the limits of the passage. As they edit out these references, however, much of the transitional material that made the passage readable in the first place is taken out as well. What they're left with is a pretty dense passage, chock full of details, with choppy or sometimes even nonexistent transitions from one subject to the next.

What's on This Section?

The Reading Comprehension section contains four passages (three single passages and one set of dual passages). Each passage has five to eight questions attached to it, for a total of 26 to 28 questions. The passages are typically between 55 and 65 lines long.

Before we begin, take a moment to read the instructions to this section.

> Directions: Each set of questions in this section is based on a single passage or a pair of passages. The questions are to be answered on the basis of what is stated or implied in the passage or pair of passages. For some questions, more than one of the choices could conceivably answer the question. However, you are to choose the best answer; that is, the response that most accurately and completely answers the question, and blacken the corresponding space on your answer sheet.

These are the directions that will appear on your LSAT. As usual on the LSAT, the official directions provide very little help. Review them now. They will not change. Don't waste time reading them in the test room.

### What Does This Section Test?

More than anything, Reading Comprehension tests your ability to answer questions about the logic of the author's argument and to find specific details scattered throughout the passage. Because the passages are presented in such a way as to hinder comprehension, this section also tests your ability to manage these tasks efficiently in a short period of time.

### Why Is This Section on the LSAT?

Reading Comprehension is on the LSAT to test your ability to read carefully and manage large amounts of information in a short period of time. This section also tests your ability to answer questions about a passage without bringing in any information from outside the passage.

## READING COMPREHENSION: GENERAL STRATEGIES

The following text is a list of general strategies that you should use when you are working on the Reading Comprehension section. Make sure you take these strategies seriously.

## It's Your Section: Prioritize

The people who write this test are not your friends. Therefore, they may not give you the easiest passage first or the hardest passage last. Fortunately, you don't have to work the passages in the order that they appear. It is important to take a few seconds to assess the difficulty level of a passage before you dive in. Quickly read the first few sentences to get a sense of how tough the passage text will be, and glance over the questions. Abstract, theoretical language and ideas will make a passage hard to understand, while concrete and descriptive passages will be much easier to follow. Long question stems and answer choices, as well as questions that ask you to apply new information to the passage, will usually be much more challenging than short and straightforward questions. Don't overreact to unfamiliar topics; remember that all the information you need to answer the questions will be included right there in the passage text. If a passage looks especially formidable, nobody says that you have to do it now, or at all. Leave the hardest passage for last, or randomly guess on it and spend your time getting the other questions right.

Do the same within each passage, assessing the difficulty of the individual questions. Does the third question look especially formidable? Move past it and come back once you've worked the others on that passage. Are you having a horrible time deciding between two answer choices? Pick the one that looked right to you the first time, move on, and come back to that question one more time before going on to the next passage. You'd be amazed what a few minutes away from a question that's giving you trouble can do to clear your head. However, don't get bogged down on one question, reading it over and over. If you are really stuck, take your best shot and move on.

Your mantra: *I will remember that I am in control of the section. If a passage or question seems likely to be especially difficult, I will move past it. If a question frustrates me, I will work on a different one and return to it later with a fresh perspective. If I am still stuck, I will pick the most likely choice and move on.*

## Take Control of the Passage: Read Actively

Reading Comprehension is probably the section of the test that feels the most familiar; you have been reading things and answering questions about those things for most of your life. However, doing well on LSAT Reading Comprehension requires reading in a way that is different from how you handle material for school, work, personal enjoyment, or even for other standardized tests. Too many test takers read the passage the first time through like a text book, scrutinizing every word and trying to remember all of the details. This approach uses up too much of your limited time. You gain points by correctly answering the questions, not by memorizing the passage. Be willing to slow down when a question gives you trouble. Going back to the passage to make a tough decision between two answer choices isn't wasted time; it's what Reading Comprehension is all about.

However, you do need to have a basic understanding of the author's argument in the passage in order to effectively address the questions. This involves knowing where key ideas are located, understanding the logical structure of the passage, and defining the purpose of the passage as a whole. Each passage has several big ideas, which will be illustrated or expanded upon. As you read, actively separate the core ideas, or claims, from the evidence used to support those claims. Focus your energy on identifying and understanding the claims, and leave the details for later (if and when they become necessary for answering the questions). The passage isn't going anywhere; if a question asks you for a detail that you skimmed over, you can always go back to find it. If you feel yourself getting bogged down, don't read troublesome text multiple times. Instead, push forward and keep an eye out for something else that helps you understand the content or purpose of that confusing part of the passage. Most fundamentally, as you read you should think about how the major claims relate to each other and how they finally add up to the main point and purpose, or bottom line, of the entire passage.

Many people find it useful to quickly preview the questions before reading the passage. This can help you decide which parts of the passage to read more carefully, and which sections you can skim through more quickly.

Your mantra: *I will get through the passage efficiently, concentrating on the big ideas and logical structure, leaving the details for later.*

## Bubble in Blocks: Transfer Your Answers After Each Passage

Work on all the questions on a particular passage and then transfer your answers to the answer sheet. You need a few seconds to regroup after each passage, and transferring your answers allows your brain to do something mindless for a few seconds. When you're down to five minutes, make sure you've filled in an answer for every single question. Then, go back and work on remaining questions you have time for, changing bubbles one at a time as you go. That way, if time is mistakenly called early, you've got an answer for every single question.

Your mantra: *I will transfer my answers in groups after each passage until five minutes are left.*

## Breathe

After you've completed each passage and transferred your answers, take three deep breaths. You've cleared your mind, and you're ready to push on to the next passage.

Your mantra: *I will take time after each passage I complete to take some deep breaths.*

Here Are Your Reading Comprehension Mantras

*I will remember that I am in control of the section. If a passage or question is difficult, I will move past it to work on a different one. I'll come back later with a fresh perspective. If I am still stuck, I will pick the most likely choice and move on.*

*I will get through the passage efficiently, concentrating on the big ideas and logical structure, leaving the details for later.*

*I will transfer my answers in groups after each passage until five minutes are left. In the last five minutes, I will make sure to fill in an answer for each question.*

*I will take time after each passage I complete to take some deep breaths.*

# READING COMPREHENSION: A STEP-BY-STEP PROCESS

We're about to give you a four-step process that will help you with the Reading Comprehension section of the LSAT. Whenever you do a passage, or set of passages, follow these steps exactly. This process is designed to help you read the passage actively, searching for what you'll need to answer the questions. That's the key to working efficiently and effectively through this section of the LSAT.

## Step 1: Prepare

In your first read-through of the passage, you are laying the groundwork for the process of answering the questions. If you have little or no understanding of what you have just read, you will have very little to work with in the following steps, and your accuracy and overall efficiency will suffer as a result. However, if you plod through the passage text, paying equal attention to every word and trying to memorize every fact, you will be overwhelmed by the mass of information (and will spend too much time in the passage before you get to what is really important: answering the questions). Remember that the test writers are not going to make it easy for you. Passages are often densely packed with detail, oddly organized, and, let's admit it, deadly boring.

So, what can you do? Think of the passage as a long argument, made up of moving parts that perform different functions. Within each paragraph, separate the major claims from the supporting evidence. Even though the passages may be written or edited in a way that makes them difficult to follow, they will still often include wording that indicates the purpose and relative importance of certain parts of the passage. For example, the word *therefore* in a sentence is a clue that the sentence presents a major claim that is important to the main point of the passage. A word like *however* alerts you to a potential shift or contrast within the passage that will also be logically important. A sentence that begins with *for example* indicates that what follows is supportive evidence for a larger claim; what you should be thinking about, then, is the larger claim that is being supported or illustrated rather than the details of the evidence.

After you read each paragraph, pause and define the main point and purpose of that chunk of information. As you move through the passage, describe to yourself how the different paragraphs relate to each other; pay special attention to changes in direction and to any expression of the author's opinion. Many passages include multiple points of view. Keep close track of when the passage shifts from one view to another. Also be alert to shifts in the author's own argument. It is common for an author to describe a theory or claim in detail, only to go on to criticize or discount it in the next sentence or paragraph.

Finally, before you move on to answer the questions, articulate the bottom line of the passage by stating the main point and purpose of the passage as a whole.

Annotating Passages

Pay attention to the structure of the passage and create a visual map so that you can quickly locate the answers to questions.

Here are some suggestions for annotating the passage.

| | |
|---|---|
| **Circled text** | Circle words that indicate the logical structure of the passage, the author's point of view, and key terminology. |
| **Brackets** | Bracket topic sentences in the margin. |
| **+/–** | Note statements that indicate the author's positive or negative attitude toward the subject matter. |
| * | Note words or phrases that you saw when you previewed the questions. |
| **MP** | If the main point of the passage is summed up for you by the author (often in the first or last paragraph), note it in the margin. |

## Annotation

You need to squeeze everything you can out of the limited amount of time you have to read the passage. Therefore, as you read, you should annotate (mark up) the passage to create a visual map that you can use as you are answering the questions. If the passage is at all complex or confusing, break it down for yourself by making notes in the margin defining the main point of each paragraph. Be especially careful to note and label where different points of view are described, or where shifts in the author's own argument occur. Also, circling key words in the text is much more effective than underlining. Underlining is too passive; it is easy to underline large chunks of text without thinking about the importance and meaning of what you are underlining. Then, as you are answering the questions, you will have to reread huge chunks of text to remind yourself of why you underlined it in the first place. Have a purpose when you circle (and think about the logical purpose or function of the words and phrases that you are circling), rather than simply underlining anything that "sounds important."

How do you decide what is truly important? The followingare the key things to circle in the passage text:

- words that indicate the author's opinion or attitude
- words that indicate conclusions (such as *therefore* or *thus*)
- words that indicate a shift in direction or contrast (such as *however, but, yet,* or *on the other hand*)
- words that indicate a continuation of or elaboration on an argument (such as *furthermore* or *additionally*)
- words that indicate a sequence of events or items on a list (such as *first, next,* or *final*)
- words that indicate examples or other supportive evidence (such as *for example, because,* or *since*) (Note: Circle these words so that you can easily locate these details later if you need to, but read through the details of the supportive evidence very quickly.)
- words or phrases that you saw while previewing the questions before you read the passage

Additionally, use symbols in the margin to note crucial parts of the author's argument. Put a plus or minus sign next to places where the author expresses a positive or negative attitude. Put a star next to question topics that you recognize from previewing the questions. If there is a topic sentence that expresses the main point of a paragraph, bracket it. Finally, if a sentence expresses the main point of the entire passage, mark it with an MP in the margin. (Keep in mind, however, that many passages will not have a single sentence that sums it all up for you.)

By the time you've finished working the passage in this way, you should be able to describe the overall logic of the author's argument in the passage and state the main point and purpose of the passage as a whole. Make this a distinct step; a solid understanding of the main idea or bottom line of the passage is one of the most useful tools you have in eliminating wrong answers.

This may sound like a lot to do and think about in the 3–5 minutes you have to read the passage before you attack the questions. However, if you consistently practice reading in this way, you will find that it becomes automatic, intuitive, and fast.

## Step 2: Assess

Once you have prepared the passage, you are ready to assess the questions. While you may have previewed the questions before reading the passage, and although you have read through parts of the passage relatively quickly, this is not the time to skim. Read each question word for word to understand exactly what that question is asking you to do. The LSAT writers are quite skilled at finding complicated ways to phrase what could have been a very straightforward question. Always take a moment to paraphrase the question before you take the next step.

Part of understanding the question task is identifying the question type. LSAT Reading Comprehension questions fall into four basic categories. Here are the four categories and their subtypes.

### Big Picture Questions

- Main Point
- Primary Purpose

These questions require you to take the passage (or, in some cases for a Comparative Reading passage, both passages) as a whole into account. *Main Point* questions ask you to summarize the author's central point, while *Primary Purpose* questions require you to accurately describe the author's purpose in writing the passage.

### Extract Questions

- Fact
- Inference

*Extract: Fact* questions are usually phrased, "According to the passage…." The correct answer to these questions will often be a paraphrase of something that is directly stated in the passage. *Extract: Inference* questions ask what can be inferred from the passage, or what the passage suggests, indicates, implies, or supports. Either type of *Extract* question may give you a line reference or lead words from the passage. *Inference* questions may also be phrased in more generic form, as in, "With which of the following statements would the author be most likely to agree?" Regardless of the exact wording of the question, *Extract* questions are asking you to find the answer choice that is best supported by information provided in the passage.

### Structure Questions

- Organization
- Function

*Structure: Organization* questions ask you to describe the overall structure of the passage. The correct answer will outline, step by step, what happens in each section of the passage. *Structure: Function* questions ask you for the purpose of a particular part of the passage; that is, what role is played by a specific statement made by the author. *Function* questions therefore ask about the importance of one part of the passage, rather than about the structure of the passage as a whole.

### Reasoning Questions

*Reasoning* questions ask you to apply or compare new information offered in the answer choices to the information provided by the passage. They may ask you to find the answer that most strengthens or weakens a claim described in the passage. Or, they may ask you to find the answer choice that is most similar or analogous to something in the passage.

## Step 3: Act

For each of the different question types, you'll have a particular approach to follow. Regardless of the type, however, you must go back to the passage to locate the relevant information. Whenever the question gives you lead words and/or a line reference, go back to the passage before you look at the answer choices. Read at least five lines above and below the reference, but make sure that you begin reading where the passage begins discussing the relevant topic, and that you keep reading until the author moves on to another issue. Use your annotation, and your understanding of the logical structure of the passage, actively. For example, if you have read five lines below, but the next sentence begins with a word like *however*, keep reading. What comes after that shift is highly likely to be relevant to the question and to the correct answer.

Once you have read (or reread) the relevant information, paraphrase it. Then, define what the correct answer needs to do, based on the question type and the passage text. For most questions, you should have an answer in your own words, based closely on the passage, before you begin reading the answer choices. This will save you time in the long run, as you will be able to more quickly eliminate the "close, but not quite" answers. For questions that don't give you a particular passage reference (including Big Picture questions), check back to the passage as you evaluate the choices.

Don't fall into the trap of relying on your memory. Reading Comprehension is essentially an open-book test; all the information you need is in the passage. Under the best of circumstances, no one can remember every nuance (and if you can, you are probably spending too much time memorizing the passage in the first place). The test writers are highly skilled at creating wrong answers that will "sound good" if you aren't actively rereading and relying on the exact wording of the passage text. And, the stress and fatigue you may be feeling during the test certainly don't create ideal circumstances! Use your resources wisely, and go back to the passage consistently and carefully.

### Step 4: Answer using Process of Elimination

As usual, this is the final step in our strategy. You want to compare what you said the answer needed to do in Step 3 with the choices you're given. Your goal is to eliminate things that are definitely wrong, meaning that you can pinpoint something in the choices that makes them wrong. "It sounds bad" is never a valid reason to cross off an answer choice—the choices are designed to be unappealing. Cross off answers that don't match what you came up with or that aren't supported by information in the passage. Also beware of information that's in the passage but has no relevance to the question being asked. We'll talk at greater length about Process of Elimination (POE) later in this chapter.

What you should definitely keep in mind as you go through answer choices, however, is that the one that has nothing wrong with it is the one you're looking for, whether or not it's phrased in a way that matches what you said you were looking for. We're not looking for the best-phrased answer choice; we're looking for one that does what we need it to do without having anything wrong with it. Whether we think the credited response is worded badly is beside the point.

## LET'S DO A READING COMPREHENSION PASSAGE

Okay, those are the four steps. Now, let's see how they work on a real Reading Comprehension passage. Take your time on this passage, and focus on learning and implementing the process. Eventually you may need to work on going faster, but for now, the focus should be on accuracy.

After the passage, we'll give you some extra techniques for attacking this section of the LSAT, just as we did in the Arguments and Games chapters.

# Reading Comprehension Passage: *Celebrity Law*

Recently, the right of public personalities to direct and profit from all commercial exploitations of their fame has gained widespread acceptance. Recognition of this "right of publicity," however, has raised difficult questions concerning the proper scope and duration of the right as well as its relationship to free speech and free trade interests. Often, the "type" of personality, be it an entertainer, politician, or athlete, also weighs on this decision-making process.

The right of publicity protects economic interests of celebrities in their own fame by allowing them to control and profit from the publicity values that they have created. Before courts recognized this right, celebrities' primary protection against the unauthorized commercial appropriation of their names or likenesses was a suit for invasion of privacy. Privacy law, however, proved to be an inadequate response to the legal questions presented by celebrities seeking to protect their economic interest in fame. Whereas privacy law protects a person's right to be left alone, publicity law proceeds from antithetical assumptions. Celebrities do not object to public attention—they thrive on it. However, they seek to benefit from any commercial use of their popularity.

A celebrity's public image has many aspects, each of which may be appropriated for a variety of purposes. Plaintiffs have sought to protect various attributes including name, likeness, a particular routine or act, characters made famous by their celebrity, unique style, and biographical information. In deciding whether the right of publicity applies to a particular attribute, courts consider underlying legal and policy goals.

Two goals support recognition of the right of publicity: the promotion of creative endeavor and the prevention of unjust enrichment through the theft of goodwill. Courts determine the scope of publicity rights by balancing these policies against countervailing First Amendment and free trade interests. Recognizing a celebrity's ability to control the exercise of some personal attribute may limit the "speech" of would-be appropriators and give the celebrity a commercial monopoly. Thus, the value of promoting creativity and preventing unjust enrichment must outweigh negative constitutional and commercial repercussions before courts extend the right of publicity to any particular attribute.

The value of a publicity right in a particular attribute depends, in large part, on the length of time such a right is recognized and protected by the law. Courts disagree on whether publicity rights survive the death of their creators. Some courts advocate unconditional devisability. They emphasize that the ability to control exploitation of fame is a property right, carrying all the characteristics of the title. Other courts conclude that the right of publicity terminates at the celebrity's death. These courts fear that recognizing postmortem publicity rights would negatively affect free speech and free trade.

The right of publicity, especially in the cases of well-known politicians and statesmen, often conflicts with First Amendment interests and thus should be defined with care and precision.

1. Which of the following statements best summarizes the above passage?

   (A) An assessment of privacy law reveals that publicity law is a more appropriate legal remedy for public personalities.
   (B) The promotion of creative endeavor justifies the legal recognition of the right of publicity.
   (C) The courts, rather than the celebrities themselves, must determine the relative importance of commercial and constitutional concerns.
   (D) The legal issues regarding the right to publicity are complex and have yet to be fully resolved.
   (E) Widely accepted approaches to deciding publicity law cases conflict with First Amendment interests.

2. Based on the passage, the judicial response to "right of publicity" questions has been

   (A) theoretical
   (B) inconclusive
   (C) creative
   (D) disdainful
   (E) widely respected

3. It can be inferred from the passage that a characteristic of "devisability" (line 52) is the ability to be

(A) commercially appropriated with the author's permission
(B) divided into more than one legal entity
(C) inherited
(D) recognized as a commercial monopoly
(E) structured in several equal branches

4. Which one of the following can be inferred from the information in the passage?

(A) First Amendment ramifications of extending the right of publicity to politicians should be analyzed.
(B) There is rarely any provable nexus between exploitation during life and career incentive.
(C) Celebrities invest substantial time and money to achieve uncertain success and are thus entitled to whatever value accrues from these efforts.
(D) Concerns regarding unjust enrichment from biographical data outweigh the right to disseminate information under the First Amendment.
(E) It is usually in the public interest to reward successful entertainers for their efforts and thereby encourage artists to devote their lives to creative endeavors.

5. According to the passage, privacy laws are inadequate as legal remedies for celebrities because

(A) public personalities have no redress for unauthorized commercial appropriation of their images
(B) private individuals waive privacy rights by becoming public figures
(C) stars wish to be protected from the public only when they are not successful
(D) the laws do not address the financial issues inherent in a public figure's fame
(E) celebrities have a responsibility to the public to share their created personas and not avoid public attention

6. To which one of the following situations would the "right of publicity" as discussed in the passage most clearly apply?

(A) A novelist objects to the unauthorized reprinting of a portion of his or her book in a student's paper.
(B) An athlete plans to design and market, but not promote, a line of sportswear.
(C) The well-known catchphrase of a local talk-show host is used as part of an ad campaign for a supermarket.
(D) The president of a small company bequeaths his or her business to an employee but his or her family contests the will.
(E) The work of a celebrated screen actor is re-edited after the actor's death.

**Step 1: Prepare** Below is a list of what each paragraph of the passage told us, and what we felt was important in it. Then we'll show you what we thought were the main idea and structure of the passage as a whole. Here we go!

Paragraph 1: Introduction of the concept of "right of publicity" and its problems
Paragraph 2: Why right of publicity was needed: privacy laws didn't do the job
Paragraph 3: What the right of publicity seeks to protect and courts' considerations
Paragraph 4: Courts consider pros and cons of the right of publicity
Paragraph 5: How long does right of publicity apply? Differing judicial perspectives
Paragraph 6: Right of publicity and politicians: often a problem

As you can see, we have retained few of the details here. All we have done is define the core idea of each paragraph in terms of what it contributes to the passage as a whole. From this outline, we can come up with the bottom line of the passage, and define its logical purpose. Always state the bottom line (the main idea, tone, and purpose) before you move on to answering the questions.

Bottom line: *The right of publicity, which seeks to protect the economic interest of celebrities in their own fame, may have certain benefits, but must also be weighed against other concerns.*

**Prepare**
Break up the passage into smaller chunks of information—remember that it's easier to process a little at a time and then put it all together.

Just as there are certain types of games and arguments, there are certain types of passages, as defined by their logical structure and purpose. We will discuss these types in more detail in a later section of this chapter. This passage, which describes different aspects of an issue without taking a clear stand for or against, is intended to tell a story.

**Steps 2, 3, and 4: Assess, Act, and Answer** For each question, we will define the question type and translate what the question is asking us to do, go back to the passage and decide what the correct choice needs to accomplish, and use POE on the answer choices.

Let's get started.

1. Which of the following statements best summarizes the above passage?
   (A) An assessment of privacy law reveals that publicity law is a more appropriate legal remedy for public personalities.
   (B) The promotion of creative endeavor justifies the legal recognition of the right of publicity.
   (C) The courts, rather than the celebrities themselves, must determine the relative importance of commercial and constitutional concerns.
   (D) The legal issues regarding the right to publicity are complex and have yet to be fully resolved.
   (E) Widely accepted approaches to deciding publicity law cases conflict with First Amendment interests.

## Here's How to Crack It

This is a Big Picture: Main Point question, so we'll want to remind ourselves of what we said the author's main point was. We said that the right of publicity is a relatively recent development and that its ramifications have yet to be fully worked out. We'll want to match this against the answer choices, looking for the response that in some way relates to every part of the passage.

Choice (A) is too specific. Privacy law is mentioned only briefly in the second paragraph. Choice (B) is also too narrow; the promotion of creative endeavor is mentioned only in the fourth paragraph. Although (C) may be true, the passage as a whole is not about who must determine the relative importance of these concerns—it's about right of publicity. Choice (D) looks pretty good; it mentions right of publicity and the lack of complete resolution. Choice (E) is too strong and too narrow. While the author suggests in the fourth paragraph that the two might come into conflict, the passage as a whole is not focused on this possibility. The best answer, therefore, is choice (D).

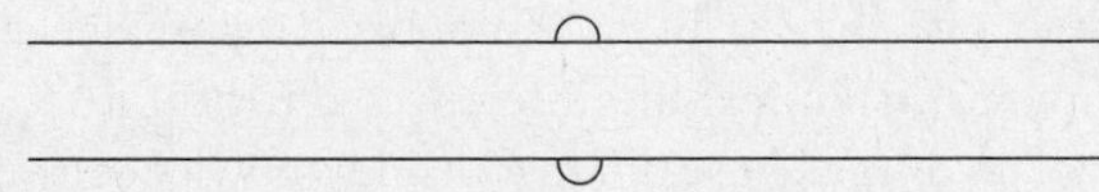

2. Based on the passage, the judicial response to "right of publicity" questions has been
   (A) theoretical
   (B) inconclusive
   (C) creative
   (D) disdainful
   (E) widely respected

## Here's How to Crack It

This is an Extract: Inference question; we are asked to characterize the judicial response to questions concerning the right of publicity. A look at our map shows that there is discussion of the judicial response in paragraphs 3, 4, and 5. Since the correct answer could come from a few different sections of the passage, it's time to look at our answer choices. The passage states that the court considered "underlying legal and policy goals" (paragraph 3). Since this indicates a more practical than purely theoretical response, choice (A) is out. The fifth paragraph describes how courts disagree on whether the right of publicity persists after death. Thus, we should keep choice (B), "inconclusive," in contention. Nothing in the passage describes the courts' response as innovative or creative, and so choice (C) is gone. The tone of choice (D) is much too negative; the author never criticizes the courts' response, nor does the passage show a lack of respect towards the courts. Finally, the passage does not indicate how widely respected the courts' actions have been (although we know that the right of publicity is widely accepted, we don't know that the same is true of the courts' decisions). Therefore, we are left with choice (B) as the best response.

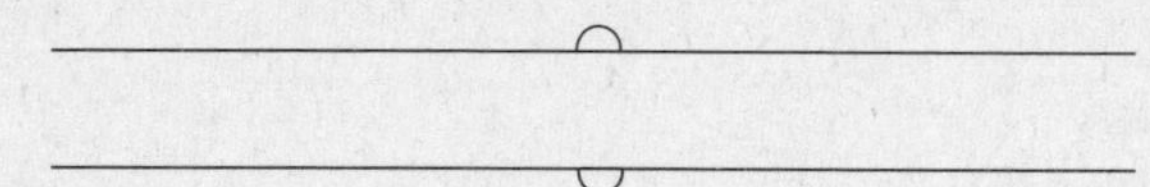

3. It can be inferred from the passage that a characteristic of "devisability" (line 52) is the ability to be
   (A) commercially appropriated with the author's permission
   (B) divided into more than one legal entity
   (C) inherited
   (D) recognized as a commercial monopoly
   (E) structured in several equal branches

## Here's How to Crack It

This is an Extract: Inference question; we are asked to decide what the concept of "devisability," as used in the passage, might mean. Note that this question begins with the phrase "It can be inferred that...." In Reading Comprehension, an inferable answer choice is one that is directly supported by evidence in the passage. You should never try to make real-life inferences on the LSAT. That is, do not speculate or extrapolate or make use of any outside knowledge you might have.

**Careful!**
When a question gives you a line reference, don't fall into the trap of reading only that one line.

We've also been given a line reference, so that helps us locate the information in the passage. Make sure to go back and read the paragraph in which it's located because context will be crucial to determining the answer. In this case, all we know is that it relates to the issue of whether the right of publicity ends with a celebrity's death or whether it continues, as would a property right. Now let's look at the answers. Choice (A) refers to a situation in which permission *has* been given by an author—this is not discussed anywhere in the passage. Choice (B) discusses division of something into multiple things, which is also not discussed.

Choice (C), "inherited," is supported by the author's connection of devisability to the question of whether or not publicity rights survive death, and the equation of it by some courts with a property right that does not terminate with death (paragraph 5). Choice (D) is too strong. While the passage mentions the risk that recognition of publicity rights may lead to commercial monopoly (paragraph 4), the author does not connect this directly to the discussion of devisabilty, or indicate that monopoly is especially likely if the right survives death. Choice (E) is out of scope—structuring something in branches is not mentioned. Therefore, choice (C) is best supported by the passage.

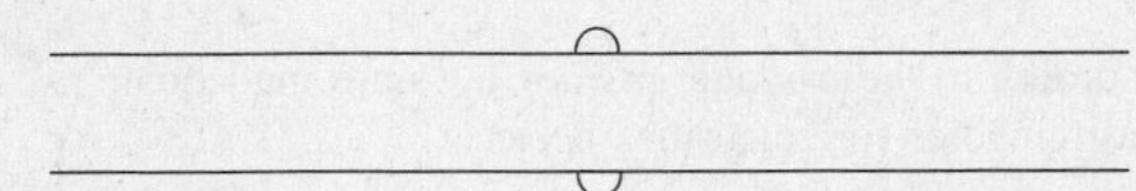

4. Which one of the following can be inferred from the information in the passage?
   - (A) First Amendment ramifications of extending the right of publicity to politicians should be analyzed.
   - (B) There is rarely any provable nexus between exploitation during life and career incentive.
   - (C) Celebrities invest substantial time and money to achieve uncertain success and are thus entitled to whatever value accrues from these efforts.
   - (D) Concerns regarding unjust enrichment from biographical data outweigh the right to disseminate information under the First Amendment.
   - (E) It is usually in the public interest to reward successful entertainers for their efforts and thereby encourage artists to devote their lives to creative endeavors.

### Here's How to Crack It

Even though this is an Extract: Inference question, there is nothing in the question stem that leads us to a particular part of the passage as a starting point. As we saw above, to infer means to find the answer that is best supported by the passage. Thus, we will have to check each answer choice against passage information. This is where our map will be a real time saver. Use POE to eliminate anything we can't find evidence for, or that takes the information in the passage too far.

Choice (A) paraphrases part of the information in the last paragraph of the passage, so we definitely want to keep it under consideration. Choice (B) is inconsistent with the passage. Take a look at paragraph 4, which suggests that there may in fact be a connection or nexus between exploitation of a celebrity's image and the incentive to undertake creative endeavors. To the extent that this choice is relevant to the passage, it is also inconsistent with it. The passage never discusses the amount of time and money invested by celebrities in their career (or how likely it is that they will achieve success); thus choice (C) is incorrect. Choice (D) definitively states that the possibility of unjust enrichment outweighs First Amendment considerations; however, the passage simply suggests that the two must be weighed against each other (paragraph 6). Finally, choice (E) is too strong. While the passage indicates that there may be some value in encouraging creative effort (paragraph 4), the author does not go so far as to argue that it is usually in the public's interest to reward successful entertainers. Therefore, choice (A) is the correct answer.

5. According to the passage, privacy laws are inadequate as legal remedies for celebrities because

(A) public personalities have no redress for unauthorized commercial appropriation of their images
(B) private individuals waive privacy rights by becoming public figures
(C) stars wish to be protected from the public only when they are not successful
(D) the laws do not address the financial issues inherent in a public figure's fame
(E) celebrities have a responsibility to the public to share their created personae and not avoid public attention

### Here's How to Crack It

This is an Extract: Fact question; we are asked why privacy laws don't adequately take care of celebrities' legal needs. If we look at our map, we see that this issue is addressed in the second paragraph. Upon rereading it, we learn that privacy laws weren't fully equipped to deal with the economic aspects of fame. We want an answer that talks about the financial side of things.

Choice (A) is a trap answer; it sounds like something argued by the author, but it takes it too far in stating that privacy law offered "no redress." Lines 16–21 discuss this concept, yet those lines indicate that privacy law did in fact provide some measure of protection, even if that protection was inadequate. Furthermore, this choice makes no mention of economic interests of celebrities, and we know from the work we did in Step 3 that this is the key issue for this question. There is no support for choice (B); even if you personally think that public figures waive their right to privacy, the passage never suggests this to be true. And, the question asks why privacy laws are inadequate, not why celebrities may or may not deserve privacy. As for choice (C), there is nothing in the passage that tells us when stars will or will not want privacy. And, there is no mention of financial issues in this answer. Choice (D) does bring in the financial issue, and does so in a way that is consistent with the relevant part of the passage. Now, this choice is looking pretty good. Choice (E), on the other hand, raises an issue (whether or not celebrities have a right to privacy) that is not relevant either to the passage or to the question. Thus, we are left with choice (D) as our correct answer.

6. To which one of the following situations would the "right of publicity" as discussed in the passage most clearly apply?

 (A) A novelist objects to the unauthorized reprinting of a portion of his book in a student's paper.
 (B) An athlete plans to design and market, but not promote, a line of sportswear.
 (C) The well-known catchphrase of a local talk - show host is used as part of an ad campaign for a supermarket.
 (D) The president of a small company bequeaths his business to an employee but his family contests the will.
 (E) The work of a celebrated screen actor is re-edited after the actor's death.

### Here's How to Crack It

This is a Reasoning question; we are asked to take the concept of "right of publicity" and apply it to a situation that is not discussed in the passage. As with any reasoning question, however, we'll still need to go back to the passage to figure out what we need to compare the answer choices to. In this case, we need a solid definition of what the right of publicity covers. Once more, we look to our map. The third paragraph discusses what the right of publicity is meant to protect, so we should look there. We also know that what's underlying this right is the desire for financial protection.

Choice (A) is not appropriate because the student is not writing the paper for financial gain. Choice (B) is not appropriate because the athlete has a right to his or her own fame. Choice (C) looks good—the supermarket is making commercial use of the talk-show host's celebrity image. Choice (D) has no direct connection to the issue of celebrity or fame. Choice (E) is attractive, but the last paragraph of the passage tells us that the courts are undecided about whether the right of publicity survives death. Thus, if we compare choices (C) and (E), the right of publicity is most clearly applicable to the scenario in choice (C).

Now that you know the basic approach, it is time to work on refining your technique in each step of the process.

**Preview the Questions**

Reading the questions first is an optional part of Step 1. Think of it like watching a preview before going to see a movie. You will already know some of the highlights and plot points, and will be better able to understand the story.

## Refining Your Technique: Read the Questions First

Many test takers find it useful to preview the questions first, before reading the passage. What does previewing the questions entail? You quickly read through the question stems (not the answer choices), picking out references to passage content. Don't worry about identifying the question types in this stage; that comes later. Knowing what the questions are asking can help you to focus on the important information as you prepare the passage, and to skim over the details that may or may not be important. If there is a line reference in the question, go ahead and put a star next to that line in the margin of the passage (but don't jump in and read that section of the passage out of context). As you read the passage, when you come across a topic you recognize from the questions or see a star in the margin, pay special attention to that section, since you know that you will need it later on. An added benefit of previewing the questions is that having some context when you start to read the passage may well help you to better understand the author's argument the first time through.

Try our four-step strategy—with and without previewing the questions—on two different sets of several passages. If you are not used to previewing, it will feel a bit strange at first. Practice it until you become comfortable with the approach, so that you can know for sure whether or not it is helpful for you. Once you have tried out both ways, choose the method that maximizes your efficiency and your accuracy, and use that approach consistently from then on.

There are a few things to keep in mind when previewing. First, it shouldn't take you more than 20–30 seconds per passage. You are not trying to memorize the questions, but rather to get a sense of what parts of the passage will be most important for answering the questions. Also, don't stop midway through the passage to answer questions, even if you think that you have the relevant information at that point. What the author says later on may affect the answer to that question. Also, for most of the questions it will be necessary to have a good understanding of the main point of the passage. If you stop reading in the middle of the process of preparing the passage, you will likely get distracted and have a harder time understanding the overall logic of the author's argument.

## Identify the Logical Purpose of the Passage

Working a game in the Analytical Reasoning section requires you to map out the structure of that game. Answering a question in the Logical Reasoning section requires that you understand the logic of the argument. In the same way, to answer many of the questions for a Reading Comprehension passage you will need to understand the logical structure of the passage itself. And, just as games and arguments fall into certain categories based on structure, so do the passages.

As you read and prepare a passage, pay close attention to the purpose of the different paragraphs and how they relate to each other. Think of each chunk of the passage as a piece of a puzzle, and fit the pieces together as you go. To do this you will have to read actively, not passively. It takes a lot of mental effort, but not necessarily more time; since active reading helps you to pick out the most important parts of the author's argument, it also helps you to avoid wasting much time on the less crucial details. Pay especially close attention to (and circle) pivotal words like *however, yet, but,* or *on the other hand.* These words often mark important shifts or contrasts, often between different points of view. Also focus on and annotate any wording that indicates the author's own opinion or point of view. When you finish reading the passage, identify the logical purpose of the passage as a whole; do this as part of articulating the bottom line. As you go through the **Act** and **Answer** steps, use your analysis of the logical structure of the passage, and your annotation that maps it out, to predict and identify wrong answers.

Passages fall into five basic categories, as listed below. If more than one category seems to apply, don't agonize over choosing one or the other; use both to describe what the author is doing.

### Tell a Story

These are the passages that sound least like arguments; the author is often simply relating a series of events with a neutral tone. The passage may, for example, describe the development of an artistic style, or the process involved in a scientific discovery, or the progression of a political movement. However, these passages are still made up of "moving parts," each of which performs a particular function. Pay close attention to words that indicate a transition between one event or issue and another. When you are answering the questions, look out for wrong answers that misrepresent the sequence of events or that attribute an inappropriate tone to the author.

### Correct the Record

These passages are similar to *Tell a Story* passages, but they do express a point of view. They explain how our understanding or interpretation of something has changed. It is particularly important in these passages to identify what the previous point of view was, and to use your annotation to distinguish the old view from the new. During POE, eliminate wrong answers that try to trick you by mixing up the old and new ideas.

### Compare/Contrast

These passages often compare and contrast different theories or points of view. What distinguishes them from passages that defend, advocate, or criticize, is that the authors themselves do not take sides. In your annotation and analysis, pay close attention to the transitions between one side and the other, and to the differences or similarities described. When answering the questions, use your prep work to help you eliminate answers that describe the wrong position or side, or that mistake a similarity for a difference or vice versa.

### Defend/Advocate

In these passages, the author will express a definitive point of view, either defending an idea or policy against its detractors, or making a recommendation about a particular point of view or course of action. As you work the passage, pay close attention to words that indicate the strength of the author's argument and make sure to carefully distinguish the author's position from any opposing positions that might be described. As you answer the questions, use this work to eliminate wrong answers that inaccurately describe the author's tone (often by making it stronger or more extreme) or that confuse the author's point of view with an opposing position.

### Criticize

*Criticize* passages do just that; they say bad things about an idea, policy, or action. What distinguishes them from *Defend/Advocate* passages is that the author does not suggest or recommend an alternative. As you read and annotate the passage, pay close attention to exactly what is being criticized, and how strong the argument is (for example, is the author denouncing something, or rather just pointing out certain drawbacks). As you answer the questions, use your understanding of this logic to eliminate choices that describe supposed author recommendations that the author did not in fact make, answers that mix up what is and is not criticized, and choices that are inappropriate to the strength of the argument in the passage.

## Refining Your Technique: Assess and Act

### Question Types

We have already touched on the different question types; now let's look at the four basic categories and their subtypes in more detail. We will also look ahead a bit to POE for each.

The question type tells you a lot. Think of it as setting out a task for you to accomplish. Identifying the type of question you are dealing with allows you to define what the correct answer needs to do, and what you need to do with the passage in order to find it. However, if you can't define the question type, don't panic. Paraphrase the question and define for yourself what that question is asking you to do.

### Big Picture

- Main Point

These questions are often worded as follows:

> *Which of the following most accurately expresses the main point of the passage?*
> *Which title best describes the contents of the passage?*

- Primary Purpose

These questions are usually phrased as follows:

> *The primary purpose of the passage is to*

Both of these are asking you to find an answer that describes the passage as a whole. In most cases, you will not need to go back to the passage before you begin assessing the choices; you have already defined the bottom line, or purpose, of the passage. However, you will need to go back to the passage as you move through the answer choices. Even on a Big Picture question, one word can be enough to invalidate an answer choice.

**Tip!**
On Big Picture questions, use the bottom line to eliminate wrong answers then refer back to the passage to confirm your response.

The most common type of attractive wrong answers for this type are statements that are too narrow; they describe the content or purpose of only one part of the passage.

## Extract

- Fact

These questions are often worded as follows:

*According to the passage*
*The author states that*
*Which of the following is mentioned in the passage?*

- Inference

These questions are phrased as some variation of the following:

*It can most reasonably be inferred from the passage that*
*Which of the following is implied/suggested/assumed?*
*Which of the following conclusions is best supported by the passage?*
*With which of the following would the author be most likely to agree?*
*Which of the following can be most reasonably concluded from the passage?*
*As it is used in the passage, X refers most specifically to*
*Which of the following does the author appear to value most?*

The answers to *Extract: Fact* questions will tend to be close paraphrases of something stated in the passage. *Extract: Inference* questions will sometimes require you to do a bit more work; the correct answer will be directly supported by one or more statements in the passage, but may not be stated outright in the text. However, the approach to any *Extract* question is the same. If the question stem gives you lead words or a line reference, go back to the passage first and read at least five lines above and below that reference. Be sure to reread all of the relevant information. If the author's discussion of that topic begins earlier or continues longer (including situations in which the topic is discussed in more than one section of the passage) you will need to read more than those 10 or 11 lines. Once you have read and paraphrased the passage information, generate an answer in your own words (based on what the passage says), defining what the correct answer needs to do. If the question stem has no reference to the passage, go back to the passage as you evaluate each answer choice. Regardless of the exact form of the question, here is where previewing the questions and annotation really pays off; if you have already circled the relevant words in the passage, your task becomes much easier.

Common types of wrong answers are those that are too extreme to be supported by the passage, choices that focus on the wrong issue (that is, they are not what the question is asking about), and choices that quote words or phrases from the passage out of context, creating a statement in the answer choice that has a different meaning than the passage text.

## Structure

- Organization

These questions may be phrased as follows:

*Which one of the following most accurately states the organization of the passage?*

- Function

These questions will be phrased as some variation of the following:

*The primary function of the second paragraph is to*
*The main function of the reference to X is to*
*The author mentions X in order to*

For both versions of *Structure* questions, use your annotation actively. Words like *therefore, for example, in contrast,* and so on tell you a lot about the purpose and function of that part of the passage.

*Structure: Organization* questions require you to describe the passage as a whole. They differ from *Big Picture* questions in that the correct choice will describe the logical structure of the passage step by step, rather than summarizing the content of the passage in a single statement. To answer these questions, break down each choice into pieces and check each piece against the passage. Here is where your articulation of the main point of each paragraph in succession will be especially useful, as the correct answer will follow the same progression.

Look out for wrong answers that describe something that the author did not in fact do, or, that mix up the progression of topics or issues.

*Structure: Function* questions have a more narrow focus. They ask you to define why the author wrote a particular paragraph or made a particular claim. Your understanding of how the parts of the passage work together will be key here.

Look out for wrong answers that describe the function of some other part of that passage that the question is not asking about.

### Reasoning

Reasoning questions can be time consuming and often require you to use the whole passage. Do these questions last within a passage.

*Reasoning* questions come in a variety of forms. What they all have in common is that they ask you to apply new information to the passage and go a step further. They may ask you to strengthen or weaken a claim made or described by the author. They may require you to find an answer choice that is most similar or analogous to something in the passage. Or they may ask you what sentence would most reasonably follow from the end of the passage (i.e., what would the author say next). All of these forms of *Reasoning* questions will give you the new information in the answer choices. Another form of *Reasoning* question will give you new information in the question stem, and then ask you to apply it to the passage.

For all *Reasoning* questions, it is still crucial to go back to the passage. Find the relevant part of the passage and paraphrase it. Then, articulate what the correct answer needs to do. While you will rarely be able to come up with the actual answer in your own words, you can still define what direction it needs to take, or what issue it needs to involve.

While all *Reasoning* questions involve working with new information, this does not mean that the correct answer will be out of the scope of the passage. Any credited response (unless it is an *Except* question) will be directly relevant to an issue raised in the passage, even if it is bringing in new facts or scenarios. Answering Strengthen and Weaken questions in Reading Comprehension, unlike in Arguments, does not require you to look for assumptions. Just define the author's argument in the passage, and find the answer choice that most supports or undermines it.

When evaluating the answer choices, be on the lookout for wrong answers that are in fact out of scope; that is, they are not relevant to the argument made by the author. This would include answers that are relevant to the wrong part of the passage. Also be careful with direction. An answer to a Strengthen or Analogy question must be consistent with the passage, while the answer to a Weaken question must be inconsistent. Strong language is not a problem for Strengthen and Weaken questions; instead, beware of answers that do not go far enough to do anything to the passage.

## Ordering the Questions

Many test takers find it useful to do the questions in a particular order (within the set of questions attached to a passage). Some find it easier to first do the *Extract* or *Structure* questions that give you some concrete reference to the passage. By going back to the passage to answer these questions, they learn more about the author's argument and have more of a foundation for answering the rest of the set. Other test takers prefer doing the *Big Picture* questions first, since they have just read the passage and defined the bottom line. Almost everyone does better by leaving the hardest questions within the set for last; these are often the *Reasoning* questions, or any question that is long, convoluted, and hard to translate. Experiment with these different ordering strategies, find the one that works best for you, and use it consistently from that point on.

## Refining Your Technique: Answer Using Process of Elimination

As you saw when working on the previous passage, going back to the passage and answering in your own words in the Act step helps you to be both more accurate and more efficient. However, using POE is fundamental on any Reading Comprehension question. The test writers are highly skilled at writing wrong answers that sound just like what you are looking for, but in fact have something wrong with them. If you are not approaching the choices critically and with a reasonable level of suspicion, looking for what is wrong with each choice, you will fall for a lot of trap answers. We have already discussed some aspects of POE for each of the question types above. Now, let's summarize the most important POE techniques.

### Wrong Part of the Passage

As we mentioned earlier in the chapter, many of the wrong answer choices do contain content consistent with the passage. The problem is that this information is from a different part of the passage. For instance, if a passage is describing the properties of three different kinds of acids, and a question asks about the properties of the second acid, many of the wrong choices will be properties of the first and third acids. As long as you focus on the information about the second acid only, you'll be able to eliminate any choices that talk about the first and third acids.

### Extreme Language

As we mentioned in the Arguments section, answer choices that make extreme claims or that use absolute wording often go beyond what can be supported by the passage. Because LSAT authors can have some strong opinions from time to time, however, you shouldn't simply eliminate choices with extreme language without checking that language against what was said in the passage. Think of extreme language as a red flag. When you see it, you should automatically look back to the passage to see whether the passage supports such a strong statement. If it doesn't, and the question hasn't asked you to strengthen or weaken the passage, then you can eliminate the answer choice.

### Too Narrow or Too Broad

Main idea and primary purpose questions often have wrong answers that are either too narrow or too broad. Remember that the main idea or primary purpose should encompass the entire passage but not more or less than that. You'll see many wrong answers that either mention something that was contained in only a part of the passage or was accomplished in only a single paragraph, or others that would include not only the main topic of the passage, but also much more beyond that (for instance, the passage discusses dolphins, but the answer choice talks about all marine mammals).

### Partially Wrong

This is a popular type of wrong answer on LSAT Reading Comprehension. Your goal is to seek out and eliminate answer choices that contain anything at all that might make them wrong. No matter how good a choice may start out, if you see anything amiss, you have to get rid of the answer. Very often, a single word may be the cause of the problem (for example, use of the word *not* to create a contradiction). In addition, it's possible that the problem with the answer choice may show up late in the choice—the test writers are hoping to lull test takers into a false sense of security. For this reason, it is imperative that you read each answer choice thoroughly and carefully all the way to its end.

### Not Supported by the Passage

As we've said many times, you must be able to prove your answer with information from the passage. Any answer choice that can't be proven in this way can't be right, even if you know it to be true from outside knowledge of a subject. Don't invent a connection between an answer choice and the passage if you can't find one already present.

## READING COMPREHENSION: DUAL PASSAGES

Beginning with the June 2007 exam, LSAC has replaced one Reading Comprehension passage with a comparative reading set comprised of two shorter passages, each with a different treatment of a similar subject. These passages require the same skills as a regular Reading Comprehension passage; in fact, analyzing these passages is very similar to analyzing a single passage with multiple viewpoints. The difference is that the questions will often ask you to compare and contrast the structure, tone, and content of the two passages. Sometimes the questions will ask you to find differences or similarities between the two passages. You may also be asked how the author of one passage would respond to a part of the other author's passage. As you read, keep an eye out for these similarities and differences so you'll be ready to answer the questions.

Let's work a comparative reading set together.

# Reading Comprehension Passage: *John Cage*

**Passage A**

John Cage's composition career began with modest innovations; for example, his imitation of a percussion orchestra by wedging various objects into his piano strings brought some new sonorities to the world. While traditional melody and harmony were never strengths for Cage, he nevertheless was willing to specify how these new sounds should be displayed.

However, around 1950, Cage ceased to be a true composer. Having resolved to remove his personality from the creative process, Cage began creating pieces that gave performers immense control over what elements to use, how to use them, or whether to use them at all. This was neither new nor innovative, since jazz composers were already structuring performer choices into musically interesting works—but Cage's greater surrender of artistic authority paradoxically gave performers many fewer ways to make pleasingly listenable music. As the anything-goes spirit of the 1960s took hold, Cage retreated further from musical responsibility. Critic Norman Lebrecht describes the *Variations* series, the directions for which consisted mostly of abstract drawings hanging above a stage, as one key point when Cage's ideas dissolved into gimmickry. The ongoing unpopularity of these "aleatoric" pieces, combined with the fact that later on he returned (in part) to composing more conventional works, demonstrates that Cage's preferred set of techniques represented a dead end for music composition. If composers had to abdicate so many opportunities to shape musical experience, where could their art go from there?

**Passage B**

In the 1950s, the composer John Cage pioneered the creation of "aleatoric music"; that is, compositional techniques that use chance procedures or that allow performers to improvise during sections of the piece (sometimes denoted in the score by brackets enclosing a blank space). The resulting opening up of possibilities for music helped many composers to think differently about the relationship between freedom and constraint in the arts. For example, the Polish composer Witold Lutosławski refused to synchronize the performers of his String Quartet (1964) as part of his commentary on the regimentation of life under Communism. In this piece, decisions by the performers about how the four independent written parts will come together yield slightly different textures for each new performance, but these are always musical and coherent—suggesting society could be similarly organized without a "master synchronizer" like the state. Lutosławski was inspired to compose such "limited aleatoric music" after attending a Cage performance in 1960.

Karlheinz Stockhausen, the German composer who is seen by many as the progenitor of electronic music, also drew inspiration from Cage's techniques but took aleatoric music in a different direction. Stockhausen is most known for his "open form" compositions (such as Klavierstück XI) which are performed using a mix of recorded and live music, played not according to a written score but rather guided by a set of general instructions provided by the composer. Stockhausen may well have been motivated by the destruction he observed during World War II, when all order and regularity in society appeared to disappear. While Stockhausen, Lutosławski, and other composers have typically not pushed Cage's procedures to the extreme levels Cage favored, it is clear that such procedures have found a lasting place in music.

1. The word "aleatoric" has which of the following meanings in both passage A (line 25) and passage B (line 2)?

   (A) Gimmicky
   (B) Influential
   (C) Electronic
   (D) Unconstrained
   (E) Fruitless

2. Which of the following CANNOT be supported on the basis of passage A?

   (A) The author of passage A finds some jazz pieces more interesting than some Cage pieces.
   (B) Percussion orchestras existed before the 1960s.
   (C) *Variations* was an aleatoric work.
   (D) The author of passage A thinks Cage's later, more conventional works were generally not harmonically strong.
   (E) The author of passage A believes removing one's personality from the creative process always leads to a dead end in music composition.

3. The authors of both passages agree that

   (A) some composers later imitated Cage's techniques
   (B) Cage used chance procedures outside human control to compose musical works
   (C) the use of indeterminacy reduces the musical quality of performances
   (D) Cage pushed his techniques further than did some other composers using those techniques
   (E) exploring the tension between freedom and constraint inspired Cage's choice of techniques

4. Which of the following best captures the relationship between passages A and B?

   (A) Both passages cite specific musical works as examples, but only passage A offers a positive view of Cage's musical compositions.
   (B) Both passages cite specific musical works as examples, but only passage B offers a positive view of Cage's musical compositions.
   (C) Multiple musical examples are mentioned in each passage, but only passage B identifies lasting value in Cage's work.
   (D) Multiple examples of Cage's techniques are mentioned, but only passage A is essentially neutral in tone.
   (E) Only one passage cites a specific musical example, but both passages examine the role of theatrical elements in Cage's career.

5. Which of the following is most likely to represent how the author of passage A would evaluate Lutosławski's *String Quartet*?

   (A) The work does not succeed because of the way Lutosławski removed his personality from the creative process.
   (B) The work succeeds because Lutosławski made use of chance procedures rather than indeterminacy.
   (C) The work succeeds because it reflects Lutosławski's own situation rather than using external gimmicks, such as the results of casting the *I Ching*.
   (D) The work does not succeed because of its similarity to Cage's *Variations*.
   (E) The work may succeed because, much like the jazz of the 1950s, it does not go to extremes in its use of performer choice.

6. Compared to the author of passage A, the author of passage B demonstrates less interest in

   (A) improvisation
   (B) the popularity of a musical work
   (C) the politics of a musical work
   (D) the coherence of a musical work
   (E) whether a technique has a place in music composition

7. Compared to the author of passage B, the author of passage A more clearly indicates that

   (A) control should be exerted over the listener's experience
   (B) control should be exerted over the composer's creative process
   (C) control should be exerted over critical reception of a musical work
   (D) control should be exerted over whether artistic elements are hanging above the stage
   (E) control should be exerted over the specific musical techniques used by performers

8. Which of the following, if it occurred, would most weaken the main point of passage A?

   (A) Discovery of archives from the 1700s indicating that Mozart experimented with indeterminacy
   (B) Discovery of archives from the early 1900s indicating that Debussy had invented Cage's *I Ching*–based chance procedures before Cage did
   (C) Discovery of archives from the early 1970s indicating a vogue for "aleatoric" composition among students at top conservatories
   (D) Discovery of, in the current day, a website where Cage enthusiasts trade homemade chance-based music in digital format
   (E) Discovery, following time travel to the year 2275, that almost all the most beloved symphonies during that century contain elements of indeterminacy

**Step 1: Prepare** Here we'll break down the two passages to figure out what's most important.

Passage A

Paragraph 1: Introduces the idea of John Cage as an innovator, but at first he had only modest innovation.

Paragraph 2: Cage ceased to become a true composer as he gave over control to performers; later he switched back to more conventional composition.

Main idea: Cage's preferred set of techniques, giving almost complete freedom to performers, resulted in a dead end for music composition.

Passage B

Paragraph 1: Describes how Cage's compositional techniques in creating "aleatoric music" influenced other composers, including Lutosławski.

Paragraph 2: Describes another composer, Stockhausen, who was also influenced by Cage's techniques, and states that Cage's techniques have had a significant influence.

Bottom line: Cage's aleatoric techniques have had a significant influence on other composers.

**Step 2: Assess** For each question, we'll not only determine what the question is asking and classify it as Big Picture, Extract, Structure, or Reasoning, but also be sure we know which passage, if not both, the question is referring to.

**Steps 3 and 4: Act and Answer** We'll go through each of these steps for every question individually. Let's get to it.

---

1. The word "aleatoric" has which of the following meanings in both passage A (line 25) and passage B (line 2)?

   (A) Gimmicky
   (B) Influential
   (C) Electronic
   (D) Unconstrained
   (E) Fruitless

### Here's How to Crack It

This is an Extract: Inference question, asking what a word means as it is used in each passage. We want to be careful to find an answer that fits with both passages, not just with one or the other. In passage A, the author uses the word "aleatoric" to refer to the *Variations* series, where the directions are "mostly abstract drawing hanging above a stage." This comes in the context of a description of how Cage's compositions "gave performers immense control" over how the piece was to be performed. The author of passage B uses the term in a similar way, to refer to compositions that allow the performers a great deal of leeway in deciding how a piece is to be presented. Although the two authors have different opinions about Cage's work, they both use the word "aleatoric" to refer to the same type of composition. Choice (A) is incorrect, as it fits with the negative tone of passage A, but not with the more positive tone of passage B. Furthermore, while according to passage A Cage's aleatoric works were gimmicky, that is not what the word itself means. Choice (B) is incorrect in part for the opposite reason. Passage B describes Cage's work as influential, but passage A describes it as a "dead end." And just like in choice (A), this answer fits with a judgment made (in this case in passage B) *about* aleatoric music; it isn't the meaning of the word itself. As for choice (C), there is no discussion of electronic music in passage A. In the context of passage B, this choice has the same problem as choice (B); Stockhausen's music was electronic, but this is not what the word "aleatoric" means. Choice (D) is promising; in both passages, the word refers to compositions whose performance is not highly constrained by the composer. Finally, choice (E) fits with the negative tone of passage A, but not with the positive tone of passage B. And, yet again, it is a judgment, not the meaning of the word. Therefore, choice (D) is the correct answer.

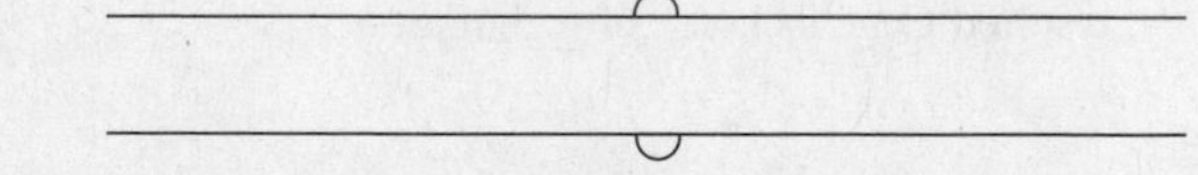

2. Which of the following CANNOT be supported on the basis of passage A?

(A) The author of passage A finds some jazz pieces more interesting than some Cage pieces.
(B) Percussion orchestras existed before the 1960s.
(C) *Variations* was an aleatoric work.
(D) The author of passage A thinks Cage's later, more conventional works were generally not harmonically strong.
(E) The author of passage A believes removing one's personality from the creative process always leads to a dead end in music composition.

**Remember!**
Always determine which passage the question is referring to before you answer the question.

### Here's How to Crack It

This is an Extract: Inference question, asking what cannot be inferred from the first passage. The best way to answer this question is to eliminate answer choices that are supported by the first passage. Choice (A) can be inferred because the author compares jazz pieces favorably to Cage's works, using the phrase "musically interesting." Choice (B) can also be inferred; if Cage was imitating percussion orchestras before 1950, they must have existed before the 1960s. After discussing *Variations*, the author refers to "these aleatoric pieces," so choice (C) can be inferred. Choice (D) can be inferred: The author says "traditional melody and harmony were never strengths for Cage." This leaves only choice (E). The author may believe this statement to be true of Cage, but never says that removing his or her personality was the problem; rather, the problem was the extreme level to which he or she pushed his procedures. There is also nothing that enables us to generalize about other composers. Choice (E) is the credited response.

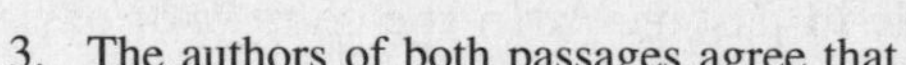

3. The authors of both passages agree that
   (A) some composers later imitated Cage's techniques
   (B) Cage used chance procedures outside human control to compose musical works
   (C) the use of indeterminacy reduces the musical quality of performances
   (D) Cage pushed his techniques further than did some other composers using those techniques
   (E) exploring the tension between freedom and constraint inspired Cage's choice of techniques

### Here's How to Crack It

This is an Extract: Inference question, asking what the authors of both passages would agree on. The author of passage A doesn't discuss later composers who imitated Cage. Jazz artists are mentioned, but the author says they were using performer choice before Cage began using it, so choice (A) can be eliminated. Passage A only discusses indeterminacy, although it does not use that term. Chance procedures are mentioned in passage B but are not discussed in passage A, so choice (B) can be eliminated. The author of passage B gives an example of how indeterminacy could enhance a work, so choice (C) can be eliminated. Both authors do describe Cage as having taken his procedures further than someone else (i.e., jazz composers, Lutosławski, Stockhausen), so choice (D) looks pretty good. Passage A cites a different source of inspiration for Cage (personality removal); passage B describes freedom/constraint as an inspiration for other composers, not for Cage himself. Therefore, choice (E) is incorrect. Choice (D), then, is the credited response.

4. Which of the following best captures the relationship between passages A and B?

(A) Both passages cite specific musical works as examples, but only passage A offers a positive view of Cage's musical compositions.
(B) Both passages cite specific musical works as examples, but only passage B offers a positive view of Cage's musical compositions.
(C) Multiple musical examples are mentioned in each passage, but only passage B identifies lasting value in Cage's work.
(D) Multiple examples of Cage's techniques are mentioned, but only passage A is essentially neutral in tone.
(E) Only one passage cites a specific musical example, but both passages examine the role of theatrical elements in Cage's career.

## Here's How to Crack It

This question is a Big Picture question. A question that asks you about the relationship between two passages is asking about similarities and differences. A lot of these answer choices seem to be focusing on tone. We can get rid of choices (A) and (D) because they discuss the author of the first passage as being positive or neutral in tone, when clearly he or she judges Cage's compositions in an essentially negative tone. Choice (E) does not match the content of the passage because theatricality is mentioned only briefly in passage A, and both passages mention specific musical examples. This leaves choices (B) and (C), which seem similar at first. Choice (B) says that the author of passage B has a positive view of Cage's musical compositions. However, passage B does not comment on Cage's compositions, but rather his techniques. Choice (C), then, matches the best; both passages cite musical examples (i.e., the specific pieces, the techniques, jazz), and only passage B identifies the lasting value of Cage's work.

5. Which of the following is most likely to represent how the author of passage A would evaluate Lutosławski's *String Quartet*?

(A) The work does not succeed because of the way Lutosławski removed his personality from the creative process.
(B) The work succeeds because Lutosławski made use of chance procedures rather than indeterminacy.
(C) The work succeeds because it reflects Lutosławski's own situation rather than using external gimmicks, such as the results of casting the *I Ching*.
(D) The work does not succeed because of its similarity to Cage's *Variations*.
(E) The work may succeed because, much like the jazz of the 1950s, it does not go to extremes in its use of performer choice.

### Here's How to Crack It

This type of question is unique to comparative reading sets. It asks us how the author of one passage would respond to a specific aspect of another passage. Go back to the passage and focus on Lutosławski. His works were coherent and successful, with a written score and yet elements of indeterminacy. We have no sense that Lutoslawski removed his personality from the creative process, so choice (A) can be eliminated. He used indeterminacy, not chance procedures, so choice (B) can be eliminated. We don't know whether or not the author of passage A believes composing from one's own situation is a criterion for success, so eliminate choice (C). *String Quartet* is not entirely similar to *Variations*, and the work does succeed according to passage B, so eliminate choice (D). Choice (E) is the credited response. The author believes that the use of performer choice is okay if it doesn't go to extremes, much like the jazz of the 1950s.

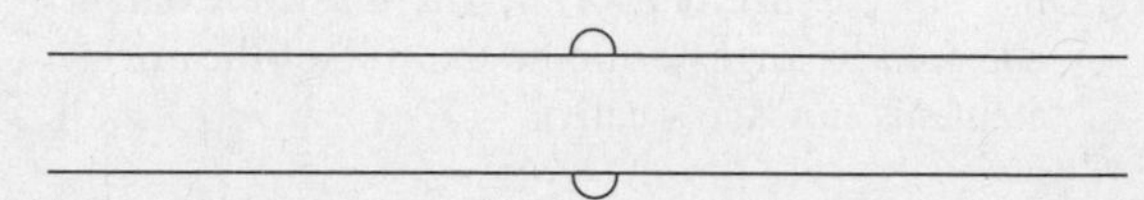

6. Compared to the author of passage A, the author of passage B demonstrates less interest in

(A) improvisation
(B) the popularity of a musical work
(C) the politics of a musical work
(D) the coherence of a musical work
(E) whether a technique has a place in music composition

### Here's How to Crack It

This is an Extract: Inference question that basically asks us to find something mentioned in passage A that's barely mentioned in passage B, if it at all. Improvisation is explicitly mentioned in the first paragraph of passage B. It is also implied by the discussion in passage A, but the author of passage B shows equal or greater interest; choice (A) can be eliminated. The author of passage A mentions that Cage's "aleatoric" works are not popular, but passage B does not address popularity at all, so choice (B) seems pretty good. Political relevance is a reason for the use of indeterminacy by Lutosławski; passage A doesn't mention it all, so eliminate choice (C). Musical coherence is a reason for the success of Lutosławski's piece. Passage A doesn't mention coherence; instead it focuses on other qualities ("musically interesting," "pleasingly listenable"), so choice (D) is not correct. As for choice (E), both passages are concerned with this issue; it's the main thing they disagree about. The level of interest is roughly equal, not significantly less for passage B. Choice (B), therefore, is the credited response.

7. Compared to the author of passage B, the author of passage A more clearly indicates that

(A) control should be exerted over the listener's experience
(B) control should be exerted over the composer's creative process
(C) control should be exerted over critical reception of a musical work
(D) control should be exerted over whether artistic elements are hanging above the stage
(E) control should be exerted over the specific musical techniques used by performers

## Here's How to Crack It

The question asks us for something that the author of passage A feels more strongly about than the author of passage B. It's another way of asking a very similar question to the previous question, even though the stems look different. Off the bat, choice (A) looks like a good choice, because the author of passage A feels Cage "surrendered" too many choices to performers and did not structure his works enough to provide a good listening experience. As for choice (B), neither author suggests anything about how the creative process should work. Also, neither author says that critics should have particular opinions, which eliminates choice (C). While the author of passage A does mention drawings hanging above the stage, the text doesn't support the idea that control over such things should be exerted. This eliminates choice (D). And, finally, the passages are concerned with composer techniques, not performer techniques, so choice (E) is out. Choice (A) is the credited response.

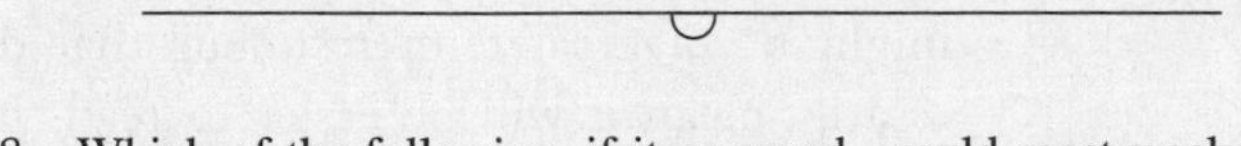

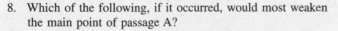

8. Which of the following, if it occurred, would most weaken the main point of passage A?

(A) Discovery of archives from the 1700s indicating that Mozart experimented with indeterminacy
(B) Discovery of archives from the early 1900s indicating that Debussy had invented Cage's *I Ching*–based chance procedures before Cage did
(C) Discovery of archives from the early 1970s indicating a vogue for "aleatoric" composition among students at top conservatories
(D) Discovery of, in the current day, a website where Cage enthusiasts trade homemade chance-based music in digital format
(E) Discovery, following time travel to the year 2275, that almost all the most beloved symphonies during that century contain elements of indeterminacy

### Here's How to Crack It

This is a Reasoning question, the first in this passage set. Note that the main idea of passage A is that Cage's techniques represented a dead end for music composition. The answer choice that most weakens that point would be the one that most clearly indicates a lasting presence in music composition for Cage's techniques. Choices (A), (B), and (C) do not provide any evidence of an effect on music composition. Choice (D) talks about Cage enthusiasts in the modern day, but doesn't discuss the extent of this trend. Choice (E) is a stronger answer. It does the best job of weakening the main point of passage A. It clearly shows that Cage's ideas have lasted for 300 years, that popular symphonies make use of his techniques, and that apparently those techniques have been in use for at least 75 years ("...during that century..."). It may be that the use of these techniques is not as extreme as it was with Cage, but extremity of application is not necessary to counteract the black-and-white conclusion of passage A.

## Reading Comprehension Technique: Passage Selection

There are many things to consider when you choose the passages to attempt on a section, but before you dive into a passage, you should always try to get a sense of its difficulty. If a passage appears hard, there may be an easier one later in the section.

What are the ingredients that will help you to determine a passage's difficulty? There are several, and what some people tend to focus on the most—subject matter—isn't as important as you might think. Given that you're planning to apply to law school, a passage on some law-related theme might be of greater interest, but that doesn't necessarily mean it will be easier to read. It's possible that it might be written in a very abstract manner, making it difficult to process. Likewise, a science passage might not be familiar territory, but the language and ideas may be very straightforward and easy to understand.

Some students also think that the number of questions a passage has should determine when they attempt it. But if a really difficult passage has a large number of questions, that doesn't mean it will be any easier to get those questions right. In fact, you could end up sacrificing more time on that passage, causing you not to attempt an easier one with fewer questions, and still end up missing half of them. If two passages appear to be of equal difficulty, however, feel free to go for the one with more questions.

### Here's What to Look for When You're Evaluating the Difficulty Level of a Passage

- Level of language and ideas: Passages that have clear, straightforward language and that have concrete, descriptive content will be easier to work than those that have abstract language and ideas.
- Sentence structure: Long, convoluted sentences don't bode well. Nor do long paragraphs, which probably contain multiple themes which will take some effort to separate from each other. Short, declarative sentences and shorter paragraphs will probably be easier to comprehend.
- Questions and answer choices: Scan the questions. Do you notice a lot of Reasoning questions? How long are the question stems and answer choices? Passages with long questions and lots of Reasoning questions will probably be more difficult to attack.

As you can see, there is not one specific characteristic that always makes a passage easier or harder. And, unlike in Games, the nature of the answer choices *can* significantly affect overall difficulty. As you work through the passages in this book and in the real LSATs you've ordered, note your impression of the passage's difficulty on the top of the page before you begin it. Afterward, check that impression against the reality of the passage—was your impression correct? If not, was there something you could have seen by reading the first few sentences and scanning the questions that would have led you to evaluate it more accurately? In this way, you will improve your skill in identifying which passages you should attempt and which you should avoid.

## APPLY WHAT YOU'VE LEARNED

Now it's time to put everything you've learned in this chapter to work on the following three Reading Comprehension passages. The goal of this drill is to see how well you've mastered the four steps and how accurately you can work, not to see how fast you can get through these passages. So, work carefully and thoroughly on these until you're sure you have them right.

If you want, you can measure the time it takes you to do each passage. By measure, we mean set your timer to count up, and then turn it away so that you can't see the clock as you work on the passage. Later you can time full sections, but this drill has only three passages, so you should only be timing up. Put the timer in a drawer or in another room if necessary. When you're done, stop the clock and note how long it took you to complete the passage and then see how accurate you were. This will help you figure out approximately how long it takes you to do a passage accurately and, by extension, how many passages you can reasonably expect to get through on a given section. Also take note of the difficulty level of each passage—if you found a passage particularly challenging, it's only natural that it would have taken longer to work on.

# Reading Comprehension Practice Drill

## Passage 1

Concern about the effects of global warming has fostered renewed interest in Earth's recurrent ice ages. Odd as it may seem to examine the possible consequences of rising global temperatures by studying past cold epochs, an understanding of long-term patterns in Earth's climate seems likely to provide key insights into a question of widespread current interest.

Earth's climate is a dynamic system influenced by many interrelated factors. Most scientists agree that three of these predominate: the amount of energy received from solar radiation, the presence of greenhouse gases such as carbon dioxide in the atmosphere, and the location of Earth's major land masses. Other factors such as cloud cover, precipitation, and volcanic activity also have significant influences on global climate because they all play major roles in the planet's water cycle and carbon cycle, both of which are instrumental in regulating Earth's surface temperature.

With all of these factors at play, what seems most surprising is that Earth's global climate follows a relatively regular cyclic pattern. Cold periods called ice ages recur roughly every hundred thousand years, punctuated by brief interglacial periods that are warmer. The current interglacial period has lasted for approximately ten thousand years so far, during which all of recorded human history has taken place. The regularity and suddenness of these changes led Milutin Milankovitch in the early twentieth century to attribute them to predictable variations in Earth's orbit, which determines the amount and distribution of solar radiation the planet receives.

Although most scientists today agree that the Milankovitch hypothesis provides at least a partial explanation of the recurrent pattern, problems with its predictions have led scientists to look elsewhere for a fuller explanation. Orbital patterns that by right should have the strongest effects on Earth's climate have been shown to have influenced it hardly at all in recent millennia. Everything from the rotation of hot spots within Earth's interior to sunspots to the orbit of Earth's solar system around the center of the Milky Way galaxy has been advanced as an explanation of the cycle, but the most widely accepted current theories focus on the level of carbon dioxide in the atmosphere, either as a precipitating factor in causation of ice ages or as a determining factor in an ice age's severity.

If they are correct, these current theories offer an alarming perspective on the effects of industrial use of fossil fuels by humans, which has increased atmospheric levels of carbon dioxide. Although on a geologic scale the redistribution of carbon from Earth's crust to its atmosphere may seem slight, there is evidence that shifts of roughly similar size due to chemical weathering during the uplift of the Himalayan massif may have helped precipitate the last ice age and led to its remarkable severity. If decreases in atmospheric carbon dioxide on this scale can cause such radical climate change, there is reason to believe that similar increases may have effects of corresponding severity, and that like ice ages, their onset may be sudden and their effects global and long lasting.

1. The primary purpose of the passage is to
   - (A) identify the likely causes of past ice ages and predict the occurrence of the next ice age
   - (B) describe efforts to understand the causes of ice ages and indicate what they suggest about the current global warming
   - (C) assess the effectiveness of Milankovitch's hypothesis at explaining past climate change and propose an alternative theory
   - (D) inventory the damage already caused by global warming and project the likely long-term consequences of this damage
   - (E) present the geological evidence indicating that Earth's past included both cold epochs and shorter interglacial periods

2. Which one of the following statements best expresses the main idea of the passage?

(A) Currently accepted theories attributing the incidence of ice ages to fluctuations in atmospheric carbon dioxide levels provide a fuller explanation of these phenomena than the orbital hypothesis advanced by Milankovitch.
(B) Currently accepted theories that describe the role of shifts in carbon distribution between Earth's crust and its atmosphere in past climate change suggest that global warming caused by human use of fossil fuels may have serious and long-lasting effects.
(C) Milankovitch's hypothesis attributing the cyclical recurrence of ice ages to changes in Earth's orbit indicates that it is possible to predict how much longer the current interglacial period will last and demonstrate that steps must be taken now to mitigate the effects of those changes.
(D) Climate scientists have concluded that popular fears about the possible effects of the industrial use of fossil fuels are exaggerated because factors unrelated to human activity have led to similarly radical climate change in the past.
(E) Climate scientists have recently recognized that the factors of land distribution, volcanic activity, and global precipitation, although they have some effects on global climate, are themselves the product of more fundamental changes in Earth's orbit and atmosphere.

3. Which one of the following, if true, would provide the strongest support for the view of Earth's climate described in lines 8–9?

(A) The temperature in localized areas of Earth's surface is correlated most strongly with the amount of solar radiation received in those areas.
(B) Fluctuations in atmospheric carbon dioxide levels on Earth appear to be primarily random and cannot be fully explained by any other factor.
(C) No existing scientific theory can explain how the orbit of Earth's solar system around the center of the Milky Way galaxy might affect Earth's climate.
(D) Snow that does not melt during an unusually cold summer reflects solar radiation back into space, leading to even colder temperatures and even more snow accumulation in future years.
(E) Volcanic activity acts to increase global temperatures by increasing atmospheric carbon dioxide but also acts to lower global temperatures by contributing to greater cloud cover and precipitation.

4. As they are described in the passage, current theories attributing climate change to shifts in atmospheric levels of carbon dioxide most directly explain which one of the following phenomena?

(A) Variations in Earth's orbit
(B) The sudden onset of past ice ages
(C) The uplift of the Himalayan massif
(D) The arrangement of land masses on Earth's surface
(E) The severity of the last ice age

5. Which one of the following, if known, would provide the strongest further evidence against the Milankovitch hypothesis as it is described in the passage?

(A) Variations in Earth's orbit cannot influence the rotation of hot spots within Earth's interior.
(B) The amount of solar radiation received by Earth's oceans is a main determining factor in the level of atmospheric carbon dioxide.
(C) Several past climate changes predicted by the hypothesis are known to have occurred shortly before the orbital variations purported to have caused them.
(D) Although glacial periods recur regularly, the length of interglacial periods in recent millennia has varied from two thousand to twenty thousand years.
(E) One orbital pattern identified by the hypothesis coincides almost perfectly with the onset of ice ages throughout Earth's geological history.

6. It can be inferred from the author's statements that each of the following influences atmospheric levels of carbon dioxide EXCEPT

(A) changes in Earth's land masses
(B) volcanic activity
(C) sunspots
(D) the actions of organisms on Earth's surface
(E) global precipitation levels

7. Which one of the following best describes the organization of the passage?

(A) A hypothesis is presented and defended with supporting examples.
(B) An issue is raised, causal factors are listed, various theoretical approaches are assessed, and future implications are suggested.
(C) A claim about a widely accepted hypothesis to explain a long-standing mystery is presented but ultimately rejected.
(D) Opposing views of a controversial subject are presented, assessed, and then reconciled.
(E) Two current theories of a past phenomenon are evaluated in light of new information relevant to that phenomenon.

## Passage 2

The English poet Richard Crashaw has long been considered an eccentric minor figure among the early seventeenth-century poets whom Dr. Johnson first characterized as "Metaphysical." In examining the poetry of those turbulent times, it is easy to understand why Donne and Herbert receive the greater share of traditional scholarship's attention: Issuing from an era when the cause of Protestantism in England became so radical that it led to the execution of King Charles I, an extended civil war, and the severe Interregnum under Oliver Cromwell, the seemingly uncomplicated devotional character of Herbert's poetry and of Donne's sermons and later sonnets lent the times an almost placid historical gloss. The intellectual inventiveness and lyric beauty of Donne and Herbert serve, as they did at the time of their writing, to convey a settled sense of orthodoxy to those most interested in finding it.

Crashaw's poetry, by contrast, seems tortured—either embarrassingly unaware of itself or actively subversive. Certainly by the standards of his day, Crashaw was a heretic: In an era when even the Anglican church was thought by many to retain too many trappings of the decadent Roman Catholic tradition, Crashaw broke with his society and his ardently Protestant father by converting to Roman Catholicism, a choice that forced him to live much of his life penniless in exile. The conflicts in which Crashaw was enmeshed manifest themselves in his poetry, which abounds with images that strike a contemporary sensibility as violent, strange, and in some cases bordering on pornographic. The energy expended by traditional scholarship to laud these strange moments as mystical, or else excuse them as manifestations of Crashaw's excessive love for rhetorical inventiveness, seems to reflect not merely a failure of interpretation, but an active determination not to interpret the poems in ways that disturb traditional views of the period but nevertheless seem patently obvious.

This failure of traditional readings of the so-called Metaphysical poets is not unique to Crashaw's work. Donne's early poetry reflects a worldliness and flirtatiousness that seem all the more surprising in light of the graceful piety of his later work; Herbert's famous image of being bound by the shackle of his faith cannot be obliterated by rhetoric and rationalization, no matter how dexterous. The tension played out in these poems is internal and intellectual, but at the time of their writing it was also profoundly political: how the human faculty of reason, an emergent interest in Renaissance England, can mediate in the traditional conflict between desire and Christian orthodoxy, and whether it can possibly tame both. It is in Crashaw's work that this tension is tuned to its highest—some might say most hysterical—pitch, and it is in critical interpretations of his work that we most distinctly see the failure of traditional scholarship to comprehend the era in which he wrote.

1. The passage suggests that the author would be most likely to agree with which one of the following statements?
   (A) Traditional readings of much English poetry of the early seventeenth century overemphasize its orthodox devotional character while neglecting the tension and turmoil it reflects.
   (B) Seventeenth-century poetry is more noteworthy for its intellectual inventiveness than it is for its lyric beauty.
   (C) Seventeenth-century poets such as Donne and Herbert are worthy of study because they were able to provide a placid historical gloss of the turbulent times in which they wrote.
   (D) The tortured quality of Crashaw's poetry and the surprise contemporary readers may feel in encountering some of his imagery were intended by Crashaw to express his mystical beliefs.
   (E) The emergence of interest in the human faculty of reason in Renaissance England is responsible for the increasingly radical nature of Protestantism during that time.

2. The author suggests that the poetry of Richard Crashaw
   (A) is superior to the poetry of Donne and Herbert
   (B) reflects an obsession with the strictures of Christian orthodoxy
   (C) was intended to convey heretical beliefs
   (D) has been routinely misinterpreted by traditional scholars
   (E) is characterized by an excessive love for rhetorical inventiveness

3. Based on the passage, traditional scholarship fails to comprehend that the poetry of early seventeenth-century England
   (A) is in part a reflection of the era in which it was written
   (B) represents a radical departure from earlier English poetry
   (C) reflects a serious interest in reason as well as Christian orthodoxy
   (D) is noteworthy only because of the work of Richard Crashaw
   (E) served as a form of political protest

4. The phrase "either embarrassingly unaware of itself or actively subversive" (lines 20–21) is used in the passage to indicate which one of the following about Richard Crashaw's poetry?

(A) its similarity to early works of Donne and Herbert
(B) its mystical and unorthodox qualities
(C) its uneven and maladroit use of imagery
(D) its difference from conventional devotional poetry
(E) its intention to confuse and distort

5. Which one of the following most accurately describes the organization of the passage?

(A) Description of a particular scholarly shortcoming; discussion of possible courses of action that could be taken to remedy that shortcoming; extension of these courses of action to other similar cases; assertion that these courses of action are unlikely to be taken seriously
(B) Description of a particular historical era and scholarly treatment of some literature of that era; discussion of the inadequacy of that scholarly treatment in one particular case; assertion that the inadequacy is not limited to that case; explanation of the reason for and the meaning of this inadequacy
(C) Description of a historical era and scholarly interpretations of it; discussion of the ways in which this interpretation neglect a key development of the era; illustration of the consequences of this neglect in a particular case; explanation of the ways scholarly errors undercut all cases of this kind
(D) Summary of the conventional view of a controversial time; discussion of a new view that contradicts the conventional view; application of the new view to a particularly troublesome instance during the time in question; rejection of the conventional view in favor of the new view
(E) Summary of two conflicting scholarly approaches to a literary problem; evaluation of the merits of the two approaches separately; application of these approaches to a particular historical case; assertion that both approaches must be used to ensure a complete understanding of all such cases

6. It can be inferred from the passage that the author interprets the famous image described in lines 46–47 to indicate

(A) that Herbert's attitude toward Christian orthodoxy is not as simple as it is interpreted to be in traditional readings
(B) that Herbert's poetry contains a veiled critique of the increasing Protestant radicalism of his time
(C) that Herbert's desire to employ the human faculty of reason is constrained by Christian orthodoxy
(D) that the turmoil of Herbert's times led him to employ inventive rhetoric that undermines the stated purpose of his poetry
(E) that the conflict between desire and Christian orthodoxy led him to question the worth of human reason in mediating between them

7. The author's position in lines 32–40 would be most weakened if which one of the following were true?

(A) Traditional views of the period do not consider the possibility that Crashaw could have intentionally employed imagery and language in his poetry that would have been interpreted as shocking or sexually suggestive at the time he wrote.
(B) None of Crashaw's other writings indicate an interest in the faculty of human reason except insofar as that faculty could be exercised in accordance with the dictates of Christian orthodoxy.
(C) Although John Donne's early poetry is sexually suggestive, his later poetry and sonnets indicate that Donne regretted the excesses of his youth and fully accepted the strictures of orthodox Christianity.
(D) The images in Crashaw's poetry that seem subversive to current-day readers employ words that have taken on violent or sexually suggestive connotations that these words did not have at the time when Crashaw wrote.
(E) Although Crashaw was forced into exile by his conversion to Roman Catholicism, both Donne and Herbert were considered models of piety in their time, and they were popular both before and during the Interregnum.

## Passage 3

**Passage A**

Modern political studies in the United States were dominated by group-centered theories of voting behavior. The prevailing model of democratic behavior posited the governmental process as one consisting of the constant struggle for control among various small groups, each with a specific agenda. This view traces its intellectual heritage back to James Madison, father of the Constitution. While a familiar definition of democracy is simply that of majority rule, Madison feared the concentration of political power in any hands, whether those hands belonged to Congress, the judiciary, the president, or the bulk of the populace. Madison believed that the only way to prevent the "tyranny of the majority" would be to allow the minority to have certain ways to check the power of the majority.

One of the finest theoretical articulations of the idea of the American political system as one of competing minority groups came from political theorist Robert Dahl. Dahl begins his formulation of democratic practices from a normative perspective, enumerating eight necessary and sufficient conditions for a true democracy. However, viewing these prerequisites as a set of limits unattained in the real world, Dahl resorts to a descriptive approach to analyze American democracy. Dahl's investigations led to an important and influential re-imagining of the idea of democracy. Democracy, despite its etymology, is not, for Dahl, the rule of the people. Instead, a more accurate definition of American democracy is that of polyarchy—rule by many small groups at various times.

**Passage B**

Anthony Downs sent shockwaves through the academic world, some of which are still reverberating today, with the publication in 1957 of his seminal work, *An Economic Theory of Democracy.* Prior to Downs, political science borrowed heavily from the more established discipline of sociology. The group, whether it be a neighborhood association, a union, or a political party, was seen as primary, the entity from which all political behavior emanated. Voters selected candidates based on how that politician would benefit the interests of the group or groups to which the individual belonged.

Such a theory of group-based voting made fine intuitive sense, but conventional wisdom does not always stand up to scientific scrutiny. Earlier, another economist, Kenneth Arrow, had used mathematical models to suggest that the democratic ideal had a near fatal pathology. Arrow demonstrated that there was no consistent way to aggregate individual preferences into a true reflection of group inclination through voting. Downs used this startling revelation to refashion theories of voting behavior. Under Downs, voting was an economic decision in which a person estimates the expected utility a certain candidate offers multiplied by the probability that the person's vote would decide the election. From this value, the individual subtracts the perceived cost of voting to determine whether it is worthwhile to cast a ballot.

1. Passage A suggests that Dahl believes that American democracy

   (A) is faithful to the Madisonian idea of using checks and balances to prevent the concentration of political power
   (B) prevents the tyranny of the majority by pitting various factions against each other in a struggle for control
   (C) resists analysis based on subscription to an idealized perspective while lending itself to a more explicative view
   (D) fails to achieve the minimum number of conditions required for designation as a democracy and therefore cannot be considered as such
   (E) transforms into a polyarchy as the necessary consequence of its inability to fully attain the eight normative conditions of true democracy

2. Downs's reformulation of voting behavior is most similar to which of the following situations?

   (A) A biologist sets out to group all animals into species designations that require certain criteria. After finding a number of animals do not fit easily into these designations, the biologist settles for cataloging the traits of each animal.
   (B) A mathematician attempts to prove a conjecture proposed by another mathematician. After years of work, the mathematician proves the conjecture and it becomes a widely accepted theorem.
   (C) An archeologist use records and diaries left by a noted anthropologist to hypothesize about the existence of a heretofore unknown civilization. Later investigations do in fact substantiate the archeologist's supposition.
   (D) A psychologist wondering about the functioning of the human brain teams with a neuroscientist to investigate the chemical processes taking place inside the cerebellum. Together, the two develop the new field of cognitive science.
   (E) An astronomer proposes an alternative theory of planetary formation after a physicist discovers a miscalculation in the models that underlie the currently favored view of celestial motion.

3. The passages are similar in that they both
   (A) discard a prior theory in favor of one that better describes reality
   (B) provide an explanation for the thought processes an individual uses when arriving at a voting decision
   (C) describe a book that had a monumental impact on the way political scientists thought of American government
   (D) indicate that the theories discussed owe something of their formulation to antecedent works
   (E) assert that the contributions of the theorists displaced the prevailing viewpoints of their respective academic fields

4. The theoretical works discussed in the two passages could best be described, respectively, as ones of
   (A) elucidation and subversion
   (B) reconstitution and recalibration
   (C) rectification and standardization
   (D) innovation and reevaluation
   (E) progression and accommodation

5. Unlike passage A, passage B contains
   (A) a description of a possible problem with using a particular theoretical model to describe actual conditions
   (B) a possible explanation for the preponderance of a certain viewpoint in one academic discipline
   (C) a description of the specific consequences of the publication of a new theoretical model of democracy
   (D) the definition of a newly coined term used to better explain the functioning of American democratic processes
   (E) information regarding the reasoning used to arrive at a behavioral model

6. Dahl and Downs would likely disagree over which of the following statements?
   (A) The importance of groups in American society has declined in recent years.
   (B) James Madison was successful in enshrining adequate protections into the Constitution against the tyranny of the majority.
   (C) Applying the term *democracy* to the American political system misrepresents the true meaning of the term.
   (D) American political behavior cannot be reduced to simple mathematical models.
   (E) Political behavior can be understood only in light of the larger society that fosters it.

7. Dahl would probably respond to Downs's theory of voting behavior by indicating that Downs had failed to consider
   (A) whether an economic theory is compatible with a normative conception of democracy
   (B) whether Madison had intended for the American political system to be dominated by small groups
   (C) to what extent societal and peer pressures affect the voting calculation made by individuals
   (D) the voting behavior of citizens of countries other than the United States
   (E) whether people make similar economic calculations when deciding the utility of joining a group or political organization

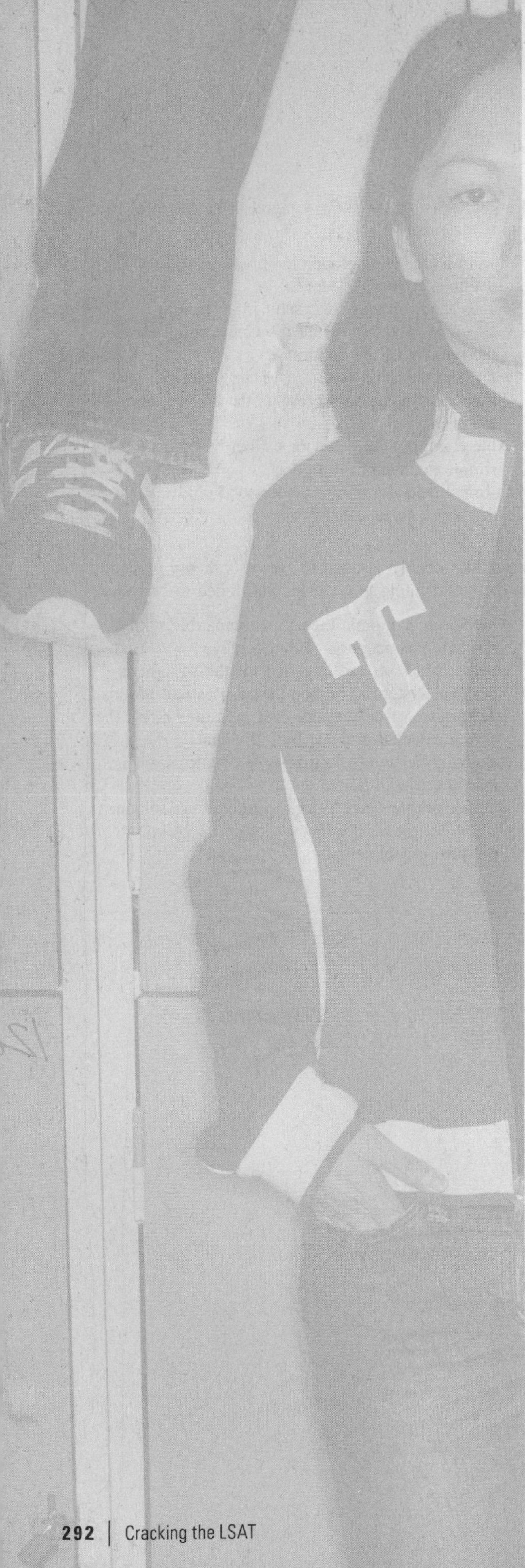

# Summary

- Here's our step-by-step approach to the Reading Comprehension section:

  Step 1: Prepare

  Step 2: Assess

  Step 3: Act

  Step 4: Answer

- Although you may be more familiar with Reading Comprehension than the other sections of this test, LSAT-style Reading Comprehension brings its own unique challenges and requires a particular strategic approach.

- Proper pacing is the key to a strong performance, and it will come only with a little experimentation and a lot of practice.

- Adjusting your everyday reading habits can also benefit your Reading Comprehension performance. Until you take the test, you should put away the trashy magazines and pick up more challenging reading.

# Chapter 5
# The Writing Sample

The Writing Sample is a 35-minute ungraded essay with an assigned topic. You'll receive a booklet containing both the topic and the space in which to write your essay. You will also receive scratch paper. You will have two lined pages on which you must write your response. Copies of these pages will be sent to law schools, along with your LSAT score, as part of your official report, so you'll want to do the best you can with the assignment you receive.

## HOW MUCH WILL MY ESSAY AFFECT MY LSAT SCORE?

Not one bit.

Only four sections contribute to your LSAT score: one Games section, two Arguments sections, and one Reading Comprehension section.

**Writing Sample**
Give this section all the time that an unscored section deserves.

## WHO WILL READ MY ESSAY?

Possibly no one.

How well or poorly you do on the Writing Sample will almost certainly not affect your admissions chances.

### If the Writing Sample Is So Unimportant, Why Discuss It?

Just for your own peace of mind. Once you have the other sections of the test under control, look over the rest of this chapter. If you are short on time, you'd be better off practicing arguments.

There's also the possibility that an admissions officer will accidentally pass his or her eyes over what you have written. If your essay is ungrammatical, riddled with misspellings, off the topic, and wildly disorganized, the admissions officer may think less of you.

Now, we're going to assume that the Writing Sample counts a little bit. You should assume the same thing, but don't lose sleep over it. No one ever got into law school because of the LSAT Writing Sample, and it's doubtful that anyone ever got rejected because of it either. Besides, good writing requires surprisingly few rules, and the rules we'll review will help your writing in general.

## THEN WHY DO LAW SCHOOLS REQUIRE IT?

Law schools feel guilty about not being interested in anything about you other than your grades and LSAT scores. Knowing that you have spent 35 minutes writing an essay for them makes them feel better about having no interest in reading what you have written.

## WILL THE TEST CHANGE?

Always be sure to check the LSAC website at www.lsac.org for any updates to the test.

## WHAT ARE THEY LOOKING FOR?

The general directions to the Writing Sample mention that law schools are interested in three things: essay organization, vocabulary, and writing mechanics. Presumably, writing mechanics covers grammar and style.

### What They're Really Looking For

Researchers at Educational Testing Service (the folks responsible for the SAT and the GRE, among other tests) once did a study of essay-grading behavior. They wanted to find out what their graders really responded to when they marked papers, and which essay characteristics correlated most strongly with good scores.

The researchers discovered that the most important characteristic, other than "overall organization," is "essay length." Also highly correlated with good essay scores are the number of paragraphs, average sentence length, and average word length. The bottom line? *Students who filled in all the lines, indented frequently, and used big words earned higher scores than students who didn't.*

We will discuss these points in more detail later. Because organization is the most important characteristic, let's start with that.

## THE PROMPT

Inside the booklet you'll find the assigned topic and two blank pages on which to write your essay. You'll also get scratch paper on which to organize your essay. The typical prompt looks something like this

Every LSAT prompt instructs you to make a decision and develop an argument for it. Use the skills you've honed from the arguments section of the test to help!

> Karen Stratton is looking into buying a property with the plan to turn it into an animal-supply store. Write an essay in support of one of two proposed properties, the cost of which would be almost exactly the same, keeping in mind Karen's needs:

- Karen needs to establish a market and begin making back her investment rather quickly, because she will put most of her money into buying the property.
- Karen wants her store to be different and memorable, so she can cultivate a loyal clientele.

> Property One is a storefront in the middle of the main drag of the bustling downtown area. The outside of the storefront looks like the fronts of most of the other stores on the block. The central location would make shopping there convenient for people who work in the downtown area, and it is accessible by all forms of public transportation.
>
> Property Two is an old, renovated Victorian house on the outskirts of town. The design of the house is unique. It is six miles from the nearest public transport, making it accessible only by car and cab. It is closer to the farm community and has space for a garden, which Karen can use to grow organic products for her store.

### What Am I Trying to Do?

You're trying to persuade your reader that one of two given alternatives is better. You cannot *prove* that one side is better; you can only make a case that it is. The test writers deliberately come up with balanced alternatives so that you can argue for either one of them.

Just choose a side and justify your choice.

## Picking Sides

The directions emphasize that neither alternative is "correct." It doesn't matter which side you choose. Pick the alternative that gives you more to work with.

Another way to decide is to compile a little list of the pros and cons on your scratch paper. Then simply pick the alternative whose list of pros is longer. Let's see how you'd do this with the sample topic we've given you.

First, list each alternative (Property One, Property Two) as a heading. Underneath each heading draw two columns, one for the pros and one for the cons. Spend the first couple of minutes brainstorming the advantages and disadvantages of each choice. The key to brainstorming is *quantity,* not quality. You can select and discard points later.

Having brainstormed for pros and cons, select the ones you intend to keep and arrange them in order of importance, from *least* to *most* important.

For the purposes of this chapter, let's assume that we intend to give the nod to Property Two.

## Don't Forget the Cons

Some students believe that if you're trying to make a case for something, you should bring up the advantages only. This is wrong.

To persuade readers that Property Two is the better choice, you must show that you have considered every argument that could be made for Property One, and found each one unconvincing.

Your argument, in other words, must show that you have weighed the pros and cons of *both* sides. The more forceful the objections you counter, the more compelling your position becomes.

## Evaluating the Pros and Cons: the Criteria

As you think of pros and cons for each position, keep in mind the given criteria. Here you have two considerations—getting money back and establishing a unique business. You must build your essay around these criteria, so don't ignore them. They give you the structure to follow.

The criteria may not be compatible. If so, weigh the pros and cons in light of this situation. In our example, an innovative-looking store might not attract other people. You may want to rank the two criteria in terms of importance. Perhaps getting money back is more important than establishing a unique business. Perhaps not. Decide which consideration is more important. If you cannot decide, state so explicitly.

## Can I Raise Other Issues?

You *must* weigh the two stated considerations, but nothing prevents you from introducing additional considerations.

You need not raise additional considerations, but if one occurs to you, and you have the time, mention it in passing. If none occurs to you, mention in the conclusion that you have evaluated the two options in view of the two stated considerations only, acknowledging that other considerations may be important.

## Property One Versus Property Two: Brainstorming the Pros and Cons

Remember: Brainstorm first. You will have blank space in your test booklet to jot down your ideas before you dive into writing the essay. Next, select the issues you intend to raise. Then, rank the final issues, beginning with the least important.

To organize your brainstorming, use a rough chart like the following one:

| | Quick money | Unique business | Other factors |
|---|---|---|---|
| Property One | possible; central location good for exposure and quick purchases | looks like every other store front | size? use of space and light? |
| Property Two | possible, but it might take a while. Harder to get to, but could be a "specialty" shop | probably; unique-looking store, customers would have to be loyal because it's farther away | size? use of space and light? |

## Beginning Your Essay: Restating the Problem

Having brainstormed the pros and cons of each choice in light of the considerations, you are ready to start writing your essay.

Your first paragraph should do little more than state your argument. Try not to use a tedious grade school opening such as, "The purpose of the essay I am about to write is to…"

There are several more interesting ways to introduce an argument. Which one you choose will influence how you organize the rest of your essay. Keep this in mind as you sketch your outline. We'll tell you more about this as we go along.

One possibility for an opening is simply to restate concisely the problem you are to address. Check out the following example:

| Karen Stratton needs to buy a property for her animal-supply business. She must turn a profit quickly, but wants to establish a unique business. The two properties both have positive and negative aspects that must be weighed in light of Karen's needs. |
|---|

This type of introduction sets up the conflict rather than immediately taking a side. The second, third, and fourth paragraphs are then devoted to weighing the specific advantages and disadvantages of each candidate. The author's preference isn't stated explicitly until the final paragraph, although a clear case for one should emerge as the essay progresses.

An essay such as this is really just an organized written version of the mental processes you went through in deciding which property to choose. In the first paragraph you say, in effect, "Here are the problems, the choices, and my decision." In the second, third, and fourth paragraphs you say, "Here are the pros and cons I weighed." In the fifth and final paragraph you say, "So you can see why I decided as I did."

Your hope is that the reader, by following your reasoning step by step, will decide the same thing. The great advantage of this kind of organization is that it *does* follow your mental processes. That makes it a natural and relatively easy method.

## Beginning Your Essay: Putting Your Cards on the Table

It's also possible to write an essay in which you begin by announcing your decision. You state your preference in the first paragraph, back it up in the middle paragraphs, and then restate your preference with a concluding flourish in the final paragraph.

Here's an example of such an opening paragraph.

| Property One is a centrally located storefront in a busy downtown area, which would probably bring in a lot of quick business. However, it looks like every other storefront, so it wouldn't stand out. Property Two, by contrast, would afford Karen Stratton an opportunity to create a unique-looking store that could be treated as a specialty shop that people would be willing to travel to. Karen should buy Property Two for her animal-supply store because it suits her needs. |
|---|

By introducing your argument in this way, you leave yourself with a great deal of latitude for handling the succeeding paragraphs. For example, you might use the second paragraph to discuss both properties in light of the first consideration, the third paragraph to discuss both properties in light of the second consideration, and the fourth and final paragraph to summarize your argument and restate your preference.

## The Body of Your Argument

We've discussed the introductory and concluding paragraphs. Depending on your preference and on the essay topic you actually confront, we recommend three variations for the middle paragraphs.

### Variation 1

Paragraph 2: Both sides in light of the first consideration
Paragraph 3: Both sides in light of the second consideration

### Variation 2

Paragraph 2: Everything that can be said about Property One
Paragraph 3: Everything that can be said about Property Two

### Variation 3

Paragraph 2: A sentence or two for Property One, followed by three or four sentences for Property Two
Paragraph 3: A sentence or two for Property One, followed by three or four sentences for Property Two

Again, if necessary, you can divide any one of the three middle paragraphs into two paragraphs.

All three variations do the job. Choose a variation you feel comfortable with and memorize it. The less thinking you have to do on the actual exam, the better.

## The Princeton Review Thesaurus of Pretty Impressive Words

The following list of words is not meant to be complete, nor is it in any particular order. Synonyms or related concepts are grouped where appropriate.

- example, instance, precedent, paradigm, archetype
- illustrate, demonstrate, highlight, acknowledge, exemplify, embody
- support, endorse, advocate, maintain, contend, espouse, champion
- supporter, proponent, advocate, adherent
- dispute, dismiss, outweigh, rebut, refute
- propose, advance, submit, marshal, adduce
- premise, principle, presumption, assumption, proposition
- advantages, merits, benefits
- inherent, intrinsic, pertinent
- indisputable, incontrovertible, inarguable, unassailable, irrefutable, undeniable, unimpeachable
- unconvincing, inconclusive, dubious, specious
- compelling, cogent, persuasive
- empirical, hypothetical, theoretical

Rules to Write By

1. Write as if you were actually making the recommendation.
2. Write naturally, but don't use abbreviations or contractions.
3. Make sure your position is clear.
4. Write as neatly as possible.
5. Indent your paragraphs.
6. Don't use first person. The assignment is formal enough that it isn't appropriate here. The objective isn't to state what "I think," but to argue in favor of one option or the other. Personal experience is not relevant.

## A Note on Diction

Make sure you don't spoil your display of verbal virtuosity by misusing or misspelling these or any other ten-dollar words. Also, get your idioms straight.

A note on a common diction error: If, as in our writing sample, your choice involves only two options, *former* refers to the first and *latter* refers to the second. You cannot use these words to refer to more than two options.

Another common diction error occurs when two or more things are compared. The first option is *better* than the second, but it is not the *best,* which is used when discussing three or more options.

## One Final Reminder

Write legibly! If you can't, at least print.

## A Sample Essay

Karen Stratton is looking for a property to buy for her animal-supply store, and has narrowed her search to two. Property One is centrally located and would allow Karen to make money quickly. Property Two is not centrally located, but would allow Karen to cultivate a special business. In view of those considerations, she should buy Property Two.

Property One would certainly be convenient for shoppers. It is also accessible by all forms of public transportation, making it even easier to get to. Karen could certainly make back some money quickly by the location alone. But her store would not be unique; it would look like every other store in the area. People would not be going there for any reason but its location, which means they might not be loyal customers. Also, being in the downtown area, the store might not be big enough for Karen to feature all of the items that would make her store unique, and the outside would not suggest uniqueness either. Costs such as labor, maintenance, security, and signage would all be higher in a downtown location, and since the main benefit of this location would be to increase walk-in business, Karen would have to stock lower-cost items; this would lead to lower profit margins.

Property Two, on the other hand, is certainly unique-looking. It is true that people would have to travel to get there, but Karen could make it into a specialty shop, by growing her own products in the garden, for example, and would make her store worth the trip. These types of stores inspire loyalty for customers looking for hard-to-find items, and though Karen might not make back her investment right away, she would over time. Her store could also serve the farm community, whose residents might not want to travel downtown. The friendlier surroundings would allow Karen to give her shop an atmosphere not found in most retail establishments, and targeting middle- and higher-income customers would allow her to realize larger profits, even on a small business level. Strategic partnerships with other local service providers, such as groomers and veterinarians, could offer ways of providing needed services and reaching a targeted audience for minimal advertising expense.

Another thing Property Two has in its favor is that it is probably bigger than Property One, or if not, it at least would afford Karen creative ways to use space and natural light that a downtown storefront would not. If Karen can afford to be a little patient money-wise, she could end up with a memorable, unique, lucrative business for herself.

Both properties have strengths and deficiencies as far as meeting Karen's needs. Karen should buy Property Two for her animal-supply store because its strengths outweigh its deficiencies.

# Summary

Don't worry about the Writing Sample. As long as you spend a little time brainstorming and outlining your essay, this inconsequential section should be no problem.

# Chapter 6
# Putting It All Together

You've worked through five pretty arduous chapters of *Cracking the LSAT*. How should you feel? Answer: CONFIDENT! Why? Because you've been given a specific process and approach for each section of the LSAT. You've got a good game plan—and the team with the good game plan usually wins the game. This chapter contains a quick review of your game plan for each section of the exam, as well as some pacing suggestions and tips for the day of the test.

## ARGUMENTS

**Step 1:** Assess the question

**Step 2:** Analyze the argument

**Step 3:** Act

**Step 4:** Answer using Process of Elimination

Pretty simple, right? Well, many people begin to get anxious and they tend to skip Step 3. They want to get right to the answer choices so they can start getting confused and frustrated. However, Step 3 is the most important step in this process. If you come up with your own ideas about what should be the right answer before looking at any of the choices, you'll be misled less often by those appealing but wrong answer choices.

## GAMES

**Step 1:** Diagram and inventory

**Step 2:** Symbolize the clues and double-check

**Step 3:** Look for links and size up the game

**Step 4:** Assess the question

**Step 5:** Act

**Step 6:** Answer using Process of Elimination

As in Arguments, many students tend to skip an essential step in the games process. That step is Step 3 (again). Students usually see how necessary it is to draw a diagram and symbolize the clues, but then they get nervous that they've spent so much time drawing and symbolizing that they go straight to the questions. However, looking at the diagram and the symbols you've drawn for 30 seconds before going to the questions will invariably make the game easier—any deduction you make will actually save you time by making you more efficient in answering the questions.

## READING COMPREHENSION

Step 1: Prepare

Step 2: Assess

Step 3: Act

Step 4: Answer

Well, here we've once again highlighted Step 3 because it's the most important step and it's the one students tend to skip most often. Again, nervousness about time is the culprit. But as you learned in the Reading Comprehension chapter, pinpointing the correct answer choice becomes much easier when you've already got an idea of what you should be looking for. Don't let the answer choices confuse you—approach the test questions by being ready for them as much as possible.

## PACING

The most important principle to keep in mind when you're planning your pacing is balance. Remember that there are two things that determine effective pacing: your speed (the number of questions you attempt) and your accuracy (the chance that, when you attempt a question, you will get it right). Generally, as your speed increases, your accuracy decreases. The challenge is to find the peak pacing strategy for yourself on each section.

The only way to do this effectively is through practice, practice, practice, and analysis, analysis, analysis. Most test takers do not perform optimally if they charge through at maximum speed. Similarly, dawdling and second-guessing yourself will not get you the most points. You need to adopt a strategy that allows you to slow down in the places you need to, but at the same time keeps you pushing through the questions that come more easily to you so you can devote time where it's needed.

The ideal way to strike this balance differs from section to section and is determined by the different natures of the questions. We have some more specific pacing guidelines for you below, but of course knowing what target you have to hit is different from knowing how it feels to hit that target. To that end, here are some general pacing thoughts on each of the sections of the exam.

## Games

Two things about Games are particularly relevant to pacing: First, getting yourself ready to work a game takes a relatively long time; second, Games questions are constructed so that with a solid approach, you can be certain of getting a right answer on any question you attempt.

For this section, you will need to lean heavily toward accuracy. Investing the time needed to make that last decision between two answer choices is unquestionably worth it, even if it seems like a fair amount of work. Take advantage of this section by working for accuracy, and then trusting your work. All you have to do on a Games question is *either* find the one right answer *or* find the four wrong ones, not both. Once you've done this on a question, pick the answer and go.

Try not to change your mind once you've started a Game. Otherwise, you're throwing away valuable time. Working a Game you've already set up, even if the questions are hard, is typically a better use of your time than working a different Game from start to finish. Of course, you want to do everything you can to pick the best Games to do, which makes spending a little time on selection eminently worth it.

## Arguments

On Arguments, the initial investment for a question is relatively small; and on many Arguments questions, there are things you can do to decide between close answer choices—but only up to a point.

The best approach here is to value speed and accuracy equally. On an easy Arguments question (there are usually many of these toward the beginning of the section), you should be able to proceed through POE and spot one that definitely looks best. In that case, pick it and go.

**Pacing**
Trust your gut. You know the difference between chipping away at a difficult question and spinning your wheels trying to comprehend what you are reading.

On a medium Arguments question, you may have two or three answer choices that seem possible. In that case, slow down—look at the conclusion of the argument, review the question if you're uncertain what it's asking you to do, look at the choices carefully, and make close comparisons. Making smart decisions in the down-to-two situation is how you make your money on the Arguments sections.

On difficult Arguments questions (many of these will be near the end of the section), mistrust answers that look extremely attractive. Keep an open mind as you look at the others, and if you're down to two here, follow the same process you use for medium questions. Look for subtle problems. If you can't find them, then go with the choice you thought was right at first and move on. However, if an answer looks too good to be true on a hard question, it probably is.

If you begin an Arguments question and it baffles you right away, move on. You can always come back to it, and you haven't lost much if you spend just a little time and then decide to do something else. Similarly, if you've done everything you can in that down-to-two situation and have nothing else to go on, pick the answer you like better and move on. It takes only one or two questions that eat up a lot of time to hurt you on an Arguments section. Be willing to slow down, but don't ever stop.

## Reading Comprehension

Speed and efficiency are important on Reading Comprehension. Remember that you don't get points for memorizing the passage; you're reading it to find the answers to the questions. Get through the initial preparation of the passage fairly quickly, without getting bogged down in the details; you can always come back for them later. In this stage, avoid reading parts of the passage over and over; keep moving and come back to difficult sections of the passage only if necessary when answering the questions. However, you *do* need to get a basic understanding of the bottom line of the author's argument. Don't read the passage so quickly that you get little or nothing out of it.

Don't just skim the questions or answer choices in the Assess, Act, and Answer steps; read them carefully, word for word. Always go back to the passage when you are answering the questions. Read for context; don't answer the questions based on only a quick glance at isolated words or phrases from the passage. When you are down to two answer choices, compare them to each other and look for relevant differences. You may need to go back to the passage again at this stage to make a final choice. If you are still stuck, take your best shot, remembering how the test writers create attractive wrong answers, and continue on. You can come back one more time before you move on to the next passage; sometimes getting a little distance from the question helps you to see what you didn't understand at first. However, don't spend a large percentage of your valuable time on a single question.

Of course, selection is important here, but not nearly as important as it is on Games. Evaluate each passage and the questions very quickly before diving in. If it looks nasty from the outset, then move to another passage; otherwise, start the passage and stick with it.

This is a general chart. Don't worry about being so exact here.

Here's a chart to help you assess your performance on the practice tests.

| Pacing Yourself | | | |
|---|---|---|---|
| **If you received…** | **Your first goal is…** | **Your intermediate goal is…** | **Your final goal is…** |
| **25–45% correct on Arguments** | Work 12–15 Arguments and try to get 10–12 right in 35 minutes | Work 15–18 Arguments and try to get 12–15 right in 35 minutes | Work 18–21 Arguments and try to get 15–18 right in 35 minutes |
| **45–65% correct on Arguments** | Work 15–18 Arguments and try to get 12–15 right in 35 minutes | Work 18–21 Arguments and try to get 15–18 right in 35 minutes | Work 21–24 Arguments and try to get 18–21 right in 35 minutes |
| **65–85% correct on Arguments** | Work 18–22 Arguments and try to get 15–18 right in 35 minutes | Work 22–24 Arguments and try to get 18–21 right in 35 minutes | Work all the Arguments and try to get 20–23 right in 35 minutes |
| **25–45% correct on Games** | Do two Games correctly in 35 minutes | Get through two full Games and halfway through a third one in 35 minutes | Do three Games correctly in 35 minutes |
| **45–65% correct on Games** | Get through two full Games and half of a third Game in 35 minutes | Get through three complete Games in 35 minutes, missing only one or two questions | Get through three full Games and half of a fourth Game in 35 minutes |
| **65–85% correct on Games** | Do three full Games in 35 minutes | Do three complete Games in 35 minutes and get halfway through the fourth game | Get through the entire section missing only a few questions in 35 minutes |
| **20–35% correct on Reading Comprehension** | Do two reading comprehension passages in 35 minutes, trying to miss only one question per passage | Do two full reading comprehension passages and get halfway through a third passage in 35 minutes | Do three full reading comprehension passages in 35 minutes |
| **35–50% correct on Reading Comprehension** | Do two full Reading Comprehension passages and get halfway through a third passage in 35 minutes | Do three full Reading Comprehension passages in 35 minutes | Do three full Reading Comprehension passages and get halfway through the fourth passage in 35 minutes |
| **50–80% correct on Reading Comprehension** | Do three Reading Comprehension passages in 35 minutes, trying to miss only one question per passage | Do three full Reading Comprehension passages and get halfway through the fourth passage in 35 minutes | Do four full Reading Comprehension passages in 35 minutes |

## EVALUATING YOUR PERFORMANCE

One of the most important things you can do to continue to improve your score is to analyze the work you do in order to better gauge both the areas in which you're making errors and the amount of time you need to spend on a given question or group of questions to ensure a high level of accuracy. Here we'll discuss several ways to accomplish this.

As we recommended for the practice drills that accompany each of the chapters on Arguments, Games, and Reading Comprehension, it's a good idea to measure how long it takes you to do a game or passage or set of arguments accurately. There's no point rushing to get to questions (and wasting brain power) if you're not going to give yourself the opportunity to get those questions right. Remember: Your score is based on how many questions you answer correctly, not on how many questions you actually get to attempt (and of course you're bubbling in answers for those you don't attempt). By measuring how long it takes, on average, to work accurately through a game, passage, or group of, say, eight arguments, you can build realistic expectations of how much you'll be able to do on a given timed section. This is important because it can help you set reachable goals for each area of the LSAT—for example, you can't expect to get to all four games if you generally need to spend 15 minutes on just one of them.

To measure your work time, set your timer to count up, not down, and then don't look at it while you're working. Put it facedown, in a drawer, or even in another room if necessary. When you've finished working, stop the clock and note the time elapsed. Then check your answers to see how accurate you were. If you missed half or more, you're definitely going too quickly. If, however, you got almost all of them correct, then you can start to think about where you might be able to speed up. Did you linger at an answer choice to convince yourself that it was really right, although you knew the other four choices were unequivocally wrong? Did you try to disprove all the choices in a Games question although you already had the answer in your diagram? As you continue to work questions, you'll eventually find that you hit your optimal speed for each section—if you go any slower, you won't get to the number of questions you know you need to answer to reach your goal, but if you work any faster, your careless errors will increase sharply.

Once you have an idea of how many questions you can reasonably expect to get to, you can start to figure out how you're going to get the score you want. Let's say you're aiming for a 160. You'd need approximately 75 correct answers to achieve that score. (You should use the conversion chart from the most recent LSAT you've ordered when making these estimates.) Perhaps Reading Comprehension is one of your strengths, so you can count on 23 out of 27 questions. Or maybe you average about 18 correct on an Arguments section. That leaves 16 that you'll need to pick up in the Games section. Are you stronger in Games? Then your goal might be 20 from Games and only 21 from Reading Comprehension, with an Arguments goal of 17 per section. Is your goal a 150? That's about 56 questions. How you break that down will be up to you, based on your own strengths and weaknesses.

As with all things on the LSAT, however, it's important not to overanalyze. Not all Games sections are the same (or Arguments or Reading Comprehension, for that matter), which means you shouldn't expect to do the same on every one of them you work. Keep this in mind while you're planning your pacing adjustments and also while you're taking your test. If you came up a little short on Games, don't panic; chances are that you'll be able to pick up the slack on Arguments as long as you give yourself the chance. Setting goals is important, and it's important to have a plan for achieving them, but always be willing to improvise. Focus on what you can control, and take the test as it comes.

Okay, you've figured out how many more questions you need to get right to achieve your goal score. How do you go about fixing your errors? You want to keep track of your progress, preferably in a notebook, on each drill or timed section you do. Analysis is the key to better performance. After each drill or timed section, write down the drill or section number, and for each question you did, note the question number, question type, whether you got it right or wrong, and what happened if you did indeed miss it. After a while you may begin to see patterns emerge: Maybe you always miss questions that ask what "must be false" because you forget the "false," or you constantly pick answer choices that go beyond the scope of a passage; or you lose focus when tackling EXCEPT questions. Or maybe there's a particular question type you keep misidentifying, or you're not picking the best questions for you to attempt. Whatever the problem is, you have to be able to diagnose it before you can fix it. Keeping track of your progress and reviewing the notes you make about questions you miss will help you further structure your preparation.

## ADDITIONAL PRACTICE TIPS

Here are a few final, extra things to think about.

- Try to time your LSAT practice to the time of day you'll be taking the real thing. At the very least, start your practice tests at the same time that the real test will be given. For a June LSAT, this means you'll want to concentrate your study time during the afternoon; for all other administrations of the test, you'll want to practice in the morning.
- Although both of the tests in this book and the real LSATs from LSAC have only four sections, the actual exam, as you know, has five. It's a really good idea to take an extra section from one of the real LSATs you've ordered and use it as an experimental section when taking full-length practice tests. It will build your stamina and it will give you a chance to practice with an extra section of each type of question because you never know what question type you could see as an experimental section on test day. Even when doing individual timed sections, try to do a couple of sections back-to-back before checking your answers. Get used to focusing for longer periods of time.

- If you've mastered what's in this book and are aiming for a score in the high 150s or above, consider purchasing our *LSAT Workout*, which focuses on higher-level skills and more difficult questions. For those students who need to get points from tougher material, this book will provide ample opportunity to practice on some challenging questions.
- Don't forget to check out our free online tools at **PrincetonReview.com/cracking**. You just need to have this book handy when you log in for the first time.

## THE DAY OF THE TEST

There is probably just as much bad advice as good advice dispensed about what to do on test day. A lot of the good advice is just common sense, but we're going to give it to you here just in case you're a bit distracted.

**Up-to-date Information:** Check out www.lsac.org for more information about specifics: locations, dates, and restrictions.

### Visit Your Test Center Before Test Day

Why worry on test day about the best way to get to the test center? Visit the test center a few weeks or days before the test so you know exactly where to go on test day. Better yet, go there with a practice LSAT and try to get into the room where you're going to take the LSAT. Work the test in that room, if possible, so you're on familiar ground the day of the test. This will do wonders for your comfort and confidence. You'll know if the room is hot or cold, what the lighting is like, whether you'll be working at an individual desk or a long table, and so on. Use the Boy Scout motto here: Be prepared.

### Eat and Drink What You Normally Eat and Drink

People have many different ideas about what to eat and drink on the morning of the test. The most important thing is not to vary dramatically from what you normally ingest. Don't eat a big, heavy breakfast that will leave you sluggish. Don't skip breakfast completely. Eat a reasonable meal that will prepare you for a grueling three-and-a-half-hour test. And don't experiment with caffeine. If you don't normally have coffee in the morning, don't start on test day. If you do normally have coffee in the morning, don't skip it on test day. The same advice applies if you get your caffeine from soda or any other caffeinated beverage.

### Take a Snack

Maybe your proctor won't let you munch on anything during the break, but maybe he or she will. If so, be prepared by taking a bottle of water and a granola bar or a banana. If you're subtle about it, chances are no one will care one way or the other. Even if you're not allowed to eat in the testing room, you can always go outside and fuel up for the second half of the test.

## Take an Analog Watch

Unlike previous years, the LSAC does not permit the use of digital timers in the testing room. We recommend that you wear an analog watch and reset it to twelve o'clock at the beginning of each section. That will take the guesswork out of determining when the section will be over. And don't forget the five-minute drill: Bubble in your "letter of the day" for any questions you haven't worked on and then change them one at a time as you pick up those last few questions.

## Take Everything You'll Need

Yes, you will need to present proper identification. You'll also need your registration ticket and a recent, passport-style photograph. Refer to the registration booklet and follow the procedures outlined there. You'll also want to have plenty of sharp (not mechanical) pencils and a separate eraser. Don't leave any room for the unexpected.

## Get There Nice and Early and Warm Up Your Brain

You're going to be stressed out enough on test day without worrying that you'll be late for the test. Get there nice and early and warm up your brain by working out a game that you've already done and perhaps by running through a few arguments. And don't bother to check the answers; the purpose is warming up, not diagnosis. That way, you'll already be in gear by the time you open up the first section. You want to hit the ground running so you won't be warming up on questions that count toward your score.

## Some Stress Is Good; Too Much Stress Is Bad

We know you're going to be stressed the day of the exam, and a little stress is not a bad thing—it will keep you on your toes. But if you tend to get *really* stressed by standardized tests, try a yoga or meditation class, or some other type of relaxation therapy, preferably a month before the test. This way, you'll have some techniques to calm you down, taught to you by people who know what they're doing. One Princeton Review student had a dream about test day—she went into the test, and the bubbles were about five feet in diameter. She hadn't even finished bubbling in one bubble before the proctor called time. If you're having dreams like this, relaxation therapy might help.

## Wear Layered Clothing

Who knows how cold or how warm the test center will be on test day? Wear your most comfortable layered clothing, so you can put more layers on if you're cold or take layers off if you're hot.

## Be Confident, and Be Aggressive

Sometimes we'll talk to students after they've taken the LSAT and they'll say, "By the time I got to section 5, I just didn't care anymore. I just filled in whatever." Don't say that, don't think that—section 5 will probably count because the experimental section is usually in the first three sections of the exam. When you open up your test to section 5, keep in mind that it's most likely a real section that will count toward your score. Your goal is to take three deep breaths and to fight your way through that last section, and approach it just as aggressively as you approached the other sections of the exam. It's going to count—don't lose your confidence and your energy here because it's almost over!

Here is another problem students have reported: "I was doing fine until I hit section 3. I didn't know how to do any of the Games, and I couldn't concentrate on the last two sections of the test." Well, guess what? That was probably the experimental section! Don't let a complex or tough section get you down, especially if it's early in the test. Remember that they are using the experimental sections to test new questions—some of them invariably will be a bit strange. And even if it is a section that ultimately counts toward your score, getting stressed out over it will only hurt your performance on that section and potentially on subsequent scored sections as well. Just roll with the punches.

## Always Keep Your Pencil Moving

Actively using your pencil will help you to stay engaged. Cross off all the wrong answer choices; circle and underline key words in Reading Comprehension and Arguments passages; always diagram and symbolize in Games. By constantly keeping your pencil moving, you'll be keeping your brain moving as well.

If you find that you're losing focus, stop working for a second and regroup. Never waste time working on a question if your mind has gone astray or if you find that you can't focus on the task at hand. The few seconds you invest in a short break will pay off in the long run.

And remember that you can always come back to a question that is giving you grief. Just mark it so that you can find it later if you have time to come back to it. Don't spend too much time on any one question. It will only lead to frustration and lost points.

Your Test Day "Top Ten"

Here are the tips mentioned above in a handy numbered list. Find some room on the fridge.

1. Visit your test center before test day.
2. Eat and drink what you normally eat and drink.
3. Take a snack.
4. Wear an analog watch.
5. Take everything you'll need.
6. Get there nice and early and warm up your brain.
7. Some stress is good; too much stress is bad.
8. Wear layered clothing.
9. Be confident, and be aggressive.
10. Always keep your pencil moving.

Good luck on test day!

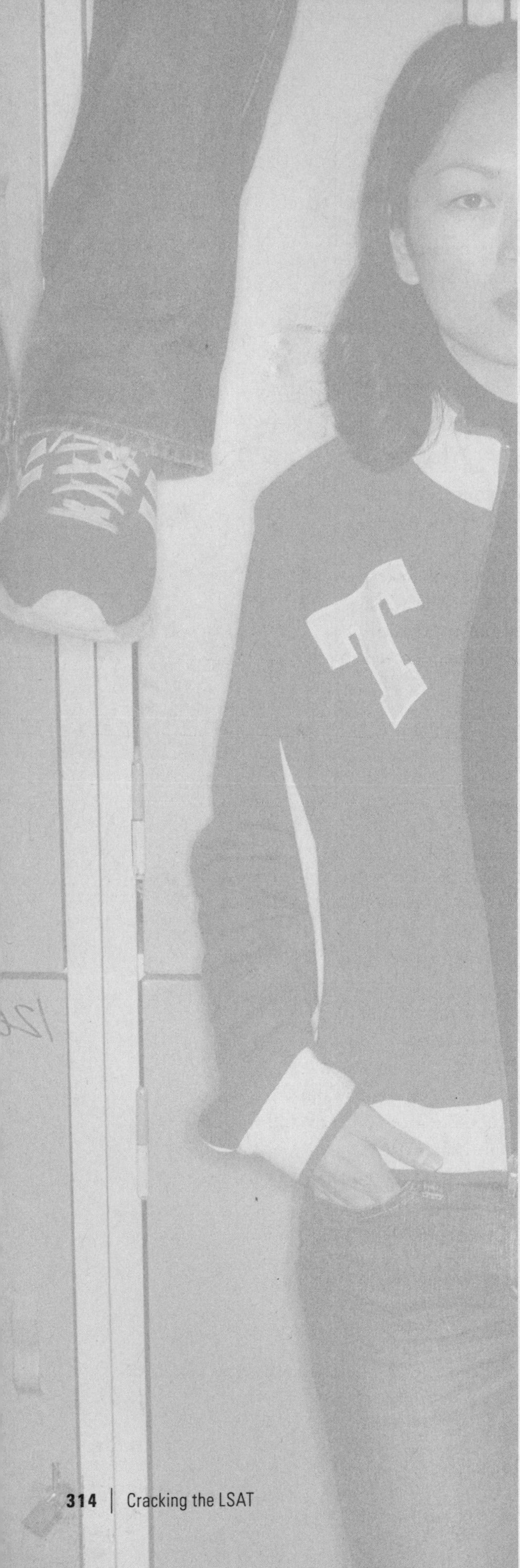

# Summary

- As you practice, your approach will become more intuitive. Until then, be sure to focus on the steps we've outlined so that you have a systematic approach for every section of the test. Most important, do not forget to do a little work before rushing to the answer choices.
- Make sure you are totally prepared for test day. You can't control the questions you will see that day, but you can make sure that you are in the best position to answer those questions.

# Chapter 7
# Law School Admissions

The process of applying to law school, although simple enough in theory, is viewed by many to be about as painful as a root canal. The best way to avoid the pain is to start early. If you're reading this in December, hope to get into a law school for the following year, and haven't done anything about it, you're in big trouble. If you've got an LSAT score that you're happy with, you're in less trouble. However, your applications will get to the law schools after the optimum time and the applications themselves, even with the most cursory glance by an admissions officer, may appear rushed. The best way to think about applying is to start early in the year, take care of one thing at a time, and be totally finished by December.

This chapter is mainly a nuts-and-bolts manual on how to apply to law school and when to do it. A checklist, information about Law School Forums, fee waivers, the Credential Asssembly Service (CAS), and several admissions calendars, which will show you when you need to take which step, are included.

LSAC, LSAT, CAS

The Law School Admission Council (LSAC), headquartered in Newtown, Pennsylvania, is the governing body that oversees the creation, testing, and administration of the LSAT (Law School Admission Test). The LSAC also runs the Credential Assembly Service (CAS), which provides information (in a standard format) on law school applicants to the schools themselves. All American Bar Association, or ABA-approved, law schools are members of LSAC.

## LSAT SCORE DISTRIBUTION

Most test takers are interested in knowing where their LSAT scores fall within the distribution of all scores. This chart should help you determine how well you did in comparison to fellow test takers over the last few years. Please be aware, however, that percentiles are not fixed values that remain constant over time. Unlike an LSAT score, a percentile rank associated with a given test score may vary slightly depending on the year in which it is reported. This chart is just to give you a roughly accurate idea where you rank compared to those competing for the same spot in law school.

| Score | % Below | Score | % Below | Score | % Below | Score | % Below |
|---|---|---|---|---|---|---|---|
| 180 | 99.9 | 165 | 93.2 | 150 | 44.9 | 135 | 5.3 |
| 179 | 99.9 | 164 | 91.4 | 149 | 41.0 | 134 | 4.4 |
| 178 | 99.9 | 163 | 89.7 | 148 | 37.0 | 133 | 3.5 |
| 177 | 99.8 | 162 | 87.3 | 147 | 33.4 | 132 | 2.9 |
| 176 | 99.7 | 161 | 84.9 | 146 | 29.6 | 131 | 2.3 |
| 175 | 99.6 | 160 | 82.2 | 145 | 26.4 | 130 | 1.9 |
| 174 | 99.5 | 159 | 79.1 | 144 | 23.3 | 129 | 1.5 |
| 173 | 99.3 | 158 | 76.5 | 143 | 20.2 | 128 | 1.2 |
| 172 | 99.0 | 157 | 72.6 | 142 | 17.7 | 127 | 0.9 |
| 171 | 98.5 | 156 | 68.7 | 141 | 15.2 | 126 | 0.7 |
| 170 | 98.1 | 155 | 65.7 | 140 | 12.9 | 125 | 0.6 |
| 169 | 97.5 | 154 | 61.5 | 139 | 10.9 | 124 | 0.5 |
| 168 | 96.7 | 153 | 57.3 | 138 | 9.2 | 123 | 0.4 |
| 167 | 95.7 | 152 | 53.2 | 137 | 7.8 | 122 | 0.3 |
| 166 | 94.6 | 151 | 49.1 | 136 | 6.5 | 121 | 0.3 |
| | | | | | | 120 | 0.0 |

## WHEN TO APPLY

Consider these application deadlines for fall admission: Yale Law School, on or about January 10; New York University (NYU) Law School, on or about February 1; Loyola University Chicago School of Law, on or about April 1. Although some of this information may make starting the application process in December seem like a viable option, remember that law schools don't wait until they've received every application to start selecting students. In fact, the longer you wait to apply to a school, the worse your chances are of getting into that school. Maybe your chances will go only from 90 percent to 85 percent, but you shouldn't take an unnecessary risk by waiting.

Additionally, some schools have "early admissions decisions" options, so that you may know by December if you've been accepted (for instance, NYU's early admission deadline is on or about October 15). This option is good for a few reasons: It can give you an indication of what your chances are at other schools; it can relieve the stress of waiting until April to see where you're going to school; and if you're put on the waiting list the first time around, you might be accepted a bit later on in the process—i.e., when everyone else is hearing from law schools for the first time. However, not every school has an early admission option, and not every school's option is the same, so check with your prospective institutions' policies before you write any deadlines on your calendar.

Law School Forums

Law School Forums are an excellent way to talk with representatives and gather information on almost every law school in the country simultaneously. More than 150 schools send admissions officers to these forums, which take place in major cities around the country between February and October. If at all possible, GO. For information about forum dates and locations, check the LSAC website at **www.lsac.org.**

Let's take a look at the major steps in the application process.

- **Take the LSAT.** All ABA-approved and most non-ABA-approved law schools in the United States and Canada require an LSAT score from each applicant. The LSAT is given in February, June, October (occasionally very late September), and December of each year.
- **Register for CAS.** You can register for the Credential Assembly Service at the same time you register to take the LSAT—both forms are contained in the *LSAT Registration Information Book* (hence the name).
- **Select approximately seven schools.** After you've selected your schools, you'll be able to see which schools want what types of things on their applications—although almost all of them will want three basic things: a personal statement, recommendations, and a résumé. Each applicant should be thinking about putting law schools into three categories: (1) "reach" schools, (2) schools where you've got a good chance of being accepted, and (3) "safety" schools. As a minimum, each applicant should apply to two to three schools in each category. (Most admissions experts will say either 2-2-3 or 2-3-2.) It is not uncommon for those with extremely low grades or low LSAT scores (or both) to apply to 15 or 20 schools.
- **Write your personal statement(s).** It may be that you'll need to write only one personal statement (many schools will ask that your personal statement be about why you want to obtain a law degree), but you may need to write several—which is why you need to select your schools fairly early.
- **Obtain two or three recommendations.** Some schools will ask for two recommendations, at least one of which should be academic (both if you are a recent graduate). Others want more than two recommendations and want at least one of your recommenders to be someone who knows you outside traditional academic circles.

- **Update/create a résumé.** Most law school applications ask that you submit a résumé. Make sure yours is up to date and suitable for submission to an academic institution.
- **Get your academic transcripts sent to CAS.** A minor administrative detail, seemingly, but then again, if you forget to do this, CAS will not send your information to the law schools. CAS helps the law schools by acting as a clearinghouse for information—CAS, not you, sends the law schools your undergraduate and graduate school transcripts, your LSAT score(s), and an undergraduate academic summary.

Those are the major steps in applying to law school. From reading this chapter, or from reading the *LSAT Registration Information Book*, you might discover that there are other steps you need to take—such as preparing an addendum to your application, asking for application fee waivers, applying for a special administration of the LSAT, and so on. If you sense that you might need to do anything special, start your application process even earlier than what is recommended in the *LSAT Registration Information Book*, which is unquestionably the most useful tool in applying to law school. This information book not only contains the forms to apply for the LSAT and CAS, but also has a sample LSAT, admissions information, the Law School Forum schedule, and two sample application schedules. These schedules are very useful. For instance, one sample schedule recommends taking the June LSAT for fall admission. This schedule allows you to focus on the LSAT in the spring and early summer and then start the rest of your application process rolling. That's good advice—as mentioned in the LSAT portion of this book, the LSAT is one of the most important factors in getting into the best law school possible.

The sample schedule also indicates that you should research schools in late July/early August. While you are doing this, go ahead and subscribe to CAS and send your transcript request forms to your undergraduate and any other educational institutions—there's no reason to wait until September to do this (you should pay CAS for seven law school applications, unless you're positive you want to apply to only a few schools). Why do this? Because undergraduate institutions can and will make mistakes and delay the transcript process—even when you go there personally and pay them to provide your records. This is essential if you're applying for early decision at some law schools—the transcript process can be a nightmare.

Finally, you should send your applications to law schools between late September and early November. Naturally, if you bombed the LSAT the first time around, you're still in good shape to take the test again in October. Another good piece of news on that front is that more and more law schools are now just simply taking the highest LSAT score that each applicant has, rather than averaging multiple scores. If you have to take the LSAT again, this is good news—but with proper preparation, you can avoid having to spend too much quality time with the LSAT.

## A Simple Checklist

The following is a simple checklist for the major steps of the application process. Each shaded box indicates the recommended month during which you should complete that action.

| | Jan. | Feb. | Mar. | Apr. | May | June | July | Aug. | Sept. | Oct. | Nov. | Dec. |
|---|---|---|---|---|---|---|---|---|---|---|---|---|
| Take practice LSAT | ■ | | | | | | | | | | | |
| Research LSAT prep companies | | ■ | | | | | | | | | | |
| Obtain Registration Information Book* | | | ■ | | | | | | | | | |
| Register for June LSAT | | | | ■ | | | | | | | | |
| Take LSAT prep course | | | | ■ | ■ | ■ | | | | | | |
| Take LSAT | | | | | | ■ | | | | | | |
| Register for LSDAS | | | | | | | ■ | | | | | |
| Research law schools | | | | | | | ■ | | | | | |
| Obtain law school applications | | | | | | | | ■ | | | | |
| Get transcripts sent to LSDAS | | | | | | | | ■ | | | | |
| Write personal statement(s) | | | | | | | | | ■ | | | |
| Update/create résumé | | | | | | | | | ■ | | | |
| Get recommendations | | | | | | | | | ■ | | | |
| Send early decision applications | | | | | | | | | | ■ | | |
| Finish sending all applications | | | | | | | | | | | ■ | |
| Relax | | | | | | | | | | | | ■ |

* The *LSAT & LSDAS Registration Information Book* is traditionally published in March of each year. Call 215-968-1001 to order your materials.

**25 to 75 Percentile LSAT Scores**

| Law School | Scores |
|---|---|
| Widener University, School of Law, Harrisburg | 147–152 |
| Gonzaga University, School of Law | 153–157 |
| Rutgers University—Newark, School of Law | 155–160 |
| University of Pittsburgh, School of Law | 155–160 |
| University of Arizona, James E. Rogers College of Law | 157–164 |
| Temple University, James E. Beasley School of Law | 158–163 |
| University of Florida, Levin College of Law | 160–164 |
| The University of Tennessee, College of Law | 156–161 |
| Case Western Reserve University, School of Law | 156–161 |
| The University of Alabama, School of Law | 158–167 |
| Southern Methodist University, Dedman School of Law | 157–165 |
| Loyola University Chicago, School of Law | 156–160 |
| University of San Diego, School of Law | 158–162 |
| Emory University, School of Law | 161–166 |
| The College of William & Mary, Marshall-Wythe Law School | 161–166 |
| The George Washington University, Law School | 162–168 |
| University of California—Berkeley, School of Law | 164–170 |
| Georgetown University, Law Center | 165–170 |
| Stanford University, School of Law | 168–173 |
| The University of Chicago, Law School | 167–173 |
| Yale University, Law School | 170–176 |

Source: *The Best 169 Law Schools, 2014 Edition.*

## HELPFUL HINTS ON PERSONAL STATEMENTS, RECOMMENDATIONS, RÉSUMÉS, AND ADDENDA

Although your LSAT score is one of the most important factors in the admissions process, you should still present a professional résumé, get excellent recommendations, and hone your personal statement when preparing your law school applications.

Many law schools still employ the "three-pile" system in the application process.

Pile 1 contains applicants with high enough LSAT scores and GPAs to admit them pretty much automatically.

Pile 2 contains applicants who are "borderline"—decent enough LSAT scores and GPAs for that school but not high enough for automatic admission. Admissions officers look at these applications thoroughly to sort out the best candidates.

Pile 3 contains applicants with "substandard" LSAT scores and GPAs for that school. These applicants are usually rejected without much further ado. There are circumstances in which admissions officers will look through pile 3 for any extraordinary applications, but it doesn't happen very often.

What does this mean? Well, if you're lucky, you are in pile 2 (and not pile 3!) for at least one of your "reach" schools. And if you are, there's a good possibility that your application will be thoroughly scrutinized by the admissions committee. Consequently, make sure the following four elements of your application are as strong as you can possibly make them.

### Personal Statement

Ideally, your personal statement should be two pages long. Often, law schools will ask you to identify exactly why you want to go to law school and obtain a law degree. "I love *Boston Legal*" is not the answer to this question. There should be some moment in your life, some experience that you had, or some intellectual slant that you are interested in that is directing you to law school. Identify that reason, write about it, and make it compelling.

Then you should have three or four people read your personal statement and critique it. You should select people whom you respect intellectually, not people who will merely give it a cursory read and tell you it's fine. Also, your personal statement is not the place to make excuses, get on your soapbox, or try your hand at alliterative verse. Make it intelligent, persuasive, short, and powerful—those are the writing and analytical qualities law schools look for.

## Recommendations

Most law schools ask for two or three recommendations. Typically, the longer it has been since you've graduated, the tougher it is to obtain academic recommendations. However, if you've kept your papers and if your professors were tenured, chances are you'll still be able to find them and obtain good recommendations—just present your prof of choice with your personal statement and a decent paper you did in his or her course. That way, the recommender has something tangible to work from. And that's the simple secret to great recommendations—if the people you're asking for recommendations don't know anything specific about you, how can the recommendation possibly be compelling? Getting the mayor of your town or a state senator to write a recommendation helps only if you have a personal and professional connection to them in some way. That way, the recommender will be able to present to the admissions committee actual qualities and accomplishments you have demonstrated.

If you've been out of school for some time and are having trouble finding academic recommendations, choose people from your workplace, from the community, or from any other area of your life that is important to you. You should respect the people you choose—you should view them as quality individuals who have in some way shaped your life. If they're half as good as you think they are, they will know, at least intuitively, that they in some way were responsible for part of your development or education, and they will then be able to talk intelligently about it. Simply put, these people should know who you are, where you live, what your background is, and what your desires and motivations are—otherwise, your recommendations will not distinguish you from the 10-foot-high pile that's on an admissions committee desk.

### Fee waivers

Even though the cost of taking the LSAT, subscribing to CAS, paying for LSAT prep materials, and paying application fees will probably be one-hundredth of your total law school outlay, it's still not just a drop in the bucket. The LSAT is $160 (late registrants must pay an additional $69), CAS is $155 (includes one report sent to a CAS-requiring law school and three letters of recommendation), plus $21 for each additional school you are applying to when ordered at the time that you register for CAS, and $21 for each additional report ordered after you register for CAS. And law school applications themselves are typically around $50 each. As a result, LSAC, as well as most law schools, offers a fee waiver program. If you're accepted into the LSAC program, you get two free LSATs per year, one CAS subscription, four CAS law school reports, and one TriplePrep Plus (which contains three previously administered LSATs). With proper documentation, you can also waive a good portion of your law school application fees. You can request a fee waiver packet from LSAC at 215-968-1001, or write to them at Law School Admission Council, Attn.: Fee Waiver Packet, Box 2000, 661 Penn Street, Newtown, PA, 18940-0998.

You can also download a packet at **www.lsac.org.**

## Résumés

Résumés are a fairly simple part of your application, but make sure yours is updated and proofed correctly. Errors on your résumé (and, indeed, anywhere on your application) will make you look as if you don't really care too much about going to law school. Just remember that this should be a more academically oriented résumé, because you are applying to an academic institution. Put your academic credentials and experiences first—no matter what they are.

## Addenda

If your personal and academic life has run fairly smoothly, you shouldn't need to include any addenda with your application. Addenda are brief explanatory letters written to explain or support a "deficient" portion of your application. Some legitimate addenda topics are academic probation, low/discrepant GPA, low/discrepant LSAT score, arrests/convictions, DUI/DWI suspensions, a leave of absence or other "time gaps," and other similar circumstances.

The addenda are not the place to go off on polemics about standardized testing—if you've taken the LSAT two or three times and simply did not do very well, after spending time preparing with a test prep company or private tutor, merely tell the admissions committee that that's what you've done—you worked as hard as you could to achieve a high score and explored all possibilities to help you achieve that goal. Then let them draw their own conclusions. Additionally, addenda should be brief and balanced—do not go into detailed descriptions of things. Explain the problem and state what you did about it. Simply put, do not whine.

# GATHERING INFORMATION AND MAKING DECISIONS

There are some key questions that you should ask before randomly selecting law schools around the country or submitting your application to someone or other's list of the "top ten" law schools and saying, "If I don't get in to one of these schools, I'll go to B-School instead." Here are some questions to think about.

## Where Would You Like to Practice Law?

For instance, if you were born and bred in the state of Nebraska, care deeply about it, wish to practice law there, and want to someday be governor, then it might be a better move to go to the University of Nebraska School of Law than, say, the University of Virginia, even though UVA is considered a "top ten" law school. A law school's reputation is usually greater on its home turf than anywhere else (except for Harvard and Yale). Apply to the schools in the geographic area where you wish to practice law. You'll be integrated into the community, you may gain some experience in the region doing clinics during law school, and it should be easier for you to get more interviews and position yourself as someone who already knows, for instance, Nebraska.

## What Type of Law Would You Like to Practice?

Law schools *do* have specialties. For instance, if you are very interested in environmental law, it might be better to go to Vermont Law School than to go to NYU. Vermont Law School is one of the most highly regarded schools in the country when it comes to environmental law; so look at what you want to do in addition to where you want to do it.

## Can You Get In?

Many people apply to Harvard. Very few get in. Go right ahead and apply, if you wish, but unless you've got killer scores and/or have done some very outstanding things in your life, your chances are, well, *slim*. Apply to a few reach schools, but make sure they are schools you really want to go to.

## Did You Like the School When You Went There?

What if you decided to go to Stanford, got in, went to Palo Alto, California, and decided that you hated it? The weather was horrible! The architecture was mundane! There's nothing to do nearby! Well, maybe Stanford wasn't the best example—but you get the point. Go to the school and check it out. Talk to students and faculty. Walk around. *Then* make a decision.

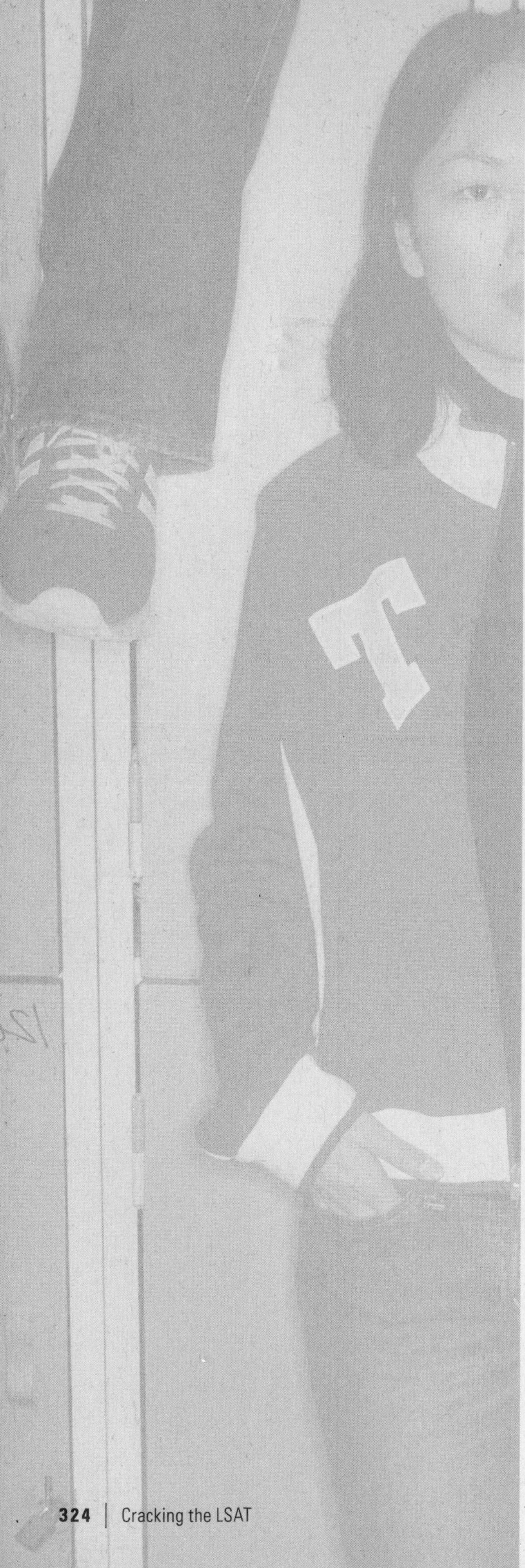

# Summary

- The application process, although detailed, is much easier than taking the extremely stressful LSAT, which in turn will be much easier than your first year of law school—no matter where you go. However, you've still got to want to go to law school. Applying to law school is a demanding process, and if you're not committed to doing it well, it will almost certainly come across in your applications. Be as thorough in preparing your applications as you were in preparing for the LSAT; otherwise you run the risk of turning in applications that are late or contain errors, thereby hurting your chances of getting accepted by the schools to which you really want to go.
- If all this administrative stuff seems overwhelming (i.e., you're the type of person who dreads filling out a deposit slip), the major test-prep companies have designed law school application courses that force you to think about where you want to go and make sure you've got all your recommendations, résumés, personal statements, addenda, and everything else together.
- Whatever your level of administrative faculty, the choice of where you want to go to school is yours. You'll probably be paying a lot of money to go, so you should really make sure you go to the place that's best for you. Take the time to do research on the schools because you'll be paying for law school for a long, long time.

# Chapter 8
# Drill Answers and Explanations

## CHAPTER 2: ARGUMENTS

### Answers for Arguments Practice Drill (Pages 118–123)

1. C
2. E
3. A
4. D
5. D
6. A
7. B
8. D
9. D
10. A
11. D
12. C
13. E

## Explanations for Arguments Practice Drill (Pages 118–123)

1. C Weaken

The conclusion here is that many people use over-the-counter pain medications instead of seeking medical help for serious ailments. This is an interpretation of a key piece of evidence: A study has shown some correlation between frequent use of over-the-counter pain medications and a high incidence of heart disease, cancer, and liver disease. There are a number of gaps here, but the argument draws attention to one in particular: These same people also had very high rates of health insurance coverage. The question we have, after reading the argument, is how we know that these people actually didn't seek medical help for these conditions. We'd like a choice that indicates that these people aren't using medications instead of going to their doctors.

We can eliminate (A) because it doesn't provide the needed information. This choice draws a possible causal connection between the use of these medications and one of the serious ailments listed, but it doesn't relate to the question of whether these people sought medical help.

We can eliminate (B) because it talks about people who actually do consult doctors. It's difficult to see how this could weaken the conclusion.

We can eliminate (D) because it makes no reference to seeking medical help. Although this casts slight doubt on the tightness of the correlation between use of medications and serious medical conditions, this is not nearly strong enough to be a good choice.

We can eliminate (E) because it merely provides further explanation of why someone with adequate health coverage wouldn't seek care for serious conditions. At best, this strengthens the conclusion.

Choice (C) is good because it casts new light on the evidence and is clearly related to seeking medical help. It indicates that many of those who use the medications frequently do so on the instructions of their doctors, which helps explain why so many of those who use the medications have serious conditions.

2. E Main point

This argument deals with carbon dioxide emissions by industry, the rise in average ocean temperatures, and whether the first factor is responsible for the second. The argument indicates that many scientists believe it is, but the argument also includes the information that there have been past fluctuations in both that cannot be attributed to humans. The argument is clearly calling the scientists' belief into question, although it isn't going as far as to state that they are definitely wrong.

We can eliminate (A) because it overstates the argument's conclusion.

We can eliminate (B) because it focuses on the time lag between changes, which is not the primary interest of this argument.

We can eliminate (C) because, like (A), it overstates the argument's case. It would be more correct to say that there is evidence that human industry may not be responsible.

We can eliminate (D) because, although it is a key item of evidence in the argument, the argument's purpose is not to establish this conclusion. It makes use of this information in arriving at its conclusion.

Choice (E) is good because it is consistent with the argument, deals with its primary focus—the cause of the rise of average ocean temperatures—and is appropriately qualified to match the argument's strength without overstating it.

3. **A** Strengthen

This causal argument concludes that legal costs cannot be responsible for price increases by insurance companies. The main piece of evidence offered is that prices have increased much more quickly than legal costs have. We want a choice that reinforces the argument's judgment, either by identifying a potential alternative reason for the increases or by addressing a potential weakness of the argument. No such weakness is readily apparent, but that doesn't mean it doesn't exist.

We can eliminate (B). Although it seems very close, it is not as strong as choice (A). This choice does identify what may be seen as a possible alternative reason for the increase—profit motive—but the chronology and strength of this choice are a little off. This choice says that price increases "are followed" by increases of a "fixed amount," which doesn't exactly explain why legal costs have increased at only "a fraction of the rate" of prices. Even if this choice is true, it's also arguable whether it eliminates legal costs as the real cause of these increases, since this choice at best sheds light on what size the increases should be, not what's ultimately responsible for them.

We can eliminate (C) because it slightly weakens the argument by eliminating a potential alternate cause of the price increase.

We can eliminate (D) because it explains the reason that awards have risen in size but does not relate to whether the increase in the size of awards is primarily responsible for the increase in prices.

We can eliminate (E) because it merely relates to the question of whether the increase in legal costs for the insurance industry is unusual, not whether those increases are primarily responsible for the increase in rates.

Choice (A) is a good answer because it definitively rules out a potential weakness of the argument. If the prices charged by insurance companies take into account likely future increases in legal costs (which, according to the argument, have so far increased at an "accelerating rate"), then this would perhaps explain why prices have increased so much faster than legal costs have thus far. With this possibility eliminated, the argument's conclusion, that legal costs are not the cause of the price increases, gains added strength.

4. **D** Assumption EXCEPT

The conclusion here is that if the restaurant increases the size of its wine list, it will become more popular. The main evidence for this claim is a comparison with the more popular restaurant next door, which is identified as having three potential advantages over the restaurant in question. The argument reaches its conclusion by indicating that two of these advantages are irrelevant to current customers. As one would expect on an EXCEPT question, there are many potential problems with this argument: Most notably, it is possible that some factor other than the three mentioned is responsible for the restaurant's lack of popularity. It also seems odd that the views of the restaurant's customers are a primary factor in making the recommendation because, after all, these are people whom the restaurant is already attracting, and to become more popular the restaurant must attract others. We're looking for four things that are necessary to make the conclusion true; the fifth will be the answer choice we pick.

Choice (A), although convoluted, is an assumption of the argument. This addresses the problem of surveying only the restaurant's current customers.

Choice (B) is an assumption of the argument. If its popularity doesn't depend at all on the wine list, then the manager's conclusion can't possibly be right.

Choice (C) is an assumption of the argument. It isn't as direct as the previous two answers, but this choice does involve a factor not considered in the argument that may be important enough to prevent the manager's plan from working.

Choice (E) is an assumption of the argument. Even if we concede that the wine list could potentially attract more customers, this choice points out the possibility that these customers might demand other things of the restaurant that its current customers do not.

Choice (D) is the answer we want. This weakens the argument and therefore can't be an assumption.

5. **D** Reasoning

Identify the reasoning in Michiko's response. Juan's conclusion is that the candidates are not making enough of an effort to address the issues. His evidence for this claim concerns the content of advertisements during the campaign. Michiko's response, which is the one we're interested in, claims implicitly that the candidates are, on the contrary, devoting enough attention to the issues. Her evidence is a survey demonstrating that voters know the candidates' positions on the most important issues.

Eliminate (A) because Michiko does not identify an internal contradiction in Juan's argument. Although her evidence and conclusion do contradict Juan's position, that isn't what this answer choice says.

Eliminate (B) because it overstates Michiko's strategy. She doesn't completely dismiss the relevance of advertising in considering the question, although she does introduce new evidence that indicates it might not be the best gauge of what the electorate knows.

Eliminate (C) because Michiko never makes a personal statement about Juan's qualifications.

Eliminate (E) because Michiko doesn't dispute the correctness of Juan's evidence, which is his statement about advertising during the campaign.

Choice (D) is the one we want here. The alternative criterion she introduces is whether the voters actually know the candidates' positions on the major issues.

6. **A** Flaw

The conclusion here is that quantum mechanics provides the only correct explanation of the behavior of matter at the subatomic level. The main premise here is that classical mechanics predicts that every experiment should have the same result, whereas quantum mechanics predicts that some experiments should have contradictory results. Because at the subatomic level experiments have contradictory results, the argument decides that quantum mechanics is the only correct theory. The main potential weakness here is that there may be some alternative theory not mentioned that also makes the prediction that some experiments should have contradictory results.

Eliminate (B) because it's pointing in the wrong direction. The upshot of the argument is that the contradictory results are not the result of error; they're unavoidable.

Eliminate (C) because the argument uses all of its key terminology in a consistent manner.

Eliminate (D) because the argument doesn't insist that these contradictory results are always found, only that it is inevitable that they will in some cases be observed.

Eliminate (E) because the opinions of scientists at large aren't relevant to the argument's conclusion.

Choice (A) is the one we want because it identifies a key problem here. Because the conclusion insists that quantum mechanics provides the "only" correct explanation, the argument needs to address all possible alternatives. Because classical mechanics is the only other theory mentioned, the argument falls short of that requirement.

7. **B** Flaw

The editor's conclusion is that the newspaper's coverage of the ballot initiative is not irresponsible. The support for this conclusion is, basically, that to be responsible, coverage must treat all points of view on the issue equally and that by not covering the ballot initiative at all, the newspaper met this requirement. The problem here is that meeting one requirement necessary for coverage to be responsible does not guarantee that the coverage actually was responsible; there may be further requirements as well. This argument confuses a necessary condition with a sufficient one.

Eliminate (A) because the adequacy of the coverage is never addressed. Also, the problem here is that the argument doesn't succeed in establishing that the newspaper's coverage wasn't irresponsible.

Eliminate (C) because the coverage afforded the ballot initiative by other media outlets isn't relevant to this argument. Also, the argument doesn't include any means for determining with certainty whether coverage is responsible, which is the whole problem with the argument.

Eliminate (D) because the question of how "controversial" the ballot initiative is has no relevance to the conclusion.

Eliminate (E) because it gets the argument backward: It doesn't attempt to conclude that the coverage was "not responsible."

Choice (B) is good because it correctly describes the argument's main premise as a necessary condition and also identifies this premise as having been misused to reach the conclusion.

8. D Reasoning

Identify the role of the statement in the argument's reasoning; this is a variant type of Reasoning question. The conclusion here is that reliance on eyewitness testimony results in the conviction of innocent defendants. The main support for this conclusion is that an eyewitness's memory may not be accurate; support for this fact is in turn provided by the general statement that memory of an event can be influenced by information received about the event after the fact. The instance of a criminal wearing sunglasses provides an example of the claim that an eyewitness's memory may not be accurate, which is the statement we're asked to work with. This is a premise of the argument, but it is also supported by another premise and is illustrated with an example.

Eliminate (A) because it incorrectly identifies the direction of support in the argument. The fact that memory can be influenced by subsequent information supports the claim we're asked to work with, not the other way around.

Eliminate (B) because it too incorrectly identifies the direction of support here. The claim we're asked to work with supports the conclusion that the legal system's reliance on eyewitness testimony is problematic, not the other way around.

Eliminate (C) because its direction is also wrong. The example of the perpetrator's appearance illustrates the claim we're asked to work with, not the other way around.

Eliminate (E) because the claim we're asked to work with, although it is supported by others in the argument, is not the main conclusion of the argument.

Choice (D) is the one we want. The term *subsidiary conclusion* refers to a premise that is itself supported by other premises in the argument, and this correctly describes the statement we're asked to work with in this case.

9. D Inference

We're given general information about a habitat's carrying capacity and what determines it: Basically, the carrying capacity is the maximum population of a kind of animal the habitat can support, and it's determined by the availability of the resource with the greatest relative scarcity. We're then given information about a particular habitat supporting snowy egrets and told that there are many unoccupied nesting sites over a long period of time. The conclusion we should be able to draw from this is that nesting sites aren't the resource that has the greatest relative scarcity in the habitat.

Eliminate (A) because it misinterprets the term *carrying capacity*. The carrying capacity of the environment is evidently smaller than the number that could be accommodated by all of the habitat's nesting sites.

Eliminate (B) because it is too specific. We know there's some other resource that's scarcer, relative to the egrets' needs, than nesting sites, but we don't know for certain that food is that resource.

Eliminate (C) because it's too strong. The key resource can't be completely absent—otherwise no egrets would live there.

Eliminate (E) because it's too strong. It is possible that the introduction of additional resources could increase the habitat's capacity to support egrets.

Choice (D) is the best answer here. Because we know that the lack of availability of some other resource is responsible for the fact that not all nesting sites are used, the number of nesting sites that remain unused is a consequence of how relatively scarce some other resource is.

10. A Resolve/Explain EXCEPT

The company conducts an anonymous employee satisfaction survey after a series of layoffs and cutbacks. Despite grumblings, average satisfaction measured by the survey is higher than it has been in any previous survey conducted by similar means. We're looking for four choices that explain why the survey could have turned out this way; the remaining choice will be our answer.

Choice (B) explains the results by indicating that the most dissatisfied employees no longer work for the company.

Choice (C) explains the results by indicating that these surveys are conducted only when satisfaction is at its lowest; thus, the fact that average satisfaction is higher now than it was during past surveys doesn't necessarily mean that it is particularly high.

Choice (D) explains the results by indicating that even though the survey was supposedly anonymous, employees may nevertheless not have responded honestly out of fear that they would be identified.

Choice (E) explains the results by indicating that those who were left to answer the survey were relieved to be employed still.

Choice (A) is the best answer here. It seems to make the paradox worse by indicating that there are more dissatisfied employees than ever; this doesn't help explain why the average satisfaction should have been the highest ever measured.

11. D Similar to Inference or Principle

The passage describes rules governing the handling of nonmajors who register for a course. The only registration options are early or late, and, in each of these cases, a different rule applies. Take them one at a time. For early nonmajors, the rule is this: If there's still space in the course after all the majors have registered early, then the nonmajor is guaranteed a space. For late nonmajors, the rule is this: Only if there's still space after all the early registrants and the late-registering majors are counted is there a possibility of the nonmajor getting a space. Don't be thrown off by the use of the word *assured* in the original statement of this second rule; it is used correctly, but the rule as stated never truly assures a late-registering nonmajor of a space. Finally, it's worth noting that we have no way of knowing when a major is assured of a space in the course.

Eliminate (A) because it guarantees a late-registering nonmajor a space. As discussed above, the rules we have can never do that. Consider what happens if Kim is one of a very large number of late-registering nonmajors, all of who are in the same circumstances.

Eliminate (B) because it guarantees a major a space. As discussed above, the rules we have can't do that. Consider what happens if Joe is one of a very large number of late-registering majors, all of who are in the same circumstances.

Eliminate (C) because it doesn't provide all of the needed information. In the original rules, we're provided information that would assure an early-registering nonmajor a space as long as there are still some spaces left in the course after all the early-registering majors are counted; because we're told in this choice that the number of early-registering majors "does not exceed" the number of spaces in the course, it remains possible that the two numbers are equal. It's tricky, but this one is just a hair short of assuring Wendy a space.

Eliminate (E) because it deals with a late-registering major. We don't have any information that tells us what the registrar does in this case (perhaps the class size is allowed to exceed the number of spaces allocated to it), so we can't definitively conclude that Philip won't get a seat.

Choice (D) is the one we want. Dorothy, a late-registering nonmajor, definitely fails to meet the criterion that is required in order for her to receive a space, so we can conclude with certainty that she won't get one.

12. C Principle

The conclusion here is that the highway patrol's stated reason for stopping Mr. Smith cannot be the only reason he was stopped. The evidence here is that others were in an identical situation at the time and yet were not stopped. We're looking for the general statement that matches the reasoning of this argument as closely as possible while supporting the conclusion.

Eliminate (A) because it mentions whether the highway patrol's actions were justified. The issue here is whether the stated reasons for stopping Mr. Smith constitute a complete explanation of the highway patrol's actions.

Eliminate (B) for the same reason. The issue in this argument is not whether the actions of the highway patrol were justified.

Eliminate (D) for the same reason. Our argument deals with the highway patrol's stated reasons for stopping Mr. Smith.

Eliminate (E), although it's close. Mostly, this is just too much to conform to the argument's reasoning: The argument doesn't demand a complete accounting of all the things the highway patrol could have done but didn't. It only insists that the explanation take into account the fact that the same thing was not done in other cases.

Choice (C) is the best answer here. It pertains directly to the question of whether or not the explanation was complete, and the mention of the explanation applying "equally to some other situation in which no action was taken" precisely matches the evidence used in the argument.

13. E Inference

The passage describes the need for a sterile environment in manufacturing integrated circuits and the danger posed by environmental contaminants. These factors are identified as reasons that conventional petroleum-based lubricants are not used in the moving parts of robots involved in manufacturing them. We can't predict what the inference drawn here will be, so we have to evaluate the choices one at a time and find the one that we can be certain is true.

Eliminate (A) because at best it goes too far, and at worst it contradicts the passage. We don't know that the robots are even potentially a "major source" of contamination; also, it seems safer to conclude in this case that, thanks to the lubricants used, the robots are not a source of contamination at all.

Eliminate (B) because we have no information at all about the nonmoving parts of these robots.

Eliminate (C) because it demands too much. We aren't told how the conventional petroleum-based lubricants pose a threat to the sterile environment, only that they do.

Eliminate (D) because it goes too far. We aren't told that any amount of contaminant will always lead to malfunction; in fact, we're told that it "often" does, which leaves open the possibility that sometimes it doesn't.

Choice (E) is the best answer here. It is qualified, and it seems an easy consequence of the passage material. Because some other lubricant is used for the moving parts of robots, it must be true that there exists some other lubricant that is both suitable for robots and less likely to compromise the sterile environment.

# CHAPTER 3: GAMES

## Answers for Game 1 (Pages 236–237)

1. C
2. C
3. E
4. E
5. B
6. A

## Explanations for Game 1 (Pages 236–237)

**Diagram and inventory** The task in this game is to order the software updates from 1 to 6 and determine what priority each update is given. We'll use a standard two-tier diagram for this, with 1 to 6 as the core of the diagram, the updates in the top row, and the priorities in the bottom row. Here's what it looks like.

| | 1 | 2 | 3 | 4 | 5 | 6 |
|---|---|---|---|---|---|---|
| GHJKLM | | | | | | |
| tssrrr | | | | | | |

**Symbolize and double-check the clues** Clue 1 is a global rule, which we can symbolize this way.

1. p p

Clue 2 is the sort of clue we expect to see in an ordering game. We note that clue 4 gives us further information about G and H, which are also mentioned in this clue. We'll combine all this information in a single symbol.

2. & 4. G/t — H/s — K/r

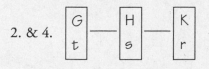

Clue 3 is an antiblock.

Clue 5 can be represented directly in our diagram.

**Look for links and size up the game** We've already done some linking by making a combined symbol for clues 2 and 4 above. There are a few other things we can deduce here: Because the fourth update is rush priority, and we can't have consecutive files with the same priority, we know that the third and fifth files can't have rush priority. There are two other rush-priority files to place and only three spaces left they can occupy. Because two of these are the first and second spaces, one of the rush-priority files has to be last; the other one will be either first or second.

Now look at our large combined symbol. G has to have at least two other files after it, and it must be the top-priority update, so the absolute latest it could be updated is third. In particular, then, this means that the fifth file to be updated not only can't be rush priority, but can't be top priority either. The only option remaining is for it to be standard priority. This large clue also allows us to restrict the placement of files G, H, and K somewhat: We've already seen that G can't be later than third; H can't be first because G has to be before it, and it also can't be fourth or sixth because of its priority; finally, K can't be first or second because of other files that must go before it, and it can't be third or fifth because of its priority, which leaves fourth or sixth as the only two possible locations for it.

Here's our final full diagram.

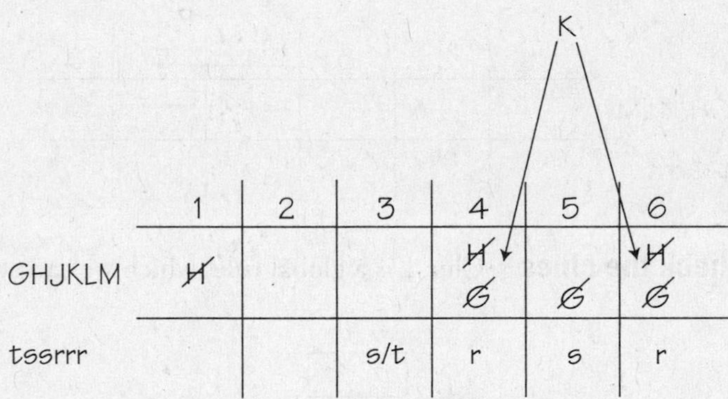


**Questions** We'll work the Specific questions on a first pass, and then the General questions on a second.

2. C Specific

M is third.

M third means that G can't be second. Because G can be only first, second, or third, we conclude that G must be first. This forces the second file to have rush priority and the third to have standard priority. Given these facts, we see that H must be the fifth file updated because that is the only standard-priority position left. H fifth means that K must be sixth. The only remaining elements are J and L, which we see are both unrestricted, and therefore identical: They can go in the remaining spaces—second and fourth—in either order.

Here's the diagram we've just come up with.

②

| 1 | 2 | 3 | 4 | 5 | 6 |
|---|---|---|---|---|---|
| G | J/L | M | L/J | H | K |
| t | r | s | r | s | r |

Choices (A), (B), (D), and (E) are all deductions we've made in our diagram. Choice (C) is the one that doesn't have to be true, and it's the answer we want.

4. **E** Specific

We're given a new block—ts—to add to our diagram.

We already know that G, the top-priority file, can be only first, second, or third, so let's focus on where we can put it. Clearly third is impossible—the fourth file has to be a top-priority file. Second looks okay. First may look all right at a glance, but remember that either the first or second file must be a top-priority file, and putting G in first would occupy both of them, forcing us to put two top-priority files next to each other. So, G must be the second file updated. This makes the second file top-priority, the third file standard-priority, and the first file top-priority. We can also conclude from G's placement that M cannot be first or third. It appears that there is still enough room to put K in either of its possible spots, so there isn't anything more definite that we can conclude here.

The following is the diagram we're working with:

④

| 1 | 2 | 3 | 4 | 5 | 6 |
|---|---|---|---|---|---|
| ~~M~~ | G | ~~M~~ | | | |
| r | t | s | r | s | r |

Not only *can* choice (A) be true, it *has* to be. Choices (B), (C), and (D) are possibilities that aren't excluded by our diagram. Choice (E), however, is excluded by our diagram, and it's the one we want.

5. **B** Specific

This question gives us a new block—JL—to work with.

Unfortunately, it isn't immediately clear how this block fits into our diagram or what other deductions it leads to. The best strategy in this case is to work the choices one at a time.

Because this is a must-be-true question, we have to do our POE carefully. Simply plugging in the choice as it is written will tell us only whether that choice *could* be true. To do POE on a must-be-true question, we must attempt to show that the choice we're working on *doesn't* have to be true. For example, in working on (A), what we want to check is whether G could be in some place other than third. Let's try first, which seems like it would be pretty easy to do; here's a diagram that demonstrates G can, in fact, be first while still keeping our JL block intact.

⑤

| 1 | 2 | 3 | 4 | 5 | 6 |
|---|---|---|---|---|---|
| G | J | L | M | H | K |
| t | r | s | r | s | r |

Because G evidently doesn't have to be third, this diagram eliminates choice (A). Happily, this diagram also shows that K doesn't have to be fourth—eliminate (C); that L doesn't have to be sixth—eliminate (D); and that M doesn't have to be second—eliminate (E). The only remaining choice is (B), which is the one we should select.

1. C General

We're looking for something that has to be true in all cases.

A quick scan of the choices shows that (C) is one of our initial deductions, and it's the choice we should select.

3. E General

We're looking for something that can't be true.

A quick scan of the choices may get us to the answer immediately. If so, great! If not, there are still plenty of other things we can try. Prior work can sometimes be helpful in these cases because it's possible that we've already generated an example of one or more of these answer choices. In this case, the only choice we've seen before is (D), in our example in question 5.

At this point, we try the choices one at a time. Choice (A) can be done; here's an example that demonstrates it; we've left open the fact that r and s can switch between the first and second spaces, and we've also left open the fact that J and L can be switched between second and fourth. Hopefully, some of these possibilities can help us with later answer choices or questions.

③ (A)

| 1 | 2 | 3 | 4 | 5 | 6 |
|---|---|---|---|---|---|
| M | J/L | G | L/J | H | K |
| r/s | s/r | t | r | s | r |

We try (B) and find that it, too, can be done. As before, we leave open the positions of our identical elements J and L.

③ (B)

| 1 | 2 | 3 | 4 | 5 | 6 |
|---|---|---|---|---|---|
| J/L | G | H | K | L/J | M |
| r | t | s | r | s | r |

A little foresight in generating this example allows us to use it to verify (C) as well. At this point, (E) is the only remaining choice. You may have noticed on your initial pass that putting M second would prevent us from putting G either first or third, and so because G can be only first, second, or third, M can never be second. However you get there, we see that (E) is the choice we have to pick here.

6. A General

We're asked to find the answer that can't be false—in other words, the one that must be true. Choice (A) is one of our initial deductions, and it's the answer we should pick here.

Lest you wonder, at this point we've generated counterexamples to all of the other choices here in our prior work. Our work from question 2 shows that (B) can be false; our work from question 3 choice (A) shows that (C) can be false; our work from question 5 shows that (D) can be false; and every example we've generated shows that (E) can be false—in fact, it can never be true.

## Answers for Game 2 (Pages 238–239)

1. A

2. C

3. E

4. D

5. C

6. E

## Explanations for Game 2 (Pages 238–239)

**Diagram and inventory** The task in this game is to place the seven board members into three groups—K (3 elements), M (4 elements), and O (4 elements). We should make sure to include the sizes of the groups in our initial diagram. There are two types of elements, so we'll use uppercase for the founding members and lowercase for the recent members. We also should indicate the rules for using the elements here: Because we have eleven spaces but only seven elements, multiple uses of some elements will be necessary. We are told, however, that no element can be in all three groups. A quick summary—"1 or 2 uses of each"—gets all this information across nicely. Finally, we are told that at least one founding member is in each group, so we can reserve spaces for them to start with. Here's our initial diagram.

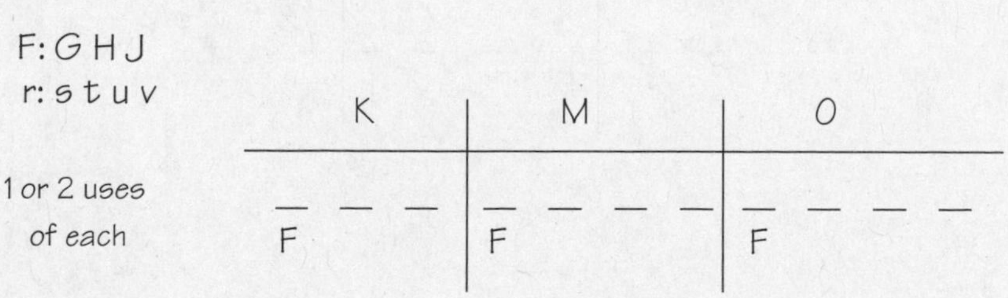

F: G H J
r: s t u v

1 or 2 uses of each

| K | | | M | | | | O | | | |
|---|---|---|---|---|---|---|---|---|---|---|
| _ | _ | _ | _ | _ | _ | _ | _ | _ | _ | _ |
| F | | | F | | | | F | | | |

**Symbolize and double-check the clues** Clue 1 may be a little difficult to symbolize clearly, but what it means is relatively easy to see. Because we have at least one founding member in group O, we must have at least two founding members in group M. Moreover, because there are only three founding members in the game, this is the only combination that satisfies the clue. Thus O consists of one founding member and three recent members, and M consists of two founding members and two recent members. This is pretty easy to reflect in our diagram.

Clue 2 is conditional. Here's a symbol for it and its contrapositive.

2.
K: FFr ⟶ ~~[GH]~~ and ~~[GJ]~~

[GH] or [GJ] ⟶ ~~K: FFr~~

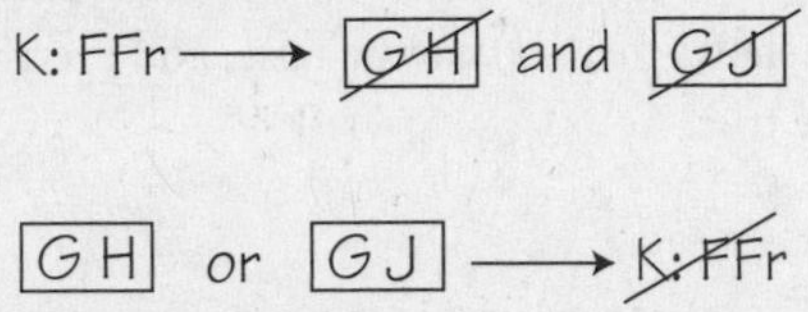

Clue 3 sounds like a conditional, but further examination shows it can be symbolized more easily. Because having either s or u in a group prevents us from putting the other in the same group, this is simply an antiblock, which we symbolize this way.

3. ~~[su]~~

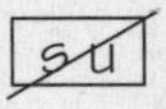

Clue 4 truly is a conditional. Having t in a group forces us to have G, but not, it's worth noting, vice versa. This clue also has a contrapositive, so we'll use this symbol.

4.
t ⟶ [Gt]

Ø ⟶ ~~t~~

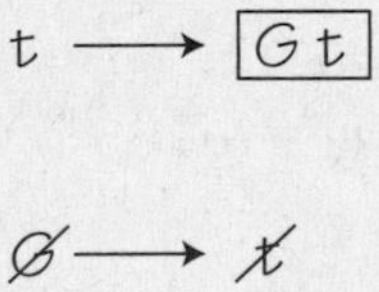

**Look for links and size up the game** We've already done some linking by figuring out what clue 1 means for the makeup of groups M and O, but there's a little more we can do here. Look at group O, which must contain three recent members. Because s and u can't be in the same group as one another, we know that the three recent members here must be t, v, and one of s or u; because t is in the group, then G must be as well. We know, basically, the makeup of group O to start with. Beyond that, it's difficult to predict what the most important factors in working this game will be. Here's our final diagram.

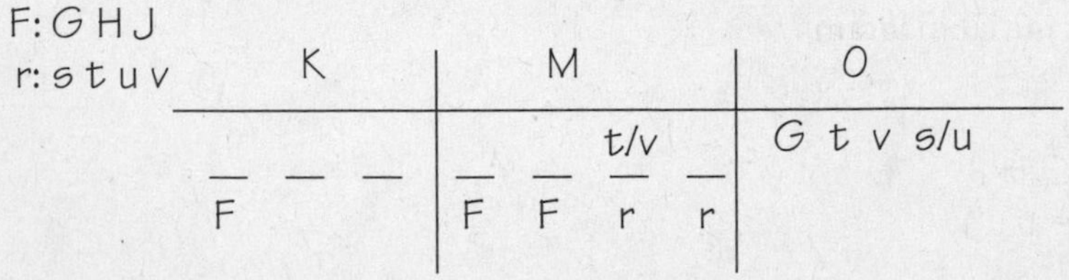

F: G H J
r: s t u v

| K | M | O |
|---|---|---|
| _ _ _ | _ _ t/v _ | G t v s/u |
| F | F F r r | |

**Questions** We'll work the Specific questions on a first pass, and then the General and Complex questions on a second.

2. C Specific

v is not in group M.

If v is not in group M, then t must be; otherwise, we would be forced to put s and u in the same group. Thus, the recent members in group M are t and one of either s or u, and because t is in this group, then G must be as well. Either J or H is the remaining founding member in this group.

Consider what this means for group K. Either J or H is in group M with G, so we can't have exactly two founding members in group K. We also can't have three founding members in group K because that would put G in all three groups. Now group K includes one founding member and two recent members, and the founding member is the other of H or J who wasn't used in group M; everyone, after all, has to be in at least one of the groups.

Who are the recent members in group K? It can't be t because G isn't there, and also putting t in group K would have that element in all three groups. Because s and u can't be together, we must put v in group K and fill the remaining space with one of s or u. We aren't sure which exact groups s and u are in, but we know that one of them fills two of the spaces reserved for them and the other fills one. Here's the full diagram.

②

| K | M | O |
|---|---|---|
| H/J v s/u | J/H G t s/u | G t v s/u |

The choice here that must be true is (C). Choice (D) could be true, but s may be in either one or two of our groups; none of the rest of the choices could ever be true.

5. C Specific

J is in group K but in no other groups.

This tells us right away that G and H are the founding members in group M. Because G and H are together, we can't have two founding members in group K; also, we can't have three founding members in that group because that would put G in all three groups. Now group K includes J and two recent members.

Who are the recent members in group K? They can't include t because G isn't in this group; to prevent s and u from being together, we'll have to use v and one of s or u. Now consider group M: We have two recent members to place there; v is in two of the groups already, so we can't include it. Again, because s and u can't be together, we'll have to choose t and one of s or u. Our diagram is filled out; here's what it looks like.

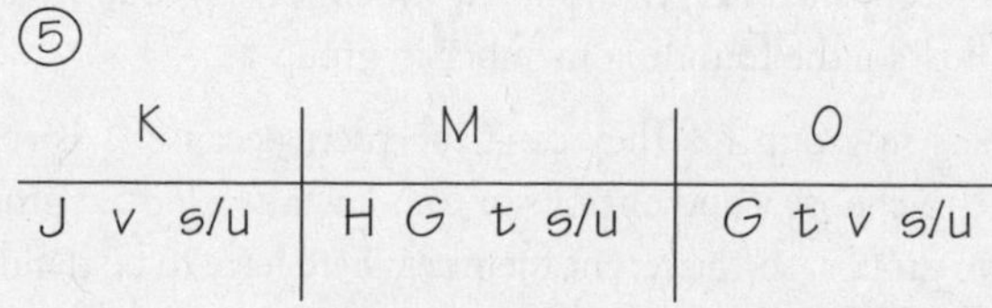


The choice here that could be true is (C). All of the rest are contradicted by our deductions.

1. **A** General

Which could be a listing of the members of group K?

The first strategy to try here is to eliminate choices that blatantly violate rules. Choice (B) violates clue 2: It has two founding members in group K but shows G and J together. Choice (E) violates clue 3: It has s and u in the same group. Choice (C) violates clue 4: It has t in a group without G. That leaves only (A) and (D) to consider.

The best thing to do at this stage is try choice (A), which we find can actually work. Here's how.

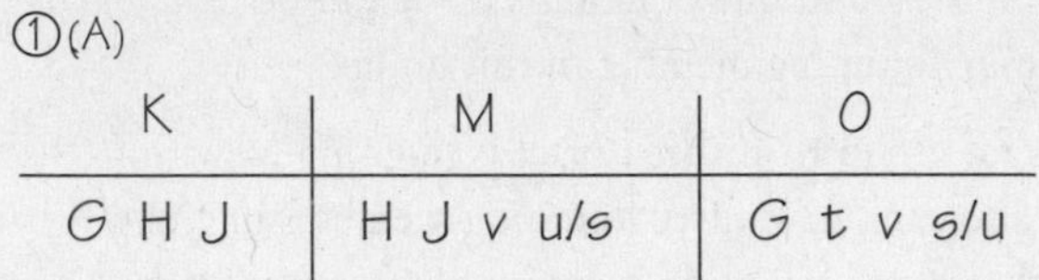

①(A)
K
M
O
G H J
H J v u/s
G t v s/u


As to why (D) doesn't work, that's a little more difficult to see (if you've figured out that (A) works, then you shouldn't waste time checking (D)—trust your work). Choice (D) shows two founding members in group K, which means that G can never be with either H or J; that means the two founding members in group M must be H and J. But consider who the recent members in that group must be: It can't be t because G isn't there; it can't be v either because that would put v in all three groups. Choice (D) forces us to put s and u together in group M, which isn't allowed.

However you get there, (A) is the choice we want on this question.

3. **E** General

What must always be true?

On a game in which we have initial deductions, it's a fair bet that a question like this will involve one of them. Sure enough, we see on a quick scan that (E) is one of the things we found to start with.

You can also eliminate on a question like this by looking at prior work. Choice (A) doesn't have to be true; we saw a counterexample in our work for question 1 choice (A); that counterexample also allows us to eliminate choice (C). We saw a counterexample for choice (B) in our work for question 2, and we've seen numerous potential counterexamples for (D).

Whichever way we go, we have to pick (E) on this one.

4. **D** Complex

G appears at least once with J but doesn't appear with H.

We classified this one as complex because of its task: *Count the ways* questions are often time consuming, but they may be a little easier once you're familiar with the game.

The fact that G and J are together means we can't have two founding members in group K. The fact that G doesn't appear with H means we can't have three founding members in that group, either. In other words, we have one founding member and two recent members in group K, which leaves group M as the only place where G and J can appear together. H, then, must be the founding member in group K.

Who are the recent members in group K? They can't include t because G isn't there, so to prevent s and u from appearing together, we have to choose v and one of s or u. Now take a look at group M, which also needs two recent members; v is already in two groups, so the recent members here have to be t and one of s or u again. Here's the full diagram, which may look a little familiar from some previous questions.

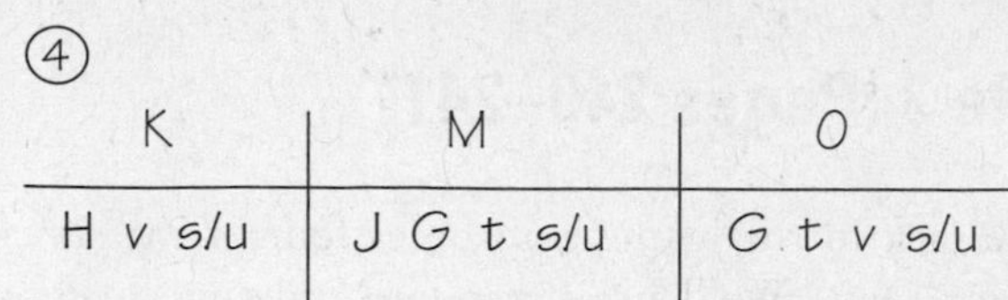

4
K
M
O
H v s/u
J G t s/u
G t v s/u


All that's left is to count how many possibilities this represents. There are two basic cases: Either we have two s's and one u or two u's and one s. Nothing constrains us when it comes to choosing which groups these elements appear in, so we just have to make sure we count correctly: If we have two s's and one u, then all we're basically doing is choosing which one of the three groups the u will go in. That's three possibilities. We see that the same situation arises when we have two u's and one s, which gives us three more possibilities.

That's a grand total of six possibilities, which is answer choice (D).

6. E General

What can't be true?

Prior work may be helpful on this one. Our work for question 2 includes examples of (A) and (B), both of which we can eliminate off the top. We saw an example of (D) in our work for question 1 choice (A). That leaves (C) and (E) as possibilities. If we try (C), we'll find that it works.

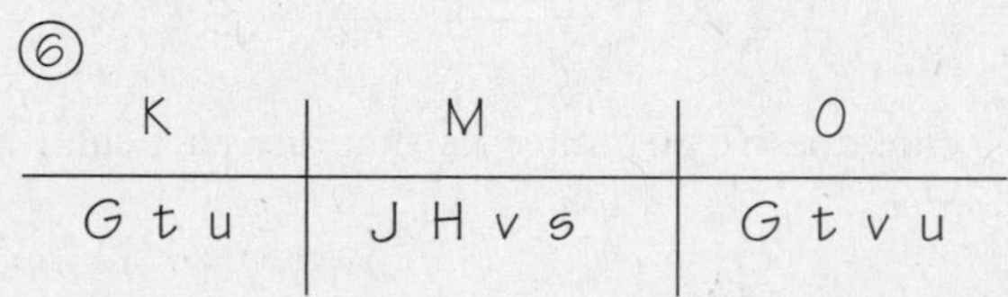


The only remaining choice is (E), and we should choose it at this stage. In case you're curious, the reason that (E) can't work is a little complicated. If t and v are in group M, then G must be in group M as well, leaving either J or H to fill out the group as its remaining founding member. Think about what that means for group K: Because G, t, and v are all in two groups already, none of them is available for use in group K, which means among other things that we can't have all three founding members in group K. Because G is already in group M with one of J or H, we can't have two founding members in group K. That means group K includes one founding member and two recent members, but the only two recent members available to put in group K are s and u, which can't go together. No matter how you slice it, the answer here has to be (E).

## Answers for Game 3 (Pages 240–241)

1. C
2. B
3. E
4. E
5. A
6. D

## Explanations for Game 3 (Pages 240–241)

**Diagram and inventory** The task in this game is to order four of the six chess players from first through fourth, with the other two being "Out." We'll use a standard ordering diagram with two spaces in an "Out" column.

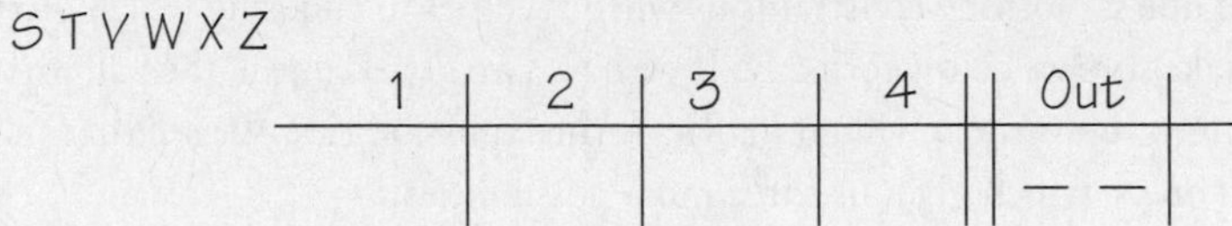


**Symbolize and double-check the clues** Clues 1, 2, and 3 are a little difficult to interpret and symbolize until you look at them together. Because there's no assurance that all of the four elements mentioned in these clues are "In," these clues are less straightforward than we'd like, but what they add up to is that whichever of these elements are In have to go in the order V, T, X, S, with other elements possibly thrown in. For the sake of clarity, we'll symbolize these three clues together this way.

1. 2. & 3. V — T — X — S

We need to understand that this clue doesn't guarantee us that any particular elements are In—only that the ones that are must occur in this order.

Clue 4 is a fairly straightforward conditional.

4. $W \longrightarrow X_2$

$\not{X}_2 \longrightarrow \not{W}$

Clue 5 is a little more complicated. When Z is In, T is also In, with Z before T; the most useful contrapositive of this would be that if T is Out, then Z must also be Out, although there are other circumstances in which we might be able to deduce that Z is Out (for instance, if T is the first seed). Here's the simplest and most useful symbol we can come up with for now.

5. Z ⟶ Z — T (both in)

$\not{T} \longrightarrow \not{Z}$

**Look for links and size up the game** It's difficult to make any more deductions at this stage, although there do turn out to be at least a few. Because they depend on thinking about several "what-if" scenarios, however, we'll move to the questions under the assumption that we don't have these deductions in hand. The one thing we can see right away that we'll need to look out for in working the questions is when we've filled up our "Out" column; once the four players participating are set, our ordering clues should provide us some very good guidance on how players have to be seeded.

**Questions** On our first pass, we'll work the Grab-a-Rule question followed by the Specific questions; on our second pass, we'll work the General and Complex questions.

1. **C** Grab-a-Rule

   Always a nice way to start out a game. Our composite ordering symbol (clues 1 through 3 combined) gets rid of choice (D), which violates clue 1, and choice (E), which violates clue 2. Clue 4 gets rid of choice (A), which has W In but X not second. Clue 5 gets rid of choice (B), which has Z In but T Out. That leaves us with the answer, (C).

3. **E** Specific

   T is seeded second.

   T second tells us that X can't be second, so W must be Out. It also leaves only one slot with a higher seed than T; although this space could be occupied by either V or Z, because there's only one available, we know that the other of Z or V has to go Out. That leaves our remaining elements—X and S—to receive the third and fourth seeds, respectively. Here's the diagram.

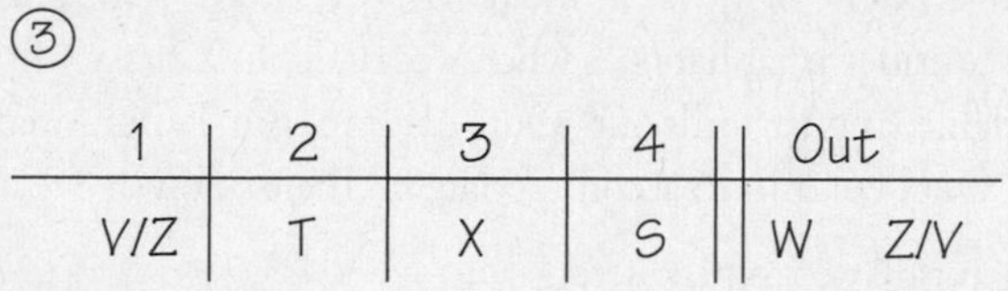

③

| 1 | 2 | 3 | 4 | Out |
|---|---|---|---|---|
| V/Z | T | X | S | W Z/V |

The only choice that could be true, given the information in our diagram, is (E), and that's the choice we want.

5. **A** Specific

   X is In; S is Out.

   The main deduction here is pretty tough; it depends on looking at what happens if we put W In. W In would force X to go In second, which would leave only one space open in front of it. V and T can only be ranked above X, so one of them would have to receive the first seed, and the other would have to go Out, filling that area of our diagram. But then what about Z? Putting it In forces us to use T, but then both Z and T would have to be seeded higher than X, and there simply isn't room for them both. The upshot of all of this is that there's no way, in this case, that we can put W In.

   Once you've made that deduction, the rest is pretty straightforward. With both S and W Out, we're left with V, Z, T, and X In. V and Z go in higher seeds than T, and X has to go in a lower seed than T, leaving V and Z to occupy the first and second seeds in either order, T In the third seed, and X In the fourth seed. Here's the diagram.

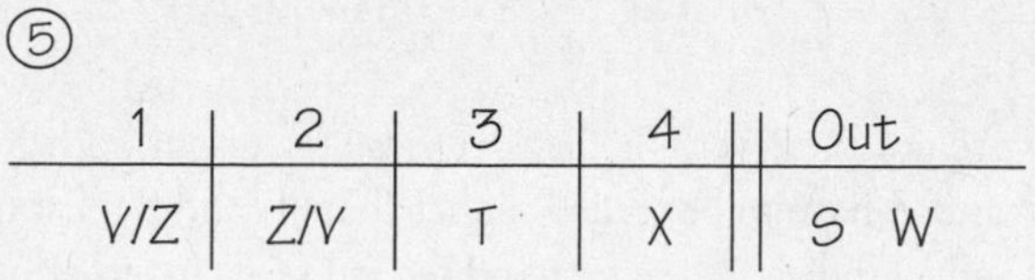

⑤

| 1 | 2 | 3 | 4 | Out |
|---|---|---|---|---|
| V/Z | Z/V | T | X | S W |

The one that has to be true here is (A), the choice we want.

2. **B** General

Complete and accurate list of players who could be first.

It's a judgment call as to whether you want to work this one before or after question 4, but we'll go ahead and do it at this point in the order.

We've already seen examples in which V and Z are first; unfortunately, all of the choices include both of these elements. The first thing to try is looking for differences: T seems like a key one because there's a 2:3 split of choices that involve it. We check to see whether T can be first. T first forces both V and Z Out because there's no higher seed available. That means that we're left with X, S, and W to go In with T. W In forces X into the second seed, but there's no problem with that: S and W can go In the third and fourth seeds in either order. Here's the diagram.

(2)

| 1 | 2 | 3 | 4 | Out |
|---|---|---|---|---|
| T | X | S/W | W/S | V Z |

Because we now know that T can be first, we eliminate (A), (C), and (E). The only difference between our remaining answer choices is X, so we consider what happens when we try to put X first. X first forces both V and T Out because there's no higher seed available, and that fills our "Out" column. But T Out forces us to put Z Out as well, and there isn't enough space in the "Out" column to accommodate it. There's no way we can have X first.

That leaves us with (B) as the answer to pick here.

4. **E** General

A pair of elements, at least one of which must be In.

This amounts to asking us to find the choice that lists a pair of elements that can't both be Out. A quick scan may allow you to see the answer, and if so, that's great. Otherwise, prior work is a good place to start. We've seen S and W Out together in question 5, so we can eliminate (A). We've seen V and W Out together in question 3, so we can eliminate (C). We haven't seen relevant examples of any of the other cases, so now we have to do a little work.

To check (B), we try to put both T and Z Out. That leaves us with S, V, W, and X all In. W In means X must be second; V, then, has to go in front of it In first. That leaves S and W to go In either order in third and fourth. Here's the diagram.

(4) (B)

| 1 | 2 | 3 | 4 | Out |
|---|---|---|---|---|
| V | X | S/W | W/S | T Z |

That eliminates (B), but we're not there yet. To check (D), we try to put both X and W Out. That leaves us with S, T, V, and Z all In. Both V and Z have to be seeded higher than T, and S must be seeded lower. Thus T is the third seed, S is the fourth seed, and V and Z are the first and second seeds in either order. Here's the diagram.

(4) (D)

| 1 | 2 | 3 | 4 | Out |
|---|---|---|---|---|
| V/Z | Z/V | T | S | W X |

That eliminates (D), leaving us with (E) as the only remaining answer. We should definitely pick it at this stage; no need to spend time trying it out as well.

In case you're curious, a moment's inspection shows why we can't have both X and Z Out. X Out forces W Out, but there's no room for it in the Out column. Choice (E) is definitely the right answer here.

6. D Complex

Substitute a rule.

Beware! When you see a question like this on a game, always work it last. You want to be as familiar as possible with how the game works before you attempt this kind of question. You also want to have as much previous work as possible to help you out. On the other hand, don't be overly scared of these questions. Some are tough, but some are pretty straightforward; this one falls into the latter category.

We already know from our deductions that V if seeded, is before S, T, and X if any of them are also seeded. And we know that S is not seeded lower than X from our third rule. If we replace the rule that T cannot be seeded lower than X with the new rule in choice (D), we end up with exact same constraints as we had originally. This gives us (D) as the correct answer. All of the other answers either fail to give us the deduction that T cannot be seeded lower than X as in choices (A) and (B), give us additional constraints that did not exist with our original clue as in choice (C), or both as in choice (E).

## Answers for Game 4 (Pages 242–243)

1. B

2. A

3. E

4. D

5. D

## Explanations for Game 4 (Pages 242–243)

**Diagram and inventory** This is a distribution game with two groups. The qualifying fight and title bout form the core of the diagram. Elements B, E, I, S are eligible to go in group Q; elements B, C, D, E are eligible to go in group T.

Clue 1 & Clue 2 give you the two possible distributions: Either Q has 3 spaces and T has 2 spaces, or Q has 2 spaces and T has 4.

Clue 3 & Clue 4 give you the elements that are eligible to go in each group.

Clue 5: [1+ In Common]

Clue 6 goes in the diagram in both possible distributions.

**Deductions** Clue 5 combined with the elements lists gives you a B/E placeholder in each group in both possible distributions.

In the scenario in which Q has 3 spaces, there is an I/S placeholder in group Q, and Group T must contain D and B/E only.

In the scenario in which Q has 2 spaces, all four eligible elements are in group T.

Here is the diagram.

| | Q (B, E, I, S) | T (B, C, D, E) |
|---|---|---|
| 0. | B/E I/S __ | D B/E |
| 0. | B/E __ | B C D E |
| 2. | B/E I/S | B C D E |
| 3. | B/E I/S __ | D B/E |
| 4. | B E | B C D E |
| 5. | B/E __ | B C D E |

**Questions** We'll work the Grab-a-Rule question first, followed by the Specific questions on a first pass; and then finish the second pass off with the General question from this game.

1. B Grab-a-rule

    Clue 1 eliminates choice (A); Clue 2 eliminates choice (C); Clue 5 eliminates choice (E); Clue 6 eliminates choice (D).

2. A Specific

    In order for five different elements to be used, Group T must contain B, C, D, and E; Group Q must contain B/E and I/S. The other possible distribution won't work without the two groups failing to have at least one in common. Choice (A) must be false.

3. E Specific

    Eliminate answer choices that must be true. For C to not be in group T, the first possible distribution must apply. That is, Q must contain three of the four elements B, E, I, S; T must contain D and B or E. Choices (A), (B), (C), and (D) must be true. Choice (E) could be false since the cage match could consist of D and B.

5. D Specific

Eliminate answer choices that could be true. If the qualifying fight is the cage match, the second distribution must apply, so group Q contains two spaces, at least one of which must be occupied by B or E, and group T contains B, C, D, and E. Choice (A) could be true if both B and E are in both groups. Choice (B) could be true if group Q contains E and either I or S. Choices (C) and (E) could be true if group Q contains E and I. Choice (D) must be false because it would violate rule 5.

4. D General

Find the answer choice that could be true. Choices (A), (B), (C), and (E) must be false from the zero line. Choice (D) could be true if Group Q contains only B and E, and Group T contains B, C, D, and E. This is possible because Clue 5 says "at least one," not "exactly one."

## Answers for Game 5 (Pages 244–245)

1. C
2. D
3. E
4. C
5. C
6. A

## Explanations for Game 5 (Pages 244–245)

**Diagram and inventory** This is a Group game with an "Out" column. The two panels form the core of the diagram, and the four friends are the elements. The goblins can be represented with capital letters: L, N, O, S; the elves can be represented with lowercase letters: a, c, d, f.

Clue 1: [dL antiblock] We can use an antiblock because there is room for only one in the "Out" column.

Clue 2: [dO antiblock] Again, room for only one in the "Out" column.

Clue 3: a —> O; ~O —>~a

Clue 4: $f_2$ —> $L_1$; ~$L_1$ —> ~$f_2$

Clue 5: [SN antiblock]

**Deductions** Besides the antiblock [da antiblock], there are not many deductions to make here, but d is heavily restricted, and c is completely unrestricted. Test writers are probably hoping that you will take the two conditional clues as a block and an antiblock, so it is useful to notice that they allow for f and L to be together on panel 1, and for O to exist without a when a is Out. Noticing this may lead you to one more deduction: O cannot be Out.

Here is the diagram.

| G: LNOS<br>e: acdf | Panel 1 | Panel 2 | Out ~O |
|---|---|---|---|
| 3. | d _ _ _<br>~L, ~O, ~a | O _ _ | _ |
| 4. | ~~LcNS~~ | ~~fOa~~ | ~~d~~ |
| 6. | a L O | d | N |
| 6. | d c f s | a L O | N |

**Questions** We'll work the Grab-a-Rule question first, followed by the Specific questions on a first pass, and then finish the second pass off with the General question from this game.

1. C Grab-a-Rule

   Clue 1 eliminates choice (E); Clue 2 eliminates choice (B); Clue 3 eliminates choice (D); Clue 4 eliminates choice (A).

3. E Specific

   Look for what must be false. Place d in panel 1. This rules L, O, and a out of Panel 1. Thus, (E) must be false.

4. C Specific

   If f and O are in the same group, they must be in either panel 1 or panel 2. Try f and O in panel 2, since it is smaller, and therefore more restricted. Now L will be on panel 1, by Clue 4. Since O is on panel 2 and L is on panel 1, d must be Out. Thus, a must be on panel 2 with O, and c, N, and S will be on panel 1. But this violates Clue 5. So f and O cannot be together on panel 2. Thus, they must be on panel 1 if they are together.

6. A Specific

   N is Out, which means that the highly restricted element, d, must be In. Since d cannot be with a, L, or O, these three must be together, regardless of whether d is on panel 1 or panel 2.

2. D General

   If O were not included in either panel, then a could not be included either, so we would need room for two elements in the Out column. This was one of the deductions.

5. C General

   Look for the pair that cannot be together on panel 2. Use your work from question 4: f and O cannot be together on panel 2, so f and a cannot be together on panel 2 either, since this would force f and O to be together.

# CHAPTER 4: READING COMPREHENSION

## Answers for Passage 1 (Pages 286–287)

1. B
2. B
3. D
4. E
5. C
6. C
7. B

## Explanations for Passage 1 (Pages 286–287)

### Prepare

The main point of this natural science passage is that recent theories advanced to explain Earth's ice ages have ominous things to say about the possible consequences of human industrial use of fossil fuels. The first paragraph describes why understanding ice ages may be important to studying the effects of global warming and human roles in causing it. The second paragraph describes the complexity of the climate system, outlining the many factors that are involved. The third paragraph indicates the regularity of past climate change and introduces the Milankovitch hypothesis, which says that changes in Earth's orbit are responsible for these changes. The fourth paragraph indicates why most believe that the Milankovitch hypothesis is incomplete, and it says that currently accepted theories emphasize the role that atmospheric carbon dioxide plays in climate change. The last paragraph ties these theories to the likely effect of fossil fuels, pointing out that decreases in carbon dioxide have led in the past to severe changes, and that this may mean that increases of similar size may have similarly drastic effects. The logical purpose of the passage as a whole is to *Tell a Story.*

### Questions

Although you might have chosen to leave some of these questions for a second pass, here we address them in the order in which they appear.

1. **B** Big Picture: Primary Purpose. The passage describes scientific efforts to understand ice ages and possible consequences of this work for the question of global warming.

   Eliminate (A) because it concerns the prediction of when the next ice age will arrive, which is not a purpose of the passage.

Eliminate (C) because it focuses too narrowly on the Milankovitch hypothesis and its potential alternatives.

Eliminate (D) because it focuses too narrowly on global warming; it needs to mention something relating to ice ages. Furthermore, the purpose of the passage as a whole is to consider theories about climate change.

Eliminate (E) because it focuses on what evidence there is for past ice ages, which isn't really even mentioned in the passage.

Choice (B) is the best answer here because it includes both ice ages and global warming and properly describes the passage's association between them.

2. B Big Picture: Main Idea. Efforts to understand the occurrence of ice ages have led to theories with ominous implications for the human use of fossil fuels and the current problem of global warming.

Eliminate (A) because it focuses completely on the question of which theory to explain ice ages is right without any mention at all of their implications for the global warming issue.

Eliminate (C) because it focuses completely on Milankovitch's theory and brings in the question of preventing the next ice age, which is not mentioned in the passage at all.

Eliminate (D) because it characterizes concern about fossil fuel use as "exaggerated," which is not consistent with the passage material.

Eliminate (E) because it focuses too narrowly on the factors affecting climate change and has nothing to do with fossil fuels or global warming.

Choice (B) is worded a little oddly, but it works. The passage indicates that "shifts in carbon distribution" involve changes to the atmosphere's carbon dioxide levels, and although this choice doesn't mention ice ages by name, it does talk about "past climate change," which is a decent paraphrase. Its focus on what this scientific work means for global warming and fossil fuel use makes it the best of the choices we have.

3. D Reasoning. Strengthen the statement that "Earth's climate is a dynamic system influenced by many interrelated factors." We want a choice that illustrates this idea.

Eliminate (A) because it identifies one primary factor rather than the dynamic and interrelated operation of factors.

Eliminate (B) because it is not consistent with the claim. Being "random" isn't the same as being "dynamic."

Eliminate (C) because it is far off the reference. This doesn't seem to lend any support to the dynamic, interrelated nature of the climate.

Eliminate (E) because, although it does talk about interrelated factors, it isn't clear what real "influence" this describes. It seems to be saying that volcanic activity is basically a nonissue for climate, with competing factors canceling one another out. If anything, this would be evidence against the claim that volcanic activity changes climate at all.

Choice (D) is the best of this group. It describes an interrelationship of snowfall, solar radiation, and temperature that shows how these factors work on one another to influence climate.

4. E Extract: Retrieval. Which specific thing do the theories focusing on carbon dioxide most directly explain? A search of the passage really turns up only one key piece of evidence in favor of these theories: the chemical weathering that led to the unusual severity of the last ice age.

Eliminate (A). This one has to do with the Milankovitch hypothesis.

Eliminate (B). This feature is more explicitly tied to the Milankovitch hypothesis, and we aren't told how the carbon dioxide theories explain it.

Eliminate (C). Although this is mentioned in connection with the chemical weathering argument, this is something the carbon dioxide theories use, not something they purport to explain.

Eliminate (D). Like (C), this may be a cause taken into account in the carbon dioxide theories, but it isn't something those theories attempt to explain.

Choice (E) is the best answer here. It comes pretty directly from the last paragraph of the passage.

5. **C** Reasoning. Weaken the Milankovitch hypothesis. Milankovitch is the one who said that changes in Earth's orbit lead to changes in the amount of solar radiation Earth receives, which in turn leads to climate change. We're looking for something that works against that cause-and-effect chain.

   Eliminate (A). The Milankovitch hypothesis does not attempt to explain the rotation of hot spots in Earth's interior; that's an alternative hypothesis that has been advanced to explain climate change.

   Eliminate (B). Although this has to do with carbon dioxide, if anything it strengthens the Milankovitch theory against the carbon dioxide theories by showing that orbit variations are ultimately responsible for changes in Earth's atmospheric carbon dioxide.

   Eliminate (D). The Milankovitch hypothesis doesn't purport to explain the length of interglacial periods, as far as we know.

   Eliminate (E). This would definitely help the Milankovitch hypothesis, rather than weaken it.

   Choice (C) is the best answer here. If some of the changes that the hypothesis attributes to orbital variations started before the orbital variations took place, this would definitely call the causal role of orbital variations into question.

6. **C** Extract: Inference. Which can influence atmospheric carbon dioxide levels? We'll need to search for each of these; we'll be able to tie four of them to carbon dioxide levels. The fifth is our answer.

   There is passage support for (A). In the last paragraph, "chemical weathering during the uplift of the Himalayan massif" is associated with decreases in carbon dioxide levels in the atmosphere.

   There is passage support for (B). In the second paragraph, volcanic activity is described as playing a "major" role in "the planet's...carbon cycle." It takes a step of reasoning, but because the distribution of carbon "between Earth's crust... [and] its atmosphere" is treated as being intimately related to atmospheric carbon dioxide levels, this is a warranted paraphrase of passage material.

   There is passage support for (D). Because humans are organisms on Earth's surface, the increase in carbon dioxide levels caused by burning fossil fuels definitely qualifies.

   There is passage support for (E). Like volcanic activity, global precipitation is identified as being involved in the "carbon cycle," which evidently involves atmospheric carbon dioxide somewhere along the way.

   Choice (C) is the only one that can't be even remotely related to carbon dioxide. Sunspots are mentioned in connection with alternative theories to explain climate change.

7. **B** Structure: Organization. We want something that corresponds as closely as possible to our paragraph-by-paragraph summary of the passage.

   Eliminate (A). This passage is not concerned with defending a single hypothesis.

   Eliminate (C). You might say that the passage rejects the Milankovitch hypothesis (although it isn't a wholesale rejection), but it's difficult to see the entire passage as rejecting a claim about that hypothesis. The passage really is more interested in the carbon dioxide hypothesis, for which it seems to have at least some sympathy.

   Eliminate (D). The passage doesn't really reconcile the various theories mentioned.

   Eliminate (E). None of the information presented in the passage is described as new.

   Choice (B) is the best answer; it follows the progression of the major topics. It is also the only choice that includes "future implications," which is a crucial issue in this passage.

## Answers for Passage 2 (Pages 288–289)

1. A
2. D
3. C
4. D
5. B
6. A
7. D

## Explanations for Passage 2 (Pages 288–289)

### Prepare

The main point of this humanities passage is that the poetry of English writer Richard Crashaw provides a particularly useful example both of the interests and conflicts of the time in which he wrote and of the routine misunderstandings of that period by traditional scholarship. The first paragraph introduces Crashaw in comparison to the better-known poets of his period and indicates how tense those times were, and it also suggests why scholars have paid more attention to the other poets. The second paragraph describes what makes Crashaw's poetry and life unusual and points to serious shortcomings in traditional approaches to his poetry. The third paragraph indicates that these shortcomings are also present in traditional approaches to the more famous poets of the period and identifies what traditional scholars fail to understand about the period. The logical purpose of the passage is to criticize.

### Questions

Although you might have chosen to leave some of these questions for a second pass, here we address them in the order in which they appear.

1. A Extract: Inference. With which statement would the author agree? Whichever one we pick, we should be able to find passage support for it.

   Eliminate (B). Although both are identified as characteristics of the poetry of Donne and Herbert, no preference for one characteristic over the other is expressed. It would be too much of a stretch to say that the author's interest in the poetry as portraying human reason indicates a preference because the ideas of desire and religious orthodoxy are also identified as being very important to the poems.

   Eliminate (C). This is identified as the reason traditional scholarship prefers seventeenth-century poets such as Donne and Herbert, but this is not something with which the author agrees.

   Eliminate (D). For one thing, *mystical* is a word used by traditional scholars, not our author, to describe Crashaw's strange imagery; for another, we know nothing really about Crashaw's intentions.

Eliminate (E). This claim ties together two statements made in the passage about the historical period, and although they're both supported, we don't know that there's a causal link here.

Choice (A) is consistent with the author's viewpoint. The first paragraph indicates that traditional scholarship has focused on Donne's and Herbert's works because of the "placid historical gloss" and "settled sense of orthodoxy" they provide, placing too little emphasis on how they reflect their "turbulent times."

2. D Extract: Inference. What is true of Crashaw's poetry? Again, we're looking for the statement with the most direct passage support.

Eliminate (A). Although the author finds Crashaw's poetry interesting, it isn't clear that the author considers it "superior."

Eliminate (B). *Obsession* is too strong a word to be justified by the passage text.

Eliminate (C). Although Crashaw is identified as being a heretic by the standards of his day, there is no evidence that his intention in writing poetry was to convey heretical beliefs.

Eliminate (E). This is something that traditional scholars say about Crashaw, but it isn't clear that the author agrees with them that his poetry is "excessive."

Choice (D) is by far the safest answer here. This is a straight paraphrase of one of the passage's central claims.

3. C Extract: Inference. What does traditional scholarship fail to comprehend about poetry of the era? This is most likely a reference to the material in the final paragraph, in which the author claims that traditional scholars fail to emphasize properly the tension between desire and religion mediated by reason.

Eliminate (A), although it's tricky. The substance of the author's objection isn't that scholars fail to understand the link between the poetry and the times; it's that they misunderstand the nature of each of them.

Eliminate (B). The passage does seem to think that the poetry is noteworthy and somehow new, but to say it's a "radical departure" is almost certainly too strong a characterization of the passage's statements.

Eliminate (D). This is an overstatement of the passage's interest in Crashaw.

Eliminate (E). Although the passage does say that the ideas behind this poetry were political, to say that they were written as a form of protest is too strong an interpretation of that fact.

Choice (C) is the safest answer here. It mentions reason and religion, and outlines what the author seems to feel is the most serious shortcoming of traditional criticism.

4. D Structure: Function. Which is the best paraphrase of the meaning or purpose of the cited text in reference to Crashaw's poetry? This follows the passage's description of the poetry's "tortured" quality, and also seems to refer to the strange imagery mentioned later in the same paragraph.

Eliminate (A). Similarity between Crashaw and the other poets is not brought up until later, and certainly the phrase in question doesn't seek to highlight any such similarity.

Eliminate (B). This choice isn't completely awful, but because it uses the terms that are associated, in the passage, with the same critics the author thinks are misguided, we'd like to have something that's a bit closer to the author's own opinion here.

Eliminate (C). The negative connotations of "uneven and maladroit" are not consistent with the author's attitude toward Crashaw's poetry.

Eliminate (E). There is no statement here that the poetry was ever intended to confuse or distort.

Choice (D) is a safe answer. It seems a bit mild, given the text in question, but the purpose of this statement is to describe how Crashaw's poetry is different from the poetry usually referred to by traditional scholars.

5. **B** Structure: Organization. We'll use our paragraph-by-paragraph summary to pick the answer that most closely matches the passage.

Probably the clearest reason to eliminate (A) is its identification of an "assertion that these courses of action are unlikely to be taken seriously." No such statement is included in the passage.

Probably the clearest reason to eliminate (C) is its identification of the primary topic of this passage as a "historical era." The times are certainly crucial to the passage, but this downplays the poetry of the time far too much to be a good description of the passage.

Probably the clearest reason to eliminate (D) is similar to the one used above in (C). Again, this choice focuses on the time without giving proper emphasis to the poetry of that time.

Probably the clearest reason to eliminate (E) is its identification of an "assertion that both approaches must be used to ensure a complete understanding of all such cases." The passage argues vehemently against one of the approaches discussed in the passage.

Choice (B) is the closest answer to be found. It mentions the times, the poetry, and the scholarly treatment of it, and it generally matches the flow of the passage topic by topic.

6. **A** Extract: Inference. We need to find the meaning of the shackle image in the last paragraph. This is used as an example of an indication from Herbert's poetry that conventional readings of it as orthodox are a bit too reductive.

Eliminate (B) because the passage doesn't go so far as to say that Herbert's image is a political critique. It might conceivably be seen that way, but the passage doesn't actually say so.

Eliminate (C) because this reads a bit too much into the later statements into this particular image. It seems just as likely, if not more so, that the more properly applicable material from this later statement is desire, not reason.

Eliminate (D) because it relies on Herbert's "stated purpose," which is never mentioned in the passage, and because "inventive rhetoric" is attributed to Crashaw, but not directly to Herbert.

Eliminate (E) because it reads far too much into the text. These things are mentioned in the same paragraph as the cited text, but we can't say that the passage supports any statement this specific or elaborate about Herbert.

Choice (A) is a good answer because it is fairly nonspecific—a virtue because the meaning of the image in the passage is not explained very fully—and because it is consistent with the author's main point throughout the passage.

7. **D** Reasoning. Weaken the cited statement. The statement in question claims that the failure of traditional scholars to interpret some of the more provocative statements in Crashaw's poetry in ways that "seem patently obvious" is an example of critics letting their preconceived ideas distort their readings. We want something that indicates these readings might not be so bad.

Eliminate (A) because it seems to strengthen the passage statement, not weaken it. This is certainly a statement about the scholars in question with which the author would agree.

Eliminate (B) because it relates to statements made in the third paragraph, not here.

Eliminate (C) because it concerns Donne, not Crashaw. This isn't specifically focused on the statement cited in the question.

Eliminate (E) because it is primarily focused on Donne and Herbert, who aren't clearly related to the question.

Choice (D) is a good answer because it attacks the linchpin of the author's interpretation of these moments in Crashaw. Although the readings supported by the author are said to be "patently obvious," they might not be correct if their subversive character is attributable to changes in the language since Crashaw wrote his poetry.

## Answers for Passage 3 (Pages 290–291)

1. C
2. E
3. D
4. A
5. B
6. E
7. C

## Explanations for Passage 3 (Pages 290–291)

### Prepare

Passage A describes the prevailing model of American democracy as many groups struggling for power. The passage focuses on Robert Dahl, who provides the theoretical background for polyarchy as central to American democracy. Passage B centers on Anthony Downs, who shook up the intuitive group-centered model and created an economic model based on individual calculations. As a comparative reading set, the logical purpose of the passage is to compare/contrast.

### Questions

Although you might have chosen to leave some of these questions for a second pass, here we address them in the order in which they appear.

1. **C** Extract: Inference. Find something that Dahl says about American democracy.

   Eliminate (A). There is no mention of the concentration of power in Dahl's description of American democracy.

   Eliminate (B). This is Madison's view of American democracy, not Dahl's.

   Eliminate (D). Dahl doesn't say America is not a democracy; it may not be a true democracy as outlined in the passage, but it is still a democracy.

   Eliminate (E). This is not stated in the passage.

   (C) is the best choice. The passage states that Dahl begins his study of American democracy with a normative approach but then switches to a descriptive one.

2. **E** Reasoning. We need an analogy to Downs's reformulation. Passage B describes how Downs used Arrow's discovery of a mathematical theorem to recast the dominant theory of voting behavior.

Eliminate (A). This is similar to Dahl's approach.

Eliminate (B). This doesn't match because Downs didn't prove the theorem; Arrow did.

Eliminate (C). There is no evidence in the passage that Downs's theory was vindicated.

Eliminate (D). Downs did not work with anyone or create a new field.

(E) is the best choice. The astronomer proposes a new system after another researcher exposed a flaw in the previous view.

3. **D** Extract: Inference. Find an answer choice that describes a similarity between the two passages.

Eliminate (A). The first passage doesn't discard a theory.

Eliminate (B). This happens in passage B but not passage A.

Eliminate (C). The passages are about voting behavior.

Eliminate (E). Passage A does not do this.

Choice (D) is what we're looking for. Passage A references Madison and passage B references Arrow as a person who contributed to the development of the theories.

4. **A** Extract: Inference. Choose the answer choice that could describe the theoretical works referenced in both passages.

Eliminate (B). Recalibrate means to adjust measurements, which is not close to Downs's theory.

Eliminate (C). Downs's theory did not standardize anything.

Eliminate (D). Dahl's theory gave democracy a more accurate name.

Eliminate (E). Downs's theory is not one of accommodation.

Choice (A) is the best answer here. The first passage states that Dahl's view is an "articulation" that provides a "more accurate" definition of democracy. Downs demonstrated that "conventional wisdom" doesn't always hold true and was able to "refashion" theories of voting behavior.

5. **B** Extract: Retrieval. Find an answer choice that contains a statement made in passage B but not in passage A.

Eliminate (A). Passage A shows how a normative view of democracy doesn't match the real world.

Eliminate (C). No mention is made of specific consequences.

Eliminate (D). This is in passage A, not passage B.

Eliminate (E). Passage A explains why Madison wanted checks on power in the U.S. Constitution.

Choice (B) is the credited response. Passage B states that political science "borrowed heavily from sociology," which may explain why it used group-centered explanations.

6. E Extract: Inference. Find the answer choice that Dahl and Downs would disagree over.

   Eliminate (A). While this passage says Downs doesn't think groups are the key to voting behavior, it doesn't say that groups aren't important in other ways.

   Eliminate (B). Downs's view on this subject is not mentioned.

   Eliminate (C). Downs's view on this subject is not mentioned.

   Eliminate (D). It is unclear what Dahl thinks about this statement.

   Choice (E) is the correct response. Downs sees political behavior as an individualistic calculation while Dahl sees it as tied to group goals.

7. C Reasoning. This question is basically asking how Dahl might weaken Downs's theory. Remember that Dahl prefers a group-oriented view of political behavior while Downs contends individualistic concerns are paramount.

   Eliminate (A). Dahl is not concerned with economic theories.

   Eliminate (B). What Madison intended is not at issue.

   Eliminate (D). This is not addressed in the passages.

   Eliminate (E). This is not relevant to Downs's voting theory.

   Choice (C) is the best answer here. If this were the case, voting behavior would depend on group issues as Dahl suggests.

# Chapter 9
# The Princeton Review LSAT Practice Test 1

## ABOUT OUR PRINCETON REVIEW LSAT PRACTICE TESTS

If you can't get your hands on some actual LSATs, our practice tests are the next best thing. As we said in Chapter 1, you should practice on real LSATs. Don't be fooled by the sample questions in the other books, which are only superficially similar to actual LSAT questions.

We have constructed our practice test using the same sophisticated procedures and statistical methods used in creating actual LSATs. Thousands of Princeton Review students have taken these tests, so we know they are an excellent predictor of LSAT scores. They include the four sections that contribute to your LSAT score; we have spared you the trouble of taking the unscored experimental section and Writing Sample.

### How to Take These Tests

Be sure to review the chapters in this book before sitting down to take these tests. Clear some table space, turn off your phone and try to complete each test in one sitting. You may want to take a break after completing the first three sections. If possible, have a friend time you. Trust us: Timing yourself is not nearly the same experience as having someone else do it for you.

# SECTION I
Time—35 Minutes
24 Questions

Directions: Each group of questions in this section is based on a set of conditions. In answering some of the questions, it may be useful to draw a rough diagram. Choose the response that most accurately and completely answers each question and blacken the corresponding space on your answer sheet.

Questions 1–5

A veterinarian will be using four large animal cages for transport: Cage 1, Cage 2, Cage 3, and Cage 4. Each cage has an upper berth and a lower berth, and each berth will be occupied by exactly one animal, either male or female. The following rules govern assignment of animals to cage berths:

Exactly three berths will contain males.
The upper berths of Cages 1 and 2 will contain females.
If a cage has a male in one of its berths, it will carry a female in the other.
If a male is assigned to the lower berth of Cage 3, then the upper berth of Cage 4 will contain a male.

1. If a female is assigned to both berths of Cage 3, then which one of the following could be two other berths that also contain females?

(A) the upper berth of Cage 1 and the lower berth of Cage 2
(B) the lower berth of Cage 1 and the upper berth of Cage 4
(C) the lower berth of Cage 1 and the upper berth of Cage 2
(D) the upper berth of Cage 2 and the lower berth of Cage 4
(E) the lower berth of Cage 2 and the lower berth of Cage 4

GO ON TO THE NEXT PAGE.

2. It CANNOT be true that females are assigned to both

(A) the lower berth of Cage 1 and the lower berth of Cage 4
(B) the lower berth of Cage 1 and the lower berth of Cage 2
(C) the lower berth of Cage 1 and the upper berth of Cage 3
(D) the lower berth of Cage 2 and the lower berth of Cage 4
(E) the upper berth of Cage 3 and the lower berth of Cage 4

3. If the upper berth of Cage 4 contains a female, then a female must also be assigned to which one of the following berths?

(A) the lower berth of Cage 1
(B) the lower berth of Cage 4
(C) the lower berth of Cage 2
(D) the lower berth of Cage 3
(E) the upper berth of Cage 3

4. If a male is assigned to the lower berth of Cage 3, which one of the following is a complete and accurate list of the berths that CANNOT be assigned males?

(A) the upper berth of Cage 1, the upper berth of Cage 2
(B) the upper berth of Cage 1, the upper berth of Cage 2, the upper berth of Cage 3
(C) the upper berth of Cage 1, the upper berth of Cage 2, the lower berth of Cage 4
(D) the upper berth of Cage 1, the upper berth of Cage 2, the upper berth of Cage 3, the lower berth of Cage 4
(E) the upper berth of Cage 1, the lower berth of Cage 1, the upper berth of Cage 2, the upper berth of Cage 3, the lower berth of Cage 4

5. If the lower berth of Cage 2 contains a female, then it could be true that females are assigned to both

(A) the lower berth of Cage 1 and the upper berth of Cage 4
(B) the lower berth of Cage 1 and the lower berth of Cage 4
(C) the upper berth of Cage 3 and the upper berth of Cage 4
(D) the lower berth of Cage 3 and the lower berth of Cage 4
(E) the lower berth of Cage 3 and the upper berth of Cage 3

GO ON TO THE NEXT PAGE.

Questions 6–11

In a single day, exactly seven airplanes—J, K, L, M, N, P, and Q—are the only arrivals at an airport. No airplane arrives at the same time as any other plane, and no plane arrives more than once that day. Each airplane flies either a domestic flight or an international flight. The following conditions apply:

No two consecutive arrivals are international flights.
P arrives some time before both K and M.
Exactly two of the planes that arrive before P are international flights.
J is the sixth arrival.
Q arrives sometime before L.

6. Which one of the following could be the order, from first to last, in which the airplanes arrive?

(A) N, Q, L, P, M, J, K
(B) N, P, Q, L, M, J, K
(C) Q, M, L, K, P, J, N
(D) Q, L, K, P, M, J, N
(E) L, Q, P, K, J, M, N

GO ON TO THE NEXT PAGE.

7. For which one of the following pairs of airplanes is it the case that they CANNOT both be international flights?

(A) J and N
(B) K and J
(C) L and M
(D) M and K
(E) N and Q

8. If N is the third arrival, then which of the following airplanes must be a domestic flight?

(A) J
(B) K
(C) L
(D) M
(E) Q

9. If exactly three of the arrivals are domestic flights, then which one of the following airplanes must be a domestic flight?

(A) J
(B) K
(C) L
(D) M
(E) Q

10. For how many of the seven airplanes can one determine exactly how many airplanes arrived before it?

(A) 1
(B) 2
(C) 3
(D) 4
(E) 5

11. Which one of the following pairs of airplanes CANNOT arrive consecutively at the airport?

(A) L and P
(B) N and P
(C) P and K
(D) P and M
(E) P and Q

GO ON TO THE NEXT PAGE.

Questions 12–18

A total of six pieces of fruit are found in three small baskets: one in the first basket, two in the second basket, and three in the third basket. Two of the fruits are pears—one Bosc, the other Forelle. Two others are apples—one Cortland, one Dudley. The remaining two fruits are oranges—one navel, one Valencia. The fruits' placement is consistent with the following:

There is at least one orange in the same basket as the Bosc pear.

The apples are not in the same basket.

The navel orange is not in the same basket as either apple.

12. Which of the following could be an accurate matching of the baskets to the pieces of fruit in each of them?

(A) basket one: Forelle pear
basket two: Dudley apple, navel orange
basket three: Bosc pear, Cortland apple, Valencia orange

(B) basket one: Dudley apple
basket two: Bosc pear, navel orange
basket three: Forelle pear, Cortland apple, Valencia orange

(C) basket one: navel orange
basket two: Cortland apple, Bosc pear
basket three: Forelle pear, Dudley apple, Valencia orange

(D) basket one: Valencia orange
basket two: Cortland and Dudley apples
basket three: navel orange, Bosc and Forelle pears

(E) basket one: Valencia orange
basket two: Bosc pear, navel orange
basket three: Forelle pear, Cortland and Dudley apples

GO ON TO THE NEXT PAGE.

13. Which one of the following CANNOT be true?

(A) A pear is in the first basket.
(B) An apple is in the same basket as the Forelle pear.
(C) An orange is in the first basket.
(D) The oranges are in the same basket as each other.
(E) Neither apple is in the first basket.

14. Which one of the following must be true?

(A) An apple and a pear are in the second basket.
(B) An orange and a pear are in the second basket.
(C) At least one apple and at least one pear are in the third basket.
(D) At least one orange and at least one pear are in the third basket.
(E) At least one orange and at least one apple are in the third basket.

15. If both pears are in the same basket, which one of the following could be true?

(A) The Cortland apple is in the third basket.
(B) An orange is in the first basket.
(C) Both oranges are in the second basket.
(D) The Bosc pear is in the second basket.
(E) The Cortland apple is in the first basket.

16. Which one of the following must be true?

(A) An apple is in the first basket.
(B) No more than one orange is in each basket.
(C) The pears are not in the same basket.
(D) The Dudley apple is not in the same basket as the Valencia orange.
(E) The Valencia orange is not in the first basket.

17. If the Bosc pear is not in the third basket, which of the following could be true?

(A) The Cortland apple is in the second basket.
(B) The Forelle pear is in the second basket.
(C) The Dudley apple is in the third basket.
(D) The navel orange is in the third basket.
(E) The Valencia orange is in the second basket.

18. If the Forelle pear and the Cortland apple are in the same basket, which one of the following must be true?

(A) The Cortland apple is in the second basket.
(B) The Valencia orange is in the second basket.
(C) The Dudley apple is in the second basket.
(D) The Dudley apple is in the first basket.
(E) The Valencia orange is in the third basket.

GO ON TO THE NEXT PAGE.

Questions 19–24

A live radio show features five bands—the Foghorns, the Geriatrics, the Hollowmen, the Inkstains, and the Jarheads—that will sing ten songs. Each band performs exactly two of the songs: One band performs songs 1 and 6, one band performs songs 2 and 7, one band performs songs 3 and 8, one band performs songs 4 and 9, and one band performs songs 5 and 10. The following conditions apply:

Neither of the Geriatrics' songs is performed immediately before either of the Hollowmen's.

The Foghorns do not sing the ninth song.

The Jarheads' first song is after (but not necessarily immediately after) the Inkstains' first song.

At least one of the Foghorns' songs is immediately after one of the Jarheads' songs.

19. Which one of the following could be an accurate list of the bands performing the first five songs, in order from song 1 to song 5?

(A) Foghorns, Geriatrics, Inkstains, Hollowmen, Jarheads

(B) Geriatrics, Inkstains, Jarheads, Foghorns, Hollowmen

(C) Hollowmen, Inkstains, Foghorns, Geriatrics, Jarheads

(D) Jarheads, Geriatrics, Inkstains, Hollowmen, Foghorns

(E) Inkstains, Jarheads, Foghorns, Geriatrics, Hollowmen

GO ON TO THE NEXT PAGE.

20. If the Foghorns sing the eighth song, then for exactly how many of the ten songs can one determine which band sings the song?

(A) ten
(B) eight
(C) six
(D) four
(E) two

21. If the Jarheads sing the fourth song, then which one of the following could be true?

(A) The Foghorns sing song 1.
(B) The Foghorns sing song 3.
(C) The Geriatrics sing song 5.
(D) The Hollowmen sing song 3.
(E) The Inkstains sing song 5.

22. Which one of the following could be true?

(A) The Foghorns sing song 4.
(B) The Geriatrics sing song 5.
(C) The Hollowmen sing song 5.
(D) The Inkstains sing song 10.
(E) The Jarheads sing song 6.

23. The Foghorns CANNOT perform which one of the following songs?

(A) song 1
(B) song 2
(C) song 3
(D) song 6
(E) song 10

24. Which one of the following could be an accurate list of the bands performing the last five songs, in order from song 6 to song 10?

(A) Foghorns, Inkstains, Geriatrics, Jarheads, Hollowmen
(B) Geriatrics, Hollowmen, Inkstains, Jarheads, Foghorns
(C) Hollowmen, Geriatrics, Inkstains, Jarheads, Foghorns
(D) Inkstains, Geriatrics, Jarheads, Foghorns, Hollowmen
(E) Jarheads, Foghorns, Geriatrics, Inkstains, Hollowmen

# STOP

**IF YOU FINISH BEFORE TIME IS CALLED, YOU MAY CHECK YOUR WORK ON THIS SECTION ONLY. DO NOT WORK ON ANY OTHER SECTION IN THE TEST.**

## SECTION II
Time—35 Minutes
25 Questions

Directions: The questions in this section are based on the reasoning contained in brief statements or passages. For some questions, more than one of the choices could conceivably answer the question. However, you are to choose the best answer; that is, the response that most accurately and completely answers the question. You should not make assumptions that are by commonsense standards implausible, superfluous, or incompatible with the passage. After you have chosen the best answer, blacken the corresponding space on your answer sheet.

1. Educator: By itself, the expert advice delivered in a workshop setting does not cause a young writer to be able to craft short stories; rather, the repeated effort of writing new stories in the context of a short-story workshop can be a cause. When any individual writes many short stories, the quality of that person's stories inevitably increases. As a result, the new short-story workshops offered by this school will increase the quality of short stories written by its students.

The conclusion drawn by the educator follows logically if which one of the following is assumed?

(A) The new short-story workshops offered by the school will increase the number of its students who write a significant number of new short stories.
(B) The advice delivered by instructors in the new short-story workshops will be superior to the advice previously offered by writing teachers in the school.
(C) The new short-story workshops will be attended by a large number of the school's students.
(D) The introduction of writing workshops represents a new emphasis in the school curriculum.
(E) Any young writer, regardless of his or her ability to craft short stories, can improve through repeated efforts at writing.

2. Last year, the challenger in this election proposed a plan to solve the city's waste-disposal problems. Just recently, the incumbent proposed a plan that is nearly the same. The incumbent claims that he was not aware of the challenger's plan and that their similarities are due to the fact that the solution is merely a matter of common sense. Yet both plans involve similar increases in spending on recycling, both recommend the decommissioning of the same waste incinerators, and both rely on a system of so-called "green landfills," a revolutionary theory not employed by any other city in the world.

The main point of the argument is that

(A) the challenger's plan and the incumbent's plan have many similarities
(B) both plans have been advanced in an effort to attract the same large bloc of votes
(C) the incumbent's plan is similar to the challenger's in ways that suggest that this similarity is the product of more than coincidence
(D) the incumbent proposed his plan only after it was learned that the challenger's plan had wide popular support
(E) new plans that are introduced by political candidates sometimes take their opponents' plans into account

GO ON TO THE NEXT PAGE.

3. Kristen: Compared to a direct business tax cut, a personal income tax cut is a better way to stimulate our state's economy. A personal income tax cut would give residents greater in-pocket income. With this increase in income, individuals will be encouraged to start their own businesses. In addition, individuals will be more likely to spend more money at existing businesses.

Mark: A personal income tax cut is not the most effective way to help business. There is no guarantee that individuals will in fact start new businesses, and the additional income may be used to purchase products from a different state or even a different country.

Mark objects to Kristen's argument by

(A) suggesting that a personal income tax cut is no more important than a direct business tax cut
(B) claiming that Kristen has reached a premature conclusion based on an inadequate understanding of the consequences of a business tax cut
(C) demonstrating that the negative impact of a personal income tax outweighs the positive effects
(D) questioning Kristen's use of the ambiguous phrase "in-pocket income"
(E) indicating that the positive consequences that Kristen predicts may not occur

4. Concerned citizen: The county government's new ordinance limiting the types of materials that can be disposed of in trash fires violates our rights as citizens. The fact that local environmental damage results from the burning of certain inorganic materials is not the primary issue. The real concern is the government's flagrant disregard for the right of the individual to establish what is acceptable on his or her own property.

Which one of the following principles, if accepted, would justify the concerned citizen's conclusion?

(A) Legislative violation of an individual's right to privacy is not justifiable unless the actions of that individual put others at risk.
(B) The right of an individual to live in a safe environment takes precedence over the right of an individual to be exempt from legislative intrusion.
(C) An individual's personal rights supersede any right or responsibility the government may have to protect a community from harm.
(D) An individual has a moral obligation to act in the best interest of the community as a whole.
(E) A compromise must be found when the right of an individual to act independently conflicts with the responsibility of the government to provide protection for the local environment.

GO ON TO THE NEXT PAGE.

5. As part of a new commitment to customer satisfaction, an electronics company sent a survey to all customers who had purchased its electronic personal organizer in the previous month. The survey, which was sent through the mail, asked customers to give personal information and to rate their satisfaction with the product. Of customers who returned the survey, more indicated that they had a negative opinion of the product's performance than indicated a neutral or positive opinion. On the basis of these results, the company, hoping to increase customer satisfaction, decided to allocate a large amount of capital to redesigning the product.

Which one of the following, if true, indicates the most serious flaw in the method of research used by the company?

(A) The company relied on a numerical system of rating responses rather than on open-ended questions that allow for more detailed feedback.
(B) Customers who were dissatisfied with the information display of the organizer outnumbered customers who were dissatisfied with the variety of functions offered by the organizer.
(C) Studies show that customer dissatisfaction with a new product is highest during the first year of the product's release and gradually decreases over the following years.
(D) The marketing division has found that responses to their mail-in surveys are generally accurate.
(E) People who are satisfied with a product or have no strong opinion about it are less likely to be motivated to return a mail-in questionnaire.

6. Adolphus: The proposed system of computer control for the city's subway traffic, once it is implemented, will lead to greater on-time service and fewer accidents. We must secure whatever resources are required to implement the new system immediately.

Jean: The current financial state of the transit authority is such that the immediate implementation of the new system would require an increase in fares, which the public would not support. We should delay the implementation of the new system until the transit authority can set money aside for the transition and build support for it among riders.

Adolphus and Jean disagree with each other over whether

(A) the system of computer control will achieve its anticipated benefits
(B) the public would support higher fares to increase on-time service and reduce accidents
(C) it is possible to implement the proposed system of computer control quickly
(D) the proposed system of computer control could be implemented without increasing subway fares
(E) the existing system of control for the city's subways should be retained for some period of time

GO ON TO THE NEXT PAGE.

7. Because the consequences of an action intended to conserve the environment cannot be fully predicted, a wise principle is that such an action should be taken only when the likely consequence of inaction is less acceptable than any foreseeable negative consequence of the action.

Which one of the following provides the best illustration of the principle above?

(A) A system of canals is proposed to preserve threatened wetlands. Without the canals, the wetlands will vanish, so the objections of area farmers should not be allowed to prevent the canal system from being built.

(B) New roads are proposed to make it easier for conservationists to reach the areas inhabited by an endangered bird species. Because these same roads would increase the access of logging companies to these sensitive areas, the roads should not be built.

(C) A threatened moss thrives in a remote, uninhabited area that is not currently protected by law. Because the area is not important for either residential or industrial purposes, there is no possible negative consequence of passing a law to limit access to the area. Thus, such a law should be passed to protect the moss.

(D) A rare species of mink is found only in one area and has long been hunted for its fur. The proposal that all hunting be banned in the area, however, should not be implemented. Mule deer living in the same area contribute to destruction of the mink's habitat, and without hunting to limit the mule deer population, it is possible that the mink will die out completely.

(E) Tailings—the waste left over from mining—lead to severe water pollution in some mountain areas. Because most of the mining companies responsible for this pollution no longer exist, it is impossible to demand that they clean it up. Therefore, no matter how negatively taxpayers may react, taxes must be used to fund the cleanup of mine tailings.

8. Columnist: Our local public schools are desperately in need of community support, not just from tax revenues, but also from sources such as auxiliary fund-raisers and volunteer work. Although the mayor has often been seen participating in these activities and claims that the public schools are our community's most important assets, there is no reason to believe that his participation is sincere. After all, his own children attend a local private school instead of the public schools.

The columnist's reasoning is most vulnerable to criticism on the grounds that it presumes, without providing justification, that

(A) the mayor's participation in fund-raising activities for local public schools is motivated solely by a desire for positive public perception

(B) the mayor could lend greater support to the local public schools by having his children attend them

(C) the mayor sends his children to a local private school so that they will not contribute to the serious problems of overcrowding in the local public schools

(D) no politician can plausibly profess support for any public institution which the politician does not use

(E) there is no reason to believe that the mayor's support for the public schools is sincere if he has no direct personal interest in seeing their needs met

GO ON TO THE NEXT PAGE.

9. A recent study seems to suggest that, contrary to popular perception, vocational and technical programs do a better job of preparing their students for the workforce than traditional four-year colleges do. This study indicated that just below 60 percent of vocational and technical school graduates found full-time employment within two years of graduation, whereas only 50 percent of those who graduated from four-year colleges did. Nevertheless, the study's official conclusion was that four-year colleges are in fact better at preparing their students for the workforce than are vocational and technical programs.

Which one of the following, if true, most helps to resolve the apparent discrepancy between the study's findings and its official conclusion?

(A) Presidents and trustees of four-year colleges work to shape public perceptions of their institutions.
(B) The study investigated a wide variety of both four-year colleges and vocational and technical programs over a period of a decade.
(C) Most graduates of vocational and technical programs who find employment within two years of graduation work in the professions for which they were trained.
(D) Increased demand for health care workers, nearly all of whom attend schools that were classified by the study as vocational, caused the employment rate among graduates of these schools to exceed 90 percent.
(E) More than 20 percent of the graduates of four-year colleges go on to professional schools that require more than two years to complete but only admit graduates of four-year colleges, and the vast majority of these students find employment when they seek it.

10. Howard: Why is it that, in physics, the direction of electric field is defined as the direction in which a positive charge experiences force? Electrons, which are negatively charged, are the particles that move in electric current, yet by the standard definition, they move in a direction opposite to the electric field.

Linda: The standard definition was developed at a time when it was known that two types of charge existed, but not that only one of them was involved in the conduction of electric current. The definition of electric field, by chance, depends upon positive charge, which generally does not move in an electric circuit.

Howard: Your explanation cannot be correct. It has been known for some time now that electrons are the only charges involved in the conduction of current, yet the definition of electric field has remained unchanged.

Which one of the following additional items of information, if true, could best be used by Linda to counter Howard's objection to her explanation?

(A) Subsequent development of physical theories related to electricity led to the wide adoption of the standard definition before its shortcomings were known, and to change it now would cause widespread confusion.
(B) Theories of magnetism, which is related to electricity, also incorporate standard definitions that take the behavior of positive charge as their bases.
(C) Students who learn the theory of electricity may initially be frustrated by its conventional dependence on the behavior of positive charge, but it does not prevent students from comprehending and correctly using that theory.
(D) There exist presentations of the theory of electricity that base their definitions around the behavior of negative charge, but anyone learning physics according to these presentations must be aware of the standard definitions in order to interpret the scientific literature surrounding electricity correctly.
(E) The choice of either positive charge or negative charge as the basis for standard definitions in the physical theory of electricity is arbitrary, and has no effect on the accuracy or completeness of the results of that theory.

GO ON TO THE NEXT PAGE.

11. Once, dieticians advocated radically reducing the proportion of total dietary calories from fat and increasing the proportion from carbohydrates as a method of aiding weight loss. One result of this advice has been an increased incidence of diabetes. Now, dieticians advocate radically reducing the proportion of dietary calories from carbohydrate and increasing the proportion from proteins and fat as a method of aiding weight loss. There is already evidence that this advice is leading to an increase in the incidence of heart disease and certain kinds of cancer. There can be little doubt that, whatever dieticians may recommend, radical changes to diet made for the purpose of losing weight do not contribute to overall health.

The reasoning in the argument is flawed because the argument

(A) takes for granted that the only possible reason for making radical dietary changes is to increase overall health
(B) takes for granted that diabetes is a less serious condition for those who suffer from it than is heart disease or cancer
(C) fails to consider the role of exercise in conjunction with dietary changes as an important factor in successful weight loss
(D) ignores the possibility that, even without advice from dieticians, many people who do not change their eating habits will develop serious health problems
(E) fails to consider that a radical reduction in calories consumed from all dietary sources may lead both to weight loss and to improved overall health

12. Dentist: Many children today eat so much sugary processed food that tooth decay has become a more serious problem than ever. Periodic brushing can protect children's teeth only if they also receive regular twice-yearly professional cleanings. Hence, the dental reimbursement plans offered by most companies are inadequate to protect the dental health of at least some children.

Which one of the following is an assumption required by the dentist's argument?

(A) In the past, children did not require twice-yearly professional cleanings to protect their teeth from decay.
(B) Some dental reimbursement plans offered by companies are adequate to protect the dental health of children who do not consume sugary processed food.
(C) No single dental reimbursement plan suits the dental health needs of all families.
(D) The dental reimbursement plans offered by some companies do not provide for regular twice-yearly professional cleanings for children.
(E) Children now are more likely than ever before to experience serious problems as the result of tooth decay.

GO ON TO THE NEXT PAGE.

13. Recent media coverage indicates that the incidence of malfeasance and fraud among securities traders has increased over the past decade. Economists believe that this is due to changes in how securities traders are compensated. Whereas ten years ago most traders were paid only a fixed percentage of the value of each transaction, now virtually all of them also receive commissions on the basis of profit generated for their employers.

Which one of the following statements is most strongly supported by the information above?

(A) An increased incentive for trader malfeasance is associated with payment based on a fixed percentage of each transaction.
(B) A decreased risk of trader fraud is associated with paying traders an increased percentage of each transaction.
(C) A decreased propensity for malfeasance and fraud is caused by changes in trader compensation that place greater emphasis on making profit for their employers.
(D) Fraud by a securities trader may lead to an increased profit-related commission that more than offsets any loss in compensation associated with the decreased value of that transaction.
(E) Fraud and malfeasance would no longer be a problem if traders were compensated solely on the basis of the value of each trader's transactions.

14. A study of former college athletes revealed that, as a group, they are five times less likely to die before the age of fifty than are members of the population at large. The advice to derive from this is clear: Colleges should vastly expand their athletic departments so as to allow a greater proportion of all students to participate in athletics, thereby increasing the overall life expectancy of their student population.

Which one of the following, if true, most seriously weakens the argument above?

(A) Because participation in college athletics requires tremendous academic discipline, college athletes are better suited to succeed in society than are students who do not participate in college athletics.
(B) The students who voluntarily compete in college athletics are more predisposed to good health than are those who do not.
(C) Few colleges have the resources to increase spending on athletics, a nonessential university program.
(D) People who become active after leading sedentary lives can remarkably decrease their chances of contracting heart disease.
(E) Women, whose average life expectancies exceed men's by seven years, have traditionally had fewer opportunities to participate in college athletics than have men.

GO ON TO THE NEXT PAGE.

Questions 15–16

To determine the suitability of candidates for this position, the human resources director evaluates each candidate's advantages; job candidates with greater advantages are more likely to be offered the position. Factors such as work experience and relevant job skills are important in these evaluations, yet age should also be an important consideration. Younger candidates demand lower salaries and are less likely to have family obligations that would interfere with job responsibilities.

15. Which one of the following, if true, most undermines the argument?

(A) Younger workers are more likely to miss work due to social activities than they are to miss work due to family obligations.
(B) Younger workers are more likely to change jobs or quit on short notice if they do not like a new job than are older workers.
(C) Younger workers are more likely to be willing to work long hours and travel frequently than are older workers.
(D) Older workers are more likely to insist on regular working hours and reasonable compensation than are younger workers.
(E) Older workers without family obligations are more similar to younger workers in their professional behavior and expectations than they are to older workers with family obligations.

16. The claim that age should be an important consideration in evaluating job candidates plays which one of the following roles in the argument?

(A) a premise of the argument
(B) the conclusion of the argument
(C) support offered for one of the argument's premises
(D) a consideration that potentially calls the argument's conclusion into question
(E) an explanation of circumstances under which the argument's conclusion is true

17. An airline representative announced the introduction of a new pricing system that uses sophisticated computer technology. Based on up-to-the-minute information on sales, the system identifies and continually updates peak times of high demand and off-peak times of low demand, keeping prices high when demand is high and lowering prices to attract customers when demand is low. As a result, the airline anticipates that large numbers of customers will choose to travel off-peak to experience savings, whereas those who wish to travel at peak times will enjoy greater availability due to higher prices. The airline therefore anticipates that the majority of customers will experience significant benefits as a result of the new system.

Which one of the following indicates an error in the reasoning on the part of the airline?

(A) The airline's conclusion is based on an unproven premise.
(B) The airline displays a naive trust in the possibilities of technology.
(C) The airline fails to factor in the cost of implementing the new system.
(D) The airline's conclusion rests on a result that would potentially cancel out the anticipated benefit.
(E) The airline fails to establish the exact number of customers who would benefit from the change.

GO ON TO THE NEXT PAGE.

18. A physicist theorized that the present distribution of matter in the universe was largely determined by random clumping of primeval particles during the early stages of the universe's formation. When computer simulations developed by the physicist showed that several different clumping patterns led to substantially similar distributions of matter, the physicist did not report the results. A journalist who learned about the results of the simulations reported them and accused the physicist of suppressing experimental findings that contradict her theory. The physicist countered that the computer simulations were inconclusive because they depended in part upon present theories of the universe's formation.

Which one of the following, if true, most strengthens the physicist's counterargument?

(A) Other experiments conducted by the physicist showed that clumping of primeval particles could influence the later distribution of matter in the universe.
(B) The clumping patterns used by the physicist in the computer simulation were not randomly generated.
(C) Present theories of the universe's formation include principles that allow only slight variations in the distribution of matter.
(D) Every computer simulation yet devised to model the formation of the universe depends to some degree upon present theories of the universe's formation.
(E) It is impossible to determine the theoretical accuracy of the assumptions used in developing any computer simulation of the universe's formation.

19. Scholar: Only those who can tell the difference between right and wrong should be held responsible for their wrong actions. It is for this reason that defendants who have serious developmental disabilities or mental illnesses cannot be held responsible for their crimes. However, many children are able to tell the difference between right and wrong and yet are not held responsible for their crimes. Therefore, ______.

Which one of the following most logically completes the last sentence of the scholar's argument?

(A) it is the ability of the parent or parents to tell the difference between right and wrong that is most relevant to determining responsibility when a child is accused of a crime
(B) not all those who are held responsible for a wrong action can tell the difference between right and wrong
(C) it cannot be true that the ability to distinguish between right and wrong is sufficient to hold a defendant responsible for his or her criminal actions
(D) it is unjust for children, or for those who have serious developmental disabilities or mental illnesses, to be found guilty of any crime
(E) only those who can be held responsible for their criminal actions are able to tell the difference between right and wrong

GO ON TO THE NEXT PAGE.

20. Statistics show that there is a direct correlation between the ammonia content and the cleaning power of industrial-strength floor and tile cleaners; simply stated, the more ammonia, the better the cleaner. However, in a nationwide survey of commercial food services, cleaning supervisors uniformly replied that for any floor and tile cleaner to be effective, it must be used on a given surface twice a day with the right proportion of cleaner to water, and must be applied with well-maintained mops. The survey thus proves that ammonia content is not relevant to the efficacy of floor and tile cleaners after all.

Which one of the following best identifies the flawed reasoning in the passage above?

(A) There is no reason to assume that effective floor and tile cleaning is the only use for floor and tile cleaner.
(B) It cannot be assumed that industrial-strength floor and tile cleaners contain comparable levels of ammonia.
(C) It is unreasonable to conclude that the ammonia content is not relevant to a cleaner's efficacy just because there are requirements for the proper use of industrial-strength floor and tile cleaners.
(D) It cannot be assumed that the efficacy of all industrial-strength floor and tile cleaners depends on the same procedures for use.
(E) It is unreasonable to assume that the makers of industrial-strength floor and tile cleaners are unaware that food services don't always use them properly.

21. Products containing naproxen sodium produce relief from pain and fever by blocking prostaglandins. As a consequence of recent technological advances, production costs for pain and fever medications containing naproxen sodium, allowing for both packaging and marketing costs, are one-fifth of what they were ten years ago, while the corresponding cost for medications using the ingredient ibuprofen, which is produced by different means, has increased. Therefore, naproxen sodium is a less costly ingredient to use in medication for the prevention of pain and fever relief than ibuprofen.

The conclusion of the argument is properly drawn if which one of the following is assumed?

(A) The cost of producing pain and fever medication containing ibuprofen has increased over the past ten years.
(B) Ten years ago, ibuprofen was used more than five times as often as naproxen sodium.
(C) None of the recent technological advances in producing pain and fever medication with naproxen sodium can be applied to the production of medication using ibuprofen.
(D) Ten years ago, the cost of producing pain and fever medication with the ingredient naproxen sodium was less than five times the cost of producing medications with ibuprofen.
(E) The cost of producing pain and fever medication with naproxen sodium is expected to decrease further, while the cost of producing similar medications using ibuprofen is not expected to decrease.

GO ON TO THE NEXT PAGE.

22. Some critics of Western medicine blame medical schools for encouraging doctors to treat sick people as defective machines rather than as feeling humans. These critics believe that if medical schools dedicate a greater portion of their curriculum to teaching compassion and medical ethics, the overall quality of medical treatment will improve. But if doctors are trained to identify with their patients too strongly, they may be reluctant to recommend courses of treatment that, although painful, are necessary to maximize the patients' chances of recovery.

The critics' reasoning provides grounds for accepting which one of the following statements?

(A) It is easier for a doctor to recommend painful chemotherapy to a cancer patient when that doctor has an understanding of his or her ethical responsibilities to the patient.
(B) It is more difficult to know what course of treatment is appropriate for a patient with a liver disorder if a doctor does not identify with that patient as a defective machine.
(C) It is easier for a doctor to recommend a transplant for a patient who is experiencing kidney failure if the doctor feels sympathy for the difficulty that patient will experience in recovering from surgery.
(D) It is easier for a doctor who feels compassion for a patient experiencing chronic pain to treat that patient effectively, particularly when the chronic pain does not seem to be caused by any known medical disorder.
(E) It is easier for doctors to think of their patients as defective machines than it is to think of them as feeling humans.

23. Increasing the starting pay for our sales agents will allow us to attract and hire more new sales agents next year; unfortunately, such an increase would anger experienced sales agents, causing more of them to quit next year. The increase in new hires we would be able to attract at the higher pay rate does not exceed the increase in the number of experienced sales agents who would quit, so increasing the starting pay of our sales agents will not increase the overall number of sales agents we employ.

The reasoning in the argument above most closely parallels that in which one of the following?

(A) Building a dam on this river would decrease the incidence of flooding in the lowlands downstream, but a dam would destroy the river's natural beauty. Tourism is an important component of the area's economy, so the building of a dam on this river is not justified.
(B) Spending additional money on safety training would result in greatly increased costs for our manufacturing operation; because accidents in our manufacturing operation cost more on an annual basis than the increased costs associated with better safety training, improving that training will increase company profits.
(C) Increasing the speed of our assembly line will increase the rate at which goods are produced; at the same time, an increase in the speed of our assembly line will increase the rate of defects. The number of additional losses due to defects will be greater than the number of additional goods produced by the assembly line, so increasing the speed of our assembly line will not increase the number of finished goods we produce.
(D) A new interstate highway will allow travelers to bypass the downtown area, leading to an increase in the rate at which travelers pass through our city; the increased rate of travel will encourage travelers to select routes passing through our city, leading to an increase in patronage of local businesses outside downtown. Therefore, we should build a new interstate highway.
(E) An earlier harvest will allow our tomatoes to reach market shelves more quickly, and will also decrease the number of our tomatoes that spoil before they are sold. However, an earlier harvest will lead to unripe tomatoes being put on market shelves. Because an unripe tomato can be safely eaten, whereas a spoiled tomato cannot, an earlier harvest will make our tomatoes safer for consumers.

GO ON TO THE NEXT PAGE.

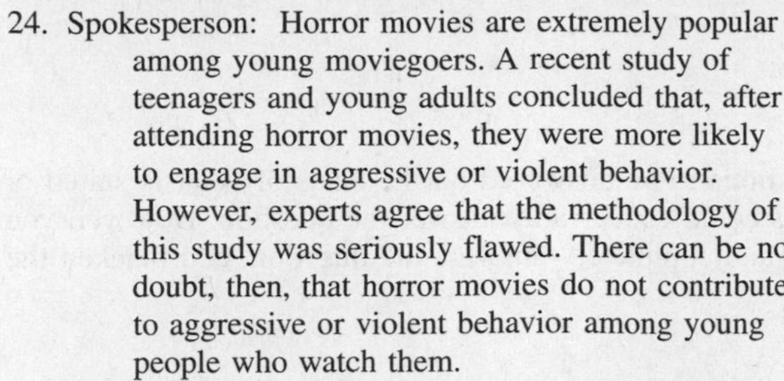

24. Spokesperson: Horror movies are extremely popular among young moviegoers. A recent study of teenagers and young adults concluded that, after attending horror movies, they were more likely to engage in aggressive or violent behavior. However, experts agree that the methodology of this study was seriously flawed. There can be no doubt, then, that horror movies do not contribute to aggressive or violent behavior among young people who watch them.

The reasoning in the spokesperson's argument is flawed because that argument

(A) takes one failure to prove a contention as confirmation of the falsity of that contention
(B) treats the occurrence of one event preceding a change in behavior as sufficient proof that the event contributed to causing the change in behavior
(C) accepts the judgment of experts as definitive proof of a contention when evidence suggests that the contention is untrue
(D) fails to consider the possibility that a lack of proof for one contention may constitute proof requiring the acceptance of some other contention
(E) neglects to specify that those conducting the study did not have an ulterior motive in reaching the study's erroneous conclusions

25. Those who read a book without having been exposed to any reviews of it are more likely to say they enjoyed the book than they are to say that they did not. Yet when readers who previously claimed to enjoy a book are exposed to several negative reviews of it and then are asked whether they would read the book again, a majority of them say they would not. Thus, exposure to reviews about a book may cause readers to change their opinions of that book.

Which one of the following is an assumption required by the argument?

(A) Readers with favorable opinions of a book they have read are not unlikely to say they would read that book again.
(B) Exposure to reviews of a book they have previously read causes readers to notice flaws in the book that they did not notice on a first reading.
(C) Readers are not more likely to enjoy reading a book they have purchased than they are to enjoy reading a book they have borrowed from a library or a friend.
(D) Readers who claim to have enjoyed a book and are subsequently exposed to positive reviews of it are also likely to say they will not read the book again.
(E) Whether a book receives positive or negative reviews is an accurate reflection of that book's quality.

# STOP

IF YOU FINISH BEFORE TIME IS CALLED, YOU MAY CHECK YOUR WORK ON THIS SECTION ONLY. DO NOT WORK ON ANY OTHER SECTION IN THE TEST.

## SECTION III

Time—35 minutes
27 Questions

Directions: Each passage in this section is followed by a group of questions to be answered on the basis of what is stated or implied in the passage. For some questions, more than one of the choices could conceivably answer the question. However, you are to choose the best answer, that is, the response that most accurately and completely answers the question, and blacken the corresponding space on your answer sheet.

Questions 1–5 are based on the following passage:

One of the most prolific authors of all time, Isaac Asimov was influential both in science fiction and in the popularization of science during the twentieth century, but he is also justly famous for the scope of his interests. Although the common claim that Asimov is the only author to have written a book in every category of the Dewey decimal system is untrue, its spirit provides an accurate picture of the man: a dedicated humanist who lauded the far-reaching power of reason. His most famous work, the *Foundation* trilogy, can be read as an illustration of Asimov's belief in reason and science, but even while he expressed that belief, science itself was calling it into question.

*Foundation* describes a time in which a vast empire spanning the galaxy is on the verge of collapse. Its inevitable doom is a consequence not of its size, but of the shortsightedness of its leaders. In this environment, a scientist named Hari Seldon devises an all-encompassing plan to help human civilization recover from the trauma of the empire's coming collapse. Using mathematics, Seldon is able to predict the future course of history for thousands of years, and he takes steps that are geared toward guiding that future in a beneficial direction. The trope of the benevolent and paternalistic scientist shaping existence from behind the scenes, present in much of Asimov's fiction, is never more explicit than in the *Foundation* series, which describes with an epic sweep the course and progress of the Seldon Plan.

As naïve and, perhaps, self-serving as the conceit of *Foundation* may seem to contemporary readers, it retains to some degree its ability to comfort by offering an antidote to the complex and unpredictable nature of experience. Science in Asimov's time was, in popular conceptions, engaged in just this pursuit: discerning immutable laws that operate beneath a surface appearance of contingency, inexplicability, and change. But even while Asimov wrote, science itself was changing. In physics, the study of matter at the subatomic level showed that indeterminacy was not a transitory difficulty to be overcome, but an essential physical principle. In biology, the sense of evolution as a steady progress toward better-adapted forms was being disturbed by proof of a past large-scale evolution taking place in brief explosions of frantic change. At the time of Asimov's death, even mathematics was gaining popular notice for its interest in chaos and inexplicability. Usually summarized in terms of the so-called "butterfly effect," chaos theory showed that perfect prediction could take place only on the basis of perfect information, which was by nature impossible to obtain. Science had dispensed with the very assumptions that motivated Asimov's idealization of it in the Seldon Plan. Indeed, it was possible to see chaos at work in *Foundation* itself: As sequels multiplied and began to be tied into narrative threads from Asimov's other novels, the urge to weave one grand narrative spawned myriad internal inconsistencies that were never resolved.

GO ON TO THE NEXT PAGE.

1. Which one of the following most accurately expresses the main point of the passage?

(A) Isaac Asimov's greatest work, the *Foundation* trilogy, is an expression of the common trope of the benevolent and paternalistic scientist.
(B) Popularizations of science are always to some degree dependent on idealizations and simplifications of that science, as Isaac Asimov's work demonstrates.
(C) The impossibility of the conceit on which Isaac Asimov's *Foundation* trilogy is based demonstrates that Asimov's fiction was based on imperfect understandings of science.
(D) The central figure of Hari Seldon in Isaac Asimov's *Foundation* trilogy is a manifestation of humanism's idealization of reason and science.
(E) Isaac Asimov's idealization of science as revealed in his *Foundation* series was called into question by the science of his time, which was increasingly focused on chaos and indeterminacy.

2. Which one of the following statements most accurately expresses the purpose of the final paragraph?

(A) The ultimate failure of the *Foundation* series as a coherent scientific narrative is discussed.
(B) A claim is made about the purpose of Asimov's writing and then is finally rejected.
(C) A key theme of Asimov's *Foundation* series is described and discoveries in science that seem contrary to that theme are outlined.
(D) The history of science is used to demonstrate the falsity of a widely believed claim about the power of human reason.
(E) The works of Asimov are used as evidence against a popular belief that Asimov encouraged but may not have personally held.

3. The author's reference to a common claim made about Isaac Asimov (lines 5–8) serves to

(A) demonstrate that many untrue beliefs are held about him
(B) illustrate the broad scope of his interests and writings
(C) undermine the claim that he was a prolific writer
(D) substantiate his belief in the power of human reason
(E) indicate that he was interested only in science

4. With respect to the Seldon Plan, the author's attitude can most properly be described as

(A) amused at the naïve conception of history it implies
(B) uncertain of the practical impossibility of its application
(C) ambivalent because of the reliance on human reason it requires
(D) convinced that it illustrates Asimov's attitude toward science
(E) confident that continued scientific progress will make it practicable

5. Which one of the following statements best illustrates the "butterfly effect" as it is described in the passage's third paragraph?

(A) A system implemented to predict the weather worldwide for the next century is soon found to be inaccurate because it was supplied with incomplete data.
(B) Efforts to predict the result of a nuclear reaction fail because of indeterminacy inherent in the behavior of subatomic particles.
(C) The fossil record indicates that certain adaptations found in many organisms appeared soon after a past catastrophic event.
(D) Scientific predictions about the future course of human history are found to be reasonably accurate once existing social theories are reconciled.
(E) A map that is less detailed than the area it represents is found not to include all the important features of that area.

GO ON TO THE NEXT PAGE.

Questions 6–12 are based on the following passage:

Renowned for its canals and rich history, the Italian city of Venice is most famous for the singular peril it faces: The city is sinking. Situated in a lagoon, in the midst of a marsh bordering on the Adriatic Sea, Venice remained a capital of Mediterranean trade for centuries, in part because the few navigable channels through the lagoon were a closely guarded secret, and without that knowledge no enemy could hope to invade. In more recent times, Venice's distinctive character has become a threat to the city's future even as it draws millions of visitors every year.

In the fourteenth century, city leaders became concerned that silt deposited by the four rivers that once emptied into Venice's lagoon was threatening to clog the deep channels on which their trading ships depended. The solution was a public works project of staggering scope: Over the course of two centuries, the rivers were diverted through canals so that they emptied elsewhere. Although this expedient preserved the deep channels leading to the city itself, it had an unanticipated effect: The main source of new sediment entering the lagoon was cut off, removing one major contributor in the dynamic reformation of the lagoon's landscape.

The "bedrock" on which Venice is built is a mile-thick layer of river sediment, deposited over a period of millennia. Such sediments naturally compact under the weight of the material above, and as a result, the land in Venice's lagoon has been sinking throughout its history. With the rivers diverted, the major source of replenishment for the area's land is no longer operating, giving the upper hand to storm and tide in their efforts to reclaim the lagoon. But even were the rivers' former courses to be restored—an action no one seriously recommends—that by itself would not constitute a solution to Venice's problem.

Archaeological data indicate that Venice's residents have historically coped with the land's subsidence by rebuilding. Multiple layers of old foundations demonstrate that Venice has been racing against the loss of land throughout its history; some floors from Roman times are now five feet below sea level. Although such solutions worked well in an atmosphere where historical preservation was not a priority, Venice's economic strength rests now on the foundation of tourism. The fact that modern-day Venice has become more a museum than a working city lends particular urgency and difficulty to the efforts to preserve it.

There is reason to believe that these efforts must be undertaken soon. Even while the land sinks, sea levels in the Adriatic Sea rise. Prediction is difficult, but most estimates put the water-level rise in the next century in the range of fifteen to thirty inches. A century ago, Venice's signature landmark—St. Mark's Square—was flooded an average of nine times a year; now, after roughly ten inches of loss versus sea level, it is flooded one hundred times in an average year. Unless radical steps are taken, within another century, most experts agree that it will be submerged year-round.

6. The primary purpose of the discussion in the second paragraph is to

   (A) argue that the blame for Venice's current problems rests with its past leaders
   (B) provide historical context that describes one contributing factor in Venice's dilemma
   (C) explain why the problem Venice faces is unique among the world's cities
   (D) show that human intervention in Venice's environment has taken place throughout its history
   (E) prove that the landscape of Venice's lagoon is being dynamically reformed

7. Given the descriptions in the passage, which one of the following is most analogous to the method by which Venetians have historically coped with their sinking land?

   (A) A Japanese shrine has stood in the same location for centuries, but because it has traditionally been constructed of materials that are not durable, it has been periodically rebuilt throughout its history.
   (B) A German castle was originally built on a river island that experienced severe erosion, so within the past century, the castle was moved to more stable ground on the riverbank.
   (C) A Roman temple was originally built of quarried marble, but since then, local residents have largely dismantled the building to use its marble in other construction.
   (D) An American armory built in the nineteenth century is no longer used for its original purpose but has instead been converted into a convention hall.
   (E) A Russian hotel that was a symbol of the former Soviet regime is demolished both because of its history and because contemporary residents now believe the building is an eyesore.

GO ON TO THE NEXT PAGE.

8. The passage's predictions about the likely future incidence of flooding in St. Mark's Square would be most weakened if which one of the following were found to be true?

(A) Variations in water level attributable to storm surge are primarily responsible for the current flooding in St. Mark's Square.
(B) The flooding in St. Mark's Square could be mostly prevented by the installation of inflatable gates in the channels leading into the lagoon, a massive project opposed by environmentalists.
(C) Steps taken in the Low Countries of Europe, many parts of which are below sea level, are effective at preventing flooding there.
(D) A moderate increase in the height of the canal walls at the edges of St. Mark's Square would prevent flooding, even if sea levels were to rise substantially.
(E) Although many proposed plans exist to halt the flooding of St. Mark's Square, most are controversial either because they are too radical or because they are likely to be ineffective.

9. Each of the following can be inferred from the passage EXCEPT:

(A) The earliest buildings constructed in the lagoon of Venice are now below sea level.
(B) River sediments deposited in the lagoon of Venice compacted over time even before humans settled in the area.
(C) Venice's primary source of economic viability is no longer Mediterranean trade.
(D) Water levels in the Adriatic Sea are rising at a faster rate than are water levels in other large bodies of water worldwide.
(E) Some factor other than secrecy surrounding the navigable channels of the lagoon has contributed to Venice's economic security.

10. The passage's author would be most likely to agree with which one of the following statements concerning modern-day Venice?

(A) The preservation of its historic buildings should be a priority.
(B) The environmental health of the salt marshes in its lagoon must be protected.
(C) Its survival depends on stopping the subsidence of land on which it is built.
(D) Moderate measures are adequate to protect it from rising sea levels.
(E) It must become more of a working city than it currently is to survive.

11. Based on the passage, the author most likely holds which one of the following opinions concerning past alterations to Venice's environment?

(A) They are solely responsible for Venice's current difficulties.
(B) They were undertaken without full knowledge of their consequences.
(C) They must be reversed for Venice to survive.
(D) They have contributed to the rise in water levels in the Adriatic Sea.
(E) They could have been prevented by responsible city leadership.

12. From the passage, it can be inferred that

(A) water levels in the Adriatic Sea will rise more than twenty inches in the next century
(B) the level of land in Venice's lagoon will sink more than ten inches in the next century
(C) St. Mark's Square will flood fewer than one hundred times per year over the next century
(D) Venice is likely to lose more elevation versus sea level in the next century than it did in the previous century
(E) some of Venice's historical landmarks will be lost in the next century

GO ON TO THE NEXT PAGE.

Questions 13–19 are based on the following passage:

The work of Amartya Sen, winner of the Nobel Prize for economics in 1998, has helped usher in a new era in the field as it is practically applied throughout the world. Institutions such as the United Nations have adopted his ideas in measuring and aiding the development of emerging economies, and the consequences of the social-choice theory he employs have garnered much public attention.

The classic defining work of social choice theory is Ken Arrow's careful investigation of voting through a series of thought experiments. The result—Arrow's Impossibility Theorem—showed that no method of conducting a majority-decision vote can be guaranteed to conform to the basic requirements of democracy. A simple example illustrates Arrow's idea: For an electorate of three voters—1, 2, and 3—there are three candidates—A, B, and C. Voter 1 prefers A to B, and B to C; voter 2 prefers B to C, and C to A; voter 3 prefers C to A, and A to B. In such an electorate, a runoff between A and B declares A the winner; a runoff between B and C is won by B; and a runoff between A and C is won by C. Whichever candidate wins, that candidate is actually less preferable to the electorate than the candidate who was not involved in the runoff.

The work for which Sen was awarded his Nobel Prize is, in essence, an application of such methods to national economies, politics, and public welfare. Just as Arrow focused on paradoxes within democratic systems, Sen investigated instances such as famine in which capitalist market systems seem not to function properly, according to traditional economic public-choice principles. Public choice focuses on self-interest as the driving factor in economics; Sen, in a famous quote, shows the flaw in this view: "'Can you direct me to the railway station?' asks the stranger. 'Certainly,' says the local, pointing in the opposite direction, toward the post office, 'and would you post this letter for me on your way?' 'Certainly,' says the stranger, resolving to open it to see if it contains anything worth stealing." Factors other than self-interest exert their influence at every level within a society, and only by incorporating them can a theory truly describe how economies function.

This departure from traditional views has made Sen's work a subject in the ongoing debate over globalization. Partisans who advocate the spread of capitalism and democracy have called Sen everything from an anarchist to a Marxist; opponents of globalization use his work as proof that these institutions are not the boon they are supposed to be. By doing so, both sides misrepresent Sen's concerns. One of his early works demonstrated the conditions under which Arrow's Impossibility Theorem does not apply to democratic elections, and Sen is most famous for his notion of "capability" as an antidote to economic injustice. The specific forms "capability" takes—education and equal access—are precisely those that are called for in theoretical formulations of how choice-driven markets and democracies are supposed to function. Sen's work is an examination of the failures of these core systems, but it is also a roadmap to realizing their promise.

13. Which one of the following most accurately expresses the main idea of the passage?

(A) Although the work of Amartya Sen has been viewed as opposing democracy and global capitalism, in fact it is a defense of these ideas.
(B) Amartya Sen's revolutionary use of social choice theory in economics has been widely misinterpreted but nevertheless offers hope that social justice can be achieved in capitalist and democratic systems.
(C) The work of social choice theorists such as Ken Arrow and Amartya Sen has helped their theories supplant public choice theory as the most widely accepted theoretical approach to economics.
(D) Amartya Sen's work delineates the circumstances under which commonly accepted notions of how economic and democratic systems operate can be said to be correct.
(E) Social choice theory does not include considerations of self-interest in its evaluation of economic and democratic institutions.

14. Which one of the following titles provides the most complete and accurate summary of the passage's contents?

(A) "Nobel Prizewinner Amartya Sen: Reluctant Economic Rebel"
(B) "Social Choice Theory: Moving Beyond Self-Interest"
(C) "Arrow's Impossibility Theorem: Why No Election Is Fair"
(D) "Economics and Social Justice: Amartya Sen's Groundbreaking Work"
(E) "Fighting the Future: The Rising Opposition to Globalization"

GO ON TO THE NEXT PAGE.

15. The passage supports the inference that the author most likely holds which one of the following views?

(A) Existing economic theories are incapable of explaining why self-interest fails to prevent famine and social injustice.
(B) No majority-decision election conducted under any circumstances is capable of fulfilling even the most basic promises of democracy.
(C) Those who believe that Amartya Sen's work is intended to oppose economic globalization misunderstand it.
(D) Social choice theory does not constitute a legitimate alternative to traditional theoretical explanations of economic action.
(E) Amartya Sen is the first economist to take social considerations into account in the analysis of institutions such as democratic elections and the free market.

16. As it is described in the passage, Ken Arrow's method for investigating democratic elections is most analogous to which one of the following?

(A) To discern universal physical principles, a physicist imagines what it would be like to ride a beam of light.
(B) To evaluate existing theories of evolution, a paleontologist undertakes a survey of the fossil record.
(C) To learn about daily life in an ancient civilization, an anthropologist studies the traditional culture of the civilization's descendants.
(D) To evaluate the success of market reforms, an economist studies changes in key indicators.
(E) To discover political attitudes within a local area, a sociologist interviews religious leaders in the area.

17. The author's attitude toward social choice theory can be described most accurately as

(A) skeptical that it will ever gain wide acceptance
(B) uncertain whether it correctly describes economic realities
(C) ambivalent about its critique of globalization
(D) satisfied that it represents an advance in economic understanding
(E) enthusiastic about its usefulness in reforming democratic elections

18. The passage suggests that which one of the following would provide the best definition of Sen's idea of "capability"?

(A) willingness to fill multiple economic roles
(B) access to legal redress for injustice
(C) capacity to exercise democratic and economic choice
(D) knowledge of underlying principles of economics
(E) assistance through the redistribution of wealth

19. Each of the following is stated or implied by the passage EXCEPT:

(A) Arrow's Impossibility Theorem does not hold for all democratic elections.
(B) Public choice theory does not provide a complete description of all economic transactions.
(C) The policies of the United Nations are not primarily concerned with aiding developing nations to achieve social justice.
(D) Amartya Sen's economic beliefs cannot properly be called Marxist.
(E) The precepts of social choice theory have not always informed economic policies.

GO ON TO THE NEXT PAGE.

Questions 20–27 refer to the following passages:

**Passage A**

While *The Origin of Species* created a great stir when it was published in 1859, Darwinian thought was almost completely out of vogue by the turn of the twentieth century. It took Ronald Fisher's "Great Synthesis" of the 1920s, which combined the genetic work of Gregor Mendel with Darwin's ideas about natural selection, and Theodosius Dobzhansky's "Modern Synthesis" of the 1930s, which built upon Fisher's work with genetics within a species by focusing on how genetic variation could cause the origin of a new species, to begin to rehabilitate Darwin.

Yet what is remarkable is how very prescient Darwin, working without knowledge of the mechanisms of heredity, proved to be. As prominent biologist Ernst Mayr notes, what made Darwin's theory so remarkable was his emphasis on "population thinking." This contrasts to Jean-Baptiste Lamarck's theory of evolution, popular throughout the nineteenth century, which posited that individuals changed through personal actions and will. Lamarckian theory is often exemplified by a giraffe constantly reaching up to eat leaves off high branches and passing on its lengthened neck to its children.

Such explanations bore a strong resemblance to children's fables (and indeed Rudyard Kipling's late nineteenth century *Just So Stories* build upon Lamarckian theories). Where Darwin differed was his insistence that significant variation was not based within one particular individual, but rather in the breeding population as a whole. Natural selection was not based on the actions or goals of one individual, but variations in the average character of the species.

**Passage B**

As Peter Bowler points out in his aptly named *The Non-Darwinian Revolution: Reinterpreting a Historical Myth,* nineteenth-century Darwinism was quite different from the Darwinism of today. Thomas Huxley, "Darwin's Bulldog," so called because of his tireless public campaigning for Darwinian thought, exemplifies this difference. As a result of his advocacy, by the end of the nineteenth century Huxley was the vehicle for Darwinian thought. Noted science fiction writer H. G. Wells, for instance, garnered all of his information about natural selection and evolution through Huxley's lectures. Yet Huxley's theories varied significantly from those of Darwin, focusing on the will of humankind.

In the preface to *Evolution and Ethics*, Huxley wrote that "we cannot do without our inheritance from the forefathers who were the puppets of the cosmic process; the society which renounces it must be destroyed from without. Still less can we do with too much of it; the society in which it dominates must be destroyed from within." According to Huxley, humankind has moved past physical evolution to the realm of self-directed moral evolution. Huxley, then, acknowledges that humankind has evolved under the pressure of natural selection and must remain aware of that fact or be "destroyed from without," but he argues that a society that continues in the path that Nature has placed it will be "destroyed from within" because it will no longer be adapted to itself.

20. Based on the information in the passage, Rudyard Kipling most likely wrote stories
    - (A) dedicated to enlightening humans by using animals as positive examples of proper behavior
    - (B) based on futuristic worlds which were populated by evolved subjects
    - (C) featuring individuals developing variation through the power of their desires
    - (D) seeking to exhibit the effects of population thinking in breeding populations
    - (E) portraying the effects of parental inheritance through examining the lives of children

21. Which of the following best represents Huxley's beliefs?
    - (A) Focusing on physical evolution leaves man as nothing more than a "puppet" of forces beyond his control; to succeed in life it is necessary to reject physical evolution in favor of moral change.
    - (B) The ideas of Charles Darwin needed to be carefully delineated through lectures so that his ideas about individual variation could be fully understood.
    - (C) By exerting personal will, humankind will be able to enact significant, lasting variation which will be demonstrated through the bodies of the children of those who seek change.
    - (D) While humankind is inescapably linked to its physical past and the material conditions of its evolution, it must be wary of being too attached to the path dictated by natural selection.
    - (E) Certain elements of Darwin's theory about evolution had to be discarded so that the public would be willing to accept the thrust of the theory as a whole.

22. The authors of passage A and passage B would most likely agree that which of the following are most closely aligned in their thinking?
    - (A) Lamarck and Huxley
    - (B) Kipling and Wells
    - (C) Mayr and Bowler
    - (D) Mendel and Huxley
    - (E) Dobzhansky and Wells

GO ON TO THE NEXT PAGE.

23. Which of the following statements about Darwin is supported by both passages?

(A) Darwin differed significantly from other theorists of evolution because he focused on breeding populations as a whole.
(B) The modern understanding of Darwin varies significantly from nineteenth-century beliefs about his theories.
(C) It was not until the early twentieth century that Darwinism as we know it began to emerge.
(D) Fiction writers were particularly interested in disseminating ideas about Darwin.
(E) Delineating the specific inheritance of the child is crucial to understanding how natural selection proceeds.

24. Which of the following best represents the difference between the two passages?

(A) The first passage begins with current understandings of Darwinism and moves back in time, while the second passage begins with older understandings and moves forward in time.
(B) While the first passage focuses on the difference between two theories of evolution, the second paragraph traces differences between two individual interpreters of evolution.
(C) The first passage introduces a general theory, offers specific evidence, and then considers the ramifications of that theory, while the second paragraph does not consider the ramifications of the evidence it presents.
(D) The first passage is concerned with demonstrating a way in which Darwin is closely linked with modern thinkers, while the second passage is focused on how he differed from one of his contemporaries.
(E) The first passage provides a historical retrospective of the primary interpreters of Darwin, and the second passage centers on one particular interpreter.

25. Based on the information in passage B, Thomas Huxley would be most likely to object to which of the following claims in passage A?

(A) It is impossible to truly understand natural selection without the benefit of modern genetic theory.
(B) It is likely that the giraffe developed a long neck due to the fact that it constantly stretched it to gain access to food.
(C) There are different ways to understand how evolution functions to change individuals.
(D) Variations in the average character of a population are the most crucial factor in the proper evolution of man.
(E) Allowing natural selection to dominate our society will lead to the destruction of humankind.

26. Which of the following best describes how variation is characterized in the two passages?

(A) In passage A it is discussed in both individual and group situations, and in passage B it is seen as purely individual.
(B) In passage A it is discussed in both individual and group situations, and in passage B it is seen as focused on the group.
(C) In passage A it is discussed in physical terms, and in passage B it is discussed in moral and physical terms.
(D) In passage A it is discussed in terms of how breeding occurs, and in passage B it is discussed in moral terms.
(E) In passage A it is discussed in terms of how breeding occurs, and in passage B it is discussed in moral and physical terms.

27. Which one of the following situations is most closely analogous to the Lamarckian mode of variation?

(A) An adult bird tries to change the environment for the benefit of its children.
(B) Seeking to morally adapt to its environment, a chimpanzee changes the way it woos its mate.
(C) A giraffe's bodily shape changes because it is unable to fit into the caves it traditionally sleeps in.
(D) Because of a change in the environment, a number of chimpanzees die out while others thrive and pass on their genes.
(E) Because it hunts for salmon with its mouth wide open, a bear gradually develops a straining mechanism between its teeth.

**S T O P**

**IF YOU FINISH BEFORE TIME IS CALLED, YOU MAY CHECK YOUR WORK ON THIS SECTION ONLY. DO NOT WORK ON ANY OTHER SECTION IN THE TEST.**

## SECTION IV
Time—35 Minutes
25 Questions

Directions: The questions in this section are based on the reasoning contained in brief statements or passages. For some questions, more than one of the choices could conceivably answer the question. However, you are to choose the best answer; that is, the response that most accurately and completely answers the question. You should not make assumptions that are by common sense standards implausible, superfluous, or incompatible with the passage. After you have chosen the best answer, blacken the corresponding space on your answer sheet.

1. In France, children in preschool programs spend a portion of each day engaged in a program of stretching and exercise. Preschool programs in the United States, however, seldom devote time to a daily stretching and exercise program. In tests designed to measure cardiovascular fitness, children in the United States were outperformed by their French counterparts. It can therefore be determined that children attending preschool programs in the United States can achieve cardiovascular fitness only by engaging in a daily school program of stretching and exercise.

Which one of the following is an assumption on which the argument depends?

(A) A daily program of stretching and exercise will allow all children to achieve cardiovascular fitness.
(B) Cardiovascular fitness is integral to one's overall health.
(C) It has been proven that children who participate in stretching and exercise programs in preschool have better cardiovascular fitness than adults.
(D) Stretching and exercise are necessary components of French children's superior cardiovascular fitness programs.
(E) United States preschool children could make healthful dietary changes as well as changes to their daily fitness regimens.

2. In an effort to lessen the risk of liability, fertility clinics are seeking new methods of record keeping and storage that would help avoid donor sperm that might contain dangerous genes. Toward this end, a database is being developed to aid the clients in their screening of donor sperm. The database is exhaustively thorough, containing the medical histories of more than twenty thousand people, approximately half of them men.

Which one of the following, if true, best explains why the database contains the records of almost ten thousand women?

(A) Small fertility clinics, located in remote areas, wish to have access to a large selection of donor sperm.
(B) Keeping genetic information on women is a standard procedure for many scientific clinics.
(C) Some genetic disorders are not expressed until the onset of puberty.
(D) Some genetic disorders may be carried by, but not manifested in, men who inherited the dangerous gene from their mothers.
(E) Some genetic disorders are due to the effects of drugs and alcohol during puberty.

GO ON TO THE NEXT PAGE.

3. If the Food and Drug Administration (FDA) does not relax some of its regulations governing the testing of experimental drugs, tens of thousands of U.S. citizens are sure to die as a result of certain diseases before an effective treatment is found and made generally available.

   It can be concluded from the statement above that if the FDA does relax some of its regulations governing the testing of experimental drugs, then tens of thousands of U.S. citizens

   (A) will definitely die of certain diseases
   (B) will probably die of certain diseases
   (C) will probably not die of certain diseases
   (D) will not die of certain diseases
   (E) may still die of certain diseases

4. The level of blood sugar for many patients suffering from disease *Q* is slightly higher than the level of blood sugar in the general population. Nonetheless, most medical professionals believe that slightly increasing blood sugar levels is a successful means by which to treat disease *Q*.

   This apparently contradictory argument can best be resolved by which one of the following statements?

   (A) Blood sugar levels for patients who have been cured of disease *Q* are virtually identical to the levels of blood sugar found in the general population.
   (B) Many of the symptoms associated with severe cases of disease *Q* have been recognized in laboratory animals with experimentally induced high blood pressure, but none of the animals developed disease *Q*.
   (C) The movement from inactive to advanced states of disease *Q* often occurs because the virus that causes *Q* flourishes during periods when blood sugar levels are slightly low.
   (D) The blood sugar level in patients with disease *Q* fluctuates abnormally in response to changes in blood chemistry.
   (E) Low levels of blood sugar are symptomatic of many other diseases that are even more serious than disease *Q*.

5. Activist: There are countries in which the number of handgun deaths per capita is less than one-tenth of the number in our country. Although not all of these countries outlaw handguns, most of them do. Therefore, to reduce the number of handgun deaths in our country, we must outlaw handguns.

   Which one of the following is an assumption on which the activist's argument depends?

   (A) The number of handgun deaths in a country is primarily determined by the rate of handgun ownership in that country.
   (B) Some countries in which handguns are not outlawed have low numbers of handgun deaths per capita because of conditions that cannot be replicated in all other countries.
   (C) The number of handgun deaths in a country may be reduced without a corresponding decrease in the number of per capita handgun deaths in that country.
   (D) Laws forbidding the ownership of handguns are justified only insofar as those laws are effective in preventing handgun deaths.
   (E) Accidents are not a significant cause of handgun deaths in countries where the number of per capita handgun deaths is relatively low.

6. Medical studies indicate that the metabolic rates of professional athletes are substantially greater than those of the average person. So, most likely, a person's speed and strength are primarily determined by that person's metabolic rate.

   Which one of the following, if true, most strengthens the argument?

   (A) Some professional athletes are either faster or stronger than the average person.
   (B) Some professional athletes do not have higher metabolic rates than some people who are not professional athletes.
   (C) The speed and strength of people who are not professional athletes are not primarily determined by choices of diet and exercise.
   (D) Intensive training such as that engaged in by professional athletes causes an increase in metabolic rate.
   (E) Drugs that suppress metabolic rate have been shown to have the side effect of diminishing the speed and strength of those who are not professional athletes.

GO ON TO THE NEXT PAGE.

7. Environmentalist: In most land ecologies, grasses are the basis of the food chain. Desertification of several North African areas over the past decade has caused the grasses there to die, leading to serious disruption of the ecology in those areas. Now it has been shown that warming in Antarctic waters is causing a die-off of krill there. Because krill is the basis of the food chain in ocean ecologies, we can anticipate that there will be serious disruption of the ecology in these waters.

The environmentalist's argument proceeds by

(A) demonstrating that ocean ecologies are more delicate than land ecologies
(B) using an analogy to reach the conclusion that some ocean ecologies are in danger
(C) proving that the population of krill in Antarctic waters is decreasing
(D) asserting the role that grasses play in the health of land ecologies
(E) demonstrating that changes in temperature have categorically negative effects on all ecologies

8. Some residents of Woodbridge work the late shift at the nearby factory. Because of the fact that all of the residents of Woodbridge who own cars are also members of the Area Auto Club, the Woodbridge city manager concluded that none of the residents who work the late shift at the nearby factory own cars.

The city manager's conclusion is properly drawn if which one of the following is assumed?

(A) None of the residents of Woodbridge who work the late shift at the nearby factory are members of the Area Auto Club.
(B) None of the residents of Woodbridge who owns a car has failed to join the Area Auto Club.
(C) Some of the residents of Woodbridge who do not work the late shift at the nearby factory do not own cars.
(D) All residents of Woodbridge who do not work the late shift at the nearby factory own cars.
(E) All residents of Woodbridge who are members of the Area Auto Club own cars.

9. Naturalist: It was once believed that only modern humans were capable of learning to use tools for obtaining food. Decades ago, archaeological evidence showed that extinct species of hominids closely related to modern humans also used tools for these purposes. What remained in doubt, however, was whether any existing nonhuman species could also learn to use tools. Some populations of chimpanzees use dried grasses to "fish" for termites, a high-protein delicacy. Moreover, evidence shows that this behavior is not instinctive but must be taught to and practiced by young chimpanzees. Some populations in the same area do not "fish" for termites in this way, although dried grasses and termite mounds are available to them.

Which one of the following most accurately expresses the conclusion of the naturalist's argument?

(A) At least some behaviors of chimpanzees are learned, not instinctive.
(B) Certain past assumptions about the uniqueness of modern humans have been shown to be false.
(C) Evidence exists that animals other than modern humans and their closest relatives are capable of learning to use tools.
(D) Only modern humans are capable of learning to use tools in ways that are not directly related to obtaining food.
(E) Some species of hominids became extinct for reasons unrelated to their ability to use tools.

GO ON TO THE NEXT PAGE.

10. Victor: Auto manufacturers report strong profit growth this year. This should not be taken to mean, however, that sales of new cars are increasing. Closer examination shows that the growth in auto manufacturers' profits is attributable solely to financing the sale of new cars.

Kim: I don't think that's right. After all, if they were not continuing to sell new cars, auto manufacturers could not profit from financing them, could they?

Kim's reply suggests that she misinterprets Victor's point to be that

(A) overall sales of new cars are not increasing
(B) auto manufacturers' profits this year were derived solely from financing
(C) the financing of the past year's sales is not solely responsible for this year's profit growth
(D) auto manufacturers should place increased emphasis on the sale and financing of used cars
(E) only sales of new cars should be considered in evaluating the financial health of auto manufacturers

11. Most people believe that obtaining a master's in business administration (MBA) leads to increased pay. A recent survey, however, suggests that this belief is unfounded. Among the top executives at the nation's most prominent companies, there is no indication that pay rates are any higher for employees with an MBA than they are for employees in similar positions without one.

The argument above is flawed because it neglects the possibility that

(A) an employee with an MBA may be more likely to attain a top executive position than a similarly able employee without one
(B) the pay of top executives in the nation's most prominent companies may be higher than the pay of other employees in those same companies
(C) pay rates for top executives may differ from company to company, even among the most prominent companies
(D) an employee who obtains an MBA may learn job skills that are critical to success in a top executive position
(E) top executives who obtain MBAs while holding their jobs may be better able than other executives to find similar positions in other companies in the event that they are laid off

12. Since Oscar received extensive training in how to repair motorcycles, he is able to repair many of their most common mechanical problems. However, Oscar does not understand how internal combustion engines work. When Oscar was given Lucy's motorcycle to repair, he was able to fix the problem, despite the fact that he did not understand what was causing it.

From the statements above, which one of the following can be properly inferred?

(A) The problem with Lucy's motorcycle involved its engine.
(B) Not all mechanical problems can be repaired only by mechanics who understand how an internal combustion engine works.
(C) At least some good mechanics are able to fix mechanical problems without an understanding of what is causing them.
(D) Oscar's mechanical training in how to repair motorcycles was incomplete.
(E) Those common mechanical problems that Oscar cannot fix require an understanding of how an internal combustion engine works.

GO ON TO THE NEXT PAGE.

13. Dr. Jackson: Many people criticize the advertisement of prescription drugs because they believe it causes patients to form mistaken beliefs about how their conditions should be treated. Surveys show, however, that in more than 60 percent of cases when a patient requests a prescription for a particular drug from a doctor, the doctor writes a prescription for the drug he or she has requested.

Dr. Morris: True, patients often receive the treatment they request. But this is most often because patients refuse to follow medical advice that does not agree with the beliefs they form about how they should be treated, not because the treatment they request is correct.

Which one of the following, if true, most supports Dr. Morris's counter to Dr. Jackson?

(A) More than half of patients are sufficiently knowledgeable about their condition to request the correct treatment for it.
(B) Many national organizations that work on behalf of doctors are opposed to the advertisement of prescription drugs.
(C) Studies show that more than half of patients receive incorrect or excessive treatment for their medical problems.
(D) More than half of patients who receive the prescriptions they request from their doctors have previously requested the same prescription from another doctor and have been refused.
(E) Only a very few of the most common medical maladies for which patients seek treatment are most appropriately treated with prescription drugs.

14. It cannot be true that the lack of success of third-party candidates in national elections is due to the difficulties such candidates encounter in securing space on national ballots. Everyone who identifies him- or herself as a supporter of a third party has voted for a major-party candidate in at least one national election when a third-party candidate was listed on the ballot.

Which one of the following most accurately describes a reasoning flaw in the argument?

(A) The argument overlooks the possibility that the lack of success of third-party candidates in national elections may be due to the fact that their views on major issues prevent them from gaining broad support.
(B) The argument takes for granted that the media coverage devoted to third-party candidates for national office is comparable to that devoted to major-party candidates for those same offices.
(C) The argument treats as contradictory to some claim evidence that may instead provide support for that claim.
(D) The argument draws its conclusion through the use of a set of facts, not all of which can be true.
(E) The argument derives a statement about the behavior of all voters on the basis of partial information about the past voting preferences of only a few voters.

GO ON TO THE NEXT PAGE.

15. Sara: Our government devotes billions of tax dollars every year to foreign aid, although most experts agree that our social and economic infrastructure is badly in need of that money. It is unconscionable that our elected representatives consider the needs of our own citizens less important than the needs of citizens of other countries.

Ross: Foreign aid helps our country by assuring its security. If money were not spent on foreign aid to the most threatened governments in the world, we would need to spend a great deal more in military interventions when those governments collapsed.

From their statements, it can most properly be inferred that Sara and Ross disagree about whether

(A) their country's spending on foreign aid ought to be increased
(B) failed governments pose a security threat to their country
(C) their country's social infrastructure is in need of additional investment
(D) their country's spending on foreign aid serves its citizens' needs
(E) decreased spending on foreign aid would necessitate additional military spending

16. In communities heavily affected by environmental regulation where such regulation directly benefits neither the companies that are most important to the community's economy nor the residents of that community, the government is perceived as being insensitive to the community's economic welfare. For this reason, the people in some communities heavily affected by environmental regulation are in favor of decreased taxes. When people believe that government considers the interests of others more important than their own, they tend to favor decreased taxes, believing this will limit the government's power over their lives.

Which one of the following is an assumption on which the argument depends?

(A) When government policy is perceived as being sensitive to a community's economic welfare, the people of that community do not wish to limit the government's power over their lives.
(B) Environmental regulation that directly benefits the companies that are most important to a community's economy leads to greater government support than environmental regulation that directly benefits only the residents of that community.
(C) A government's power over the lives of a community's residents depends on taxes collected from those residents.
(D) People in a community tend to believe that their government considers others' interests more important than their own unless that government is perceived as being sensitive to the community's economic welfare.
(E) Community members do not consider indirect benefits to themselves or to the companies that are most important to the community's economy in formulating their response to environmental regulation.

GO ON TO THE NEXT PAGE.

17. Researcher: Heavily insulated homes trap radon gas much better than do poorly insulated homes. Therefore, those who live in heavily insulated homes are at greater risk for certain types of brain cancer because evidence shows that those who are being treated for brain cancer have high blood levels of the radioactive compounds that are found in those who are exposed to high levels of radon gas.

Which one of the following, if true, most undermines the researcher's argument?

(A) Radon gas is commonly found even in homes that do not trap it well.
(B) Exposure to radiation is known to lead to an increased incidence of cancer of all kinds.
(C) Young people are particularly susceptible to the negative consequences of high levels of radon exposure.
(D) Radioactive compounds are used in many cases to help develop an initial diagnosis of medical problems.
(E) The most common brain cancer therapy involves radiation and leads to high blood levels of many radioactive compounds.

18. Food critic: Consumers should buy only wild salmon, not farmed salmon. Whereas the environmental damage associated with harvesting wild salmon is slight, salmon farms are significant causes of water pollution, and salmon that escape from the farms displace wild varieties, threatening biodiversity. The fact that farmed salmon is cheaper than wild varieties has led to a large increase in the popularity of salmon, which may eventually pose a threat to wild populations because of overfishing.

Which one of the following most accurately describes a flaw in the food critic's argument?

(A) At least one of the potential disadvantages cited in arguing against a course of action applies at least as strongly to the alternative course of action the argument recommends.
(B) The argument is constructed in such a way that it precludes the possibility of reaching any logical conclusion, if all of its premises are accepted as true.
(C) It overlooks the possibility that some unspecified benefit of the choice argued against may outweigh any possible benefit of the choice argued for.
(D) It concludes that one course of action is not permissible on the basis of a principle that is in greater need of support than the conclusion it is advanced to defend.
(E) Its premises are presented in such a way that the argument presupposes the truth of the conclusion it is intended to support.

GO ON TO THE NEXT PAGE.

19. Resentment is not a reasonable response to rejection because rejection is merely an expression of preference: Either a preference is purely personal, in which case the rejection could not have been anticipated, or else that preference is commonly held, in which case steps should have been taken in advance to avoid rejection.

Which one of the following, if assumed, enables the argument's conclusion to be properly drawn?

(A) No emotional response to any action that could not have been anticipated is reasonable.
(B) Resentment is not a reasonable response to any action which steps should have been taken in advance to avoid.
(C) Resentment is not a reasonable response to any preference that is either purely personal or commonly held.
(D) Responses to resentment indicate preferences that either could not have been anticipated or else could have been avoided.
(E) No response to an expression of preference that steps should have been taken to avoid could reasonably have been anticipated.

20. According to newspaper reviews, some of the films released this year were of superior artistic quality. According to audience surveys, some of the films released this year involved exciting plots. Therefore, some of the films this year that involved exciting plots were also of superior artistic quality.

The flawed reasoning in the argument above is most similar to that in which one of the following?

(A) Judging from automotive magazines, some of the cars released this year were exceptionally fast, but according to automotive enthusiasts, none of the cars released this year is likely to become a classic. Thus not even the fastest car released this year is likely to become a classic.
(B) According to consumer magazines, some of the new refrigerators introduced this year are exceptionally energy efficient. According to consumer surveys, energy efficiency plays some role in determining whether a customer is satisfied with a new refrigerator. Therefore, the reason some customers are satisfied with their new refrigerators is that they are exceptionally energy efficient.
(C) Art says that snow is forecast for some parts of our area tomorrow, and Lois says that rain is forecast for some parts of our area tomorrow. Thus, tomorrow it will neither snow nor rain in some parts of our area.
(D) Doctors say that some vaccines need be administered only once in a patient's lifetime, and drug companies say that some vaccines prevent measles, so some vaccine that prevents measles need be administered only once in a patient's lifetime.
(E) According to publishers, most of the works of fiction published this year were novels. According to book reviewers, most of the works of fiction published this year were of inferior quality. Therefore, some of the novels published this year were of inferior quality.

GO ON TO THE NEXT PAGE.

21. Stock options are the only investments that allow an individual investor to achieve high returns with limited liability. With relatively small risk, an individual investing in stock options can make profits of several hundred percent over a short period of time. Thus stock options represent a more efficient use of an individual's money than any other investment option.

Which one of the following, if assumed, enables the argument's conclusion to be properly inferred?

(A) Investments other than stock options do not allow an individual investor to achieve high returns with limited liability.
(B) The efficient use of an individual investor's money requires the possibility of achieving profit over a short period of time.
(C) A profit of several hundred percent over a short period of time is considered a high return on an individual's investment.
(D) An investment cannot be considered efficient unless it returns several hundred percent profit.
(E) Investments that allow an individual to achieve high returns with limited liability represent a more efficient use of money than any other potential use.

22. Only corporate executives who behave ethically are likely to be promoted, but no corporate executive who makes wise business decisions is a poor employee. All corporate executives who behave ethically are both well respected and make wise business decisions, qualities lacking in many corporate executives who do not behave ethically.

If all of the statements above are true, which one of the following must also be true?

(A) No corporate executive who makes wise business decisions but does not behave ethically is well respected.
(B) All corporate executives who are well respected but do not behave ethically make wise business decisions.
(C) No corporate executive who is likely to be promoted is a poor employee.
(D) All corporate executives who are not well respected are poor employees.
(E) All corporate executives who are good employees behave ethically.

23. It cannot be true that everyone who donates money to charity is concerned with the well-being of others. After all, it is possible that donating money to charity may help some people lessen their own feelings of guilt.

Which one of the following arguments employs a principle of reasoning most similar to that illustrated by the argument above?

(A) It cannot be true that the only reason for space exploration is scientific discovery. After all, there have been many space missions that have not contributed to scientific knowledge at all.
(B) It cannot be true that income taxes are justified by the government's obligation to redistribute wealth. After all, many government programs paid for by tax money benefit wealthy individuals.
(C) It cannot be true that Columbus was the one who discovered that Earth was not flat. After all, ancient mathematicians had calculated Earth's circumference centuries before Columbus was born.
(D) It cannot be true that all those who become actors desire wealth and fame. After all, some actors may perform so that they can share their artistic vision with others.
(E) It cannot be true that a meteor impact caused the extinction of the dinosaurs. After all, it is possible that climatic conditions similar to those following a meteor impact could have been created by a massive volcanic eruption.

GO ON TO THE NEXT PAGE.

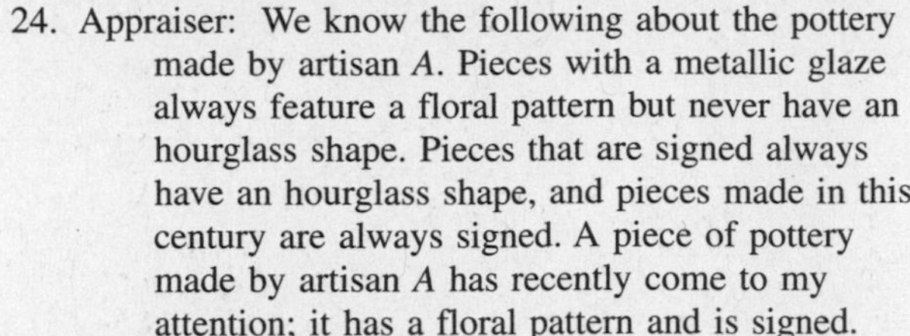

24. Appraiser: We know the following about the pottery made by artisan *A*. Pieces with a metallic glaze always feature a floral pattern but never have an hourglass shape. Pieces that are signed always have an hourglass shape, and pieces made in this century are always signed. A piece of pottery made by artisan *A* has recently come to my attention; it has a floral pattern and is signed.

From the appraiser's statements, which one of the following can be properly concluded about the piece of pottery by artisan *A* that has recently come to the appraiser's attention?

(A) It has an hourglass shape and was made in this century.
(B) It has an hourglass shape but was not made in this century.
(C) It has an hourglass shape but does not have a metallic glaze.
(D) It has a metallic glaze and was made in this century.
(E) It lacks both an hourglass shape and a metallic glaze.

25. No doubt the presidential candidate who wins an election deserves credit for persistence and political aplomb, but the advisers who develop campaign strategy are often overlooked. Although presidential candidates sometimes take the lead in shaping their campaign's policy positions, most often it is political professionals who, in service to the campaign, devote their time and energy to crafting the candidate's message and persona. Campaign strategists play a crucial role in virtually every successful candidacy.

The claim that presidential candidates sometimes take the lead in shaping their campaign's policy positions plays which one of the following roles in the argument?

(A) It indicates the circumstances to which the argument's conclusion is to be understood to apply.
(B) It concedes that the shortcoming the argument intends to address does not exist in every instance.
(C) It supports the argument's contention that political professionals devote time and energy to crafting the candidate's message and persona.
(D) It suggests that the relationship between a candidate's policy and that candidate's persona is not as essential as some may believe it to be.
(E) It is a premise on which other premises supporting the conclusion is based.

**STOP**

IF YOU FINISH BEFORE TIME IS CALLED, YOU MAY CHECK YOUR WORK ON THIS SECTION ONLY.
DO NOT WORK ON ANY OTHER SECTION IN THE TEST.

The Princeton Review

Completely darken bubbles with a No. 2 pencil. If you make a mistake, be sure to erase mark completely.

**1. YOUR NAME:** ______________________________
(Print) Last First M.I.

**SIGNATURE:** ______________________________ **DATE:** ___ / ___ / ___

**HOME ADDRESS:** ______________________________
(Print) Number

______________________________
City State Zip Code

**PHONE NO.:** ______________________________
(Print)

**IMPORTANT:** Please fill in these boxes exactly as shown on the back cover of your test book.

## 2. TEST FORM

## 3. TEST CODE

| | | | | |
|---|---|---|---|---|
| 0 | A | 0 | 0 | 0 |
| 1 | B | 1 | 1 | 1 |
| 2 | C | 2 | 2 | 2 |
| 3 | D | 3 | 3 | 3 |
| 4 | E | 4 | 4 | 4 |
| 5 | F | 5 | 5 | 5 |
| 6 | G | 6 | 6 | 6 |
| 7 | | 7 | 7 | 7 |
| 8 | | 8 | 8 | 8 |
| 9 | | 9 | 9 | 9 |

## 4. REGISTRATION NUMBER

| | | | | | |
|---|---|---|---|---|---|
| 0 | 0 | 0 | 0 | 0 | 0 |
| 1 | 1 | 1 | 1 | 1 | 1 |
| 2 | 2 | 2 | 2 | 2 | 2 |
| 3 | 3 | 3 | 3 | 3 | 3 |
| 4 | 4 | 4 | 4 | 4 | 4 |
| 5 | 5 | 5 | 5 | 5 | 5 |
| 6 | 6 | 6 | 6 | 6 | 6 |
| 7 | 7 | 7 | 7 | 7 | 7 |
| 8 | 8 | 8 | 8 | 8 | 8 |
| 9 | 9 | 9 | 9 | 9 | 9 |

## 5. YOUR NAME

| First 4 letters of last name | | | | | FIRST INIT | MID INIT |
|---|---|---|---|---|---|---|
| A | A | A | A | | A | A |
| B | B | B | B | | B | B |
| C | C | C | C | | C | C |
| D | D | D | D | | D | D |
| E | E | E | E | | E | E |
| F | F | F | F | | F | F |
| G | G | G | G | | G | G |
| H | H | H | H | | H | H |
| I | I | I | I | | I | I |
| J | J | J | J | | J | J |
| K | K | K | K | | K | K |
| L | L | L | L | | L | L |
| M | M | M | M | | M | M |
| N | N | N | N | | N | N |
| O | O | O | O | | O | O |
| P | P | P | P | | P | P |
| Q | Q | Q | Q | | Q | Q |
| R | R | R | R | | R | R |
| S | S | S | S | | S | S |
| T | T | T | T | | T | T |
| U | U | U | U | | U | U |
| V | V | V | V | | V | V |
| W | W | W | W | | W | W |
| X | X | X | X | | X | X |
| Y | Y | Y | Y | | Y | Y |
| Z | Z | Z | Z | | Z | Z |

## 6. DATE OF BIRTH

| Month | Day | | Year | |
|---|---|---|---|---|
| JAN | | | | |
| FEB | | | | |
| MAR | 0 | 0 | 0 | 0 |
| APR | 1 | 1 | 1 | 1 |
| MAY | 2 | 2 | 2 | 2 |
| JUN | 3 | 3 | 3 | 3 |
| JUL | | 4 | 4 | 4 |
| AUG | | 5 | 5 | 5 |
| SEP | | 6 | 6 | 6 |
| OCT | | 7 | 7 | 7 |
| NOV | | 8 | 8 | 8 |
| DEC | | 9 | 9 | 9 |

## 7. SEX

MALE

FEMALE

The Princeton Review

FORM NO. 00001-PR

## Test 1

Start with number 1 for each new section.
If a section has fewer questions than answer spaces, leave the extra answer spaces blank.

| Section 1 | Section 2 | Section 3 | Section 4 |
|---|---|---|---|
| 1. A B C D E | 1. A B C D E | 1. A B C D E | 1. A B C D E |
| 2. A B C D E | 2. A B C D E | 2. A B C D E | 2. A B C D E |
| 3. A B C D E | 3. A B C D E | 3. A B C D E | 3. A B C D E |
| 4. A B C D E | 4. A B C D E | 4. A B C D E | 4. A B C D E |
| 5. A B C D E | 5. A B C D E | 5. A B C D E | 5. A B C D E |
| 6. A B C D E | 6. A B C D E | 6. A B C D E | 6. A B C D E |
| 7. A B C D E | 7. A B C D E | 7. A B C D E | 7. A B C D E |
| 8. A B C D E | 8. A B C D E | 8. A B C D E | 8. A B C D E |
| 9. A B C D E | 9. A B C D E | 9. A B C D E | 9. A B C D E |
| 10. A B C D E | 10. A B C D E | 10. A B C D E | 10. A B C D E |
| 11. A B C D E | 11. A B C D E | 11. A B C D E | 11. A B C D E |
| 12. A B C D E | 12. A B C D E | 12. A B C D E | 12. A B C D E |
| 13. A B C D E | 13. A B C D E | 13. A B C D E | 13. A B C D E |
| 14. A B C D E | 14. A B C D E | 14. A B C D E | 14. A B C D E |
| 15. A B C D E | 15. A B C D E | 15. A B C D E | 15. A B C D E |
| 16. A B C D E | 16. A B C D E | 16. A B C D E | 16. A B C D E |
| 17. A B C D E | 17. A B C D E | 17. A B C D E | 17. A B C D E |
| 18. A B C D E | 18. A B C D E | 18. A B C D E | 18. A B C D E |
| 19. A B C D E | 19. A B C D E | 19. A B C D E | 19. A B C D E |
| 20. A B C D E | 20. A B C D E | 20. A B C D E | 20. A B C D E |
| 21. A B C D E | 21. A B C D E | 21. A B C D E | 21. A B C D E |
| 22. A B C D E | 22. A B C D E | 22. A B C D E | 22. A B C D E |
| 23. A B C D E | 23. A B C D E | 23. A B C D E | 23. A B C D E |
| 24. A B C D E | 24. A B C D E | 24. A B C D E | 24. A B C D E |
| | 25. A B C D E | 25. A B C D E | 25. A B C D E |
| | | 26. A B C D E | |
| | | 27. A B C D E | |

## COMPUTING YOUR SCORE

**Directions**

1. Use the Answer Key on the next page to check your answers.
2. Use the Scoring Worksheet below to compute your raw score.
3. Use the Score Conversion Chart to convert your raw score into the 120–180 LSAT scale.

**Your scaled score on this virtual test is for general guidance only.**

Scores obtained by using the Score Conversion Chart can only approximate the score you would receive if this virtual test were an actual LSAT. Your score on an actual LSAT may differ from the score obtained on this virtual test.

In an actual test, final scores are computed with an equating method that makes scores earned on different editions of the LSAT comparable to one another. This virtual test has been constructed to reflect an actual LSAT as closely as possible, and the conversion of raw scores to the LSAT scale has been approximated.

What this means is that the Conversion Chart reflects only an estimate of how raw scores would translate into final LSAT scores.

**Scoring Worksheet**

1. Enter the number of questions you answered correctly in each section.

| | **Number Correct** |
|---|---|
| Section I . . . . . . . . . . . . . | ______ |
| Section II. . . . . . . . . . . . . | ______ |
| Section III . . . . . . . . . . . . | ______ |
| Section IV. . . . . . . . . . . . | ______ |

2. Enter the sum here: ______

**This is your raw score.**

**SCORE CONVERSION CHART**

**For Converting Raw Scores to the 120–180 LSAT Scaled Score**

| Reported Score | Raw Score Lowest | Raw Score Highest |
|---|---|---|
| 180 | 99 | 102 |
| 179 | —* | —* |
| 178 | 98 | 98 |
| 177 | 97 | 97 |
| 176 | 96 | 96 |
| 175 | —* | —* |
| 174 | 95 | 95 |
| 173 | 94 | 94 |
| 172 | 93 | 93 |
| 171 | 92 | 92 |
| 170 | 91 | 91 |
| 169 | 89 | 90 |
| 168 | 88 | 88 |
| 167 | 87 | 87 |
| 166 | 85 | 86 |
| 165 | 84 | 84 |
| 164 | 83 | 83 |
| 163 | 81 | 82 |
| 162 | 79 | 80 |
| 161 | 78 | 78 |
| 160 | 76 | 77 |
| 159 | 74 | 75 |
| 158 | 73 | 73 |
| 157 | 71 | 72 |
| 156 | 69 | 70 |
| 155 | 67 | 68 |
| 154 | 66 | 66 |
| 153 | 64 | 65 |
| 152 | 62 | 63 |
| 151 | 60 | 61 |
| 150 | 58 | 59 |
| 149 | 57 | 57 |
| 148 | 55 | 56 |
| 147 | 53 | 54 |
| 146 | 51 | 52 |
| 145 | 50 | 50 |
| 144 | 48 | 49 |
| 143 | 46 | 47 |
| 142 | 44 | 45 |
| 141 | 42 | 43 |
| 140 | 41 | 41 |
| 139 | 39 | 40 |
| 138 | 37 | 38 |
| 137 | 36 | 36 |
| 136 | 34 | 35 |
| 135 | 33 | 33 |
| 134 | 31 | 32 |
| 133 | 29 | 30 |
| 132 | 28 | 28 |
| 131 | 27 | 27 |
| 130 | 25 | 26 |
| 129 | 24 | 24 |
| 128 | 22 | 23 |
| 127 | 21 | 21 |
| 126 | 20 | 20 |
| 125 | 19 | 19 |
| 124 | 18 | 18 |
| 123 | 16 | 17 |
| 122 | 15 | 15 |
| 121 | —* | —* |
| 120 | 0 | 14 |

* There is no raw score that will produce this scaled score for this form.

# ANSWER KEY

## SECTION I

1. D
2. B
3. D
4. D
5. D
6. A
7. B
8. C
9. A
10. B
11. E
12. B
13. A
14. D
15. E
16. E
17. C
18. E
19. A
20. A
21. D
22. B
23. B
24. C

## SECTION II

1. A
2. C
3. E
4. C
5. E
6. E
7. D
8. E
9. E
10. A
11. E
12. D
13. D
14. B
15. B
16. B
17. D
18. C
19. C
20. C
21. D
22. D
23. C
24. A
25. A

## SECTION III

1. E
2. C
3. B
4. D
5. A
6. B
7. A
8. D
9. D
10. A
11. B
12. D
13. B
14. D
15. C
16. A
17. D
18. C
19. C
20. C
21. D
22. A
23. B
24. D
25. D
26. C
27. E

## SECTION IV

1. D
2. D
3. E
4. C
5. B
6. E
7. B
8. A
9. C
10. B
11. A
12. B
13. D
14. C
15. D
16. D
17. E
18. A
19. C
20. D
21. E
22. C
23. D
24. C
25. B

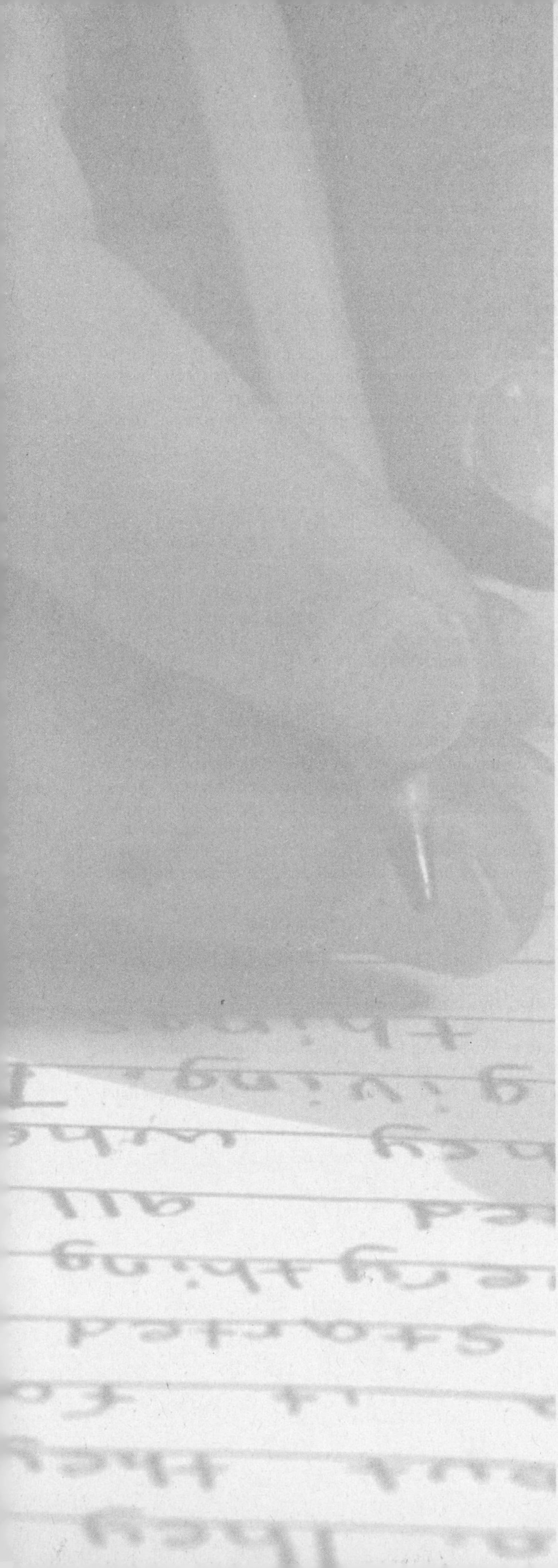

# Chapter 10
# Answers and Explanations to Practice Test 1

# SECTION I

Questions 1–5

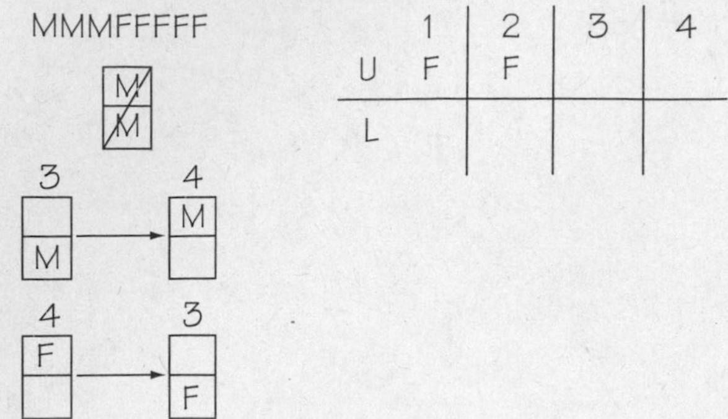


*The only deduction of note in this game is a distribution deduction: Since there are three M's, and M's cannot be in the same cage together, three cages will contain one M and one F each, and exactly one cage will contain two F's.*

1. **D** Do this on the first pass through the game. If 3 contains two F's, then all the rest of the cages must contain one M and one F apiece. That makes the membership of Cages 1 and 2 clear. The conditional clue doesn't provide us any information about the arrangement in Cage 4; if you don't understand this, then you definitely need to review the material on conditional clues. Here's the diagram for this question.

| | 1 | 2 | 3 | 4 |
|---|---|---|---|---|
| U | F | F | F | M/F |
| L | M | M | F | F/M |

Only (D) is possible.

2. **B** Do this on the second pass through the game. If you do, then you realize that you hit the jackpot in question 4. That diagram shows that (A), (C), (D), and (E) are all possible, leaving us with only (B), the right answer.

   A quick inspection shows why: We deduced initially that exactly one cage can have two F's in it; choice (B) would force us to make two such cages, which in turn would force two M's together in a cage.

3. **D** Do this on the first pass through the game. You should recognize that the new information in this question triggers the contrapositive of clue 4: F in the upper berth of 4 requires us to put an F in the lower berth of 3 to keep from violating the rule. This is answer choice (D); it's also the only deduction we can make from the information in this question.

4. **D** Do this on the first pass through the game. An M in the lower berth of 3 requires us to put an M in the upper berth of 4, because of the conditional clue. Then the remaining berths in 3 and 4 must be occupied by F's. This leaves us one M and one F to place in the open spaces in Cages 1 and 2; they can go in either arrangement. Here's the diagram.

| | 1 | 2 | 3 | 4 |
|---|---|---|---|---|
| U | F | F | F | M |
| L | F/M | M/F | M | F |

   The berths that cannot contain males are those that must contain females. The choice that lists all of these slots, and only these slots, is (D).

5. **D** Do this on the first pass through the game. Putting F in the lower berth of Cage 2 means that all the other cages have to contain one M and one F; then the lower berth of Cage 1 contains an M. From there, we know that Cages 3 and 4 must each contain one F and one M, and we have to watch out for the conditional clue. Be careful about jumping to conclusions, though: There are three different ways the remaining elements could be arranged in Cages 3 and 4.

   It's best to proceed by POE from here.

   (A) Wrong. The lower berth of Cage 1 must contain an M.
   (B) Wrong. The lower berth of Cage 1 must contain an M.
   (C) Wrong. An F in the upper berth of 4 would require us to put an F in the lower berth of 3.
   (D) This is possible; make sure you use the conditional clue carefully.
   (E) Wrong. Cages 3 and 4 must each contain one M and one F to follow rule 3.

# SECTION I

Questions 6–11

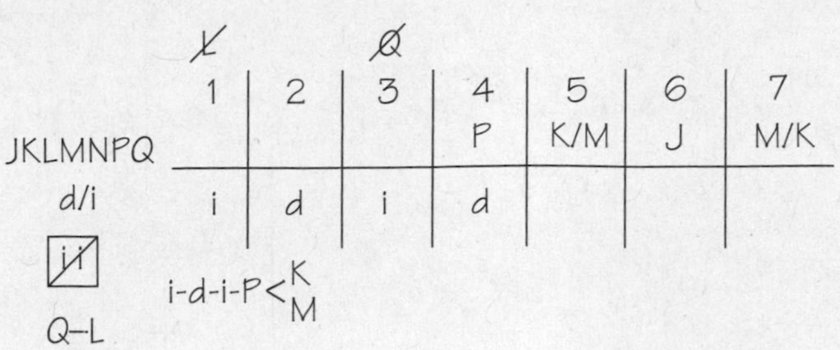


The key deductions for this game involve combining the two large clues about P. In clue 2, we learn that P must be followed by at least two elements: K and M; in clue 3, we learn that at least two i's must precede P, but since i's cannot arrive consecutively, this means at least one d must separate them. Thus P must have at least 3 arrivals before it, forcing P to appear no earlier than 4. But the fact that J must be the sixth arrival means that P also cannot arrive later than 4; otherwise, there wouldn't be enough room to K and M. Thus, P must arrive fourth.

The other deductions flow from this one. With P fourth, 1 must be i, 2 must be d, and 3 must be i. Since i's cannot arrive consecutively, the fourth arrival—P—must be d. K and M must occupy 5 and 7, although we do not know in which order. Finally, since Q must arrive before L, L cannot be in 1, and Q cannot be in 3, the last space that remains open in the top tier. With all these deductions, the questions should go quickly.

6. **A** Do this first for this game; it's a Grab-a-Rule question. With this many deductions, we can scan and quickly eliminate anything that doesn't have these last four entries: P, then K or M, then J, then M or K. The only choice that remains is (A).

7. **B** Do this on the second pass through the game. At this stage of the game, you probably recognize that the only way a pair of planes could never both be international flights is if they always have to be next to one another in the diagram. If you see this, then (B) stands out as the answer, since this is the only pair listed that has to arrive consecutively.

   POE will also get you to the answer, although more slowly:

   (A) Your work from question 8 can be adapted to show that J and N can both be i's.
   (B) This is the answer, for reasons described above.
   (C) Your work from question 9 can be adapted to show that L and M can both be i's.
   (D) Your work from question 9 shows that M and K can both be i's.
   (E) Your work from question 8 shows that N and Q can both be i's.

8. **C** Do this on the first pass through the game. N third leaves only spaces 1 and 2 open on the top tier; Q must go in 1 and L must go in 2 to fit with the ordering clue we're given about them. Here's the diagram.

| 1 | 2 | 3 | 4 | 5 | 6 | 7 |
|---|---|---|---|---|---|---|
| Q | L | N | P | K/M | J | M/K |
| i | d | i | d | | | |

The only airplane listed that has to be a domestic flight is L, so choice (C) is the answer.

9. **A** Do this one on the first pass through the game. We already know that two have to be d's; if there's only one more, then the remaining d has to go in 6 to prevent i's from appearing consecutively. Here's the diagram.

| 1 | 2 | 3 | 4 | 5 | 6 | 7 |
|---|---|---|---|---|---|---|
| | | | P | K/M | J | M/K |
| i | d | i | d | i | d | i |

The only airplane listed that has to be a domestic flight is J, so choice (A) is the answer.

10. **B** Do this on the second pass through the game. Knowing how many planes arrived before a given plane is equivalent to knowing where it appears in the diagram. We know the locations of only two planes—P and J—so the answer here is (B).

11. **E** Do this on the second pass through the game. We actually deduced enough to choose (E) from the outset: P must be fourth, either K or M must be fifth, and Q can't be third, so Q can never appear next to P. A quick scan can get you this answer if you have all those deductions. As usual, POE can also yield the correct answer, although more slowly.

(A) Your work from question 9 can be adapted to show that we can have L in 3; P, of course, is always in 4.

(B) Your work from question 8 shows that N can be in 3; P, of course, is always in 4.

(C) All of your work on this game indicates that K can be in 5; P, of course, is always in 4.

(D) Since K and M are identical elements, this answer is the same as (C).

(E) This is the correct answer, for reasons discussed above.

# SECTION I

Questions 12–18

p : BF
a : CD
o : NV
N/Vo Bp

| 1 | 2 | 3 |
|---|---|---|
| Ca/Da/No | Ca/Da/No _ | Ca/Da/No _ _ |

The key deduction for this game is noticing that there are three elements—the two apples and the navel orange—that have to be kept apart from one another. Since there are only three groups, exactly one of these elements must occupy a space in each group. Beyond that, the only real clue is the one forcing Bp to appear with an orange; note that, since No is one of the triad that is spread out over the three groups, it is possible for Bp to appear in group 2.

12. **B** Do this Grab-a-Rule question first in this game.

(A) This puts Da and No together in group 2.
(B) This is the answer; it doesn't violate any rules.
(C) This doesn't put Bp with an orange.
(D) This puts the two apples together.
(E) Like (D), this puts the two apples together.

13. **A** Do this on the second pass through the game. This is actually quite simple if you have the deduction that exactly one space in each group must be occupied by Ca, Da, or No. If you happen to peek on the first pass and see that (A) is the answer, that's great. If you wait for the second or don't have the deduction, trying the choices in order will quickly lead you to discover that (A) can't work.

14. **D** Do this on the second pass through the game. We can easily eliminate choices by finding counterexamples in our prior work. In fact, as it turns out, our work from question 15 alone eliminates (A), (B), (C), and (E). The only choice we can pick here is (D).

15. **E** Do this on the first pass through the game. Since Bp has to appear with an orange, the only way we could also have it appear with a pear is to put it into basket 3. That forces No into basket 3 also; the two apples occupy the reserved spaces in baskets 1 and 2, in either arrangement, leaving Vo for the remaining space in basket 2. Here's the diagram.

| 1 | 2 | 3 |
|---|---|---|
| Ca/Da | Da/Ca Vo | No Bp Fp |

The only choice that's possible, given this diagram, is (E).

16. **E** Do this on the second pass through the game. If you happen to spot that (E) would violate our crucial deduction about Ca, Da, and No, then you can pick it directly. Otherwise, we can do POE using prior work. Our work from question 18 shows that (A), (B), and (D) don't have to be true all the time; our work from question 15 shows that (C) doesn't have to be true all the time. You can get to (E) easily either way.

17. **C** Do this on the first pass through the game. If Bp isn't in basket 3, then it can only go into basket 2; it must appear there with No. That forces the apples into the two remaining reserved spaces, in either arrangement, leaving Vo and Fp to occupy the two open spaces in basket 3. Here's the diagram.

| 1 | 2 | 3 |
|---|---|---|
| Ca/Da | No Bp | Da/Ca Vo Fp |

The only choice that's possible, given this diagram, is (C).

18. **E** Do this on the first pass through the game. Fp and Ca in the same basket can happen either in basket 2 or in basket 3. Since this is a must-be-true question, it's probably easier to map out the two possible scenarios than it is to try POE.

If Fp and Ca are in basket 2, then Bp must go into basket 3. The only open space in our diagram is in basket 3; this space must contain Vo. Now Bp is in the same basket with an orange, so Da and No can occupy the reserved spaces in baskets 1 and 3 in either order.

If Fp and Ca are in basket 3, then Bp must go into basket 2 with No. Once again, Vo goes into basket 3; this time, Da has to go into basket one. This diagram summarizes all the deductions for this question.

| | 1 | 2 | 3 |
|---|---|---|---|
| i. | Da/No | Ca Fp | No/Da Bp Vo |
| ii. | Da | No Bp | Ca Fp Vo |

The only choice that has to be true in both scenarios is (E), the correct answer.

# SECTION I

Questions 19–24

FGHIJ

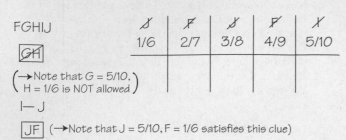

| ~~J~~ | ~~F~~ | ~~J~~ | ~~F~~ | ~~I~~ |
|---|---|---|---|---|
| 1/6 | 2/7 | 3/8 | 4/9 | 5/10 |
| | | | | |

~~GH~~ (→Note that G = 5/10, H = 1/6 is NOT allowed)

I— J

JF (→Note that J = 5/10, F = 1/6 satisfies this clue)

Be sure to note the irregularities with clues 1 and 4. Since the order "wraps around," we have to be careful with these clues. There are only a few deductions. Since F can't be 4/9, we can't have J in 3/8; otherwise, there would be no way to make the JF block. Since I must always perform before J, we know J cannot be 1/6, and I cannot be 5/10. Since J cannot be 1/6, F cannot be 2/7, since that would prevent us from making the JF block.

19. **A** This is a Grab-a-Rule question; do it first on this game.

    (A) This follows all the rules; note that it satisfies the JF block by making J perform fifth and F perform sixth. This is the answer we want.
    (B) This puts F in 4/9.
    (C) This doesn't have J perform immediately before F.
    (D) This doesn't have J perform immediately before F; it also doesn't have J perform after I.
    (E) This has G perform immediately before H.

20. **A** Do this on your second pass through the game. Although it is a specific question, the task here looks like a difficult one, since you must directly deduce the answer.

    It turns out not to be as difficult as it looks. F in 3/8 means J must be in 2/7, so that we preserve the JF block. This forces I to be in 1/6 to stay in front of J. To prevent G from coming immediately before H, we must put G in 5/10 and H in 4/9, the only two spaces remaining. Here's the diagram.

| 1/6 | 2/7 | 3/8 | 4/9 | 5/10 |
|---|---|---|---|---|
| I | J | F | H | G |

We've deduced the position of every element, so (A) is the answer here.

21. **D** Do this on your first pass through the game. J in 4/9 means F must be in 5/10 to preserve the JF block. Many arrangements of I, G, and H will work from here, but we must always be certain to keep G from coming immediately before H. Although we have only one real deduction, the only choice this deduction doesn't eliminate is (D).

22. **B** Do this on your second pass through the game. As it turns out, our work on question 20 leads us directly to (B), the answer here.

    If instead you worked this one by POE, the initial deductions from the game would eliminate (A), (D), and (E). You can see the reason (C) doesn't work if you play with it a bit: H in 5/10 means that G can't be in 4/9; we have a clue that tells us F can't appear in 4/9; in order to make the JF block, we couldn't put J in 4/9. The only element left for this space is I, but this would force I to appear after J, violating a rule.

    However you arrive there, (B) is the choice to pick.

23. **B** Do this on your second pass through the game. One of our initial deductions was that F can't be in 2/7, so (B) is the answer here.

24. **C** Do this on your first pass through the game. It's unusual to find more than one Grab-a-Rule question on a game, but there is on this one.

    (A) This doesn't have J perform immediately before F.
    (B) This has G perform immediately before H.
    (C) This follows all the rules; it's the answer we want.
    (D) This puts F in 4/9.
    (E) This has J performing before I.

# SECTION II

1. **A Conclusion:** Workshops will increase the quality of the short stories written by students.

   **Premise:** Anyone who repeatedly writes new stories will write better-quality stories.

   **Assumption:** The workshops will cause an increase in the number of students who repeatedly write new stories.

   This is a SUFFICIENT ASSUMPTION question. We want to pick the answer that, if true, guarantees the truth of the conclusion—most likely by filling the gap.

   (A) Yes. This choice links the premise to the conclusion and fills the argument's main gap.
   (B) This choice refers to advice; the argument states that advice isn't important for improving quality.
   (C) Because the conclusion involves a comparison, we need to know how the number of students writing many new stories will compare to the number doing so now.
   (D) This is too wishy-washy to guarantee the truth of the conclusion.
   (E) This is a restatement of the main premise; it doesn't provide additional support to the conclusion. It could be a decent Assumption answer, but this isn't an Assumption question.

2. **C** This is a MAIN POINT question. We want to find the single thing the argument is constructed to make us believe.

   (A) The argument wants to explain the reasons for this similarity; this is a premise of the argument.
   (B) What the politicians hope to gain by introducing their plans isn't the issue here.
   (C) Yes. This is a gentle restatement of what the argument wants to say: The incumbent copied the challenger's plan.
   (D) Like (B), this choice goes to what gain the politicians hope to get.
   (E) This is far too general to the main point of this argument, which deals with a single situation.

3. **E** This is a REASONING question. Come up with your own description of how Mark objects to Kristen before you go to the answer choices, and then try to match your description to the choices.

   (A) Importance is not the issue here—effectiveness is. Eliminate it.
   (B) No, she's making a mistake with regard to the personal income tax cut—not the business one. Eliminate it.
   (C) He doesn't point out any negative impacts of the personal income tax. He just shows that Kristen's positive points may not be so positive.
   (D) He doesn't ever question that.
   (E) Exactly. He shows how it's possible that neither of Kristen's good outcomes could occur. It's the correct answer.

4. **C** This is a PRINCIPLE question. We are given five principles in the answer choices for this specific question, so we should come up with our own principle for the actions in the argument and match it to the answer choices. The conclusion we are trying to justify is that the real concern over the new ordinance is about the government's disregard for individual property rights.

   (A) If this were true, it would not match with the actions in the argument, because the argument says the local environmental risk isn't as important as individual rights.
   (B) This has the same problem as answer choice (A). It's the opposite of what the argument is saying.
   (C) Bingo. An individual's rights (such as privacy) are more important than environmental rights.
   (D) This would also go in the opposite direction from the argument.
   (E) This is nice, but it's not something that would strengthen the citizen's viewpoint. This is the politically correct response. Watch out—it's a trap.

5. **E Conclusion:** The company is going to redesign the product.

   **Premise:** The surveys indicate that more people have a negative opinion of the product than have a neutral or positive one.

   **Assumption:** The survey is representative of the opinions of all people who have used the product.

   This is a WEAKEN question. Try to see which answer choice has the most negative impact on the conclusion of the argument. Remember to assume the hypothetical truth of each choice and apply it to the argument.

   (A) We have no idea whether a numerical system or an open-ended system would be more appropriate for this survey.
   (B) We're not concerned with the specific feature these customers didn't like about the product. We're looking for something that would show why the conclusion might be wrong.
   (C) This looks okay, but it doesn't really show that we should ignore the dissatisfaction of the customers. Let's eliminate it.
   (D) This would strengthen the argument by showing how the survey was representative. It's the opposite of what we want in this case.
   (E) This shows how the survey was not representative because there's a lot of happy, or at least not unhappy, people who aren't sending back the questionnaires, thereby skewing the data. It's the answer.

# SECTION II

6. **E** This is basically an INFERENCE question. We want a statement about which both Adolphus and Jean definitely express different views.

   (A) Jean never says that the new system won't do what Adolphus says it will.
   (B) Adolphus does not address the issue of public support.
   (C) Jean doesn't think it can't be implemented quickly; she just doesn't think that would be a good idea.
   (D) Adolphus doesn't address the question of how to pay for the change.
   (E) This is correct. Adolphus would say no: replace it immediately; Jean would say yes: secure funding and build public support first.

7. **D** This is a PRINCIPLE question, although because we are asked to apply a principle, it's actually very similar to an INFERENCE question. Take the stated principle as truth: Take action only when the likely consequences of inaction are worse than the foreseeable negative consequences of the action. Note that the condition used in this principle is a necessary ("only-if") condition.

   (A) This choice does not address possible negative consequences of the canal system at all.
   (B) This choice doesn't state that the negative consequences outweigh the consequences of inaction.
   (C) Tough one. This demonstrates that the necessary condition in the principle is satisfied; however, that condition can tell you only when *not* to pass the law ("pass it only if…"). There may be further requirements we aren't told about.
   (D) Yes. If the ban is instituted, it is possible that the mink will die out; if the ban is not instituted, it seems likely that the mink will continue to survive because it has been hunted for a long time. Because this doesn't satisfy the necessary condition, the ban should *not* be implemented. This is a correct use of the principle.
   (E) This choice talks about funding for an environmental policy, which isn't relevant to the principle.

8. **E** **Conclusion:** The mayor's support for public schools is insincere.

   **Premise:** The mayor sends his or her own children to private school.

   **Assumption:** It is impossible for someone who doesn't send his or her own children to public schools to be sincere in his support for them.

   This is an ASSUMPTION question. We want to pick something the argument needs for its conclusion to be correct.

   (A) This is too specific in its description of the mayor's motives; some other factor may explain his behavior.
   (B) Very close, but this doesn't go to the question of the mayor's sincerity in professing support, which is the issue in this argument.
   (C) This is far too specific to be an assumption required by this argument.
   (D) This is rather too sweeping to be an assumption required by this argument.
   (E) Yes. This includes both the main issues: public schools and the mayor's sincerity. "No direct personal interest" is a reasonable paraphrase of the idea of sending his or her own children to public schools.

9. **E** This is a RESOLVE/EXPLAIN question. We want to find the choice that tells us why the study's official conclusion appears to contradict its statistic about employment rates.

   (A) "Public perception" isn't clearly relevant to how the study's conclusion was reached.
   (B) This makes the paradox worse by indicating that the study was properly conducted.
   (C) This makes the paradox slightly worse by suggesting the vocational schools are successful in training students.
   (D) This explains why the numbers for vocational schools were so high but not where the study's official conclusion came from.
   (E) Yes. Many graduates of four-year colleges do not seek employment within two years because they go on to other schools, an option not open to anyone else. The number of students is large enough to account for the difference.

## SECTION II

10. **A** This is most nearly a WEAKEN question. Howard claims that Linda's explanation cannot be correct because it has been known for some time that electrons are the only charges involved in the conduction of current. We want the choice that indicates why Howard's objection doesn't get to the heart of the matter.

    (A) Yes. The standard definition, although inconvenient, was not changed once further evidence came to light because changing it would have caused problems.

    (B) This is similar to (A), but it doesn't contain an explicit explanation of why the definition was not changed.

    (C) This shows that the standard definition isn't unworkable, but it doesn't explain why the definition wasn't changed.

    (D) This is similar to (A), but again it doesn't contain as explicit of a statement of why the definition wasn't changed.

    (E) This is like (C); it explains that the standard definition isn't absolutely unworkable, but nothing more.

11. **E Conclusion:** Radical dietary changes made to lose weight do not improve health.

    **Premises:** Past radical dietary changes recommended for weight loss had negative health consequences; current ones are certain to do so as well.

    **Assumption:** No radical change other than the ones discussed could improve health.

    This is a FLAW question. We want a choice that indicates or describes the assumption.

    (A) The argument accepts that people make changes for other reasons—weight loss; it claims that changes made for this purpose do not improve health.

    (B) The relative severity of the problems discussed in the premises doesn't affect the conclusion.

    (C) The issue in this argument is overall health, not whether weight-loss efforts are successful.

    (D) The argument doesn't try to blame all health problems on dietary changes.

    (E) Yes. Here is a diet plan that would reduce weight while improving health.

12. **D Conclusion:** Dental plans don't protect the dental health of children.

    **Premise:** Dental health of children cannot be protected unless they receive regular twice-yearly cleanings.

    **Assumption:** To be adequate, dental reimbursement plans must provide what is required to protect children's dental health.

    This is a NECESSARY ASSUMPTION question. The correct answer will be something necessary for the conclusion to be true, and if made false, will make the argument fall apart.

    (A) What was true in the past isn't relevant to this conclusion.

    (B) The children for whom dental plans are adequate aren't relevant to this conclusion.

    (C) This is far too sweeping to be an assumption required by this argument.

    (D) Yes. If this is untrue, then the argument no longer makes sense.

    (E) The argument says that tooth decay is a serious problem, but the problems that result from tooth decay aren't directly relevant to the conclusion.

13. **D** This is an INFERENCE question. The answer should be a logical consequence of the material in the passage.

    (A) This is the opposite of the passage; this is the method of compensation that was used before fraud began to grow.

    (B) Although the fixed-percentage method is associated with less fraud, we aren't told that a bigger percentage would give us even less fraud.

    (C) This is the opposite of the passage; this is the method of compensation that appears to have caused fraud to increase.

    (D) Yes. If fraud causes a decrease in one kind of compensation, then it must at least sometimes increase the other kind of compensation by a greater amount, or else the new compensation method wouldn't encourage fraud.

    (E) The problem here is the word *problem*; we're told that changes have increased the amount of fraud, but we don't know that it wasn't a problem before it increased.

# SECTION II

14. **B** **Conclusion:** Colleges should expand their athletic departments.

    **Premises:** College athletes are less likely to die young; expanded departments would allow more people to participate in college athletics.

    **Assumption:** Participation in athletics makes people live longer, rather than something inherent in the people who currently compete in college athletics.

    This is a WEAKEN question. Figure out which answer choice has the most negative impact on the conclusion of the argument. Remember to assume the hypothetical truth of each choice and apply it to the argument.

    (A) Succeeding in society has no impact on this argument. Eliminate this choice.
    (B) This is it. It seems to be saying that the existing athlete population is different health-wise from the college population at large, which would weaken the argument that if we included more people in the program, more people would be healthy.
    (C) This doesn't impact the argument that if colleges were able to expand athletic departments, people would be healthier.
    (D) This would strengthen the argument, if anything, if we made nonathletes into athletes when they entered college.
    (E) Comparing women to men is not relevant. There could be biological (or other) reasons that women live longer than men—reasons that are completely unrelated to athletics. For this answer to be relevant, it would need to compare women athletes to women nonathletes.

<u>Questions 15–16</u>

**Conclusion:** Youth should be considered an advantage in hiring.

**Premises:** Younger workers can be paid less; younger workers have fewer other commitments that detract from their jobs.

**Assumption:** The identified advantages of youth are not more than compensated for by disadvantages that are not mentioned.

15. **B** This is a WEAKEN question. We want something that tells us why youth shouldn't really be considered an advantage.

    (A) This compares two reasons a young employee might miss work; it doesn't involve a comparison between young workers and older workers.
    (B) Yes. This identifies a disadvantage of younger workers that doesn't apply to older workers.
    (C) This strengthens the argument by identifying an additional advantage of young workers.
    (D) This strengthens the argument by identifying a disadvantage of older workers.
    (E) This weakens the argument very slightly by showing that not all older workers have the cited disadvantages, but it isn't as clear or direct as (B).

16. **B** This is a REASONING question. The claim mentioned is the conclusion of the argument. (B) is the only possible choice here.

    (A) No. The claim mentioned is the conclusion, not a premise.
    (B) Yes. This is the primary thing that the argument wants to establish.
    (C) No. Anything that supports a premise would also be a premise of the argument; the claim mentioned is the conclusion.
    (D) No. It states the conclusion, so it certainly doesn't call it into question.
    (E) No. This statement is the conclusion, not a stipulation or a qualification of the conclusion.

## SECTION II

17. **D Conclusion:** The majority of customers will experience significant benefits as a result of the new system.

    **Premise:** The computer will set the prices so that they are high when demand is high and low when demand is low.

    **Assumptions:** Prices will stay low at off-peak times, even though lots of people will want tickets, and will stay high at peak times, even though fewer people will want tickets.

    This is a FLAW question. Come up with your own description of why the author's conclusion is flawed before you go to the answer choices. Then try to match your description to the choices.

    (A) No, we are allowed to accept premises as facts. Eliminate it.
    (B) Assuming that the technology will work is not what's wrong with this line of reasoning. Eliminate it.
    (C) This has no impact on the goal of the airline—to pass savings on to its customers. Eliminate it.
    (D) Yes. The result, that a large number of people would choose to travel at off-peak times, would cancel the benefit that off-peak times would be cheaper because the system would increase the number of flights as a larger number of people sought to buy tickets.
    (E) We're not concerned with the exact number here. Eliminate it.

18. **C** This is a STRENGTHEN question. We want the choice that provides the most additional support for the physicist's contention that the results were inconclusive.

    (A) This provides only weak support; it doesn't deal with the results of the simulations.
    (B) The issue here is whether changes in clumping could cause changes in the distribution of matter; the "random" factor in this choice is a red herring.
    (C) Yes. This supports the physicist's explanation by reinforcing it; the results were very similar because the theories used do not allow for much variation.
    (D) The fact that this is a common attribute of all models doesn't support the physicist's statement about this case.
    (E) This doesn't appear to affect the physicist's statements either way.

19. **C** This is most similar to an INFERENCE question. We want to pick the statement that most clearly sums up the rest of the passage.

    (A) This goes far beyond the material in the passage.
    (B) This is the opposite of the direction the passage is going: Children can tell the difference, yet they aren't always held responsible.
    (C) Yes. If everyone who could tell the difference were held responsible, then many children would be held responsible.
    (D) This brings in the concept "unjust," which isn't explicitly used in the passage.
    (E) This contradicts the passage, which identifies some people who can tell the difference but aren't held responsible.

20. **C Conclusion:** Ammonia content is not relevant to a cleaner's efficacy.

    **Premise:** For a cleaner to be effective, it must be used with the right proportion of water and applied with a mop twice a day.

    **Assumption:** Because you must do other things to make a cleaner effective, ammonia has nothing to do with a cleaner's effectiveness.

    This is a FLAW question. Come up with your own description of why the author's conclusion is flawed before you go to the answer choices. Then try to match your description to the choices.

    (A) This answer choice is an excellent example of LSAT gibberish. Eliminate it.
    (B) Why not? Because you know that's true in life? We're talking about the argument. Eliminate it.
    (C) That's right. The other requirements don't just make the ammonia issue evaporate. No pun intended.
    (D) The author is flawed in assuming that ammonia content isn't relevant, not in discussing procedure.
    (E) The awareness of the cleaner makers is out of the scope of this argument.

## SECTION II

21. **D Conclusion:** Naproxen sodium is less costly than is ibuprofen.

    **Premises:** Naproxen sodium costs one-fifth what it did ten years ago, while ibuprofen costs somewhat more.

    **Assumption:** Naproxen sodium was not five times as expensive or more than was ibuprofen ten years ago.

    This is a SUFFICIENT ASSUMPTION question. Figure out which answer choice has the most positive impact on the conclusion of the argument. Remember to assume the hypothetical truth of each choice and apply it to the argument.

    (A) Nope. We need something that links the price of naproxen and ibuprofen. Eliminate it.
    (B) The frequency of use of either product is outside the scope of the argument.
    (C) Bummer, but we're not trying to help the ibuprofen makers here anyway. Eliminate it.
    (D) Bingo. If you work out the math, you'll see that it's now a certainty that naproxen is less costly than ibuprofen.
    (E) But if naproxen were *really* expensive as compared to the possibly super-cheap ibuprofen originally, this wouldn't necessarily make the conclusion work.

22. **D** This is an INFERENCE question. We want something that is a correct conclusion from the passage material.

    (A) "Medical ethics" is mentioned in the passage, but we aren't told how this would change a doctor's behavior.
    (B) This mixes up the "identifying with a patient" and "defective machine" claims in the passage. There's no way we can conclude this.
    (C) The only passage material about sympathy in treatment indicates it might be harder for a sympathetic doctor to recommend difficult treatment.
    (D) Yes. This is a case in which sympathy leads to better care than treating the patient as a defective machine would.
    (E) We have no information about which way of viewing a patient is easier for a doctor.

23. **C Conclusion:** Increasing starting pay wouldn't increase the overall number of sales agents.

    **Premises:** Increasing starting pay would increase the number of new hires, but it would also increase the number of existing employees who leave; the number of additional new hires is no greater than the number who would be induced to quit.

    This is a PARALLEL question. We want a choice that also talks about a measure that has two effects—one causing an increase and the other causing a decrease—in which the sizes of the two effects are compared.

    (A) The comparison here isn't between similar quantitative things.
    (B) The comparison here is between the increase in spending on training and the overall amount spent on accidents; this might have a chance if the anticipated *change* in the amount spent on accidents were mentioned, but it isn't.
    (C) This is it. The increase due to faster production is offset by a decrease due to defects, so speeding up production wouldn't help.
    (D) This one doesn't compare an increase and a decrease to the same quantity. This isn't quite parallel.
    (E) This one brings in the issue of safety, which isn't quantitative.

## SECTION II

24. **A Conclusion:** Horror movies don't contribute to the bad behavior of young people.

    **Premises:** A study concluded that horror movies contribute to bad behavior of young people; experts agree that the study was flawed.

    **Assumption:** No evidence other than the mentioned study links horror movies to bad behavior; a contention that has not been proven cannot be true.

    This is a FLAW question. We want a choice that exploits or describes the argument's assumptions.

    (A) Yes. The argument does this, and this is indeed its problem.
    (B) This relates to the flawed study, not to the spokesperson's argument.
    (C) No evidence suggests that the experts' judgment about the study is incorrect.
    (D) On the contrary, the argument doesn't fail to consider this fact; it's the (incorrect) method the argument uses to reach its conclusion.
    (E) The motives of those who conducted the flawed study aren't relevant to the spokesperson's conclusion.

25. **A Conclusion:** Exposure to reviews of a book can change a reader's opinion of it.

    **Premises:** Most people say they enjoy a book when they read it without having read reviews; most people who say they enjoyed a book say they will not reread it after having read some reviews.

    **Assumptions:** Willingness to reread a book is a reliable indicator of whether a reader has a favorable opinion of that book.

    This is a NECESSARY ASSUMPTION question. We want to pick the choice that the argument requires for its conclusion to be correct.

    (A) Yes. If this is untrue—if a reader who likes a book is unlikely to say that he or she will reread it—then the argument's reasoning falls apart.
    (B) This would strengthen the argument, but it's too specific to be something the argument needs.
    (C) This brings in questions of how the reader got the book; this doesn't have any clear impact on the argument's reasoning.
    (D) This might weaken the argument, but it isn't an assumption.
    (E) How good the book actually is isn't relevant to the argument's conclusion.

# SECTION III

Questions 1–5

1. **E** This is a BIG PICTURE: MAIN POINT question. We're looking for the main idea of the passage as a whole.

   (A) This is too narrow; it leaves out the material in the third paragraph.
   (B) The emphasis here is wrong; it focuses on popularizations of science and Asimov merely as one example, whereas the passage is primarily concerned with Asimov's work. Furthermore, this statement is too strong to be supported by the passage.
   (C) The tone here is wrong; the passage isn't concerned with showing that Asimov didn't understand science.
   (D) This is too narrow; it's too focused on Seldon specifically and leaves out the larger implications from the third paragraph.
   (E) Yes. This has pieces from all three paragraphs and is consistent with the author's tone.

2. **C** This is a STRUCTURE: FUNCTION question. We're looking for a good summary of the third paragraph.

   (A) The tone here is wrong; "ultimate failure" is too strong.
   (B) This isn't similar to the paragraph. No claim about Asimov's fiction is considered and rejected.
   (C) Yes. This contains the two main topics of the paragraph, and the tone matches the author's.
   (D) This is too general. It needs to include some reference to Asimov's work specifically.
   (E) This is contrary to the passage; the themes of Asimov's works are represented as ones he definitively believed in.

3. **B** This is a STRUCTURE: FUNCTION question. We're working with the statement that Asimov wrote at least one book in every Dewey Decimal category.

   (A) The statement is untrue, but this isn't identified as one of many untrue things that are believed about him.
   (B) Yes. Although the statement is untrue, the passage says that "its spirit provides an accurate picture of the man."
   (C) The passage itself states that Asimov was prolific.
   (D) This isn't directly related to the cited statement about the diversity in his works.
   (E) This contradicts passage information, which suggests that he had a wide range of interests.

4. **D** This is an EXTRACT: INFERENCE question. We're dealing with statements in the second paragraph.

   (A) "Amused" is the wrong tone here.
   (B) On the contrary, the passage's whole point is to show that it's blatantly impossible.
   (C) "Ambivalent" is the wrong tone here.
   (D) Yes. This is a primary piece of evidence in the passage's description of Asimov's beliefs about the power of science.
   (E) No. The passage suggests that it is impossible to achieve.

5. **A** This is a REASONING question. We're looking for an illustration of the effect described in the third paragraph.

   (A) Yes. The referenced area of the passage explains the effect as showing that perfect prediction is impossible when knowledge is imperfect.
   (B) This has to do with described advances in physics, which are in a different part of this paragraph.
   (C) This has to do with described advances in biology, which are in a different part of this paragraph.
   (D) This contradicts the idea described in the passage.
   (E) This doesn't have to do with inevitable errors in predictions.

Questions 6–12

6. **B** This is a STRUCTURE: FUNCTION question. We want the choice that provides a good summary of the second paragraph.

   (A) The tone here is wrong; the material in this paragraph describes one source of the problem, but the purpose is not to lay blame.
   (B) Yes. History is used to describe one reason for the severity of the current problem, the canals.
   (C) The problem's uniqueness is described most clearly in the first paragraph; this is the wrong emphasis.
   (D) The emphasis here is wrong; certainly the discussion supports this contention, but this isn't the purpose of the paragraph.
   (E) The emphasis here is wrong; this has always been true of the lagoon, but this paragraph describes a past event that influenced how it is happening.

## SECTION III

7. **A** This is a REASONING question. We're looking for a situation similar to the one described in the fourth paragraph.

    (A) Yes. This describes another situation in which loss is compensated for by new building on the same spot.
    (B) This describes a situation in which loss is compensated for by moving a building elsewhere.
    (C) This describes a situation in which new building leads directly to loss, rather than rebuilding what exists.
    (D) This describes a situation in which an old building is adapted to suit new purposes.
    (E) This describes a situation in which intentional demolition leads to loss of a building.

8. **D** This is a REASONING question. We want a statement that weakens the last sentence of the passage.

    (A) This doesn't tell us that radical measures may not be required to prevent flooding.
    (B) This strengthens the statement by indicating that radical measures may be required.
    (C) This suggests that the problem may be prevented, but we don't know how radical the preventive measures will need to be.
    (D) Yes. This describes a relatively modest measure that, according to the choice, would solve the problem.
    (E) This strengthens the statement by suggesting that effective solutions may have to be radical.

9. **D** This is an EXTRACT: INFERENCE question. Four of these statements will be supported by the passage, and the fifth will be our answer.

    (A) This can be concluded from the statements about Roman construction in the fourth paragraph.
    (B) This can be concluded from the statements about natural compaction of river sediments in the third paragraph.
    (C) This can be concluded from the statements about Venice's current economy in the fourth paragraph, or alternatively from statements about its history in the first paragraph.
    (D) Yes. We're told that water levels are rising, but not how the rate of the rise compares to the rate elsewhere.
    (E) This can be concluded from the statements in the first paragraph describing the factors that "in part" led to Venice's trade success, or the statement in the fourth paragraph that "Venice's economic strength rests now on the foundation of tourism."

10. **A** This is an EXTRACT: INFERENCE question. The phrase *modern-day* points to the last sentence in the fourth paragraph.

    (A) Yes. This relates to the nearby claim about the "foundation" of "Venice's economic strength."
    (B) Environmental effects on the salt marshes aren't discussed in the passage.
    (C) The passage indicates that this can't be stopped.
    (D) This contradicts statements in the last paragraph.
    (E) This is not a recommendation the author ever makes.

11. **B** This is an EXTRACT: INFERENCE question. The stem points us to the discussion in the second paragraph of diverting rivers.

    (A) No. The passage says that this contributes to the problem but is not solely responsible for it.
    (B) Yes. This comes from the comment that diverting the rivers had "an unanticipated effect."
    (C) The passage says that no one has seriously recommended restoring the rivers' courses and that this change wouldn't solve the problem anyway.
    (D) This is not said anywhere in the passage.
    (E) The tone here is wrong. The author's point in this paragraph isn't to show that past city leaders were irresponsible.

12. **D** This is an EXTRACT: INFERENCE question. We're looking for direct passage support for one of the choices.

    (A) The passage says that the water-level rise will most likely be from fifteen to thirty inches.
    (B) Although the passage talks about the loss of elevation versus sea level, it focuses on rising water as the cause of this, rather than sinking land.
    (C) On the contrary, the passage predicts it will flood more often if nothing is done.
    (D) Yes. The passage says that sea level rises are likely to be in the range of fifteen to thirty inches; taking the sinking land into account, the loss versus sea level would be larger. The passage says it lost ten inches versus sea level in the last century. This leaves us plenty of wiggle room.
    (E) This is a danger identified by the passage, but it doesn't predict that this will definitely happen.

# SECTION III

Questions 13–19

13. **B** This is a BIG PICTURE: MAIN POINT question. We're looking for the main point of the entire passage.

(A) The tone here is wrong. It's too much to say that the passage represents Sen's work as a "defense" of these ideas.
(B) This is it. It includes all the major components of the passage and is appropriately qualified to fit the tone of the passage.
(C) The emphasis here is wrong; the passage isn't just about social choice. Also, we're never told that it's replaced other theories.
(D) The tone here is wrong. This is too neutral to represent the author's views correctly.
(E) The emphasis here is wrong; it's too narrowly focused on one issue in the passage, and it overstates the passage's treatment of that issue.

14. **D** This is a BIG PICTURE: MAIN POINT question. We're looking for a title that comes closest to encapsulating the passage.

(A) The tone here is wrong; calling Sen a "rebel" isn't consistent with the passage's treatment of him.
(B) This is too general. It would be nice to have a choice that focuses on Sen.
(C) The emphasis here is really wrong. The passage isn't primarily about Arrow.
(D) Yes. This has Sen, social justice, and a positive spin on both.
(E) This is far too general, has the wrong emphasis, and doesn't even mention Sen or social choice.

15. **C** This is an EXTRACT: INFERENCE question. We'd like direct passage support for our answer.

(A) "Incapable" is an overstatement of information about Sen's work in the third paragraph.
(B) This contradicts statements about Sen's work in the fourth paragraph, which in part says that Arrow's theorem doesn't always apply.
(C) Yes. This is directly supported by statements in the fourth paragraph.
(D) This contradicts the passage's third paragraph.
(E) This contradicts the passage's second paragraph, in which we learn that Arrow worked in social choice before Sen.

16. **A** This is a REASONING question. The reference is to the second paragraph.

(A) Yes. Arrow's work is described as "a series of thought experiments."
(B) This choice involves using evidence from the past, not thought experiments.
(C) This choice involves using specific observations, not thought experiments.
(D) This choice involves using measurement tools, not thought experiments.
(E) This choice involves using personal statements, not thought experiments.

17. **D** This is an EXTRACT: INFERENCE question. We need to find direct support in the passage for our answer.

(A) This is inconsistent with the statements made in the first paragraph.
(B) The tone here is wrong; the author seems to think that social choice theory is pretty nifty.
(C) The tone here is inappropriate; the author expresses an entirely positive attitude, not ambivalence, towards Sen's ideas.
(D) Yes. This is indicated in the first and third paragraphs.
(E) Practical applications for election reform are not addressed in the passage.

18. **C** This is an EXTRACT: INFERENCE question. The reference is to the fourth paragraph.

(A) Mobility and adaptability aren't really the ideas described here.
(B) *Access* and *justice* are key terms in the description, but *legal redress* doesn't really come out of the passage.
(C) Yes. Markets and democracies are described as *choice-driven* in this area of the passage.
(D) The passage doesn't require that everyone be an economist.
(E) This goes too far; the passage doesn't say that Sen believes equal access entails redistribution of wealth.

19. **C** This is an EXTRACT: INFERENCE question. We'll find passage support for four of the choices, and the fifth will be our answer.

(A) This is stated in the fourth paragraph, in a description of Sen's early work.
(B) This is stated at the end of the third paragraph.
(C) Yes. We aren't given complete enough information about the United Nations to know this.
(D) This is stated near the beginning of the fourth paragraph.
(E) This is stated right at the beginning of the passage.

## SECTION III

Questions 20–27

20. **C** This is an EXTRACT: INFERENCE question. The passage states that Kipling's stories "build upon Lamarckian theory." If you look in the previous paragraph, you find that Lamarckian theory suggests that individuals can change through will.

    (A) While fables use stories about animals to create morals, there is no evidence in the passage that Kipling writes fables.
    (B) Futuristic worlds most likely appear in science fiction stories; while the second passage mentions science fiction, the first does not.
    (C) Yes. This is a good paraphrase of Lamarckian ideas.
    (D) Population thinking is a key element of Darwinian, rather than Lamarckian, ideas.
    (E) While the example of Lamarckian change depicts the change of the parent giraffe in the body of the child, this answer is too specific; there is no evidence that Kipling focused on the parent-child relationship.

21. **D** This is an EXTRACT: INFERENCE question. Passage B offers a lengthy quote from Huxley followed by several lines of explanation. Basically, you can paraphrase this paragraph as stating that we can't ignore our physical past, but we must morally evolve beyond it so we won't destroy ourselves.

    (A) This is too strong; while Huxley urges moral change, he states that the cost of ignoring physical evolution would be destruction.
    (B) Individual variation is a major factor of the first passage, not the second one, in which Huxley's ideas are discussed.
    (C) This paraphrases Lamarckian ideas rather than Huxleyian ones.
    (D) Yes. This is a good paraphrase of the second paragraph of the second passage.
    (E) Huxley argues for discarding certain elements of "our inheritance from our forefathers," not Darwin's theory.

22. **A** This is an EXTRACT: INFERENCE question. Find a statement that both authors would likely agree on.

    (A) Yes. Both Lamarck and Huxley are described as believing in self-directed evolution: of an organism (Lamarck) or humankind (Huxley).
    (B) Both Kipling and Wells are writers, but there is no information about Wells's particular beliefs.
    (C) Both Mayr and Bowler are modern commentators, but Mayr discusses "population thinking," while Bowler writes about the differences between current and nineteenth-century Darwinism.
    (D) Mendel focuses on genetic issues, while Huxley is interested in moral evolution.
    (E) Dobzhansky was a scientist who focused on change between species, while Wells was a science fiction writer.

23. **B** This is an EXTRACT: INFERENCE question. Both passages suggest that Darwinism has been understood differently at different times: The first passage demonstrates how the introduction of genetics changed Darwinism in the 1920s, and the second passage summarizes Peter Bowler's argument about changes in the meaning of Darwinism.

    (A) Breeding populations are discussed in the first passage, but not the second.
    (B) Yes. This focuses on Darwinism varying in different time periods.
    (C) While the first passage states that the early twentieth century is when modern Darwinian ideas began, the second passage does not offer a specific time period.
    (D) Both passages mention a fiction writer, but there is no evidence that fiction writers focused on Darwin in particular.
    (E) Passage A argues that focusing on the inheritance of the child, rather than the population as a whole, is a Lamarckian rather than Darwinian idea.

24. **D** This is a BIG PICTURE: PRIMARY PURPOSE question regarding the difference between the passages.

    (A) The second passage stays focused on nineteenth-century understandings of Darwin, so it is inaccurate to say that it moves forward in time.
    (B) The first passage does mention Lamarckian theory as a different theory of evolution, but its primary focus is demonstrating how Darwinian theory was prescient, or predictive, of modern understandings of evolution.
    (C) There is no discussion of the ramifications of Darwin's similarity to modern understandings of evolution in passage A, so this is not the correct answer.
    (D) This is true. The first passage demonstrates that Darwin's theories, without the benefit of modern genetics, still focused on very similar issues of population change, and the second passage shows how Huxley varied in his understanding of the path of evolution.
    (E) The first passage focuses a great deal on Lamarck, who had his own theory about evolution, rather than being a primary interpreter of Darwin, so this answer choice is not correct.

# SECTION III

25. **D** This is an EXTRACT: INFERENCE question. Passage B details Huxley's views on evolution: While man was physically shaped by evolution, he must now move to "self-directed moral evolution." Thus we can infer that he is somewhat Lamarckian in his beliefs, since Lamarck believed "that individuals changed through personal actions and will."

(A) Because Huxley lived in the nineteenth century, he was unaware of modern genetic theory, which passage B indicates came into play during the 1920s; he would not object to a theory he didn't know about.
(B) This is a description of Lamarckian ideas, which Huxley basically agreed with.
(C) Passage B is dedicated to showing how Huxley differed from Darwin; thus you can assume that Huxley would not object to this idea.
(D) Yes. This is Darwin's idea about population, rather than individual, change. In contrast, Huxley believed in self-directed evolution.
(E) This is a paraphrase of Huxley's own statement in the second paragraph.

26. **C** This is an EXTRACT: INFERENCE question. The first passage discusses how understandings of genetic variation revitalized Darwinian theory, as well as how variation was differently understood by Darwin and Lamarck. In all cases the variation discussed is physical. The second passage is focused mainly on how Huxley viewed variation: He stresses that the physical inheritance of our past cannot be ignored, but that humanity must now move to individual moral evolution.

(A) Huxley discusses "our inheritance from the forefathers who were the puppets of the cosmic process," so there is a group element to Passage B.
(B) Because Huxley emphasizes the need for individual moral evolution, this answer can be eliminated.
(C) Yes. This summarizes the difference between the two passages.
(D) Passage A does stress the importance of variation in breeding populations, but it is not claiming that the method of breeding varies.
(E) This can be eliminated for the same reason that choice (D) can.

27. **E** This is a REASONING question. Lamarck argued that individuals changed through "personal actions and will" and then passed these changes on to their children.

(A) The bird tries to change the environment rather than itself.
(B) Moral adaptation is a concern of Huxley, not Lamarck.
(C) You are told the giraffe can't fit into the cave, but not that it takes any specific action to get into the cave, so this is not a Lamarckian change.
(D) This is a traditionally Darwinian model of evolution, which focuses on change in environment rather than the individual's actions.
(E) Yes. This example shows an individual taking an action (hunting with its mouth open) and then physically changing as a result.

# SECTION IV

1. **D Conclusion:** U.S. children can achieve cardiovascular fitness only by engaging in daily stretching and exercise.

   **Premises:** French children are more fit than are U.S. children, and French children engage in daily stretching and exercise.

   **Assumptions:** There is no other reason that French children have greater cardiovascular fitness; if U.S. children start such a program, they will achieve greater fitness; the reason French children are more fit has something to do with daily stretching and exercise.

   This is a NECESSARY ASSUMPTION question. The correct answer will be something necessary for the conclusion to be true, and if made false, will make the argument fall apart.

   (A) This certainly strengthens the conclusion that stretching and fitness, applied to children anywhere, will help them achieve cardiovascular nirvana. Is it necessary though? We're concerned only with kids in the United States, so "all" is too extreme.

   (B) We're not concerned with the overall health of the children in this argument. Eliminate it.

   (C) We're not concerned with how fit the children will become when they are adults. Eliminate it.

   (D) If stretching *weren't* a necessary part of the French children's fitness, then the argument that doing the same thing in the United States would have the same result would fall apart. Thus, it's the answer.

   (E) Dietary changes are outside the scope of the argument. Eliminate it.

2. **D** This is a RESOLVE/EXPLAIN question. The paradox is that half of the medical histories on file are of women, while the goal is to track dangerous genes in sperm donors. Look for an answer choice that allows both parts of the argument to be true, and remember to assume the hypothetical truth of each of the answer choices.

   (A) This doesn't explain why half the records are of women. Eliminate it.

   (B) This looks pretty good, but it doesn't actually explain why this is "standard procedure." Also, it's a bit too general because it says "scientific clinics," and we're talking specifically about fertility clinics. Eliminate it.

   (C) Puberty is outside of the scope of the argument. Eliminate it.

   (D) Ah, so we have an example of why the records of the same number of women are kept as of men. Here is our answer.

   (E) Puberty is outside of the scope of the argument. Eliminate it.

3. **E** This is an INFERENCE question. Your goal is to find the one choice that must be true based on the information in the passage.

   (A) We don't know for sure what will happen if they do relax regulations, only what will happen if they don't. This one is too extreme. Therefore, look for a wishy-washy answer.

   (B) This is less extreme than (A), so let's leave it in for right now.

   (C) This has a similar structure to (B), so we now have to eliminate both (B) and (C).

   (D) Too extreme. Eliminate.

   (E) This is the most wishy-washy choice; therefore, it's the best answer.

4. **C** This is a RESOLVE/EXPLAIN question. The paradox is that doctors treat disease *Q* by increasing blood sugar levels even though patients with disease *Q* already have slightly elevated blood sugar levels. Look for an answer choice that allows both parts of the argument to be true, and remember to assume the hypothetical truth of each of the answer choices.

   (A) This would exacerbate the paradox, if anything. Eliminate it.

   (B) This doesn't do anything to explain the paradox, and blood pressure is out of the scope here. Eliminate it.

   (C) If we are always making sure to keep our blood sugar levels high, then we won't ever have these slightly low periods where the virus will flourish. This is the answer.

   (D) We don't care why the blood sugar fluctuates. We just want to know why we should keep it high.

   (E) Other diseases are outside of the scope of the argument.

## SECTION IV

5. **B Conclusion:** We must outlaw handguns to reduce handgun deaths.

   **Premise:** Most of the countries in which handgun deaths are substantially lower outlaw handguns.

   **Assumptions:** Other countries are similar enough that a ban may have similar effects; no means other than a ban will work.

   This is a NECESSARY ASSUMPTION question. We're looking for something that's necessary for the argument's conclusion to be true.

   (A) The rate of ownership isn't relevant to the conclusion in the strictest sense; the argument doesn't depend on bans working in this specific way.
   (B) Yes. If this isn't true—if the result of few gun deaths can be replicated in all countries without banning handguns—then the conclusion is definitely wrong.
   (C) Although there is a language shift like this in the argument, the conclusion doesn't depend on this statement being true.
   (D) The question of the basis on which a ban is justified is not relevant to the conclusion, which concerns only the ban's effect.
   (E) Like (A), this one tries to deal with how a ban would work; the argument doesn't depend on anything that specific.

6. **E Conclusion:** A person's speed and strength are determined mostly by metabolic rate.

   **Premise:** The metabolic rates of professional athletes are higher than those of average people.

   **Assumptions:** Speed and strength are determining factors in whether a person is a professional athlete; no third factor is responsible for speed and strength as well as metabolic rate.

   This is a STRENGTHEN question. We want something that supports the conclusion.

   (A) This provides very weak support for the argument's causal conclusion.
   (B) This choice weakens the argument slightly.
   (C) At best, this provides exceptionally weak support for the conclusion.
   (D) This choice seems to weaken the conclusion by suggesting that the causation may be reverse.
   (E) Yes. This makes a strong causal connection between metabolic rate and the other factors discussed.

7. **B** This is a REASONING question. We're looking for a choice that refers to the similarity between past developments on land and likely future developments in the ocean.

   (A) The two are presented as similar, not different, in this way.
   (B) Yes. The analogy is between grasses in land ecologies and krill in ocean ecologies.
   (C) This is a premise of the argument; this choice leaves out the conclusion.
   (D) Like (C), this choice covers only a part of the argument, leaving out the conclusion.
   (E) The argument doesn't make any statement that is this sweeping.

8. **A Conclusion:** work late shift → ~own car

   **Premise:** own car → AAC member

   ~AAC member → ~own car

   This is a SUFFICIENT ASSUMPTION question. We're looking for the additional item of information that would most strongly support the conclusion.

   (A) Yes. This choice—work late shift → AAC member—gives us a piece that, when connected to the contrapositive of the premise, guarantees us that the conclusion is correct.
   (B) This is a restatement of our premise; it doesn't provide any additional strength.
   (C) This tells us about people who don't work the late shift—information that isn't relevant to our conclusion.
   (D) Like (C), this tells us about people who don't work the late shift. We need definite information about those who do.
   (E) This includes no information about those who work the late shift.

9. **C** This is a MAIN POINT question. We're looking for the best statement of the single thing the argument wants us to believe.

   (A) This choice leaves out the notion of using tools.
   (B) This choice is a bit too general to be the best available expression of the point.
   (C) Yes. This includes the two main pieces of the argument: using tools and animals other than humans.
   (D) Tool use not related to getting food isn't addressed by this argument.
   (E) This isn't what the argument is trying to prove.

## SECTION IV

10. **B** This is a REASONING question; it doesn't fit well in any strict category. We want the choice that correctly describes what Kim seems to think Victor is saying.

   (A) This is Victor's point. Kim interprets Victor to be saying something stronger.
   (B) Yes. Kim appears to think that Victor's comments apply to profits, not the *growth* in profits.
   (C) This choice introduces considerations of chronology that aren't included in the argument.
   (D) Used cars aren't mentioned by either of them.
   (E) "Financial health" isn't an issue that either of them addresses.

11. **A** **Conclusion:** Having an MBA doesn't lead to increased pay.

   **Premise:** A recent survey shows that top executives with MBAs are paid the same amount as top executives without MBAs.

   **Assumption:** Pay rates among top executives reliably show what effect having an MBA has on the salaries of all workers.

   This is a WEAKEN question. We're looking for new information suggesting that the conclusion may not be true.

   (A) Yes. If this is the case, then having an MBA might have the effect of increasing pay because it's a matter of common sense that top executives get paid more than other workers.
   (B) This choice doesn't provide us any new information about the effect of having an MBA.
   (C) This choice doesn't provide us any new information about the effect of having an MBA.
   (D) The success of those who already have a top job doesn't have a clear impact on pay rates.
   (E) This involves a comparison of those who already have top executive positions.

12. **B** This is an INFERENCE question. We want the choice that must be true, given the information in the passage.

   (A) We know that Oscar didn't understand the cause of Lucy's problem, but that doesn't guarantee us that the problem was with the engine.
   (B) Yes. Oscar repaired Lucy's problem; Oscar doesn't understand engines; this has to be true.
   (C) We don't know enough about "good" mechanics from the passage to conclude this.
   (D) We can't judge the completeness of Oscar's training just because he doesn't understand engines.
   (E) We don't know that the only problems Oscar can't fix pertain to engines.

13. **D** This is a STRENGTHEN question. We're looking to provide further support for Dr. Morris's part of the conversation. Dr. Morris attributes the results of the surveys to patient stubbornness as opposed to correct treatment.

   (A) This would weaken Dr. Morris's argument.
   (B) The opinions of organizations aren't relevant to Dr. Morris's point.
   (C) This is suggestive, but it doesn't strengthen Dr. Morris's argument directly.
   (D) Yes. This provides further support for Dr. Morris's contention that patients refuse to accept any treatment other than the one they request.
   (E) The impact of this choice isn't clear; certainly it doesn't directly support Dr. Morris's point about what patients will accept as treatment.

14. **C** **Conclusion:** The difficulty third-party candidates have in getting on the ballot in national elections isn't the reason they haven't had much success.

   **Premise:** All self-identified supporters of third parties have at some point voted for a major-party candidate in a national election when a third-party candidate was listed on the ballot.

   **Assumption:** The third-party candidates listed on the ballot in national elections are always members of the party supported by the voters mentioned in the premise.

   This is a FLAW question. We're looking for a choice that describes or exploits the argument's assumption.

   (A) On the contrary, the argument concludes that some factor other than difficulty getting on the ballot must be responsible.
   (B) As with (A), this choice concerns a possible reason other than difficulty getting on the ballot that may be responsible; that's the argument's point!
   (C) Yes. The fact that third-party supporters sometimes vote for major-party candidates may well be explained by the fact that candidates they support can't get on the ballot.
   (D) There are no internal contradictions here.
   (E) The behavior of all voters isn't relevant to the conclusion here.

# SECTION IV

15. **D** This is an INFERENCE question. We're looking for a statement about which Sara and Ross definitely express different views.

    (A) Ross doesn't go so far as to say that foreign aid spending should be increased.
    (B) Sara registers no opinion on this question.
    (C) Ross registers no opinion on this question.
    (D) Yes. Sara would say it doesn't; Ross would say it does.
    (E) Sara registers no opinion on this question.

16. **D Conclusion:** People in communities affected by environmental regulation often favor decreased taxes.

    **Premises:** When environmental regulation doesn't have direct economic benefits for the community, the government is perceived as being insensitive; when government seems to consider other people's interests more important, people in an area tend to favor less taxation.

    **Assumption:** The perception that government is insensitive leads to the belief that the government considers others' interests more important.

    This is a NECESSARY ASSUMPTION question. We're looking for a statement that is needed for the conclusion to be true.

    (A) This concerns what happens when government is perceived as being sensitive, but it includes no information about what happens when it's insensitive; this doesn't provide the needed link.
    (B) This compares two possible sources of perceived insensitivity in a way that isn't essential to the argument.
    (C) This relates to the beliefs that people have about the results of decreased taxation, but those beliefs could be wrong without affecting the argument.
    (D) Yes. Suppose this isn't true and that people may not hold this belief even if the government is perceived as being insensitive. Under those circumstances, the argument doesn't work.
    (E) Even if they do consider indirect benefits, the reasoning in the argument may still stand. This isn't a factor that's essential to the argument's reasoning.

17. **E Conclusion:** Those who live in heavily insulated homes are at greater risk for brain cancer.

    **Premises:** Heavily insulated homes trap more radon gas; radon gas exposure leads to high blood levels of radioactive compounds found in those who are being treated for brain cancer.

    **Assumptions:** The radioactive compounds are somehow involved in the causation of brain cancer.

    This is a WEAKEN question. We want to break the assumption or otherwise make the conclusion seem less likely.

    (A) The argument concerns only those exposed to high levels of radon; the fact that everyone is exposed to some radon doesn't hurt the argument.
    (B) This would slightly strengthen the argument.
    (C) The relative susceptibility of certain people to these problems isn't relevant here.
    (D) This seems to be trying to identify an alternate source of the compounds, but it's a weak answer; why, if these are used only initially, do patients with brain cancer continue to have them in their blood?
    (E) Yes. The brain cancer treatment is the source of these radioactive compounds, suggesting that they aren't involved in causing brain cancer.

18. **A Conclusion:** People should buy wild salmon instead of farmed salmon.

    **Premises:** Farmed salmon have many more bad environmental effects than wild salmon; cheapness of farmed salmon has increased the popularity of the fish, which may eventually threaten wild populations.

    **Assumption:** Buying only wild salmon could somehow prevent these bad effects; especially notable in this regard is the strange assumption that buying only wild salmon could somehow prevent them from being overfished.

    This is a FLAW question. We're looking for the choice that describes or exploits an assumption.

    (A) Yes. This refers to the strange idea that buying more wild salmon could help prevent it from being overfished.
    (B) The premises aren't contradictory; they just don't support the conclusion the argument is trying to draw from them.
    (C) It's not evident what these benefits may be.
    (D) No questionable principle is employed here.
    (E) The argument is not circular.

## SECTION IV

19. **C Conclusion:** Resentment isn't a reasonable response to rejection.

**Premise:** Rejection is the expression of either a purely personal preference or else a commonly held one; if purely personal, it could not have been predicted; if commonly held, it could have been taken into account.

This is a SUFFICIENT ASSUMPTION question. We're looking for the statement that makes our conclusion certain.

(A) This gets only one of the two possibilities mentioned; it leaves out the question of commonly held preferences.
(B) This gets only one of the two possibilities mentioned; it leaves out the question of purely personal preferences.
(C) Yes. This assures us the conclusion is right in both of the possible cases.
(D) This describes responses to resentment, not rejection.
(E) This mixes up the two possibilities described in the argument.

20. **D Conclusion:** Some things with quality A also have quality B.

**Premises:** Some things in a group have quality A; some things in the same group have quality B.

**Flaw:** "Some" is too small a proportion to guarantee that there is a member of the group with both qualities.

This is a PARALLEL-THE-FLAW question. We're looking for another argument that has the problem described above.

(A) The premises here involve one "some" statement and one "none" statement.
(B) The premises here don't involve two things that are each true of "some refrigerators."
(C) The conclusion here isn't similar; it talks about cases in which neither quality is present.
(D) Yes. Quality A is "prevents measles;" quality B is "needs to be administered only once."
(E) The premises here involve two "most" statements.

21. **E Conclusion:** Stock options are the most efficient use of an individual's investment money.

**Premise:** Stock options are the only investment in which an individual can get high returns with limited liability.

This is a SUFFICIENT ASSUMPTION question. We're looking for the choice that makes the argument's conclusion certain.

(A) This is a restatement of the argument's premise and provides no further support.
(B) This strengthens the argument somewhat, but it doesn't make the conclusion airtight. A short time period is identified as an advantage, but we don't know that this is the only investment with that advantage.
(C) This seems to be a fact that's indicated by the premises; restating it doesn't offer further support to the conclusion.
(D) We're told that this is an attribute of stock options, but we don't know that options are the only investment with this attribute.
(E) Yes. In addition to our premise, this fact would guarantee the truth of the conclusion.

22. **D** likely to be promoted → behave ethically

makes wise decisions → ~poor employee

behave ethically → well respected AND makes wise decisions

This is an INFERENCE question. We're looking for a statement that's definitely true, given the facts in the passage.

(A) The only thing we know for certain about executives who don't behave ethically is that they're not likely to be promoted. The last phrase of the passage guarantees us that there are some who lack both the quality of being well-respected and the quality of making wise decisions, but it leaves open the possibility that there are some executives who don't behave ethically who have either one or even possibly both of these qualities.
(B) See the explanation in (A) above.
(C) Yes. This is a correct use of this chain from the passage: likely to be promoted → behave ethically → makes wise decisions → ~poor employee.
(D) The only things we know about executives who aren't well respected is that they don't behave ethically and aren't likely to be promoted.
(E) We aren't able to draw any definite conclusions about executives who aren't poor employees.

# SECTION IV

23. **D Conclusion:** It cannot be true that everyone who engages in an activity (donating to charity) does so out of the same motive (concern for others).

    **Premise:** Another motive (lessening guilt) may also be a reason to engage in the activity.

    This is a PARALLEL question. We're looking for the choice that uses the same basic method of reasoning as the original argument.

    (A) The premise here is that the purpose wasn't achieved in all cases; it doesn't have to do with another possible purpose.
    (B) Like (A), the premise here has to do with the purpose not being achieved.
    (C) This doesn't have to do with motives at all.
    (D) Yes. One motive (wealth and fame) is rejected as the explanation for all cases because another possible motive (sharing artistic vision) could explain it as well.
    (E) This has to do with causes, which seems close, but this argument talks about a single instance, whereas our original argument talks about a whole group of instances.

24. **C** metallic glaze → floral pattern AND ~hourglass shape

    signed → hourglass shape

    made this century → signed

    This piece: floral pattern AND signed

    This is an INFERENCE question. We can predict the answer on this one using the conditionals. We cannot conclude anything for certain from the fact that the piece has a floral pattern. From the fact that the piece is signed, we can conclude that it has an hourglass shape; from the fact that it has an hourglass shape, we can conclude that it does not have a metallic glaze. We cannot conclude anything more about the piece.

    The only choice that's consistent with our conclusions is (C).

25. **B** This is a REASONING question. We're looking for the choice that correctly describes the cited statement.

    (A) On the contrary, the statement in question describes the cases when the conclusion *doesn't* apply.
    (B) Yes. In cases when the candidate takes the lead on policy, you can't say that strategists don't get the credit they deserve. In every other case, however, you can.
    (C) This statement doesn't provide support for any other statement in the argument.
    (D) This doesn't seem to be an accurate description of the argument's contents.
    (E) This is similar to (C). This statement doesn't provide support for any other.

# Chapter 11
# The Princeton Review LSAT Practice Test 2

# SECTION I

Time—35 Minutes
27 Questions

Directions: Each passage in this section is followed by a group of questions to be answered on the basis of what is stated or implied in the passage. For some questions, more than one of the choices could conceivably answer the question. However, you are to choose the best answer, that is, the response that most accurately and completely answers the question, and blacken the corresponding space on your answer sheet.

Questions 1–8 are based on the following passage:

Perhaps no figure from the Reconstruction era in the aftermath of the U.S. Civil War exemplifies the failed promise of those times better than Tunis Campbell. Campbell, born free in New Jersey, came to postwar Georgia as a superintendent in the Freedmen's Bureau. He was assigned to organize the settlement of three of the sea islands off Georgia's coast, in accordance with General William T. Sherman's Special Field Order 15, which famously granted forty acres and a mule to each of forty thousand freed slaves in the coastal areas of Georgia and South Carolina.

Campbell, a champion of black equality and self-determination, set up one of the islands—St. Catherine's—as an effectively independent black principality. Taking possession of the abandoned plantation lands granted by Sherman's order, the residents of St. Catherine's set up their own constitution, education system, and militia, and allowed no whites on the island. Within a year, however, the effects of Lincoln's assassination were felt throughout the occupied South, and the Union army seized the land back from residents, either returning it to its former owners or selling it to white investors in the North. A sharecropping system was instituted, whereby many of the practical realities of slavery, if not their precise form, took hold again. Campbell himself was exiled.

Determined to continue fighting for the freed slaves, Campbell worked tirelessly on their behalf. Resettling in MacIntosh County, he organized farm labor to help them gain power in negotiations with white landowners, and he worked tirelessly to register black voters. Within a few years his efforts paid off, and he became one of three African Americans to be elected to the Georgia state senate, where against all odds he managed to secure some few legal protections for black Georgians. His stature, however, was a serious irritant to the white power structure of the state, and Campbell was eventually driven out of the senate as the result of a concerted campaign of election fraud and the preferment of false charges against him.

Campbell continued to work on the former slaves' behalf, but the rising power of white supremacists and the indifference of the federal government to the fate of former slaves steadily eroded what progress he was able to make. Eventually, with the help of a judge sympathetic to their cause, Campbell's enemies were able to convict him on a trumped-up charge, and Campbell was sentenced to a year of hard labor on a chain gang. The plantation owner who bought his labor for that year paid the state of Georgia the meager sum of $8.75. Annual mortality rates for chain-gang laborers then averaged between 16 and 25 percent, and at age 63, it seems almost miraculous that Campbell survived. After his release Campbell left Georgia and returned only once more before his death in 1891. In Georgia as in most of the former Confederate states, efforts to implement reform during Reconstruction were systematically foiled by those who sought to preserve white power and relegate black Americans to a permanent underclass.

1. The passage is primarily concerned with

    (A) assessing the accomplishments of a well-known historical figure
    (B) criticizing conventional views of a contentious historical era
    (C) correcting mistaken understandings of an important geographical region
    (D) detailing the obstacles faced by a leader who sought self-determination for a group
    (E) asserting the importance of laws in reevaluating views of a historical era

2. The passage supports which one of the following statements concerning the lives of freed slaves in South Carolina and Georgia soon after the conclusion of the Civil War?

    (A) Some owned land and were able to participate in government.
    (B) Many were able to live independent of white influence.
    (C) Most were forced to continue working for their former owners.
    (D) All were able to exercise the freedoms afforded to other citizens.
    (E) No effort was made to assure their representation in national government.

GO ON TO THE NEXT PAGE.

3. Which one of the following best describes the function of the second paragraph of the passage?
   (A) It describes developments during Reconstruction that led to Campbell's eventual failure.
   (B) It describes an effort to establish self-determination for freed slaves and the ways in which that effort was foiled.
   (C) It summarizes the reasons Sherman's Special Field Order 15 was not fully implemented and indicates its limited effects.
   (D) It shows an instance of efforts to maintain freed slaves as a permanent underclass not being entirely successful.
   (E) It describes the outcome of the only effort during Reconstruction to respect the freed slaves' new legal equality.

4. In the fourth paragraph, the author mentions that a plantation owner paid $8.75 for a year of Campbell's labor while he was imprisoned primarily to
   (A) demonstrate the ways in which institutions of slavery remained operative during Reconstruction
   (B) quantify the dangerous conditions under which chain-gang laborers worked
   (C) suggest that Campbell's punishment was demeaning
   (D) prove the claim that the state of Georgia profited from Campbell's imprisonment
   (E) indicate why Campbell returned to Georgia only once after he had served out the term of his imprisonment

5. Which one of the following, if true, would provide the LEAST support for the author's statements concerning the sharecropping system that was instituted after the Civil War?
   (A) Black farmers were often subject to violence and intimidation by white landowners, both as slave laborers and as sharecroppers.
   (B) The rents that white landowners demanded from black sharecropping farmers were so high that it was impossible for most of them to accumulate any property or money of their own as the result of their labor.
   (C) The children of sharecropping farmers only rarely had access to education, and most of them were forced to work in the fields from a young age, just as they had during slavery.
   (D) Legal means were used to prevent sharecropping farmers from organizing to demand lower rents and better treatment from the white landowners whose land they farmed.
   (E) Sharecropping farmers were able to keep their families together and make other significant life decisions that were not available to slaves.

6. It can be inferred from the passage that each of the following is true of the political system in Georgia during the initial stages of Reconstruction EXCEPT:
   (A) Some freed slaves cast votes in state elections.
   (B) African American legislators were able to pass laws protecting some rights of freed slaves.
   (C) No white legislators supported Campbell's efforts to extend important freedoms to freed slaves.
   (D) White leaders were not all pleased at the stature achieved by some black politicians.
   (E) White judges at times served purposes approved of by white supremacists.

7. The passage does NOT provide an answer to which one of the following questions?
   (A) Was land ever given to freed slaves as a result of Special Field Order 15?
   (B) Was forced labor used as a means of punishment during Reconstruction?
   (C) Were African Americans elected to positions in state government at any time during Reconstruction?
   (D) For how long did the sharecropping system remain the primary means by which Southern landowners profited from their land?
   (E) Did the laborers who were former slaves negotiate with white landowners?

8. The author would most likely agree with which one of the following statements about Campbell's importance to a full understanding of Reconstruction?
   (A) Campbell was the only leader during Reconstruction who attempted to secure a full range of citizens' rights for freed slaves.
   (B) Campbell's story is emblematic of the reasons that Reconstruction did not deliver on its promise of freedom and equal rights for former slaves.
   (C) Campbell did not succeed in Georgia because he himself was not a freed slave and was not fully trusted by those he sought to help.
   (D) Campbell's effort at protecting freed slaves in Georgia from white supremacists exemplifies the fact that Southern state governments were weak during Reconstruction.
   (E) The analysis of Reconstruction requires that its failures as well as its successes be studied in detail, and Campbell provides ample illustrations of both.

GO ON TO THE NEXT PAGE.

Questions 9–14 are based on the following passage:

The crucial discovery that opened the way for modern advances in biochemistry was the role of DNA and protein in the biological activity of cells. After much debate and experimentation, it was eventually learned that DNA serves as the genetic blueprint for proteins, which are the compounds upon which all cellular activity depends. Thus, although no living cell can function without protein, DNA and its chemical cousin RNA serve as the driving force for its organization and use. This led to a proper understanding of viruses. Although pathogens such as parasites and bacteria are cellular and are thus by conventional definitions living organisms, viruses are not. They have no cells of their own; instead, they are composed of DNA or RNA material accompanied by only a small amount of protein. A virus uses its genetic instruction set to commandeer the machinery of other cells, and therefore was thought to demonstrate that although a pathogen can exist without protein, it must at a bare minimum include DNA or RNA.

In 1982, however, the biologist Stanley Prusiner hypothesized that there might exist proteins that were themselves pathogenic. Prusiner's idea of "prions" (proteinaceous infectious particles) was controversial because it contradicted the central dogma of modern biology. This hypothesis was, however, strengthened by further study of a class of encephalopathies that exist in many mammals: Called scrapie in sheep and goats, chronic wasting disease in elk and mule deer, and bovine spongiform encephalopathy in cattle ("mad cow disease"), these diseases are also found in humans—kuru, Creutzfeldt-Jakob Disease (CJD), and Fatal Familial Insomnia, to name a few. The fact that all of these diseases lead to similar types of brain damage was interesting, but even more interesting was the fact that material from infected individuals could transmit disease even after sterilization in an autoclave. DNA could not survive such treatment, but some proteins could, leading to the speculation that the pathogens in these cases were special forms of protein acting alone, without genetic direction.

A prion protein is not a foreign protein, but a variant conformation of a protein normally produced by cells. Because a protein's conformation—its folding and physical shape—determines its biological activity, the prion protein no longer serves its normal purpose. Instead, prion proteins replicate themselves by catalyzing the conversion of normal copies of the protein into the prion conformation, and they may also alter the synthesis of new protein to favor that conformation. This mechanism helps explain why a disorder such as scrapie may develop spontaneously in a sheep that has never been exposed to an external source of the prion protein that causes it because a normal protein may slip into its prion conformation by chance. This mechanism also explains how humans exposed to cattle prion proteins in their food may subsequently develop disease because it has been shown that cattle prions can cause a similar human protein to shift from its normal conformation into a prion form.

9. Which one of the following best expresses the main idea of the passage?

(A) Recent discoveries suggest that the understandings of DNA and protein on which modern biochemistry is based are incomplete.
(B) The hypothesis that prions cause certain classes of disease shows that there may be pathogens that do not possess genetic material.
(C) The central dogma of modern biology is that the presence of genetic material is necessary for an organism to be considered alive.
(D) Although pathogens have been found that are composed primarily of DNA or RNA with little protein, no pathogen can exist completely without protein.
(E) The discovery that prions cause certain encephalopathies holds out hope that hitherto untreatable diseases may soon be cured.

10. The passage indicates that one consequence for a person who ingests food products derived from cattle with bovine spongiform encephalopathy may be

(A) the contraction of a virus
(B) the spontaneous development of scrapie
(C) the contraction of a prion disease
(D) resistance to certain types of parasites
(E) the expression of genes that do not operate normally

GO ON TO THE NEXT PAGE.

11. Which one of the following best describes the organization of the passage?

(A) A commonly held belief is introduced, scientific evidence against the belief is offered, and the belief is finally rejected as untrue.
(B) A new area of biology is described, possible benefits of study in this area are hypothesized, and further directions for study in this area are recommended.
(C) One potential cause of a class of diseases is hypothesized, evidence both for and against this hypothesis is presented, and the hypothesis is finally accepted.
(D) The basis of a scientific belief is introduced, a class of diseases this belief may not be adequate to explain is described, and a proposed cause of the diseases that do not conform to the belief is outlined.
(E) An alternative mechanism for a commonly observed phenomenon is posited, evidence in favor of that mechanism is considered, and arguments against the mechanism are ultimately accepted.

12. The author refers to the fact that material from individuals infected with certain encephalopathies may remain infectious even after sterilization in an autoclave primarily in order to

(A) provide evidence that the conventional belief that all pathogens contain genetic material may not be true
(B) reinforce the claim that the class of encephalopathies discussed are all caused by the same prion
(C) indicate that it remains possible that these encephalopathies may be caused by viruses
(D) undermine conventional views of encephalopathy that state that these diseases can develop only spontaneously
(E) show how normal proteins may in some cases become pathogenic

13. By the author's statements, it can be inferred that the author would be most likely to agree with which one of the following statements?

(A) Not all diseases are caused by parasites, bacteria, viruses, or prions.
(B) Not all prion diseases involve changes to the conformation of a naturally produced protein.
(C) Not all proteins that exist in a prion form have detrimental biological effects in that form.
(D) Most diseases that are thought to be caused by prions can be spread from one species to another.
(E) Not all cases of prion disease can be explained by exposure to an external source of the pathogen that causes it.

14. Which one of the following is most analogous to the proposed mechanism by which a prion replicates itself, as that mechanism is described in the passage?

(A) A teacher who advocates a new method of teaching reading to students is more successful with her method than are other teachers using more conventional methods.
(B) An artisan who produces works that other artisans consider to be of inferior quality is nevertheless successful because he can produce his works very cheaply.
(C) A scientist who has always accepted the theory that protein is involved in heredity changes her mind when it is discovered that genetic traits cannot be transmitted by a cell with its DNA removed.
(D) A criminal who has developed a safe and lucrative scheme for cheating investment banks convinces many other individuals who have previously obeyed the law to use the same scheme to make money, who then convince others to do so.
(E) A high-school graduate who goes into business for himself instead of going to college is extremely successful and becomes a role model for other graduates who chose not to attend college.

GO ON TO THE NEXT PAGE.

Questions 15–20 are based on the following passages:

**Passage A**

According to W. Dale Mason, the issue of tribal sovereignty is especially pertinent to contemporary debates regarding Indian gaming. Since American law recognizes tribal sovereignty, many tribes are responsible, to varying degrees, for generating revenue for their communities. As such, many have turned to gaming as a source for much-needed income. With the passage of the Indian Regulatory Gaming Act (IRGA) in 1988, the United States Supreme Court recognized the right of tribes to own and operate gaming facilities without state interference. However, the issue of Indian gaming is still a controversial one.

Judy Zellio is a scholar of Indian gaming who focuses, for the most part, on numbers. She examines the number of Indian gaming facilities in the United States and the amount of money they now generate for Native communities. Drawing on statistical evidence, she examines the rapidly increasing trend of Indian gambling enterprises, pointing out that roughly half of the 560 tribes in the United States now operate gambling facilities of some kind or another. Most notably, some of the resort-like casinos located in densely populated coastal areas rival the "big boys" of Las Vegas and Atlantic City in terms of size and the money that they generate. According to Zellio, there is a complicated relationship among Indian tribes, surrounding communities, and government officials. Despite the passage of the IRGA, government officials endeavor to find ways of "cashing in" on these initiatives as they become more and more lucrative. Typically, they attempt revenue-sharing agreements or taxation. While Zellio clearly favors casinos and their multiple benefits to Native communities, she ultimately displays a cautious "wait-and-see" attitude regarding these communities, their gambling enterprises, and the relationships they might have with the American government in the future.

**Passage B**

In his examination of the relationship between Native communities, casinos, and the state, Ronald Andrade is quite polemical. He focuses his attention on California governor Arnold Schwarzenegger, particularly for his position on Indian casinos and for his negative representation of Native peoples. Schwarzenegger insists that Native peoples pay the state of California for their income generated in the gambling industry, arguing that they both live off of society and do not pay their "fair share." By drawing on historical examples, Andrade tries to show that Schwarzenegger's policies toward Native peoples is the latest in a long line of governmental attempts to prevent Indian communities from becoming self-sustaining and successful. For Andrade, Schwarzenegger's inflammatory language is designed to turn the general population of California against Native casinos, divide Indian communities, and like political leaders before him, undermine Native people's attempts to better themselves. Andrade's language may be forceful, but his language is in response to Governor Schwarzenegger's equally strong words, and is indicative of the anger that many Native people feel.

15. In the context of the second passage, which one of the following phrases could best be substituted for the word "polemical" (line 3) without substantially changing the author's meaning?

(A) agreeable but cautious
(B) derisive and contemptuous
(C) inflammatory and misleading
(D) aggressive and argumentative
(E) conciliatory and mollifying

16. It can be inferred that Zellio would probably agree with each of the following statements regarding Native casinos EXCEPT:

(A) Increasingly, Native communities throughout the United States turn to various forms of gambling enterprises as a way to raise revenue for their communities.
(B) Some of the larger gambling facilities along the east and west coast of the United States are comparable to those found in more established gaming areas like Las Vegas and Atlantic City.
(C) The relationship between Native communities and government officials is, at times, an uneasy one, as the latter wish to partake in gambling revenues to which they are not, by law, entitled.
(D) While some Native gaming facilities have been successful in generating revenue for their community, roughly half of the tribes in the United States do not operate gaming enterprises.
(E) Because of the success that some Indian gambling facilities have experienced, most Native communities will turn to gaming enterprises as a way of generating revenue for themselves.

GO ON TO THE NEXT PAGE.

17. It is likely that both Zellio and Andrade would agree that

(A) despite the passage of the Indian Gaming Regulatory Act, American government officials often attempt to find ways of involving themselves in the revenues of these lucrative businesses
(B) Arnold Schwarzenegger's inflammatory language on the issue of Native casinos is designed to turn the general population of California against Native casinos, divide Indian communities, and like political leaders before him, undermine Native attempts to better themselves
(C) Native communities should contribute their "fair share" to society by giving profits from gaming facilities to the government through revenue-sharing agreements or taxation
(D) while gaming facilities can be profitable businesses and can raise much-needed revenue for Native communities, social problems, such as gambling addiction, increase as the number of gaming facilities do
(E) government officials must respect the law and leave the operation of gaming facilities to Native communities

18. The discussion of Native gaming facilities in both passages focuses on

(A) how Native gaming facilities have changed the relationship between Native communities and government officials
(B) the relationship between Native communities and the government, especially on the government's interest in sharing the wealth of profitable gambling enterprises
(C) examining the positive and negative effects of the Indian Regulatory Gaming Act
(D) criticizing the Indian Regulatory Gaming Act
(E) examining the positive and negative effects of Native gaming facilities

19. Unlike Andrade, Zellio is primarily concerned with

(A) examining the negative social effects of Native gaming facilities
(B) considering the effects of Native gaming facilities on the surrounding communities
(C) criticizing a governmental official for his stance on Native gaming facilities
(D) comparing Native gaming facilities with those found in Las Vegas and Atlantic City
(E) providing statistical information on the prevalence of Native gaming, and outlining some of the key issues involved with these enterprises

20. Which of the following, if true, would most clearly weaken the view expressed in the second passage?

(A) There is evidence to suggest that in previous years governmental officials successfully taxed other profitable Native businesses, and after doing so, these enterprises quickly failed.
(B) Many provincial governments in Canada also have plans to tax lucrative gambling enterprises.
(C) Many Native communities that operate gaming enterprises enjoy a comfortable and peaceful relationship with the surrounding communities.
(D) Through education and financial support, the California government is currently assisting a number of Native communities to become successful and self-sustaining.
(E) Statistics show that gambling facilities in the central states are not as profitable as the ones located on the east and west coasts of the United States.

GO ON TO THE NEXT PAGE.

Questions 21–27 are based on the following passage:

Like many aspects of public life in the former Soviet Union, the production of visual art was sanctioned and closely controlled by the central government and the Communist party. Most Soviet-era work is thus dismissed by critics as mere propaganda, not worthy of the same consideration due to Western works of the same period. Interest in Soviet artists has traditionally focused on those who resisted the regime and in many cases, were persecuted for doing so. Yet it is difficult to avoid seeing, in this interest, not an objection to art as propaganda, but rather a preference for one kind of propaganda over another. In the highly charged political atmosphere of the Cold War, works produced both inside and outside the Soviet Union tended to take on ideological dimensions, whether or not the artist intended them to.

Soviet art took shape at a time when governments worldwide were beginning to make full use of the power of propaganda. Although the Nazi regime in Germany is typically identified as leading the way in this pursuit, over the same period Stalin was expanding the Soviet Union's propaganda apparatus. With regard to visual arts, this apparatus operated in the contexts of both "high culture" and "low culture." Stalin's government sponsored a style of painting called Socialist Realism, which used conventional sentimental tropes and a lexicon of Communist imagery to portray life in the Soviet Union, and Stalin himself, in idealized and inspirational ways. At the same time, the production of posters was vastly expanded; these posters used cartoonish and overblown imagery to evoke such ideas as the greed of capitalism, the savagery of fascism, and the bravery of factory workers and collective farmers. Today, the Soviet-era posters that survive are collector's items, and a modest market remains for the high-culture works of painting and sculpture that survived the overthrow of the Soviet regime.

An examination of cultural production in the United States over the same period yields surprising similarities. Throughout the thirties, the government sponsored production of public art through the Works Progress Administration. Often these works celebrated the dignity of work and the enduring spirit of the people. World War II poster propaganda yielded images that linger in the popular culture even now: Rosie the Riveter, Uncle Sam, and caricatured racist portrayals of people living in fascist countries. Even the most famous high-culture painting in the United States—the abstract expressionist work of such painters as Pollock and Rothko—took on political dimensions that are striking in light of their apparent lack of ideological content. Triumphal showings of these artists' work, represented as "cultural exchange," were organized within the Soviet Union during the Cold War with the purpose of lauding freedom of expression. Soviet officials, at the same time, pointed to them as proof of capitalist decadence. Even these works, meant to exemplify the aesthetic in its purest form, became weapons in an arms race of propaganda that mirrored other political contests taking place throughout the Cold War.

21. According to the passage, which one of the following opinions would art critics be most likely to hold concerning Socialist Realist paintings produced in the Soviet Union under Stalin's regime?

(A) They cannot be considered as artistically valuable as other works produced during the same period because of their status as government propaganda.
(B) They are at least as ideologically motivated as paintings made under the Works Progress Administration during the same time.
(C) Their market value exceeds the market value of some serious paintings made outside the Soviet Union during the same time.
(D) Their popularity in the contemporary market indicates that they are of less artistic value than other paintings made during that time.
(E) Although they are propaganda, they cannot be completely dismissed because much of the art made during that period served similar purposes.

22. Which one of the following, if true, would most undermine the author's interpretation of the fact that the U.S. government sponsored the production of art through the Works Progress Administration?

(A) U.S. painters who produced government-sponsored works were not subject to direct oversight by government representatives during the planning stages of their work.
(B) Soviet painters who worked in the officially approved style were paid for their work only after it had been accepted by the Communist party.
(C) U.S. painters were free to choose whether they wished to seek government funding for works that might have been considered subversive.
(D) Soviet painters were able to gain at least some public attention for paintings produced outside the auspices of the government and the Communist party.
(E) U.S. painters who were funded by the Works Progress Administration were not prevented from producing work critical of the U.S. government, and they often did.

GO ON TO THE NEXT PAGE.

23. Which one of the following best describes the organization of the second paragraph?

(A) A general claim about a historical period is presented and then illustrated with the use of supporting examples from several countries.
(B) A contention concerning one country is used as proof of the truth of this contention for all countries.
(C) A particular strategy by a government is shown to operate in two separate contexts for similar purposes.
(D) The ongoing popularity of the results of a particular policy is used to demonstrate the efficacy of that policy.
(E) Two governments that are considered similar in one way are shown to be dissimilar in other important ways.

24. According to the passage, which one of the following is true of abstract expressionist paintings?

(A) They were aesthetically superior to any paintings being produced in the Soviet Union at the same time.
(B) Their apparent lack of ideological content did not prevent them from being used as propaganda.
(C) The artists intended for them to be interpreted as lauding free expression.
(D) Their production was sponsored by the U.S. government through the Works Progress Administration.
(E) Their decadence is a primary reason they are considered among the greatest paintings of the twentieth century.

25. It can be inferred that the author would most likely agree with which one of the following statements concerning posters produced in the Soviet Union during World War II?

(A) They dealt with the same subjects used in propaganda posters produced in Nazi Germany during the same time.
(B) They employed the same deceptive practices that Socialist Realist paintings of the period employed.
(C) They attributed characteristics to factory and farm workers that those workers normally did not possess.
(D) They served similar purposes to the purposes served by some posters produced in the United States during the same period.
(E) These posters are not as desirable to collectors today as are propaganda posters produced in other countries during the same period.

26. Which one of the following is most analogous to the passage's discussion of the "preference" (line 11) ascribed to art critics?

(A) Literary reviewers prefer literary novels to popular novels because the tastes of literary reviewers are more refined than the tastes of most readers.
(B) Economists who prefer capitalism to socialism focus on the inefficiencies of a socialist government's policies and the successes of a rich venture capitalist who has been imprisoned by that government.
(C) Fashion designers who prefer creativity to practicality make garments that are exceptionally inconvenient to wear and maintain.
(D) Archaeologists who subscribe to a particular view of a civilization's history commence an investigation of a major site inhabited by that civilization with hopes of finding support for their view.
(E) A landscape designer who prefers shrubs to flowers nevertheless must accommodate a client's wishes to have a substantial number of flowers in a garden she is designing.

27. Which one of the following best expresses the main idea of the passage?

(A) The use of propaganda in both high-culture and low-culture contexts was prevalent in many countries during the twentieth century.
(B) Critics who dismiss Soviet art as being excessively ideological are incapable of seeing the ideological content of art produced at the same time in the United States.
(C) Paintings and posters were the primary means by which the governments fighting World War II sought to motivate their public to endure hardships associated with that war.
(D) Those who dismiss visual art produced in the Soviet Union as propaganda reveal their biases by doing so because even the greatest works by U.S. artists during the same period could also be used as propaganda.
(E) All art, regardless of the time and place of its production, has a political dimension that may be exploited by governments in their effort to produce propaganda.

# STOP

**IF YOU FINISH BEFORE TIME IS CALLED, YOU MAY CHECK YOUR WORK ON THIS SECTION ONLY. DO NOT WORK ON ANY OTHER SECTION IN THE TEST.**

# SECTION II
Time—35 Minutes
26 Questions

Directions: The questions in this section are based on the reasoning contained in brief statements or passages. For some questions, more than one of the choices could conceivably answer the question. However, you are to choose the best answer; that is, the response that most accurately and completely answers the question. You should not make assumptions that are by common sense standards implausible, superfluous, or incompatible with the passage. After you have chosen the best answer, blacken the corresponding space on your answer sheet.

1. Some analysts believe that changes in the price of oil are never appreciably influenced by long-term weather forecasts. Last year, however, the prediction of an especially violent hurricane season for this year was followed by a sharp increase in oil prices because in the past large hurricanes have been known to disrupt oil production in the Gulf of Mexico. Hence, the predicted incidence of hurricanes—only one of many aspects of long-term weather forecasts—can cause changes in the price of oil, which means that other aspects of weather forecasting can as well.

   The statement that large hurricanes in the past have disrupted oil production in the Gulf of Mexico is intended to support the contention that

   (A) the predicted violence of the upcoming hurricane season is the most important weather-related factor in determining oil prices
   (B) long-term weather forecasts usually do not influence oil prices at the time they are issued
   (C) any long-term weather forecasting must take into account the likely effect of fluctuations in the price of oil
   (D) a variety of predictions made in long-term weather forecasts can influence the price of oil
   (E) the usual effect of long-term predictions concerning the severity of the next year's hurricane season is to cause a sharp increase in the price of oil

2. In an experiment, first-year college students were asked to listen to a tape of someone speaking French. When asked to repeat the sounds they had heard, students who had studied French in high school could repeat more of the sounds than could students who had no knowledge of French. When asked to listen to a tape of only meaningless sounds, none of the students were able to repeat more than a few seconds' worth of the sounds made on the tape.

   Which one of the following conclusions is best supported by the information above?

   (A) Knowledge of a foreign language interferes with one's ability to repeat unfamiliar sounds.
   (B) People who have a knowledge of French have better memories than do people who have no knowledge of French.
   (C) The ability to repeat unrelated sounds is not improved by frequent practice.
   (D) The ability to repeat sounds is influenced by one's ability to comprehend the meaning of the sounds.
   (E) Learning a foreign language requires an ability to distinguish unfamiliar sounds from gibberish.

GO ON TO THE NEXT PAGE.

3. Many species of animals that have evolved poison as a protection from predators contain extremely large amounts of those poisons. It might seem that a poisonous animal would need to contain only enough poison to sicken or kill most animals, but there are some amphibians whose bodies contain enough poison to kill an elephant. This can be explained by the fact that the most common predators of these amphibians have evolved resistance to the defensive poisons, so that over time the prey has continually become more poisonous, while the predator has developed ever greater resistance to the poison.

Which one of the following most accurately expresses the main conclusion of the argument?

(A) The seemingly excessive amount of poison contained in some prey animals' bodies can be explained by the co-evolution of predator and prey.
(B) Some animals that protect themselves from predation by being poisonous contain more than enough poison to kill any predator.
(C) An animal that protects itself against predators by being poisonous is likely to contain much more poison than is a predator that kills its prey with the use of poison.
(D) The evolution of poison is not completely effective at preventing an animal from being preyed upon.
(E) Poison is the most effective method available for prey animals to protect themselves from predators.

4. Gardener *M*: High levels of nitrogen-containing compounds are necessary for any plant to grow well. Therefore, to aid in this plant's growth, you must be sure to add plenty of fertilizer.

Gardener *O*: That would be pointless. The soil in which this plant is growing already contains a high level of nitrogen-containing compounds, and it is also receiving plenty of light and water.

Which one of the following, if true, provides the strongest basis for Gardener *M* to respond to the objection raised by Gardener *O*?

(A) The fact that the plant is receiving all of the things necessary for its growth does not necessarily ensure that it will grow well.
(B) Without the addition of plenty of fertilizer, the plant will soon deplete the supply of nitrogen-containing compounds currently found in its soil.
(C) A steady supply of light and water, although important for a plant's growth, is not as essential to a plant's growth as the supply of nitrogen-containing compounds.
(D) No measure that guarantees a plant's growth should be neglected, even if it is possible that the plant may grow without that measure being taken.
(E) The addition of excessive amounts of fertilizer may harm a plant, even if that plant requires nitrogen-containing compounds to grow.

GO ON TO THE NEXT PAGE.

5. Medical Researcher: If I don't get another research grant soon, I'll never be able to discover a cure for phlebitis.

Assistant: But that's great. If your grant does come through, that dreaded disease will finally be eradicated.

Which one of the following statements best describes the flaw in the assistant's reasoning?

(A) The assistant believes the researcher will be unable to cure phlebitis unless the grant comes through.
(B) The assistant thinks the researcher will use the grant to find a cure for phlebitis, rather than for some other purpose.
(C) The assistant believes it is more important to cure phlebitis than to eradicate other, more deadly conditions.
(D) The assistant believes that all the researcher needs to cure phlebitis is another research grant.
(E) The assistant thinks the researcher will cure phlebitis even if the grant does not come through.

6. Commentator: Projections indicate that our nation's Gross Domestic Product (GDP) will shrink next year, leading to a 2 percent loss in tax revenues collected by the federal government. Therefore, we should pass a 2 percent cut in all federal taxes for next year. That way, the federal government's lost tax revenue will at least serve to stimulate the economy.

Which one of the following indicates a flaw in the commentator's argument?

(A) A cut in federal taxes may necessitate a decrease in federal spending, which in turn may necessitate further tax cuts.
(B) The economic stimulus offered by the proposed tax cut may not be great enough to ensure that the loss in federal taxes collected is no greater than 2 percent.
(C) Tax cuts that are adequate to increase the rate of GDP growth in a healthy economy may not suffice to prevent the shrinkage of GDP when the economy is weak.
(D) Money that is spent for one purpose cannot also be spent for another purpose.
(E) There is no assurance given that the benefits of the proposed tax cut will not accrue primarily to the wealthiest individuals in society.

7. Due to the increasing number of part-time adjuncts hired to teach university courses, it has become increasingly difficult for people who have recently earned PhDs to find full-time employment in universities.

Which one of the following conforms most closely to the principle illustrated above?

(A) Because the number of trees cut down in this area exceeds the number of new trees that have been planted, deforestation is a growing problem in the area.
(B) Because the number of teachers who are qualified to teach science and math is declining, the quality of instruction students receive in those subjects is suffering.
(C) Because individual songs can now be downloaded cheaply and easily from the internet, sales of new albums in record stores have significantly declined.
(D) Because two new computer programs appeal to the same market and include the same features, neither of these programs will be cost-effective for the companies that sell them.
(E) Due to the increasing number of coffee growers who are going out of business, it has become increasingly difficult for those who supply equipment to coffee growers to find a market for their products.

8. Sheet for sheet, Brand A paper towels cost less than Brand B paper towels and are more absorbent. Yet a roll of Brand A paper towels costs more than a roll of Brand B paper towels.

Which one of the following, if true, explains how the statements above can both be true?

(A) Both Brand A and Brand B towels are manufactured by the same company, which often creates artificial competition for its expensive products.
(B) A roll of Brand B paper towels is more absorbent than a roll of Brand A paper towels.
(C) A roll of Brand A paper towels is more absorbent than a roll of Brand B paper towels.
(D) The cost of a roll of Brand A towels has risen every year for the last five years.
(E) A roll of Brand A paper towels has more sheets than a roll of Brand B paper towels.

GO ON TO THE NEXT PAGE.

9. State agricultural officials are hoping to save California's $30 billion-a-year fruit industry from destruction by the Mediterranean fruit fly by releasing nearly one billion sterile female fruit flies throughout the state. In the past, this has been shown to be the only effective means of limiting the spread of this destructive pest, outside of large-scale pesticide spraying.

   Which one of the following best explains the intended effect of the program described above?

   (A) to drastically increase the number of potential mates for the male fruit flies, requiring them to devote more of their energies to mating rather than eating fruit
   (B) to saturate a given area with fruit flies, creating greater competition for food and thereby containing the damage done by the fruit fly to a smaller area
   (C) to ensure that a large number of fruit flies in succeeding generations are born infertile
   (D) to limit the growth of the population by reducing the number of successful matings between fruit flies
   (E) to encourage overpopulation of the fruit fly in the hopes that nature will correct the situation itself

10. Small businesses, which are essential to our country's economy, are more likely to fail when the price of health insurance increases unexpectedly. A recent bill introduced in parliament would reimburse health insurers who agree to limit the growth of the prices they charge to a set amount each year. Although this would effectively control the price of health insurance, there is no reason to pass the bill because only a small proportion of the small businesses that fail in this country do so because of sudden increases in insurance rates.

    Which one of the following, if true, most seriously weakens the argument?

    (A) Sudden increases in costs not associated with health insurance are equally harmful to small businesses.
    (B) Changes to the market that result from lowering the risk of sudden increases in health insurance prices will increase the vulnerability of small businesses to sudden increases in other costs.
    (C) Employees of small businesses who become unemployed as the result of the failure of the companies they work for are less likely to accept employment in other small businesses.
    (D) The reimbursements to health insurers mandated by the bill will be funded by increased taxation that will significantly harm the overall economy.
    (E) Decreasing the risk to employers associated with sudden increases in health insurance costs would induce many more people to start their own small businesses.

GO ON TO THE NEXT PAGE.

11. Marie: I just found out that it is cheaper for me to heat my home with gas or oil than for me to use any of the alternative methods available. I don't understand why environmentalists insist that the cost of fossil fuels is so high.

Louise: That's because you are confusing the price of fossil fuels with their cost. Gas and oil release tremendous amounts of pollution into the water and air, causing great damage to the environment. Not only does this pose a threat to the ecological balance that will affect the quality of life for future generations, but it also causes health problems that may be related to the consumption of these fuels. Once you add in these factors, it is clear that there are many alternatives that are actually cheaper than gas or oil, and consumers should adopt them.

According to her argument above, if an alternative energy source were to be found, under which one of the following conditions would Louise definitely object to its use?

(A) if its price and cost were equal
(B) if its cost were higher than the price of fossil fuels
(C) if its cost were higher than the cost of fossil fuels
(D) if the price of fossil fuels were to fall
(E) if it were less efficient than fossil fuels

12. Company president: Many shareholders believe that rather than developing products of our own to compete in new markets, our company should instead acquire existing companies that offer products of that type. This would be unwise. Any company that is willing to be acquired cannot be in a healthy competitive position in its market, and any company that is unwilling to be acquired would cost too much for our company to acquire without incurring substantial risk.

The company president's argument proceeds by

(A) advocating one course of action because a potential alternative course of action offers fewer advantages
(B) determining that a course of action is unwise because it cannot be undertaken without incurring unacceptable costs
(C) arguing against a course of action because there exist potential alternative courses of action that have not been definitively ruled out
(D) dismissing the course of action recommended by a group of shareholders because the members of that group do not have the best interests of the company at heart
(E) rejecting a course of action because the two possible situations in which it could be pursued are both unacceptable

GO ON TO THE NEXT PAGE.

13. Pollster: In one survey of the electorate, a representative sample of likely voters was initially presented with information about the candidates' positions on several important issues. Months later in a second survey, these same voters were presented with information concerning the positions held by these candidates on the same issues, which in some cases had changed substantially. Despite this fact, the proportion of the sample that supported each candidate remained virtually unchanged. It can be concluded, therefore, that new information received about the candidates cannot appreciably change a voter's decision of which candidate to support.

Which one of the following, if true, most undermines the pollster's argument?

(A) The number of issues on which either candidate had completely reversed his or her earlier position was relatively small.
(B) It is not reasonable to expect voters to remember every detail of a political candidate's position on every significant issue.
(C) The issues covered by the survey were not those that had been most widely reported in media coverage of the election.
(D) More than a third of the survey group indicated that they supported a different candidate at the time of the second survey than they had at the time of the initial survey.
(E) At the time of the initial survey, a majority of the survey group indicated that the candidates' positions on issues were not the most important determining factor in their decision of which candidate to support.

14. Oil exploration cannot be efficiently conducted by geological methods alone. The information gained through geological methods is useful for obtaining an accurate estimate of the likelihood of finding oil in a particular area, but only invasive surveys can determine with certainty the quantity of oil that will be produced by any area where it is found, and geological methods of oil exploration never include invasive surveys.

Which one of the following is an assumption on which the argument depends?

(A) Oil exploration, to be successful, must include considerations of how practical it is to extract oil from a given area where it is found.
(B) Oil exploration in an area cannot be conducted efficiently without an accurate estimate of the likelihood of finding oil in that area.
(C) Knowledge of both the likelihood of finding oil in an area and the quantity of oil produced by that area are required by most oil companies before they will decide to drill there.
(D) Oil exploration can be efficiently conducted only with certain knowledge of the quantity of oil that will be produced by any area where oil can be found.
(E) Certain knowledge of the amount of oil that will be produced by any area where oil is likely to be found can be obtained solely through geological methods.

GO ON TO THE NEXT PAGE.

15. Although all societies have some form of class system, there are systems that are based on neither wealth nor power. Still, there is no society that does not divide its population into the privileged and the common.

    If the above statements are correct, it can be properly concluded that

    (A) making distinctions between haves and have-nots is a part of human nature
    (B) there are some people in all cultures who are considered privileged
    (C) every society has its own unique hierarchy
    (D) privileged people must have money
    (E) all societies have a tradition of seeing themselves as either privileged or common

Questions 16–17

On the basis of our understanding of ancient geography, it has long been accepted that the Americas were initially settled by people from eastern Asia who crossed into North America on a land bridge that once spanned the Bering Strait. Under this belief, all the native peoples of North and South America have been thought to be descendents of these first colonists. Yet genetic analysis of surviving native populations in the Americas indicates that most of them are much more closely related to the native populations of the Philippines and other Pacific islands. It seems clear that Pacific islanders must have been the first to reach the Americas. It has been shown that, using traditional construction methods, a group could have crossed the Pacific Ocean and reached South America.

16. Which one of the following is the main conclusion of the argument?

    (A) The native populations in the Americas are no longer generally thought to be descended from settlers who came from eastern Asia.
    (B) The genetic makeup of native populations in the Americas is substantially similar to that of native populations in the Philippines and other Pacific islands.
    (C) The first human settlers in the Americas were Pacific islanders.
    (D) At least some Pacific islanders reached the South American continent by traveling on boats that were constructed using traditional methods.
    (E) Pacific islanders originating in the Philippines were the ancestors of all native populations in North and South America.

17. The reasoning in the argument is most vulnerable to which one of the following criticisms?

    (A) That a stated belief has been traditionally held to be true is taken as evidence that the belief must, in fact, be false.
    (B) That a given explanation of a set of facts is possible in some cases is taken as positive proof that this explanation is correct in all cases.
    (C) The statement of a set of conditions under which some correction to a set of long-held beliefs would be required is confused with the establishment of the fact that such a set of conditions actually arose.
    (D) The historical cause of a particular set of facts is mistakenly assumed to be the only possible cause of a similar set of facts elsewhere.
    (E) Facts that may support only the claim that a particular historic event occurred are taken to show that this event occurred before other similar events that could possibly have occurred earlier.

18. The current method of powering aircraft, the burning of fuel by internal-combustion engines, cannot be maintained indefinitely. Internal-combustion engines now burn refined petroleum, and the world's supply of petroleum is necessarily limited.

    Which one of the following is an assumption required by the argument?

    (A) Some means of powering aircraft other than the burning of fuels in internal-combustion engines could be successfully adopted.
    (B) Internal-combustion engines cannot be designed so that they burn some fuel not derived from limited resources.
    (C) Products from refined petroleum other than those currently burned in aircraft engines could not be chemically modified to replace the fuels used in aircraft today.
    (D) Engines that do not operate by internal combustion could not be designed to operate using fuels derived from petroleum.
    (E) No method of powering aircraft that relies on a finite resource is practical.

GO ON TO THE NEXT PAGE.

19. Evidence seems to indicate that people's faith in some mystical practices increases when these practices offer relief in frightening or challenging situations. One significant piece of evidence is the observation that the use of "healing crystals" is more prevalent among people who suffer from life-threatening diseases such as cancer than it is among people who have minor health problems such as colds or the flu.

Which one of the following, if true, would most seriously weaken the conclusion drawn in the passage above?

(A) Rapid social change has alienated people and has led to an overall increase in people's adoption of mystical practices.
(B) Many mystical practices are never used by more than a small number of extremely ill people.
(C) Those who are diagnosed with life-threatening diseases may seek nontraditional treatments for those diseases without having faith in their effectiveness.
(D) Psychics and mediums do not experience a surge in business after the occurrence of earthquakes and plane crashes.
(E) The use of crystals is one of the most ancient methods utilized for healing.

20. Executive: Nearly everyone can become a consultant, for there are no formal requirements that must be satisfied to be called a consultant. Anyone who convinces a company to hire him or her to perform an advisory function—no matter what its nature—is by definition a consultant.

The executive's conclusion can be properly drawn if which one of the following is assumed?

(A) Nearly everyone can convince a company to hire him or her to perform an advisory function.
(B) Some consultants satisfy a set of formal requirements not directly related to any advisory function they perform for a business.
(C) Those who convince companies to hire them to perform advisory functions satisfy their employers' requirements for the performance of those functions.
(D) Every consultant has convinced some company that he or she satisfies a set of informal requirements.
(E) Some consultants could convince any company to hire them to perform certain advisory functions.

21. An editor found that the manuscript of a new novel contained many grammatical errors and misused words. Despite this fact, the editor did not recommend that the manuscript be rejected.

Each of the following, if true, would explain the editor's decision EXCEPT:

(A) The manuscript in question had already been accepted by the publisher, a decision that could not be reversed on the editor's advice.
(B) The author of the manuscript was a first-time author whose work was not expected to attract much critical notice.
(C) The prose style used in the manuscript, although unorthodox, was groundbreaking and enjoyable to read.
(D) The errors in the manuscript could easily be corrected in the editing process, and the novel's story was gripping and dramatic.
(E) Correct grammar and word usage are not the most important factors in an editor's decision of whether to recommend a manuscript's rejection.

22. If a candidate is to win an election easily, that candidate must respond to the electorate's emotional demands—demands that the opponent either does not see or cannot act upon. Although these emotional demands are often not directly articulated by the electorate or by the candidate responding to them, they are an integral part of any landslide victory.

Which one of the following conclusions can most logically be drawn from the passage above?

(A) If neither candidate responds to the emotional demands of the electorate, either candidate might win in a landslide.
(B) If an election was close, the emotional demands of the electorate were conflicting.
(C) If a candidate responds to the emotional demands of the electorate, that candidate will have a landslide victory.
(D) An election during which neither candidate responds to the emotional demands of the electorate will not result in a landslide.
(E) Emotional demands are the only inarticulated issues in an election.

GO ON TO THE NEXT PAGE.

23. A well-known philosopher once articulated the method by which an action can be judged to be unethical: Imagine the consequences of everyone in society taking that action; if those consequences would be harmful to society, then the action is unethical. Yet it cannot be denied that, at times in the past, the intentional breaking of laws to draw attention to injustice has had beneficial effects in many societies. By the philosopher's standard, however, these actions would be judged unethical because if everyone in a society disregarded its laws, chaos would result. Because it is every person's ethical responsibility to fight against injustice in society, the philosopher's method must be incorrect.

The argument is flawed because it

(A) confuses what is ethically impermissible with what is merely not forbidden
(B) treats actions that have characteristics in common with a larger class as members of that class without recognizing a relevant distinction
(C) derives a conclusion about all the actions of a certain class on the basis of a principle whose relevance to those actions is doubtful
(D) mistakenly ascribes a characteristic to a class of actions that can properly be said to apply only to the individual actions that make up that class
(E) incorrectly assumes the truth of its conclusion that the philosopher's method is flawed

24. For every known physical phenomenon, physicists have posited laws that govern the occurrence of that phenomenon. It can be concluded, therefore, that every known physical phenomenon is governed by the same law.

The flawed reasoning in the argument above is most similar to that in which one of the following?

(A) The trunk of every tree is a body of tissue that contains both xylem and phloem. Therefore, any body of tissue that contains both xylem and phloem is the trunk of a tree.
(B) Every house has a unique mailing address. Therefore, because these packages are all marked with the same mailing address, they will all be sent to the same house.
(C) Because every action taken by a person can be explained by unconscious motives, a single motive explains all of the actions taken by any person.
(D) No violin that was made in the twentieth century is remarkably valuable. Because this violin is remarkably valuable, it must not have been made in the twentieth century.
(E) For every known star, astronomers can determine that star's elemental composition. Because a star's elemental composition determines its exact color, no two stars are the same exact color.

25. No iconoclasts are public figures, and all politicians are public figures. It follows that no politicians are fanatics.

The conclusion above follows logically if which one of the following is assumed?

(A) All fanatics are public figures.
(B) All fanatics are iconoclasts.
(C) All public figures are politicians.
(D) No fanatics are iconoclasts.
(E) No iconoclasts are politicians.

26. Wendy: Young people in our country are lagging behind the young people in other countries in science and math. With the increasing importance of technology in the world economy, it seems all but certain that our country's economic stature is in jeopardy.

Thomas: You forget that our country's strong economy allows us to attract new immigrants easily. Although the young people in our country may not fill the need for employees in technology companies, we will always be able to satisfy it by allowing those with the needed skills to emigrate from other countries, thereby maintaining our crucial competitive position in the world economy.

By their statements, it can be most reasonably inferred that Wendy and Thomas would agree with which one of the following statements?

(A) Efforts should be made to encourage the growth of the country's economy in areas that do not rely as heavily on technical knowledge.
(B) Continued efforts to ensure that the country's future workforce includes those who have the skills needed by technology companies are warranted.
(C) The quality of math and science education offered to the country's young people can be improved only if the rate of immigration is limited.
(D) In the future, the country's economic stature is likely to decline.
(E) Technology companies will adapt their business operations so that they can successfully employ people in many different countries who have needed skills.

**STOP**

**IF YOU FINISH BEFORE TIME IS CALLED, YOU MAY CHECK YOUR WORK ON THIS SECTION ONLY. DO NOT WORK ON ANY OTHER SECTION IN THE TEST.**

NO TEST MATERIAL ON THIS PAGE

SECTION III
Time—35 Minutes
25 Questions

Directions: The questions in this section are based on the reasoning contained in brief statements or passages. For some questions, more than one of the choices could conceivably answer the question. However, you are to choose the best answer; that is, the response that most accurately and completely answers the question. You should not make assumptions that are by commonsense standards implausible, superfluous, or incompatible with the passage. After you have chosen the best answer, blacken the corresponding space on your answer sheet.

1. Senator: For economic issues, I base my responses on logic. For political issues, I base my responses either on logic or gut instinct. For moral issues, I never base my responses on logic.

Which one of the following can be correctly inferred from the statements above?

(A) If the senator relies on logic, he may be responding to a moral issue.
(B) If the senator relies on logic, he is not responding to an economic issue.
(C) If the senator does not rely on logic, he is responding to a political issue.
(D) If the senator does not rely on logic, he must be responding to an economic issue.
(E) If the senator does not rely on logic, he might be responding to a political issue.

2. Social institutions are organized in such a way that they reinforce the need for their continued existence. Thus, although many political candidates claim that they will do away with certain social institutions that are not universally supported, it is unlikely that these candidates will be able to deliver on their promises.

The statement that social institutions are organized in such a way that they reinforce the need for their continued existence functions in the argument in which one of the following ways?

(A) It is a premise offered to lend support to the claim that political candidates may be unable to deliver on their promises to eliminate certain social institutions.
(B) It is a conclusion supported by the premise that many political candidates claim that they will do away with some social institutions.
(C) It is an assertion despite which the argument says that political candidates will succeed in doing away with the least popular of social institutions.
(D) It is offered as evidence against the belief that political candidates are sincere when they promise to do away with certain social institutions.
(E) It is the main conclusion of the argument.

3. An electronics manufacturer in financial trouble decided last year that, to survive, it needed to eliminate its least popular product lines to save on production costs. The product lines it eliminated accounted for 20 percent of all products produced by the manufacturer at that time. Yet, one year after their elimination, production costs directly related to the manufacture of their products have decreased by only 15 percent.

Which one of the following, if true, contributes most to an explanation of the difference between the reduction in manufacturing output and the cost savings achieved as a result of that reduction?

(A) The product lines eliminated by the manufacturer were also the most expensive products to produce.
(B) Production of products in the lines that were not eliminated were significantly cut back over the past year.
(C) Raw materials for the manufacturer's products constitute a far greater share of the products' direct production costs than expenses such as labor and maintenance.
(D) The total direct production costs associated with manufacturing components used in all of the manufacturer's products were not changed by the elimination of some product lines that used those components.
(E) The manufacturer's contract with the union to which its employees belong required the reassignment of workers who had previously been employed in producing the eliminated product lines to administrative departments not directly related to manufacturing operations.

GO ON TO THE NEXT PAGE.

4. Advertisement: Professional exterminators will tell you that to rid your home of roaches, you must do more than kill all the roaches you see. This is why the system that professional exterminators use most includes a poison that inhibits the development of roach eggs already laid, as well as a chemical that kills all adult roaches. This same combination is now available to the nonprofessional in new Extirm. When you're ready to get rid of roaches once and for all, get Extirm in your corner.

All of the following are implied by the advertisement above EXCEPT:

(A) Professional exterminators asked about roach extermination recommended Extirm.
(B) Extirm contains a chemical that inhibits the development of roach eggs.
(C) More than one chemical is required to rid a home of roaches.
(D) Inhibiting the development of roach eggs may not eliminate roaches from the home.
(E) Roaches reproduce by laying eggs.

5. The use of genetically engineered bacteria to process some types of radioactive waste is preferable to the traditional method of burying it in sealed containers. Whereas waste disposed of by traditional means remains radioactive for thousands of years, the engineered bacteria can render radioactive waste safe within a matter of months. Also, breaches or flaws in the containment of buried waste can lead to harmful contamination of soil and water that may be extremely difficult to detect.

Which one of the following statements, if true, most weakens the argument?

(A) The byproducts generated by the genetically engineered bacteria in processing radioactive waste are not more harmful to the environment than the radioactive waste itself would be.
(B) No type of genetically engineered bacteria has yet been discovered that can process all types of radioactive waste.
(C) The processes that produce radioactive waste also lead to radioactive contamination of equipment that cannot be reduced through the use of genetically engineered bacteria.
(D) The environmental conditions required by the genetically engineered bacteria in processing radioactive waste make harmful soil and water contamination likely.
(E) There is a risk that some of the genetically engineered bacteria, when used, will give rise to mutant progeny that are unable to process radioactive waste.

6. On Tuesday night, we observed that comet X was moving in the direction of star P. On Wednesday night, a flare was observed that could have been caused by a comet colliding with a star. Therefore, the flare that was observed on Wednesday night was caused by comet X colliding with star P.

The questionable method of reasoning in the argument above is most similar to that in which one of the following arguments?

(A) At three o'clock, a trash can was standing upright at the corner of the intersection of Myrtle and Carleton. At four o'clock, a trash can was lying in the center of that same intersection. Because at four o'clock there was no longer a trash can standing upright on the corner, it is likely that a passing automobile collided with the trash can and knocked it into the intersection.
(B) This morning, Stewart was in downtown Frostburg. This afternoon, Stewart was in downtown Augusta. Because Stewart could not have traveled so far in so short a time without traveling by airplane, Stewart must have traveled in an airplane today.
(C) Yesterday, Misty expressed her intention to make an offer on a house that is for sale through realtor V. Today, an offer was made on a house that is for sale through a realtor. Therefore, that offer was made by Misty on a house that is for sale through realtor V.
(D) Either May or Kathleen will be the next CEO of Thiscorp. Because media reports suggest that the one chosen will not be May, Kathleen is certain to be the next CEO of Thiscorp.
(E) Ten minutes ago, a red car was moving down this country road at excessive speed. No one else has used the road all day. A car has just collided with a large tree along this country road; there can be no doubt that the car involved in the collision is red.

GO ON TO THE NEXT PAGE.

7. Sales representative: Our nutritional supplement treats mold allergies at least as well as any prescription drug does. Unfortunately, we have no study results to prove this claim, but the supplement is clearly effective: Our customer satisfaction surveys show that people with mold allergies who take our supplement all report a lessening of symptoms. No study conducted by any maker of a prescription drug has ever refuted this evidence.

   The sales representative's argument is flawed because it reasons that

   (A) the fact that the supplement is effective does not necessarily imply that it is as effective as any prescription drug
   (B) the results of a survey conducted by an organization with commercial interest in its findings may be biased
   (C) because no evidence demonstrates that a survey's results are inaccurate, the results must therefore be accurate
   (D) the experiences of those who seek treatment for a condition are relevant to an evaluation of the relative efficacy of those treatments
   (E) the lessening of symptoms does not necessarily constitute effective treatment of the malady responsible for those symptoms

8. It is widely believed that the consumption of certain cold medicines may impair a driver's ability to operate a vehicle safely. However, the results of examinations administered during the process of obtaining a driver's license show that this is a misconception. The rate at which examinees who were taking cold medicines were awarded driver's licenses was no different from the rate at which examinees in the population at large received driver's licenses.

   The reasoning above is fallacious because it fails to consider the possibility that

   (A) the number of those taking cold medicines during the examination process represented a relatively small proportion of the total number of examinees
   (B) not all cold medicines have similar effects on a driver's ability to operate a vehicle safely
   (C) an individual who is able to operate a vehicle safely may fail one or more of the examinations on which the decision to award a driver's license is based
   (D) the belief that cold medicines impair coordination has been refuted by other studies not directly related to operating vehicles
   (E) an individual who takes cold medicine may be able to operate a vehicle more safely than that individual would if he or she left the cold untreated

9. The fact that many animals preyed upon by large carnivores are herd animals does not therefore imply that their herding behavior confers protection from predation. When hunting prey that lives in herds, large carnivores routinely target the weakest members of the herd, and unless the targeted animal is a juvenile, even the closest relatives of the targeted animal do not act to protect it. The closest relatives of most juvenile animals, whether or not they live in herds, will most often act to protect them from predators.

   Which one of the following most accurately expresses the main conclusion of the argument?

   (A) The closest relatives of juvenile animals most often act to protect those animals from predators.
   (B) Living in herds offers advantages that do not stem from the decreased likelihood of being killed by a predator.
   (C) Large carnivores tend to prefer prey that lives in herds.
   (D) The reason that many animals live in herds cannot be that herding behavior increases the number of animals that will act to protect the herd's members from large carnivores.
   (E) The confusion engendered when a herd flees from a large carnivore provides protection for the targeted member of that herd, even when no other herd member actively protects that animal.

GO ON TO THE NEXT PAGE.

10. Recent history in many former dictatorships suggests that the introduction of democratic reforms and market reforms at the same time is ultimately counterproductive. Although many countries in which one of these types of reform was carried out independent of the other have in time embraced liberalization of both types, almost all countries in which both political and economic continuity are interrupted eventually slip back into authoritarian styles of government that exert strong control over the market. It can be concluded that the best strategy for reform in a country that was formerly a dictatorship is to promote increased democracy, or more freedom in the market, but not both.

Which one of the following statements, if true, would provide the greatest additional support for the argument above?

(A) Economic reform in countries that were not formerly dictatorships is usually more difficult to promote than is political reform.
(B) Some authoritarian governments oppress their populations by exerting control over their countries' markets.
(C) Reform efforts that do not address the fundamental humanitarian needs of a country's citizenry are unlikely to succeed.
(D) Reform in a former dictatorship cannot be successful without including aspects of political or economic continuity as well as political or economic liberalization.
(E) Countries with both democratic governments and market economies may also benefit from reform to one or the other of these systems.

11. In mathematics, different definitions of key concepts may be advanced, but no new definition is considered correct if it conflicts with the accepted definition. In some cases, however, it is possible that a new correct definition is able to solve some problem that the accepted definition cannot. In this case, because the accepted definition should always be the correct definition that is capable of solving the greatest number of problems, the new definition should become the accepted definition.

Which one of the following principles, if valid, most helps to justify the reasoning above?

(A) Any new definition of a mathematical concept that can solve some problem that the accepted definition cannot must be correct.
(B) No new correct definition that is able to solve some problem that the accepted definition cannot solve fails to solve any problem that the accepted definition can solve.
(C) It is possible that a new incorrect definition of some mathematical concept is capable of solving problems that the currently accepted definition cannot.
(D) The definitions of mathematical concepts cannot be evaluated in terms of their truth, only their correctness.
(E) Any existing correct definition of a mathematical concept that is not the accepted definition must fail to solve at least one problem that the accepted definition can.

12. Computer Technician: This system has either a software problem or a hardware problem. None of the available diagnostic tests has been able to determine where the problem lies. The software can be replaced, but the hardware cannot be altered in any way, which means that if the problem lies in the hardware, the entire system will have to be scrapped. We must begin work to solve the problem by presupposing that the problem is with the software.

On which one of the following principles could the technician's reasoning be based?

(A) In fixing a problem that has two possible causes, it makes more sense to deal with both causes rather than spend time trying to determine which is the actual cause of the problem.
(B) If events outside one's control bear on a decision, the best course of action is to assume the "worst-case" scenario.
(C) When the soundness of an approach depends on the validity of an assumption, one's first task must be to test that assumption's validity.
(D) When circumstances must be favorable in order for a strategy to succeed, the strategy must be based on the assumption that conditions are indeed favorable until proved otherwise.
(E) When only one strategy can be successful, the circumstances affecting that strategy must be altered so that strategy may be employed.

13. To become a master at chess, a person must play. If a person plays for at least four hours a day, that person will inevitably become a master of the game. Thus, if a person is a master at the game of chess, that person must have played each day for at least four hours.

The error in the logic of the argument above is most accurately described by which one of the following?

(A) The conclusion is inadequate because it fails to acknowledge that people who play for four hours each day might not develop a degree of skill for the game that others view as masterful.
(B) The conclusion is inadequate because it fails to acknowledge that playing one hour a day might be sufficient for some people to become masters.
(C) The conclusion is inadequate because it fails to acknowledge that if a person has not played four hours a day, that person has not become a master.
(D) The conclusion is inadequate because it fails to acknowledge that four hours of playing time each day is not a strategy recommended by any world-champion chess players.
(E) The conclusion is inadequate because it fails to acknowledge that most people are not in a position to devote four hours each day to playing chess.

GO ON TO THE NEXT PAGE.

14. Prescriptive grammar is not a natural science. We know this because prescriptive grammar relies upon a set of axiomatic principles, and no science that relies upon a set of axiomatic principles depends primarily on experimentation.

The conclusion of the argument follows logically if which one of the following is assumed?

(A) Some natural sciences rely on a set of axiomatic principles.
(B) All natural sciences depend primarily on experimentation.
(C) No science that depends primarily on experimentation relies on a set of axiomatic principles.
(D) All sciences that depend primarily on experimentation are natural sciences.
(E) No grammar that relies on a set of axiomatic principles is a science.

15. Last year, Marcel enjoyed a high income from exactly two places: his sporting goods store and his stock market investments. Although Marcel earns far more from his store than from his investments, the money he earns from the stock market is an important part of his income. Because of a series of drops in the stock market, Marcel will not earn as much from his investments this year. It follows then that Marcel will make less money this year than he did last year.

Which one of the following is an assumption necessary to the author's argument?

(A) Increased profits at Marcel's sporting goods store will not offset any loss in stock market income.
(B) Sporting goods stores earn lower profits when the stock market drops.
(C) Drops in the stock market do not always affect all of a particular investor's stocks.
(D) Marcel's stock market investments will be subject to increased volatility.
(E) If his income is lower, Marcel will not be able to meet his expenses.

16. Efforts to encourage conservation by individuals are unlikely to address the world's most pressing energy problems, for although individuals have some knowledge of the amount of energy they use directly, there are hidden energy costs to everything an individual does. Every product purchased and every service received has an attendant energy cost, and the cumulative total of these costs far exceeds the amount of energy used directly by individuals.

Which one of the following is an assumption on which the argument relies?

(A) The most pressing energy problems involve consumption of energy that cannot be attributed to individual behavior.
(B) The prices of goods and services do not incorporate the hidden energy costs involved in their production and delivery.
(C) Conservation efforts are most effective when individuals have control over the amount of energy they consume.
(D) The world's most pressing energy problems cannot be solved by reliance on the actions of individuals.
(E) Individuals can effectively conserve energy in only those cases when they have some knowledge of the energy costs attendant upon their actions.

17. Activist: All nations that base their economic policy on unbridled competition encourage dishonest business practices, and all nations in which dishonest business practices are common lose the trust on which international investment is based. Any nation that, because of factors beyond the government's control or because of shortsighted policies, loses the respect of its trading partners is unlikely to be able to secure needed aid in the event of economic hardship. Thus, if a nation wishes to maintain economic stability, it is essential that the activities of banks be heavily regulated.

Each of the following, if true, weakens the activist's argument EXCEPT:

(A) Moderate regulation of banks is adequate to ensure that dishonest business practices do not become commonplace.
(B) Unbridled competition, in the absence of other contributing factors, only leads to a low incidence of dishonest business practices in an economy.
(C) Those nations that lose the trust on which international investment is based do not necessarily lose the respect of their trading partners.
(D) It is possible for a nation to maintain economic stability without securing aid in the event of economic hardship.
(E) An economic policy based on unbridled competition is not the only shortsighted government policy that may lead to a loss of respect among a country's trading partners.

GO ON TO THE NEXT PAGE.

18. Columnist: Labor unions claim that they take tough negotiating positions to secure fair treatment for workers, but they have self-interested motives in doing so. A union that gets higher wages for its members can collect higher union dues, thus allowing the union to make more political contributions and gain influence. There can be little doubt that the purpose of the labor movement is primarily to amass political power and only incidentally to help workers.

The reasoning in the columnist's argument is flawed because the argument

(A) incorrectly concludes that every union is interested in gaining political power based on the fact that many unions are interested in doing so
(B) improperly derives a conclusion about the labor movement as a whole on the basis of information concerning the behavior of individual labor unions
(C) assumes without warrant that two goals are mutually exclusive when a premise of the argument states that the pursuit of one goal may be furthered by pursuit of the other
(D) makes ambiguous use of the term *labor*
(E) rejects the arguments made by a group on the basis of information concerning the political preferences of that group

19. In concluding that there has been a shift in the sense of parental responsibility in the United States since the 1960s, researchers point to the increase in the frequency with which fathers tend to the daily needs of their children. However, this increase cannot be attributed exclusively to a shift in parental mores, for during the same period there has been an increase in the percentage of mothers who have jobs. With this in mind, the increased participation of fathers in child rearing may well be only a symptom of a more fundamental change in society.

The author of the passage criticizes the conclusion of the researchers by

(A) offering a clearer definition of the researchers' premises, thereby compromising their argument
(B) attacking the integrity of the researchers rather than their reasoning
(C) showing that the researchers have reversed cause and effect in making their argument
(D) pointing out that their criteria for "parental responsibility" are not a logical basis for their argument
(E) suggesting an alternative cause for the effect cited by the researchers

<u>Questions 20–21</u>

Upon exiting an exhibit, some visitors to art museums find it difficult to describe what it was that they liked and didn't like about the paintings. Yet because these visitors feel strongly about which art they believed to be good and which art they believed to be bad, appreciating a work of art obviously does not require the ability to articulate what, specifically, was perceived to be good or bad.

20. The argument above assumes which one of the following?

(A) The fact that some people find it difficult to articulate what they like about a work of art does not mean that no one can.
(B) If an individual feels strongly about a work of art, then he or she is capable of appreciating that work of art.
(C) The vocabulary of visual art is not a part of common knowledge, but rather is known only to those who study the arts.
(D) When a person can articulate what he or she likes about a particular painting, he or she is able to appreciate that work of art.
(E) Paintings can be discussed only in general terms of good and bad.

21. According to the passage above, all of the following could be true EXCEPT:

(A) Some museum visitors can explain with great precision what they liked and didn't like about a certain painting.
(B) If a person studies art, then that person will be able to articulate her opinion about paintings.
(C) If a person can't say why she likes a piece of art, it doesn't necessarily mean that she doesn't appreciate that piece.
(D) Some visitors can explain what they liked about a piece, but are unable to explain what they didn't like.
(E) The inability to express the reason for a particular preference indicates that the preference must not be strong.

GO ON TO THE NEXT PAGE.

22. Evan: Earlier this year, the *Stockton Free Press* reported that residents consider Mayor Dalton more concerned with his image than with advancing the cause of the less fortunate of Stockton.

Dalia: But the mayor appointed a new director of the public television station, and almost immediately the station began running a documentary series promoting the mayor's antipoverty program.

Evan: Clearly the mayor has, by this appointment, attempted to manipulate public opinion through the media.

Evan's second statement counters Dalia's argument by

(A) disputing the relevancy of her statement
(B) suggesting that Dalia is less informed about the issue than he
(C) confusing the argument she presents with his own
(D) appealing to popular opinion that the mayor should not misuse his access to the media
(E) claiming that Dalia's argument is an example that actually strengthens his own argument

23. Naturalist: Every year, thousands of animals already on the endangered species list are killed for their hides, furs, or horns. These illegal and often cruel deaths serve to push these species further toward the brink of extinction. The products made from these animals, such as articles of clothing and quack medical remedies, are goods no one really needs. What is needed is a large-scale media campaign to make the facts of the killings known and lessen the demand for these animal products. Such a campaign would be a good start in the effort to save endangered species from extinction.

Environmentalist: For the overwhelming majority of currently endangered species, the true threat of extinction comes not from hunting and poaching, but from continually shrinking habitats. Concentrating attention on the dangers of poaching for a very few high-visibility species would be counterproductive, leading people to believe that a boycott of a few frivolous items is enough to protect endangered species, when what is needed is a truly global environmental policy.

The point at issue between the naturalist and the environmentalist is which one of the following?

(A) whether the poaching of some endangered species actually increases that species' chances of becoming extinct
(B) whether a large-scale media campaign can affect the demand for some products
(C) whether more endangered species are threatened by poaching and hunting or shrinking of habitat
(D) whether some species could be saved from extinction by eliminating all commercial demand for that species
(E) whether a large-scale media campaign that lessens the demand for products made from endangered species is a good strategy for saving endangered species

GO ON TO THE NEXT PAGE.

24. Historian: Excavations in the ancient city of Ouz have uncovered a massive bronze statue. No other bronze object has ever been found in the city's ruins. Thus, because it appears that the ancient inhabitants of Ouz lacked either the ability to make bronze or the knowledge of how to shape it, it seems clear that the statue was looted and brought back during one of its many raids on neighboring cities.

Which one of the following, if true, most seriously weakens the historian's argument?

(A) Although all of Ouz's neighboring cities have been excavated, none has been found to include any bronze objects.
(B) The bronze statue is of a peacock, an animal that was widely found throughout the geographic region where Ouz was situated.
(C) No historical or archaeological evidence indicates that smaller bronze objects made in Ouz were removed by subsequent visitors to the site.
(D) A nearby city known to be frequently at war with Ouz contains signs that its inhabitants were able to shape bronze.
(E) Bronze was used in many regions as a material for making weapons throughout the era in which the city of Ouz was inhabited.

25. Studies of fighter pilots reveal the surprising fact that they are much less likely to die of heart attacks than are members of the population at large, despite the stressful nature of their work and the rigorous selection process to which they are subjected. These results hold even when the data are adjusted to compensate for the fact that piloting fighter jets is dangerous work and leads to some premature deaths. It seems doubtful, then, that recent studies purporting to show that job stress leads to an increased risk of heart attack can be correct.

Which one of the following, if true, lends the strongest support to the argument's conclusion?

(A) The average life expectancy of male fighter pilots is nearly five years shorter than the life expectancy of the general male population.
(B) The characteristics that allow fighter pilots to pass through the rigorous selection process to which they are subjected do not also allow them to avoid suffering the negative consequences of stress.
(C) Fighter pilots are in general fitter and more physically strong than are the members of the population at large, allowing them to survive more of the heart attacks they experience.
(D) Other studies of high-stress jobs outside the military have shown that the risk of heart attack triples for people who hold those jobs.
(E) Factors other than job stress, such as heredity, exercise, and diet, are known to be more important determining factors in whether or not an individual suffers a heart attack than is job stress.

**S T O P**

IF YOU FINISH BEFORE TIME IS CALLED, YOU MAY CHECK YOUR WORK ON THIS SECTION ONLY.
DO NOT WORK ON ANY OTHER SECTION IN THE TEST.

## SECTION IV
Time—35 Minutes
23 Questions

Directions: Each group of questions in this section is based on a set of conditions. In answering some of the questions, it may be useful to draw a rough diagram. Choose the response that most accurately and completely answers each question and blacken the corresponding space on your answer sheet.

Questions 1–6

An interior decorator is designing a color scheme using at least one of the following colors: red, orange, yellow, indigo, green, and violet. No other colors will be used. The selection of colors for the scheme is consistent with the following conditions:

If the scheme uses orange, then it does not use indigo.
If the scheme does not use green, then it uses orange.
If the scheme uses yellow, then it uses both indigo and violet.
If the scheme uses violet, then it uses red or green or both.

1. Which one of the following could be a complete and accurate list of the colors the scheme includes?

(A) yellow, indigo
(B) indigo, green
(C) yellow, indigo, violet
(D) yellow, green, violet
(E) orange, yellow, indigo, violet

GO ON TO THE NEXT PAGE.

2. Which one of the following could be the only color the scheme uses?

(A) red
(B) yellow
(C) indigo
(D) green
(E) violet

3. Which one of the following CANNOT be a complete and accurate list of the colors the scheme uses?

(A) orange, green
(B) green, violet
(C) red, orange, violet
(D) yellow, indigo, green, violet
(E) red, orange, yellow, indigo, violet

4. If the scheme doesn't use violet, then which one of the following must be true?

(A) The scheme uses orange.
(B) The scheme uses at least two colors.
(C) The scheme uses at most three colors.
(D) The scheme uses neither yellow nor indigo.
(E) The scheme uses neither yellow nor orange.

5. If the scheme uses violet, then which of the following must be false?

(A) The scheme does not use red.
(B) The scheme does not use green.
(C) The scheme does not use indigo.
(D) The scheme uses indigo but not yellow.
(E) The scheme uses indigo but not green.

6. If the condition that if the scheme doesn't use green then it does use orange is suspended, and all the other conditions remain in effect, then which one of the following CANNOT be a complete and accurate list of the colors the scheme uses?

(A) indigo
(B) red, indigo
(C) yellow, indigo, violet
(D) red, indigo, violet
(E) red, yellow, indigo, violet

GO ON TO THE NEXT PAGE.

Questions 7–13

Five runners—Fanny, Gina, Henrietta, Isabelle, and Mona—are assigned to lanes numbered 1 through 5 on a track. Each runner has the option of wearing a knee brace during the competition. Two of the runners are from Palo Alto, two are from San Jose, and one is from Newcastle. The following conditions must apply:

Isabelle and Mona are assigned to the first two lanes, but not necessarily in that order.

The runner in the third lane is from Newcastle and wears a knee brace.

Neither runner from San Jose wears a knee brace.

Both Gina and Fanny are assigned higher-numbered lanes than that of Henrietta.

Neither Mona nor Fanny comes from San Jose.

7. Which one the following could be an accurate list of the runners, in order from lane 1 to lane 5?

(A) Isabelle, Henrietta, Fanny, Mona, Gina
(B) Isabelle, Mona, Gina, Henrietta, Fanny
(C) Mona, Gina, Henrietta, Isabelle, Fanny
(D) Mona, Isabelle, Gina, Henrietta, Fanny
(E) Mona, Isabelle, Henrietta, Fanny, Gina

8. Which one of the following could be true?

(A) Fanny runs in lane 5.
(B) Gina runs in lane 1.
(C) Henrietta runs in lane 2.
(D) Isabelle runs in lane 3.
(E) Mona runs in lane 5.

GO ON TO THE NEXT PAGE.

9. If the runner in lane 1 is from San Jose, then which one of the following could be true?
   (A) Fanny runs in a lane numbered one higher than Isabelle's.
   (B) Henrietta runs in a lane numbered one higher than Fanny's.
   (C) Henrietta runs in a lane numbered one higher than Mona's.
   (D) Henrietta runs in a lane numbered one higher than Isabelle's.
   (E) Isabelle runs in a lane numbered one higher than Mona's.

10. If a runner with a knee brace runs in lane 1, then which one of the following CANNOT be true?
    (A) Fanny runs in lane 4.
    (B) Gina runs in lane 5.
    (C) A runner with a knee brace runs in lane 2.
    (D) A runner with a knee brace runs in lane 3.
    (E) A runner with a knee brace runs in lane 4.

11. Which one of the following must be true?
    (A) Gina runs without a knee brace.
    (B) Henrietta runs without a knee brace.
    (C) Mona runs without a knee brace.
    (D) Fanny runs with a knee brace.
    (E) Isabelle runs with a knee brace.

12. If runners wearing knee braces do not run in consecutively numbered lanes, and runners not wearing knee braces do not run in consecutively numbered lanes, then in exactly how many distinct orders could the runners be assigned to lanes?
    (A) 1
    (B) 2
    (C) 3
    (D) 4
    (E) 5

13. If a runner with a knee brace runs in lane 2, then which one of the following CANNOT be true?
    (A) The runner in lane 1 is from San Jose.
    (B) The runner in lane 1 is from Palo Alto.
    (C) The runner in lane 4 is from San Jose.
    (D) The runner in lane 5 is from San Jose.
    (E) The runner in lane 5 is from Palo Alto.

GO ON TO THE NEXT PAGE.

Questions 14–18

The Paulson, Rideau, Stevenson, Tisch, Van Pelt, and Wong families have each rented a time-share in a six-unit condominium. The condominium has three floors, labeled first to third from bottom to top. Each floor has an identical layout consisting of two units: a garden view apartment on the west side of the building and an ocean view apartment on the east side of the building. The following conditions must apply:

The Rideaus rent the unit immediately beneath the Paulsons's ocean-view unit.

If the Wongs rent an ocean-view apartment, the Rideaus occupy the same floor as the Van Pelts.

If the Paulsons and the Tisches occupy the same floor, the Wongs rent the unit immediately and directly beneath the Stevensons's unit.

If the Tisches rent a garden-view unit, the Wongs occupy a unit on the first floor.

If the Tisches occupy a first-floor unit, the Stevensons occupy a third-floor unit.

14. Which of the following could be true?

(A) The Stevensons occupy a second-floor unit, whereas the Tisches occupy a first-floor unit.
(B) The Paulsons occupy a unit immediately and directly below the Wongs, and share a floor with the Tisches.
(C) The Paulsons rent a garden-view unit on the same floor as the Van Pelts.
(D) The Wongs rent an ocean-view unit on the same floor as the Van Pelts.
(E) The Tisches and Wongs both occupy the third floor.

15. If both the Van Pelts and the Tisches rent garden-view units, then which of the following could be true?

(A) The Wongs rent the first-floor ocean-view unit.
(B) The Stevensons rent the first-floor garden-view unit.
(C) The Paulsons and the Tisches occupy the same floor.
(D) The Paulsons and the Wongs occupy the same floor.
(E) The Van Pelts and the Wongs occupy the same floor.

GO ON TO THE NEXT PAGE.

16. If the Wongs rent a third-floor unit, then which of the following must be true?

    (A) The Rideaus rent a second-floor unit.
    (B) The Stevensons rent a second-floor unit.
    (C) The Stevensons rent a first-floor unit.
    (D) The Tisches rent a third-floor unit.
    (E) The Van Pelts rent a first-floor unit.

17. If the Tisches rent the first-floor ocean-view unit, then each of the following must be true EXCEPT:

    (A) The Paulsons and the Stevensons occupy the same floor.
    (B) The Rideaus and the Van Pelts occupy the same floor.
    (C) The Van Pelts rent a garden-view unit.
    (D) The Wongs rent a garden-view unit.
    (E) The Paulsons rent a third-floor unit.

18. If neither the Paulsons nor the Stevensons rent a third-floor unit, then which one of the following could be true?

    (A) The Rideaus rent a second-floor unit.
    (B) The Tisches rent a second-floor unit.
    (C) The Wongs rent a second-floor unit.
    (D) The Stevensons rent an ocean-view unit.
    (E) The Wongs rent an ocean-view unit.

GO ON TO THE NEXT PAGE.

Questions 19–23

Four racehorses and their four jockeys are assigned to consecutive tracks at a racetrack—tracks 1, 2, 3, and 4. Each horse has exactly one jockey, and each pair is assigned to exactly one track. The horses are Ficklehoof, Galloper, Knackerbound, and Lackluster; the jockeys are Ramos, Simon, Tonka, and Urbach. The following conditions apply:

Ficklehoof is assigned to a lower-numbered track than is Galloper, and at least one track separates the two.

Knackerbound is assigned to track 2.

Lackluster's jockey is Urbach.

19. Which one of the following horse and jockey teams could be assigned to track 1?

(A) Ficklehoof and Ramos
(B) Ficklehoof and Urbach
(C) Galloper and Ramos
(D) Galloper and Urbach
(E) Lackluster and Tonka

GO ON TO THE NEXT PAGE.

20. If Ramos is assigned to a higher-numbered track than is Urbach, which one of the following statements CANNOT be true?

(A) Ficklehoof is assigned to a lower-numbered track than is Simon.
(B) Knackerbound is assigned to a lower-numbered track than is Ramos.
(C) Knackerbound is assigned to a lower-numbered track than is Tonka.
(D) Simon is assigned to a lower-numbered track than is Ramos.
(E) Tonka is assigned to a lower-numbered track than is Knackerbound.

21. If Lackluster is assigned to a lower-numbered track than is Galloper, which one of the following statements could be false?

(A) Ficklehoof is assigned to a lower-numbered track than is Urbach.
(B) Galloper is assigned to track 4.
(C) Either Ramos or Tonka is assigned to a lower-numbered track than is Urbach.
(D) Simon is assigned to a lower-numbered track than is Urbach.
(E) Urbach is assigned to track 3.

22. What is the maximum possible number of different horse and jockey teams, any one of which could be assigned to track 4?

(A) 2
(B) 3
(C) 4
(D) 5
(E) 6

23. If Simon is assigned to a higher-numbered track than is Lackluster, then which one of the following statements could be false?

(A) Galloper is assigned to a higher-numbered track than is Ramos.
(B) Galloper is assigned to a higher-numbered track than is Tonka.
(C) Lackluster is assigned to a higher-numbered track than is Tonka.
(D) Tonka is assigned to a higher-numbered track than is Ramos.
(E) Urbach is assigned to a higher-numbered track than is Ramos.

**STOP**

IF YOU FINISH BEFORE TIME IS CALLED, YOU MAY CHECK YOUR WORK ON THIS SECTION ONLY. DO NOT WORK ON ANY OTHER SECTION IN THE TEST.

The Princeton Review

**Completely darken bubbles with a No. 2 pencil. If you make a mistake, be sure to erase mark completely.**

**1. YOUR NAME:** ______________________________
(Print) Last First M.I.

**SIGNATURE:** ______________________ **DATE:** ___/___/___

**HOME ADDRESS:** ______________________________
(Print) Number

______________________________
City State Zip Code

**PHONE NO.:** ______________________________
(Print)

IMPORTANT: Please fill in these boxes exactly as shown on the back cover of your test book.

## 2. TEST FORM

______________________________

## 3. TEST CODE

| | | | | |
|---|---|---|---|---|
| 0 | A | 0 | 0 | 0 |
| 1 | B | 1 | 1 | 1 |
| 2 | C | 2 | 2 | 2 |
| 3 | D | 3 | 3 | 3 |
| 4 | E | 4 | 4 | 4 |
| 5 | F | 5 | 5 | 5 |
| 6 | G | 6 | 6 | 6 |
| 7 | | 7 | 7 | 7 |
| 8 | | 8 | 8 | 8 |
| 9 | | 9 | 9 | 9 |

## 4. REGISTRATION NUMBER

| | | | | | |
|---|---|---|---|---|---|
| 0 | 0 | 0 | 0 | 0 | 0 |
| 1 | 1 | 1 | 1 | 1 | 1 |
| 2 | 2 | 2 | 2 | 2 | 2 |
| 3 | 3 | 3 | 3 | 3 | 3 |
| 4 | 4 | 4 | 4 | 4 | 4 |
| 5 | 5 | 5 | 5 | 5 | 5 |
| 6 | 6 | 6 | 6 | 6 | 6 |
| 7 | 7 | 7 | 7 | 7 | 7 |
| 8 | 8 | 8 | 8 | 8 | 8 |
| 9 | 9 | 9 | 9 | 9 | 9 |

## 5. YOUR NAME

| First 4 letters of last name | | | | FIRST INIT | MID INIT |
|---|---|---|---|---|---|
| A | A | A | A | A | A |
| B | B | B | B | B | B |
| C | C | C | C | C | C |
| D | D | D | D | D | D |
| E | E | E | E | E | E |
| F | F | F | F | F | F |
| G | G | G | G | G | G |
| H | H | H | H | H | H |
| I | I | I | I | I | I |
| J | J | J | J | J | J |
| K | K | K | K | K | K |
| L | L | L | L | L | L |
| M | M | M | M | M | M |
| N | N | N | N | N | N |
| O | O | O | O | O | O |
| P | P | P | P | P | P |
| Q | Q | Q | Q | Q | Q |
| R | R | R | R | R | R |
| S | S | S | S | S | S |
| T | T | T | T | T | T |
| U | U | U | U | U | U |
| V | V | V | V | V | V |
| W | W | W | W | W | W |
| X | X | X | X | X | X |
| Y | Y | Y | Y | Y | Y |
| Z | Z | Z | Z | Z | Z |

## 6. DATE OF BIRTH

| Month | Day | | Year | |
|---|---|---|---|---|
| JAN | | | | |
| FEB | | | | |
| MAR | 0 | 0 | 0 | 0 |
| APR | 1 | 1 | 1 | 1 |
| MAY | 2 | 2 | 2 | 2 |
| JUN | 3 | 3 | 3 | 3 |
| JUL | | 4 | 4 | 4 |
| AUG | | 5 | 5 | 5 |
| SEP | | 6 | 6 | 6 |
| OCT | | 7 | 7 | 7 |
| NOV | | 8 | 8 | 8 |
| DEC | | 9 | 9 | 9 |

## 7. SEX

MALE

FEMALE

The Princeton Review

FORM NO. 00001-PR

## Test 2

Start with number 1 for each new section.
If a section has fewer questions than answer spaces, leave the extra answer spaces blank.

1. A B C D E
2. A B C D E
3. A B C D E
4. A B C D E
5. A B C D E
6. A B C D E
7. A B C D E
8. A B C D E
9. A B C D E
10. A B C D E
11. A B C D E
12. A B C D E
13. A B C D E
14. A B C D E
15. A B C D E
16. A B C D E
17. A B C D E
18. A B C D E
19. A B C D E
20. A B C D E
21. A B C D E
22. A B C D E
23. A B C D E
24. A B C D E

1. A B C D E
2. A B C D E
3. A B C D E
4. A B C D E
5. A B C D E
6. A B C D E
7. A B C D E
8. A B C D E
9. A B C D E
10. A B C D E
11. A B C D E
12. A B C D E
13. A B C D E
14. A B C D E
15. A B C D E
16. A B C D E
17. A B C D E
18. A B C D E
19. A B C D E
20. A B C D E
21. A B C D E
22. A B C D E
23. A B C D E
24. A B C D E
25. A B C D E

1. A B C D E
2. A B C D E
3. A B C D E
4. A B C D E
5. A B C D E
6. A B C D E
7. A B C D E
8. A B C D E
9. A B C D E
10. A B C D E
11. A B C D E
12. A B C D E
13. A B C D E
14. A B C D E
15. A B C D E
16. A B C D E
17. A B C D E
18. A B C D E
19. A B C D E
20. A B C D E
21. A B C D E
22. A B C D E
23. A B C D E
24. A B C D E
25. A B C D E
26. A B C D E
27. A B C D E

1. A B C D E
2. A B C D E
3. A B C D E
4. A B C D E
5. A B C D E
6. A B C D E
7. A B C D E
8. A B C D E
9. A B C D E
10. A B C D E
11. A B C D E
12. A B C D E
13. A B C D E
14. A B C D E
15. A B C D E
16. A B C D E
17. A B C D E
18. A B C D E
19. A B C D E
20. A B C D E
21. A B C D E
22. A B C D E
23. A B C D E
24. A B C D E
25. A B C D E

## COMPUTING YOUR SCORE

**Directions**

1. Use the Answer Key on the next page to check your answers.
2. Use the Scoring Worksheet below to compute your raw score.
3. Use the Score Conversion Chart to convert your raw score into the 120–180 LSAT scale.

**Your scaled score on this virtual test is for general guidance only.**

Scores obtained by using the Score Conversion Chart can only approximate the score you would receive if this virtual test were an actual LSAT. Your score on an actual LSAT may differ from the score obtained on this virtual test.

In an actual test, final scores are computed using an equating method that makes scores earned on different editions of the LSAT comparable to one another. This virtual test has been constructed to reflect an actual LSAT as closely as possible, and the conversion of raw scores to the LSAT scale has been approximated.

What this means is that the Conversion Chart reflects only an estimate of how raw scores would translate into final LSAT scores.

**Scoring Worksheet**

1. Enter the number of questions you answered correctly in each section.

| | **Number Correct** |
|---|---|
| Section I . . . . . . . . . . . . . | ______ |
| Section II. . . . . . . . . . . . . | ______ |
| Section III . . . . . . . . . . . . | ______ |
| Section IV. . . . . . . . . . . . | ______ |

2. Enter the sum here: ______

**This is your raw score.**

SCORE CONVERSION CHART

**For Converting Raw Scores to the 120–180 LSAT Scaled Score**

| Reported Score | Raw Score Lowest | Raw Score Highest |
|---|---|---|
| 180 | 99 | 102 |
| 179 | —* | —* |
| 178 | 98 | 98 |
| 177 | 97 | 97 |
| 176 | 96 | 96 |
| 175 | —* | —* |
| 174 | 95 | 95 |
| 173 | 94 | 94 |
| 172 | 93 | 93 |
| 171 | 92 | 92 |
| 170 | 91 | 91 |
| 169 | 89 | 90 |
| 168 | 88 | 88 |
| 167 | 87 | 87 |
| 166 | 85 | 86 |
| 165 | 84 | 84 |
| 164 | 83 | 83 |
| 163 | 81 | 82 |
| 162 | 79 | 80 |
| 161 | 78 | 78 |
| 160 | 76 | 77 |
| 159 | 74 | 75 |
| 158 | 73 | 73 |
| 157 | 71 | 72 |
| 156 | 69 | 70 |
| 155 | 67 | 68 |
| 154 | 66 | 66 |
| 153 | 64 | 65 |
| 152 | 62 | 63 |
| 151 | 60 | 61 |
| 150 | 58 | 59 |
| 149 | 57 | 57 |
| 148 | 55 | 56 |
| 147 | 53 | 54 |
| 146 | 51 | 52 |
| 145 | 50 | 50 |
| 144 | 48 | 49 |
| 143 | 46 | 47 |
| 142 | 44 | 45 |
| 141 | 42 | 43 |
| 140 | 41 | 41 |
| 139 | 39 | 40 |
| 138 | 37 | 38 |
| 137 | 36 | 36 |
| 136 | 34 | 35 |
| 135 | 33 | 33 |
| 134 | 31 | 32 |
| 133 | 29 | 30 |
| 132 | 28 | 28 |
| 131 | 27 | 27 |
| 130 | 25 | 26 |
| 129 | 24 | 24 |
| 128 | 22 | 23 |
| 127 | 21 | 21 |
| 126 | 20 | 20 |
| 125 | 19 | 19 |
| 124 | 18 | 18 |
| 123 | 16 | 17 |
| 122 | 15 | 15 |
| 121 | —* | —* |
| 120 | 0 | 14 |

* There is no raw score that will produce this scaled score for this form.

# ANSWER KEY

## SECTION I

| | | | |
|---|---|---|---|
| 1. D | 8. B | 15. D | 22. E |
| 2. A | 9. B | 16. E | 23. C |
| 3. B | 10. C | 17. A | 24. B |
| 4. C | 11. D | 18. B | 25. D |
| 5. E | 12. A | 19. E | 26. B |
| 6. C | 13. E | 20. D | 27. D |
| 7. D | 14. D | 21. A | |

## SECTION II

| | | | |
|---|---|---|---|
| 1. D | 8. E | 15. B | 22. D |
| 2. D | 9. D | 16. C | 23. B |
| 3. A | 10. E | 17. E | 24. C |
| 4. B | 11. C | 18. B | 25. B |
| 5. D | 12. E | 19. C | 26. B |
| 6. B | 13. D | 20. A | |
| 7. C | 14. D | 21. B | |

## SECTION III

| | | | |
|---|---|---|---|
| 1. E | 8. B | 15. A | 22. E |
| 2. A | 9. D | 16. E | 23. E |
| 3. D | 10. D | 17. E | 24. A |
| 4. A | 11. B | 18. B | 25. B |
| 5. D | 12. D | 19. E | |
| 6. C | 13. B | 20. B | |
| 7. C | 14. B | 21. E | |

## SECTION IV

| | | | |
|---|---|---|---|
| 1. B | 8. A | 15. A | 22. C |
| 2. D | 9. C | 16. D | 23. D |
| 3. E | 10. C | 17. B | |
| 4. C | 11. A | 18. C | |
| 5. E | 12. A | 19. A | |
| 6. C | 13. B | 20. C | |
| 7. E | 14. E | 21. D | |

# Chapter 12
# Answers and Explanations to Practice Test 2

# SECTION I

Questions 1–8

1. **D** This is a BIG PICTURE: PRIMARY PURPOSE question. We're looking for a description of the passage's purpose.

   (A) The tone here is off; the passage focuses on Campbell's failures.
   (B) Conventional views aren't discussed in the passage.
   (C) The primary emphasis in the passage is less on a region than it is on a person and an era.
   (D) Yes. This has the proper emphasis and tone.
   (E) Laws are not the primary focus of this passage.

2. **A** This is an EXTRACT: INFERENCE question. It seems to be referring to the end of the first paragraph.

   (A) Yes. St. Catherine's does provide an example of each of these.
   (B) This is too strong. "Many" and "independent" are both overstatements of passage material.
   (C) This is also too strong. Although it seems clear that some did, we aren't told that most did.
   (D) This is far too strong; nothing this positive took place.
   (E) National government is not explicitly dealt with by the passage.

3. **B** This is a STRUCTURE: FUNCTION question. We want the choice that matches our summary of the second paragraph.

   (A) This choice is too broad. The paragraph describes only some of the developments that led to Campbell's eventual failure.
   (B) Yes. This is similar to (A), but it includes both a description of what St. Catherine's was and limits its scope to just that part of Campbell's story.
   (C) This statement is too broad. The passage does not suggest that St. Catherine's was the only instance of the attempted implementation of Sherman's Order 15.
   (D) The second paragraph shows an instance of a failed attempt to create an independent community of freed slaves, not an attempt to maintain freed slaves as an underclass.
   (E) This is an overstatement. We don't know that this was the only such effort.

4. **C** This is a STRUCTURE: FUNCTION question. We're looking for the choice that's most consistent with passage material.

   (A) This is an overstatement. It is not an example of slavery *per se*.
   (B) The following statement about mortality rates, not the reference to money, does this.
   (C) Yes. Although this isn't by any means perfect, this choice is consistent with the passage's tone.
   (D) The passage doesn't claim that Georgia profited from Campbell's punishment—not monetarily, anyway.
   (E) The author does not suggest a connection between the amount paid to the state and Campbell's decision to return only once.

5. **E** This is a REASONING question. Eliminate the four choices that lend additional support to the statement at hand, and pick the one that does not support it.

   (A) This identifies a similarity between slavery and sharecropping: Conditions were terrible.
   (B) This identifies a similarity between slavery and sharecropping: It was impossible to earn money with work under either system.
   (C) This identifies a similarity between slavery and sharecropping: Education was very difficult to obtain.
   (D) This identifies a similarity between slavery and sharecropping: Laws prevented workers from organizing to demand better conditions.
   (E) Yes. This is the odd choice out; it identifies an improvement, however slight, in sharecropping over slavery.

6. **C** This is an EXTRACT: INFERENCE question. Four of these answers will have direct passage support; the odd one out is the answer.

   (A) This is stated in the passage's third paragraph.
   (B) This is stated in the passage's third paragraph.
   (C) Yes. This is the odd choice out. We aren't told that absolutely no white legislators supported these measures.
   (D) This is stated in the passage's third paragraph.
   (E) This is stated in the passage's fourth paragraph.

7. **D** This is an EXTRACT: RETRIEVAL question. The passage will provide answers to four of these questions; the fifth will be the answer.

   (A) This question is answered in the second paragraph.
   (B) This question is answered in the fourth paragraph.
   (C) This question is answered in the third paragraph.
   (D) Yes. This question is not answered in the passage.
   (E) This question is answered in the third paragraph.

8. **B** This is an EXTRACT: INFERENCE question. The correct answer will be directly supported by information in the passage.

   (A) This is too strong; we aren't told that Campbell was the only one.
   (B) Yes. This is a reasonable statement of the passage's main point.
   (C) This is said nowhere in the passage.
   (D) The weakness of state governments seems not to have been the problem.
   (E) The tone here is off. The passage focuses on his eventual failure, not his successes.

# SECTION I

Questions 9–14

9. **B** This is a BIG PICTURE: MAIN POINT question. We're looking for the main idea.

(A) The emphasis here is wrong; we'd like something that mentions prions and disease.
(B) Yes. This is a succinct statement of the passage's contents.
(C) This is far too general.
(D) The emphasis here is wrong; the passage's purpose is not to indicate that protein is absolutely necessary.
(E) Cures for these diseases are not discussed.

10. **C** This is an EXTRACT: INFERENCE question. The reference is to the final sentence of the passage.

(A) According to the passage, this disease is not caused by a virus.
(B) Scrapie is a disease of sheep, not humans.
(C) Yes. This is consistent with the statement in question.
(D) Parasites are mentioned only briefly in the first paragraph.
(E) Abnormal genes are not discussed in the passage.

11. **D** This is a STRUCTURE: ORGANIZATION question. We're looking for the choice that best agrees with a paragraph-by-paragraph summary of the passage.

(A) No belief is rejected at the end of the passage.
(B) No further directions for study are recommended.
(C) Evidence against the prion hypothesis is never mentioned.
(D) Yes. This is the closest fit to the contents and structure of the passage.
(E) No argument against the mechanism is even mentioned.

12. **A** This is a STRUCTURE: FUNCTION question. We're looking for the answer that's most consistent with the cited statement, which is in the second paragraph.

(A) Yes. The key is that sterilization in an autoclave destroys DNA and RNA.
(B) This is an overstatement of the passage's identification of similarities among these diseases.
(C) This is inconsistent with the passage. Viruses, which are composed of DNA and RNA, would be destroyed by sterilization.
(D) This is not described in the passage as the conventional belief about them; note the word "only."
(E) The mechanism of a prion's action is not described until the following paragraph.

13. **E** This is an EXTRACT: INFERENCE question. We're looking for direct passage support of our answer.

(A) No other potential cause of disease is mentioned.
(B) This would contradict material in the third paragraph.
(C) The passage does not mention the possibility that prions may be either harmless or beneficial.
(D) This is too strong a conclusion to draw from the passage's discussion of mad cow disease; note the word "most."
(E) Yes. The passage mentions in the third paragraph that scrapie can develop spontaneously.

14. **D** This is a REASONING question. We're looking for something that's similar to the mechanism described in the third paragraph, which describes the conversion of a normal into an abnormal, harmful form.

(A) This does not involve conversion from one thing to another.
(B) Like (A), this doesn't include any kind of conversion.
(C) This talks about an individual changing his or her mind in the face of evidence; there is no sense of spreading or replication here.
(D) Yes. This talks about a pathological change caused by a single example and indicates that the change spreads from that individual.
(E) This does not describe a conversion or change.

Questions 15–20

15. **D** This is an EXTRACT: INFERENCE question. Find the answer choice that provides a good substitute for the word *polemical* as it is used in the passage.

(A) This answer choice mixes up information in the passage, describing Zellio's position on Native gambling facilities and governmental interference.
(B) While Andrade's position is strong, the passage doesn't suggest that he is hateful or scornful of politicians or their positions.
(C) Again, this answer choice mixes up information in the passage. These are words that Andrade would use to describe Schwarzenegger's position.
(D) Yes. These words define the term *polemical,* and they appropriately describe Andrade's argument. Near the end of the passage, the author refers to Andrade's forceful language and says that his tone is indicative of the anger felt by many Native communities.
(E) These terms contradict Andrade's position. In no way is he trying to soothe or make concessions.

## SECTION I

16. **E** This is an EXTRACT: INFERENCE question. Since this is an EXCEPT question as well, you will find support in the passage for each of the answer choices except the correct one. This question focuses on the first passage, so you only need to look for support for the answer choices there.

    (A) This is supported in the passage. In the second sentence, the author mentions that statistical evidence indicates a trend in Native gaming enterprises. Zellio as described in the second paragraph would agree that this is true.
    (B) This is supported in the passage. The author describes Zellio's direct comparison between some Native gaming enterprises and similar facilities in Las Vegas and Atlantic City.
    (C) This is supported in the passage. The author refers to Zellio's claim that there is a complicated relationship between Native communities and governmental officials. The first paragraph also states that the IRGA recognized the right of tribes to operate gaming facilities without state interference. The second paragraph then states that Zellio discusses how the government tries to cash in "despite the passage of the IRGA."
    (D) This is supported in the passage. In the second paragraph, the author refers to Zellio's statistical evidence that shows that roughly half of the tribes in the United States operate gaming facilities. Thus, roughly half of them do not.
    (E) Yes. This is not supported in the passage. Because it makes predictions about the future, it is too broad in scope to be supported by the author's description of Zellio's argument.

17. **A** This is an EXTRACT: INFERENCE question. Find a statement that is supported by both Andrade and Zellio.

    (A) Yes. This is supported in both passages. While there are a number of differences between the passages, both deal with, to varying degrees, governmental interference in Native gaming enterprises.
    (B) This is a partial answer; eliminate it. While this is something that Andrade is likely to assert, nothing in the passage suggests that this is a position that Zellio would agree with.
    (C) This contradicts both passages; eliminate it.
    (D) There is no support for this answer choice in either passage; eliminate it.
    (E) Zellio withholds judgment—this statement is too strong to be supported by her. Andrade does not discuss the IRGA; rather, he criticizes a certain political figure for his statements and possible policies.

18. **B** This is a BIG PICTURE: PRIMARY PURPOSE question. Find a similarity between the purpose of each passage.

    (A) While both passages discuss the complicated relationship between Native communities and governmental officials, neither passage examines how this relationship has changed over time.
    (B) Yes, this is a commonality between both passages.
    (C) Neither passage discusses negative effects of the IRGA.
    (D) Neither passage criticizes the IRGA. Also, this would contradict both positions.
    (E) If anything, both passages suggest that gambling facilities are positive for Native communities, and neither one considers their possible drawbacks.

19. **E** This is an EXTRACT: INFERENCE question. Find a statement supported by Zellio and not Andrade.

    (A) This is not supported in the text. Zellio never considers the negative effects of gaming.
    (B) While Passage A indicates that Zellio may consider these effects, Zellio's primary focus is on statistics.
    (C) This is something that Andrade does, and not Zellio.
    (D) This answer choice has the wrong scope. While Zellio compares Native gaming facilities to the ones in Las Vegas and Atlantic City, this isn't her primary concern.
    (E) Yes, this is a good summary of the first passage. Andrade, on the other hand, is not described as concerned with statistics.

20. **D** This is a REASONING question. Since this question is based on the second passage, identify the central argument in this passage and determine which answer choice goes the furthest to undermine it. The second passage as a whole describes Andrade's view.

    (A) This strengthens Andrade's argument.
    (B) This has no effect on Andrade's argument about California.
    (C) Again, this is irrelevant to Andrade's argument.
    (D) Yes. This answer choice weakens his argument. Essentially, he argues that currently and historically, governments act in ways that prevent Native communities from advancing. This answer choice is inconsistent with this assertion.
    (E) The second passage doesn't discuss comparative profitability of different facilities.

# SECTION I

Questions 21–27

21. **A** This is an EXTRACT: FACT question. There is a dual reference here—to the critics in the first paragraph and to Socialist Realism in the second.

(A) Yes. This is a good paraphrase of the material in the first paragraph.
(B) The passage does not suggest that Socialist Realist paintings are less ideological. The author's argument in the passage is that both Socialist Realist and Works Progress Administration art has some ideological or political dimension.
(C) The passage says the market is "modest" but nothing more.
(D) The critics mentioned in the passage don't base their judgment of the painting's value on their popularity, but rather on their ideological dimensions.
(E) This is the author's idea, not the critics'.

22. **E** This is a REASONING question. We're looking for something that goes against the author's purpose in including the cited information, which appears in the third paragraph.

(A) This is suggestive of a difference, but we don't know that the Soviet Union controlled the art that was produced in this way, either.
(B) This is suggestive of a difference, but it doesn't very directly undermine the passage's suggestion that the works produced under WPA could be considered propaganda.
(C) This is suggestive of a difference, but it isn't clear that absolutely every artist working in the Soviet Union had to seek government funding.
(D) This doesn't really attack the idea we're looking for: that the government in the United States also exerted some control over the production of art.
(E) Yes. This is the best choice. Although the government sponsored production of art, this choice lets us know that it didn't exert control over its content.

23. **C** This is a STRUCTURE: FUNCTION question. We're looking for the choice that best fits a general summary of the second paragraph.

(A) We don't have specific examples from several countries here.
(B) The paragraph isn't concerned with proving something about all countries.
(C) Yes. The contexts mentioned here are "high culture" and "low culture."
(D) The tone here is off. The purpose isn't to praise the popularity of the works and the effectiveness of the policy.
(E) Dissimilarities between the Soviet Union and Germany are not discussed. Rather, the paragraph emphasizes a similarity only.

24. **B** This is an EXTRACT: FACT question. The reference is to the third paragraph.

(A) The passage makes no judgment regarding their comparative aesthetic value.
(B) Yes. This is a safe paraphrase of the text in the third paragraph.
(C) This is how they were used as propaganda, but we're not sure that this was the artists' intent in producing them.
(D) No connection is made between the Works Progress Administration and these particular artworks.
(E) Decadence is a quality ascribed to these paintings by Soviet officials, not the author.

25. **D** This is an EXTRACT: FACT question. The cited text is in the second paragraph.

(A) We aren't told that the subjects were the same.
(B) The tone here is wrong; "deceptive" is a judgment that the author doesn't make.
(C) The tone here is wrong; we don't know that these workers didn't deserve their portrayals in the posters.
(D) Yes. At the very least, both are said to have been against fascism.
(E) This is not a comparison that the passage makes.

26. **B** This is a REASONING question. The cited text is in the first paragraph.

(A) We're not looking for refined tastes; we're looking for preferences that can be interpreted as political.
(B) Yes. This is a political preference that influences the decision of what positive and negative aspects will be emphasized.
(C) This has to do with making things, not with making judgments about them.
(D) This is too neutral to be similar to the situation described in the passage.
(E) This has to do with going against preferences. It isn't similar.

27. **D** This is a BIG PICTURE: MAIN POINT question. We're looking for the central point of the passage as a whole.

(A) This is too general to be the main point of this passage, which is not about the use of propaganda as a whole.
(B) This is too focused on the failings of the critics to be the best choice available.
(C) This choice leaves out the issue of the author's evaluation of the critics.
(D) Yes. This has the Soviet/U.S. comparison on which the passage is focused, the notion of propaganda, and the author's evaluation of the critics.
(E) This is too general to be the main point of the passage, which is not about all art at all times.

## SECTION II

1. **D** This is a REASONING question. The statement mentioned is a premise of the argument, and we're looking for what it supports.

   (A) It's too much to say that hurricane forecasts are the most important factor.
   (B) This contradicts information in the argument.
   (C) This is not a conclusion stated anywhere in the argument.
   (D) Yes. This is the main conclusion of the argument, and even if the cited statement doesn't support it directly, nevertheless the statement is part of the reasoning supporting this conclusion.
   (E) The argument doesn't conclude that every forecast causes an increase in prices.

2. **D** This is an INFERENCE question. Your goal is to find the one choice that must be true based on the information in the passage.

   (A) No, because none of the students was able to repeat the sounds for more than a few seconds.
   (B) General memory is not related to an ability to speak French.
   (C) Maybe, but we don't know about practice.
   (D) Do we have proof of this? Yes—the French-speaking students remembered more of the sounds that were the French language than they did of the gibberish language. Plus, it's nice and wishy-washy—"is influenced by." This is the answer.
   (E) Maybe, but we don't know about learning a foreign language.

3. **A** This is a MAIN POINT question. We're looking for the statement of the single thing the argument most wants us to accept.

   (A) Yes. "Coevolution" seems a good paraphrase of the escalating increases in the amount of poison in the prey's body along with the predator's resistance to that poison.
   (B) This is a premise of the argument, not its conclusion.
   (C) Predators that use poison are not even mentioned.
   (D) This is not the thing that the argument is trying to get us to believe.
   (E) No comparison to other methods is made.

4. **B** This is most nearly a WEAKEN question. We're looking for something that would counter Gardener *O*'s objection to Gardener *M*.

   (A) This does not address *O*'s primary objection, which concerns nitrogen-containing compounds.
   (B) Yes. This lets us know that although there are enough nitrogen-containing compounds in the soil now, fertilizer must nevertheless be added.
   (C) This does not address *O*'s objection, which is that enough of these compounds are currently present.
   (D) The addition of fertilizer is not presented as guaranteeing growth; also, this doesn't directly address *O*'s statement that there would seem to be no purpose in adding fertilizer.
   (E) If anything, this would help *O*'s argument.

5. **D** **Conclusion:** If the researcher gets the grant, the disease will be eradicated.

   **Premise:** If the researcher doesn't get the grant, she'll never discover a cure.

   **Assumption:** There's no other factor preventing her from discovering a cure.

   This is a FLAW question. Come up with your own description of how the assistant made a mistake before you go to the answer choices, and then match your description to the choices.

   (A) No. This is what the medical researcher said. Look for something that mentions how the assistant thinks the researcher said that the grant was sufficient to ensure success.
   (B) This isn't a flaw in the argument—it's accurate.
   (C) Other diseases weren't mentioned by anyone.
   (D) Yes. He confused *necessary* with *sufficient* in this case—the researcher said it was necessary for her to get the grant, and the assistant assumed that the grant will be sufficient to effect the cure.
   (E) No. Neither person said this.

# SECTION II

6. **B Conclusion:** Cutting taxes by 2 percent will allow lost revenue to help stimulate the economy.

**Premise:** Tax revenues are projected to decline by 2 percent next year because of shrinkage in GDP.

**Assumption:** The commentator appears to think that a cut in taxes of 2 percent will somehow result in a loss of only 2 percent to tax revenues, although the GDP is projected to decrease.

This is a FLAW question. We're looking for a choice that describes or exploits the argument's assumption.

(A) The argument doesn't depend on the fact that no further tax cuts will be required.
(B) Yes. This is the best available statement of the flaw here.
(C) It isn't clear how this choice is relevant to the particular tax cuts under discussion here.
(D) Very interesting. It's difficult to see how this expresses the argument's problem.
(E) To whom the benefits of a tax cut primarily accrue is not a relevant issue in this argument.

7. **C** This is a PARALLEL-THE-PRINCIPLE question. We're looking for the argument that illustrates the same principle that the initial argument illustrates.

(A) This has to do with competing factors, but whereas the initial argument involves things of different types (full-time jobs versus part-time jobs), this one involves only one thing: trees.
(B) This does not deal with competing factors.
(C) Yes. This reproduces the competing factors—downloading of individual songs versus buying complete albums—and indicates that the cheaper option that includes less is displacing the more expensive one that includes more.
(D) This involves competing factors, but it does not have one winning out over another.
(E) This does not involve competing factors.

8. **E** This is a RESOLVE/EXPLAIN question. Look for an answer choice that allows both parts of the argument to be true, and remember to assume the hypothetical truth of each of the answer choices.

(A) This doesn't explain the discrepancy in the per sheet versus overall price issue.
(B) Absorbency is totally out of the scope here. Eliminate it.
(C) This has the same problem as (B). Eliminate it.
(D) What about Brand B? Without anything to compare this information to, it's useless. Eliminate it.
(E) Can this explain why the overall price is higher? Yes. There are more sheets on Brand A. It's the answer.

9. **D** This is a MAIN POINT question. Look for the answer that is the goal of the agricultural officials. What are they trying to do here?

(A) This looks okay, but they're still going to eat some fruit. Let's see if there is something better.
(B) This is still not all that great, is it? At least part of the state isn't going to have any fruit left at all. Let's keep looking.
(C) But if we're releasing sterile flies, there won't be succeeding generations. Eliminate it.
(D) This looks really good. By releasing sterile flies, we should be able to reduce the population of fruit flies. It's the answer.
(E) Overpopulation is the opposite of what we want here. Eliminate it.

10. **E Conclusion:** There is no reason to pass the bill.

**Premise:** The bill would prevent a problem that is responsible for only a small proportion of small-business failures.

**Assumptions:** The bill would not help the economy in other ways than preventing the failure of a small proportion of small businesses.

This is a WEAKEN question. We're looking for the choice that attacks the assumption or, failing that, gives us a reason to believe the conclusion might not be right.

(A) At best, this would strengthen the conclusion.
(B) This would strengthen the conclusion.
(C) This doesn't seem to be relevant to the bill at the center of this argument.
(D) This would strengthen the conclusion.
(E) Yes. Because we're told that small businesses are crucial to the country's economy, this would be a beneficial effect of the bill in question.

11. **C** This is most like a WEAKEN or STRENGTHEN or RESOLVE/EXPLAIN question because you're looking for the one thing in the answer choices that, if known, will have the most IMPACT on the argument. So let's go looking for that.

(A) It depends. Were they equal at current cost levels? No. At current price levels? Maybe. Eliminate it.
(B) This confuses "cost" and "price." Eliminate it.
(C) Correct We know she doesn't like the current situation, and this would make it worse. She would therefore object.
(D) This would have no impact on the argument either way. Eliminate it.
(E) Efficiency is not the issue—cost is.

## SECTION II

12. **E** This is a REASONING question. We're looking for the choice that correctly describes the argument.

(A) It's not the advantages, but the disadvantages, of the course of action that are mentioned.
(B) One of the bad results concerns cost, but not both of them.
(C) Failure to eliminate other possibilities is not the reason the course of action mentioned is considered unwise.
(D) The motives of the shareholders are not discussed.
(E) Yes. This mentions the two possibilities discussed in the argument and matches the argument's conclusion.

13. **D** **Conclusion:** New information received about candidates doesn't affect a voter's decision of which candidate to support.

**Premises:** An initial survey in which information was presented yielded the same proportion of voters who support each candidate as a later poll in which further information was presented to the same voter.

**Assumptions:** The primary assumption here is that we can conclude that voters didn't change their opinions on the basis of the fact that the proportion of the group that supported each candidate didn't change.

This is a WEAKEN question. We're looking for a choice that attacks the assumption, or else generally contradicts the conclusion.

(A) Although this suggests that the new information wasn't of too major a nature, it doesn't contradict the conclusion very strongly.
(B) This doesn't have a definite impact on the question of whether new information changes opinions.
(C) If anything, this strengthens the conclusion by showing that the information conveyed in the survey was in fact new.
(D) Yes. This indicates that although the proportions were the same, many individual voters changed their mind. Although this doesn't definitively contradict the conclusion, it does destroy the evidence's relevance to it.
(E) This doesn't attack the relevance of the evidence to the conclusion; new information other than that provided in the survey may still have changed the voters' decisions.

14. **D** **Conclusion:** Oil exploration can't be efficiently conducted if it uses only geological methods.

**Premises:** Geological methods can find oil, but they can't tell you how much is there.

**Assumption:** Efficient oil exploration requires being able to tell how much oil is in a place where you find it.

This is a NECESSARY ASSUMPTION question. We're looking for something that the conclusion requires in order to be correct.

(A) The practicality of extraction isn't clearly related to either geological or invasive methods.
(B) Geological methods give you this, so this isn't really relevant to the conclusion.
(C) The issue here is conducting exploration efficiently, not making the decision to drill.
(D) Yes. If efficient exploration can be conducted without this knowledge, then it remains possible that it could be conducted with geological methods alone.
(E) This contradicts a premise of the argument.

15. **B** This is an INFERENCE question. Your goal is to find the one choice that must be true based on the information in the passage.

(A) "Human nature" is a little too general here. Eliminate it.
(B) "Some" is nice and wishy-washy. Let's leave it — is our best answer here.
(C) It doesn't have to be true that every society's hierarchy is "unique." Eliminate it.
(D) Money is out of the scope of the argument. Eliminate it.
(E) Each society has BOTH privileged and common categories. Eliminate it.

# SECTION II

Questions 16–17

16. **C** **Conclusion:** Pacific Islanders were the first humans to settle the Americas.

**Premise:** The vast majority of native peoples are much more closely related to Pacific Islanders than they are to the group widely believed to have been the first to settle the Americas.

**Assumption:** The group from which a majority of the native inhabitants are descended must have been the first one to arrive.

This is a MAIN POINT question. We're looking for the thing that the argument wants us to believe.

(A) The conclusion here doesn't explicitly say that this belief is no longer held.
(B) This is a premise of the argument, not its conclusion.
(C) Yes. This is a good paraphrase of the main point as it is stated in the argument.
(D) The conclusion here isn't concerned with how they got here first, only that they did.
(E) This is more extreme than the similar statement made in the argument, and it isn't its main conclusion.

17. **E** This is a FLAW question. We want the choice that describes or exploits an assumption of the argument.

(A) Acceptance of the other theory is not the reason that the argument concludes it is false.
(B) The fact that this is a possible explanation is not the reason that the argument concludes it is correct.
(C) There is no hypothetical statement anywhere in the argument similar to the one described in this choice.
(D) The argument doesn't use a conclusion about one place to draw conclusions about another.
(E) Yes. The evidence supports only the conclusion that descendents of Pacific Islanders came to the Americas; it doesn't directly show that they came to the Americas first.

18. **B** **Conclusion:** Internal-combustion engines cannot be indefinitely used to power aircraft.

**Premises:** Current internal-combustion engines burn refined petroleum; the supply of petroleum is limited.

**Assumption:** Internal-combustion engines cannot burn, instead of petroleum, some resource whose supply is not limited.

This is a NECESSARY ASSUMPTION question. We're looking for something that the argument needs for its conclusion to be correct.

(A) This is not within the scope of the argument; the conclusion concerns only internal-combustion engines.
(B) Yes. If this is untrue—if internal-combustion engines can be designed to burn fuel from renewable resources—then it's possible that they could be used to power aircraft indefinitely.
(C) Other fuels derived from petroleum have no effect on the force of this argument.
(D) Other types of engines are not strictly relevant to this argument's conclusion.
(E) Practicality is not an explicit issue of this argument.

19. **C** **Conclusion:** Faith in mystical practices increases in life-threatening situations.

**Premise:** People are more likely to use healing crystals for cancer than for a cold or flu.

**Assumption:** The people who use healing crystals actually believe they will work.

This is a WEAKEN question. Figure out which answer choice has the most negative impact on the conclusion of the argument. Remember to assume the hypothetical truth of each choice and apply it to the argument.

(A) We're concerned more with crystals and specific diseases—this is a little too general.
(B) Mystical practices that are not used are not the issue.
(C) Ah, so while they are trying these cures, their faith in them hasn't necessarily increased—this would weaken the argument. This is the answer.
(D) None of this is talking about anything in the argument. Eliminate it.
(E) The ancientness of crystals has no impact on the argument. Eliminate it.

# SECTION II

20. **A Conclusion:** Nearly everyone can become a consultant.

    **Premise:** Anyone who convinces a company to hire him or her to perform an advisory function is a consultant.

    This is a SUFFICIENT ASSUMPTION question. We're looking for the choice that makes the conclusion certain.

    (A) Yes. If we assume this, then the conclusion definitely follows.
    (B) The argument says that no formal requirements are relevant to the issue.
    (C) This wouldn't help us conclude that nearly everyone can do this.
    (D) This restates a premise, and as such provides no additional support to the conclusion.
    (E) This doesn't help us conclude that nearly anyone can become a consultant.

21. **B** This is a RESOLVE/EXPLAIN EXCEPT question. Four of these choices will explain the decision; the odd choice out is our answer.

    (A) This would help to explain why the editor didn't suggest that the manuscript be rejected. The suggestion wouldn't have mattered.
    (B) Yes. This doesn't offer a clear reason for not rejecting a manuscript with so many problems.
    (C) This would help to explain why the editor didn't suggest that the manuscript be rejected. Although it contained what could be called errors, the errors were features of a good style.
    (D) This would help to explain why the editor didn't suggest that the manuscript be rejected. Its good qualities were very good, and the errors were easy to correct.
    (E) This would help to explain why the editor didn't suggest that the manuscript be rejected. Its flaws didn't relate to the important factors for making the decision.

22. **C** This is an INFERENCE question. Your goal is to find the one choice that must be true based on the information in the passage.

    (A) No, because if candidates don't respond, there can't be a landslide.
    (B) We have no idea what would happen if the election were close. Eliminate it.
    (C) This is the invalid contrapositive of the first sentence. Eliminate it.
    (D) Bingo! It's the contrapositive of the first sentence: if you don't respond, you can't have a landslide.
    (E) "Only" is too extreme here. Eliminate it.

23. **B Conclusion:** The philosopher's rule for deciding when an action is unethical is incorrect.

    **Premises:** Sometimes, disobeying laws serves to fight injustice in society; it is everyone's ethical responsibility to fight injustice; by the philosopher's rule, however, breaking laws is unethical.

    **Assumption:** The philosopher's rule, when applied to the cases in question, would consider only the fact that they are examples of breaking the law, rather than examples of breaking the law for the purpose of fighting injustice.

    This is a FLAW question. We're looking for a choice that either describes or exploits an assumption of the argument.

    (A) This is not a distinction that is relevant to the argument's conclusion.
    (B) Yes. The relevant distinction is that these instances of breaking the law are intended to help society.
    (C) The relevance of the principle isn't in doubt; the method of its application is.
    (D) This argument does not confuse characteristics of an individual with characteristics of a group or collection.
    (E) No. The argument attempts to support its conclusion with premises that differ from it.

## SECTION II

24. **C** **Conclusion:** All known physical phenomena are governed by the same law.

    **Premise:** Each known physical phenomenon is governed by physical laws.

    **Flaw:** There may be more than one physical law, yet all are called "the same law."

    This is a PARALLEL-THE-FLAW question. We're looking for the answer choice that has the same problem.

    (A) No. This one is flawed because it misuses the conditional "all" statement: The fact that all tree trunks have xylem and phloem doesn't exclude the possibility that some tissues with xylem and phloem are not tree trunks. This is not the same as the problem with the original argument.
    (B) No. This argument is not flawed.
    (C) Yes. In this argument, "action taken by a person" corresponds to "known physical phenomenon," and "can be explained by unconscious motives" corresponds to "is governed by physical laws."
    (D) No. This argument is not flawed.
    (E) No. The conclusion of this argument is not at all similar to the conclusion of the original argument.

25. **B** **Conclusion:** politician → ~fanatic

    **Premises:** iconoclast → ~public figure; politician → public figure

    This is a SUFFICIENT ASSUMPTION question. We're looking for the choice that makes the conclusion certain by completing a chain of conditional statements leading from "politician" to "~fanatic."

    Note that the two premises given allow us to form part of such a chain, using the contrapositive of the second statement listed above. We have this chain: politician → public figure → ~iconoclast. We need to extend it by one link to "fanatic."

    (A) Fanatic → public figure. Neither this statement nor its contrapositive allows us to extend the chain.
    (B) Fanatic → iconoclast. This is it. Note its contrapositive: ~iconoclast → ~fanatic. This allows us to extend the chain to reach the desired conclusion.
    (C) Public figure → politician. This doesn't involve the missing term—"fanatic"—at all.
    (D) Fanatic → ~iconoclast. Neither this statement nor its contrapositive allows us to extend the chain.
    (E) Iconoclast → ~politician. We already know this from our premises; also, this doesn't include the missing term: "fanatic."

26. **B** This is most closely related to an INFERENCE question. We're looking for a choice about which Wendy and Thomas would both express the same opinion.

    (A) Neither participant expresses this opinion.
    (B) Yes. Both Wendy and Thomas would say that this is true.
    (C) Neither participant expresses this opinion.
    (D) It seems as though Wendy would say this is true; Thomas would definitely say it isn't.
    (E) Neither participant expresses this opinion.

# SECTION III

1. **E** This is an INFERENCE question. Your goal is to find the one choice that must be true based on the information in the passage.

    (A) No. The senator never bases moral issue responses on logic. Eliminate it.
    (B) No. The senator may very well be responding to an economic issue. Eliminate it.
    (C) No. The senator could be responding to a moral issue. Eliminate it.
    (D) No. The senator always uses logic to respond to economic issues. Eliminate it.
    (E) Bingo. Nice and wishy-washy—, and accurate. With political issues, the senator might respond with a gut instinct. This is the answer.

2. **A** This is a REASONING question. We want the choice that correctly describes the purpose of the indicated statement.

    (A) Yes. The statement in question is the only premise of the argument.
    (B) The statement in question is not supported by any other premise.
    (C) This choice contradicts the argument's conclusion.
    (D) The sincerity of political candidates is not an issue in this argument.
    (E) The main conclusion of the argument is that politicians will not make good on their promises.

3. **E** This is a RESOLVE/EXPLAIN question. We're looking for the choice that describes how 20 percent of production could be eliminated while only reducing direct manufacturing costs by 15 percent.

    (A) If anything, this would make the paradox worse.
    (B) If anything, this would make the paradox worse. Cutbacks in addition to the ones mentioned should result in more savings, not less.
    (C) This doesn't seem to offer a clear explanation of the unexpectedly low cost savings.
    (D) Yes. This tells us that the costs of some part of the production process associated with the eliminated products were impossible to reduce.
    (E) This choice describes costs not directly related to manufacturing, which are not relevant to the paradox here.

4. **A** This is an INFERENCE question. It is also an EXCEPT question, so your goal is to find the one choice that doesn't have to be true based on the information in the passage.

    (A) We have no idea what they recommend. It's never mentioned in the passage. This is the answer.
    (B) Yes. This is mentioned in the second sentence. Eliminate it.
    (C) Yes. This is mentioned in the second sentence. One for eggs; one for adults. Eliminate it.
    (D) This is why we need two chemicals—see the second sentence again and eliminate it.
    (E) This is a major part of sentence two. Eliminate it.

5. **D** **Conclusion:** Engineered bacteria is a better way to dispose of some radioactive waste than is burying it in sealed containers.

    **Premises:** Buried waste remains radioactive for much longer; burying waste can lead to contaminated soil or water.

    **Assumption:** The cited advantages of bacteria are not outweighed by an unstated disadvantage.

    This is a WEAKEN question. We're looking for the choice that tells us why bacteria might not be a better solution.

    (A) This would strengthen the argument, if only slightly.
    (B) This argument's conclusion doesn't state that bacteria are suitable for all types of radioactive waste.
    (C) Like (B), this choice indicates that there are some types of radioactive contamination for which bacteria won't work, but the argument doesn't claim that they will work for all types of contamination.
    (D) Yes. Bacteria have a more serious negative effect on soil and water than burying waste does, which casts doubt on the conclusion.
    (E) As long as these mutants aren't harmful and don't render the method completely ineffective, this isn't relevant to the conclusion.

## SECTION III

6. **C Conclusion:** The flare was caused by comet X colliding with star P.

**Premises:** Comet X was observed heading toward star P. Then later a flare was observed; a flare could have been caused by a comet colliding with a star.

**Flaw:** The fact that an observation could have had a particular cause is treated as positive proof that it did.

This is a PARALLEL-THE-FLAW question. We're looking for the choice that makes the same mistake.

(A) The conclusion in the original is definite; the conclusion here is qualified.
(B) This is a good argument.
(C) Yes. This reproduces all of the features of the original.
(D) This argument involves an either/or that isn't similar to anything seen in the original argument.
(E) This is a good argument.

7. **C Conclusion:** The supplement is at least as effective at treating mold allergies as any prescription drug.

**Premises:** Surveys show that all mold allergy sufferers who took the supplement improved; these surveys have never been refuted by the drug companies.

**Assumption:** The fact that the study has never been refuted indicates that its findings are correct; the improvement found in the study was at least as great as the improvements associated with those who are treated with prescription drugs.

This is a FLAW question. We're looking for a choice that describes or exploits an assumption.

(A) Careful. This would be a great answer to a weaken question, but this isn't something the argument says.
(B) Like (A), this is related to an error in the reasoning but doesn't correctly describe what the argument is saying.
(C) Yes. This indicates something that the argument does incorrectly.
(D) This doesn't seem like an incorrect thing to do.
(E) Again, this is a great answer to a weaken question, but doesn't fit the question asked.

8. **B Conclusion:** It is not true that certain cold medicines impair the ability to operate a car.

**Premise:** Applicants on cold medicine are no less likely to pass driver's license exams than are applicants generally.

**Assumption:** Performance on driver's license exams measures ability to operate a car; the cold medicines mentioned in the conclusion are the same ones the applicants in the survey were taking.

This is a FLAW question. We're looking for a choice that exploits an assumption of the argument.

(A) The size of the group taking cold medicine isn't relevant unless the number is very small.
(B) Yes. It's possible that only a few cold medicines have a detrimental effect; it seems likely that you wouldn't take them before taking a driver's license test, doesn't it?
(C) Close, but this indicates that those who fail may nevertheless operate a vehicle safely; it seems that this possibility would affect both groups equally.
(D) This doesn't appear to have any effect on the argument's conclusion.
(E) This is a side issue.

9. **D** This is a MAIN POINT question. We're looking for what the argument wants us to believe.

(A) This is a premise of the argument.
(B) The issue here is not what advantages herding behavior offers so much as it is one particular advantage that it does not offer.
(C) The preferences of carnivores aren't what this argument is trying to tell us about.
(D) Yes. This is the choice that gets all of the significant pieces of the argument and tells us what the argument wants us to get from them.
(E) This would weaken the argument. It's certainly not the main point.

## SECTION III

10. **D Conclusion:** The best strategy to reform former dictatorships is to propose democratic reform or market reform, but not both.

    **Premises:** Many countries where one was introduced ended up adopting the other; most countries where the two were introduced simultaneously adopted neither.

    This is a STRENGTHEN question. Because there are no obvious flaws, it's likely that our answer will directly support the conclusion.

    (A) The difficulty of one route versus the other has no effect on this conclusion.
    (B) The details of how authoritarian governments work do not appear to be relevant to this conclusion.
    (C) Humanitarian needs are not directly relevant to the conclusion.
    (D) Yes. This provides additional support for the fact that some type of reform must be advocated for, but advocating both will not be successful.
    (E) These countries are not relevant to the conclusion.

11. **D Conclusion:** A new correct definition that is able to solve some problems that the currently accepted definition cannot should become the accepted definition.

    **Premise:** The accepted definition should be the correct definition that solves the greatest number of problems.

    **Assumption:** A new correct definition that solves some problems that the currently accepted definition cannot must solve a greater number of problems than the currently accepted definition does.

    This is a PRINCIPLE question. We're looking, more specifically, for the principle that would justify the conclusion.

    (A) Determining whether a definition is correct is irrelevant to the conclusion; it covers only correct definitions.
    (B) Yes. This would guarantee that the new definition really does solve more problems than the previously accepted definition.
    (C) Incorrect definitions are not relevant to the conclusion.
    (D) Truth is not relevant to this conclusion.
    (E) This is a side issue; definitions of this sort are not relevant to the conclusion.

12. **D** This is a PRINCIPLE question. We are given five principles in the answer choices for this specific question, so we should come up with our own principle for the actions in the argument and match it to the answer choices.

    (A) But they're not dealing with both causes—only the software cause. Eliminate it.
    (B) They're not assuming that—if they were, they'd go out and replace the hardware. Eliminate it.
    (C) They're not testing assumptions; they can't test anything. They just have to hope it's the problem that's cheaper to fix. Eliminate it.
    (D) They're hoping that it's the software until it's really obvious it's not. This is the answer.
    (E) They're not altering any strategy in the argument. Eliminate it.

13. **D Conclusion:** If a person is a master, he or she must have played chess at least four hours each day.

    **Premise:** If a person plays four hours each day, he or she will become a master.

    **Assumption:** Playing four hours each day is the only way to become a master.

    This is a FLAW question. Try to come up with your own description of why the author's conclusion is flawed before you go to the answer choices, and then match your description to the choices.

    (A) Whether other people think the player is a master is irrevelant. According to the argument, anyone who plays at least four hours a day "will inevitably become a master."
    (B) Bingo. The author makes an invalid contrapositive in the argument. This is the answer.
    (C) We have no idea whether this is true. Eliminate it.
    (D) We don't care about chess champion recommendations. Eliminate it.
    (E) We don't care about most people. The argument doesn't say everyone. Eliminate it.

## SECTION III

14. **B Conclusion:** prescriptive grammar → ~natural science

**Premises:** prescriptive grammar → set of axiomatic principles; set of axiomatic principles → ~experimentation

This is a SUFFICIENT ASSUMPTION question. We want the choice that guarantees the truth of the conclusion by completing the chain from "prescriptive grammar" to "~natural science."

Note that the two premises given allow us to form part of such a chain: prescriptive grammar → set of axiomatic principles → ~experimentation. The most likely link we'll find in the choices is "~experimentation → natural science."

(A) No "some" statement can provide us the needed link.
(B) Yes. This reads "natural science → experimentation." Its contrapositive provides the link we're looking for.
(C) This reads "experimentation → set of axiomatic principles," which is the contrapositive of one of our premises. This choice doesn't add any new information.
(D) This reads "experimentation → natural science." This does not allow us to extend the chain.
(E) No grammar that does not rely upon a set of axiomatic principles is a science.

15. **A Conclusion:** Marcel will make less money this year than last year.

**Premise:** He made less from his investments.

**Assumption:** His other sources of income did not increase by enough to offset the decrease in profit from investments.

This is a NECESSARY ASSUMPTION question. The correct answer will be something necessary for the conclusion to be true, and if made false, will make the argument fall apart.

(A) If they did offset, then Marcel could make just as much, which would make the argument fall apart. This is the answer.
(B) There is no connection between these two things except for the fact that Marcel is interested in both of them. Eliminate it.
(C) But we are specifically told in the argument that his portfolio WILL be affected. Eliminate it.
(D) Bummer, but we already know he's not going to make as much. Eliminate it.
(E) Bummer, but the argument never mentions his expenses. This is out of the scope of the argument.

16. **D Conclusion:** Efforts to encourage conservation by individuals are unlikely to solve the world's most pressing energy problems.

**Premise:** The greatest proportion of energy consumption by individuals is in the form of hidden energy costs associated with products and services.

**Assumption:** Individuals cannot act to conserve energy usage in forms where they cannot tell how much they are using; solving the most pressing energy problems involves reducing energy usage in forms that consume more energy than individuals directly consume.

This is a NECESSARY ASSUMPTION question. We're looking for something on which the conclusion's truth depends.

(A) The consumption that needs to be reduced is associated with individual behavior; the individuals just don't know how much they're consuming.
(B) The prices of the goods with hidden energy costs aren't clearly relevant to the conclusion here.
(C) Like (A), this choice doesn't make the needed distinction.
(D) Like (A) and (C), this choice misses the fact that individuals are really consuming the energy; they just aren't aware of how much they're consuming.
(E) Yes. If it's possible for individuals to engage in effective conservation even without this knowledge, then the argument's reasoning doesn't work.

## SECTION III

17. **E** **Conclusion:** Banks must be heavily regulated if a nation wants to remain economically stable.

    **Premises:** Unbridled competition encourages dishonest business practices; when dishonest business practices are common, a nation loses trust; a nation that loses respect cannot secure aid in times of economic trouble.

    **Assumptions:** If banks are not heavily regulated, unbridled competition results; encouraging dishonest business practices leads to those practices becoming common; losing the trust of investors leads to losing the respect of trading partners; aid in times of economic hardship is needed to maintain economic stability.

    This is a WEAKEN EXCEPT question. Four of these choices will attack assumptions of the argument; the odd choice out will be the answer.

    (A) This weakens the argument by pointing out that unbridled competition may not result even if banks are not heavily regulated.
    (B) This weakens the argument by pointing out that unbridled competition doesn't necessarily lead to dishonest business practices becoming common.
    (C) This weakens the argument by pointing out that a nation could lose trust without losing the respect of trading partners.
    (D) This weakens the argument by pointing out that securing aid in times of hardship isn't necessary to economic stability.
    (E) Yes. Other shortsighted policies do not appear to be relevant to the conclusion.

18. **B** **Conclusion:** The labor movement's purpose is primarily to secure power and only secondarily to help workers.

    **Premise:** Unions that secure better pay for workers serve their own interests by increasing their ability to wield political power.

    **Flaw:** One of two potential motives for an effort is singled out as being the primary one; attributes of labor unions are ascribed to the labor movement as a whole.

    This is a FLAW question. We're looking for a choice that describes or exploits an assumption.

    (A) The relevant question isn't whether political power is in the unions' interest, but whether this is their primary interest.
    (B) Yes. This refers to the part/whole flaw in the argument.
    (C) The argument does not say that the two goals discussed are mutually exclusive.
    (D) This term appears to be used in a consistent manner.
    (E) No political preference is mentioned here.

19. **E** This is a REASONING question. Come up with your own description of how the author makes the argument and then match your description to the choices.

    (A) Their argument is clear; it's their conclusion that stinks. Eliminate it.
    (B) The author doesn't say that they are liars, just that their conclusion is wrong.
    (C) No. The author is saying that there is a different cause. Eliminate it.
    (D) Their criteria and premises are fine; it's their conclusion that is bad. Eliminate it.
    (E) Yes. It's not that fathers care more; it's just that they are exposed more to their children because mothers now work. This is the answer.

## SECTION III

Questions 20–21

20. **B Conclusion:** Appreciating art does not depend on your ability to say what was good or bad.

    **Premise:** Many visitors can't say what they liked or didn't like about art, yet they feel strongly about it.

    **Assumption:** Strong feelings about art are the same as appreciating art.

    This is a NECESSARY ASSUMPTION question. The correct answer will be something necessary for the conclusion to be true, and if made false, will make the argument fall apart.

    (A) We're looking for a connection between articulation and appreciation. This isn't it.
    (B) Bingo. If it were not true that strong feelings can lead to appreciation, the argument would totally fall apart. This is the answer.
    (C) This is classic LSAT babble. Vocabulary of visual art? Eliminate it.
    (D) Always? What if the person hates it? Is that appreciation?
    (E) We're not talking specific or general here; we're more concerned with whether we merely can or can't say anything at all. (B) is the best choice.

21. **E** This is an INFERENCE question. Because it is also an EXCEPT question, your goal is to find the one choice that can't be true based on the information in the passage.

    (A) This can be true—the argument says only that some can't. Eliminate it.
    (B) This can be true—there could be some people who can do this. Eliminate it.
    (C) As long as they feel strongly about it, they can still appreciate it. Articulation isn't necessary.
    (D) This can be true also—there is no contradiction in the argument.
    (E) This is the answer. It is the opposite of the argument, which says you can feel strongly and appreciate without expressing a reason.

22. **E** This is a REASONING question. Come up with your own description of how Evan's second statement counters Dalia, and then match your description to the choices.

    (A) No. He attacks it directly, so he does think it's relevant. Eliminate it.
    (B) He doesn't call into question the amount of information she possesses, but rather her interpretation of that information. Eliminate it.
    (C) No. He's not confused at all. He's actually saying that her argument supports his argument.
    (D) He doesn't appeal to anyone. Eliminate it.
    (E) Bingo. He twists it around so it supports his argument. This is the answer.

23. **E** This is a REASONING question. Come up with your own description of what they're arguing about, and then match your description to the choices.

    (A) Both agree that poaching is bad; they're arguing about whether it's the primary cause of extinction.
    (B) Not whether this campaign will affect the demand, but whether it will affect extinction.
    (C) We don't know the numbers. Eliminate it.
    (D) They're arguing over the best method for saving as many species as possible.
    (E) Yes. The environmentalist thinks that the strategy of saving habitats is more important than the naturalist's strategy of a media campaign. This is the answer.

# SECTION III

24. **A Conclusion:** The statue found in the ancient city of Ouz was looted from a neighboring city.

**Premises:** There is no sign that the inhabitants of Ouz made anything out of bronze; the inhabitants at Ouz frequently raided other cities.

This is a WEAKEN question. Because there doesn't seem to be an obvious flaw to the argument, our choice will most likely attack the conclusion directly.

(A) Yes. Although this doesn't tell us with any certainty how the statue got there, it does cast significant doubt on the argument's explanation.
(B) This may lend slight strength to the conclusion; it doesn't weaken it.
(C) This may lend slight strength to the conclusion; it doesn't weaken it.
(D) This strengthens the conclusion.
(E) This is too general to have much impact on the conclusion.

25. **B Conclusion:** It seems unlikely that job stress leads to increased risk of heart attack.

**Premise:** Despite the stresses to which they are exposed, fighter pilots are less likely to die of heart attack than are most people.

**Assumptions:** Comparisons concerning the likelihood of dying of a heart attack provide useful information about the incidence of heart attack; fighter pilots are representative of all those who have stressful jobs.

This is a STRENGTHEN question. We want a choice that will either shore up an assumption of the argument or support the conclusion directly.

(A) This seems most likely to be an effect of the hazardous nature of their work, which according to the argument was compensated for in the study. At best, this might weaken the conclusion.
(B) Yes. This concerns a characteristic of fighter pilots that may not be shared by the rest of the population. By eliminating a potential alternative explanation of the survey results, this strengthens the argument.
(C) This weakens the argument.
(D) This weakens the argument.
(E) Because the conclusion concerns only whether job stress increases the likelihood of heart attack, the fact that other factors may have more of an effect isn't truly relevant.

# SECTION IV

Questions 1–6

ROYIGV

* ** { O → ~~I~~ ; I → ~~O~~ }

* { ~~G~~ → O ; ~~O~~ → G }

** { Y → I AND V ; ~~I~~ OR ~~V~~ → ~~Y~~ }

** { V → R OR G ; ~~R~~ AND ~~G~~ → ~~V~~ }

| IN | OUT |
|---|---|
| G/O | O/I |

The most important thing with an in/out game is to make sure that you symbolize and use your clues correctly. Note that the first two conditional clues form a chain (I in means that O is out, which means that G is in), as do the last two conditional clues; the third clue is also connected to the first. It is usually better to mark the connected clues but not clutter your diagram by writing out full chains, which can become long and complicated. It is also useful to note two either/or's that arise from these clues: Because of the first clue, either O or I must be out, and it is possible that both are out; because of the second clue, either G or O must be in, and it is possible that both are in.

Conditional clues are incredibly important on the LSAT. If any of the discussion above seems perplexing to you, be sure to review the material on conditional statements.

1. **B** This is a Grab-a-Rule question; it should be the first one you work on this game.
   - (A) This one has Y in, but not V.
   - (B) This one does not violate any rules, and thus is our answer.
   - (C) This one has V in, but neither one of R or G.
   - (D) This one has Y in, but not I.
   - (E) This one has both O and I in.

2. **D** Do this one on your second pass through this game. Our deduction, that either G or O has to be in, is useful here: Since at least one of them has to be in, only G or O can possibly be the answer to this question. Only G is listed, so choice (D) must be the answer.

3. **E** If you notice that this is effectively a Grab–a–Rule question, you should do it on your first pass through the game. We want to pick the choice that violates a rule. In this case, that's clearly (E).

4. **C** Do this one on your first pass through this game. V out means that Y must be out, but we cannot tell anything else about the position of the other colors. This is actually enough to find the answer: We know that V, Y, and at least one of I or O must be out. Since the game includes only 6 elements, and at least 3 must be out, there can be no more than 3 in.

   If you resort to POE on this question, you have to be careful. Since this is a must-be-true question, you have to find counterexamples for the choices you work on—in other words, you have to try to make them false; if you cannot, then you've found the answer.

   For your reference, the diagram below includes counterexamples for the incorrect choices on this question.

| | IN | OUT |
|---|---|---|
| (A), (B), (D) | RIG | OVY |
| (E) | GO | IVY |

   In order to make (C) false, you would have to put at least 4 elements in; since this can never be done without violating a rule, (C) is the answer.

5. **E** Do this one on your first pass through this game. V in means that R or G must be in; we can make no further deductions. Since this is a must-be-false question, the simplest way to proceed is by POE: Try to make the choices true; the one you can't make true is the answer. The diagram below shows examples that make (A), (B), (C), and (D) true.

| | IN | OUT |
|---|---|---|
| (A), (D) | IVG | ORY |
| (B), (C) | RVO | IGY |

   Why can't (E) work? I in forces O out; O out forces G in, which contradicts this choice. If you scanned and spotted this contradiction, then you saved yourself a good deal of time.

6. **C** This is a Rule-Changer question; do it after you've done all the others on this game. This one removes the assurance that either G or O must be in. Fortunately, this question is basically another Grab-a-Rule; as in question 3, we want to pick the one that violates one of the rules we have left. Choice (C) has V in but doesn't include either R or G. Thus (C) is the answer we want.

# SECTION IV

Questions 7–13

| I | G | M | F |
|---|---|---|---|
| s | s | p | p |
| X | X | K/X | K/X |

| 1 | 2 | 3 | 4 | 5 |
|---|---|---|---|---|
| I/M | M/I | H | G/F | F/G |
| | | n | | |
| | | K | | |

A large number of deductions make the questions on this one go quickly. The clues directly place I and M, in either order, in spots 1 and 2. Since H must go before both F and G, and there are only two spaces remaining, H must be in 3, and F and G must go in 4 and 5, in either order. We're told that spot 3 is from n, which leaves only two runners from s and two from p. We're told that neither M nor F is from s, which means both must be from p; that leaves both I and G to be from s, and we now know which town each runner comes from. Finally, we know that both of the runners from s do not use knee braces (symbolized by X above). As a result, the game breaks down into four vertical blocks, with the top tier determining their placement.

7. **E** This is as close to a Grab-a-Rule question as you're likely to get on a game like this; since you have so many deductions, you should do this one first. The only choice that matches our diagram is (E).

8. **A** Do this one on your second pass through this game. It's clear from our deductions that (A) can happen, and the others can't.

9. **C** Do this one on your first pass through this game. If the runner in 1 is from s, then that runner is I; the runner in 2 is M. The only choice that fits with this case is (C).

10. **C** Do this one on your first pass through the game. If the runner in 1 has a brace, then it must be M; I is in 2. Since I doesn't wear a brace, (C) cannot happen, and is therefore the answer we want.

11. **A** Do this one on your second pass through the game. (A) is one of our initial deductions, so this is the answer we want here.

12. **A** Do this one on your second pass through the game; although it is a specific question, the question task here looks rather difficult. Fortunately, we have a large number of deductions to help. The fact that runners with the same entry in the bottom tier cannot be next to one another means, first of all, that both M and F must wear braces, since they will definitely be next to I and G, respectively. Moreover, since H wears a brace, the runners that do not—I and G—must be next to H. Thus there is only one arrangement that works, making (A) is the answer here.

13. **B** Do this one on your first pass through the game. If a runner with a brace is in 2, it must be M; that puts I in 1. Then (B) can't be true, and that's the answer we want.

## SECTION IV

Questions 14–18

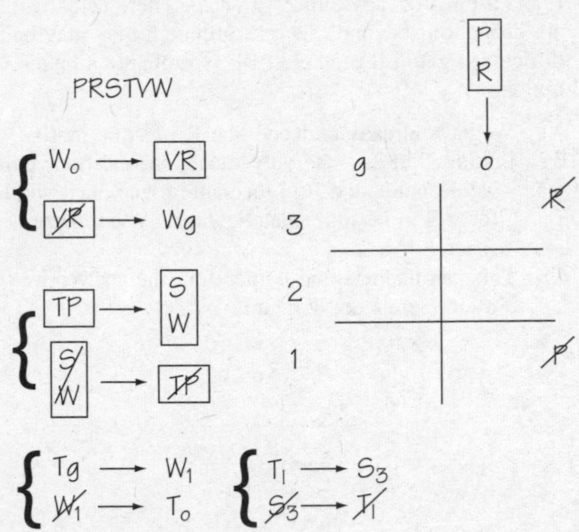


With such open-ended conditionals, there isn't much to deduce here. The PR block is the most concrete clue here—and the one we'll probably rely on most. Realize that there is only one space open in the o column, so anytime we learn who the third element in this column is, the other three must go in the g column.

14. **E** Do this one on your second pass through this game. On this pass, you're hoping for your prior work to help you out, and it does: We have previously seen an example of (E) in question 16, so this is the choice we want.

15. **A** Do this one on your first pass through this game. T in the g column means that W is on the first floor. We also know that one of S or W must be on each side, which means that S cannot be immediately above W; T, then, cannot be on the same floor with P. Beyond this, we have to do POE to find the answer.

(A) Fortunately, we find the answer on the first try; here's the diagram.

| | g | o |
|---|---|---|
| 3 | S | P |
| 2 | V | R |
| 1 | T | W |

(B) S in 1g would force W into 1o. That forces the PR block into 3o and 2o. With W in the o column, we must have V and R on the same floor, so V must be in 2g. But that would force T into 1g—the same floor with P, which we know we can't have.

(C) This contradicts our deduction that T and P cannot be on the same floor.

(D) W has to be in the first floor; P can never be on the first floor.

(E) In order to do this, V would have to be in 1g while W is in 1o. But W in 1o requires V and R to be on the same floor, so this can't work.

16. **D** Do this one on your first pass through this game. W on the third floor means that it isn't on the first floor, so T must be in the o column. The o column is now full, so W, S, and V must all be in the g column. In particular, then, W is in g3. Since g3 is occupied, S can't be on the third floor, which means T can't be on the first floor. In order to accommodate the PR block, then, T must be in o3, P must be in o2, and R must be in o1. S and V can be in the remaining spaces in either order. Here's the diagram.

| | g | o |
|---|---|---|
| 3 | W | T |
| 2 | S/V | P |
| 1 | V/S | R |

The only choice that's consistent with our diagram is (D).

# SECTION IV

17. **B** Do this one on your first pass through this game. T in 1o means that P is in 3o, R is in 2o, and the remaining elements—W, S, and V—must be in the g column. T on the first floor means that S is on the third floor; it must be 3g. Here's the diagram.

| | g | o |
|---|---|---|
| 3 | S | P |
| 2 | W/V | R |
| 1 | V/W | T |

The only choice listed that doesn't have to be true is (B), the choice we want here.

18. **C** Do this one on your first pass through the game. P not on the third floor means that P is in 2o, and R is in 1o. S not on the third floor means that T is not on the first floor; S must occupy either 1g or 2g. There actually are deductions beyond this one, although they may be difficult to get at this stage. POE is probably a better option.

(A) We have already deduced that R must be in 1o.

(B) Putting T in 2g—the only vacant second-floor unit—would put T and P in the same row, which would force S to be immediately above W, but there is no space for this.

(C) This can happen, and is therefore the answer we want. Here's the diagram.

| | g | o |
|---|---|---|
| 3 | V | T |
| 2 | W | P |
| 1 | S | R |

(D) We've already deduced that S can go only in 1g or 2g.

(E) The only open slot in the o column is 3o. W in o would force T into column g, but we have a clue that tells us anytime T is in column g, W must be on the first floor.

# SECTION IV

Questions 19–23

The only real deduction here involves the clue with F and G; since there must be at least 1 space between them, and since K must be in 2, the only place F can go is in 1. G and L go in either order in 3 and 4, and L must go with u. The other three jockeys are identical.

19. **A** Do this one on the second pass through this game. F has to be in 1; the only jockey F can't be paired with is u, who must be with L. (A) is the only choice that works here.

20. **C** Do this one on the first pass through this game. Since u has to go with L, and L must be one of the last two, the only way r can be assigned to L is if L and u are in 3, and G and r are in 4. s and t are in the remaining positions. Here's the diagram.

| 1 | 2 | 3 | 4 |
|---|---|---|---|
| F | K | L | G |
| s/t | t/s | u | r |

The only choice that isn't possible, according to the diagram, is (C).

21. **D** Do this one on the first pass through this game. This one puts L and u in 3 and G in 4; we don't know anything else about the locations of r, s, and t. Thus, (D) is the answer; s could be in 4 with G.

22. **C** Do this one on the second pass through this game. As count-the-ways questions go, this one isn't bad. Either L or G must be assigned to 4. If L is in 4, we have only one possibility: u must go with L. If G is in 4, then any of r, s, or t may also appear there: That's three more possibilities. The total number of possibilities is 4, which is answer choice (C).

23. **D** Do this one on the first pass through this game. This is identical to number 20, except that now it's s in 4 instead of r. Here's the diagram.

| 1 | 2 | 3 | 4 |
|---|---|---|---|
| F | K | L | G |
| r/t | t/r | u | s |

The only choice that doesn't have to be true, according to the diagram, is (D).

# About the Authors

Adam Robinson was born in 1955. He lives in New York City.

Kevin Blemel started working with The Princeton Review in 1994. Over the years, he has served as a teacher, tutor, and Master Trainer throughout the United States as well as in Bangkok, Thailand. In addition to creating written materials, Kevin has developed educational content for a Distance Learning program that provides web-based instruction. He makes his home in Austin, Texas, but can often be seen traveling here and abroad to feed his addictions to taking risks outdoors and to eating anything strange he can get his hands on.

# Have you gone online yet!?

Go online to PrincetonReview.com/cracking to type in your answers for these tests and get a score report.

The score report will tell you what areas you need to work on the most. After learning about these topics in the book, you can use your online lessons and drills to reinforce what you've learned.

You can also take a practice test online and enjoy the luxury of automatic grading!

Why are you still here? Go online!

princetonreview.com

## NOTES

# NOTES

# NOTES